MANAGEMENT ACCOUNTING
A Decision Emphasis

fourth edition

MANAGEMENT ACCOUNTING
A DECISION EMPHASIS

Don T. DeCoster

Seattle University, Seattle

Eldon L. Schafer

Pacific Lutheran University, Tacoma

Mary T. Ziebell

Seattle University, Seattle

WILEY

John Wiley & Sons

New York   Chichester   Brisbane   Toronto   Singapore

Library of Congress Cataloging in Publication Data:

DeCoster, Don T.
    Management accounting.

    Bibliography: p.
    1. Managerial accounting.   2. Decision-making
I. Schafer, Eldon L.   II. Ziebell, Mary T.
III. Title.
HF5657.4.D43   1988   658.1'511   87-29427
ISBN 0-471-63713-0

Printed in the United States of America

10 9 8 7 6 5 4 3 2 1

about the authors

DON T. DeCOSTER, Ph. D., C.P.A., is Professor of Accounting at Seattle University in Seattle. He holds a Ph.D. in Business Administration from The University of Texas and a Ph.D. in Counseling Psychology from the University of Oregon. He wrote, with William J. Bruns, Jr., *Accounting and Its Behavioral Implications* and with Kavasseri V. Ramanathan and Gary L. Sundem, *Accounting for Managerial Decision Making.* He has published articles in *The Accounting Review, The Journal of Accounting Research, Cost and Management, The Journal of Accountancy, Business Budgeting, The Journal of Vocational Behavior,* and other professional journals. Teaching interests include management accounting and cost accounting at both the graduate and undergraduate level. He has served as both Editor of the Educational Research Section of *The Accounting Review* and Editor of *The Accounting Review.* Research interests focus on the interactions of human beings with the accounting function.

ELDON L. SCHAFER, Ph.D., C.P.A., is Professor of Accounting at Pacific Lutheran University in Tacoma, Washington. He holds a Ph.D. in Business Organization and Management from the University of Nebraska. He taught previously at the University of Washington, Syracuse University, San Jose State University, and the University of Nebraska. A member of the American Accounting Association, the Washington Society of Certified Public Accountants, and the National Association of Accountants, he has been active in professional development programs in management accounting throughout the United States. He has been engaged in research and writing on financial management of ambulatory health care organizations under a grant from the Center for Research in Ambulatory Health Care Administration.

MARY T. ZIEBELL, Ph.D., is Associate Professor of Accounting at Seattle University in Seattle. She holds a Ph.D. in Business Administration from the University of Washington. She has published articles in *Health Care Management* and *The Women's C.P.A.* A member of the American Accounting Association and the American Society of Women Accountants, she has also been active at both the local and national level of Beta Alpha Psi, the national accounting fraternity. She has served on a number of Boards of Directors in the health-care field, engaged in the development of professional health care programs and drawn many of her cases from this area which have been printed in accounting and marketing textbooks. Her teaching and research interests are focused on management and cost accounting and management control systems in public service organizations.

preface

This book is an introductory text in management accounting. We assume that students have had an introduction to the basic accounting process of measuring and summarizing business transactions and preparing financial statements. While it is not necessary that previous exposure to accounting theory and practice be extremely rigorous, it is important for the student to have been exposed to the accounting cycle, including journal entries.

It is our goal to take the student as deeply into management accounting theory and practice as feasible within the constraints of a one-quarter or one-semester course. To accomplish this goal we have adopted a number of pedagogical goals. First the organization of this book focuses the student's attention on the primary purpose of management accounting data, decisions by management, as contrasted with external reporting.

Second, the textual material is presented in a thematic form. The backbone of the theme is decision making and the flesh is the role of extant or possible accounting systems in providing relevant data. In this sense the book can be viewed as both normative and real world-oriented.

Third, when material is presented we try to provide both the theory and the technique. In many cases this makes the coverage more complete and involved than in other texts.

Fourth, we have included accounting theory, economic theory, quantitative methods, and organizational theory as appropriate. No attempt has been made to make this a "traditional" record keeping book, or a "quantitative" book, or a "behavioral" book. Rather, necessary tools and techniques have been covered when they blend into the overall theme of management accounting for decision making.

Fifth, we have tried to keep the content and explanations clear and understandable without sacrificing depth. To assist in the students' understanding there are many problems at the end of each chapter. We believe that the students will find these problems challenging and that their ability to handle "real-world" settings will be significantly advanced by their active participation in the problem solving. Some problems are basic; some require considerable thought and effort; some have a range of suitable approaches; some compound and integrate previous material. There are some "teaching" problems where the content pushes beyond the text. Finally, we have included teaching cases for those applications where the instructor wants to take the student beyond problem solving into complex, real-world settings where the solutions are judgmental as well as numerical.

CONTENT OF THIS EDITION

Part One is entitled "Accounting Data for Decision Making." Its three chapters introduce the student to the decision process by discussing the planning and control process and the role of fixed and variable costs in decision making.

Chapter 1, "The Planning and Control Process for Decision Making," sets the stage by providing a planning and control framework through a review of the nature of the decision process and the types of decisions that business management must make.

Chapter 2, "Determining Cost Behavior Patterns," includes definitions of fixed and variable costs and a detailed discussion of the methods accountants use to measure and evaluate cost behavior patterns.

Chapter 3, "Cost-Volume-Profit Interaction for Operating Decisions," discusses the role of fixed and variable costs in decision making by focusing on the breakeven point and the contribution margin.

The second part is entitled "Variable Costing Systems." Its three chapters introduce the student to the accounting methodologies of data gathering and selection. These chapters represent a departure from the more traditional textbook presentation. Because it is generally accepted among management accountants that variable costing is preferred for management decision making, these chapters emphasize variable costing for data collection. The instructor is spared the embarrassing position of first teaching absorption costing and then having to say "this is a less valuable system for decision making than variable costing, which we haven't emphasized."

Chapter 4, "Cost Flows for Product Costing," has two purposes. Beginning with the distinction between product and period costs, it serves the traditional role of giving the student the accounting terminology needed. Second, the chapter discusses the differences between variable and absorption costing and their strengths and weaknesses.

Chapter 5, "Variable Job Order and Process Costing Systems," concentrates on how historical accounting creates the flow of costs necessary for measuring production costs. Both job order and process costing are illustrated using variable costing.

Chapter 6, "Variable Standard Costing for Cost Efficiency," introduces standard cost systems. Emphasis is placed on setting standards, operating a standard cost system, and understanding variable standard cost variances.

Part Three is entitled "Absorption Costing Systems and Cost Allocations." There are two chapters in this section.

Chapter 7, "Overhead and Absorption Costing," introduces the problems of fixed overhead costs in absorption costing. Special emphasis is placed on predetermined overhead rates for absorption costing and the analysis of overhead variances. A comparison of variable and absorption standard costing summarizes the chapter. In the chapter appendix the methodology of converting a variable costing system to an absorption costing system is explained and demonstrated.

Chapter 8, "The Allocation of Indirect Costs," shows how indirect costs are allocated between products and departments in both manufacturing and non-manufacturing settings. An Appendix to the chapter illustrates how reciprocal allocations can be used.

Part Four is entitled "The Use of Data in Making Decisions." The three chapters in this section focus on the data needed for both short-range and long-range decisions.

Chapter 9, "Revenue and Pricing Decisions," contains a discussion of both economic and accounting approaches to pricing decisions. There is also coverage of governmental "cost-based" pricing.

Chapter 10, "Relevant Costs and Production Decisions," covers a number of short-range decisions that affect production output and costs including make or buy, sell or process, and linear programming. The chapter also includes coverage of inventory control methods.

Chapter 11, "Long-range Decisions," introduces long-range decisions. After a discussion of the measurement of costs and benefits for long-range decisions, both discounted cash flow methods and techniques that do not use the time value of money are explained. ACRS is used as the example of how income taxes can affect the cash flows. The chapter closes with an illustration of how discounted cash flow methods can be used to cope with inflation.

Part Five, "Planning and Control Systems for Decision Implementation," uses the budgetary process to show how the integration of decision data can be grouped into a meaningful, coordinated package.

Chapter 12, "Budgeting: A Systematic Approach to Planning," has been rewritten. Using a simple example, this chapter shows how the sales forecast is converted into sales and production budgets for both quantities and costs, culminating in the Profit Plan. Next the Cash Budget and the Statement of Financial Position are shown. Finally, end-of-the-period performance reports are shown using both the Profit Plan and the flexible budget.

Chapter 13, "Responsibility Accounting and Budgetary Control," takes a different approach from chapter 12. Here the focus is on how the budgeting process can be accomplished through responsibility centers. Emphasis is placed on relating the budgetary process to the reporting system necessary to achieve good responsibility accounting.

Chapter 14, "Measurement of Divisional Performance," deals with problems that are unique to larger, decentralized organizations. Problems discussed are divisionalization, divisional profit measurement, intercompany transfer pricing, and divisional rates of return.

Overall, the revisions in this Fourth Edition should provide for a systematic and logical coverage of management accounting. Some chapters, notably Chapters 6, 7, 8, 11, 12, and 13, have been substantially rewritten. There are also other major changes such as strengthening the statistical methods in a Chapter 2 Appendix, the addition of material on the learning curve in an Appendix to Chapter 6, and the movement of the conversion from variable to absorption costing to an Appendix at the end of Chapter 7. We believe that these changes will make the text material flow smoothly for the student without sacrificing breadth or depth.

We have also made substantial changes in the problem materials. Each chapter now has a large number of problems ranging from the very simple to the complex. With careful use of the problem assignments, it is possible for an instructor to teach a very straightforward course for the sophomore or a more complex course for the M.B.A. The problem materials are also diverse in their settings: There are manufacturing, service, retail, profit-oriented, nonprofit, and governmental and personal settings.

We have been encouraged and supported in our writing by many people. We would like to offer a special word of thanks to our colleagues and friends who have read and commented on the manuscript:

Michael F. Thomas, Oklahoma State University; Wayne G. Bremser, Villanova University; David P. Franz, San Francisco State University; John H. Salter, University of Central Florida; Richard Arvey, Seattle University; Jack O. Hall, Jr., Western Kentucky University; Douglas A. Johnson, Arizona State University; John A. Dettman, University of Minnesota-Duluth, Bobbe Barnes, University of Texas.

Each of these reviewers made valuable comments and suggestions. We have given serious consideration to each suggestion, and we believe their efforts strengthened the manuscript. Of course, we must take full responsibility for the text.

We are also indebted to the American Institute of Certified Public Accountants, the National Association of Accountants, the Institute of Certified Management Accountants, the Society of Industrial Accountants of Canada, and many publishers and companies for their permission to quote from their publications and examinations. Problems from the Uniform CPA Examinations are designated *CPA adapted*; problems from the examinations administered by the Society of Industrial Accounts are designated *Canada SIA adapted*; and problems from the Certified Management Accountant examination given by the Institute of Certified Management Accountants are designated *CMA adapted*.

The authors and the publisher welcome comments from users.

Don T. DeCoster
Eldon L. Schafer
Mary T. Ziebell

contents

part **1**

ACCOUNTING DATA FOR DECISION MAKING

chapter **1**

THE PLANNING AND CONTROL PROCESS FOR DECISION MAKING

The primary purpose of an economic system is to satisfy the wants and needs of its members by generating and allocating resources. In the not-for-profit segment of the economy, particularly governmental entities, the plans for resource allocation are made through the budgetary process. The legislative and executive branches decide what resources will be used for national defense, maintenance of law and order, and recreational and park activities, among others. Once these needs have been determined and budgeted, taxes are levied to support them. It is through the collection of taxes and subsequent governmental expenditures that economic resources are allocated in the public sector.

The decisions of investors and business managers allocate resources in the profit-oriented segment of the economy. Business resource allocations take place at two levels. First, and most visible, are interfirm decisions made in the capital markets, such as the stock and bond exchanges. The flow of resources between firms is determined in part by these markets. Investors commit their resources (funds) to those firms where they believe they can earn an acceptable rate of return on their investment.[1] Second, and less visible, are intrafirm decisions. Once resources have been invested in a firm, its managers must make decisions about how best to use them to earn a satisfactory rate of return.

The role of accounting is to provide meaningful information for both of these resource allocation decisions. In the broadest sense, accounting is a vehicle for communicating the data necessary for making intelligent economic decisions.

THE ROLE OF ACCOUNTING IN DECISION MAKING

Because accounting provides a data base for both interfirm and intrafirm decisions, it is logical to assume that accounting data must be multipurpose. The focus of accounting data for *interfirm* resource allocations is termed **financial accounting.** The focus of accounting data for *intrafirm* allocations through the planning and control process is termed **management accounting.** There is much common ground between financial and management accounting. There are, however, important differences in both data requirements and philosophical approaches to these data.

INTERFIRM ALLOCATION DECISIONS

Financial accounting data serve two distinct purposes. First, these data serve as an information source for investors and creditors making their investing and lending decisions. Financial reports (Statement of Financial Position, Income Statement, Statement of Retained Earnings, and Statement of Changes in Financial Position) are used by prudent investors in selecting investments. They provide clues to the financial security and stability of a firm and point toward the possible results of future operations. Second, for society at large, financial

---

[1]Rate of return on investment is measured by: Income ÷ Investment. A discussion of rate of return for performance evaluation will be found in Chapter 14; the role of the rate of return on asset additions is discussed in Chapter 11.

data are used to ensure that a firm has complied with societal regulations and laws.

When financial accounting data are made available to the public, certain requirements are imposed. First, the users, whether they are stockholders, bond-holders, or governmental agencies, typically use these data in their decision-making activities without access to the detailed transactions that are the basis of the summary reports. They must have assurance of a fair and objective presentation of facts. The independent auditor (Certified Public Accountant) serves the function of attesting to the general fairness of the data.

Second, because the financial data serve many diverse interests and people, there is a need for uniformity and standardization. This need has generated many accounting activities seeking to develop a common base of knowledge and, hence, communication. For example, the Financial Accounting Standards Board seeks to develop a common theory of identifying, measuring, and reporting financial and economic events to the public.

INTRAFIRM ALLOCATION DECISIONS

Intrafirm operating decisions begin when resources have been committed to the firm. The goal of management accounting is to provide the information necessary to facilitate management's choices about how to optimize the use of these financial resources. The data demands of the manager are more specific than the data demands of the investor. There must be allocations between products, asset structures, territories, departments, and management responsibility centers.[2] The nature of a specific decision is often well defined so that the data can be pinpointed and decision rules developed. It should be pointed out that it may be relatively simple to determine what data are needed for a decision. This does not mean, however, that the gathering of this information is simple or easy. It may be difficult, and at times impossible, to isolate the data necessary for a particular decision. But management has one advantage that people outside the firm may not have. With access to the sources of events, management can modify the accounting system and reports to meet its unique specifications. This accessibility makes the data flexible and allows the development of specific data for specific decisions.

This text emphasizes management accounting, that is, information that management needs to make specific intrafirm resource allocations. Such emphasis assumes that accounting must perform the two separate, distinct functions of financial and management reporting and that the data needs for each are often different. However, there are common threads that run through both financial

---

[2] We will use the term *responsibility center* a few times in a general sense before we give a detailed definition. A responsibility center is an organizational unit where there is specific managerial responsibility for a specific activity and, therefore, for the related costs, revenues, and/or resources.

and management accounting. Moreover, the societal and legal requirements of financial accounting often act to limit the flexibility of management accounting.

THE PLANNING STAGE

Business owners and managers cannot avoid making decisions, even if the decision is to do nothing. They must choose whether to focus their decision making toward specific goals or merely to react to events as they take place. Without goals, and without data about these goals, decisions will lack purpose. A good management decision will be both effective and efficient. An **effective** decision accomplishes the goals management seeks. An **efficient** decision consumes the minimum amount of resources necessary to achieve the goal.

The following section discusses the nature of business decisions. Three assumptions are implicit in this discussion. First, it is assumed that the firm has scarce, but unallocated, resources at its disposal. These resources may be financial, such as cash; physical, such as material, equipment, and buildings; or human, such as the time, skill, and energy of people. Second, it is assumed that management desires to make decisions about how to use these resources in an effective and efficient way. Third, it is assumed that the planning process can be generalized and applied to all types of economic entities. Each firm or organization will approach the steps in the process somewhat differently, but we can isolate and study the common thread running through the planning process. Exhibit 1–1 provides a generalized overview of the planning and decision process.

The first step in making a decision is **planning,** which involves the selection of enterprise goals and the development of programs to allocate resources to achieve these goals. Planning is the backbone of effective decision making. It is through the planning process that management formulates courses of action that reduce uncertainty about the future and assimilate the many pressures that bear on the firm.

The planning process may be formal or informal. Formal planning is generally superior to informal planning, but informal planning is better than no planning at all. Formal planning should begin with the development of the firm's goals and a recognition of the individual and societal limitations the firm faces in accomplishing its goals.

ORGANIZATIONAL GOALS

Before there can be purposeful decisions, there must be a goal—a direction. The goal is the basic aim of the decision maker. In capitalistic countries such as the United States and Canada, it is generally held that business activity has the common goal of making a profit. Springing from traditional economic the-

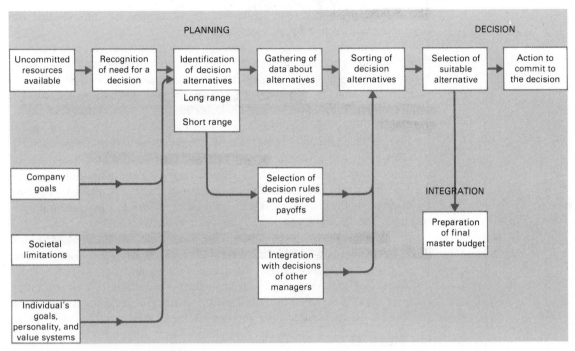

EXHIBIT 1–1   The planning and decision process

ory, this fundamental goal is often stated directly. At other times the profit goal is implied within broader statements such as ''providing a public service'' or ''providing for the long-run existence of the firm.'' The assumption is that if a firm provides a useful, sought-after service, it will receive a fair price and profits will result. Similarly, the long-run existence of a firm is assured if it can continue to provide a desired service with an acceptable profit. Certainly, the common element that links all business firms, from the smallest to the largest, is the profit motive.

It would be too simplistic to say that the *only* goal of a business firm is to *maximize* profits. There are many goals other than profit. Some managers seek to establish a power base and build an empire. Others seek social prestige and peer-group or public approval. Another goal is security. The removal of uncertainty or ambiguity about the future can often override the pure profit motive. Finally, many individuals and firms have humanitarian goals. Hiring disabled workers, maintaining a clean environment, and providing an enjoyable place to work are examples of humanitarian goals.

Not all enterprises have a profit motive. The federal and state governments; charitable organizations such as the Red Cross, the Salvation Army, and the Good Neighbor Funds; and community service activities such as hospitals, art museums, and symphony orchestras do not have a profit motive. The goals of these not-for-profit organizations are to provide the maximum services within the resources available. Thus, while they do not have a profit motive, they do need to make effective and efficient decisions.

The problems of combining many diverse yet separate goals into a unified whole should be apparent. Within the overriding requirement that the firm earn a satisfactory profit to maintain its existence, managers and workers strive to meet their own goals. These owners', managers', and workers' goals must be combined within the framework of the legal, political, and economic objectives of society. Unless managers are successful in blending the majority of goals, the firm will operate at cross purposes with society or the workers or the owners. The firm must find a way to achieve adequate **goal congruence.** This need is complicated by the fact that most goals are subjective and unspoken. Further, they are broad and rarely capable of being quantified. Perhaps it is because of the vagueness of many goals that decision makers emphasize a more quantifiable objective—the profit motive.

When a firm has uncommitted resources, or resources that may be shifted from one use to another, a decision about their use is necessary. The goals of the firm, as well as any external limitations, act as guides for the managers' decisions. Beginning with these goals there are several planning steps that management should take to ensure an effective and efficient decision. As shown in Exhibit 1–1, once the need for a decision has been recognized the next step is to define the problem and list decision alternatives.

TYPES OF DECISIONS

Some decisions call for the commitment of company resources to plant and equipment. Usually these decisions are termed **long-range** or **capacity decisions.** Long-range decisions have two unique characteristics. First, they involve changes in the productive or service potential of the firm. Second, and equally important, they cover a relatively long time span, so their effect on the firm is best measured in terms of cash flow, adjusted for the time value of money. The **time value of money** is a formal recognition of the simple fact that a dollar invested today will earn a return and be worth more later. Conversely, a dollar to be received in the future in worth less today.

Decisions involving production output, competitive pricing, additions to the product line, and temporary shutdown are **short-range** or **operating decisions.** Each of these decisions spans a short enough time period so the time value of money is not considered significant, although it is present. Further, none involves adding to or reducing production facilities; rather, they involve obtaining the best results possible from existing facilities or resources.

BENEFITS AND COSTS RELEVANT TO DECISIONS

As shown in Exhibit 1–1, after the decision alternatives have been identified, the next step in the planning process is the development of data on benefits and costs of the alternatives. The accounting system is a valuable source of data about the possible alternatives, although it is not the only source. The accounting system accumulates financial data resulting from past decisions. Such data are useful for subsequent decisions if management is interested in data measured in dollars and believes that past results are useful in predicting the future.

To make an effective and efficient decision, management requires estimates of all benefits and costs relevant to the alternatives being considered. A **relevant benefit** or **cost** is one affected by the decision. A benefit or cost not affected by the decision is **nonrelevant.** A nonrelevant benefit or cost can be ignored in making a decision because it will not change as a result of that decision. The ability to distinguish between which benefits and costs are relevant and which are nonrelevant underlies any effective decision.

To illustrate the concept of relevant benefits and costs, let's take a simple example. John is currently working in a lumber yard. He is considering returning to college. What data are relevant to his decision? Obviously, the added costs of tuition, books, and school fees are relevant. How about his room and board? Since he is self-supporting, he would incur room and board costs whether he went to school or continued working at the lumber yard. Only the difference, if any, in room and board between the two alternatives would be relevant. If he could continue to live in the same boardinghouse, his costs of room and board would be nonrelevant. More difficult to estimate are the benefits of the two alternatives. If he goes to college, he must forego the revenue he would earn at the lumber yard. Economists and accountants call this foregone revenue an **opportunity cost.** However, if he continues to work at the lumber yard, he might earn less in later years than he would if he were a college graduate. It is the difference in income across time that is relevant to his decision.

To illustrate relevant and nonrelevant benefits and costs in a business setting, let's assume that the Bradford Company recently spent $100,000 to purchase a building with an estimated useful life of 10 years. The firm has two alternative uses for the building. One alternative is to lease it to another company for a flat monthly rental fee. The second alternative is to store inventory in the building. In this illustration, the depreciation charges are nonrelevant because they will not be affected by either choice. Only the differences in maintenance and operating costs are relevant costs to compare with the alternative benefits of a monthly rental fee or the value of the warehouse as storage space.

Another way of thinking about benefits and costs that is useful for decision making is that of differential benefit or differential cost. A **differential benefit** is the difference in benefits between any two available, acceptable alternatives. A **differential cost** is the difference in cost between any two available, acceptable alternatives. This approach compares the two alternatives directly by looking at the differences between them. The difference in benefits between receiving a commission rather than a fixed salary is a differential benefit. The difference in cost between operating a large car and a small car is a differential cost. The difference in cost between leasing and purchasing a car is a differential cost. Many accountants also call this process **incremental anal-**

ysis, because they are measuring the total "additional" benefits or costs of one alternative over another.

As shown in Exhibit 1–1, the next step in the planning process, after scanning the decision alternatives, is the sorting of alternatives by determining which benefits and costs are relevant. This sorting requires the development of decision criteria or rules. Because short-range decisions are conceptually different from long-range decisions, accountants have developed different decision rules for each. In the next two sections we will develop an overview of these two decision rules. Then, in later chapters, we will look at them in more detail.

RELEVANT BENEFITS AND COSTS FOR OPERATING DECISIONS

Operating (short-range) decisions involve choosing alternatives that best use the existing capacity to maximize net income. These short-run choices revolve around three types of decisions: what quantity to produce, what price to charge, and what costs must be incurred. If the firm can optimize the selling price per unit and the quantity of units sold, while simultaneously controlling costs, it will maximize net income.

Experience and study have shown that one of the best methods accountants have for determining which costs are relevant and which costs are nonrelevant in operating decisions is to view costs from a perspective of how they change as activity levels change. Some costs change with output variations; others do not. Costs that change with variations in output (**variable costs**) are relevant to output decisions; costs that do not change (**fixed costs**) are not relevant to output decisions.

The understanding of a firm's fixed and variable costs facilitates the measurement of differential costs in operating decisions. In most differential production decisions involving volume output, the variable costs are relevant and the fixed costs are nonrelevant. The identification and reporting of fixed and variable cost behavior patterns is a major contribution that the management accountant can make to management decision making.

To measure benefits from operating decisions, the accountant uses the selling price of the items being produced. The difference between the average revenue per unit and the average variable cost per unit is the **contribution margin per unit.** To illustrate the concept of the contribution margin, let's assume that the Terry Company produces 10,000 units of a single product that sells for an average of $5.00 per unit. Variable cost to produce and sell the product is $3.00 per unit. Total fixed costs for production and selling are $15,000 per year. The selling price of $5.00 less the total variable cost of $3.00 gives a contribution margin of $2.00 per unit. The **total contribution margin** is 10,000 units × $2.00 per unit, or $20,000. The **contribution margin ratio** is $2.00 ÷ $5.00, or 40%.

The contribution margin approach assumes that the selling price per unit is constant over a range of activity and, therefore, that total revenue is proportional to volume. Total variable costs will also increase in proportion to volume. Thus, the total contribution margin is also proportional to volume.

TERRY COMPANY COMPARATIVE INCOME STATEMENTS				
	10,000 Units		15,000 Units	
Sales Revenue				
($5 per unit)	$50,000	100%	$75,000	100%
Variable Costs				
($3 per unit)	30,000	60%	45,000	60%
Contribution Margin				
($2 per unit)	$20,000	40%	$30,000	40%
Fixed Costs				
($15,000 per year)	15,000		15,000	
Income	$ 5,000		$15,000	

EXHIBIT 1–2
Comparative
contribution margin
income statements

We can see the contribution margin approach in the comparative income statements of the Terry Company presented in Exhibit 1–2. The income at 10,000 units is $5,000; at 15,000 units income is $15,000. This $10,000 increase in income with a 5,000-unit increase in sales volume is the result of 5,000 units of differential sales at $2.00 contribution margin per unit. The fixed costs are not relevant because they do not change with volume. The use of the contribution margin recognizes that both sales revenue and variable costs change in linear proportion to volume.

Much of this text is concerned with short-run, or operating, decisions. Chapters 2 and 3 deal specifically with defining and using fixed and variable costs in decisions. Chapters 4 through 8 focus on accounting systems that generate decision-making information—both historical and planned. In Chapters 9 and 10 we focus directly on pricing and production decisions.

RELEVANT BENEFITS AND COSTS FOR CAPACITY DECISIONS

Long-range decisions involve adding to or decreasing the productive capacity of the firm. Typically, long periods of time must elapse before the benefits of the decision are fully realized by the firm. This time element makes the time value of money a significant factor in long-range decisions. Money, like any other resource, has a cost. In long-range decisions this cost is significant; therefore accountants use cash inflow and cash outflow to measure benefits and costs.

From this perspective, the concepts of out-of-pocket and sunk costs are meaningful. An **out-of-pocket-cost** is one that requires an expenditure of cash as a result of a decision. The expenditure of cash has already been made for a **sunk cost**[3] and a current cash expenditure is not required. Out-of-pocket and

---

[3]The economist often uses the terms *fixed costs* and *sunk costs* interchangeably. In this text they have different meanings.

sunk costs are opposites. A sunk cost is a prior investment of cash resources; an out-of-pocket cost is a current or near-future cash expenditure.

Some decision makers assume that all variable costs are out-of-pocket costs and that all fixed costs are sunk costs. This is not so. The president's salary may be fixed, but it is still an out-of-pocket cost. The cost of supplies may be sunk because cash resources have already been expended in obtaining them, but it could be a variable cost. However, in most instances the costs of depreciation, depletion, and the amortization of intangibles are sunk costs. Likewise, in most instances the costs of material and production labor are out-of-pocket costs and are also variable. It is imperative that the decision maker keep in mind that the perspective of fixed and variable costs is different from the perspective of out-of-pocket and sunk costs. While at times they may appear synonymous, they are not the same view of cost.

A long-range decision must consider both the time value of money and the timing of the investment and recovery of cash. The long-range decision rule is that an investment decision is favorable if incremental benefits, measured by cash inflows directly attributable to the decision and adjusted for the time value of money, are at least equal to incremental costs, measured by cash outflows directly attributable to the decision and adjusted for the time value of money. The specific techniques of this analysis will be covered in detail in Chapter 11.

DECISIONS EXPRESSED THROUGH BUDGETS

As managers begin to select possible alternatives and collect data to facilitate their decisions, they are preparing a **tentative budget.** While they sort the decision alternatives (see Exhibit 1–3) leading to an ultimate selection, they rely upon a forecast of what they believe would happen if they made a certain decision. These forecasts are not final until there is a commitment to a specific decision. They are tentative budgets.

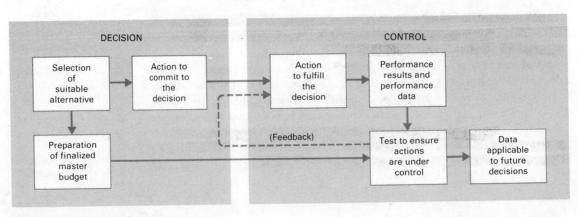

EXHIBIT 1–3   The control process

Budgets express management's plans in quantitative terms. Budgets show the probable impact upon the responsibility centers and the firm if plans are committed to action. A budget may be limited to a particular activity, as is an advertising budget or a capital additions budget. It may deal with total operations including expected income, expenses, and assets, or it may be in terms of anticipated cash flow, as in a cash budget.

The planning process begins to take final shape when all tentative budgets for the responsibility centers are integrated. Budgets for each individual decision ultimately must be combined into a coordinated whole called the **master budget.** The master budget expresses the anticipated total impact of all the responsibility centers' decisions upon revenues, expenses, assets, liabilities, and owners' equity. In this function the master budget is the principal coordinating vehicle for the firm's plans. A master budget is shown in Chapters 12 and 13.

The master budget also serves another important role. By requiring a formal, written commitment to coordinated decisions, it serves as a benchmark against which actual performance can be compared. This control function acts to ensure that plans and performance are congruent.

POST-DECISIONAL CONTROL STAGE

Control is the process of measuring, evaluating, and correcting actual performance to ensure that the firm's goals and plans are accomplished. Control presupposes the existence of plans. There is no way to know whether the firm is meeting its goals without a previous statement of what is desirable and some feedback on operating results.

PERFORMANCE DATA

The old adage, it's too late to shut the barn door after the horse has run away, is particularly applicable to the control process. A manager cannot control what is past. A manager may study the effects of past actions, but the focus should be to find ways to avoid unwanted actions in the future. The best control process a manager can install is one that forestalls deviations. The next best control process is one that detects deviations as they happen. The later the report of a need for correction is received after the actual event, the weaker the control system.

Exhibit 1–3 shows the sequence of the control process, which begins with selection of suitable alternatives, and expression of these plans in the form of a final budget. Comparing Exhibit 1–3 with Exhibit 1–1, we can see that the control process begins with the completion of the planning process. Once the desired alternatives have been chosen, there must be definitive action to commit the firm to the decision. Contracts are signed, employees hired, production scheduled, and raw materials purchased.

As these actions are taken, the firm begins to build performance data. Accounting, as a data base, is a major source of performance data. The control process evaluates actual performance by comparing it with the plans. This comparison ensures that actions are under control. Any deviations are communicated to management for corrective action. Simultaneously, a comparison of planned and actual performance serves as the beginning of the next planning process, and the cycle starts again. The control function of budgeting is shown in Chapters 12 and 13.

NONFINANCIAL CONTROLS

The preceding discussion may be misleading in that it focuses on quantified plans and controls. It is dangerous to assume that *all* plans are quantifiable into a master budget and that *all* performance data are financial in nature. Many activities are planned and controlled through nonfinancial data. The planning process (Exhibit 1–1) and the control process (Exhibit 1–3) are general statements applicable to both quantifiable and nonquantifiable control systems.

One broad class of nonfinancial planning and control data is composed of physical measures. These are particularly applicable at the lower organizational levels where materials are used, labor and services are consumed, machine hours are operated, ton-miles of freight are carried, kilowatt hours are consumed, units are produced per direct labor hour, customers are served, or employee turnover exists. The number of possible physical measures is almost infinite.

Many other aspects of crucial importance to the firm's existence cannot be expressed in financial terms. How do you measure, in dollars, an employee's morale or the value of a ''team'' attitude within a department? How do you measure the competence of an accountant in minimizing the company's tax liability? What quantitative measures can be used to assess the goodwill customers feel toward personnel? These questions show how difficult it is to establish quantitative plans and controls for *all* phases of business activities.

THE MANAGEMENT ACCOUNTANT'S RESPONSIBILITIES

The management accountant, often called the **controller,** is the manager of the accounting information used in decision planning and in the subsequent control of operations. The management accountant must bear in mind that different decisions require different data. Short-run production decisions require different data than long-run decisions do, and external reports require different data than do internal reports. Decisions affecting the total company, such as product lines to be produced, require more aggregate data than do decisions affecting the optimum use of a particular machine. The generation of different data for different decisions requires a high degree of flexibility.

The management accountant is also a decision maker and must therefore gather data applicable to others' decisions and data for his or her own use as well. The accounting system must be structured to meet both financial and management accounting requirements. The development of the data base consumes resources of the firm that could be used in other ways. Accounting is an economic activity requiring economic resources. As such, a good accounting system is one where the benefits of having the data exceed the cost of gathering it. Unless data generated by the accounting system are relevant, no effort should be expended in gathering them. Unfortunately, the determination of benefits from accounting data are vague and difficult to measure. An area called **information economics,** which is beyond the scope of this book, deals with this difficult topic of benefits and costs of accounting data.

SUMMARY

Management's role is to make decisions about how to use the firm's resources effectively and efficiently so the firm will have a satisfactory rate of return on its investment. These decisions can be classified as either long-range or short-range. Long-range decisions involve adding to or deducting from the firm's service potential. Because long-range decisions span a long period of time, the time value of money is important. The manager's long-range decision rule is to add to productive capacity whenever the cash inflows resulting from the decision, adjusted for the time value of money, are equal to or greater than the cash outflows resulting from the decision, adjusted for the time value of money.

Short-range decisions are concerned with how best to use existing capacity. They span a short time period, so the time value of money need not be considered. The accountant assumes that within the relevant range of activity both the revenue and variable costs are linear and that revenue minus variable costs is the contribution margin. The short-run decision rule that will maximize net income is, "Maximize the total contribution margin of the firm."

The process of planning focuses management's attention on needed decisions. Planning involves the determination of the firm's goals and the selection of specific courses of action to achieve these goals. The summary of management's plans is the master budget. The master budget serves as a way of coordinating the firm's plans and as a benchmark to control the effectiveness and efficiency of actual performance.

PROBLEMS AND CASES

1-1 *(Pricing Strategy).* The Dunn Corporation has the following projected sales volumes at each of three selling prices.

Selling Price	Sales in Units
$8	50,000
$7	140,000
$6	260,000

In addition, variable costs are $5 per unit and fixed costs are $140,000.

REQUIRED:

A. What price should be charged to maximize dollar sales?

B. What price should be charged to maximize profits?

C. Why do the answers for parts A and B differ?

1-2   *(Differential and Incremental Revenues and Costs).* The Scott Corporation prepared the following schedule.

Units	Variable Costs	Fixed Costs	Total Costs	Total Revenue
300	$300	$200	$ 500	$ 900
301	$301	$200	$ 501	$ 903
400	$400	$200	$ 600	$1,200
800	$800	$500	$1,300	$1,600

All units produced are sold.

REQUIRED:

A. At 300 units, what is the differential revenue from selling one more unit? What is the differential cost?

B. What is the difference in costs of a change from producing and selling 300 units to producing and selling 800 units? What is the difference in revenue? Is this an advantageous move to the firm? Explain.

C. As production increases to 800 units, the fixed costs rise and the revenue per unit decreases. What might be the causes for each of these occurrences? If these fixed costs rise, are they really fixed costs?

1-3   *(Decision Making Using Differential Revenues and Costs).* The Hammond Company has an idle production line after discontinuing a losing product. After careful study, the company has narrowed potential new products to two: Zeon and Trion. Only one of the two products may be manufactured on the production line. Revenue and cost estimates for the two products are presented below. In addition to the variable costs for each product, fixed costs associated with the production line are $500.

	ZEON			TRION	
Output in Units	Total Revenue	Total Variable Costs	Output in Units	Total Revenue	Total Variable Costs
50	$ 7,500	$ 6,000	2,000	$4,000	$3,000
60	$ 8,400	$ 6,600	2,100	$4,200	$2,520
70	$ 9,100	$ 7,000	2,200	$4,400	$2,200
80	$ 9,600	$ 7,200	2,300	$4,600	$2,990
90	$ 9,900	$ 9,000	2,400	$4,800	$3,840
100	$10,000	$11,000	2,500	$5,000	$4,750

REQUIRED:

What recommendations would you make to management about the production and sale of Zeon and Trion?

1-4 *(Long- and Short-run Decisions).* Indicate whether the following are long-range or short-range decisions. Give the reasons for your choice.

L 1. A manufacturing company is trying to decide whether or not plant expansion is economically justifiable.

S 2. A wholesaler is considering a decrease in selling price to regain lost markets. Competitors have increased their share of the market.

L 3.S The unemployment rate has increased substantially. The state legislature is trying to decide whether to create jobs through a park renovation project.

L 4. Technological advancements in new equipment will drastically decrease production costs. A factory manager is trying to decide whether to purchase the new equipment and change production methods.

S 5. An analysis of last period's sales shows that some products are declining in sales volume while others are showing growth. The marketing manager is trying to decide which products should be advertised.

L 6. The price of feed grain has tripled in the past year. A chicken farmer is trying to decide whether to sell his flock or continue to produce eggs.

S 7 L The profit picture looks good for the year. Sales have risen and costs have remained stable, but the increased production has caused a drain on cash. The board of directors is trying to decide how much in cash dividends can be paid without placing the firm in a dangerously low cash position.

S 8. Demand for the company's product has fallen almost to zero. The president is trying to decide whether to shut down the plant until demand increases or another product is developed.

L 9. A research institute has found a cure for a disease. The board of trustees is now considering new goals and challenges.

L 10. The city council of a small town is attempting to decide whether to grant a permit for a new regional shopping center.

1-5   *(Long- and Short-run Goals).* You have just accepted a position as assistant manager of the Brookside Neighborhood Health Center. You will be responsible for nonmedical administration and financial management. The center was organized four months ago to serve the health needs of a low-income neighborhood including a public housing project. About 75% of the family heads in the housing project are employed, but many have low incomes.

   The center was started with a federal grant and has provided health care for slightly more than two months. The grant will reimburse the center for service provided to low-income families not covered by Medicaid or Medicare.

   On your first day of work you are notified by the bank that the center's account is overdrawn. You find that the financial records are limited to a desk drawer full of documents supporting the transactions and a checkbook that has not been reconciled. The federal grant requires a financial report in two months, including cost and utilization data to support the billing rate.

REQUIRED:

A. What should you do? Your answer should cover actions aimed at both the short-range and long-range concerns of the center.

B. State the primary goal of the center as completely as you can.

1-6   *(Goals and Performance Assessment).* The Mayor of Midline City formed a Citizens' Task Force to study the operations of the city and make suggestions for better service to the people. He was particularly interested in being able to improve services.

   The Citizens' Task Force suggested the following measures of accomplishment for the fire department.

   Reduction of fires in the city.

   Reduction of losses from fires.

   Reduction of fire-related injuries or deaths.

   Modernization of fire equipment.

   Reduction of fire insurance rates in the city.

   Improvement in fire prevention programs in the area.

   Presentation of fire prevention programs through the schools.

   Development of a first-aid unit for the district.

   Reduction of number of fund-raising events needed to supplement funding from taxes.

   Intensification of training for fire combat units.

   Expansion of fire permit and inspection service.

   The fire chief feels that the list is confusing, conflicting, and excessive. He has asked your help in ranking these performance measures and preparing a statement of objectives for the fire department.

REQUIRED:

A. Rank these performance measures in *your* order of priority.

B. State each performance measure as an objective that will provide specific targets for the fire department. (You will not be able to provide specific quantities or dates; therefore use *x* amount, etc.)

1-7   *(Long- and Short-run Goals).* Samuel Johnson founded his business many years ago and through hard work has expanded it to include a manufacturing plant, three retail outlets, and a consulting branch. He now owns 75% of the outstanding stock and acts as general manager. Because of his many years of experience, Sam has a "feel" for the business. He knows approximately how the firm is doing throughout the year. When he feels production is not acceptable, he goes down to the manufacturing department and applies pressure on the employees. Sam believes that each time he purchases a new piece of equipment production should become more efficient and monthly output should increase. Unfortunately, these gains have not occurred.

   As the firm has grown, Sam has found it increasingly difficult to keep track of what everyone is doing and where everything is kept. Errors have begun to increase. To make matters worse, the lease on his main retail outlet is about to expire, and it cannot be renewed. As a final straw, an economic slump has reduced sales by 20%. Sam obviously has several problems and is faced with some decisions, both long-run and short-run.

REQUIRED:

A. Discuss Sam's methods of managing the firm up to this point.

B. Discuss some decisions, both long-run and short-run, that Sam should be concerned about.

C. What steps would you recommend that Sam take to ensure that his decisions are made wisely?

1-8   *(Determination of Unit Costs).* The Nipper Company manufactures a barking toy dog. Their income statement for 19X7, when they sold 90,000 units, was as shown in the box. During the planning cycle for 19X8, management forecasted a sales volume of 110,000 units.

REQUIRED:

A. Prepare a profit plan (budgeted income statement) for 19X8.

B. Calculate:

   1. The contribution margin per unit.

   2. The differential cost per unit.

   3. The differential revenue per unit.

   4. The average cost per unit at a sales volume of 90,000 units.

5. The average cost per unit at a sales volume of 110,000 units.

6. Explain why the average cost per unit in items *4* and *5* differ.

THE NIPPER COMPANY
INCOME STATEMENT
For the Year 19X7

Sales		$360,000
Variable costs:		
Materials	$54,000	
Labor	90,000	
Sales commissions	36,000	
Total variable costs		180,000
Contribution margin		$180,000
Fixed costs:		
Rent on building	$30,000	
Depreciation of machinery	45,000	
Administrative salaries	65,000	
Total fixed costs		140,000
Income		$ 40,000

1-9 *(Financial Statements and Decisions by Financing Agencies).* The Loss Leader Sales Company had the financial statements shown at the bottom of this page and on the top of page 21.

Management is anticipating a 100% expansion of sales activity, which would require an additional $30,000 in capital. This capital could be raised either through increased borrowing or through the sale of capital stock.

REQUIRED:

A. What data included in the financial statements might a bank loan officer use? What additional data would the loan officer likely want?

B. What data included in the financial statements might be used by an investor in the company's stock? What additional data would an investor likely want?

BALANCE SHEET
December 31, 19X6

Assets:		Liabilities:	
Cash	$ 5,000	Accounts payable	$10,000
Accounts receivable	20,000	Notes payable	15,000
Inventory	10,000		$25,000
Equipment (net)	15,000	Owners' equity:	
Building (net)	35,000	Common stock	$40,000
		Retained earnings	20,000
			$60,000
Total assets	$85,000	Total liabilities and owners' equity	$85,000

INCOME STATEMENT
Year Ending December 31, 19X6

Sales		$80,000
Cost of sales		20,000
Gross margin		$60,000
Operating expenses:		
Administrative expense	$20,000	
Selling expense	5,000	
Depreciation	5,000	
Other	10,000	
Total operating expenses		40,000
Income before taxes		$20,000
Income tax (25%)		5,000
Net income after taxes		$15,000

1-10 *(Data Needs for Decision Making).* The Black Manufacturing Company achieved a technological breakthrough in one of its products. With a limited capital investment, it could double the productive capacity of the main plant while reducing production costs by about one-fourth. The implementation of this breakthrough will require that the plant be closed for about three months. Because Black Manufacturing Company exists in a highly competitive market, the sooner it starts this new process, the bigger the jump it will have on its competitors, who are also working to perfect the same technique.

At this time it is impossible to determine the long-run environmental impact, but there is some evidence to suggest that it may be substantial. To complicate matters further, if Black's competitors implement this new process and Black does not, many of Black's sales will be lost and it will have to lay off 350 to 400 workers. Because unemployment is already high in this area, members of the city council are pressuring Mr. Jason Fleece, Black's owner, to proceed with the new process and worry about the societal consequences later.

REQUIRED:

A. What quantitative and nonquantitative factors should Mr. Fleece consider in his decision?

B. Discuss what accounting data he might need to help him in his decision.

C. How would you go about helping Mr. Fleece in the selection of an alternative from among his possible courses of action?

1-11 *(Individual and Company Goal Congruence.)* Duval, Inc. is a large publicly held corporation that is well known throughout the United States for its products. The corporation has always had good profit margins and excellent earnings. However, Duval has experienced a leveling of sales and a reduced market share in the past two years which has resulted in a stabilization of profits rather than growth. Despite these trends, the firm has maintained an excellent cash and short-term investment position. The president has called a meeting of the treasurer and the vice-presidents for sales and production to develop alternative strategies for improving Duval's performance. The four individuals form the nucleus of a well-organized management team that has worked together for several years to bring success to Duval, Inc.

The sales vice-president suggests that sales levels can be improved by presenting the company's product in a more attractive and appealing package. He also recommends that advertising be increased, and that the current price be maintained. This latter step would have the effect of a price decrease because the prices of most other competing products are rising.

The treasurer is skeptical of maintaining the present price when others are increasing prices because it will curtail revenues, unless this policy provides a competitive advantage. She also points out that the repackaging will increase costs in the near future, because of the start-up costs of a new packing process. She does not favor increasing advertising outright because she is doubtful of the short-run benefit.

The sales vice-president replies that increased, or at least redirected, advertising is necessary to promote the price stability and to take advantage of the new packaging; the combination would provide the company with a competitive advantage. The president adds that the advertising should be studied closely to determine the type of advertising to be used—television, radio, newspaper, magazine. In addition, if television is used, attention must be directed to the type of programs to be sponsored—children's, family, sporting events, news specials, etc.

The production vice-president suggests several possible production improvements, such as a systems study of the manufacturing process to identify changes in the work flow that would cut costs. He suggests that operating costs could be further reduced by the purchase of new equipment. The product could be improved by employing a better grade of raw materials and by engineering changes in the fabrication of the product. When queried by the president on the impact of the proposed changes, the production vice-president indicates that the primary benefit would be product performance, but that appearance and safety would also be improved. The sales vice-president and treasurer comment that this would result in increased sales.

The treasurer notes that all the production proposals would increase immediate costs, and this could result in lower profits. If profit performance is going to be improved, the price structure should be examined closely. She recommends that the current level of capital expenditures be maintained unless substantial cost savings can be obtained.

The treasurer further believes that expenditures for research and development should be decreased, reasoning that previous outlays have not prevented a decrease in Duval's share of the market. The production vice-president agrees that the research and development activities have not proven profitable, but thinks that this is because the research effort was applied in the wrong area.

The sales vice-president cautions against any drastic reductions because the packaging change will provide only a temporary advantage in the market; consequently, more effort will have to be devoted to product development.

Focusing on the use of liquid assets and the present high yields on securities, the treasurer suggests that the firm's profitability can be improved by shifting funds from the currently held short-term marketable securities to longer-term, higher-yield securities. She further states that cost reductions would provide more funds for investments. She recognizes that the restructuring of the investments from short-term to long-term would hamper flexibility.

In his summarizing comments, the president observes that they have a good start and the ideas provide some excellent alternatives. He states, "I think we ought to develop these ideas further and consider other ramifications. For instance, what effect would new equipment and the systems study have on the labor force? Shouldn't we also consider the environmental impact of any plant and product change? We want to appear as a leader in our industry—not a follower.

"I note that none of you considered increased community involvement through such groups as the Chamber of Commerce and the United Fund.

"The factors you mentioned plus those additional points all should be considered as we reach a decision on the final course of action we will follow."

REQUIRED:

A. Discuss the implied corporate goals being expressed.
B. Compare the type of goals discussed above with the corporate goal(s) postulated by the economic theory of the firm.

(CMA adapted)

1-12 *(Organization and Strategy of Budgeting).* Springfield Corporation operates on a calendar year basis. It begins the annual budgeting process in late August when the president establishes targets for the total dollar sales and net income before taxes for the next year.

The sales target is given to the Marketing Department where the marketing manager formulates a sales budget by product line in both units and dollars. From this budget, sales quotas by product line in units and dollars are established for each of the corporation's sales districts.

The marketing manager also estimates the cost of the marketing activities required to support the target sales volume, and prepares a tentative marketing expense budget.

The executive vice-president uses the sales and profit targets, the sales budget by product line, and the tentative marketing expense budget to determine the dollar amounts that can be devoted to manufacturing and corporate office expense. The executive vice-president prepares the budget for corporate expenses and then forwards to the Production Department the product line sales budget in units and the total dollar amount that can be devoted to manufacturing.

The production manager meets with the factory managers to develop a manufacturing plan that will produce the required units when needed within the cost constraints set by the executive vice-president. The budgeting process usually comes to a halt at this point because the Production Department does not consider the financial resources allocated to be adequate.

When this standstill occurs, the vice-president of finance, the executive vice-president, the marketing manager, and the production manager meet together to determine the final budgets for each of the areas. This normally results in a modest increase in the total amount available for manufacturing costs while the marketing expense and corporate office expense budgets are cut. The total sales and net income figures proposed by the president are seldom changed. Although the participants are seldom pleased with the compromise, these budgets are final. Each executive then develops a new detailed budget for the operations in his or her area.

None of the areas has achieved its budget in recent years. Sales often run below the target. When budgeted sales are not achieved, each area is expected to cut costs so that the president's profit target can still be met. However, the profit target is seldom met because costs are not cut enough. In fact, costs often run above the original budget in all functional areas. The president is disturbed that Springfield has not been able to meet the sales and profit targets. He hired a consultant with considerable experience with companies in Springfield's industry. The consultant reviewed the budgets for the past four years. He concluded that the product line sales budgets were reasonable, and the cost and expense budgets were adequate for the budgeted sales and production levels.

REQUIRED:

A. Discuss how the budgeting process as employed by Springfield Corporation contributes to the failure to achieve the president's sales and profit targets.

B. Suggest how Springfield Corporation's budgeting process could be revised to correct the problems.

C. Should the functional areas be expected to cut their costs when sales volume falls below budget? Explain your answer.

(CMA adapted)

1-13 The Retired Teachers Association (RTA) had as one of its primary goals the establishment of an active plan for its members' retirement where, as older people, the retired teachers could continue to contribute to the community while also living within their means. As one vehicle of creating an active retirement the RTA directors decided to build a retirement home for its members. The Eastside Home Association (EHA) was established by the RTA to serve as the operational organization to construct and manage the home. The by-laws of EHA stated simply: "Housing facilities operated by the corporation shall be open to all aged and infirm persons, and not be restricted to members, but the trustees may give preference to members of the RTA in lists of occupancy."

The organizational structure of the EHA placed control of operations with the Board of Trustees. The president and secretary of the board were authorized to "perform such duties in the management of the property and the affairs of the corporation as are ordinarily performed by the president of a corporation, and as otherwise prescribed by the trustees." The decision-making power was placed in the hands of the Board of Trustees with the purpose of facilitating the operation of the EHA. It allowed the Board of Trustees to formulate plans, make decisions, and activate those decisions without having formally to poll the membership.

The EHA Board of Trustees applied for funding for the retirement home through Housing and Urban Development (HUD), specifically Section 231. The requirements of Section 231 funding were written loosely and would have fit well with the objectives of EHA to build affordable housing for its members. One of the advantages of Section 231 funds was that they were not restricted by low-income requirements.

The Section 231 program did place some restrictions on EHA, however. In terms of possible tenants, Section 231 stated that whereas the development of the rental housing was to be primarily for the elderly and handicapped, they would not have exclusive rights of occupancy. It also stated that there could be no income requirements for tenants and that there were to be no restrictions due to race, creed, color, national origin, or sex. In terms of construction and financial requirements, HUD specified that the home had to conform to their property standards, that it must involve new construction, that HUD would restrict the profits of contractors to 10%, and that HUD would retain the rights to regulate rents, rates of return, and methods of operations.

In response to the application HUD determined the EHA to be insufficiently knowledgeable in construction and operations of a retirement home. In addition, HUD required an initial cash outlay of $150,000 to $200,000, which was far in excess of the $30,000 EHA had raised. This opened to question the financial stability of EHA. HUD officials also expressed doubt about EHA capabilities of supporting the requirement of equality of treatment for all elderly and handicapped of low-income status without regard to their ability to pay.

Stalemated in their funding attempts and uncertain about how to continue, the Board of Trustees contacted United Marketing. United Marketing had experience with HUD through the operation of several retirement homes and associated experience in the operation of condominiums and office buildings. United Marketing saw their role as a service organization providing operational expertise. United Marketing assured EHA board members that all of their operations would be in strict adherence to HUD regulations regarding operations and tenancy. United Marketing would use its own operating policies, financial controls, employment policies, and follow their established business practices. A contract with United Marketing would allow EHA board members to avoid direct involvement in the day-to-day operations. Rather, the trustees would act as broad policy setters who would review United Marketing operations. Performance evaluations, financial analysis, statements of financial positions, and cash analysis would be provided by United Marketing to the board at their prescribed meetings.

With a tentative agreement with United Marketing and new financial data, EHA reapplied to HUD for funding. However, federal program cutbacks had eliminated Section 231 funding, and Section 202 funding was the only federal funding available. The Section 202 funding requirements were very detailed as to the mode of operation, stipulation for tenancy, and financial backing of the requesting organization. Because this program was primarily a subsidized rent program, HUD had a larger vested interest and concern over the use of monies. HUD requirements included certified financial statements, a comprehensive management plan for the operation of the retirement home, periodic on-site inspections by HUD to ensure compliance, submission of all contractual agreements of the mortgagor including agreements with the marketing agent, and formal agreements to take on as charity all eligible people complete with plans showing how this support would come from the operating funds of the retirement home.

Because this was the only funding available, and because of their commitment to the retired teaching professionals, the Board of Trustees decided to proceed with the building of the retirement home by using Section 202 funding. With an approved commitment from HUD for $4.5 million, EHA was ready to enter into the final negotiation stages for construction and operation of the retirement home. The requirements imposed by HUD, coupled with the contractual requirements of United Marketing, formed the basic operating structure of the Hutchinson House. In a factual sense, EHA involvement was not so much purposely designed as it was what was left after the sponsoring organizations applied their constraints. Before completing the final negotiations, the Board of Trustees called a meeting to review the progress to date and to adopt policy statements for the future. The following agenda was proposed:

1. Evaluate the success of EHA and RTA in meeting their original goals.
2. What level of involvement in the project should EHA and RTA have in this project? Explain.
3. What new Board policies, if any, should EHA develop?

chapter **2**

DETERMINING COST BEHAVIOR PATTERNS

Many factors cause changes in costs and hence in profits. Costs change because of inflationary trends in the economy, changes in the labor market, technological advances, or changes in size or quality of production facilities. Each of these represents a unique, sporadic change. Regular, recurring events also cause costs to change. One of the most significant causes of variations in costs is a change in the volume of activity. In this chapter we will study how the accountant defines and determines which costs are variable and therefore change with volume, and which costs are fixed and therefore remain constant over volume changes. Then in the next chapter we will study how knowledge of fixed and variable costs helps in understanding cost-volume-profit interrelationships and how the contribution margin can be used in making operating decisions.

DEFINITIONS OF COST BEHAVIOR PATTERNS

VARIABLE COSTS

Variable costs are costs that vary in total dollar amount in direct proportion to changes in volume. Increases in production output result in proportionate increases in variable costs. Raw materials used in production typically are variable costs. If raw materials cost $1.00 per unit of product produced, it would take a total cost of $1.00 to produce one unit, $2.00 to produce two units, $6.00 to produce six units, and $12 to produce twelve units.

Although the total variable cost increases proportionately to volume, the variable cost per unit of output is constant. Exhibit 2–1 is a graphic presentation of a variable cost that increases at the rate of $1.00 per unit of output. Exhibit 2–2 shows this same cost from a different perspective—that of cost per unit. When the total dollar amount of a cost varies in direct proportion to changes in volume, then the unit cost is constant per unit of production.

FIXED COSTS

Fixed costs are costs whose total dollar amount is unaffected by changes in volume. In the short run they remain the same regardless of changes in production output. For example, assume that plant maintenance is contracted with an outside firm at $600 per month, or $7,200 per year. Regardless of the plant output, this cost will not change. The greater the plant output, the lower the maintenance cost *per unit* of output. If the firm produces 2 units per month, maintenance cost will be $300 per unit. If the firm produces 6 units per month, the cost per unit will be $100. Thus, fixed costs are constant in total as volume levels change, but vary per unit inversely with changes in volume. Exhibit 2–3

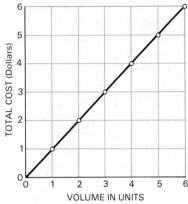

EXHIBIT 2–1
Total variable cost

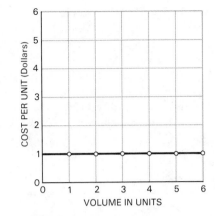

EXHIBIT 2–2
Variable cost per unit

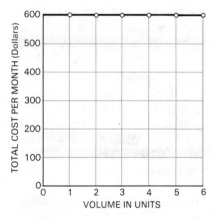

EXHIBIT 2–3
Total fixed cost

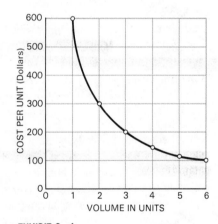

EXHIBIT 2–4
Fixed cost per unit

shows a total fixed cost of $600 per month. Exhibit 2–4 shows the same fixed cost from a cost-per-unit perspective.

When looking at costs in terms of their behavior patterns (how they change with changes in volume), the time period is held constant. Ordinarily this time span is one year, although it could be any time period selected by management. This consideration puts limitations on the interpretations of fixed and variable costs. Let's assume that a firm has a machine with a depreciable cost of $1,000 and a useful life of five years. We can see the effect of the assumption of a constant time period when considering cost variability. Management is considering the two alternative depreciation methods of straight-line and sum-of-the-year's digits in accounting for the machine. Exhibit 2–5 shows the annual depreciation charge for each of these assumptions.

	STRAIGHT-LINE DEPRECIATION		SUM-OF-THE-YEARS' DIGITS DEPRECIATION	
Year	Annual Proportion of Total Cost	Annual Depreciation	Annual Proportion of Total Cost	Annual Depreciation
1	1/5	$200	5/15	$333
2	1/5	$200	4/15	$267
3	1/5	$200	3/15	$200
4	1/5	$200	2/15	$133
5	1/5	$200	1/15	$ 67

EXHIBIT 2–5
Comparative
depreciation schedules

In Year 1 the *fixed cost* would be $200 under the straight-line depreciation method, whereas under the sum-of-the-years'-digits method the *fixed cost* would be $333. Since the amount of depreciation is not related to the volume of production, the costs from either schedule would be fixed although they change from year to year. Thus, costs are fixed or variable only in relationship to volume changes within a given time period.

SEMIVARIABLE COSTS

Not all costs are perfectly fixed or perfectly variable. Many costs change with changes in volume, but not in direct proportion. These costs are called **semivariable costs.** They have both fixed and variable cost attributes. Some people call then **semifixed,** although *semivariable* is more commonly used.

Among the factors that can make costs semivariable are the following:

1. It is frequently necessary to have a minimum organizational structure or to consume a minimum quantity of supplies or services in order to maintain productive readiness. Beyond this minimum cost, which is fixed, additional costs may vary with changes in volume.

2. The accounting classification system may group fixed and variable costs together. For example, by accumulating all insurance premiums into an account entitled "Insurance Expense," the accounting system may group together various types of policy premium costs having different behavior patterns.

3. Often production factors are not divisible into infinitely small units. For example, moving from a single-shift to a double-shift production schedule will cause some costs to change in stairstep fashion.

In general, there are three broad classes of semivariable costs. Perhaps the easiest to visualize is the **stairstep cost** shown in Exhibit 2–6. Supervisory

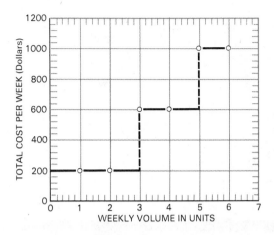

EXHIBIT 2–6
A stairstep cost

salaries often behave in this way. One supervisor may supervise 10 production line workers. As the number of workers increases because of increased production volume, another supervisor is added.

Stairstep semivariable costs further illustrate the nature of fixed costs and how they differ from other cost behavior patterns. One way to think about fixed costs is that they are stairstepped costs. For example, assume that a company has a machine with a maximum capacity of 6,000 units per year. The firm will have to buy a new machine to increase production beyond 6,000 units per year. In this sense, all fixed costs are stairstepped.

Exhibit 2–7 shows two different cost patterns. Both Costs A and B vary with changes in volume. Cost B, however, varies over smaller incremental changes in volume than does Cost A. If during the coming year the company plans to produce between 2,000 and 6,000 units, Cost A would be considered fixed and Cost B would be semivariable. If the company's volume ranges between 2,000 and 10,000 units, both costs would be semivariable. Both costs would be fixed if the production plans were between 3,001 and 5,000 units.

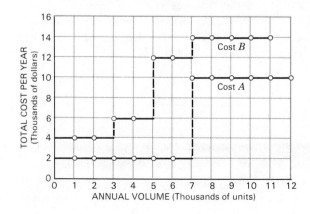

EXHIBIT 2–7
Comparison of two
stairstepped costs

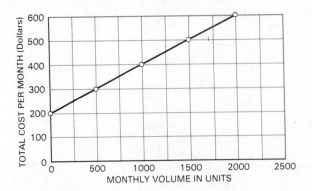

EXHIBIT 2–8
A mixed cost

This illustration shows that costs can be viewed as fixed or variable only within a volume range. Beyond that activity range it is likely that the fixed and variable cost patterns will change. Accountants call this the relevant range of activity.

Another type of semivariable cost is one that includes both a fixed and a variable component. Maintenance is an example of such a cost. If the company produces nothing, maintenance will still be required. As the volume of production increases, the amount of required maintenance will increase. The common name of a cost with both fixed and variable cost attributes is **mixed cost.** A mixed cost is shown in Exhibit 2–8. In this illustration the fixed component is $200 and the variable costs increase at the rate of $.20 per unit of volume.

Other costs change with production volume, but in a nonlinear way. Costs such as utilities often increase at a decreasing rate. For example, assume that a manufacturing process requires one gallon of water per unit of output, and that the cost per gallon of water is $.03 for consumption between 1,000 and 3,000 gallons; $.02 for consumption between 3,001 and 5,000 gallons; $.01 for consumption between 5,001 and 10,000 gallons; and $.005 per gallon for consumption over 10,000 gallons. This cost is shown graphically in Exhibit 2–9.

A few costs increase at an increasing rate. These costs are really fines and penalties. Examples include demurrage charges on rail cars, pollution fines, and in some instances, the costs of labor. One effect of the energy crisis is to shift the semivariable costs of energy from costs that decrease per unit with increased usage to costs that increase per unit as usage increases.

DETERMINING FIXED AND VARIABLE COSTS

Fixed and variable are specific ways of viewing costs. However, the typical accounting system does not record or classify costs as fixed or variable. Traditionally, accounting summarizes costs by the nature of the expenditure. For

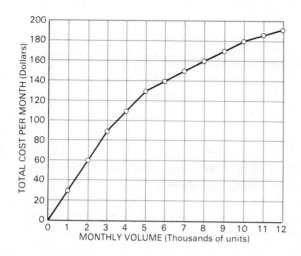

EXHIBIT 2–9
Curvilinear
semivariable cost

example, when an invoice for the purchase of insurance on the factory is received, the amount is recorded in overhead as factory insurance, not as a fixed or variable cost. In a very real sense the classification of costs into their fixed and variable components requires a special study above and beyond routine accounting procedures. It is a different perspective of costs that requires different measuring tools.

CHOOSING A VOLUME MEASURE

The first step in measuring the variability of costs is to find a suitable measure of volume or activity. When only one type of product is produced, it is possible to express volume in terms of physical units. However, when a company produces many different products, it may be difficult to find a single measure of volume. The following considerations are important when selecting a volume measure.

1. The unit of measurement must measure fluctuations in the activity level, or volume, which cause costs to vary. There must be a definite, positive relationship between the incurrence of costs and the activity measure.

2. The volume measure should be simple and easy to understand. Thus, measures such as sales dollars, labor hours, labor dollars, units of product, and machine hours are particularly attractive.

3. The activity figures should be attainable without undue additional clerical expense. The cost of gathering accounting information must be kept in mind.

MEASURING VARIATIONS OF COST WITH VOLUME

There are three widely practiced ways of determining cost behavior patterns: inspection of contracts, engineering cost estimates, and analysis of past cost behavior patterns. The first two are prospective in that they consider what cost patterns will be in the future. The last is retrospective in that it deals with past cost patterns.

INSPECTION OF CONTRACTS

The most intuitive method of determining whether a cost is fixed or variable is to examine the production activities and existing contracts. Some costs are fixed or variable by their nature, and their behavior patterns are readily determined. For example, depreciation by any method except the units-of-output basis would be fixed for any one year. Many salaries, such as the president's, are fixed. At the same time, there are many costs that are inherently variable. Costs such as raw materials and production labor paid on a piecework wage plan are variable. A special warning is necessary. The examination must cut beneath the surface and seek the basic contract. *All* depreciation charges are *not* necessarily fixed, and *all* workers' salaries are *not* necessarily variable.

ENGINEERING COST ESTIMATES

Where the contracts are unclear or where there is no past experience to use in estimating cost variability, there is no recourse but to make estimates. The technical expertise of industrial engineers can be drawn upon to estimate the quantities of materials, labor, and production facilities needed to produce a new product or to estimate the behavior patterns of many costs. Work measurement techniques can provide reliable estimates of some fixed and variable costs. As actual production takes place and a base of experience is developed, refinements can be made and more objective methods used to examine the cost behavior patterns. This process not only increases the reliability of the cost behavior patterns, but also allows an after-the-fact measure of the accuracy of engineering cost estimates.

ANALYSIS OF PAST COST BEHAVIOR PATTERNS

Past data can provide empirical evidence of cost behavior patterns. Although past experience may not always be the best guide, it can be useful. The analysis of experience assumes that future cost behavior will be like past cost behavior. Where this assumption seems justified, there are systematic ways of determining how costs have varied with volume.

Earlier, variable costs were defined as costs that vary proportionately with volume. Underlying this definition is a linear, or straight-line assumption of the relationship between cost and volume. As long as this simplifying assumption is realistic, the relationship will apply to any volume level.

In order to measure the cost–volume relationship from past data, the accountant fits a straight line to the data. We may fit a straight line to any set of two or more points. The mathematical statement of a straight line is the equation $y_c = a + b(x)$ where:

y_c = Total cost at a specified volume

a = Amount of cost where the straight line intercepts the cost axis at the zero activity level (total fixed cost)

b = Amount of change in cost with a change in volume or the rate of slope in a straight line (average variable cost per unit of activity)

x = Measure of activity level (volume)

This equation may be illustrated as follows:

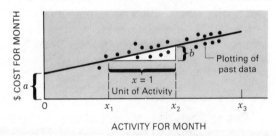

The equation allows us to describe the behavior of individual costs and sum them into one pattern of total costs. For example, a variable cost of $1.00 per direct labor hour would be expressed by the formula $y_c = \$0 + \$1.00(x)$, and graphed as

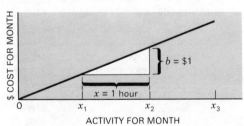

A fixed cost of $1000 per month would be expressed as $y_c = \$1,000 + \$0(x)$, and graphed as

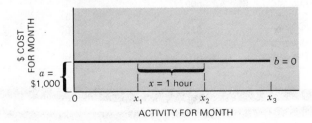

A mixed cost that includes both a fixed and a variable cost component, such as $2,500 per month fixed cost and a variable cost of $.20 per direct labor hour, would be expressed as $y_c = \$2,500 + \$.20(x)$ and graphed as

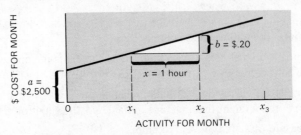

Since the volume measure on each of the three costs is direct labor hours, it is possible to add them together:

$$y_c = \$0 \qquad + \$1.00(x)$$
$$y_c = \$1,000 + \$0 \quad (x)$$
$$\underline{y_c = \$2,500 + \$\ .20(x)}$$
$$y_c \quad\ \$3,500 + \$1.20(x)$$

The formula for the total of the individual costs is $y_c = \$3,500 + \$1.20(x)$. This can be used to estimate total costs at any volume level inside the relevant range of activity.

To illustrate the separation of past cost data into fixed and variable costs, let's assume that an examination of the accounting records for the past year's maintenance costs of the Clark Manufacturing Company provides cost and volume information as shown in the accompanying tabulation.

	Hours of Activity	Total Cost of Maintenance
January	100	$185
February	150	$255
March	300	$258
April	400	$300
May	600	$350
June	700	$390
July	800	$430
August	500	$344
September	300	$251
October	300	$265
November	200	$233
December	600	$362

From these data we can see that in general maintenance costs increase as activity increases and fall as activity decreases. However, it is extremely difficult to draw an accurate mental image of this relationship when the data are presented in this form.

There are three general methods of fitting a straight line to these past data: the scattergraph, which relies on a visual fitting; the high-low point method, which fits a line to two points of data; and regression analysis, which statistically fits a line to the observations.

Scattergraph Estimates. **Scattergraph estimates** are made by plotting actual cost experiences at the various volume levels on graph paper and then fitting a line by visual inspection. The scattergraph allows the drawing of a mental image of the relationship. Exhibit 2–10 shows the data for the Clark Manufacturing Company plotted on graph paper. The horizontal axis (x axis) represents the volume, measured by hours of activity, and the vertical axis (y axis) represents the total cost of maintenance. The graph shows the general relationship of the total cost of maintenance to the hours of activity and allows visual examination to reveal unusual observations as well as nonlinear patterns.

The simplest way to fit a line on the scattergraph is to draw a line from visual inspection so that about half the dots lie above the line and half lie below the line. The point where the "fitted" line intersects the cost axis (vertical axis) is the estimate of the fixed costs designated by a. In this case fixed costs are estimated at approximately $160. Variable costs may be determined at any given activity level by subtracting fixed costs from total costs on the line at that activity level. The variable cost per unit (b) of activity (x) is determined by dividing the total variable cost by the measure of activity at the selected level. For example, at 560 hours of activity, the total cost estimate on the line is $350. Subtracting the fixed cost estimate of $160 from the $350 total cost provides a variable cost

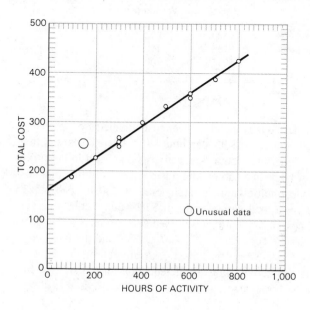

EXHIBIT 2–10
Scattergraph to
determine fixed and
variable cost
components

of $190. Dividing this $190 by the activity measure ($190 ÷ 560 hours) provides the variable cost of $.339 per hour.

A closer examination of the data on the scattergraph reveals that the February costs of $255 at the activity level of 150 hours seem out of line with the other costs. Something unusual happened that month. Perhaps extraordinary repairs were incurred, or the company made major repairs before the activity increase during summer months. Certainly, the unusually high cost calls for further analysis. If the $225 is considered abnormal, it could be excluded from the analysis of cost variability. Then, when the company forecasts February costs, it can consider the "abnormality" as a separate issue.

High-Low Point Estimates. The **high-low point** method of segregating fixed and variable costs uses only the highest and lowest volumes and their related costs to determine a straight-line relationship between costs and volume. It is the easiest way to relate past cost patterns objectively. The highest and lowest activity levels are isolated, along with their related costs. The change between the high and low levels of activity is divided into the change in cost to provide the measure of variable cost per unit of activity. The variable rate is then used to determine the total variable costs at either the high or low activity level. Finally, the variable costs are subtracted from the total costs to arrive at fixed costs. For example, for the Clark Manufacturing Company, the lowest activity level was 100 hours when the cost was $185; the highest activity level was 800 hours when the cost was $430. The differences in costs and volume for the high-low point method would be

	Costs	Volume (Activity)
Highest (July)	$430	800 hours
Lowest (January)	$185	100 hours
Difference	$245	700 hours

The variable cost per hour is the change in costs divided by the change in volume ($245 ÷ 700 hours) or $.35 per hour. The fixed costs are then estimated by multiplying either the high or low activity, expressed in hours, by the variable rate ($.35 per hour) and subtracting this product from the total cost at that level. For example, multiplying the high level of 800 hours by $.35 variable cost per hour gives a total variable cost of $280. Subtracting this variable cost from the total cost of $430 provides a fixed cost estimate of $150. At the 100-hour level the variable costs are $35 (100 × $.35), and the fixed costs are again $150 ($185 − $35). Notice that fixed costs are determined by substituting the variable rate and activity level in the equation for the straight line and solving for fixed costs. For example,

$$y_c = a + b(x)$$
$$\$430 = a + \$.35(800)$$
$$a = \$430 - \$280$$
$$a = \$150$$

The high-low point method of segregating fixed and variable costs is simple and easy to use, but it does have some weaknesses. It assumes that the cost and patterns at the highest and lowest points of activity are typical of other cost–volume experiences. In our example, the answer would differ considerably if the costs at the 150-hour activity level had been used in lieu of those at the 100-hour level. Judgment should be exercised to select a representative low and a representative high point. In spite of these weaknesses, the high-low method does have an apparent objectivity that is not assured in the scattergraph method.

Statistical Regression Analysis. Statistical regression analysis is a more sophisticated and reliable method of estimating fixed and variable costs than either the scattergraph or the high-low method. **Regression analysis** is a systematic way of determining whether the y values (costs) are related to the x values (volume measures).[1] The method of regression analysis using the least-squares approach provides two mathematical properties that are missing in the lines drawn by inspection or high-low methods. First, the algebraic sums of the positive and negative deviations from the fitted line equal zero. Second, the sum of the squares of these deviations is less than the sum of the squared vertical deviations from any other line.

The method of least squares uses two equations to determine the a value (fixed cost) and the b value (variable rate). These equations are[2]

$$b = \frac{\Sigma xy - (\Sigma x\, \Sigma y/n)}{\Sigma x^2 - [(\Sigma x)^2/n]}$$

---

[1] It should be pointed out that the accountant assigns a cause-and-effect relationship to regression analysis. The accountant says, in essence, that the cost is the "effect" resulting from the "cause" of volume. The pure statistician, on the other hand, is not willing to assign cause and effect to regression analysis. The statistician speaks only in terms of whether the x and y values are related.

[2] Students who are interested in the mathematical aspects of the least-squares method and proof of the equations should consult a statistics book. For our purposes we can accept the mathematical validity of the equations. Many statistical texts calculate a and b with a set of normal equations that are solved simultaneously. These equations are

I. $\Sigma y = na + b\Sigma x$
II. $\Sigma xy = a\Sigma x + b\Sigma x^2$

The equations in the text above are these normal equations recast so that it is possible to go to a direct solution thereby avoiding the mathematical complexities of simultaneous equations. This section, for illustrative purposes, calculates the data manually. However, in today's world with computers and calculators these calculations would be "inside the machine." The Appendix to this chapter shows one typical computer printout.

where

Σy = Total costs a = Total fixed costs
Σx = Total volume b = Variable cost per unit of volume
   n = Number of time periods Σxy = Costs times volume summed

Once b is determined, then a can be found by

$$a = \frac{\Sigma y - b\Sigma x}{n}$$

     Using the data for the Clark Manufacturing Company, let's develop the cost estimates for the regression line. The first step is the development of the factors found in the formulas, as shown in the worksheet in Exhibit 2–11.

Substituting these data in the formula for b provides:

$$b = \frac{1,671,750 - \dfrac{(4,950)(3,623)}{12}}{2,602,500 - \dfrac{(4,950)^2}{12}}$$

$$b = \$.316$$

Month	Hours x	Costs y	xy	x^2
January	100	185	18,500	10,000
February	150	255	38,250	22,500
March	300	258	77,400	90,000
April	400	300	120,000	160,000
May	600	350	210,000	360,000
June	700	390	273,000	490,000
July	800	430	344,000	640,000
August	500	344	172,000	250,000
September	300	251	75,300	90,000
October	300	265	79,500	90,000
November	200	233	46,600	40,000
December	600	362	217,200	360,000
Total	4,950	3,623	1,671,750	2,602,500

Σx = 4,950
Σy = 3,623
Σxy = 1,671,750
Σx^2 = 2,602,500

EXHIBIT 2–11
Least-squares regression line worksheet

Using the cost estimate of $.316 for b,

$$a = \frac{3,623 - .316(4,950)}{12}$$

$$a = \$171.56; \text{ rounded to } \$172.00$$

Using the 12-months data for the Clark Manufacturing Company, the least-squares regression line used for cost estimation would be $y_c = \$172 + \$.316(x)$. This solution differs from the high-low point method, which estimated the fixed costs at $150 and the variable costs at $.35 per hour. One reason for these differences is the effect of the month of February. The high-low point method excluded all months except January and July; the regression line method used all 12 months. Inclusion of the unusual month of February acted to increase the fixed cost estimate and reduce the slope of the line (variable rate). A regression line excluding February, to test for the effect of that month, provides a regression equation of $y_c = \$159 + \$.337(x)$. The exclusion of February in the regression analysis results in fixed and variable cost estimates that are close to the estimates obtained from the scattergraph and high-low methods.

THE RELEVANT RANGE OF ACTIVITY

Unless the concepts of cost variability allow the decision maker to be more precise and flexible in making decisions, the effort and money spent in developing fixed and variable cost patterns are wasted. The range of volume over which the cost behavior patterns can reasonably be expected to hold true is termed the **relevant range.** No analysis of fixed and variable costs should be made without specifying the relevant range of activity.

It would be a mistake to believe that the relevant range of activity extends from zero activity to maximum volume capacity. In the event of a drastic decrease in volume, management would take a different set of actions than it would if production continued at a normal pace. As volume declined, past policies and decisions would be reexamined. Perhaps executive salaries would be lowered, production lines closed, insurance policies cancelled or reduced, or products dropped from the production schedule. On the other end of the scale, as production increased to reach maximum capability, there would be "diminishing returns." Storerooms would become crowded and inefficient, machines would require additional maintenance, workers in the second shift or on overtime would be less productive, and production facilities would become overworked.

GOODNESS-OF-FIT TESTS

When the relation between cost and volume is perfect, each point representing actual cost will fall exactly on the estimation (regression) line and there will be no unexplained variations. In the analysis of cost–volume interactions it would be rare to find a regression line that perfectly fits the data. This lack of perfect relationships could result from variations due to reasons other than volume (e.g., variations caused by changes in management policy), errors or imprecisions in collecting and measuring the data, or the failure of a straight line to adequately describe the relationship. The greater the vertical distances of the actual observations to the regression line, the less reliable the line is in predicting the costs. The least-squares regression line was constructed on the premise that a line that minimizes the sum of the squared distances will serve as a better predictor than any other line. To test the quality and reliability of the regression line, a measure of the goodness of fit is necessary. (The Appendix at the end of this chapter demonstrates a computer program that provides goodness-of-fit tests.)

A special warning seems appropriate here. Statistical decision-making methods are objective, and they carry an aura of accuracy that must be approached with caution. Statistical methods do *not* remove the necessity for the decision maker to make personal judgments about the usefulness of the data. Even though the regression line and measures of goodness of fit for the Clark Manufacturing Company are known, subjective judgment is still required to determine whether or not to use the data. One way to give the manager a basis for subjective judgment is to prepare a scattergraph on each cost, regardless of the statistical methods of analysis. As a matter of fact, most computer programs do this automatically.

There are occasions when it is impossible to fit a satisfactory estimation line. Exhibits 2–12 and 2–13 illustrate two scattergraphs that defy a segregation of the cost into its fixed and variable components, given the activity base chosen. In both cases variability would be so large as to negate the meaning of the flexible budget equation. In those cases where cost patterns do not lend themselves to fixed and variable cost analysis, management has no recourse but to use its intuitive judgment in planning future costs. Usually the direct establishment of the levels of these costs will result in treating them as fixed.

There are other costs that are not susceptible to fixed and variable cost analysis. Research and development costs (R&D) and advertising costs are two excellent examples. These costs cannot be directly related to either production or sales volume. The proper amount that should be incurred for these costs depends on factors other than volume. Among these factors are the marketplace and its structure, the projected need for new products, the probability of success in developing product innovations, the projected cash flow patterns of the firm, and the competitors' behavior. As a result, these costs are established by management choice, or discretion. Accountants call them **discretionary costs.** Typ-

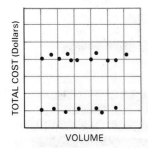

EXHIBIT 2–12
Scattergraph where
cost–volume
relationship is unclear

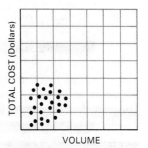

EXHIBIT 2–13
Scattergraph where no
cost–volume
relationship exists

ically, control of discretionary costs depends more on measuring the results of
the cost expenditure than on cost variability.

EXPRESSING COST BEHAVIOR PATTERNS: THE FLEXIBLE BUDGET

Whatever the technique used to determine cost behavior patterns, the end result
is an equation $y_c = a + b(x)$ that can be used to estimate total costs at any
volume level within the relevant range. Accountants call this statement of fixed
and variable costs the **flexible budget.** Assume that a company has only three
costs: a fixed cost, a variable cost, and a mixed cost. The flexible budget for
each individual cost and for total costs follows.

Cost	FLEXIBLE BUDGET $(y_c = a + bx)$	
	a	b
Fixed	$500 +	$0 (x)
Variable	$ 0 +	$.25(x)
Semivariable	$ 50 +	$.10(x)
Total cost	$550 +	$.35(x)

For estimating and planning individual costs the company could use the
flexible budget for each type of cost. For example, if 150 units of volume were
planned, the budgeted semivariable cost would be $65 [$50 + $.10(150)]. When
planning the costs for the company as a whole, the flexible budget of $550 +
$.35(x) would be appropriate. Assume the firm planned 200 units of volume the

coming accounting period. The total budgeted costs would be $620 [$550 + $.35(200)].

The flexible budget is also valuable in performance assessment. For example, assume that the firm spent $78 for the semivariable cost, when the actual volume was 240 units. The flexible budget adjusted to the actual volume would be $74 [$50 + $.10(240)]. This would represent a target expenditure, given the volume of 240 units. Thus, the firm spent $4 more than allowed.

In order to combine the individual cost elements, it is important to seek a single measure of volume that fits all costs. The volume measures must be the same if the individual flexible budget formulas are to be additive. When we think about the activities of a manufacturing company, we can visualize two distinct types of activities. First, the firm must manufacture the products to be sold. Second, they must undertake the sales and distribution of the products. For manufacturing costs the volume measure (x) would relate to manufacturing; possible measures of volume would be units produced, direct labor hours, or machine hours. For selling costs the volume measure (x) would relate to selling; possible volume measures would be units sold, units shipped, or dollars of sales. When the firm uses two flexible budgets, one for manufacturing costs and another for selling and distribution costs, the two budgets will not be additive if they used different volume measures (x).

SUMMARY

Basic to profit planning and control is the knowledge of how costs change with changes in volume. Fixed costs are costs that do not change with changes in volume; variable costs vary in direct proportion to change in volume. Costs that change with changes in volume, but not in direct proportion, are semivariable costs. There are three types of semivariable costs: stairstepped, mixed, and curvilinear. The flexible budget is the formal statement of how costs vary with volume.

The simplest and most straightforward way of determining fixed and variable costs is to examine the firm's contracts. Where there are no contracts, fixed and variable costs can be estimated directly through special studies. Historical costs, when available, can be used to estimate fixed and variable costs. One way to separate historical costs into their fixed and variables components is to plot the data on a scattergraph; volume is shown on the horizontal axis and costs are shown on the vertical axis. A line is then drawn that bisects this plotted history. Fixed costs are determined where the line intersects the vertical axis; the variable cost rate is determined by measuring the slope of the line. Similar to the scattergraph approach is the high-low point method, which measures the variable cost rate between costs at the highest and lowest activity levels. A third method of analyzing historical costs is regression analysis. It is similar in effect to the scattergraph, but is more objective in separating costs into their fixed and variable components.

APPENDIX

STATISTICAL METHODOLOGY FOR GOODNESS-OF-FIT TESTS

GOODNESS-OF-FIT TESTS

Least-squares regression analysis is a statistical procedure that may be used to estimate the flexible budget equation. When this method is used it is also possible to tell how well the flexible budget fits the past data, how statistically significant the equation is, and how much variation should be expected between estimated and actual data.

Because of the number of calculations required to perform the goodness-of-fit tests, the computer is an important tool. Virtually all computer centers have programs available to perform the necessary calculations. For example, one program is the Interactive Data Analysis (IDA) program using the HP2000/Access System.[3] Another widely available program is a subprogram of the *Statistical Package for the Social Sciences* (SPSS).[4] Another easy-to-use computer package is the *Minitab,* developed at Penn State University.[5] All of these programs provide the scattergraph (for visual observation); the intercept point (*a*); the slope (*b*); and tests for goodness of fit—the correlation coefficient, the coefficient of determination, and the standard error of the estimate.

The Minitab output for the Clark Manufacturing Company illustration used in the text is presented in Exhibit A2–1. In the exhibit, the scattergraph shows the observations by a star, or if more than one by a number. The horizontal axis is labor hours; and the vertical axis is total cost. The column headed COEFFICIENT gives the values of *a* and *b* in the linear model. In this printout

---

[3]Harry V. Roberts, *Conversational Statistics* (Cupertino, Calif.: Hewlett-Packard Company, 1974).

[4]Norman H. Nie, C. Hadlai Hull, Jean G. Jenkins, Karin Steinbrenner, and Dale H. Brent, SPSS (New York: McGraw-Hill Book Company, 1975).

[5]Thomas A. Ryan, Jr., Brian L. Joiner, and Barbara F. Ryan, *Minitab Student Handbook* (North Scituate, Mass.: Duxbury Press, 1976).

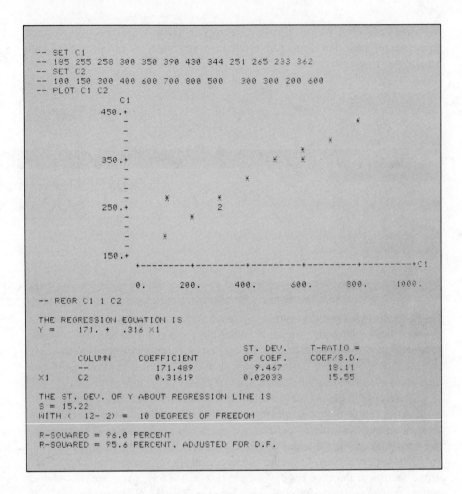

```
-- SET C1
-- 185 255 258 300 350 390 430 344 251 265 233 362
-- SET C2
-- 100 150 300 400 600 700 800 500  300 300 200 600
-- PLOT C1 C2
              C1
         450.+                                        *
              -
              -
              -                                *
              -                             *
         350.+                         *    *
              -                   *
              -
              -
              -         *        *
         250.+                   2
              -              *
              -
              -         *
         150.+
              +---------+---------+---------+---------+---------+C1
              0.       200.      400.      600.      800.     1000.

-- REGR C1 1 C2

THE REGRESSION EQUATION IS
Y =     171. +  .316 X1

                                       ST. DEV.     T-RATIO =
          COLUMN      COEFFICIENT      OF COEF.     COEF/S.D.
          --          171.489         9.467        18.11
X1        C2          0.31619         0.02033       15.55

THE ST. DEV. OF Y ABOUT REGRESSION LINE IS
S = 15.22
WITH ( 12- 2) =   10 DEGREES OF FREEDOM

R-SQUARED = 96.0 PERCENT
R-SQUARED = 95.6 PERCENT, ADJUSTED FOR D.F.
```

EXHIBIT A2–1
Clark Manufacturing
Co. minitab output

the value of the constant a is \$171.49 and the value of b is \$.316. Allowing for rounding error, this is the same linear equation determined from the manual computations in the chapter.

Three tests of the goodness of fit are also available: the r^2 value, the r value, and the standard error of the estimate. The r^2 value (called R-SQUARED on the minitab output), is the **coefficient of determination.** It is a measure of the proportion (percentage) of variance in the one variable "explained" by the variance in the other. r^2 can range from a minimum of 0 to a maximum of 1.0. The r^2 of .956 for the Clark Manufacturing Company shows that approximately 96% of the variance in total cost is explained by the variance in labor hours.

The r value is not given directly on the minitab output but may be found by taking the square root of the adjusted R-SQUARED, which is shown. The r value is the Pearson product-moment **correlation coefficient.** When there is a perfect fit, r will be $+1.0$ or -1.0. A positive correlation means that the two variables tend to increase (or decrease) together. A negative correlation does not mean a bad fit; rather it shows that as one variable becomes larger the other tends to be smaller. When the linear regression line is a poor fit to the data, the value of r will be closer to zero. Adjusted r value for the Clark Manufacturing Company of .978 indicates a strong, positive relationship.

The **standard error of the estimate** (called STD. DEV. OF Y ABOUT REGRESSION LINE on the output) shows how far the actual observations deviate from the regression line. The further the past costs differ from the flexible budget predictions, the larger the standard error. Conversely, the closer the actual data are to the estimates of the flexible budget line, the smaller the standard error of the estimate. The standard error of the estimate is determined by measuring the variation of each actual observation from the corresponding predicted value given by the linear equation to obtain the total variance or **residual sum of the squares.** If we divide the residual sum of the squares by $n - 2$ (number of observations $-$ 2), we obtain a measure known as the **residual variance.** The standard error of the estimate is the square root of the residual variance. For the Clark Manufacturing Company, the standard error of the estimate of 15.2 is small.

In sum, with approximately 96% of the variation in cost explained by the variation in hours, and a small standard error of the estimate, the goodness of fit tests show a very strong relationship between total cost and hours for the Clark Manufacturing Company.

In least-squares regression analysis, the signficance of a deviation from the regression line increases with its size. Therefore, any outlier observation will pull the regression line toward them. Observations that are not the result of normal operations should be excluded from the analysis. For example, if we exclude the data for February because it did not represent normal operations, an even stronger fit is indicated. The minitab output for the Clark Manufacturing Company (this output is not shown) shows the constant (a value) is $158.92, the b value is $.3375, the adjusted r is .9933, the r^2 is .9866, and the standard error of the estimate is 8.67. This means that slightly less than 99% of the variation in cost is explained by the variation in hours and the standard error is slightly more than half the standard error when all observations are included in the analysis.

USING PROBABILITY ESTIMATES

If we can make four assumptions about our data in this example, we can use a table of probabilities to evaluate further the flexible budget equation. First we have assumed that the relationship between costs and volume is linear. When this is not true, a straight line will not fit the actual data. Second, it is assumed that the actual data are normally distributed (i.e., bell-shaped) around the estimated line; that is to say, all the differences between the actual costs at a given volume level and the estimates made by the flexible budget at the same volume level would create a normal, bell-shaped curve. Third, it is assumed that there is a uniform dispersion of actual costs around the estimated line. At a high-volume level the actual data are distributed around the estimated line in the same way they are at lower volumes. Finally, it is assumed that the cost measures are independent of each other. For example, the costs reported in May are not dependent on those reported in April.

In statistics the normal distribution is the familiar bell-shaped curve. This curve has the property that 68.27% of all observations fall between the mean ($\bar{x}$) plus or minus one standard deviation; within the range of $\bar{x} \pm 2$ standard deviations, 95.45% are included; and within $\bar{x} \pm 3$ standard deviations, 99.73% or nearly all of the items are included. The normal distribution allows the manager to assess how well the regression line fits the observed data and to make probability statements about the fit to the data. We must, however, exercise care in the use of these relationships when the number of observations upon which our estimates are based is small. Our observations represent only a sample of the possible observations and we face the risk of sampling error with a small number of observations. When the number of observations is small it is common to use the Student's t-distribution rather than the normal distribution. The t-distribution compensates for a small number of observations.

When using regression analysis it is assumed that the estimated coefficients a and b each have a normal distribution. The estimated standard deviations (SD) of these two coefficients are shown in the column headed ST. DEV. OF COEF. The estimated standard deviation of a is 9.467 and the estimated standard deviation of b is .020. These standard deviations may be used for two additional analyses.

One way to utilize these estimated standard deviations is to test whether the computed coefficient is statistically different from zero. To test this null hypothesis the following general formula is used to determine the t-statistic.[6]

$$t = \frac{\text{Coefficient} - \text{Hypothesized value}}{\text{Estimated standard deviation}}$$

When the hypothesized value is zero, this t is simply the coefficient divided by the estimated standard deviation. For the Clark Manufacturing Company these are

$$t = \frac{171.489}{9.467} = 18.11 \text{ for } a$$

$$t = \frac{.31619}{.02033} = 15.55 \text{ for } b$$

These values are shown on the computer output in the column T-RATIO.

---

[6]The student is referred to any elementary statistics book for a discussion of the use of t-tests.

The interpretation of these t-statistics requires a table of critical values of t. An abbreviated table is provided below.

Degrees of Freedom	.05 Level of Significance (Two-tailed Test)
5	2.571
10	2.228
15	2.131
20	2.086
25	2.060
30	2.042

With 10 degrees of freedom (see the computer output), the t values of 18.11 and 15.55 are highly significant. This provides statistical evidence that the coefficients are probably not zero. This, in turn, implies that the changes in volume (x) is a useful predictor of the changes in cost (y). (It should be noted that this t-test is exactly the same as testing whether the population correlation is zero.)

A second way to use the estimated standard deviations is to develop confidence intervals around the coefficients. The general formula for a t-confidence interval is:

$$\text{Coefficient} \pm \left(\begin{array}{c}\text{Value from}\\t\text{-table}\end{array}\right) \times \left(\begin{array}{c}\text{Estimated standard}\\\text{deviation}\end{array}\right)$$

For the Clark Manufacturing Company with 10 degrees of freedom the 95% confidence level—that is, the range within which the actual costs are expected to fall 95% of the time—for a is

$$171.49 \pm (2.228) \times (9.467)$$

This implies that 95% of the time we would expect the cost neither to exceed 192.58 (the upper limit) nor to go below 150.40 (the lower limit).

For b the 95% confidence intervals are an upper limit of .3615 and a lower limit of .2709 [$.31619 \pm (2.228) \times (.02033)$]. We would expect that 95% of the time the actual variable cost rate is between .3615 and .2709.

This same confidence level technique can be used to establish confidence intervals for the predicted values at a specific level. For example, assume that the Clark Manufacturing Company used their flexible budget to estimate costs at the 400-hour level as follows:

$$y_c = \$171.49 + \$.316(400)$$
$$= \$298.4; \text{ rounded to } \$298.$$

When the sample size (n) is fairly large, approximately 50 observations, it is possible to assume a normal distribution. In a normal distribution about 95% of all observations should fall within $\pm$ 2 SD. Using the standard deviation of y about the regression line ($15.22), we could estimate that the actual cost should fall between $328.44 [$298 + (2 × 15.22)] and $267.56 [$298 − (2 × 15.22)] about 95% of the time. This shows that the smaller the standard error, the more confidence the decision maker can have in the flexible budget equation for prediction purposes.

In our example of the Clark Manufacturing Company the number of observations was 12, resulting in 10 degrees of freedom. This opens to question the use of the normal distribution to establish confidence intervals. When there are too few degrees of freedom to justify the use of the normal distribution, statisticians use the following formula:

$$\text{Predicted } y \pm \frac{t\text{-Table}}{\text{value}} \sqrt{\frac{1}{n} + \frac{(x_o - \bar{x})^2}{\Sigma(x - \bar{x})^2} + 1}$$

It is possible to recast this general formula into the following:

$$\text{Predicted } y \pm \frac{t\text{-Table}}{\text{value}} \sqrt{\left(\begin{array}{c}\text{Estimated SD of} \\ \text{predicted } y\end{array}\right)^2 + \left(\begin{array}{c}\text{SD of } y \text{ about} \\ \text{regression line}\end{array}\right)^2}$$

The **estimated standard deviation of the predicted** y, shown under the radical sign, is a correction factor recognizing that a particular individual event is never as predictable as averages—that is, that we can expect more uncertainty in any prediction at a specific level.

It is beyond the scope of this text to show the methodology of determining the estimated standard deviation of the predicted y. (A discussion may be found in the minitab manual or any elementary statistics textbook.) In some minitab programs (specified as NOBRIEF), this statistic is given for the actual observations. From this minitab output, which is not shown in Exhibit A2–1, this amount was calculated as 4.40 for our example.

Using this estimate the following confidence levels can be determined:

$$\$298 \pm 2.228 \sqrt{(4.40)^2 + (15.2)^2}$$
$$\$298 \pm 2.228 \sqrt{250.40}$$
$$\$298 \pm 2.228 \times 15.82$$

This gives an upper confidence level of $333 and a lower confidence level of $263.

OTHER STATISTICAL TECHNIQUES

The straight-line measure of cost variability is the method most widely used by accountants. It is not universally applicable, however. In some instances a linear regression line will result in an unsatisfactory fit. In other instances the relationship may be curvilinear. As discussed in the chapter, some of the semi-variable costs behave this way. To estimate this cost behavior pattern, a second-degree curve, expressed by the following formula, might be appropriate:

$$y_c = a + bx + cx^2$$

The solution of this formula requires three normal equations. With this and other higher-order curves that might be useful, the mathematics become complex. Without a computer these studies would be difficult if not infeasible.

The decision maker may find that the cost being studied is related to one or more factors in addition to volume, or that there are two or more different measures of volume. For some cost predictions there may be two or three independent measures, such as machine hours, labor hours, product dimensions, and labor skills. In this case the decision maker may find the techniques of multiple regression useful. Multiple regression measures the change in cost (y) for one of these variables, while holding all of the other variables constant. The formula to express the relationships among many variables is

$$y_c = a + bx_1 + cx_2 + dx_3 \ldots$$

where y_c is the cost to be predicted; x_1, x_2, and x_3 are the different volume measures; a is constant, and b, c, and d are coefficients.

If in preparing goodness-of-fit tests there is an apparent lack of cost–volume relationships, the curvilinear or multiple regression discussed above might prove useful.

The goal of these statistical methods is quite singular—to allow the decision maker confidence in the cost estimates obtained from the flexible budget.

PROBLEMS AND CASES

2-1 (*High-Low Methods*). The Hill Company had the following cost and volume experiences for employee fringe benefit costs.

	Direct-Labor Hours	Actual Costs
January	8,000	$18,000
February	7,000	$17,000
March	10,000	$22,000
April	12,000	$27,000
May	8,000	$17,000
June	9,000	$20,000

REQUIRED:

A. Determine the flexible budget equation using the high-low method.

B. Comment on the validity of the flexible budget formula.

2-2 (*High-Low Method*). The Charter Distributing Company is in the process of analyzing its cost structure. The company has determined that the following mixed cost exists at various levels of production.

Month	Units Produced	Total Costs
January	25	$45
February	18	$22
March	21	$40
April	15	$36
May	12	$32
June	19	$40

The company is anxious to break the mixed cost into the basic variable and fixed cost elements to assist in planning and control of operations. They have asked you to assist in this task.

REQUIRED:

A. By means of the high-low method, break the total costs into their fixed and variable elements. Express the answer as a linear equation.

B. Assuming that the least-squares regression technique resulted in the cost equation of $y_c = \$17.50 + \$1.00(x)$, compare this equation with the answer you obtained in part A. Which cost analysis would you choose for this cost? Explain. Would your choice hold true for all other variable and fixed cost separations? Explain.

2-3 (*Flexible Budgets and Cost Planning*). The following are flexible budget equations for the Crane Corporation.

Rent	$\$4,700 + \$0\ (x)$
Indirect labor	$\$0 \quad + \$.40(x)$
Repairs	$\$1,800 + \$.25(x)$

REQUIRED:

A. Develop flexible budget cost estimates for 7,000, 8,000, and 9,000 units. (Assume that the volume measure x is units.)

B. Calculate the per-unit cost for each level of activity. Why does the per-unit cost change as volume increases?

C. Explain why it is desirable to find a single volume measure for all production costs.

2-4 *(Determining the Flexible Budget)*. The India Company had the following average unit costs at several different volume levels as follows.

Units Sold	Unit Costs
100	$280
200	$230
400	$205
500	$200
1,000	$190

The unit sales price and the unit variable cost, and hence the contribution margin per unit, are the same at each of the levels.

REQUIRED:

A. Determine the variable costs per unit.

B. Determine the total fixed costs.

C. What average unit cost would you estimate if 800 units were sold?

2-5 *(Identification of Cost Patterns)*. Select the graph that matches the numbered factory cost or expense data.

The vertical axes of the graphs represent *total* dollars of expense, and the horizontal axes represent production. In each case the zero point is at the intersection of the two axes. The graphs may be used more than once.

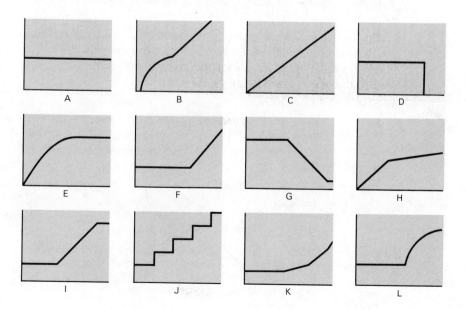

1. Depreciation of equipment, where the amount of depreciation charged is computed by the machine-hours method.

2. Electricity bill—a flat fixed charge, plus a variable cost after a certain number of kilowatt-hours are used.

3. City water bill, which is computed as follows:

First 1,000,000 gallons or less	$1,000 flat fee
Next 10,000 gallons	$.003 per gallon used
Next 10,000 gallons	$.006 per gallon used
Next 10,000 gallons	$.009 per gallon used
etc., etc., etc.	

4. Cost of lubricant for machines, where cost per unit decreases with each pound of lubricant used (e.g., if 1 pound is used, the cost is $10.00; if 2 pounds are used, the total cost is $19.98; if 3 pounds are used, the total cost is $29.94; with a minimum cost per pound of $9.25).

5. Depreciation of equipment, where the amount is computed by the straight-line method. When the depreciation rate was established, it was anticipated that the obsolescence factor would be greater than the wear-and-tear factor.

6. Rent on a factory building donated by the city, where the agreement calls for a fixed fee payment unless 200,000 man-hours are worked, in which case no rent need be paid.

7. Salaries of repair personnel, where one repairman is needed for every 1,000 hours of machine hours or less (i.e., 0 to 1,000 hours requires one repair person, 1,001 to 2,000 hours requires two repair people, etc.).

8. Unemployment compensation taxes for the year, where labor force is constant in number throughout the year. Assume unemployment taxes are computed at .5% of the first $10,000 earned. Average annual salary is $18,000 per worker.

9. Cost of raw material used.

10. Rent on a factory building donated by the county, where agreement calls for rent of $100,000 less $1.00 for each direct labor hour worked in excess of 200,000 hours, but minimum rental payment of $20,000 must be paid.

(CPA adapted)

2-6 *(Determining Flexible Budgets by Examining Contracts)*. Assume the following independent cost behaviors:

1. *Rent*—The factory building lease calls for monthly payments of $2,000 for the next five years.

2. *Salespersons' salaries*—The team of five salespersons each receive a salary of $750 per month plus a commission of 6% of their net sales.

3. *Production workers' wages*—Production workers receive an average hourly wage of $8.00 per hour. Production output remains constant at the rate of two finished units per direct labor hour.

4. *Depreciation of drill press*—The company uses a straight-line depreciation method to depreciate the drill presses. Each drill costs $10,000 and has an estimated useful life of five years. The maximum capacity per drill press is 5,000 units per year. Output is budgeted at 6,000 units next year.

5. *Factory workers' wages*—The 15 factory workers receive a monthly salary of $1,000 each. Production is stable at 1,200 units per month and worker efficiency is stable at two hours per finished unit.

6. *Supervisor's salaries*—Front-line supervisors average $1,800 per month each. It is company policy to provide a ratio of 15 production workers per supervisor. Planned output for the coming year will require 75 production workers.

7. *Production worker vacation pay*—The union contract calls for the company to fund production workers' vacations. Each of the 100 production workers receives an hour of paid vacation for each 20 hours worked. Production workers average $7.00 per labor hour in wages.

8. *Maintenance costs*—The firm employs a four-person maintenance crew. The crew averages $6.00 per hour for regular time, plus time and one-half for overtime. Each worker averages 2,000 hours regular time plus 200 hours overtime per year.

REQUIRED:

Prepare flexible budget formulas on an annual basis for each of these costs.

2-7 *(Determining Flexible Budget Formulas)*. The King Company prepared the following cost reports for two different activity levels:

	MACHINE HOURS	
	80,000	110,000
Indirect materials	$ 37,600	$ 51,700
Indirect labor	187,200	257,400
Utilities	41,200	56,200
Maintenance	141,500	192,500
Supervision	13,000	13,000
Depreciation	14,000	14,000
Rent	28,000	28,000
Total	$462,500	$612,800

REQUIRED:

A. Using the above data, determine the flexible budget formula for each individual cost and for the total costs.

B. Prepare a schedule of budgeted costs assuming the planned activity level is 95,000 machine hours.

2-8 *(Determining Flexible Budgets).* Quicktest Laboratories, Inc. performs laboratory tests for hospitals and medical clinics. The current average unit cost for tests is $6.50 per test when 12,000 tests are performed and $5.25 per test when 24,000 tests are performed. Recently several hospitals have requested a new lab test for a communicable disease. This new test would require additional equipment as well as another technician. Considering all costs, the equipment supplier has assured Quicktest that these new tests could be done for an average unit cost of $4.00 per test when 10,000 tests are made and $2.50 per test when 20,000 tests are made.

REQUIRED:

A. What is the flexible budget for the current tests?

B. What is the flexible budget for the new test?

C. In your opinion, would it be acceptable for these flexible budgets to be added together to provide a flexible budget for the laboratory as a whole? Explain.

2-9 *(Cost Determination).* Total average unit costs for the Beta Company at output levels of 400 and 500 units are shown below.

	TOTAL AVERAGE UNIT COST	
Cost	400 Units Produced	500 Units Produced
A	$3.75	$3.00
B	$2.90	$2.60
C	$1.75	$1.75
D	$ .50	$ .40
E	$4.15	$4.07

REQUIRED:

Prepare a table to show:

A. Per-unit variable cost.

B. Total fixed cost.

C. Type of cost (i.e., variable, fixed, semivariable).

2-10 *(Selection of Volume Base).* The Snohomish Corporation, a manufacturer of high-quality fishing reels, gathered the following historical data concerning their manufacturing process:

Total Costs	Direct Labor Hours	Machine Hours
$20,000	2,000	2,000
$23,000	3,100	2,500
$34,000	2,650	3,250
$35,000	3,600	3,900
$37,000	4,100	3,650
$43,000	3,300	4,350
$43,000	4,200	4,900
$46,000	5,000	4,900
$48,000	4,000	4,600
$50,000	4,600	5,100
$53,500	3,950	4,700
$54,000	4,550	5,600
$54,500	3,000	5,250
$55,000	5,350	6,000
$61,000	5,250	6,300

Management was attempting to develop this data for future cost estimation purposes. They could not decide between direct labor hours and machine hours for the activity base and asked your help in determining which base would be most appropriate.

REQUIRED:

Choose the appropriate activity base and support your decision.

2-11 *(Choosing a Volume Measure via Goodness-of-Fit Tests).* Top management of the Marathon Company has decided to institute a flexible budget for cost planning and control. As a first step in the process they need to choose a volume base. The accountant gathered the following data:

Machine Hours	Labor Hours	Maintenance Costs	Utilities Costs	Indirect Labor
1,000	2,500	$2,000	$10,000	$5,100
1,600	3,000	$2,900	$12,200	$6,100
1,200	2,000	$2,200	$ 8,200	$4,100
1,500	2,800	$2,800	$11,500	$5,700

This data was run through a computer program with the following results from the regression analysis:

	Flexible Budget	SD of y about Regression Line	r^2	t-RATIO (COEFF. ÷ SD) a	b
Regression on machine hours					
Maintenance costs	364 + 1.59x	70.3	98.3	1.83	10.81
Utilities costs	4,112 + 4.80x	1,446.0	55.6	1.01	1.58
Indirect labor	2,309 + 2.22x	758.0	49.4	1.08	1.40
Regression on labor hours					
Maintenance costs	444 + .79x	342.5	60.1	0.38	1.73
Utilities costs	4.85 + 4.07x	150.0	99.5	0.01	20.42
Indirect labor	100 + 2.00x	.000	100.0	—	—

REQUIRED:

A. Using the above data, what recommendations would you make regarding choosing a proper volume base? Justify your position.

B. Compare the regression analysis results shown above with results you obtain using the high-low method. Comment on any significant differences.

2-12 *(Planning and Control with Flexible Budget).* The Sound Foundry has prepared flexible budget equations for each cost. For maintenance the flexible budget is

$$y_c = \$5,600 + \$.25(x)$$

where

y_c is the estimate of total maintenance costs.

x is direct machine hours.

REQUIRED:

A. Prepare a cost estimate for 6,000 machine hours: for 9,000 hours.

B. Management believes that there will be a general 10% price increase for maintenance costs that will affect both fixed and variable costs. Prepare a new flexible budget equation.

C. Prepare cost estimates for 6,000 and 9,000 machine hours using the revised budget equation obtained in part *B*.

D. Using the original equation of $\$5,600 + \$.25(x)$, can you tell if management controlled costs effectively if actual costs of maintenance were $7,000 last year when the actual activity level was 4,000 machine hours?

E. Discuss the statement: "Fixed costs don't change with changes in volume, so it is impossible for management to control them." Do you agree or disagree? Why?

F. What would be the budget allowance if the department was in a "stand-by" position (zero activity but ready to produce if asked to do so)? Do you feel this allowance is realistic? Why?

G. Management is planning an activity level of 8,000 machine hours. Because of cash management difficulties, management would like a possible cost range. What cost estimate should encompass the high- and low-cost experiences 68% of the time? Assume a standard error of $150.

2-13 *(Flexible Budget and High-Low Method)*. The Peter Pan Company produces lawn games. Last year, production varied from a high of 25,500 games in June to a low of 8,000 in January. Production costs were $77,100 and $42,100, respectively.

REQUIRED:

A. Determine the flexible budget using the high-low method.

B. Using the flexible budget determined in part *A*, calculate the budgeted costs at 10,000 and 30,000 units. How reliable do you believe those estimates are?

C. In other months the costs were

Units of Production	Cost
8,000	$42,100
9,000	$44,100
25,000	$76,100
25,500	$77,100

Determine a new flexible budget using the high-low method. Would a scattergraph aid in improving accuracy? Explain.

D. Assume that 8,500 games are produced during January of the next year at a cost of $42,000. How well did the firm control its costs? (Assume that the flexible budget in part *C* was accepted by management.)

E. What are the shortcomings of using the high-low method for determining cost behavior? How can they be remedied?

2-14 *(Multiple Choice on Regression Analysis)*. Armer Company is accumulating data to be used in preparing its annual profit plan for the coming year. The cost behavior pattern of the maintenance costs must be determined. The accounting staff has suggested that regression be employed to derive an equation in the form of $y = a + bx$ for maintenance costs. Data regarding the maintenance hours and costs for last year and the results of the regression analysis are as follows:

	Hours of Activity	Maintenance Costs
January	480	$ 4,200
February	320	3,000
March	400	3,600
April	300	2,820
May	500	4,350
June	310	2,960
July	320	3,030
August	520	4,470
September	490	4,260
October	470	4,050
November	350	3,300
December	340	3,160
Sum	4,800	$43,200
Average	400	3,600

Average cost per hour ($43,200 ÷ 4,800) = $9

Intercept	684.65
b coefficient	7.2884
Standard error of the intercept	49.515
Standard error of the b coefficient	.12126
Standard error of the regression	34.469
r^2	.99724
t-value intercept	13.827
t-value b	60.105

REQUIRED:

Answer the following multiple-choice questions.

a. In the standard regression equation of $y = a + bx$, the letter b is best described as the

1. Independent variable.
2. Dependent variable.
3. Constant coefficient.
4. Variable coefficient.
5. Coefficient of determination.

b. The letter y in the standard regression equation is best described as the

1. Independent variable.
2. Dependent variable.
3. Constant coefficient
4. Variable coefficient.
5. Coefficient of determination.

C. The letter x in the standard regression equation is best described as the

1. Independent variable.
2. Dependent variable.
3. Constant coefficient.

4. Variable coefficient.

5. Coefficient of determination.

D. If the Armer Company uses the high-low method of analysis, the equation for the relationship between hours of activity and maintenance cost would be

1. $y = 400 + 9.0x$.

2. $y = 570 + 7.5x$.

3. $y = 3,600 + 400x$.

4. $y = 570 + 9.0x$.

5. Some equation other than those given above.

E. Based upon the data derived from the regression analysis, 420 maintenance hours in a month would mean the maintenance costs would be budgeted at

1. $3,780.

2. $3,461.

3. $3,797.

4. $3,746.

5. Some amount other than those given.

F. The coefficient of corrrelation for the regression equation for the maintenance activities is

1. $34.469 \div 49.515$.

2. .99724.

3. $\sqrt{.99724}$.

4. $(.99724)^2$.

5. Some amount other than those given above.

G. The percentage of the total variance that can be explained by the regression equation is

1. 99.724%.

2. 69.613%.

3. 80.982%.

4. 99.862%.

5. Some amount other than those given above.

H. What is the range of values for the marginal maintenance cost such that Armer can be 95% confident that the true value of the marginal maintenance cost will be within this range? (Use $t = 2.23$.)

1. $7.02–$7.56.

2. $7.17–$7.41.

3. $7.07–$7.51.

4. $6.29–$8.29.

5. Some range other than those given above.

(CMA adapted)

2-15 *(Regression Analysis)*. The Alene Company, in its annual review of the flexible budget, determined the following data about machinery repair costs.

Costs	Volume in Hours
$1,800	100
$5,010	320
$3,450	210
$1,790	130
$1,810	180
$5,020	340
$1,850	150
$3,380	200
$3,500	270
$5,000	350
$4,900	310
$3,050	280

Sum of hours $(\Sigma x) = 2,840$
Sum of costs $(\Sigma y) = 40,560$
Sum of hours times costs $(\Sigma xy) = 10,794,500$
Sum of hours squared $(\Sigma x^2) = 753,800$

REQUIRED:

A. From the given data determine the total fixed costs and variable costs per hour using the regression method.

B. Your management, while appreciating your effort, does not understand the least-squares method. You are asked to plot the original data on a scattergraph. Does this scattergraph give you any insights into the cost behavior pattern of repair costs? Discuss.

2-16 *(Regression Analysis)*. The controller of the Market Corporation is studying the cost behavior patterns of indirect labor in relationship to units produced. She believes that a knowledge of fixed and variable costs will help her to budget future costs as well as control actual expenditures. Past cost and production data show the following:

Units Produced	Cost
10	$ 5,400
20	$ 7,500
50	$13,300
80	$20,000
60	$15,400
10	$ 5,600
30	$ 9,300
50	$14,000
60	$15,500

Sum of units (Σx) = 370
Sum of costs (Σy) = 106,000
Sum of units times costs (Σxy) = 5,358,000
Sum of units squared (Σx^2) = 20,100
Sum of variance from regression line $\Sigma(y - \bar{y})^2$ = 479,185

REQUIRED:

A. Using the least-squares regression technique, determine the flexible budget showing total fixed costs and the variable rate per unit.

B. Compare the flexible budget from the regression method with a cost estimate using the high-low method.

2-17 (*Interpreting Goodness-of-Fit Tests of Flexible Budgets*). The controller of the Lewis Company had just completed a regression study of five costs. The regressions were based on the following data:

Machine Hours	Cost 1	Cost 2	Cost 3	Cost 4	Cost 5
100	$ 350	$ 50	$ 350	$350	$200
200	$ 700	$ 300	$ 580	$355	$200
400	$1,400	$ 150	$ 920	$350	$400
500	$1,750	$ 750	$1,150	$330	$400
600	$2,100	$ 400	$1,365	$365	$400
800	$2,800	$1,200	$1,735	$350	$600
900	$3,150	$ 700	$1,950	$360	$600

The computer output is summarized below:

	Flexible Budget	SD of y about Regression Line	r^2	t-RATIO (COEFF. ÷ SD) a	t-RATIO (COEFF. ÷ SD) b
Cost 1	.000 + 3.50(x)	.0000	100%	3.37	—
Cost 2	−26.5 + 1.07(x)	273.80	61.2%	−.12	2.81
Cost 3	159 + 1.98(x)	20.47	99.9%	9.82	69.86
Cost 4	348 + .0077(x)	11.87	4.2%	37.07	0.47
Cost 5	131 + .538(x)	42.97	94.2%	3.85	9.04

REQUIRED:

For each cost give a specific recommendation to the controller about whether the regression output should prove useful in predicting future costs. Justify your recommendations.

2-18 (*Three Approaches to Flexible Budget*). The Sally Manufacturing Company has decided to make a study of its manufacturing overhead to see if it can determine what portion of overhead is variable and what portion is fixed. To begin this study, the accountant gathered the following cost and production data.

	Total Costs of Overhead	Total Labor Hours of Production
January	$1,950	500
February	$1,900	450
March	$2,150	600
April	$3,100	800
May	$3,450	900
June	$4,600	1,350
July	$3,750	1,100
August	$3,550	750
September	$2,300	550
October	$1,950	400
November	$2,400	3,000
December	$3,000	950

REQUIRED:

A. Prepare a scattergraph of these data. From this scattergraph develop an estimate of the flexible budget showing total fixed costs and the variable cost rate per hour of production.

B. Which month(s) might bear closer examination? Why? Could this be a normal occurrence? Why?

C. What are some of the assumptions made when this cost behavior pattern is used to forecast the future?

D. When using the scattergraph for forecasting, is there any way to remove the effects of unusual occurrences? Should this be done? Discuss some of the consequences.

E. Determine the fixed and variable cost estimates using the high-low method.

F. Discuss some of the weaknesses in using this method of determining fixed and variable costs.

G. Using your estimates of fixed and variable costs prepared in part E above, what is your estimate of the overhead costs at 2,750 hours?

H. Determine the fixed and variable costs using the least-squares regression method.

I. Discuss why the least-squares regression method could be considered superior to the scattergraph or high-low method.

2-19 (*Determination of Flexible Budgets from Financial Statements*). The Nothing-for-Everyone Company manufactures an adjustable television antenna. Since the company was founded in 19X1, sales and profits have had an upward trend, as shown in the following income statements.

	19X1	19X2	19X3	19X4	19X5
Sales					
Units	10,000	15,000	12,000	14,000	16,000
Dollars	$100,000	$150,000	$144,000	$168,000	$192,000
Costs					
Materials	$ 20,000	$ 30,000	$ 24,000	$ 28,000	$ 32,000
Labor	30,000	45,000	42,000	49,000	56,000
Maintenance	11,000	16,000	13,000	15,000	17,000
Building rent	7,000	8,000	8,000	8,000	8,000
Administration	15,000	20,000	25,000	30,000	35,000
Depreciation	5,000	5,000	6,000	6,000	6,000
Sales commissions	10,000	15,000	14,400	16,800	19,200
Total	98,000	139,000	132,400	152,800	173,200
Income	$ 2,000	$ 11,000	$ 11,600	$ 15,200	$ 18,800

Management has just started a formal planning system and has asked you to assist them. The president, N. Minnow Gray, has heard of the flexible budget and the master budget from his accountant but is not certain of their meaning. He has also heard of fixed and variable costs but, when he examined the income statements, he was uncertain as to which costs were fixed and which were variable.

One of the things that confused Mr. Gray was whether a cost is fixed or variable when there have been management policy or economic changes. For example, Mr. Gray had raised the sales price in 19X3 when the new union contract called for an across-the-board pay raise. In the same year management had purchased new equipment, which caused depreciation expense to increase. Further, while management had been able to keep material prices the same for the past five years through careful purchasing policies, there was an announced price increase for 19X6 of 10% that Mr. Gray could not avoid.

REQUIRED:

A. Using only the information in the income statements, prepare a flexible budget for each cost item using the high-low method.

B. How would you modify the flexible budget equations from part A using all of the information available. Explain your choices.

C. Using the flexible budget prepared in part B, prepare a budgeted income statement for 19X6 assuming that the planned sales volume is 18,000 units.

2-20 *(Determination of Flexible Budget).* The Ramon Company manufactures a wide range of products at several different plant locations. The Franklin Plant, which manufactures electrical components, has been experiencing some difficulties with fluctuating monthly overhead costs. The fluctuations have made it difficult to estimate the level of overhead that will be incurred for any one month.

Management wants to be able to estimate overhead costs accurately in order to plan its operation and financial needs better. A trade association publication to which Ramon Company subscribes indicates that, for companies manufacturing electrical components, overhead tends to vary with direct labor hours.

One member of the accounting staff has proposed that the cost behavior pattern of the overhead costs be determined. Then overhead costs could be predicted from the budgeted direct labor hours.

Another member of the accounting staff suggested that a good starting place for determining the cost behavior pattern of overhead costs would be an analysis of historical data. The historical cost behavior pattern would provide a basis for estimating future overhead costs. The methods proposed for determining the cost behavior pattern included the high-low method, the scattergraph method, and simple linear regression. Data on direct labor hours and the respective overhead costs incurred were collected for the past two years. The raw data are as follows:

19X3	Direct Labor Hours	Overhead Costs	19X4	Direct Labor Hours	Overhead Costs
January	20,000	$84,000	January	21,000	$86,000
February	25,000	$99,000	February	24,000	$93,000
March	22,000	$89,500	March	23,000	$93,000
April	23,000	$90,000	April	22,000	$87,000
May	20,000	$81,500	May	20,000	$80,000
June	19,000	$75,500	June	18,000	$76,500
July	14,000	$70,500	July	12,000	$67,500
August	10,000	$64,500	August	13,000	$71,000
September	12,000	$69,000	September	15,000	$73,500
October	17,000	$75,000	October	17,000	$72,500
November	16,000	$71,500	November	15,000	$71,000
December	19,000	$78,000	December	18,000	$75,000

Using a service bureau's statistical package, the following output was obtained using linear regression:

Coefficient of determination r^2	.9109
Coefficient of correlation (r)	.9544
Coefficients of regression equation:	
Constant	39,859
Independent variable	2.1549
Standard error of the estimate	2,840

REQUIRED:

A. Of the three proposed methods (high-low, scattergraph, linear regression), which one should Ramon Company employ to determine the historical cost behavior pattern of Franklin Plant's overhead costs? Explain your answer completely, indicating the reasons why the other methods should not be used.

B. During April 19X5, the Franklin Plant scheduled production requiring 23,000 hours. The company has been approached by Burden's Supply, a new customer, for 5,000 electrical switches that will require an additional 3,000 hours of production. The added production is well within the technical capability and capacity of the Franklin Plant. What amount of variable overhead should be considered in pricing the contract?

C. During August 19X5, the Ramon Company is again approached by Burden's Supply for 5,000 electrical switches that will require an additional 3,000 hours of production. What is the amount of variable overhead cost that should be considered in pricing the second contract? Explain any differences in the two cost estimates or why there are no differences.

(CMA adapted)

chapter **3**

COST-VOLUME-PROFIT INTERACTIONS FOR OPERATING DECISIONS

In this chapter the ways in which fixed and variable cost information can be used by the manager to assist in making operating decisions are explored. These decisions involve the interaction of cost behavior patterns, production volume, and sales volume and revenue.

FIXED AND VARIABLE COSTS AND REVENUE

The study of cost-volume-profit relationships is most commonly called **breakeven analysis.** This term can be misleading. Firms do not seek to break even. They seek acceptable rates of return on their investments. However, breakeven analysis need not be limited merely to seeking the point at which the firm's revenue equals its costs. It can span all volumes within the relevant range of activity. Central to cost-volume-profit studies is an understanding of which costs are fixed and which are variable, as developed in the previous chapter.

Cost-volume-profit analysis is a term used by accountants to span a wide number of possible management decisions. Examples of decisions covered in this chapter are: "What volume must be sold to break even?" "What volume must be sold to achieve a specific profit?" "What effects do changes in costs or cost structures have on the firm's income?" and "What products should be emphasized or deemphasized in a multiproduct firm?" In later chapters we will look at other cost-volume-profit issues, including whether to sell or process a product further, whether to make or buy a product, and which departments to expand or contract, to name a few.

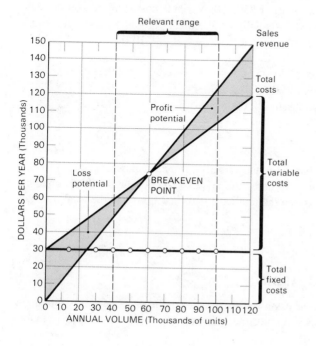

EXHIBIT 3—1
Breakeven graph for the Gordon Manufacturing Company

COST-VOLUME-PROFIT ANALYSIS THROUGH GRAPHS

The easiest way to see breakeven analysis is graphically. Exhibit 3–1 is a graphic presentation of cost-volume-profit relationships with the breakeven point indicated. This breakeven analysis of the Gordon Company was built upon a study of its cost behavior and revenue patterns. The Gordon Manufacturing Company produces a single product, a teak-handled can opener, which it sells to souvenir stores for $1.25 each. The firm's flexible budget shows that total fixed costs are estimated to be $30,000 per year and that variable costs per unit are estimated to be $.75. Management believes that the relevant range of activity is between 40,000 and 100,000 units per year. In constructing the graph, the fixed costs were plotted as a straight horizontal line at the $30,000 level. Variable costs were plotted at the rate of $.75 per unit of volume, providing the total cost line. The sales line was plotted at the rate of $1.25 per unit of volume.

The **breakeven point** is where the sales revenue line intersects the total cost line. At this volume, total revenues equal total expenses; the firm will make neither a profit nor a loss. For the Gordon Manufacturing Company the break-even point, determined from the vertical axis of the graph, is $75,000 in sales. This point occurs at a volume of 60,000 units, which is found on the horizontal axis. The distance between the sales revenue line and the total cost line at a volume below the breakeven point represents the loss potential of the firm. If the company operates at a volume beyond the breakeven point, the distance between the sales revenue line and the total cost line represents the profit potential of the firm.

If the company sells 40,000 units, what will be their loss? Sales will be 40,000 units × $1.25 per unit, or $50,000. Variable costs will be 40,000 units × $.75, or $30,000. Fixed costs will be $30,000. Combining these figures into an income statement, we can see that the loss will be $10,000.

Sales (40,000 × $1.25)	$ 50,000
Variable costs (40,000 × $.75)	30,000
Contribution margin (40,000 × $.50)	$ 20,000
Fixed costs	30,000
Loss	$(10,000)

The loss could also be found directly on the breakeven graph. Moving out the volume axis to 40,000 units, the loss of $10,000 may be determined by taking the difference between the total cost line ($60,000) and the total revenue line ($50,000).

COST-VOLUME-PROFIT ANALYSIS THROUGH EQUATIONS

The graphic method is an easy way to see the implications of a cost-volume-profit relationship, but expressing the relationships in equation form is much more precise and rapid. A general form of expressing cost-volume-profit relationships that can be adapted to any situation is

$$Sales - Fixed\ costs - Variable\ costs = Income$$
or
$$Sales = Fixed\ costs + Variable\ costs + Income$$

Because the total dollar amount of sales and variable costs are a function of the level of activity, the equation must be restated as follows:

$$SP(x) = FC + VC(x) + I$$

where

$$SP = \text{Selling price per unit.}$$
$$x = \text{Number of units sold.}$$
$$FC = \text{Total fixed costs.}$$
$$VC = \text{Variable cost per unit.}$$
$$I = \text{Total income.}$$

The Gordon Manufacturing Company's breakeven point, in number of units sold, may now be computed.

$$
\begin{array}{lll}
SP(x) & = FC + VC(x) + I & (1)\\
\$1.25(x) & = \$30,000 + \$.75(x) + 0 & (2)\\
\$.50x & = \$30,000 & (3)\\
x & = \$30,000 \div \$.50 & (4)\\
x & = 60,000 \text{ units needed to break even} & (5)
\end{array}
$$

Notice that step (4) is the fixed costs ($30,000) divided by the contribution margin per unit ($1.25 − $.75). The breakeven equation could be stated as:

$$\text{Breakeven point in units} = \frac{\text{Total fixed costs}}{\text{Contribution margin per unit}}$$

COST-VOLUME-PROFIT ANALYSIS
THROUGH THE CONTRIBUTION MARGIN

Many decision makers think in terms of a contribution margin income statement for cost-volume-profit analysis. Because we assume the revenue per unit is constant and the variable cost per unit is constant, the contribution margin per unit is constant. For the Gordon Manufacturing Company the contribution margin per unit is:

	Dollars	Percentage
Unit sales price	$1.25	100%
Unit variable cost	.75	60%
Unit contribution margin	$ .50	40%

Each unit generates a contribution margin that is available to cover fixed costs and, after they are covered, to contribute to profit. It should be apparent that if there is a negative contribution margin, the firm will *never* break even, because the variable costs will always exceed the sales revenue. In this case the more the company sells, the more it loses.

Alongside the income statement in dollars is a percentage analysis. If sales are considered 100%, then variable costs are 60% of each sales dollar. This relationship is called the **variable cost ratio.** The sales percentage minus the variable cost percentage is the **contribution margin ratio.** For the Gordon Manufacturing Company this ratio is 40% (100% − 60%). The fixed costs divided by the contribution margin ratio ($30,000 ÷ 40%) is the breakeven point in dollars of sales ($75,000). This is the same as the formula:

$$\text{Breakeven in dollars} = \frac{\text{Fixed costs}}{1 - \dfrac{\text{Variable costs}}{\text{Sales}}}$$

The denominator, $1 - \dfrac{\text{Variable costs}}{\text{Sales}}$, is the contribution margin ratio.

In summary, the breakeven point is:

$$\text{Breakeven in units} = \frac{\text{Fixed costs}}{\text{Contribution margin per unit}}$$

or

$$\text{Breakeven in dollars} = \frac{\text{Fixed costs}}{\text{Contribution margin ratio}}$$

The contribution margin and the contribution margin ratio allow another useful graphic technique called the **profit–volume chart** (PV chart). Exhibit 3–2 shows the PV chart for the Gordon Manufacturing Company. On this graph the vertical axis represents the annual income. The horizontal line at zero income level is that point where there are no profits or losses. The diagonal line is the

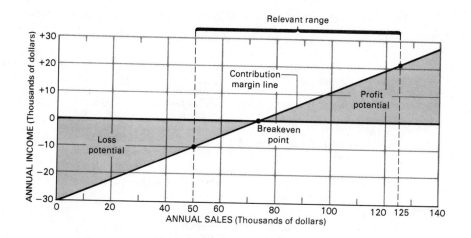

EXHIBIT 3–2
Profit–volume chart for
the Gordon
Manufacturing
Company

total contribution margin of the firm. The breakeven point occurs where the total contribution margin line crosses the zero income line.

Remember the question asked earlier about the amount of loss if the company sold 40,000 units at $1.25? At sales of $50,000 (40,000 × $1.25), the loss of $10,000 can be read directly from the PV chart.

CONTRIBUTION MARGIN APPROACH IN NONMANUFACTURING ACTIVITIES

The contribution margin approach is valid in any setting. In fact, the contribution margin is easy to apply in a nonmanufacturing setting, where inventory consists of purchased goods—all of which are variable costs.

To illustrate the contribution approach for a retail firm, let's assume the following traditional income statement for a florist's shop.

ROSIE'S FLOWER SHOP
INCOME STATEMENT

Sales		$200,000
Cost of goods sold		120,000
Gross margin		$ 80,000
Operating expenses:		
Salaries	$30,000	
Supplies	10,000	
Utilities	5,000	
Depreciation	13,000	
Other	2,000	60,000
Income		$ 20,000

Assume that a study of the cost–volume relationships supplied the following cost behavior patterns for the shop.

Variable Costs		Fixed Costs	
Cost of goods sold	$120,000	Salaries	$10,000
Salaries	$ 20,000	Utilities	$ 5,000
Supplies	$ 10,000	Depreciation	$13,000
Other	$ 2,000		

The income statement that follows uses the contribution margin format.

ROSIE'S FLOWER SHOP
INCOME STATEMENT

Sales		$200,000	100%
Cost of goods sold		120,000	60%
Contribution margin from trading		$ 80,000	40%
Variable operating costs:			
Salaries	$20,000		
Supplies	10,000		
Other	2,000	32,000	16%
Contribution margin from operations		$ 48,000	24%
Fixed operating costs:			
Salaries	$10,000		
Utilities	5,000		
Depreciation	13,000	28,000	
Income		$ 20,000	

By identifying the contribution margin, questions that concern change in volume, such as the following, may be answered.

1. How much additional income will result from a 10% increase in volume? Revenue and variable costs will each increase by 10%. Since fixed costs will remain unchanged, the increased contribution margin of $4,800 ($48,000 × 10%) will increase income by $4,800. This question cannot be answered from the traditional income statement.

2. What is the volume of sales at breakeven?

$$\frac{\text{Sales at}}{\text{breakeven}} = \frac{\text{Fixed costs}}{\text{Contribution margin ratio}}$$

$$= \frac{\$28,000}{24\%}$$

$$= \$116,667$$

The contribution margin approach is not limited to the private, profit-seeking sector of the economy. There are many situations where not-for-profit organizations will find the contribution margin approach useful. For example, consider the following income statement for the Eastside Community Health Center, a not-for-profit organization.

EASTSIDE COMMUNITY HEALTH CENTER INCOME STATEMENT		
	August	*September*
Patient visits	2,000	2,400
Revenue from patients	$20,000	$24,000
Operating costs:		
Personnel costs:		
Consulting physicians	$10,000	$12,000
Nurses and lab technicians	6,500	6,500
Administration	3,200	3,200
Medical supplies	2,000	2,400
Rent and occupancy costs	1,800	1,800
Service bureau (medical records)	600	700
Total operating costs	24,100	26,600
Loss from operations	$ (4,100)	$ (2,600)

The following cost behavior patterns were determined using the high-low method assuming 2,000 patient visits in August and 2,400 visits in September.

Variable Cost Per Visit		*Fixed Costs Per Month*	
Consulting physicians	$5.00	Nurses and lab technicians	$ 6,500
Medical supplies	1.00	Administrative salaries	3,200
Service bureau (records)	.25	Occupancy costs	1,800
		Service bureau (records)	100
Total	$6.25	Total	$11,600

The service bureau fee for maintenance of medical records is a mixed cost that includes a fixed monthly charge of $100 plus a variable charge of $.25 per patient visit.

The monthly income statements may now be recast to a contribution margin approach (Exhibit 3–3). The amount of loss does not change, but the income statements are much more useful. The director of the health center now has the financial information to answer a number of questions.

EASTSIDE COMMUNITY HEALTH CENTER
INCOME STATEMENT

	AUGUST		SEPTEMBER	
	Amount	Per Patient Visit	Amount	Per Patient Visit
Revenue from patients	$20,000	$10.00	$24,000	$10.00
Variable operating costs:				
Consulting physicians	$10,000	$ 5.00	$12,000	$ 5.00
Medical supplies	2,000	1.00	2,400	1.00
Medical records	500	.25	600	.25
Total variable costs	12,500	6.25	15,000	6.25
Contribution margin	$ 7,500	$ 3.75	$ 9,000	$ 3.75
Fixed costs:				
Nurses and lab technicians	$ 6,500		$ 6,500	
Administration	3,200		3,200	
Occupancy costs	1,800		1,800	
Medical records	100		100	
Total fixed costs	11,600		11,600	
Loss from operations	$(4,100)		$(2,600)	

EXHIBIT 3–3
Contribution margin income statement of the Eastside Community Health Center

1. One of the goals of the health center is to become financially self-sufficient. Assuming that the cost–revenue relationships do not change, how many patients must the center serve in order to break even?

$$\text{Breakeven in number of patients} = \frac{\text{Fixed costs}}{\text{Contribution margin per patient}}$$

$$= \frac{\$11,600}{\$3.75}$$

$$= 3,094 \text{ patient visits}$$

2. Assuming that the health center considers a volume of 2,500 patient visits per month to be a normal level that can be served within the present cost structure, what average billing rate per patient visit must be charged to break even?

$$\text{Revenue} = \text{Fixed costs} + \text{Variable costs}$$
$$2,500(SP) = \$11,600 + \$6.25 \ (2,500)$$

where SP is the desired billing rate to break even.

$$2,500(SP) = \$11,600 + \$15,625$$
$$2,500(SP) = \$27,225$$
$$(SP) = \$10.89$$

If the health center is to break even at a level of 2,500 patients with the present cost structure, the average billing rate must be raised to $10.89 per patient visit.

The contribution margin approach can be useful in any setting where the impact of volume change on revenue and costs is needed for management decisions.

EFFECTS OF CHANGING FACTORS

A breakeven graph shows the relationship among four variables: sales price, fixed costs, variable costs, and volume. In this section we will look at how changes in the three variables of sales price, fixed costs, and variable costs interact with volume to create a profit.

EFFECTS OF CHANGES IN SELLING PRICE

Let's assume that the management of the Gordon Manufacturing Company (an earlier example) has the opportunity to increase the unit selling price of its can opener from $1.25 to $1.50. It believes that no other factor will change by a significant amount. The immediate effect on the breakeven point is that it will be reached sooner. In this case the breakeven point in units would be:

$$\frac{\text{Fixed costs}}{\text{Contribution margin per unit}} = \frac{\$30,000}{\$1.50 - \$.75} = 40,000 \text{ units}$$

At the old selling price of $1.25 the breakeven point was 60,000 units. It is apparent that an increase in the selling price will raise the contribution margin if the variable costs are unchanged, and that an increase in the per-unit contribution margin will decrease the sales volume necessary to cover fixed costs.

What happens if the company has to lower the selling price to $1.00 per unit because of increased competition? The breakeven point will be increased to 120,000 units [$30,000 ÷ ($1.00 − $.75)]. At this output level the company will have to reassess its cost and revenue patterns completely, because 120,000 units is beyond the relevant range of activity.

EFFECTS OF CHANGES IN VARIABLE COSTS

Assume there have been changes in variable costs. Teak has been in short supply; due to increased demand around the world, the price increased. The teak used in the product has increased in price by $.05 per unit. Also, because of inflationary pressures, the wages of the production workers increased an average of $.20 per unit. These changes increased the total variable costs from $.75 per unit to $1.00 per unit. The new contribution margin becomes $.25 ($1.25 − $1.00), and the breakeven point in units would be:

$$\frac{\text{Fixed costs}}{\text{Contribution margin per unit}} = \frac{\$30,000}{\$.25} = 120,000 \text{ units}$$

Again, 120,000 units is beyond the relevant range.

Any time the selling price per unit decreases or the variable cost per unit increases, the contribution margin per unit will decline and the volume necessary to achieve breakeven will increase. Of course, increases in the selling prices or decreases in the variable costs will reduce the volume necessary to achieve the breakeven point.

EFFECTS OF CHANGES IN FIXED COSTS

Assume that it is becoming clear to management that it will be necessary to add $6,000 for advertising if the company is to maintain its selling price of $1.25 per unit. The new breakeven point would be

$$\frac{\text{Fixed costs} + \text{Additional fixed cost}}{\text{Contribution margin per unit}} = \frac{\$30,000 + \$6,000}{\$1.25 - \$.75}$$
$$= 72,000 \text{ units}$$

Notice that the one-fifth increase in fixed costs (from $30,000 to $36,000) resulted in a one-fifth increase in the breakeven point (from 60,000 to 72,000 units). Changes in fixed costs will always result in proportional changes in the breakeven point.

VOLUME NECESSARY TO ACHIEVE DESIRED INCOME

The examples so far have stressed the effect of changes in costs on the breakeven point. Of course, management seeks an income. What the desired income will be is determined by many factors, including stockholder goals, economic environments, and desired growth rates.

To illustrate how a desired income can be incorporated into the planning process, what volume must the Gordon Manufacturing Company achieve to obtain an income of $12,000 if it sells its can openers for $1.25 each, incurs

$.75 per unit for variable costs, and has fixed costs of $30,000? The desired sales volume would be

$$\frac{\text{Sales necessary for}}{\text{desired income}} = \frac{\text{Fixed costs} + \text{Desired income}}{\text{Contribution margin per unit}}$$

$$= \frac{\$30,000 + \$12,000}{\$1.25 - \$.75} = 84,000 \text{ units}$$

There is another way to approach the same question. If management has already calculated the breakeven point, it can approach the volume needed to earn a desired income by determining the increment in sales beyond the breakeven point. In the Gordon Manufacturing Company the breakeven point is 60,000 units, or $75,000 of sales, assuming $30,000 of fixed costs and a contribution margin of $.50 per unit. At this level all fixed costs would be recovered. Beyond the breakeven point, the entire contribution margin per unit adds to the income. For each unit sold beyond 60,000, the income would be increased by $.50, the contribution margin per unit. Thus, to achieve an income of $12,000, the company would have to sell 24,000 units ($12,000 ÷ $.50) beyond breakeven, or a total of 84,000 units (60,000 + 24,000).

The income in the previous illustrations has been the income *before* income taxes. Management may want to state its net income objectives *after* income taxes. In this case the analysis must be expanded slightly. Assume that the company wants a net income after taxes of $14,000 and that its current tax rate is 30%. In this example the net income after taxes is 70% of the income before taxes. The formula to calculate the sales *volume* necessary to earn $14,000 after taxes is

$$\frac{\text{Fixed costs} + \dfrac{\text{Desired income after taxes}}{1 - \text{Tax rate}}}{\text{Contribution margin per unit}} = \frac{\$30,000 + \dfrac{\$14,000}{1 - .30}}{\$1.25 - \$.75}$$

$$= \frac{\$30,000 + \$20,000}{\$.50}$$

$$= 100,000 \text{ units}$$

To find the sales *dollars* needed to achieve an after-tax income of $14,000, the formula would be adjusted to divide by the contribution margin ratio (.40). This calculation is

$$\frac{\$30,000 + \$20,000}{.40} = \$125,000$$

UNDERLYING ASSUMPTIONS OF COST-VOLUME-PROFIT RELATIONSHIPS

A thoughtful look at the breakeven graph provides insight into the underlying assumptions of cost-volume-profit analysis. Among them are the following.

1. The breakeven graph shows costs separated into fixed and variable components. This classification implies that the decision maker has been successful in finding and using a method of segregating fixed and variable costs. Within this assumption lie the problems and limitations of cost–volume analysis discussed in Chapter 2.

2. The fixed costs are constant across the changes in volume, and the variable costs change in direct proportion to volume. Inherent in this assumption is the concept of the relevant range. It is apparent that fixed costs will stairstep at some volume. Some variable costs are not linear. Labor will meet with diminishing returns at some activity level and raw materials may involve quantity discounts if used in large amounts. All these issues, and others like them, have been resolved via a linear relationship within the assumption of a relevant range.

3. The revenue line is also linear. Throughout the relevant range it assumes that management is not granting price concessions to obtain higher sales volume. This is the economist's definition of pure competition.

4. When both costs and revenues are plotted on the same volume (x) axis, the assumption of a single volume measure is made.

5. Since the time implied by such a cost-volume-profit graph is an accounting period, for example, the fiscal year, the cost-volume-profit graph assumes no price-level changes and no significant changes in production methods, products, or managerial policies during the accounting period.

6. Because the graph assumes a constant contribution margin per unit, it implies that there is only one product or, if more than one, that the combination of products sold provides a constant average contribution margin ratio.

A CURVILINEAR APPROACH TO COST-VOLUME-PROFIT ANALYSIS

The contribution margin approach assumes the selling price and variable cost per unit are constant. This decision model leads to producing and selling at the maximum plant capacity as long as the contribution margin per unit is positive. This assumption is valid only as long as the firm does not find it necessary to reduce the selling price per unit to increase sales volume or the variable costs per unit do not increase because of diminishing returns.

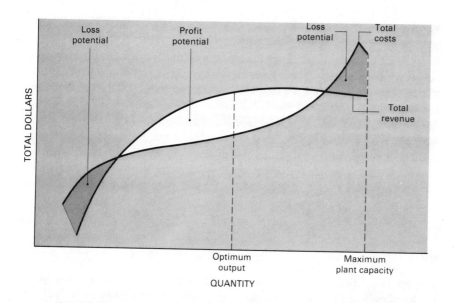

EXHIBIT 3—4
Economist's total
revenue and cost
curves.

The economist, in developing a theoretical model for decisions about pricing of products and the level of production output, takes into account the possibility of decreasing sales price per unit and increasing costs per unit. In this sense the economist's curvilinear model is more generalizable than the accountant's linear model. In economic theory total costs increase at a declining *rate* per unit, then at a constant *rate* per unit, and finally at an increasing *rate* per unit. This behavior pattern of costs recognizes that gains in operating efficiencies act to reduce costs per unit to a certain point (**economies of scale**) and that as the level of production continues to increase, operating inefficiencies take effect (**diminishing returns**). Furthermore, economics assumes that the price per unit must be reduced to sell more units. The firm must offer price concessions to obtain increased sales volume.[1]

The effect of the decreasing price per unit and the increasing cost per unit is to have an income figure that increases to a point and then decreases until it becomes a loss. Thus, the optimum production level is where the total revenue line exceeds the total cost line by the largest amount. The total revenue and cost curves, with the optimum volume level, are shown in Exhibit 3–4.

Economists also state this decision rule on a per-unit basis. Using a per-unit analysis the optimum output by the economist's rule is the point at which the added cost of producing the next unit (**marginal cost**) equals the added revenue from the next unit sold (**marginal revenue**). These are concepts that relate the changes in cost and revenue effected by adding *one* unit. It is beyond the scope of this book to demonstrate that this economic principle is true. For

---

[1]This statement is true in all cases except pure competition. In pure competition the selling price per unit is assumed to be constant over the output range because the individual producer cannot offer a large enough amount to influence the price.

our purposes we will use total revenue and cost, which provides the same results, rather than marginal revenue and cost analysis.

The economist, in developing a model that is descriptive over wide ranges of activity, allows unit quantities, unit prices, and cost inputs to vary. The accountant, on the other hand, uses a model where only the quantities vary; unit prices and cost inputs are held constant. Because of these limiting constraints the accountant stresses the **relevant range of activity** over which these linear assumptions are valid. Outside the relevant range of activity the entire cost and revenue patterns of the accountant must be reassessed. Thus, when we say that the decision rule for operating (short-run) decisions is to maximize the total contribution margin of the firm we are consistent with economic theory, assuming the constraints of the relevant range of activity.

MULTIPRODUCT SITUATIONS

The previous illustrations assumed that the Gordon Manufacturing Company produced only one product. However, many manufacturers make more than one type of product. The relative combination of the quantities of each product sold is called the **sales mix.** If each product has an identical contribution margin, changes in the product mix will not affect the breakeven point or the profit from operations. However, when the products have different contribution margins, changes in the product mix will affect the breakeven point and the results from operations.

To explore the effect of sales mix, let's assume that the management of the Gordon Manufacturing Company added two new items to its product line—a bottle opener and a corkscrew. Projected selling prices, cost patterns, and volume of sales are shown in Exhibit 3–5. Exhibit 3–6 shows the projected income statements for each product and for the company as a whole.

The breakeven point for the Gordon Manufacturing Company, given the sales mix of 50,000 can openers, 25,000 bottle openers, and 15,000 corkscrews, is $36,000 ÷ 35.83%, or $100,474. The 35.83% is the aggregate contribution margin ratio based upon the specific sales mix. At the bottom of Exhibit 3–6 the sales for each product are shown as a percentage of total sales. Given the

	Can Opener	Bottle Opener	Corkscrew
Sales price per unit	$1.25	$2.00	$2.50
Variable cost per unit	.75	1.30	1.75
Contribution margin per unit	$ .50	$ .70	$ .75
Contribution margin ratio	40%	35%	30%
Total Fixed Costs, $36,000			
Projected units to be produced and sold	50,000	25,000	15,000

EXHIBIT 3–5
Projected cost and revenue data for the Gordon Manufacturing Company

THE GORDON MANUFACTURING COMPANY
PROJECTED INCOME STATEMENT
For the Year Ended December 31, 19X6

	Can Opener	Bottle Opener	Corkscrew	Total	
Units sold	50,000	25,000	15,000		
Sales	$62,500	$50,000	$37,500	$150,000	100.00%
Variable cost	37,500	32,500	26,250	96,250	64.17%
Total contribution margin	$25,000	$17,500	$11,250	$ 53,750	35.83%
Fixed costs				36,000	
Net income before taxes				$ 17,750	
Sales as percentage of total sales	41.67%	33.33%	25.00%	100.00%	
times					
Contribution margin ratio	40.00%	35.00%	30.00%	35.83%	
equals					
Contribution margin of each product per dollar of revenue	16.67%	11.66%	7.50%	35.83%	

EXHIBIT 3–6 Projected income statements by product line for the Gordon Manufacturing Company

sales mix in Exhibit 3–6, the can openers account for 41.67% of the total sales of $150,000; the bottle openers, 33⅓%; and the corkscrews, 25%. Multiplying each product's percentage share of total sales by the contribution margin ratio for that product gives the total contribution margin *per sales dollar* for each product. Thus, the 16.67% for the can opener is its contribution margin per total dollar of revenue.

Given this setting, and other things being equal, management would stress those products with the greatest contribution margins. Assume that during the year management actually sold 25,000 additional bottle openers in place of 25,000 can openers. The income statement for the year would be as shown in Exhibit 3–7. Based upon the sales of 25,000 can openers, 50,000 bottle openers, and 15,000 corkscrews, the breakeven point would be $36,000 ÷ 34.81%, or $103,419. The shift from selling 50,000 can openers and 25,000 bottle openers to selling 25,000 can openers and 50,000 bottle openers had a curious effect. It lowered the aggregate contribution margin ratio from 35.83% (Exhibit 3–6) to 34.81% (Exhibit 3–7) while simultaneously increasing the net profit by $5,000 ($22,750 − $17,750). This income difference can be seen as:

	Budgeted	Actual
Sales	$150,000	$168,750
Average contribution margin ratio	35.83%	34.81%
Total contribution margin	$ 53,750	$ 58,750

THE GORDON MANUFACTURING COMPANY
ACTUAL INCOME STATEMENT
For the Year Ended December 31, 19X6

	Can Opener	Bottle Opener	Corkscrew	Total	
Units sold	25,000	50,000	15,000		
Sales	$31,250	$100,000	$37,500	$168,750	100.00%
Variable cost	18,750	65,000	26,250	110,000	65.19%
Total contribution margin	$12,500	$35,000	$11,250	$ 58,750	34.81%
Fixed costs				36,000	
Net income before taxes				$ 22,750	
Sales as percentage of total sales	18.52%	59.26%	22.22%	100.00%	
times					
Contribution margin ratio	40.00%	35.00%	30.00%	34.81%	
equals					
Contribution margin of each product per dollar of revenue	7.40%	20.74%	6.67%	34.81%	

EXHIBIT 3–7　Actual income statements by product line for the Gordon Manufacturing Company

The can opener has a higher contribution margin ratio (40%) than the bottle opener (35%), but the contribution margin per unit of the bottle opener is higher ($.70) than that of the can opener ($.50). The firm should move toward those products that provide the greatest *total contribution margin*, considering the product mix, rather than automatically choosing the product with the highest contribution margin ratio.

In Exhibits 3–6 and 3–7 the fixed costs are shown as a lump-sum amount deducted from the total column. Fixed costs have not been allocated or apportioned to the individual product line income statements. It is not necessary to do so because for management decisions, the question of which products to emphasize and the effect of cost-volume-revenue interactions on profits and breakeven points do not depend on allocation of fixed costs.

THE MARGIN OF SAFETY

The operating characteristics of different departments within a company, or of two different companies, can be examined through a closer study of their cost structures. Assume that a company has two decentralized departments with cost and revenue characteristics shown in the accompanying tabulation.

	Department A		Department B	
Sales	$50,000	100%	$50,000	100%
Variable costs	35,000	70%	10,000	20%
Contribution margin	$15,000	30%	$40,000	80%
Fixed costs	10,000		35,000	
Income	$ 5,000		$ 5,000	
Breakeven points in sales dollars	$33,333		$43,750	

These two departments have the same income although they have very different underlying economic characteristics. One way to examine these differences is through the **margin of safety,** which shows the difference between the actual (or budgeted) sales and the breakeven point. Two margins of safety are as follows:

	Department A	*Department B*
1. Margin of safety expressed in dollars		
($50,000 − $33,333)	$16,667	
(($50,000 − $43,750)		$6,250
2. Margin of safety expressed as a percentage of sales		
$16,667 ÷ $50,000)	33.33%	
($6,250 ÷ $50,000)		12.50%

Department B is operating closer to the breakeven point than is Department A. Department B has a narrower margin of safety. If the volume of Department B drops more than 12.50%, it will operate at a loss; Department A will not operate at a loss unless its volume drops 33.33%. In one sense the margin of safety is an inexact measure of the risks of investing in fixed costs rather than variable costs. A rise in the breakeven point reduces the margin of safety and increases managerial pressure to sustain a high sales volume.

SUMMARY

The breakeven graph is a pictorial presentation of cost-volume-profit interactions. It shows the point where total revenue equals total cost. More importantly, it shows how managerial decisions regarding revenues and volume affect the firm's profit. Inherent in cost-volume-profit analysis is the relevant range of activity. The relevant range is that volume over which the relationships can be assumed valid.

The breakeven point in dollars is the fixed costs divided by the contribution margin ratio. The breakeven point in units is the fixed costs divided by the contribution margin per unit. For firms with multiple products, the breakeven point must be built upon a specific product mix. Where there are separate departments within the firm, the effect of cost–volume changes can be seen in the margin of safety (budgeted or actual sales minus breakeven sales) and the margin of safety ratio (the difference between actual sales and breakeven sales divided by actual sales).

PROBLEMS AND CASES

3-1 *(Terminology on the Breakeven Graph).* The Eagle Company's breakeven graph is shown below.

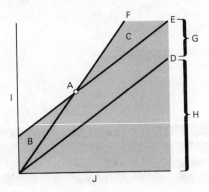

REQUIRED:

Determine the proper terminology to identify each concept labeled by a letter on the breakeven graph.

3-2 *(Terminology on the Profit–Volume Graph).* Below is the profit–volume graph of the Byrd Company.

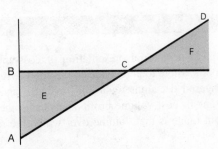

REQUIRED:

Determine the proper terminology to identify each concept labeled by a letter on the profit–volume graph.

3-3 *(Matching Graphs with Concepts).* Below are six graphs. Match the appropriate graph with the concepts listed below. (Each graph may be used more than once.)

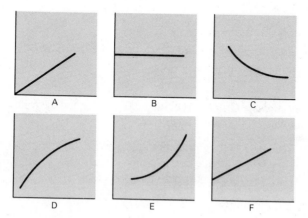

1. Total rental costs paid on a monthly basis.
2. Economists' total revenue line.
3. A mixed cost.
4. Direct labor cost per unit when workers are paid on piece-rate basis.
5. Economists' unit cost line.
6. Direct materials cost per unit where the supplier grants quantity discounts.
7. A semivariable cost with a fine or penalty clause.
8. A fixed cost, measured on a per-unit basis.
9. The total cost line on a linearly prepared breakeven graph.
10. Contribution margin per unit.
11. Contribution margin line on profit–volume graph.
12. Cost per mile for operating an automobile.
13. A variable cost per unit.
14. The total variable cost line on a linearly prepared breakeven graph.
15. Total direct labor where labor is encountering diminishing returns.

3-4 *(Breakeven Graph).* The River Company had the following income statement when 10,000 units were sold:

```
RIVER COMPANY INCOME STATEMENT

Sales                                            $20,000
Expenses:
    Variable expenses          $12,000
    Fixed expenses               6,000           18,000
Income                                          $ 2,000
```

REQUIRED:

A. Prepare a breakeven graph for the company.

B. From the graph, how many units must be sold to break even?

C. What is the margin of safety in dollars?

3-5 *(Profit–Volume Graph).* The Stream Company had the following revenue and cost data when 2,000 units were sold.

Selling price per unit	$12.00
Variable cost per unit	$ 6.00
Fixed cost per unit	$ 4.50

REQUIRED:

A. Prepare a profit–volume graph for the company.

B. Determine the breakeven point from the graph.

C. From the graph, determine how many units must be sold to generate a net income of $3,000.

3-6 *(Cost-Volume-Profit Decisions).* The Popular Paper Company produces a line of quality napkins and paper tablecloths. One particular product, a 72-inch round tablecloth, is causing disagreement between the sales department and the cost accounting department. The sales department believes that the product is selling well and contributing greatly to the profitability of the firm, stressing the fact that the product has a variable cost ratio of 55%. The cost accounting department, on the other hand, says that the yearly sales of 250,000 units at $1.00 per unit did not produce sufficient volume to cover the fixed costs of $130,000 per year.

REQUIRED:

A. What is the volume of sales necessary to break even?

B. What selling price per unit is necessary to break even at the present volume level?

C. Prepare a contribution margin income statement based upon the original data in the problem.

3-7 (*Contribution Margin, Breakeven in Dollars in a Service Concern*). The Collier Company had the following income statement for the past year:

Sales		$300,000
Operating expenses:		
Rent (100% fixed)	$30,000	
Utilities (40% fixed)	20,000	
Sales commissions (100% variable)	90,000	
Marketing expenses (50% fixed)	80,000	
General expenses (100% fixed)	40,000	260,000
Income		$ 40,000

REQUIRED:

A. The contribution margin as a percentage of sales.

B. The breakeven point in sales dollars.

C. The management of the Collier Company is under pressure to change their policy on sale's commissions. Salespeople are asking for a shift from a 30% sales commission without guarantee to a guaranteed salary plus a 10% commission. At the current level of sales the guaranteed salaries would total $60,000. Recompute the answers in parts A and B, assuming the firm would adopt this new proposal.

3-8 (*Cost-Volume-Profit Analysis Under Different Assumptions*). Going-to-Pot Productions produces, among other products, a line of 4-inch clay pots. Breakeven is currently at a sales volume of $18,000, or 36,000 clay pots. Each pot generates a contribution margin of $.20. The company desires a profit of $4,000 on the sale of these pots and is willing to increase advertising by $2,000 to obtain the needed volume increase.

REQUIRED: (Consider each case separately.)

A. How many pots beyond the breakeven point would the company have to sell to earn their desired profit without the advertising?

B. If fixed costs were to increase 10%, what volume of sales would be necessary to earn the desired profit of $4,000?

C. If the company decided to spend the $2,000 for advertising, what volume would be necessary to earn the $4,000 profit?

D. The company believes it can double sales by lowering the selling price to $.28 per unit. Would you advise doing this? Why or why not? Would your answer differ if the selling price were lowered to $.35 to achieve this volume increase?

3-9   *(Breakeven with Two Products).* The Security Lock Company manufactures two locks—keyed and combination. Relevant sales and cost data for June 19X3 are as shown below.

Product	Units Sold	Unit Price	Variable Costs
Keyed	50,000	$4.00	$2.70
Combination	60,000	$7.00	$3.50

The fixed costs for the company were $264,000.

REQUIRED:

Compute the breakeven point in units and in dollars for both products.

3-10 *(Cost-Volume-Profit Interactions).* The Huber Company estimates its sales at 500,000 units per year at $2.00 per unit. Variable costs generally equal $.40 per unit. Fixed costs for this planned sales level would equal $1.20 per unit.

REQUIRED:

A. The estimated income at the planned level of sales.

B. The breakeven point in units.

C. The margin of safety expressed as a percentage of sales.

D. The contribution margin ratio.

E. The decrease in income that would result from a 10% decrease in sales.

3-11 *(Cost-Volume-Profit Decisions Under Different Assumptions).* The Forest Manufacturing Company has the following revenue and cost characteristics on their only product.

Selling price per unit	$6.00
Variable costs per unit	$4.20
Annual fixed costs	$360,000
Annual volume	270,000 units

REQUIRED:

A. Determine the following:

   1. Variable cost ratio.

   2. Contribution margin ratio.

   3. Contribution margin per unit.

   4. Breakeven point in units and in dollars.

   5. Income at current operating level.

B. For each of the following *independent* cases, determine the new contribution margin ratio, breakeven point in dollars, and income.

1. 5% increase in selling price.
2. 20% increase in variable costs.
3. 50% increase in fixed costs.
4. 5% increase in sales and production volume.
5. Decrease of $30,000 in fixed costs.
6. Decrease in variable costs of $.20.
7. Decrease in variable costs of $.60 and 20% increase in selling price.
8. 20% decrease in fixed costs and 20% increase in variable costs.

3-12 *(Breakeven Points Using Levels of Fixed Costs).* The Red Turbin Company had the following cost data:

Production Volume in Units	Fixed Costs
0	$400,000
1–3,000	$528,000
3,001–6,000	$780,000

The unit sales price is $600. At a full capacity of 6,000 units the company's variable costs were $1,350,000.

REQUIRED:

A. Compute the company's breakeven point in sales dollars and sales units.

B. Determine the level of operations where it would be more economical to close the plant than to continue operations.

C. Assume the company is operating at 40% of capacity when it decided to reduce the sales price to $350 in an attempt to increase sales volume. What is the breakeven sales volume in units at the reduced sales price?

3-13 *(Effect of Changes in Sales Mix).* The Miniature Animal Company manufactures two pottery animal figurines—a dog and a cat. Data for the past year were:

Sales:		
Dog (30,000 units)	$ 45,000	
Cat (90,000 units)	180,000	$225,000
Variable costs:		
Dog	$ 36,000	
Cat	90,000	126,000
Contribution margin		$ 99,000
Fixed costs		99,000
Income		$ 0

The company is considering an advertising campaign to convince customers to buy cats instead of dogs. If $4,000 additional is spent on new advertising management believes the sales of cats would increase 20,000 units while sales of dogs would decrease 20,000 units.

REQUIRED:

A. Determine the income (loss) if the company undertakes the advertising campaign by preparing a new contribution margin income statement.

B. Determine the breakeven point in units of dogs and cats if the advertising campaign is undertaken.

3-14 *(Identification of Terms and Cost-Volume-Profit Decisions).* Cost-volume-earnings analysis (breakeven analysis) is used to determine and express the interrelationships of different volumes of activity (sales), costs, sales prices, and sales mix to earnings. More specifically, the analysis is concerned with the effect on earnings of changes in sales volume, sales prices, sales mix, and costs.

REQUIRED:

A. Certain terms are fundamental to cost-volume-earnings analysis. Explain the meaning of each of the following terms:

1. Fixed costs.

2. Variable costs.

3. Relevant range.

4. Breakeven point.

5. Margin of safety.

6. Sales mix.

B. Several assumptions are implicit in cost-volume-earnings analysis. What are these assumptions?

C. In a recent period Zero Company had the following experience:

Sales (10,000 units @ $200)			$2,000,000
	Fixed	*Variable*	
Costs			
Direct material	$ 0	$ 200,000	
Direct labor	0	400,000	
Factory overhead	160,000	600,000	
Administration expenses	180,000	80,000	
Other expenses	200,000	120,000	
Total costs	$540,000	$1,400,000	1,940,000
Income			$ 60,000

Each item below is independent.

1. Calculate the breakeven point for Zero in terms of units and sales dollars. Show your calculations.

2. What sales volume would be required to generate an income of $96,000? Show your calculations.

3. What is the breakeven point if management makes a decision that increases fixed costs by $18,000? Show your calculations.

D. After reading an article you recommended on cost behavior, a friend asks you to explain the following excerpts from it:

> *Fixed costs* are variable per unit of output and *variable costs* are fixed per unit of output (although in the long run all costs are variable).

> *Depreciation* may be either a fixed cost or a variable cost, depending on the method used to compute it.

For each excerpt:

1. Define the italicized terms. Give examples where appropriate.

2. Explain the meaning of the excerpts to your friend.

(CPA adapted)

3-15 *(Margin of Safety and Breakeven Point with Multiple Products).* The Oak Tree Company produces two main product lines made of oak: an old-fashioned bucket, which sells for $6.00, and a 5-gallon decorative wine cask, which sells for $7.50. The variable cost for the bucket is $4.50 per unit; for the wine cask it is $5.00. The bucket department had sales of 50,000 units, while the wine cask department had sales of 30,000 units. Identifiable fixed costs are $50,000 and $55,000 for the bucket and cask departments, respectively.

REQUIRED:

A. Prepare contribution margin income statements for each product line and for the company as a whole.

B. Calculate the breakeven point for each product and for the company as a whole.

C. Calculate the contribution margin ratio for the company as a whole.

D. For each product, and for the company as a whole, determine:

1. The margin of safety in dollars.

2. The margin of safety expressed as a percentage of sales.

E. Which line offers the least risk? Why?

3-16 *(Contribution Margin Income Statements and Margins of Safety in a Nonmanufacturing Setting).* The North Bay Mental Health Clinic operates two different programs. The outpatient clinic's clients come from the neighboring community. Clients are billed for each visit according to their ability to pay; on the average, clients pay $25 per visit. Counselors in the outpatient clinic receive $15 per patient visit on a contract basis. Variable costs of record-keeping average $1.00 per patient visit. The fixed costs, composed of rent, insurance, director's salary, and office personnel total $4,000 per month. In a typical month the clinic has 450 client visits.

The inpatient clinic operates a residential home for homeless adolescents under a state contract. The state pays North Bay $1,000 per month per approved resident. In a typical month the home has 20 residents. The clinic's total monthly staff salaries, all of which are fixed, total $14,500. The clinic's rent, which includes all operating costs of the facility, is $3,000 per month. The clinic also incurs $100 per month per resident for food purchases.

REQUIRED:

A. Prepare a separate contribution margin income statement for each program.

B. Determine the breakeven point in dollars and the margin of safety in dollars for each program.

C. Comment on the cost structures of the two programs.

3-17 (*Cost-Volume-Profit Decisions and Flexible Budget Determination*). Cider Press Company was organized at the beginning of the year to process apples grown on Vashon Island into apple cider.

The firm has three employees: a clerk, a crushing machine operator, and a bottling machine operator. All employees are paid $3.00 per hour plus $1.50 per hour for any time worked over the regular working hours of 40 hours in one week. The clerk must be on hand during regular working hours to purchase any apples brought into the plant by orchard operators. The other two employees work only if there are apples ready to be crushed. (They are not guaranteed any specific number of hours of work in a week.)

About 50 gallons of cider are processed in an hour if sufficient applies are on hand. If apples are always on hand, 2,000 gallons may be processed in a week during normal working hours.

Cider Press Company leases the machinery and building for $340 per week.

The firm purchases apples for $2.40 per bushel. About 6 gallons of cider can be produced from 1 bushel.

The cider is bottled in glass jugs that cost $.29 each (including the cap).

Maintenance costs and power costs are $2.00 for each hour the machinery is run. (The machinery is run only when apples are available.)

Summary of costs (assuming 2,000 gallons produced in a week):

Clerk's wages	$.06 per gallon
Crushing machine operator	$.06 per gallon

Bottling machine operator	\$.06 per gallon
Leasing costs	\$.17 per gallon
Apples	\$.40 per gallon
Jugs and caps	\$.29 per gallon
Maintenance and power	\$80.00 per week

The cider is immediately sold to a distributor for \$1.21 per gallon.

REQUIRED:

A. What is the breakeven point (in gallons per week)?

B. If sufficient apples are available, should the machines be run more than 40 hours in a week? (All the apples can be purchased by the clerk during regular working hours.)

C. How many gallons would have to be processed and sold to realize an income of \$300 in a week?

D. What is the contribution margin per gallon if the cost of apples falls to \$1.80 per bushel due to an unusually large harvest?

(Prepared by Eric Noreen)

3-18 *(Flexible Budgets and Breakeven Point in a Retail Setting).* Hank Rugger operates a lumberjack equipment store specializing in axes and chain saws. His income statement for 19X8 is shown in page 96.

Hank asked the bookkeeper to perform a fixed and variable cost study. The bookeeper's report was as follows.

Dear Hank:

As you requested I studied the contracts of your firm. As you know, your lease agreement calls for an annual lease payment of \$2,400. Over the years your utilities have averaged \$125 per month.

The bookkeeping service fee is as we agreed. I receive \$50 per month for the basic work plus 3% of gross sales, because the greater your sales the larger the number of sales and purchase invoices I must process.

The advertising costs result from the ads you run in the weekly newspaper. Typically you run ads 50 weeks per year at an average cost of \$36 per week.

The sales commissions are a direct percentage of sales. You pay a commission of 5% on all gross sales of axes and 10% on all gross sales of saws.

The cost-of-goods-sold percentage is a result of your pricing policy. Over the years you have used the industry-wide markup on both axes and saws. For axes the markup was 50% of cost. For example, if an axe cost \$10, the sales price was \$15. For saws the markup was 33⅓% of cost. For example, if a saw cost \$12, the selling price was \$16.

Hope this helps you Hank. Cheers.

Casper M.

```
                    HANK RUGGER
                  INCOME STATEMENT
                  FOR THE YEAR 19X8

    Sales:
      Axes                    $30,000
      Saws                     80,000      $110,000
    Cost of goods sold:
      Axes                    $20,000
      Saws                     60,000        80,000
    Gross profit                           $ 30,000
    Operating expenses:
      Rent                    $ 2,400
      Utilities                 1,500
      Bookkeeping service       3,900
      Advertising               1,800
      Sales commissions         9,500        19,100
    Income                                 $ 10,900
```

REQUIRED:

A. Recast the income statement for 19X8 using the contribution margin approach. Show both total and product line data.

B. What is Hank's breakeven point in dollars of sales? How would the breakeven point change if sales of saws increased while sales of axes decreased?

C. Prepare a profit plan (budgeted income statement) for 19X9 assuming that sales are budgeted at $48,000 for axes and $120,000 for saws.

D. Do you approve of Hank's policy on sales commissions? Explain.

3-19 (*Cost-Volume-Profit Decisions in Manufacturing Setting*). R. A. Ro and Company, maker of quality handmade pipes, has experienced a steady growth in sales for the past five years. However, increased competition had led Mr. Ro, the president, to believe that an aggressive advertising campaign will be necessary next year to maintain the company's present growth.

To prepare for next year's advertising campaign, the company's accountant has prepared and presented Mr. Ro with the following data for the current year, 19X2:

Cost Schedule	
Variable costs:	
Direct labor	$ 8.00/pipe
Direct materials	3.25/pipe
Variable overhead	2.50/pipe
Total variable costs	$13.75/pipe

Fixed costs:	
Manufacturing	$ 25,000
Selling	40,000
Administrative	70,000
Total fixed costs	$135.000
Selling price, per pipe:	$ 25.00
Expected sales, 19X2 (20,000 units):	$500,000
Tax rate: 40%	

Mr. Ro has set the sales target for 19X3 at a level of $550,000 (or 22,000 pipes).

REQUIRED:

A. What is the projected after-tax net income for 19X2? 19X3?

B. What is the breakeven point in units for 19X2? 19X3?

C. Mr. Ro believes that an additional selling expense of $11,250 for advertising in 19X3, with all other costs remaining constant, will be necessary to attain the sales target. What will be the after-tax net income for 19X3 if the additional $11,250 is spent?

D. What will be the breakeven point in dollar sales for 19X3 if the additional $11,250 is spent for advertising?

E. If the additional $11,250 is spent for advertising in 19X3, what is the required sales level in dollar sales to equal 19X2's after-tax net income?

F. At a sales level of 22,000 units, what is the maximum amount that can be spent on advertising if an after-tax net income of $60,000 is desired?

(CMA adapted)

3-20 *(Cost-Volume-Profit Decisions in Animal Husbandry Setting).* Ahmul and Ashmir raise and sell camels. They acquire the camels they sell by two methods. Half they buy from other breeders at an average price of $100. The other half is taken from their own herd. They try to maintain a stable breeding herd of 500 camels by selling their one-year-old camels. It costs them an average of $50 per camel per year to feed, watch, and maintain their herd. They have a reputation for fair dealing and quality merchandise so there is no problem selling their supply. They sell an average of 600 camels every year, at an average price of $175 each.

This year, however, due to unexpected circumstances, the slightly larger than normal crop of 340 calves consisted of 80% white camels—a most unfortunate occurrence. White camels cannot be bartered or sold as beasts of burden because of local taboos. They must keep the white camels until they are two years old and then transport them, at a cost of $72 per head, to another country. There they can receive only $27 for each camel.

To add to their troubles, their principal customer insists that they deliver their normal quantity. If they do not meet his demands, their sales will fall to

250 camels this year. The other camel raisers, knowing Ahmul and Ashmir cannot afford to lower their breeding herd below 500, are taking advantage of the supply-and-demand situation by increasing their prices from $100 to $150 per head.

REQUIRED:

A. Prepare a contribution margin income statement for a normal year for Ahmul and Ashmir.

B. Prepare a contribution margin income statement for the current year, assuming they decide to supply their normal sales volume of 600 camels.

C. Would it be better to buy the extra camels they need at current prices or allow their sales to fall to 250 camels? Support your decision.

D. Calculate the breakeven point under normal conditions. Calculate the new breakeven point, assuming they decide to buy the needed camels.

E. Assume that several zoos are intersted in the white camels. They have no money to buy the camels but have offered to take the camels at the end of the first year if Ahmul and Ashmir deliver them to the town of Abdul. They estimate it will cost $120 per head for delivery. Should Ahmul and Ashmir keep the camels for two years and then sell them in another country, or should they ship them to the zoos at the end of the first year? Support your conclusions.

3-21 *(Cost-Volume-Profit Decisions in a Restaurant Setting).* Mr. Calderone started a pizza restaurant in 19X0. A building was rented for $400 per month. Two ladies were hired to work full-time at the restaurant and six college boys were hired to work 30 hours per week delivering pizza. An outside accountant was hired for tax and bookkeeping purposes. For this service Mr. Calderone pays $300 per month. The necessary restaurant equipment and delivery cars were purchased with cash. Mr. Calderone has noticed that expenses for utilities and supplies have been rather constant.

Mr. Calderone increased his business between 19X0 and 19X3. Profits have more than doubled since 19X0. Mr. Calderone does not understand why his profits have increased faster than his volume.

A projected income statement for 19X4 prepared by the accountant is shown on page 99.

CALDERONE COMPANY
PROJECTED INCOME STATEMENT
FOR THE YEAR ENDED DECEMBER 31, 19X4

Sales		$95,000
Cost of food sold	$28,500	
Wages & fringe benefits of restaurant help	8,150	
Wages & fringe benefits of delivery boys	17,300	
Rent	4,800	
Accounting services	3,600	
Depreciation of delivery equipment	5,000	
Depreciation of restaurant equipment	3,000	
Utilities	2,325	
Supplies (soap, floor wax, etc.)	1,200	73,875
Net income before taxes		$21,125
Income taxes		6,338
Net income		$14,787

Note: The average pizza sells for $2.50. Assume that Mr. Calderone pays out 30% of his income in income taxes.

REQUIRED:

A. What is the breakeven point in number of pizzas that must be sold?

B. What is the cash flow breakeven point in number of pizzas that must be sold?

C. Mr. Calderone would like an after-tax net income of $20,000. What volume must be reached in number of pizzas in order to obtain the desired income?

D. Briefly explain to Mr. Calderone why his profits have increased at a faster rate than his sales.

(CMA adapted)

part 2
VARIABLE COSTING SYSTEMS

chapter **4**

COST FLOWS FOR PRODUCT COSTING

In the first three chapters we examined ways in which the decision maker can view costs relevant to decisions. Now we will look at the cost accumulation systems accountants use to gather data for both financial reporting and management planning and control. If the decision maker is to select relevant costs, the way historical costs are actually measured and reported must be understood.

Our emphasis will be on a manufacturing concern. This emphasis is based on the premise that the physical flow, and hence the cost flow, of a manufacturing concern is more involved than that of a retailing or service concern. With an understanding of the more involved system, the student should be able to transfer this knowledge to less complicated situations.

COSTS FROM A FINANCIAL REPORTING PERSPECTIVE

Financial accounting entails the measurement and reporting of financial position and its changes due to operations. Central to measurement of financial position and net income are the concepts of expired and unexpired costs. As resources are acquired, they are considered as **unexpired costs** (assets) on the statement of financial position. These costs are carried forward to future periods where they are expected to contribute to future revenues. When they have been consumed in the generation of revenue and have no future revenue-producing potential, they are considered as **expired costs** (expenses) on the income statement. For example, as a firm produces goods for resale, the costs incurred in production are carried in the inventory as unexpired costs on the statement of financial position. When the goods are sold, the inventory cost is matched with revenue as cost of goods sold, an expired cost.

A cost that has been consumed in the production of revenue is called an **expense.** A cost that has been consumed without providing a benefit or revenue is termed a **loss.** The problem of measuring expired and unexpired costs is important in financial accounting practice, because these costs directly affect the reported net income and statement of financial position.

In a manufacturing concern, materials flow through the factory where labor and other factory costs are expended to convert them into a finished salable product. Production costs can be thought of as adhering or attaching to the unit of product so that cost flow in the books of account parallels physical flow in the factory. Costs incurred in one form, such as materials, workers' wages, heat, light, and power, are converted and transformed into the product. **Product costs** are costs that accountants attach to the unit of product and hold as an asset in the inventory until the goods to which they are attached are sold. They are matched with revenue when the sale is measured. Costs that are not inventoried and, as a result, are treated as expenses in the period they are considered consumed, are called **period costs.**

Accountants have used the following logic in deciding which costs are product costs and which costs are period costs. In service concerns there are no inventoriable product costs because there are no tangible products; all costs are period costs. In retailing concerns there are inventoriable costs of the merchandise purchased and held for resale. All costs, other than the costs of the purchased merchandise, are related to the current period and are therefore treated as period costs. In a manufacturing firm the cost flow structure is more complex. First, the firm must produce the goods that it sells. The costs incurred in producing these goods are called **production costs** (also called **manufacturing costs**). The firm also incurs the **nonproduction costs** of selling and distributing the products, administering the operations, and financing the company.

When we classify costs as production and nonproduction, the definitions of product and period costs in a manufacturing concern parallel that of the product and period costs of a retailing concern. Product costs are those costs necessary to have a tangible product available for sale; period costs are the costs associated with the sales and administration activities of the period. Product costs are matched with revenue as cost of goods sold in the period of the sale. Period costs are matched with revenue on a time period basis.

In a manufacturing concern raw materials are purchased and then converted into a new product. Iron ore is converted into steel, aluminum into airplanes, logs into lumber, and lumber into boat hulls. The complexity of the manufacturing activity is best accounted for by using three inventory accounts. The **Raw Materials Inventory** contains the cost of the raw materials on hand but not yet processed. The **Work-in-Process Inventory** contains the costs of the raw materials, labor, and other production costs of the uncompleted goods in the process of being manufactured. The **Finished Goods Inventory** contains the costs of the completed goods awaiting sale. Each of the three inventory accounts is an unexpired cost; an asset. Thus, when raw materials are issued to Work-in-Process and combined with labor and other factory costs, the cost of manufacturing is treated as a product cost and therefore an unexpired cost until the product is sold. At the point of sale these product costs move from an asset account, Finished Goods, to the expired cost account, Cost of Goods Sold.

It is sometimes difficult to know whether a cost should be treated as a production or a nonproduction cost. Two examples should highlight this problem. The president supervises both production and distribution activities. Should the president's salary be allocated between the two activities, and if so, what basis of allocation should be used? To solve this dilemma most firms simply assign the president's salary to nonproduction costs. Another example is that of packaging the final product. Some firms wait until the item is sold and treat the packaging costs as selling costs; others assign packaging costs to production costs. Typically, cost assignment depends on *when* the packaging is done. If the packaging is done in the warehouse, it will usually be treated as a selling expense; if it is done in the factory, it will probably be considered a production cost.

PRODUCTION COSTS

Production costs can be separated into three cost elements: raw materials, labor, and overhead. In this section we will look at each of these elements.

DIRECT AND INDIRECT MATERIALS

Raw materials include the physical commodities that are consumed in making the final product. Two views of materials seem prevalent. One view takes a physical approach. **Materials** are defined as all physical commodities that become a part of the final product. This approach is useful in the engineering design of the product but poses distinct accounting problems for commodities that are either physically small or of low cost. The other view is less physical and is oriented more toward the ease of accounting for costs. Only the major materials in terms of cost per unit or the materials that involve large physical quantities justify the record-keeping necessary to trace them directly to the product. These are called **direct materials.** Minor materials are not traced to the product, although they may be vital to its production. Rather, these **indirect materials** are included in overhead.

Production materials, particularly direct materials, are typically variable costs. As more finished units are produced, more materials are used. Some of the indirect materials, such as supplies and lubricants, not physically incorporated in the finished product may behave as semivariable costs; generally, however, it would be reasonable to say production material costs are variable costs.

DIRECT AND INDIRECT LABOR

Labor costs include the wages paid to factory workers who directly or indirectly aid in converting the raw materials into a finished product. **Direct labor** costs represent labor that is expended directly on the final product and traced directly to it. For example, through accounting records, the time of the machine operators, welders, grinders, and assemblers may be traced directly to the product they produce. Other employees, such as supervisors, janitors, material handlers, and maintenance employees, do not work directly with the product. Their wages are considered **indirect labor** costs because there is no reasonable way to trace their activities directly to specific units of output. These costs are regarded as a part of overhead.

Direct labor generally is treated as a variable cost. This is obvious when the workers are paid on a piecework wage plan. Where direct labor is paid on an hourly basis, direct labor is variable if a constant productivity per labor hour can be assumed. If direct labor is paid on a salaried basis, the costs will be stairstep semivariable costs; the appropriateness of treating labor as a variable cost will depend on the size of the stairsteps.

OVERHEAD

Overhead includes all costs of operating the factory except those costs that have been designated as direct materials and direct labor. Included in overhead are indirect materials, indirect labor, and other factory costs such as depreciation of factory buildings and machinery, factory supplies, factory maintenance and repairs, insurance, property taxes, factory employees' fringe benefits, heat, light, and power. A variety of terms are used to describe these costs, including **factory overhead, factory burden, manufacturing expenses, indirect factory costs, manufacturing overhead, indirect expenses,** and **indirect manufacturing costs.** Each firm seems to select a title that communicates best to its management. We use the simple term **overhead.**

Overhead is a potpourri of costs. It includes indirect material costs, indirect labor costs, and the costs of providing and maintaining productive capacity. The one thing these costs have in common is that they are difficult, if not impossible, to trace directly to the units of product. For this reason, accountants typically use an averaging technique called an *overhead rate* to apply overhead to the product. We will explain this technique in a later chapter.

Unlike direct material and direct labor, which are variable costs, overhead is a mixture of variable costs, semivariable costs, and fixed costs. Rent, depreciation of the factory building and machinery, insurance, and property taxes are normally fixed costs. Repairs, maintenance, and many fringe benefits of labor are mixed costs. Some indirect labor costs are variable; others, such as supervisors' salaries, are fixed or stairstepped costs.

NONPRODUCTION COSTS

Accountants have emphasized production costs in their cost studies. One reason for this emphasis has been the ability to find reliable cause-and-effect relationships between production costs and production volume. This relationship is more difficult to find in the nonproduction cost area. Another reason has been the rapid growth of industrialization and mechanization in the past century. This growth has forced management to scrutinize production cost patterns. As a practical matter, the concentration on production activities has resulted in too little time and effort being spent studying nonproduction costs, yet in many firms the nonproduction costs are equal to or greater than production costs.

The elements of nonproduction costs are not as well defined as those of production costs. However, for our purposes, they can be separated into four distinct categories: selling, distribution, general and administrative, and financial.

SELLING COSTS

Often called **order-getting costs,** selling costs are the result of marketing activities. They include, for example, the salespeople's salaries, commissions, and travel costs; advertising, catalog costs; and promotional costs. Selling costs can be both fixed and variable. However, unlike production costs, which vary with production output, selling costs vary with sales volume.

DISTRIBUTION COSTS

Sometimes called **order-filling costs,** distribution costs arise from ensuring that the proper goods are in the proper location, ready to sell. Distribution costs include outbound freight and transportation, warehousing, insurance, finished-goods materials handling, packing, and shipping costs. As with selling costs, distribution costs are both fixed and variable. Distribution costs vary with the volume shipped. In most firms the volume sold and the volume shipped are the same; therefore, many firms relate distribution costs to sales volume.

GENERAL AND ADMINISTRATIVE COSTS

There are a large number of costs that are not directly associated with production, selling, or distribution. Executive and clerical salaries, home office or head-quarters costs, corporate legal costs, board of directors' fees, general accounting costs, and corporate public relation costs are all examples of general and ad-ministrative costs. Most firms find that their general and administrative costs do not vary with either production or sales volume. Because the amount of these costs depends on top management discretion rather than production or sales volume, they are often treated as discretionary fixed costs.

FINANCIAL COSTS

The costs of financing the organization's capital requirements often require spe-cial attention and are separated from administrative costs. Bank service charges, interest expense on both long-term and short-term borrowing, and the costs of underwriting stock issues comprise some of the financial costs. As with general and administrative costs, financial costs do not vary with either production or sales volume; most firms treat them as discretionary fixed costs.

PRODUCT COSTING WITH ABSORPTION AND VARIABLE COSTING

Before the advent of industrialization, with its concurrent heavy equipment in-vestments, production costs consisted primarily of material and labor costs. These **prime costs,** the sum of direct materials and direct labor, were the only production costs of any significance to be inventoried. When industrialization began requiring large investments in capacity, the growth of overhead costs was rapid. It made intuitive sense to include in the unit cost of inventory *all* the costs necessary to make it salable, including the costs of capacity. Accountants did not think of costs as fixed and variable, only as production and nonproduction costs.

By the turn of the twentieth century, accounting in the United States was solidified in the use of absorption product costing. **Absorption product costing** related the accounting cost flow system to physical activity in the plant. With absorption costing, *all production* costs are treated as product costs; all non-production costs treated as period costs. Absorption costing became generally accepted practice in external, financial reporting.

Independently of accounting, however, economists were using the nature of fixed and variable cost behavior patterns in their marginal analysis. In the 1930s, economic theory became more widely integrated with accounting thought, and an alternative to absorption costing was proposed. This alternative, which we call **variable costing,**[1] revolved around cost analysis from a fixed and variable viewpoint, rather than from a production and nonproduction view-point. With variable costing *all variable production* costs are treated as product costs. Fixed production costs and all nonproduction costs are treated as period costs.

The 1940s and World War II added impetus to the study of fixed and variable costs in accounting. The need to make efficient, economic allocation decisions was urgent, and many of our current scientific decision-making theories and models were born during this period. By the 1950s considerable discussion was going on among accountants regarding alternative methods of presenting cost data for both internal and external purposes. In this chapter we will look at the two alternatives most widely proposed for reporting inventory values: absorption costing and variable costing.

Absorption costing defines product costs as including *all* costs of production, and period costs as *all* nonproduction costs. The product "absorbs" all costs necessary to produce it and have it in salable form. Exhibit 4–1 shows the flow of costs in an absorption costing system. The white boxes represent product costs; the dark boxes are period costs. The production cost flow with absorption costing results in a unit cost that can be described as the *average unit cost to produce.*

Variable costing stems from an entirely different premise than absorption costing. Beginning with the idea that the separation of costs into their fixed and variable components provides management with information relevant for differential pricing and production decisions, variable costers redefine product and period costs. Variable costing defines the product costs as the variable costs to produce the product. Fixed production costs and all nonproduction costs are treated as period costs. The cost flow pattern for variable costing is shown in Exhibit 4–2. The white boxes represent product costs under the variable costing

---

[1]It is also called **direct costing** by many accountants in the United States, although this term is a misnomer. In England it is called **marginal costing.** We will use the more descriptive term, *variable costing,* in this text.

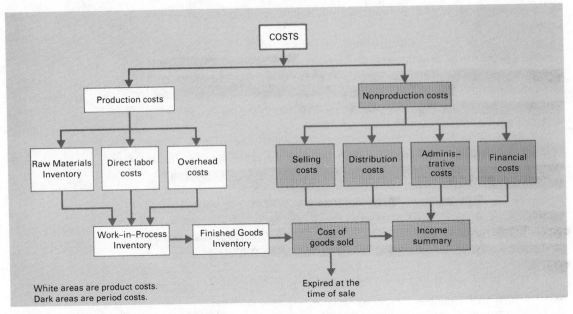

EXHIBIT 4–1   Cost flow with absorption costing

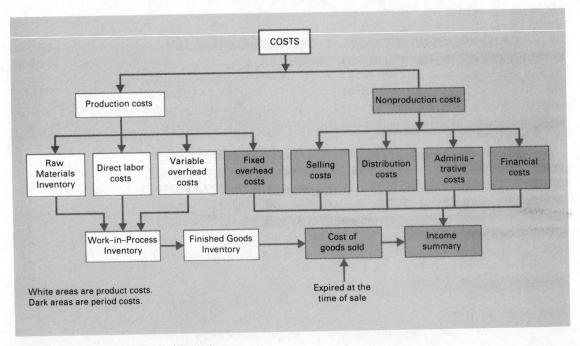

EXHIBIT 4–2   Cost flow with variable costing

method; the dark boxes are period costs. A close examination of this diagram shows that the unit cost is the *average variable cost to produce*.

VARIABLE AND ABSORPTION COSTING ILLUSTRATED

To illustrate the difference between variable and absorption costing in measuring inventory values and income, let's assume that the McKay Manufacturing Company manufactures a top-quality lawn chair of tubular steel. McKay began the current year with no beginning inventory. During the year they manufactured 20,000 chairs, they sold 18,000 of the chairs, ending the accounting period with an inventory of 2,000 completed but unsold chairs. During the year they had the following revenues and costs:

Sales revenue	$25 per chair sold
Production costs:	
Direct materials	$5 per chair manufactured
Direct labor	$6 per chair manufactured
Variable overhead	$4 per chair manufactured
Fixed overhead	$60,000 for the period
Nonproduction costs:	
Variable selling	$2 per chair sold
Fixed selling	$32,000 for the period.

The product costs per unit to be inventoried under the two costing systems are as follows:

	Absorption Costing	Variable Costing
Direct material	$ 5	$ 5
Direct labor	6	6
Variable overhead	4	4
Fixed overhead	3	0
Total product cost	$18	$15

If the firm adopted variable costing, the unit cost of production, including only variable product costs, would be $15. If the firm adopted absorption costing, the unit cost of production would be $18. Obviously the difference between the two costing systems is the inclusion of the $3.00 per unit of fixed overhead in the product under absorption costing. Fixed overhead is treated as a product cost in absorption costing, whereas in variable costing it is treated as a period cost and is not allocated to the individual products.

EXHIBIT 4–3
Absorption costing
income statement
for the McKay
Manufacturing
Company

ABSORPTION COSTING
McKAY MANUFACTURING COMPANY
INCOME STATEMENT
For the Year Ended December 31, 19X5

Sales (18,000 × $25)		$450,000	100%
Less cost of goods sold:			
Production costs (20,000 × $18)	$360,000		
Less ending inventory (2,000 × $18)	36,000	324,000	72%
Gross margin (18,000 × 7)		$126,000	28%
Less nonproduction costs:			
Selling expenses		68,000	15%
Income		$ 58,000	14%

The income statements in Exhibits 4–3 and 4–4 show the effects of these two costing systems on income. The income shown on the absorption costing income statement in Exhibit 4–3 is $6,000 larger than the income shown on the variable costing income statement in Exhibit 4–4. In variable costing, the total fixed production costs of $60,000 are treated as period costs; that is, all $60,000 are expensed in the accounting period when the costs are incurred. In absorption costing, $54,000 of the fixed costs are included in the cost of goods sold, and matched with revenue; the remaining $6,000 of costs are retained in the final inventory. The final inventory increased by 2,000 units. Under variable costing the final inventory is $30,000 (2,000 units × $15); under absorption costing the final inventory is $36,000 (2,000 units × $18).

EXHIBIT 4–4
Variable costing
income statement
of the McKay
Manufacturing
Company

VARIABLE COSTING
McKAY MANUFACTURING COMPANY
INCOME STATEMENT
For the Year Ended December 31, 19X5

Sales (18,000 × $25)		$450,000	100%
Less variable production costs:			
Production costs (20,000 × $15)	$300,000		
Less ending inventory (2,000 × $15)	30,000	270,000	60%
Contribution margin from production (18,000 × $10)		$180,000	40%
Less variable nonproduction costs:			
Variable nonproduction costs (18,000 × $2)		36,000	8%
Contribution margin from operations (18,000 × $8)		$144,000	32%
Less fixed costs:			
Fixed production costs	$ 60,000		
Fixed nonproduction costs	32,000	92,000	20%
Income		$ 52,000	12%

From this short example it can be seen that any time production volume is greater than sales volume, absorption costing will give a higher income than variable costing. This is because absorption costing retains some of the fixed costs in inventory. Conversely, when a firm sells more than it produces (there is a decrease in the inventory levels), variable costing will give a larger income than absorption costing. If the beginning and ending inventories are zero, the income under both systems would be the same.

VARIABLE AND ABSORPTION COSTING ACROSS TIME PERIODS

Some accountants have argued that variable costing should be used in external reporting in lieu of absorption costing. One argument used to support this view is that fixed costs are the result of providing capacity in general, and that this productive capacity does not relate to any one specific unit. Another argument for variable costing is that fixed costs are more closely related to the passage of time than to production and thus are properly treated as period costs. A third argument for the adoption of variable costing for income measurement is that the profits increase or decrease in direct relationship to increases or decreases in sales. With absorption costing the effects on income of increases or decreases in sales are intermingled with the effects of increases or decreases in production output.

Exhibit 4–5 compares the income under variable and absorption costing for the same company over a four-year time span. In the first year more units are produced than sold. In the second and fourth years more units are sold than produced. In the third year production and sales are equal. The selling price and cost structure remain unchanged throughout the example. For simplicity, the only costs are production costs.

Selling price	$ 10 per unit
Variable production costs	$ 6 per unit
Fixed production costs	$270 per year

In this illustration we have assumed a LIFO (last-in, first-out), flow of inventory costs. Other methods, such as FIFO or average, would also illustrate the difference between absorption and variable costing, but income and inventory values would differ. LIFO was chosen because it presents a clearer flow of costs. With LIFO, cost of goods sold includes costs from the previous year only when the inventory level is decreased.

We have assumed that the cost behavior patterns remain unchanged throughout the four years. Under variable costing all units are costed at $6.00 per unit throughout the illustration. The unit cost under absorption costing will depend on the number of units produced. When 100 units are produced, the unit cost under absorption costing is $8.70 [$6.00 variable + $2.70 fixed ($270 ÷

	FIRST YEAR		SECOND YEAR		THIRD YEAR		FOURTH YEAR		TOTAL FOR FOUR YEARS	
	Variable	Absorption	Variable	Absorption	Variable	Absorption	Variable	Absorption	Variable	Absorption
Units Sold	80	80	100	100	100	100	110	110	390	390
Units Produced	100	100	90	90	100	100	100	100	390	390
Sales	$800	$800	$1,000	$1,000	$1,000	$1,000	$1,100	$1,100	$3,900	$3,900
Current production costs:										
Variable costs	$600	$600	$ 540	$ 540	$ 600	$ 600	$ 600	$ 600	$2,340	$2,340
Fixed costs	270	270	270	270	270	270	270	270	1,080	1,080
Total costs	$870	$870	$ 810	$ 810	$ 870	$ 870	$ 870	$ 870	$3,420	$3,420
Change in inventory										
(Increase)	(120)	(174)							(120)	(174)
(Decrease)			60	87	—	—	60	87	120	174
Costs matched with revenue	750	696	870	897	870	870	930	957	3,420	3,420
Income	$ 50	$104	$ 130	$ 103	$ 130	$ 130	$ 170	$ 143	$ 480	$ 480
Beginning inventory:										
Units	0	0	20	20	10	10	10	10	0	0
Cost	—	—	$120	$174	$ 60	$ 87	$ 60	$ 87	—	—
Ending inventory:										
Units	20	20	10	10	10	10	0	0	0	0
Cost	$120	$174	$ 60	$ 87	$ 60	$ 87	—	—	—	—

EXHIBIT 4–5 Comparative income statements across four time periods

100 units)]. When production is 90 units, the cost will increase to $9.00 [$6.00 variable + $3.00 fixed ($270 ÷ 90 units)].

In the first year, production exceeded sales and the finished goods inventory increased by 20 units. The income under variable costing is lower than under absorption costing because all fixed costs are treated as period costs. Under absorption costing each of the 20 units in inventory includes $2.70 of fixed costs.

In the second year, sales exceeded production. In addition to current fixed costs for that year, the income statement for absorption costing includes the fixed costs applicable to the 10 units produced in the first year. Therefore, income under variable costing in the second year exceeds income under absorption costing by $27 (10 × $2.70).

During the third year, income is the same under the two costing systems. Because production and sales were equal, only current costs were included in the income statements.

The last year is comparable to the second year. Sales exceeded production, and the income statement for absorption costing included fixed costs from the beginning inventory.

Let's look at the differences in income determination for these four years.

1. In years where production exceeds sales, the income reported by absorption costing is greater than that reported by variable costing. This is true because some of the fixed costs remain in inventory under absorption costing.

2. In years where sales exceed production, variable costing reports a higher income than absorption costing. This is true because absorption costing matches both current, and some previously deferred fixed costs against revenue, whereas variable costing matches only current fixed costs against revenue.

3. In years where sales and production are equal, the two methods produce the same income.

4. Comparing the second and third years, we can see that in years where sales volume is constant but production fluctuates, variable costing gives identical incomes. This is so because income under variable costing is not affected by inventory changes. In absorption costing, income fluctuates with changes in the inventories, as well as with changes in sales, because fixed costs are spread over a different number of units.

5. When the total production output over the years equals total sales, the total income will be the same under either costing method, if the costs and revenues are constant over the years.

Which accounting method one chooses depends in large part on what purposes the firm has for the accounting information. If there is a major interest in incremental cost and revenue data, then the firm would choose variable costing. If, however, the financial reports are used exclusively for external reporting purposes, then absorption costing would be the system of choice. If the firm needs both sets of data, then it must adopt variable costing for internal needs and convert to absorption costing for external needs. We will show how to convert from variable to absorption costing in a later chapter.

EXTERNAL REPORTING AND VARIABLE COSTING

The controversy over the proper reporting of cost data can be examined from two perspectives: external financial statements for investors and internal reports for management. A particular reporting method may be generally accepted for one purpose and rejected as nonrelevant in another. In this and the following section we will look at the use of variable costing for external reports and internal reports, respectively.

For external reporting purposes, generally accepted accounting principles view absorption costing as the proper way to account for production costs. All authoritative organizations concerned with establishing generally accepted accounting principles and/or with financial reporting have approved absorption costing and rejected variable costing as a generally acceptable method of inventory valuation *for external reporting*. Determination of acceptable reporting practice revolves around the questions "What is a product cost?" and "What is the proper timing in matching fixed costs with revenue?" Absorption costers hold that fixed costs are necessary to produce the product and cannot be excluded from inventories. As a consequence, they believe that fixed costs should be matched with revenue on a sales basis. For external reports they hold that the users of the financial statements are taking a more global, long-range view and that for this view the "averaging" of all costs is relevant to their decisions. Because absorption costing meets these criteria, it is considered the appropriate method for external reports.

INTERNAL REPORTING AND THE CONTRIBUTION MARGIN APPROACH

There is no question among accountants that the separation of costs into their fixed and variable components is useful in management decision making. This knowledge can help management decide which products to emphasize or deemphasize, what prices to charge on special orders, the effects of price-cost-volume changes, and when to increase or decrease output. It can also serve as input to other decision models. Thus management accountants have pressed for the adoption of variable costing for internal reporting.

VARIABLE COSTING AND THE CONTRIBUTION MARGIN APPROACH

At the heart of variable costing's benefits is the contribution margin. However, there are two ways of viewing variable costing and the contribution margin.

The first view is from the standpoint of what costs are considered product costs and thus are included in the inventory, and what costs are considered period costs. This is essentially a question of income measurement. We will call this view **variable costing.** With both variable and absorption costing methods, accountants exclude all nonproduction costs from inventory. Under variable costing, fixed production costs are also excluded from the inventory; the contribution margin is sales revenue less variable production costs. This format is relevant when management is concerned with cost–volume relationships from production activities only.

The second view of contribution margin is much broader. Here the contribution margin is the amount of net revenue remaining after deducting *all* variable costs, both production and selling. It must cover fixed costs and provide a satisfactory profit. We will call this perspective the **contribution margin approach.** When management is concerned with the firm's total cost–volume relationships, the variable nonproduction costs become relevant, as well as the variable production costs.

Actually, variable costing should be considered a subset of the contribution margin approach. In this text, when we are dealing with only the production area and therefore variable costing, the contribution margin will be called **contribution margin from production,** to exclude nonproduction variable costs. However, when we are concerned with cost-volume-profit relationships for the entire firm, we will use the term **contribution margin from total operations** or simply **contribution margin.**

Let's return to the McKay Manufacturing Company in Exhibit 4–4 to examine these two views of the contribution margin. Remember that the McKay Company manufactured 20,000 chairs during the accounting period. It sold 18,000 of these at $25 each and incurred the following variable production costs per unit: direct materials $5.00, direct labor $6.00, and variable overhead $4.00. The fixed production costs totaled $60,000. The nonproduction costs were variable costs in the amount of $2.00 per unit sold plus fixed costs of $32,000.

To arrive at an inventory cost for income determination purposes, the product cost with variable costing would be

Direct materials	$ 5
Direct labor	6
Variable overhead	4
Total inventoriable cost	$15

Using the inventoriable cost, the **unit contribution margin from production** is $10 (the selling price of $25 less the variable production cost per unit of $15). The **total contribution margin from production** is the excess of total sales revenue over total variable production costs, which in our case is $180,000 (18,000 units × $10), and the **contribution margin ratio from production** is 40% ($10 ÷ $25). Remember, however, these contribution margins from the production do not include the variable nonproduction costs.

The broader view of contribution margin includes the total variable costs of the company. Total variable costs per unit of product for the McKay Company are

Direct materials	$ 5
Direct labor	6
Variable overhead	4
Variable nonproduction costs	2
Total variable costs	$17

Using the total variable costs of the firm, not just the variable production costs, the **unit contribution margin from total operations** is the selling price of $25 less the variable cost per unit of $17, or $8.00. The **total contribution margin from total operations** is $144,000 (18,000 units × $8.00) and the **contribution margin ratio from total operations** is 32% ($8.00 ÷ $25). It is the contribution margin from operations that is used in calculating the breakeven point. The breakeven point in units for the McKay Manufacturing Company is fixed costs divided by the unit contribution margin ($92,000 ÷ $8), or 11,500 units. The breakeven point in dollars of sales is the fixed costs divided by the contribution margin ratio ($92,000 ÷ .32), or $287,500.

The variable costing approach is useful in making incremental production decisions. The contribution margin approach is useful in making both incremental production *and* incremental selling decisions, in addition to its value in the study of cost-volume-profit relationships for the firm as a whole.

CONTRIBUTION MARGIN APPROACH
AND COST-VOLUME-PROFIT ANALYSIS

The breakeven graph, which was shown in Chapter 3, has been described as a graphic contribution margin income statement. The contribution margin income statement is, in fact, another mode of presenting cost-volume-profit relationships. It lends itself directly, without reinterpretation, to cost-volume-profit analysis.

Absorption costing does not fulfill the same information role as does variable costing. One of the primary differences is that under absorption costing the per-unit cost changes with changes in production volume. As a result of these volume-cost interactions, income may also vary. That is, sales could increase and income decrease, or conversely sales could decrease and income increase. Under variable costing, changes in production volume do not affect the per-unit cost, the unit contribution margin, or the contribution margin ratio. As a result there is a direct relationship between sales and income. That is, when sales increase the income will increase and when sales decrease the income will decrease.

LIMITATIONS OF THE CONTRIBUTION MARGIN APPROACH

The contribution margin approach is useful in making incremental production and distribution decisions, but it has limitations. First, it is based on the cost–volume analysis used in determining fixed and variable costs. It assumes that the accountant has determined which costs are fixed and which are variable. As we discussed in Chapter 2, this analysis requires special tools that are based on certain underlying assumptions.

Second, many accountants have felt that an overemphasis on the contribution margin may mislead the decision maker into assuming *only* a short-range decision attitude. They argue that the contribution margin approach may underemphasize the importance of the fixed costs. Proponents of the contribution margin approach counter that it actually highlights the fixed costs, since it does not ''lose'' them in the unit cost but keeps them intact instead.

Third, opponents of the contribution margin approach argue that heavy reliance upon variable costing may lead management mistakenly to overlook the need to maintain an adequate production volume. If the total contribution margin is allowed to fall too low, it will not cover the fixed costs, even though the unit contribution margin is good. That is to say, the contribution margin approach may lead management to adopt only a short-range viewpoint. In the long run the firm may go broke with a good unit contribution margin. Proponents of the contribution margin approach argue that it reports profits and operating data in a way easily understood by management, and that this understanding leads to better short- and long-range decisions.

Fourth, even the best kept records of *past* costs are not useful in decision making unless they help predict future costs. This point applies to absorption costing as well as to the contribution margin approach. Because decisions are future-oriented, past data are useful only if it is believed that the future will be similar to the past. Changes in operations, cost behavior classifications, and organizational structures cause the exact fixed and variable costs to change from year to year. If there are significant changes, neither absorption costing nor the contribution margin approach will be relevant. Decision data would have to come from special studies, not from the accounting records.

Allowing for these limitations, most accountants concerned with decision making believe that the knowledge of fixed and variable costs and the resultant contribution margin are of significant value to management, although they might advocate the use of absorption costing in external reports.

ALTERNATIVE PROPOSALS

We cannot ignore the fact that absorption costing is required for external reporting. Neither can we ignore the value that the contribution margin provides to management. An acceptable alternative is to provide each group with its data needs. Internally, the firm can use the contribution margin approach. Then, when external reports are prepared, the accountant can prepare the financial statements on an absorption costing basis. This is the approach we will take in the next two chapters. We will illustrate in Chapters 5 and 6 how the accountant can develop variable costing systems for management. Then, in Chapters 7 and 8 we will explore overhead costing for absorption costing.

SUMMARY

There are two major costing systems for determining product and period costs. Absorption costing classifies all production costs as product costs and all non-production costs as period costs. Variable costing treats the variable costs to produce the product as product costs; fixed production costs and nonproduction costs are treated as period costs. It is generally accepted accounting practice to use absorption costing for external reports. This practice has the support of most major accounting and governmental agencies.

There is wide agreement that the contribution margin is useful for management decision making. The contribution margin is sales revenue less variable costs; the contribution margin ratio is the contribution margin divided by the sales revenue. The contribution margin is particularly useful in cost-volume-profit analysis. As a matter of fact, the breakeven graph has been called a graphic variable costing income statement. The contribution margin from the variable cost flow system used in income determination can be different from that of the contribution margin approach; a contribution margin approach will include variable nonproduction costs.

To compromise between the two data needs of internal and external reports, it is possible to use the contribution margin approach within the firm, but to use absorption costing in external reports. The accountant has the opportunity to present different costs for different purposes.

PROBLEMS AND CASES

4-1 *(Cost Classification)*. Classify the following costs as (1) product or period cost; and as (2) primarily variable or fixed.

	Product	Period	Fixed	Variable
A. Direct material.				
B. Salesperson's commission.				
C. Factory manager's salary under absorption costing.				
D. President's salary.				
E. Factory rent under variable costing.				
F. Prime costs.				
G. Cost of TV ads for a new product.				
H. Interest on loan to finance the new product.				
I. Depreciation of factory equipment by the units of production method.				
J. Wages of a grape stomper in a winery.				

4-2   *(Product–Period Cost Classification)*. Below are a number of costs incurred by the Johnson Company. Indicate if the cost would be a product or a period cost under both absorption and variable costing.

	Absorption		Variable	
	Product	Period	Product	Period
A. Depreciation expense on sales people's automobiles.				
B. Plant supervisor paid on monthly salary.				
C. Production-line worker paid on an hourly basis.				
D. Board of directors' fees.				
E. Cost of advertising.				
F. Bond interest expense.				
G. Cost of crude oil in petroleum refinery.				
H. Depreciation of factory building on straight-line basis.				
I. Cost of paper supplies used in accounting department.				
J. Cost of electricity used in aluminum pot-line.				
K. Depreciation of factory machinery on a unit-of-output basis.				
L. Cost of wiping rags used on production line.				
M. Cost of freight for shipping finished goods.				

N. Cost of program-
ming the produc-
tion-line robots.

O. Cost of the mainte-
nance crew paid on
monthly salary ba-
sis.

4-3 (*Variable Versus Absorption*): The Campbell Company, which uses absorption costing, had the following data for its first year of operations.

Direct materials	$ 2.00 per unit
Direct labor	$ 3.00 per unit
Variable overhead	$ 1.50 per unit
Fixed overhead	$ .50 per unit
Variable selling expenses	$ 1.20 per unit
Fixed selling expenses	$ .80 per unit
Selling price	$10.00 per unit
Production volume	5,000 units
Sales volume	4,500 units

REQUIRED:

A. Determine ending inventory under variable costing.   3250

B. Determine ending inventory under absorption costing. 3500

C. Prepare a variable costing income statement in good form. NI = 4250

D. Determine income under absorption without using an income statement. NI = 4500

CLASS **4-4**   (*Preparation of Variable Costing Income Statement*). The Knox Company had the following budgeted revenue, cost, and volume data.

	40,000 Units	60,000 Units
Prime costs	$360,000	$540,000
Factory overhead	$162,000	$222,000
Selling expenses	$100,000	$140,000
Sales revenue	$640,000	$960,000

During the accounting period the firm produced 50,000 units; sales amounted
to 45,000 units.

REQUIRED:

A. Prepare a variable costing income statement.

B. Determine the income from absorption costing. (It is not necessary to prepare
an income statement.)

4-5   *(Absorption and Variable Costing Income Statements)*. The Elway Company's first year of operations appeared successful. During the year they produced 30,000 units, resulting in the following revenues and costs.

Sales (26,000 units)	$780,000
Total fixed production costs	$ 90,000
Total variable production costs	$420,000
Total fixed selling expenses	$104,000
Total variable selling expenses	$ 91,000

REQUIRED:

A. Prepare an income statement in good form, assuming

   1. Absorption costing

   2. Variable costing

B. Explain the difference between the income from absorption costing and the income from variable costing.

CLASS   **4-6**   *(Variable Costing)*. The Arizona Company produced 36,000 units of its product during 19X6. There were no beginning inventories. Ending inventories consisted of 6,000 units in Finished Goods Inventory. The selling price is $10 per unit.

Costs for the year were as follows.

	Fixed Costs	Variable Costs
Direct materials		$72,000
Direct labor		$54,000
Overhead	$36,000	$36,000
Selling expenses	$39,000	10% of sales
Administrative expenses	$31,600	$12,000

REQUIRED:

Compute the following:

A. Sales for the year.

B. Contribution margin from production.

C. Contribution margin from total operations.

D. Contribution margin ratio.

E. Income under variable costing.

F. Breakeven point in dollars of sales.

G. Cost of ending inventory under variable costing.

4-7 (*Absorption Costing*). The Oregon Company produced 36,000 units of its product during 19X6. There were no beginning inventories. Ending inventories consisted of 6,000 units in Finished Goods Inventory. The selling price is $10 per unit.

Costs for the year were as follows:

	Fixed Costs	Variable Costs
Direct materials		$72,000
Direct labor		$54,000
Overhead	$36,000	$36,000
Selling expenses	$39,000	10% of sales
Administrative expenses	$31,600	$12,000

REQUIRED:

Compute the following:

A. Sales for the year. 300,000
B. Gross margin. 135,000
C. Gross margin ratio. .45
D. Income under absorption costing. 22,400
E. Breakeven point in units. 26,000
F. Cost of ending inventory under absorption costing. 33,000

4-8 (*Variable and Absorption Costing Across Time Periods*). The Johnson Company had the following production and sales quantities during the past year.

	1st Quarter	2nd Quarter	3rd Quarter	4th Quarter
Units produced	50	45	50	50
Units sold	40	50	50	55

During the year the selling price was constant at $10 per unit, variable production costs were $6.00 per unit, and fixed production costs were $135 per quarter. Assume a LIFO inventory flow.

REQUIRED:

A. Prepare income statements that set forth sales, variable and fixed costs, and income for each quarter under both absorption and variable costing approaches.

B. Calculate the ending inventory values for each quarter under both absorption and variable costing.

C. Prepare a schedule that compares the ending inventory values and incomes showing how they differ under absorption and variable costing.

4-9 *(Cost-Volume-Profit Analysis and Pricing Policy).* The president of Easy Listening Corporation, which manufactures tape decks and sells them to producers of sound reproduction systems, anticipates a 10% wage increase on January 1 of next year to the manufacturing employees (variable labor). She expects no other changes in costs. Overhead will not change as a result of the wage increase. The president has asked you to assist her in developing the information she needs to formulate a reasonable product strategy for next year.

You are satisfied by regression analysis that volume is the primary factor affecting costs and have separated the semivariable costs into their fixed and variable segments by means of the least-squares criterion. You also observe that the beginning and ending inventories are never materially different.

The following data for the current year are assembled for your analysis.

Current selling price per unit	$80
Variable cost per unit:	
Material	$30
Labor	12
Overhead	6
Total	$48
Annual volume of sales	5,000 units
Fixed costs	$51,000

REQUIRED:

Provide the following information for the president, using cost-volume-profit analysis.

$82 A. What increase in the selling price is necessary to cover the 10% wage increase and still maintain the current contribution margin ratio?

5195 B. How many tape decks must be sold to maintain the current income if the sales price remains at $80 and the 10% wage increase goes into effect?

C. The president believes that an additional $190,000 of machinery (to be depreciated at 10% annually) will increase present capacity (5,300 units) by 30%. If all tape decks produced can be sold at the present price, and the wage increase goes into effect, how would the estimated income before capacity is increased compare with the estimated income after capacity is increased? Prepare income statements under the contribution margin approach *before* and *after* the expansion.

NI_B = 112,240

NI_A = 142,212

EXPAND

(CPA adapted)

4-10 *(Contribution Margin Approach in Wholesale Setting—Review of Chapter 3).* The president of Leather Products Company is not satisfied with the following income statement that was prepared by his bookkeeper. Income is lower than he thinks it should be. He doubts that all product lines are generating the income they should but does not have the information to evaluate individual product lines.

LEATHER PRODUCTS COMPANY
INCOME STATEMENT
For the Year 19X7

Sales		$600,000
Cost of goods sold	$365,000	
Sales commissions	49,000	
Delivery costs	20,000	
Salaries	70,000	
Advertising	40,000	
Rent	24,000	
Other	6,000	574,000
Income		$ 26,000

The president asks you to prepare an income statement that shows "how well he is doing" on each of his three product lines.

Additional information:

Sales for the three product lines:

Product A	$100,000
Product B	$300,000
Product C	$200,000

Cost of goods sold by product line:

Product A	60% of sales
Product B	55% of sales
Product C	70% of sales

Commissions by product line: Product A, 10% of sales; Product B, 5% of sales; Product C, 12% of sales.

Salespeople's salaries: $20,000 for Product A and $30,000 for Product B.

Delivery expense: 5% of sales for Products A and B.

Advertising: Product A, $10,000; Product B, $20,000; Product C, $10,000.

The balance of the salaries are sales management and administration.

Rent and other expenses cannot be traced to product lines.

REQUIRED:

A. Prepare an income statement by product line using the contribution margin approach.

B. What can you tell from the contribution margin income statement that you could not tell from the income statement prepared by the bookkeeper?

C. Other firms in the industry have a return on sales of 8%. Were the president's suspicions correct? Explain.

4-11 *(Contribution Margin Approach in Educational Setting—Review of Chapter 3).* The voters of Calhoun rejected the $50,000 supplemental operating levy for the city's school system. As a result, the school board must reduce budgeted expenses by $50,000. The budget proposed to the voters was as shown below.

CITY OF CALHOUN
PROPOSED BUDGET
For the Year 19X7–19X8

Revenues:	
Property taxes (regular levy)	$454,000
Property taxes (special levy)	50,000
Admission to athletic events	40,000
School lunch revenue	48,000
Total budgeted revenues	$592,000
Expenses:	
Salaries	$432,000
Material and supplies	76,000
Building repairs and utilities	36,000
Other	48,000
Total budgeted expenses	$592,000

An examination of expenses shows the following:

Salaries:		
Classroom teachers	(fixed)	$363,000
Coaching staff	(fixed)	10,000
School administration	(fixed)	40,000
Cafeteria personnel	(fixed)	15,000
Ticket takers for athletic events		
	(10% of revenue)	4,000
		$432,000

Material and supplies:		
Classroom materials	(variable)	$ 24,000
Athletic supplies	(variable)	10,000
Food	(variable)	42,000
		$ 76,000

Building repairs and utilities	(fixed)	$ 36,000
Other	($12,000 fixed; balance variable)	$48,000

Some members of the school board want to eliminate the athletic program and school lunch program because "they are a financial drain on the basic education resources."

REQUIRED:

The chairman of the school board wants you to assist the school board in its decision. What would you recommend? Why?

4-12 *(Contribution Margin Approach in a Service Concern).* The consulting firm of Coe, Roe, and Low is considering a number of changes including expansion and an increase of billing rates to clients. The following income statement does not provide the information needed by the owners.

COE, ROE, AND LOW
INCOME STATEMENT
For the Year 19X7

Revenue		$200,000
Operating expenses:		
Salaries of employees	$64,000	
Salaries of owners	75,000	
Supplies	6,000	
Equipment depreciation	2,000	
Rent and utilities	12,000	
Travel	20,000	
Other	16,000	195,000
Income		$ 5,000

A study of operating expenses revealed the following cost behavior patterns.

Salaries of employees	$2,000 per month plus 20% of revenue
Salaries of owners	$25,000 per year for each of three owners
Supplies	3% of revenue
Equipment depreciation	$2,000 per year
Rent and utilities	$1,000 per month
Travel	10% of revenue
Other	$1,000 per month plus 2% of revenue

REQUIRED:

A. Prepare an income statement using the contribution margin approach showing revenue and costs when revenue is $200,000, $220,000, and $250,000.

B. Prepare a profit–volume chart.

C. Do the income statement in part A and the profit–volume chart in part B show the same income at each of the three levels of revenue? Why or why not?

D. What kind of decisions will the income statement in part A and profit–volume chart in part B help the owners make?

4-13 *(Cost Calculations from Incomplete Data)*. The Emerson Company has the following data.

Beginning and ending inventories	None
Sales	$400
Direct materials used	$ 80
Direct labor cost	$ 70
Variable overhead	?
Contribution margin from operations	$ 65
Variable selling expenses	$ 25
Fixed selling expenses	?
Fixed overhead	?
Gross margin	$ 70
Income	$ 30

REQUIRED:

Compute the following amounts:

A. Fixed selling expenses.

B. Cost of goods sold assuming absorption costing.

C. Cost of goods sold assuming variable costing.

D. Contribution margin from production.

E. Fixed overhead costs.

F. Variable overhead costs.

G. Breakeven point in sales dollars.

H. Prime costs.

I. Total product costs assuming variable costing.

J. Total period costs assuming absorption costing.

4-14 *(Cost Concepts from Unit Cost Data)*. The Olsen Company had the following unit revenue and cost data.

Sales		$8.00
Cost of goods sold:		
Materials	$1.25	
Labor	2.75	
Variable overhead	1.00	
Fixed overhead	.60	5.60
Gross margin		$2.40
Less selling expenses:		
Variable selling	$ .80	
Fixed selling	.60	1.40
Income		$1.00

The cost data were based on the current year's production of 16,000 units. There were no beginning inventories. There were 1,000 units in the ending inventory of finished goods.

REQUIRED:

Using the above data, determine the following.

A. The flexible budget for overhead.

B. The flexible budget for selling expenses.

C. The contribution margin per unit.

D. The inventory value per unit assuming absorption costing.

E. The inventory value per unit assuming variable costing.

F. The total inventory value assuming absorption costing.

G. The total inventory value assuming variable costing.

H. Income assuming absorption costing.

I. Income assuming variable costing.

J. The breakeven point in units.

4-15 (*Contribution Margin Income Statements*). The Brian Company manufactures three principal products. During the past year it had the following cost, revenue, and production experiences.

	Product A	Product B	Product C
Units produced	5,000	10,000	1,000
Units sold	5,000	9,000	900
Unit sales price	$ 20	$ 15	$ 50
Direct material per unit	$ 5	$ 5	$ 20
Direct labor per unit	$ 6	$ 4	$ 10
Variable overhead per unit	$ 2	$ 1	$ 5
Fixed overhead per year	$2,500	$10,000	$5,000
Fixed selling expenses	$5,000	$10,000	$1,000

REQUIRED:

A. Prepare income statements for each product using the contribution margin approach.

B. Calculate for each product the contribution margin per unit and the contribution margin ratio per unit.

C. Prepare a schedule showing the ending inventory values for each product under both absorption costing and variable costing.

D. Discuss the value of the contribution margin in making incremental production decisions.

4-16 *(Income Statements with an Inventory Decrement).* The controller of the Steward Company prepared the following schedule of data for 19X4.

Sales	$180,000
Variable production costs incurred	$ 60,000
Fixed production costs incurred	$ 30,000
Variable marketing costs incurred	$ 48,000
Fixed marketing costs incurred	$ 22,000

The controller also prepared the following schedule of inventory values for Finished Goods Inventory.

	Beginning Inventory 1/1/19X4	*Ending Inventory 12/31/19X4*
Variable costs	$ 8,000	$ 6,000
Fixed costs	5,000	4,400
Total	$13,000	$10,400

REQUIRED:

A. Prepare an absorption costing income statement.

B. Prepare a variable costing income statement.

C. Reconcile the difference between the absorption and variable costing incomes.

4-17 *(Contrast of Income Statements Under Variable and Absorption Costing).* The controller of the newly formed Able Company was asked to prepare a recommendation to the board of directors concerning the inventory costing method to be adopted by the company. One member of the board is also a director of another company that uses the contribution margin approach for internal reporting. He thinks the Able Company should prepare reports for the board of directors using the contribution margin approach. Another member of the board thinks it is wrong for the company "to keep two sets of books."

Data for the first year of operations follow.

Units produced	100,000, of which 80,000 were sold at $11 per unit
Direct materials	$240,000
Direct labor	$320,000
Overhead:	
Variable costs	$ 80,000
Fixed costs	$160,000
Selling and administrative expenses:	
Variable costs	$ 48,000
Fixed costs	$180,000

REQUIRED:

A. Indicate the cost to be assigned to the inventory using:

1. Variable costing.
2. Absorption costing.

B. Prepare an income statement for the member of the board of directors who wants the company to use the contribution margin approach.

C. Prepare an income statement that will meet the requirements for reporting to the stockholders.

D. Prepare a recommendation to the board of directors concerning the costing method to be used for inventory costing. Your recommendation should consider the concerns of both directors.

4-18 *(Variable Costing and Breakeven Analysis)*. At the end of the Moore Company's first year of business the following income statement was prepared by a Certified Public Accountant.

MOORE COMPANY INCOME STATEMENT For the Year 19X7			
Sales	(20,000 units × $12)		$240,000
Cost of goods sold:			
Production costs	(25,000 units × $ 8)	$200,000	
Ending inventory	(5,000 units × $ 8)	40,000	160,000
Gross margin			$ 80,000
Selling and administrative expenses			76,000
Income			$ 4,000

Mr. Moore showed the income statement to his daughter, Wendy, who was home from college during the semester break. He was pleased that the company had shown a profit for the first year.

Wendy had just completed a course in management accounting and eagerly set about to apply the concepts from the course. From the accountant's report and other information about the company, Wendy found that the unit product cost of $8.00 included fixed costs of $2.00, and that of the $76,000 selling and administrative expenses $16,000 were fixed.

After preparing a breakeven chart, Wendy said, "Sorry pops, but my breakeven chart shows that you lost about $6,000."

REQUIRED:

A. Prepare a breakeven chart for the Moore Company. What income or loss do you show at the 20,000-unit sales level?

B. Mr. Moore is confused about whether or not his company earned a profit last year. Is either his income statement or the breakeven chart wrong? Explain.

C. Prepare an income statement using variable costing and the contribution margin approach. Does your income or loss agree with the income statement or breakeven chart? Why?

D. What is the breakeven point in units? In sales dollars?

4-19 *(Absorption and Variable Costing Compared)*. The Moon Company had prepared the following flexible budgets:

$$
\begin{aligned}
\text{Direct materials} &= \$0 && + 1.00(x) \\
\text{Direct labor} &= \$0 && + \$2.20(x) \\
\text{Factory overhead} &= \$24{,}000 && + \$ .80(x) \\
\text{Selling expenses} &= \$18{,}000 && + \$1.50(x)
\end{aligned}
$$

The firm manufactured 12,000 units during the current year. Sales were 11,000 units at $11 each.

REQUIRED:

Given the above data determine the following.

A. The prime costs per unit.

B. The product cost per unit using absorption costing.

C. The product cost per unit using variable costing.

D. The per-unit contribution margin from operations.

E. The per-unit contribution margin from production.

F. The gross margin.

G. The total period costs assuming absorption costing.

H. The total period costs assuming variable costing.

I. The total value of the ending inventory assuming absorption costing.

J. The total value of the ending inventory assuming variable costing.

K. The income assuming absorption costing.

L. The income assuming variable costing.

M. The breakeven point in units.

N. The breakeven point in sales dollars.

O. The margin of safety in dollars.

4-20 *(Contrast of Variable and Absorption Costing Across Time Periods)*. The Komfy Quilt Company manufactures a line of fine-quality patchwork quilts. Due to increased demand, the manager is faced with the decision of adding productive capacity. During the analysis of past costs, revenues, and incomes, a question was raised in staff meeting about the definition of product cost. The company is currently using absorption costing, but the manager has heard that a variable costing system might prove more informative to management. The following information was developed to facilitate a comparison between the two systems.

	19X1	19X2	19X3	19X4
Units produced	1,200	1,500	1,200	1,200
Units sold	1,000	1,200	1,300	1,600

Cost and revenue information:

Variable costs:
Raw materials	$30
Direct labor	40
Variable overhead	20
Total variable costs	$90

Other costs:
Fixed production costs	$18,000 per year
Administrative costs	$14,000 per year
Selling costs	5% of sales revenue
Sales price	$150 per unit

Assume no beginning inventory and a LIFO inventory flow.

REQUIRED:

A. Prepare a schedule that shows income for each year using both variable and absorption costing.

B. For each year reconcile the differences in income between variable and absorption costing. As a part of your reconciliation show the ending Finished Goods Inventory under both variable and absorption costing.

4-21 *(Cost Flow Systems and Management Performance Assessment).* The Leaky Tank Company presents a Plant Manager of the Month Award to the plant manager with the highest monthly income. The award is very important to the plant managers; it carries peer-group approval. Because of the high freight costs of the finished tanks, the company has several plants in strategic locations. The plants are of approximately the same size and have about the same cost structures, so top management believes that income is a fair measure to use in presenting the monthly incentive award.

The plant manager of the Mud Flats Plant distrusts the accounting system because the manager of the Green River Plant has won the award for the past two months. The Green River Plant has sold fewer units in the past month and has had labor problems. Income statements follow for the two plants.

MUD FLATS PLANT
INCOME STATEMENT

	June	July
Sales (@ $400)	$40,000	$40,000
Cost of goods sold	30,000	30,000
Gross margin	$10,000	$10,000
Operating expense	5,000	5,000
Income	$ 5,000	$ 5,000

GREEN RIVER PLANT
INCOME STATEMENT

	June	July
Sales (@ $400)	$40,000	$36,000
Cost of goods sold	25,000	22,950
Gross margin	$15,000	$13,050
Operating expense	5,000	5,000
Income	$10,000	$ 8,050

You were asked to study the income statements of the two plants. The entire company uses a full-absorption costing system to measure unit cost and a LIFO cost flow method to match inventory cost with revenue. In the process of your investigation you discover the following additional information.

MUD FLATS PLANT

	June	July
Variable production costs (per unit)	$ 150	$ 150
Fixed production costs (per month)	$15,000	$15,000
Beginning inventory	0	0
Units sold	100	100
Units produced	100	100

GREEN RIVER PLANT

	June	July
Variable production costs (per unit)	$ 150	$ 180
Fixed production costs (per month)	$15,000	$15,000
Beginning inventory	0	50
Units sold	100	90
Units produced	150	200

REQUIRED:

A. Explain to the Mud Flats Plant manager why the award was won by the Green River Plant manager.

B. To whom would you give the award? Explain.

4-22 *(Differential Income Measures).* Magnus Corporation produces speakers for sale to hi-fidelity equipment distributors. The firm was started four years ago by its current president, Maximus Leisure. Max hired an accountant during 19X6 to keep track of his operations, and the accountant filed the following report for 19X6 using Generally Accepted Accounting Principles.

Income 19X6	Amount	Percentage of Sales
Sales	$200,000	100
Cost of goods sold	180,000	90
Gross margin	$ 20,000	10
Administrative expenses	75,000	
Sales expenses	35,000	
Income	($90,000)	

Max was discouraged by this report, but hoped that next year's operating results would be better. His hope lasted only until the budget was completed. Based on assumed sales of twice this year's sales, Max's accountant developed the following projected income statement for next year.

Income 19X7 (projected)	Amount	Percentage of Sales
Sales	$400,000	100
Cost of goods sold	360,000	90
Gross margin	$ 40,000	10
Administrative expenses	75,000	
Sales expenses	35,000	
Income	($70,000)	

Downcast by this bleak projection, Max decided to hand over the firm to an investor who had agreed to take over the firm's $50,000 debt.

The accountant for the new owner prepared the following income statement at the end of 19X7.

Income 19X7		
Sales	$400,000	
Cost of goods sold	240,000	
Gross margin	$160,000	
Administrative expenses	75,000	
Sales expenses	35,000	
Income	$ 50,000	

REQUIRED:

What probably happened?

(Prepared by Eric Noreen)

4-23 *(C/V/P Analysis and Variable Costing).* Pralina Products Company is a regional firm that has three major product lines: cereals, breakfast bars, and dog food. The income statement for the year ended April 30, 19X8 is shown on page 139; the statement was prepared by product line using absorption (full) costing. Explanatory data related to the items presented in the income statement follow the statement.

OTHER DATA

1. Cost of sales. The company's inventories of raw materials and finished products do not vary significantly from year to year. The inventories at April 30, 19X8 were essentially identical to those at April 30, 19X7.

Factory overhead was applied to products at 120% of direct labor dollars. The factory overhead costs for the 19X7–19X8 fiscal year were as follows.

Variable indirect labor and supplies	$ 15,000
Variable employee benefits on factory labor	30,000
Supervisory salaries and related benefits	35,000
Plant occupancy costs	100,000
	$180,000

There was no overapplied or underapplied overhead at year-end.

2. Advertising. The company has been unable to determine any direct causal relationship between the level of sales volume and the level of advertising expenditures. However, because management believes advertising is necessary, an annual advertising program is implemented for each product line. Each product line is advertised independently of the others.

3. Commissions. Sales commissions are paid to the sales force at the rates of 5% on the cereals and 10% on the breakfast bars and dog food.

4. Licenses. Various licenses are required for each product line. These are renewed annually for each product line.

5. Salaries and related benefits. Sales and general and administrative personnel devote time and effort to all product lines. Their salaries and wages are allocated on the basis of management's estimates of time spent on each product line.

REQUIRED:

A. The controller of Pralina Products Company has recommended that the company do a cost/volume/profit (C/V/P) analysis of its operations. As a first step the controller has requested that you prepare a revised income statement for Pralina Products company that employs a product contribution margin format that will be useful in C/V/P analysis. The statement should show the

the profit contribution for each product line and the income before taxes for the company as a whole.

B. What effect, if any, would there be on income before taxes determined in requirement A if the inventories as of April 30, 19X8 had increased significantly over the inventory levels of April 30, 19X7? Explain your answer.

C. The controller of Pralina Products Company is going to prepare a report, which she will present to the other members of top management explaining C/V/P analysis. Identify and explain the following points that the controller should include in the report.

1. The advantages that C/V/P analysis can provide to a company.

2. The difficulties Pralina Products Company could experience in the calculations involved in C/V/P analysis.

3. The dangers that Pralina Products Company should be aware of in using the information derived from the C/V/P analysis.

(CMA adapted)

PRALINA PRODUCTS COMPANY
INCOME STATEMENT
For the Year Ended April 30, 19X8
(000 omitted)

	Cereals	Breakfast Bars	Dog Food	Total
Sales in pounds	2,000	500	500	3,000
Revenue from sales	$1,000	$400	$200	$1,600
Cost of sales:				
Raw materials	$ 330	$160	$100	$ 590
Direct labor	90	40	20	150
Factory overhead	108	48	24	180
Total cost of sales	528	248	144	920
Gross margin	$ 472	$152	$ 56	$ 680
Operating expenses:				
Selling expenses:				
Advertising	$ 50	$ 30	$ 20	$ 100
Commissions	50	40	20	110
Salaries and related benefits	30	20	10	60
Total selling expenses	$ 130	$ 90	$ 50	$ 270
General and administrative expenses:				
Licenses	$ 50	$ 20	$ 15	$ 85
Salaries and related benefits	60	25	15	100
Total general and administrative expenses	110	45	30	185
Total operating expenses	240	135	80	455
Operating income before taxes	$ 232	$ 17	$(24)	$ 225

chapter **5**

VARIABLE JOB ORDER AND PROCESS COSTING SYSTEMS

In the previous chapter the differences between absorption costing and variable costing were illustrated. We summarized the discussion by saying that most management accountants believe that variable costing is valuable because it provides contribution margin data for decision making. Taking a management accounting approach, we will begin by focusing on variable costing. First, we will present variable historical costing; then in the following chapter we will show the benefits of variable standard costing over historical costing in creating efficient operations. After variable costing has been illustrated we then will show absorption costing, which is required for external reporting. By approaching the topics in this order we focus on the primary intent of this text, which is to develop on data for management decisions. At the same time we will not ignore the external reporting demands.

METHODS OF CALCULATING UNIT COST OF PRODUCTION

Two general systems, with many variations, are used to trace production costs to the product: job and process costing. Both systems have the same objective of determining the unit cost of the products produced. It is through this unit cost that the accountant determines the cost to hold in the inventory or the cost to match with revenue. Job and process costing are two methods of keeping the detailed records supporting the Work-in-Process Inventory and of determining the unit cost of production. Both systems may be used with either variable or absorption costing. Both variable and absorption costing are concerned with the problem of which costs are product costs and which costs are period costs. Job order and process costing are concerned with the question of how product costs, regardless of their definition, are combined to determine the unit cost of manufacture.

Job costing is used where the products are manufactured in a series of identifiable and separate jobs, lots, or batches. Often the company has a firm sales order before it begins work on a job. Examples of industries where job costing is suitable include building construction, shipbuilding, printing, and aircraft manufacturing. In these plants each product unit is identifiable from the beginning of production. Costs are accumulated for each job, and the unit cost is the sum of all costs identified with the particular job. In these plants the **job cost sheet** serves as the focal point of costs. There is one job cost sheet for each unit or batch produced, and the sum of the costs on the job cost sheets must equal the dollars charged to the Work-in-Process Inventory.

In plants where the production is a continuous flow, or where one unit of product is indistinguishable from another, costs are assigned to the products through **process costing.** In a process cost system the costs are traced to departments during a specified time period on a **departmental cost sheet,** and the cost per unit of product is determined by dividing the production costs of the department for the accounting period by the output produced by the department during the accounting period. The result is an average unit cost for all items produced. Industries that use process costing include steel mills, petroleum refineries, meat-packing plants, lumber mills, and aluminum manufacturers.

JOB COSTING ILLUSTRATED

In a job costing system the detailed record (subsidiary ledger) supporting the Work-in-Process Inventory is the **job cost sheet.** With a large product, such as an airplane or ship, there is usually one job cost sheet for each unit. With small units there could be a job cost sheet for a number of units; the cost of a single unit of product would be determined by dividing the total cost for the lot by the number of units in the lot.

Each job cost sheet is numbered so that each cost can be traced accurately. All product costs incurred must be traced to job cost sheets, either directly, through material requisitions and labor time tickets, or indirectly through an overhead rate. The total costs charged to Work-in-Process Inventory during any specific time period will be equal to the charges on the job cost sheets. When a product is completed, the job cost sheet for that product is totaled. The total of the charges on the job cost sheet is the amount transferred to Finished Goods Inventory. Any jobs started but not completed provide the detail of the ending Work-in-Process Inventory. In a job costing system, accumulation of costs for a particular product is important. It may take two or more accounting periods before a particular job is finished and the final unit cost determined.

To illustrate the flow of costs in a job costing system, let's examine the cost system for the Roving Jack Company, a manufacturer of mobile camper units. The journal entries illustrating the flow of costs for the Roving Jack Company are keyed to the cost flow diagram shown in Exhibit 5–1. Transactions will not always be in numerical sequence. Refer to Exhibit 5–1 occasionally to maintain an overall perspective of the flow of costs through the system.

At the beginning of October the Roving Jack Company had three units in the process of construction. Inventories at the beginning of the month included $2,500 of materials in the Raw Materials Inventory, $6,542 in the Work-in-Process Inventory for the three partially completed units, and no units in the Finished Goods Inventory. The job cost sheets in Exhibit 5–2 show the following beginning inventory balances for the three jobs in process on October 1.

	101	102	103	Total
Direct materials	$1,355	$ 917	$1,080	$3,352
Direct labor	1,250	$1,040	430	2,720
Variable overhead	215	180	75	470
Total cost	$2,820	$2,137	$1,585	$6,542

The transactions of the Roving Jack Company for October follow.

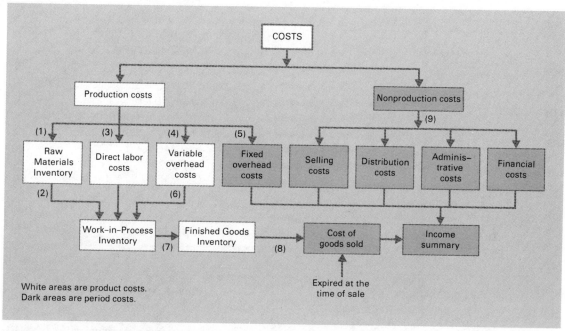

EXHIBIT 5–1   Cost flow with variable costing

PURCHASE OF RAW MATERIALS

The storeroom records indicated that the company needed additional raw materials. The storekeeper sent a **purchase requisition** to the purchasing department to advise them of the need for raw materials. Using the purchase requisition as authority, the purchasing agent issued a **purchase order** notifying the supplier of the material needs. No accounting entry was made for these two events, because no exchange with outside parties was completed.

When the supplier received the purchase order, the order was filled and the materials were shipped. At the same time, an **invoice** was sent for the selling prices of the materials. After the goods were received, inspected, and accepted by the Roving Jack Company, the accountant made the following journal entry to record the purchase of raw materials.

(1) Raw Materials Inventory $4,400
         Accounts Payable (or Cash) $4,400
   <small>To record the purchase of raw materials</small>

The Raw Materials Inventory is a control account; that is, the aggregate total is kept in the general ledger and supported by detailed records in a subsid-

ROVING JACK COMPANY				
Job Cost Sheet No.			101	

Date	Direct Material	Direct Labor	Variable Overhead	Total
Bal. 9-30	$1,355	$1,250	$ 215	$2,820
October	500	4,400	750	5,650
Total	$1,855	$5,650	$ 965	$8,470

ROVING JACK COMPANY				
Job Cost Sheet No.			102	

Date	Direct Material	Direct Labor	Variable Overhead	Total
Bal. 9-30	$ 917	$1,040	$ 180	$2,137
October	317	1,900	300	2,517
Total	$1,234	$2,940	$ 480	$4,654

ROVING JACK COMPANY				
Job Cost Sheet No.			103	

Date	Direct Material	Direct Labor	Variable Overhead	Total
Bal. 9-30	$1,080	$ 430	$ 75	$1,585
October	820	3,200	550	4,570
Total	$1,900	$3,630	$ 625	$6,155

ROVING JACK COMPANY				
Job Cost Sheet No.			104	

Date	Direct Material	Direct Labor	Variable Overhead	Total
October	$3,350	$6,200	$1,000	$10,550
Total				

EXHIBIT 5—2   Job cost sheets for the Roving Jack Company

iary ledger. For each type of raw material a subsidiary ledger card is kept to show the quantity and price of the items received, issued, and on hand. (We have not included the subsidiary ledger records for the Raw Materials Inventory account.)

ISSUE OF RAW MATERIALS

The production schedule for October called for the completion of Jobs 101, 102, and 103, and for the start of one new job: 104. On the basis of this production schedule, the production manager prepared **material requisitions** for the material necessary to perform the scheduled work.

Material requisitions serve as authority for the storeroom to release materials to the factory and as evidence to support the accounting entry. The following summation of these material requisitions for October showed direct materials issued to the jobs.

Job 101	$ 500
Job 102	317
Job 103	820
Job 104	3,350
Total direct materials	$4,987

Materials issued from the storeroom were removed from the raw materials ledger cards (not shown) and were posted to the individual job cost sheets, as shown in Exhibit 5–2. The following journal entry records the issue of this direct material.

(2) Work-in-Process Inventory $4,987
       Raw Materials Inventory......................... $4,987
    To record the issue of direct materials.

The material requisitions showed that in addition to the direct materials previously listed, $1,000 of indirect materials were issued to the factory. These are materials that are required for production but for some reason cannot be traced to a specific job. The following journal entry records this issue.

(4) Variable Overhead Control.................. $1,000
       Raw Materials Inventory......................... $1,000
    To record the issue of indirect materials.

The accounts Variable Overhead Control and Fixed Overhead Control are used by accountants to record actual overhead costs. These accounts will be discussed later in this chapter.

PURCHASE AND CONSUMPTION OF LABOR

Two distinct functions are involved in labor accounting. First, the time for which the workers are to be paid is determined by their **clock cards.** From these cards the payroll department prepared their paychecks and distributed them on payday. The clock cards used in preparing the payroll show what the workers have earned but do not indicate the activities they performed while working. To determine these activities there must be a second document. At the end of each day employees or their supervisors prepare **time tickets** that list the amount of time spent on each job (treated as direct labor) and the amount of nonproduction time (treated as indirect labor). From the details of the time tickets, the Roving Jack Company's accountants found that of the $16,700 paid to the workers, $15,700 was direct labor that could be traced to the jobs, and $1,000 was indirect labor that was treated as fixed overhead. The direct labor was used as follows:

Job 101.............	750 hours	$ 4,400
Job 102.............	300 hours	1,900
Job 103.............	550 hours	3,200
Job 104.............1,000 hours		6,200
Total direct labor		$15,700

The following journal entries record the labor costs.

(3) Work-in-Process Inventory $15,700
       Accrued Payroll $15,700
   To record direct labor cost.

(5) Fixed Overhead Control....................... $1,000
       Accrued Payroll $1,000
   To record the indirect labor cost.

The amount of the direct labor was also posted to the individual job cost sheets shown in Exhibit 5–2.

TRANSFER OF OVERHEAD TO WORK-IN-PROCESS INVENTORY

Overhead costs are diverse and difficult to trace directly to the individual jobs. Therefore, it is necessary to apportion or allocate them to the jobs. The **overhead rate** is the accountant's method of allocating these costs. Under variable costing, only the variable overhead costs are included in the overhead rate. It is possible to use either an "after-the-fact" overhead rate or a "predetermined" overhead rate to assign these costs to the jobs. In this example we will assume a "predetermined" rate. In Chapter 7 the advantages and disadvantages of both methods of overhead costing will be discussed.

At the beginning of the year the management of the Roving Jack Company estimated that the production budgeted for the year would require 32,000 direct labor hours. The accountant for the Roving Jack Company had prepared an analysis of the cost behavior pattern for overhead costs and arrived at the flexible budgets of[1]

---

[1]In our example we use direct labor hours as the volume measure. Other measures are discussed in a later chapter.

Cost Items	Annual Fixed Costs	Variable Cost per Direct Labor Hour
Indirect material	$ 0	$ .40
Indirect labor	13,200	0
Heat, light, power	0	.15
Labor-related costs	0	.45
Depreciation	18,000	0
Factory insurance	4,800	0
Miscellaneous	12,000	0
Total cost	$48,000	$1.00

This example has been simplified by omitting all semivariable costs. This allows the accountant to treat each cost, in both the planning and actual recording phases, as purely fixed or purely variable.

The variable overhead rate of $1.00 per direct labor hour was used during the previous months and will be used for the rest of the year to apply variable overhead costs to the jobs. Until the current month of October the incurrence of overhead costs and the actual direct labor hours worked for the year have been exactly as planned.

The following journal entry applies variable overhead to individual jobs in the Work-in-Process Inventory for October.

(6) Work-in-Process Inventory $2,600
      Variable Overhead Applied $2,600

    To apply variable overhead to jobs at the rate of $1.00 per direct labor hour.

The variable overhead applied to each job is listed below. The posting is also shown on the job cost sheets in Exhibit 5–2.

Job	Direct Labor Hours	×	Variable Overhead Rate per Labor Hour	=	Total Variable Overhead Applied
101	750		$1		$ 750
102	300		$1		300
103	550		$1		550
104	1,000		$1		1,000
Total overhead applied to jobs					$2,600

INCURRENCE OF OVERHEAD

We have already recorded indirect materials of $1,000 as variable overhead and indirect labor of $1,000 as fixed overhead. The classification as fixed or variable was based on the accountant's study, discussed in the previous section. Assume that the Roving Jack Company's accountant processed other actual overhead costs as listed below.

Cost	Amount	Behavior
Heat, light, and power	$ 700	Variable
Labor-related costs	1,300	Variable
Depreciation of building	1,500	Fixed
Factory insurance	200	Fixed
Miscellaneous (normally detailed)	1,200	Fixed
Total	$4,900	

The following journal entry records these actual overhead costs incurred.

(4) Variable Overhead Control $2,000
(5) Fixed Overhead Control $2,900
    Accumulated Depreciation $1,500
    Cash, or Payables, or Prepaids $3,400

To record the incurrence of overhead.

    The two previous overhead entries used two accounts that require special comment. When actual overhead costs are incurred, accountants accumulate the amounts in overhead control accounts: Variable Overhead Control and Fixed Overhead Control. When variable overhead is applied to the individual jobs with an overhead rate determined at the beginning of the accounting period, the amount of the overhead charged to the jobs is accumulated in the account, Variable Overhead Applied. The difference between the Variable Overhead Control account and the Variable Overhead Applied account results because the actual costs were not incurred in conformity with the flexible budget equation for the year. In our example, variable overhead was underapplied by $400.[2]

    To explore the Underapplied Variable Overhead and to see how well fixed costs were controlled, the management accountant prepared the report in Exhibit 5–3. In the left-hand column are the actual variable and fixed costs extracted directly from the accounting system (see entry 5). The **Performance Budget** column comes from the original flexible budgets adjusted to the actual hours worked. For example, the indirect materials were budgeted at $.40 per

---

[2]If the firm had used a historical (after-the-fact) variable overhead rate, they would have divided actual variable overhead ($3,000) by actual direct labor hours (2,600) at the close of the accounting period to obtain the overhead rate of $1.154 per direct labor hour. If this historical, or actual, overhead rate had been used there would be no Under- or Overapplied Overhead. Because the actual overhead cost equals the overhead charged to Work-in-Process, most firms using historical actual rates would not use an "applied" account. Rather, they would credit the variable Factory Overhead Control account directly.

THE ROVING JACK COMPANY
OVERHEAD COST REPORT
For the Month of October, 19X3

	Actual Overhead Costs	Performance Budget	Spending Variance
Variable Costs:			
Indirect Materials	$1,000	$1,040	$ 40 F
Heat, Light, Power	700	390	(310) U
Labor-related Costs	1,300	1,170	(130) U
Total Variable Costs	$3,000	$2,600	$(400) U
Fixed Costs:			
Indirect Labor	$1,000	$1,100	$ 100 F
Depreciation	1,500	1,500	–0–
Factory Insurance	200	400	200 F
Miscellaneous	1,200	1,000	(200) U
Total Fixed Costs	3,900	4,000	100 F
Total Overhead Costs	$6,900	$6,600	$(300) U

EXHIBIT 5–3
Overhead cost control report

direct labor hour. At 2,600 actual direct labor hours the company should have spent $1,040 ($.40 × 2,600 hours). Because actual expenses were $1,000, the management had a favorable[3] variance of $40 on indirect materials. The Performance Budget for the fixed costs was derived by assuming that the fixed costs were budgeted uniformly throughout the year ($48,000 ÷ 12 months), or $4,000 per month. For indirect labor the monthly budget was $1,100 ($13,200 ÷ 12 months). Because actual costs were $1,000 there was a $100 favorable indirect labor cost variance in October.

From management's perspective the variances are a feedback mechanism through which they are alerted to unexpected or undesired results. To report the magnitude of the variances is important, but not a complete story. To know what the variances are is one matter; identifying the causes of the variances is quite another. As an example, heat, light, and power show an unfavorable variance of $310 (Exhibit 5–3). This variance could have been caused by higher electrical rates, colder weather than expected, failure to institute conservation measures, or perhaps, poor estimations at the time the flexible budgets were determined. As another example, the Performance Budget for fixed costs was calculated as $4,000 ($48,000 ÷ 12 months). This assumes the fixed costs are incurred evenly throughout the year. Any nonuniformity during the year in the incurrence of fixed costs could result in a monthly variance. Obviously, management would want to know the causes of any variance it considers important.

---

[3]A favorable variance results when actual cost is less than the performance budget; an unfavorable variance results when the actual cost exceeds the performance budget. Throughout the book we will use **F** to show a favorable variance and **U** to show an unfavorable variance.

COMPLETION OF THE JOBS

The costs of production shown on the job cost sheets are transferred from Work-in-Process Inventory to Finished Goods Inventory when the jobs are completed and moved from the factory to the warehouse. Factory records for the Roving Jack Company indicate that Jobs 101, 102, and 103 were completed during the month and transferred to the showroom. Job cost sheets for the completed mobile units showed the following completed job costs.

Job 101	$ 8,470
Job 102	4,654
Job 103	6,155
Total cost of completed jobs	$19,279

Job 104 was uncompleted and remained in the factory. The following journal entry records the completed units.

(7) Finished Goods Inventory $19,279
　　　　Work-in-Process Inventory...................... $19,279
　　　　　To record the completion of Jobs 101, 102, and 103.

After this journal entry is posted to the Work-in-Process Inventory account, the balance will be $10,550, the accumulated costs of Job 104.

SALE OF FINISHED PRODUCTS

The **sales invoices** of the Roving Jack Company indicate that the sales personnel sold Job 102 for $8,000 cash and Job 103 for $10,500 cash. Two entries are required to recognize the sale. First, the sales revenue must be recognized.

(8a) Cash $18,500
　　　　Sales....................................... $18,500
　　　　　To record the sales revenue ($8,000 + $10,500).

Second, the cost of the units sold must be transferred from Finished Goods Inventory to Cost of Goods Sold. The amounts shown on the completed job cost sheets associated with the units sold serve as the source of the amounts for this journal entry.

(8b) Cost of Goods Sold $10,809
　　　　Finished Goods Inventory $10,809
　　　　　To record the goods sold of Jobs 102 and 103 ($4,654 + $6,155).

After this entry has been posted to the Finished Goods Inventory account, the balance will be $8,470. This is the cost of Job 101, which is still unsold.

INCURRENCE OF NONPRODUCTION COSTS

For simplicity, we will assume that the Roving Jack Company incurred $800 of selling costs and $700 of administrative costs, and that it incurred no distribution or financial costs. The following journal entry records these costs.

(9) Selling Expense Control........................ $800
        Administrative Expense Control................ $700
            Cash, or Payables, or Prepaids $1,500
    To record the incurrence of actual selling and administrative expenses.

    In an actual setting, detailed information about the selling and administrative costs would be recorded in subsidiary ledgers to the control accounts. This subsidiary ledger would be similar to the details kept for overhead. Also, if the firm had flexible budgets for these costs, a cost report similar to Exhibit 5–3 would be prepared. To simplify our exammple we have used only the total costs incurred and have omitted these details.

CLOSING THE OVERHEAD ACCOUNTS

At the end of the month, the Variable Overhead Control account, which shows the costs actually incurred, and the Variable Overhead Applied account, which shows the overhead charged to the jobs, are closed. The difference between the two accounts for variable costs is computed and transferred to an account called Under- or Overapplied Variable Overhead. If the overhead applied to production during the month is larger than the actual variable overhead incurred (shown in the Variable Overhead Control), overhead is *overapplied*. If the control balance is larger than the applied balance, the overhead is *underapplied*. The following journal entry closes the overhead accounts.

Variable Overhead Applied...................... $2,600
Under- or Overapplied Variable Overhead .... $ 400
    Variable Overhead Control........................... $3,000
To close the variable overhead accounts.

Exhibit 5–4 shows the T-accounts of the Roving Jack Company for the month of October. In Exhibit 5–5 we have presented a monthly income statement for the Roving Jack Company. This report is for management's use; it is not intended for external reporting.

    At the end of the accounting period the accountant will close the Under- or Overapplied Variable Overhead account. If this were the end of the period the following entry would be made.

Cost of Goods Sold $400
    Under- or Overapplied Variable Overhead $400
To close the Under- or Overhead Variable Overhead account.

RAW MATERIALS INVENTORY

Bal. 9-30	$2,500	(2)	$4,987
(1)	4,400	(4)	1,000
	$6,900		913
		Bal. 10-31	$6,900
Bal. 10-31	$ 913		

ACCUMULATED DEPRECIATION

	$1,500

SALES

	(8a)	$18,500

VARIABLE OVERHEAD CONTROL

(4)	$1,000	To Close	$3,000
(4)	2,000		
	$3,000		$3,000

COST OF GOODS SOLD

(8b)	$10,809

VARIABLE OVERHEAD APPLIED

To Close	$2,600	(6)	$2,600

WORK-IN-PROCESS INVENTORY

Bal. 9-30	$ 6,542	(7)	$19,279
(2)	4,987	Bal. 10-31	10,550
(3)	15,700		
(6)	2,600		
	$29,829		$29,829
Bal. 10-31	$10,550		

SELLING EXPENSE CONTROL

(9)	$800

CASH OR PAYABLES

(8a)		$18,500
(1)		15,700
(3)		1,000
(5)		3,400
(9)		1,500

Note: the debit side lists $ 4,400; 15,700; 1,000; 3,400; 1,500.

FINISHED-GOODS INVENTORY

Bal. 9-30	$ 0	(8b)	$19,279
(7)	19,279	Bal. 10-31	8,470
	$19,279		$19,279
Bal. 10-31	$ 8,470		

ADMINISTRATIVE EXPENSE CONTROL

(9)	$700

UNDER- OR OVERAPPLIED VARIABLE OVERHEAD

From Closing	$400

FIXED OVERHEAD-CONTROL

(5)	$1,000
(5)	2,900
	$3,900

EXHIBIT 5—4   General ledger accounts for the Roving Jack Company

```
                    ROVING JACK COMPANY
                INCOME STATEMENT FOR MANAGEMENT
                   For the Month of October 19X3

Sales                                        $18,500      100%
Variable Cost of Goods Sold:
  Cost of Goods Sold            $10,809
  Plus:
    Underapplied Variable Overhead   400       11,209      61%
Contribution margin                          $ 7,291       39%
Less:
  Fixed overhead                $ 3,900
  Selling expenses                 800
  Administrative expenses          700        5,400        29%
Income                                       $ 1,891       10%
```

EXHIBIT 5–5
Contribution margin
income statement for the
Roving Jack Company

Also at the end of the accounting period the Fixed Overhead Control, along with all other nominal accounts, will be closed to Retained Earnings, via Income Summary.

PROCESS COSTING ILLUSTRATED

Process costing differs from job costing in the way in which costs are traced to the factory and unit costs are determined. In a process costing system the costs are accumulated for departments or processes for a specified period of time, often one month. The unit cost of manufacturing the goods is found by dividing these departmental costs by the units produced during the time period. Process costing is used where a large quantity of similar units are produced.

To illustrate process costing, let us assume that the Hot Link Sausage Company produces a line of Polish sausage in two departments: a Mixing–Stuffing Department and a Smoking–Drying Department. In the Mixing–Stuffing Department, meat and other products are issued at the beginning of the process. These products are ground together, seasonings are added using a closely held family recipe, and the resulting mixture is stuffed into thin skins. In the Smoking–Drying Department the stuffed sausages are hung over large drying racks and rotated between the smoking and the drying rooms until the sausages are properly cured. The Smoking–Drying Department uses no materials; any supplies are included in overhead. Labor and overhead are added uniformly throughout both processes. Exhibit 5–6 shows the process diagrammatically.

The Hot Links Company follows the policy of combining direct labor and overhead in its Work-in-Process Inventory accounts. The sum of direct labor

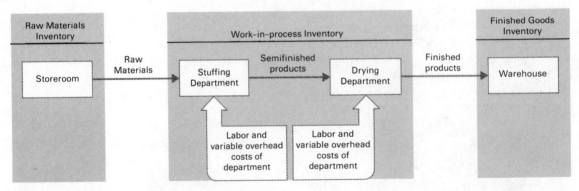

EXHIBIT 5—6   Cost and product flow diagram

and overhead is called **conversion costs,** and treated as a package, because overhead is charged to the departments on the basis of direct labor. Treating these two cost elements as a single cost enables the accountants of the Hot Links Company to simplify their calculation of unit costs.

Exhibit 5–7 shows the quantity and cost reports for the two departments for the month of March. These monthly production and cost reports are focused on the departments and serve as the data base for calculating the unit cost of units transferred out of the departments and of those left in the final inventories. The departmental production report shows the units and costs for which the department must account.

Recasting the units found on the production report into a quantity report, we find the following.

	Stuffing Department	Drying Department
Beginning units in process	0	8,000
New units started	60,000	40,000
Units available	60,000	48,000
Ending units in process	20,000	12,000
Units transferred out	40,000	36,000

This schedule shows the flow of the units throughout the factory. The 40,000 units transferred from the Stuffing Department become the prior department units for the Drying Department. The 36,000 units leaving the Drying Department are transferred to Finished Goods Inventory, where they await sale.

We will proceed systematically through the two departments to see how the unit cost of production is calculated and used as the basis of journal entries.

THE HOT LINKS COMPANY
DEPARTMENTAL PRODUCTION AND COST REPORT
For the Month of March, 19X2

	DEPARTMENTS	
	Stuffing	*Drying*
QUANTITY DATA		
Units in process, March 1		
Stuffing	None	—
Drying (100% complete as to prior department costs; 1/4 complete as to conversion costs)	—	8,000
New units started	60,000	—
Units received from prior departments		40,000
Units completed and transferred to		
Drying	40,000	—
Finished-goods inventory	—	36,000
Units in process, March 31		
Stuffing (100% complete as to materials costs; 1/5 complete as to conversion costs)	20,000	—
Drying (100% complete as to prior department costs; 1/3 complete as to conversion costs)	—	12,000
COST DATA		
Beginning inventory, March 1		
Prior department costs	None	$9,600
Conversion costs	None	$4,000
New costs incurred this period		
Raw materials	$60,000	None
Prior department costs	None	?
Conversion costs	$22,000	$114,000

EXHIBIT 5–7
Departmental production
and cost reports

STUFFING DEPARTMENT

In the Stuffing Department there was no beginning Work-in-Process Inventory. During the month of March, $60,000 of raw materials and $22,000 of direct labor and variable overhead were used.

In the Stuffing Department there are units in the final inventory in addition to the units transferred out. To calculate the unit cost for the period, it is necessary to calculate **equivalent units.** For example, two half-completed units are equivalent in cost to one totally complete unit. Equivalent units recognize that not all of the units in process shown on the quantity report are fully completed.

The equivalent unit schedules for the Stuffing Department for the month of March are as shown in the accompanying tabulation.

	Equivalent Units	
	Raw Materials	Conversion Costs
Transferred out to the drying department (100% complete)	40,000	40,000
Ending inventory		
material (20,000 × 100%)	20,000	
Conversion costs (20,000 × 20%)		4,000
Equivalent units	60,000	44,000

The ending inventory in the Stuffing Department is 100% complete as far as raw material costs are concerned. Conversion costs, on the other hand, are not 100% complete. Because the 20,000 units in the final inventory have progressed only one-fifth of the way through the process, and conversion costs are added uniformly throughout the process, the department "equivalently" completed only 4,000 of these 20,000 units. Next period the department will have to add sufficient conversion costs to finish the equivalent of 16,000 units. Of course, the 40,000 units transferred to the Drying Department were 100% as to all cost factors, or they would not have been finished and suitable to transfer.

Because each cost factor can be at a separate stage of completion, most firms determine equivalent units and, subsequently, unit costs for each type of cost element. The total unit cost is then the sum of the unit costs for the individual cost factors. The total cost, equivalent units, and unit cost for each cost element in the Stuffing Department are shown in the computations that follow.

COMPUTATION OF UNIT COST—STUFFING DEPARTMENT			
	Total Cost	÷ Equivalent Units	= Unit Cost
Raw material costs	$60,000	60,000	$1.00
Conversion costs	22,000	44,000	.50
Total cost	$82,000		$1.50

The following computations show the inventory values and the costs transferred out.

```
┌─────────────────────────────────────────────────────────────────┐
│        COMPUTATION OF COSTS INVENTORY AND TRANSFERRED OUT—        │
│                      STUFFING DEPARTMENT                          │
│ ───────────────────────────────────────────────────────────────  │
│   Ending Work-in-Process Inventory of department, March 31:       │
│     Raw material costs (20,000 × $1.00)              $20,000      │
│     Conversion costs (4,000 × $.50)                    2,000      │
│     Total ending Work-in-Process Inventory           $22,000      │
│   Transferred to Drying Department (40,000 × $1.50)    60,000      │
│   Total costs of Stuffing Department accounted for   $82,000      │
└─────────────────────────────────────────────────────────────────┘
```

The following journal entry records the transfer to the Drying Department.

> Work-in-Process Inventory—
>   Drying Department $60,000
>   Work-in-Process Inventory—Stuffing Department ... $60,000
>   To transfer production costs.

After this entry is posted, the Work-in-Process Inventory—Stuffing Department will have a $22,000 balance, which was the amount determined in the preceding computation as the value of the ending inventory.

DRYING DEPARTMENT

In the Drying Department there was a beginning inventory of 8,000 units at a cost of $13,600. These 8,000 units had all of the prior-department costs from the Stuffing Department but were only one-fourth completed with respect to the Drying Department's conversion costs. The $9,600 and $4,000, respectively, were the inventory balances determined at the end of February. During March the Drying Department received $60,000 of semicomplete products from the Stuffing Department and added $114,000 of conversion costs.

The equivalent unit schedules for the Drying Department are as shown in the following tabulation.

EQUIVALENT UNITS		
	Prior-Department Costs	Conversion Costs
Transferred out to Finished Goods Inventory (100% complete)	36,000	36,000
Plus: Ending Inventory		
Prior department costs (12,000 × 100%)	12,000	
Conversion costs (12,000 × 33⅓%)		4,000
Total	48,000	40,000
Less: Beginning Inventory		
Prior department costs (8,000 × 100%)	8,000	
Conversion costs (8,000 × 25%)		2,000
Equivalent production	40,000	38,000

The calculation of the equivalent units was based on the following logic. The 36,000 units transferred out had to be wholly complete with respect to both prior-department costs and conversion costs. This figure is added to the work on the final inventory that was accomplished this period. The final inventory of 12,000 units was wholly complete relative to prior-department costs. That is, the material received from the Stuffing Department was fully complete as far as the Stuffing Department was concerned. However, these 12,000 units had not been fully processed through the Drying Department. They were only one-third completed in Drying; this is the equivalent of 4,000 units of conversion costs in the final inventory. The beginning inventory of 8,000 equivalent units for prior-department costs and 2,000 for conversion costs represents work accomplished in the previous accounting period and is deducted to arrive at the equivalent units of work accomplished solely within this accounting period. Using these equivalent units, the unit cost computation would be as follows.

COMPUTATION OF UNIT COST—DRYING DEPARTMENT			
	Total Costs ÷	Equivalent Units =	Unit Cost
Prior-department costs:			
Beginning inventory	$ 9,600	8,000	$1.20
Current production	60,000	40,000	$1.50
Total	$ 69,600	48,000	$1.45
Conversion costs:			
Beginning inventory	$ 4,000	2,000	$2.00
Current production	114,000	38,000	$3.00
Total	118,000	40,000	$2.95
Total	$187,600		

A close examination of the unit cost computation shows that there are two layers of equivalent units and costs. Prior-department costs consist of 8,000 equivalent units in the beginning inventory at a unit cost of $1.20, and 40,000 equivalent units added this period at a unit cost of $1.50. For conversion costs there is a beginning inventory layer of 2,000 equivalent units at a unit cost of $2.00, and 38,000 equivalent units added this period at a unit cost of $3.00. Because there are two layers of units, it is possible to create the different inventory cost flows of FIFO or weighted average.

WEIGHTED AVERAGE

With weighted-average costing the two layers are combined into a single, average unit cost. For prior-department cost the weighted-average unit cost is $1.45; for conversion costs it is $2.95. Both the units in the final inventory and those transferred out are costed at this average cost. The following computations show the inventory values and the costs transferred out using the weighted-average cost flows.

WEIGHTED-AVERAGE COMPUTATION OF COSTS OF INVENTORY AND TRANSFERRED OUT—DRYING DEPARTMENT	
Ending Work-in-Process Inventory of department, March 31:	
Prior-department costs (12,000 × $1.45)	$ 17,400
Conversion costs (4,000 × $2.95)	11,800
Total ending Work-in-Process Inventory	$ 29,200
Transferred out to Finished Goods Inventory	
(36,000 × $4.40)	158,400
Total costs of drying department accounted for	$187,600

The following journal entry transfers the 36,000 units to Finished Goods Inventory with weighted average.

Finished Goods Inventory $158,400
       Work-in-Process Inventory—Drying Department ... $158,400
To record the transfer of cost of completed units to Finished Goods Inventory.

After this entry is posted, the balance of Work-in-Process Inventory—Drying Department will be $29,200.

FIFO COST FLOW

With FIFO cost flow the units in the final inventory comes from the most current production. Therefore, the final inventory should be valued at the most current costs; all other costs are transferred out. The following computation shows the inventory values and costs transferred out using FIFO cost flow.

FIFO COMPUTATION OF COSTS OF INVENTORY AND TRANSFERRED OUT—DRYING DEPARTMENT	
Ending Work-in-Process Inventory of department, March 31:	
Prior-department costs (12,000 × $1.50)	$ 18,000
Conversion costs (4,000 × $3.00)	12,000
Total ending Work-in-Process Inventory	$ 30,000
Transferred out to Finished Goods Inventory	157,600
Total costs of Drying Department accounted for	$187,600

The ending inventory was costed at the unit costs of the current period. Thus, for prior-department costs, the 12,000 units were costed at $1.50; for the

4,000 equivalent units of conversion costs, the current cost was $3.00. The $157,600 transferred to the Finished Goods Inventory was determined by deducting the value of the ending inventory ($30,000) from the total costs to be accounted for of $187,600.[4]

The following journal entry transfers the 36,000 units to Finished Goods Inventory with FIFO.

> Finished Goods Inventory $157,600
>   Work-in-Process Inventory—Drying Department ... $157,600
>   To record the transfer of cost of completed units to Finished Goods Inventory.

After this entry is posted, the balance of Work-in-Process Inventory—Drying Department will be $30,000.

SUMMARY

There are two systems of combining the product costs to determine inventory values. A job costing system is used in those industries where the product is large, identifiable, and often made to special order. In a job costing system job cost sheets serve as the focal point of cost accumulation. The unit cost is determined by summing the costs that are recorded on the job cost sheets. In a process costing system the unit cost is determined by summing the costs of a department over a period of time and dividing by the number of equivalent units. Process costing systems are used in industries where large numbers of similar units are produced.

---

[4]It is possible to prove that the $157,600 was properly calculated as follows.

Transferred out (36,000 units):	
From Beginning Inventory (8,000 units):	
Prior-department costs (8,000 @ $1.20)	$ 9,600
Conversion costs from last period (2,000 @ $2.00)	4,000
Conversion costs from this period (6,000 @ $3.00)	18,000
From new units started and completed this period (36,000 units − 8,000 units):	
Prior-department costs (28,000 @ $1.50)	42,000
Conversion costs (28,000 @ $3.00)	84,000
Total costs transferred to Finished Goods Inventory	$157,600

AN ALTERNATIVE OVERHEAD ACCOUNTING PROCEDURE

In the Roving Jack Company illustration in this chapter we made a simplifying assumption. In the development of the flexible budgets for overhead all of the costs were either purely fixed or purely variable. This assumption of having no mixed costs allowed the use of the Variable Overhead Control and Fixed Overhead Control accounts. It was assumed that when a cost was incurred and recorded it could be defined automatically as fixed or variable.

This assumption, while useful as a teaching aid, is unrealistic in a business setting. As explained in Chapter 2, the amount of the total fixed costs and the variable rate are often determined, after the costs have been recorded, by some technique such as the high-low or regression analysis. From this type of analysis we can say "costs tend to have fixed or variable attributes"; it is unlikely we can say with certainty, "this cost is absolutely fixed or that cost is absolutely variable." This implies that when costs are incurred and recorded within the accounting system from the invoices, it is impossible to know how much is fixed and how much is variable. Certainly this would be true for all mixed costs or when different transactions are combined into a single overhead subsidiary ledger account.

To illustrate an alternative accounting procedure, assume that the Tiger Company had only four overhead costs with the following flexible budgets:

	Fixed Costs per Month		Variable Cost per Direct Labor Hour
Indirect material	$ 0	+	$1.00(x)
Indirect labor	$3,600	+	$ .20(x)
Utilities	$1,200	+	$ .30(x)
Depreciation	$2,800	+	$ 0(x)

In this example there are one fixed, one variable, and two semivariable costs. Using variable costing the overhead rate would be $1.50 per direct labor hour. If we assume the firm actually worked 10,000 direct labor hours in the current month, the journal entry to apply variable overhead to Work-in-Process would be as follows:

Work-in-Process Inventory $15,000
    Variable Overhead Applied $15,000
To apply variable overhead (10,000 × $1.50).

Now assume that the firm incurred the following actual costs at the 10,000 direct labor hour level.

Indirect materials	$11,000
Indirect labor	5,200
Utilities	4,300
Depreciation	2,800
Total overhead costs	$23,300

At the time of recording these actual costs it would be impossible, for example, to know how much of the $5,200 incurred for indirect labor is fixed and how much is variable. For this reason many accountants would use only a single overhead account.

Factory Overhead Control $23,300
    Raw Materials Inventory $11,000
    Accumulated Depreciation . . . . $ 2,800
    Cash (Accounts Payable) . . . . $ 9,500

Even though the total overhead costs cannot be identified as fixed or variable, there is no reason that the firm cannot prepare a cost control report similar to Exhibit 5–3. Such a report would look like this.

	Actual Costs	Performance Budget	Variance
Indirect materials	$11,000	$10,000	$1,000 U
Indirect labor	5,200	5,600	400 F
Utilities	4,300	4,200	100 U
Depreciation	2,800	2,800	—
Total	$23,300	$22,600	$ 700 U

At the end of the accounting period the two overhead accounts would be closed with the following entry.

Variable Overhead Applied $15,000
Income Summary . . . .$ 8,300
    Factory Overhead Control $23,300

The nature of the $8,300 requires some explanation. It is composed of the variable and fixed overhead spending variance ($700) and the budgeted fixed costs ($7,600). Because the budgeted fixed costs plus or minus the fixed overhead spending variance equals the "actual" fixed costs, the $8,300 could also be defined as the actual fixed costs plus the variable overhead underapplied. Thus the effect on income is identical to the accounting procedures illustrated in the chapter. This is true because in variable costing the over- or underapplied variable overhead and the actual fixed costs are both treated as period costs. This is the result of the above treatment.

5-1   *(Journal Entries for Cost Flows)*. Prepare journal entries for the Sanford Company. The company uses a variable costing system.

A. Purchased raw materials on account, $250.

B. Issued materials to production, $200.

C. Paid employees: direct labor $180, indirect labor $20. (Indirect labor is a variable cost.)

D. Applied variable overhead to production at the rate of 60% of direct labor cost.

E. Paid actual costs: variable overhead $100, fixed overhead $50, and selling and administrative expenses $150.

F. Sold products costing $600 for $950 on account.

G. Closed the variable overhead control and variable overhead applied accounts.

5-2   *(Job Cost)*. Tasha, Inc. produces a line of copper bowls in its small roadside factory. The copper bowls are very popular with tourists visiting the area. The bowls are sold both at the factory outlet and in several retail outlets in town. To minimize the costs of production, Tasha produces the bowls in batches of 100 bowls each. Materials and labor are traced directly to individual batches, and overhead is applied at the rate of $4.50 per direct labor hour. The following material and labor costs were traced to batch 672.

Material	$286
Labor (20 hours)	$100

REQUIRED:

A. How much overhead was applied to batch 672?

B. What was the total cost of batch 672?

C. What was the unit cost per bowl for bowls produced in batch 672?

5-3   *(Under- or Overapplied Overhead)*. The Jackson Company accumulated the following data relating to labor and overhead. The company uses a variable costing system.

Flexible budget for overhead =
   $1,200 per month plus $2.40 per direct labor hour.

Actual variable overhead for April	$4,000
Actual fixed overhead for April	$1,150

Actual direct labor for April: 1,600 hours @ $5.00 per hour.

REQUIRED:

A. How much overhead was applied to products?

B. What was the amount of Under- or Overapplied Overhead for April?

C. Prepare the entry to close the Under- or Overapplied Overhead to Cost of Goods Sold.

CLASS **5-4** *(Development of Overhead Rate).* The Allison Company had the following cost and volume data.

	Direct Labor Hours	Factory Overhead
19X2	25,000	$210,000
19X3	28,000	$240,000
19X4	20,000	$190,000
19X5	35,000	$280,000

REQUIRED:

A. Using the above data, determine the firm's flexible budget for overhead.

B. Assume that in 19X6 the firm based its overhead rate on the flexible budget, actually worked 30,000 direct labor hours, and incurred total overhead costs of $264,000, of which $68,000 was fixed. Determine

  1. The variable overhead applied to Work-in-Process.

  2. Variable Overhead Over- or Underapplied.

  3. The variable and fixed overhead spending variances using a Performance Budget.

5-5   *(Job Order Entries and Documents).* Using the letter in front of the accounts or documents (e.g., *B* = Raw Materials), complete the following schedule for the Terry Company.

Accounts	Source Document	Subsidiary Ledger
A. Cash (or Payables)	L. Purchase requisition	R. Raw Material Stock Card
B. Raw Materials	M. Purchase order	S. Job Cost Sheet
C. Work-in-Process	N. Material requisition	T. Finished Goods Stock Card
D. Finished Goods	O. Labor clock card	U. Overhead Subsidiary Ledger
E. Variable Overhead Control	P. Labor time ticket	V. Selling Expense Subsidiary Ledger
F. Variable Overhead Applied	Q. Purchase invoice	
G. Fixed Overhead Control		
H. Selling Expense Control		
I. Cost of Goods Sold		
J. Sales		
K. Under- or Overapplied Variable Overhead		

Transactions	Dr.	Cr.	Source Document(s)	Subsidiary Ledger(s)
1. Purchase of direct and indirect materials	___	___	___	___
2. Issue of direct materials	___	___	___	___
3. Issue of indirect materials (variable)	___	___	___	___
4. Paid plant supervisor salary	___	___	___	___
5. Paid rent on factory building	___	___	___	___
6. Paid utilities (variable)	___	___	___	___
7. Applied overhead to Work-in-Process	___	___	___	___
8. Completed Job 306 and 307	___	___	___	___
9. Sold Job 306	___	___	___	___
10. Paid salespeople	___	___	___	___
11. Closed the overhead accounts (assume overhead is overapplied)	___	___	___	___

5-6 *(Job Cost Sheet)*. The Lamb Company uses job costing to account for its products. It applies variable overhead to the jobs on the basis of direct labor hours. The predetermined overhead rate was estimated at the beginning of the year using the following data.

Fixed overhead	$ 36,000
Variable overhead	72,000
Total estimated overhead	$108,000
Total estimated direct labor hours	12,000

Job 608 was completed during the past month. Raw materials used on Job 608 were $68 and direct labor was four hours at $5.00 per hour. Job 608 was a special order for the Lion Company consisting of 56 candlesticks.

REQUIRED:

A. Prepare a job cost sheet for Job 608 assuming variable costing.

B. Calculate the cost per candlestick.

C. Prepare the journal entries for Job 608.

D. Assume that during the year the company actually worked 20,000 direct labor hours instead of the planned 12,000, and that it incurred actual overhead of $142,000, of which $110,000 was variable. Prepare the journal entry to close the overhead accounts.

E. Determine the total cost and unit cost of Job 608 for external reporting. Explain how the cost was determined.

5-7 *(Variable Job Costing).* The Solid-State Company manufactures minicomputer components to special order. The firm uses a variable, job cost system. The variable overhead rate was based on the following flexible budget equations where the volume measure is direct labor hours. The planned level of operations for 19X7 was 10,000 direct labor hours.

Supervision	$12,000 + \$\ \ 0(x)$
Repairs	$\$\ 6,000 + \$\ .75(x)$
Utilities	$\$\ 0\ \ \ \ + \$1.00(x)$
Depreciation of machinery	$\$\ 0\ \ \ \ + \$1.25(x)$
Depreciation of building	$\$\ 9,000 + \$\ \ 0(x)$
Indirect materials	$\$\ 1,000 + \$\ .50(x)$
Fringe benefits	$\$\ 2,000 + \$1.50(x)$

At the beginning of May 19X7, there were two jobs in process–102 and 103. During May, work was begun on four jobs—104, 105, 106, and 107. Jobs 102, 103, 104, and 105 were finished in May and sent to the finished goods warehouse. Jobs 102, 103, and 105 were delivered to the customers for $26,000. The cost data on all jobs were as follows.

	102	103	104	105	106	107
Beginning inventory:						
Materials	$1,450	$ 850				
Labor	1,295	700				
Overhead	925	500				
Current Period:						
Materials	305	1,150	$1,475	$2,800	$ 200	$ 400
Labor	210	665	1,750	1,680	1,960	1,190
Overhead	150	475	1,250	1,200	1,400	850
Total	$4,335	$4,340	$4,475	$5,680	$3,560	$2,440

REQUIRED:

A. Prepare all journal entries for the month of May that can be made with the data.

B. Determine the ending balances of Work-in-Process and Finished Goods. Also determine the actual direct labor worked.

5-8 *(Cost Flows with Incomplete Data).* The West Company had the following partially complete T-accounts and additional data for the month of January. Using these data, provide the following information.

Raw Materials Inventory

Bal. 1-1	$5,000		$23,000

Finished Goods Inventory

Bal. 1-1	$8,000	

Variable Overhead Control

Indirect materials	$3,000	
Indirect labor	2,400	
Other	7,000	

Work-in-Process Inventory

Bal. 1-1	$1,800	

Payroll Payable

	Bal. 1-1	$300
	Gross wages 3,400 hours @ $6	20,400

Variable Overhead Applied

	3,000 hours @ $4 =	$12,000

The January 31 ending inventories are

Raw Materials Inventory	$3,000
Work-in-Process Inventory	$4,400
Finished Goods Inventory	$9,800

REQUIRED:

A. Raw material purchases.

B. Direct materials issued to Work-in-Process.

C. Direct labor charged to Work-in-Process.

D. Variable overhead charged to Work-in-Process.

E. The cost of goods completed and transferred to Finished Goods.

F. The Cost of Goods Sold.

G. Variable Overhead Over- or Underapplied.

5-9 *(Overhead Cost Control Reports).* As part of their overall cost studies the accountant of the Kidder Company developed the following flexible budgets for overhead.

Indirect materials	$0 + $3.25(x)
Labor fringe benefits	$18,000 + $1.30(x)
Factory depreciation	$30,000 + $ 0(x)
Factory maintenance	$25,000 + $2.05(x)
Factory supervision	$28,000 + $ 0(x)

These flexible budgets were approved and adopted for the coming year, 19X5, which had a budgeted volume of 15,000 direct labor hours. During 19X5 they actually worked 14,000 direct labor hours. To test for cost control the accountant prepared the following report.

	Master Budget	19X5 Actual	Variance
Indirect materials	$ 48,750	$ 47,250	$1,500 F
Labor fringe benefits	37,500	37,000	500 F
Factory depreciation	30,000	30,500	(500) U
Factory maintenance	55,750	54,500	1,250 F
Factory supervision	28,000	27,000	1,000 F
Total	$200,000	$196,250	$3,750 F

Overall he was quite pleased with the cost control in the factory and sent a memo to that effect to the factory manager.

REQUIRED:

A. Assuming the firm uses variable costing determine:

  1. Variable overhead application rate
  2. Variable overhead applied to work-in-process

B. Evaluate the accountant's report. What changes would you recommend?

5-10 (Journal Entries for Cost Flows). The Gregory Publishing Company had the following information in its general ledger accounts at the beginning of the current month.

Raw Materials Inventory Balance	$ 7,500
Work-in-Process Inventory Balance	$25,000
Finished Goods Inventory Balance	$12,500

During the current month the following transactions took place.

  a. Purchased raw materials of $24,000.
  b. Incurred and distributed direct labor of $42,000.
  c. Incurred fixed utilities costs of $6,400.
  d. Recorded fixed depreciation of $12,000.
  e. Incurred fixed administrative expenses of $18,000.
  f. Requisitioned $22,000 of direct raw materials from the storeroom.

g. Purchased and used $840 of variable factory supplies (indirect materials).

h. Incurred miscellaneous variable overhead of $23,900.

i. Applied variable overhead to work in the factory using a variable overhead rate of 50% of direct labor cost.

j. Completed production of $94,000 of work in the factory.

k. Sold $138,000 of products that cost $102,500.

l. Closed the overhead accounts.

REQUIRED:

A. Prepare general journal entries assuming variable costing.

B. Determine the inventory balances at the end of the month.

C. Prepare an income statement for the month.

5-11 *(Reconstructing T-accounts for Cost Flows).* The following are partially completed T-accounts and additional information for the Marc Burley Company for the month of November.

Additional information:

1. Labor time tickets totaled 200 direct labor hours. Employees are paid at the rate of $5.00 per hour.

2. Variable overhead is applied at the rate of $3.00 per direct labor hour.

3. Actual variable overhead incurred during November amounted to $500.

4. Sales during the month were $4,000.

Raw Materials Inventory

Bal. 11-1	$ 200		
	$1,000		

Finished Goods Inventory

Bal. 11-1	$ 400		

Variable Overhead Applied

Work-in-Process Inventory

Bal. 11-1	$ 300		$2,100
Material requisition	$ 700		

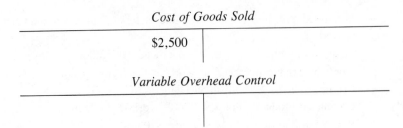

Cost of Goods Sold

$2,500	

Variable Overhead Control

REQUIRED:

Determine the following amounts.

A. The balance of Raw Materials Inventory at November 30.

B. Direct labor cost for the month.

C. The amount of variable overhead applied to products during November.

D. The balance of Finished Goods Inventory on November 30.

E. The total of the job cost sheets at the beginning of November.

F. The total of the job cost sheets at the end of November.

G. The total of the costs added to the job cost sheets during November.

H. The amount of under- or overapplied variable overhead for November.

I. Contribution margin for November before closing under- or overapplied overhead.

J. Assuming that fixed overhead and fixed selling and administrative expenses totaled $1,100, what was the income for November?

5-12 *(Reclassifying Product and Period Costs).* The Bert Cole Company was formed on January 2 and has operated for a year. The owner's wife ran the office and kept the books. Because her experience was limited, she set up a Work-in-Process account and recorded all "expenses" as debits and sales as credits. The balance of the account was closed to Retained Earnings as income or loss for the month. The owner of the company was surprised that a loss was sustained. The company had received many orders, and goods were shipped the day they were finished. The owner asked you for help. The Work-in-Process account follows:

Work-in-Process Inventory

Materials purchased	$120,000		
Payroll for year	250,000	Sales (50,000 @ $8.00)	$400,000
Depreciation expense	30,000		
Selling expense	50,000	Loss to Retained Earnings	130,000
Other factory costs	60,000		
Advertising	20,000		
	$530,000		$530,000

An analysis of the items in the Work-in-Process Inventory revealed the following.

1. There were $40,000 of raw materials in the storeroom at the end of the year.

2. Payroll included:

Owner's salary	$ 20,000
Direct labor payroll	$120,000
Other factory labor	$ 60,000
Selling and administrative payroll	$ 50,000

3. One-third of the fixed assets are used in selling and administrative activities. Depreciation is computed on the straight-line basis.

4. During the year 100,000 units were started; 60,000 were finished, of which 50,000 were sold, and 40,000 were in process one-half complete.

5. The selling expense and other factory costs are variable. All other overhead and nonproduction costs are fixed.

REQUIRED:

A. For each "expense" item recorded in Work-in-Process, indicate if it is properly recorded. If it is not properly recorded, determine the correct amount. Assume that the company uses variable costing.

B. Determine the equivalent production and cost per unit for the year.

C. Determine the proper balances at the end of the year for

1. Raw Materials Inventory

2. Work-in-Process Inventory

3. Finished Goods Inventory

D. Prepare a contribution margin income statement for the Bert Cole Company.

5-13 (*Process Costing: Weighted Average*). Kleenzit Company produces an industrial cleaner. Materials are added at the beginning of the blending process. After the product is blended, it is sent to the Packaging Department. Conversion costs are added uniformly through the process. Cost and production records for the blending process during September show the following.

September 1, 20 barrels in process, 40% complete as to conversion costs.

September 30, 30 barrels in process, 70% complete as to conversion costs.

Material was added in September to start 90 barrels.

80 barrels of Kleenzit were transferred to packaging during September.

Cost of September 1 inventory: materials $1,000; conversion costs $160.

Cost of material added during September, $4,500.

Conversion costs during September, $2,870.

REQUIRED:

A. Compute the equivalent units of production for both materials and conversion costs during September.

B. Compute the material and conversion unit costs during September assuming weighted-average costing.

C. Determine the cost of the 30 barrels in the ending inventory at the end of September.

D. Determine the cost of the 80 barrels sent to Packaging during September.

5-14 *(Process Costing: FIFO).* The Muppet Company produces piggy banks. Materials are added at the beginning of the process in the Molding Department. After the product is molded, it is sent to the Painting Department. Conversion costs are added uniformly throughout the plant. Cost and production data for the Molding Department for the month of December show the following.

December 1, 5,000 banks in process, 60% complete as to conversion costs.

December 31, 3,000 banks in process, $33\frac{1}{3}$% complete as to conversion costs.

Material was added in December to start 28,000 banks.

Cost of December 1 inventory:

| Material | $3,750 |
| Conversion costs | $1,500 |

Costs added during December:

| Material | $25,200 |
| Conversion costs | $16,800 |

REQUIRED:

A. Compute the equivalent units of production.

B. Compute the material and conversion unit costs during December assuming a FIFO cost flow.

C. Determine the cost of the banks in the ending inventory at the end of December.

D. Determine the cost of the banks sent to Painting during December.

5-15 *(Process Costing: Two Departments; No Beginning Inventories).* The Everly Company began operations on January 1, 19X6. They manufacture a chrome-plated closet organizer unit in two departments—molding and finishing. During January 19X6 they incurred the following costs.

	Molding Department	*Finishing Department*
Materials	$3,200	$ 924
Direct labor	$ 828	$2,272
Overhead applied	100% of labor cost	75% of labor cost

The Molding Department began 1,000 units in process during the month. At the end of the month 200 units were still in process. These units had 100% of the materials and 60% of the conversion costs added.

The Finishing Department, after receiving the units transferred from the Molding Department, added the chrome plating and accessories. They completed and transferred 650 units to the Finished Goods Inventory. The units still in process had 80% of the materials and 40% of the conversion costs added.

REQUIRED:

Prepare journal entries to record *all* cost flows for the month. Support your entries, where necessary, with schedules in good form.

5-16 *(Process Costing—Comparison of Weighted Average and FIFO).* The Fox Company manufactures small appliances in an assembly-line process. After receiving assembled parts from other departments, the Assembly Department completes the manufacturing process by joining them into the final product. During March the Assembly Department had the following quantities.

Beginning inventory—March 1 (All materials, 50% of labor and overhead)	10,000 units
Units transferred into department	80,000 units
Units transferred to warehouse	75,000 units
Ending inventory—March 31 (all materials and $66\frac{2}{3}\%$ of labor and overhead)	15,000 units

Costs relevant to March were:

	Beginning Inventory	Current Month
Transferred in costs	$67,000	$608,000
Material costs	$15,750	$191,250
Conversion costs	$24,000	$316,000

REQUIRED:

A. Using weighted average, prepare in good form schedules that show the equivalent units and the cost distributions.

B. Using FIFO prepare in good form schedules that show the equivalent units and the cost distributions.

5-17 *(Process Costing—FIFO).* Cost and production data for two departments are presented on page 174 for the Stick-it Glue Company. The company uses FIFO costing in its process costing system.

REQUIRED:

Assuming that 3,000 units were sold for $10 each, prepare all journal entries for February, including the transfer of costs within the factory.

QUANTITY DATA	DEPARTMENTS	
	Mixing	Cooking
Units in process, February 1:		
Mixing Department	None	
Cooking Department (100% complete as to prior-department cost, 50% as to conversion costs)		4,000
New units started	10,000	5,000
Units completed and transferred to:		
Cooking Department	5,000	
Finished Goods Inventory		6,000
Units in process, Feb. 28:		
Mixing Department (100% complete as to material, 80% complete as to conversion)	5,000	
Cooking Department (100% complete as to prior-department costs, 33⅓% as to conversion costs)		3,000
COST DATA		
Costs in beginning inventory:		
Prior-department costs	None	$11,600
Conversion costs	None	$ 7,800
New costs incurred this period:		
Raw materials	$10,000	None
Prior-department costs	None	?
Conversion costs	$18,000	$20,000

5-18 *(Process Costing with Weighted Average; Journal Entries).* Hangwell Company produces a special metal hanger for the construction industry. Metal strips are cut and shaped in the Shaping Department and finished in the Finishing Department. Because production requirements are rigorous and costs are difficult to control, the company uses a weekly period of accounting. All materials are added at the beginning of the shaping process. At the beginning of Week 23, the following inventories were on hand.

> Raw Materials, $4,800
> Work-in-Process:
> Shaping Department, 600 units
> Material (100% complete), $660
> Conversion (40% complete), $430
> Finishing Department, none
> Finished Goods, 5,000 units @ $5.50

The transactions for Week 23 follow.

1. Purchased raw materials on account, $8,600.
2. Issued materials to the Shaping Department to start 5,000 units, $6,060.

3. Paid direct labor for the week:
    Shaping Department, $6,300.
    Finishing Department, $7,420.

4. Sold 4,000 units at $9.00 each on account from beginning inventory.

5. Overhead for the week (credit Various Accounts):
    Variable overhead in Shaping Department, $2,990.
    Variable overhead in Finishing Department, $3,140.
    Fixed overhead for the company, $6,000.

6. During the week, 5,100 shaped units were transferred from the Shaping Department to the Finishing Department. This left 500 units complete as to material and 60% complete as to conversion costs in the Shaping Department.

7. During the week 4,700 units were completed in the Finishing Department and sent to finished goods. At the end of the week there were 400 units in the Finishing Department complete as to material and 25% complete as to conversion costs.

REQUIRED:

A. Prepare journal entries for the transactions assuming variable and weighted-average costing. Your entries should be supported by computations of equivalent production and unit costs in good form. (Do not compute separate unit costs for direct labor and variable overhead.)

B. Prepare T-accounts and post the transactions.

C. Prepare a contribution margin income statement.

5-19 *(Reconstruction of Journal Entries from Subsidiary Ledgers).* You are head accountant for the Rolling Roller Skate Company. Your company has the following cost system: they maintain a perpetual inventory system on all items; they maintain accounts for Raw Materials, Work-in-Process, Finished Goods, Variable Overhead Control, Variable Overhead Applied, Under- or Overapplied Variable Overhead; all inventory accounts are supported by subsidiary ledgers, as is the Variable Overhead Control; the Variable Overhead accounts are closed monthly to Under- or Overapplied Variable Overhead; and variable costing is used internally.

The subsidiary ledgers for the month of March are on pages 176–177.

REQUIRED:

Using the subsidiary ledgers as your source of information, reconstruct all of the journal entries for the month; make your entries in summary form (do not make an entry for each entry in the subsidiary ledger). Assume that no purchases are returned to the suppliers and that no materials are returned from the factory to the raw material storeroom.

JOB COST SHEET #11
Product: *Little Skates*
Started 2-25-X7　Completed 3-20-X7

Date	Material	Labor	Overhead	Total
Bal. 2-28	$2,000	$1,000	$ 500	$ 3,500
3-1	3,000			6,500
3-2	1,500			8,000
3-20		7,000		15,000
3-20			3,500	18,500
Total	$6,500	$8,000	$4,000	$18,500

JOB COST SHEET #13
Product: *Little Skates*
Started 3-15-X7　Completed

Date	Material	Labor	Overhead	Total
3-15	$2,500			$2,500
3-20		$4,250		6,750
3-31			$2,125	$8,875
Total				

RAW MATERIAL STOCK CARD
Material #1

Date	Receipts	Issues	Balance
2-28			$10,000
3-1		$3,000	$ 7,000
3-3	$4,000		$11,000
3-7		$4,000	$ 7,000
3-15		$2,500	$ 4,500
3-29		$ 500	$ 4,000

FINISHED GOODS STOCK CARD
Little Skates

Date	Receipts	Issues	Balance
2-28			$ 2,000
3-5		$ 1,000	$ 1,000
3-20	$18,500		$19,500
3-22		$ 5,000	$14,500
3-25		$12,000	$ 2,500

JOB COST SHEET #12
Product: *Big Skates*
Started 3-1-X7   Completed 3-29-X7

Date	Material	Labor	Overhead	Total
3-7	$4,000			$ 4,000
3-8	2,000			6,000
3-25	3,500			9,500
3-26		$6,200		15,700
3-29			$3,100	18,800
Total	$9,500	$6,200	$3,100	$18,800

VARIABLE OVERHEAD CONTROL
Subsidiary Ledger for March

Date	Indirect Material	Indirect Labor	Utilities	Repairs	Total
3-20		$5,300			$5,300
3-29	$ 500				5,800
3-29	700				6,500
3-31			$800		7,300
3-31				$1,200	8,500
Total	$1,200	$5,300	$800	$1,200	$8,500

RAW MATERIAL STOCK CARD
Material #2

Date	Receipts	Issues	Balance
2-28			$8,000
3-2		$1,500	$6,500
3-8		$2,000	$4,500
3-25		$3,500	$1,000
3-29		$ 700	$ 300
3-29	$6,000		$6,300

FINISHED GOODS STOCK CARD
Big Skates

Date	Receipts	Issues	Balance
2-28			$ 4,000
3-29	$18,800		$22,800
3-30		$16,500	$ 6,300

5-20 *(Comprehensive Variable Costing Flows).* On January 1, 19X6 the Beaufort Company had no beginning inventory of finished goods and the following Work-in-Process Inventory.

Job	Materials	Labor	Variable Overhead	Total
203	$11,800	$12,500	$2,000	$26,300
204	$ 500	$ 700	$ 500	1,700
	Total beginning inventory			$28,000

From its inception the Beaufort Company had made a study of its fixed and variable costs at the beginning of each year. The development of the flexible budgets was used in their budgeting process, in the development of their variable costing overhead rate applied on direct labor hours, and in their cost control. To calculate the predetermined variable overhead rate for product costing, the controller developed the following budgeted costs, based on the estimated volume of 14,000 direct labor hours per month.

Variable:		
Indirect materials	$4,900	
Indirect labor	6,300	
Utilities	4,200	$15,400
Fixed (per month)		
Depreciation	$7,200	
Supervision	5,400	12,600
Total budgeted overhead		$28,000

During January the company incurred the following costs and labor hours that were directly traceable to the jobs.

Job	Materials	Labor $	Labor Hours
203	$ 2,300	$ 3,500	750
204	4,900	15,200	3,500
205	5,900	17,200	4,100
206	8,100	24,000	4,300
207	800	2,100	350
January Total	$22,000	$62,000	13,000

Actual overhead costs incurred in January were

Indirect materials	$ 4,700
Indirect labor	6,100
Utilities	4,100
Depreciation	7,200
Supervision	5,600
Total actual overhead	$27,700

During January the factory completed Jobs 203, 204, 205, and 206 and transferred them to finished goods. Jobs 203, 204, and 205 were sold during the month. Job 203 sold for $49,065; Job 204 sold for $39,400; and Job 205 sold for $42,750.

In addition to the production costs, the Beaufort Company incurred selling expenses of $17,600; of these, $8,400 were fixed selling costs; the remainder were considered variable costs.

REQUIRED:

A. Using the above data, prepare the following journal entries.

1. The purchase of raw materials. (Assume that the Raw Materials Inventory increased $2,500 in January and that both direct and indirect materials are kept in the Raw Materials Inventory.)
2. The issue of direct materials to Work-in-Process.
3. The issue of indirect materials.
4. The purchase and consumption of labor, both direct and indirect.
5. The incurrence of other factory overhead.
6. The application of variable overhead to Work-in-Process.
7. The transfer from Work-in-Process to Finished Goods.
8. The Cost of Goods Sold.
9. The closing of the Factory Overhead Applied and Factory Overhead Control accounts to Over- or Underapplied Overhead.
10. The incurrence of selling expenses.
11. The monthly sales.

B. Prepare in good form a contribution margin income statement for management.

C. The president of the company was pleased because actual overhead of $27,700 was less than the budgeted overhead of $28,000. Show whether this is a correct or incorrect perception by preparing an overhead cost report using a Performance Budget approach.

D. Determine the ending inventory values for Work-in-Process and Finished Goods by preparing T-accounts of these two accounts

5-21 *(Decision of Product Costing System).* Grady, Omura, and Johnson is the largest architectural firm in Clovis, Nebraska. During the past 15 years the firm has grown from a "three-man shop" to more than 80 partners, staff, and support employees. Over the years they have, somewhat haphazardly, developed the organizational structure described below. Mr. Grady, the principal partner, serves as president and chief executive officer. There are five departmental managers reporting directly to Mr. Grady.

1. Residential architectural partner—Mr. Omura—has responsibility for supervising the client contact, design, and implementation of all contracts involving personal residences and homes. Twelve lead architects, six draftspeople, and two computer-assisted drafters report directly to Mr. Omura.

2. Commercial architectural partner—Mr. Johnson—has responsibility for supervising the client contact, design, and implementation of all contacts involving commercial buildings, including apartment houses, office buildings, stores and shopping malls, and high-rise buildings. Mr. Johnson has 18 lead architects, 8 draftspeople and model builders, and 3 computer-assisted drafters reporting directly to him.

3. Engineering and building materials partner—Ms. Daniels—is primarily responsible for providing engineering and materials support to Mr. Omura and Mr. Johnson. This often requires close coordination with the architects to ensure that their plans are feasible from an engineering and materials perspective. If the opportunity arises, and Ms. Daniels' staff has "idle time," she is free to contract with clients outside the firm to provide engineering or materials assistance. Four engineers, three materials specialists, one zoning code coordinator, and one real estate advisor report to Ms. Daniels.

4. On site supervisional partner—Mr. Foster—is responsible for supervising the contractors and the project's costs in those contracts where it is specifically negotiated. Four supervisors and contract coordinators and three on-site inspectors report to Mr. Foster.

5. Office manager—Mr. Crane—is responsible for the management of the office staff including the bookkeepers, the steno pool, the photocopy and duplication area, the receptionists, the auto pool, and the equipment and supplies storerooms.

Overall, Mr. Grady is pleased with the organizational structure and the firm's ability to provide a full range of services to their clients. However, he has grown increasingly troubled about his ability to measure costs and profitability of the many projects that the firm completes each year. He has asked Mr. Crane to install a cost accounting system that will allow him to trace the results on each contract and project.

Mr. Crane is somewhat overwhelmed! Each contract is different. For example, in the Residential Department some jobs call for only floor plan designs. Other contracts require "from the ground-up" planning including site surveying, floor plan designs, material consulting, and contractor supervision.

In the Commercial Department many projects are long-term, requiring two to three years' work by the firm. In many of the larger projects the engineering and on-site supervision are substantial; in many small projects engineering and supervision are minor.

The Engineering Department's contracts with outside clients are limited but not inconsequential. Their reputation for good advice has spread throughout the community and they are increasingly being asked to consult with smaller one- and two-person architectural offices.

Mr. Crane's study of the accounting data shows the following:

a. For the lead architects, draftspeople, engineers, materials specialists, on-site supervisors, and inspectors it was possible to establish time tickets allowing them to trace their "billable" hours to each project. About 90% of their time is billable to specific projects.

b. The partners and managers rarely work directly on a specific project in a technical role; rather, they tend to be "people" managers. However, each partner does assume an active role in establishing client goodwill and maintaining a public presence to obtain future clients.

c. The firm maintains a fleet of five vehicles managed by the motor pool. The two vans are used exclusively by the On-site Supervision Department. The three sedans are available to any employee for firm business when authorized by their manager.

d. The firm maintains three computers. One is assigned to the Residential Department, one to the Commercial Department, and one to the office manager.

e. In addition to the salaries and equipment costs listed above in items a–d the major costs of the firm are as follows:

1. Salaries of support help such as secretaries.
2. Employee fringe benefits.
3. Depreciation and utilities of the office building.
4. Supplies, materials, and maintenance of a reference library.

REQUIRED:

A. What recommendations would you make to Mr. Crane in the design of a cost accounting system?

B. List specific problems you see in designing such a system.

chapter **6**

VARIABLE STANDARD COSTING FOR COST EFFICIENCY

One of the weaknesses of historical costing, presented in the previous chapter, is its failure to provide criteria for judging the results of day-to-day operating decisions. A comparison of the current period's costs with those of the last period will not assure management of proper control over operations. The current period's activities could be just as inefficient as those of the previous period. Thus, management needs criteria for judging the results of operating decisions. Standard costs are one way to plan and control the costs of any repetitive task such as production, shipping, testing, or clerical activities. If management can assume that the sales price per unit of product is relatively constant within the relevant range of activity, profits will be maximized if costs are minimized.

A **standard** is a precise measure of what *should* occur if performance is efficient. Par is a standard for the golf course; 80 words per minute is a standard for typists; and a four-minute mile is a very difficult standard for runners. A **standard cost** is a measure of acceptable performance. Such a measure is derived from the expenditure of considerable thought and energy as to how a task should be accomplished and how many resources should be consumed. Although many different tasks and activities are performed in an organization, standard costs are often focused on the costs of manufacturing the product—raw materials, direct labor, and overhead costs. The focus on manufacturing activities is deliberate. These activities are repetitive and hence susceptible to the establishment of standards. Further, using standard costs in product costing allows a blending within the accounting system of the inventory costing and management control systems. However, standards can be set for any repetitive task—selling and administrative duties as well as production tasks—but most firms concentrate their standard cost control on their production activities.

There are many benefits associated with using standard costs. First, a standard cost system, once installed, can be cheaper to maintain than a historical cost system because it eliminates some bookkeeping and paperwork. Second, the time and energy expended in developing standards may highlight possible production inefficiencies *before* actual production begins. The potential benefits of these efforts are cost savings and, as a result, higher profits. Third, standard costs assist management in formally constructing plans and budgets. Fourth, standards allow management a way to focus on operational control.

The difference between actual cost and standard cost is called a variance. By frequently comparing actual results with standard costs via the variances, management can determine whether actual performance is under control. If the actual exceeds the standard, the variance is unfavorable, indicating the need for management action. The variance is favorable if the actual is equal to or less than the standard, implying that the firm's costs are under control. It is the ability to create meaningful variances by comparing actual results with a measure of what *should* happen that makes the standard cost system a potent management tool.

TYPES OF STANDARD COSTS

There is more than one philosophical approach to the scientific determination of a performance standard. One approach is to set an **ideal standard** that estimates what should happen if all conditions are perfect—no waste, no scrap, no idle time, no rest periods, and no machine breakdowns. Over any extended period of time it would be impossible for the actual activities to equal the ideal standard.

A normal, or average, standard is a widely used philosophy in establishing standard costs. **Normal standards** are achievable, but their attainment requires that activities be efficient. Sometimes they are called **currently attainable** standards. This implies that the standard is tighter than what currently exists but that achievement is possible. They allow for normal workers performing in normal settings. In a production firm, allowances would be made for normal scrap and waste, normal fatigue and breaks, normal machine breakdowns and maintenance, and normal mistakes in production.

Another concept of a standard is used by some firms. The **expected standard** is based on the most likely attainable result. Technically, this is a standard cost only if current operations are already in the range of satisfactory efficiency. It is an estimate of what *will* happen, not what *should* happen.

The difference between ideal, currently attainable, and expected standards is a philosophical one. The mental approach to the setting of standards determines the philosophy. If the standard is so tight that very few can attain it, it is an ideal standard; if it is based on an estimate of what will happen, it is an expected standard; and if it is tight but attainable, it is a normal standard. The method of establishing the standard does *not* determine whether it is ideal, normal, or expected. All may be set by past experience, by work measurement and time-and-motion studies, by engineering estimates, or by a combination of these. It is the intent that determines the type of standard.

THE SETTING OF STANDARDS

The primary purpose of a standard cost system is to keep the costs of operations as low as possible, given the current state of the industry. The system is made efficient by the achievements of the workers in using no more than the standard amount of materials, labor, and overhead to produce the product or services. Thus, a standard cost is a motivational system. Its goal is to provide a benchmark of good performance that workers will strive to achieve.

STANDARDS FOR MOTIVATION

When a standard is set at the ideal or perfect level, the employee will almost always fail to achieve the standard, and variances will be unfavorable. In the long run, this failure can be frustrating and create a feeling of hopelessness. When the standards are too loose, there is no need to perform efficiently, and performance may or may not be satisfactory. The observation that motivational factors seem to improve with tightening standards up to a point, and then drop off, has led most standard setters to believe that a tight yet attainable standard is most useful in motivating efficient performance.

The role of standards in motivating employees is a complicated subject. There are definite interactions among the tightness of the standards, employee attitudes, organizational structure, performance feedback, and employee reward systems. At this time we know far too little about these interactions. Current beliefs seem to be that standards motivate best when there is valid participation in their establishment, when they are tight but reasonable, when there is rapid performance feedback, and when employee rewards are tied to success in achieving the standard.

ESTABLISHING TECHNICAL STANDARDS

At the heart of a standard cost system is the **standard cost card,** the predetermined estimate of what one unit of product should cost if produced efficiently. It includes detailed estimates of material quantities and prices, labor quantities and prices, and overhead quantities and rates. These details serve as the benchmarks of efficiency against which actual quantities and costs are compared. This focus on the efficient cost of producing one unit requires a reemphasis of the relevant range of activity concept. When standards for material, labor, and overhead are established, there is an implicit assumption that the actual production volume will be within a relevant range of activity.

MATERIAL STANDARDS

In most compances the material quantities are determined by the industrial engineers who design the product and determine the production process. Typically, the prices paid for raw materials are the responsibility of the purchasing agent. If the quantity of raw material consumed results in price discounts, the material prices must be set through cooperation between the purchasing department and the production schedulers. For a new product, management cannot rely on past experience; the parts list must be taken from blueprints, and the material prices obtained from suppliers' quotations and bids.

LABOR STANDARDS

Labor time standards are often established from work measurement and time-and-motion studies. Performed by the industrial engineering department, these studies are often a source of conflict between the workers and management. The industrial engineer usually observes a worker in actual working conditions and then suggests ways of increasing worker efficiency. The methods of measuring labor time standards require special training and a considerable amount of professional judgment. Based on a certain amount of subjectivity, the labor time standards are often less certain and more open to variation than material standards.

Standard wage rates are often the result of collective bargaining agreements. Where union contracts exist, they can be used as the basis for establishing wage standards. In unionized plants the responsibility for wage rate standards rests with those involved in contract negotiations. In nonunion plants this responsibility often lies with the departmental managers or the personnel department. Although the wage rate for each skill level may be determined by contract negotiations, the establishment of standard costs can be complicated if the manager is able to mix worker skill levels. The standard wage rate is usually a composite of many wage rates, assuming a specific mix of employee skills.

OVERHEAD STANDARDS

The best way to develop standard overhead costs is to begin with cost–volume analysis. The separation of overhead costs into fixed and variable components allows not only more precise prediction of costs, but also a detailed examination of *how* costs behave relative to volume. With this understanding management can undertake a study of what costs *should* be at different volumes of output.

The flexible budget based on past experience cannot automatically be considered a standard. It becomes a standard only when energy and thought have been applied to see if these are what costs *should* be. Only when management is satisfied that the flexible budget expresses what costs should be if operations are efficient can it serve as standard for overhead.

ACCEPTANCE OF STANDARDS

The value of a standard cost system may be negated if the standards are constantly under attack by the managers and workers. Acceptance of the standards is necessary for at least two reasons. First, the workers must believe that they are reasonable. If the standards set are considered unfair, the workers may not attempt to achieve them and may try to subvert the system. The results are misdirected energy and, ultimately, misused resources—the antithesis of the goal of standard costs.

Second, the standards must be accepted if the variances are to have meaning. If the standards are open to question, then so are the variances. When the workers consider the standard cost to be ''incorrect,'' the automatic implication is that actual cost is ''correct'' and the variance becomes a measure of the inaccuracy of the standard cost. Thus, there is no attitude of measuring or correcting inefficiencies. Let's look at the nature of the variance if the standard cost is accepted as "correct" by the workers. Here, the actual cost is "incorrect." (It is not necessarily incorrect in terms of its measurement. We assume the actual cost has been accounted for correctly.) It is "incorrect" because it is not what it *should* be. The unfavorable variance is the measure of resources wasted through inefficiency; the favorable variance is a measure of resources saved through efficiency.

REVISION OF STANDARDS

Standards must be revised whenever the conditions upon which they are based change. Most firms find that a continual program of revision is necessary. A typical policy is to review the standards whenever quantity or prices change significantly, but at least once per year. Failure to revise them periodically can result in the standards becoming unfair for evaluating performance.

Typically, price standards are more subject to change than quantity standards. New contracts and inflation are regular occurrences in most firms. With a significant change, the price standards must be adjusted. Changes in the quantity standards are required when there are improvements in performance, new production specifications or methods, or changes in product mixes. If a long-range decision results in the purchase of new production equipment, the standards may have to be modified.

Many firms trace the direction of variance details to glean information about production efficiency and about the existing standards. If the variances are continually unfavorable, employees may begin to reduce their effort, believing that the standards are unattainable. If, on the other hand, the variances are always favorable, the standards may be too loose and thus ineffective in stimulating efficient performance. The amount and the direction of the variances can point to the need for revising the standard costs.

A VARIABLE STANDARD COST SYSTEM ILLUSTRATED

The standard cost system is not only a method of controlling operating efficiency by the reporting of variances, but also a system of income determination. When it is used as an inventory costing system, each unit of product in the Work-in-Process Inventory, Finished Goods Inventory, or Cost of Goods Sold is costed at standard cost. The resources actually used will be recorded at their actual cost. The differences between standard and actual—the variances—typically are treated as period costs in the income statement. Exhibit 6–1 summarizes the flow of costs for a variable standard costing system.

To explain the way standard costs are used within an accounting system, let's assume that the Forddon Furniture Company established the standard cost

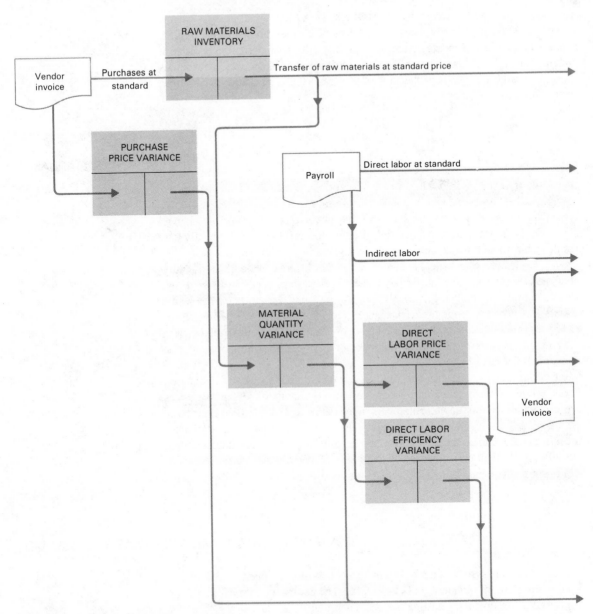

EXHIBIT 6–1   Variable standard cost system

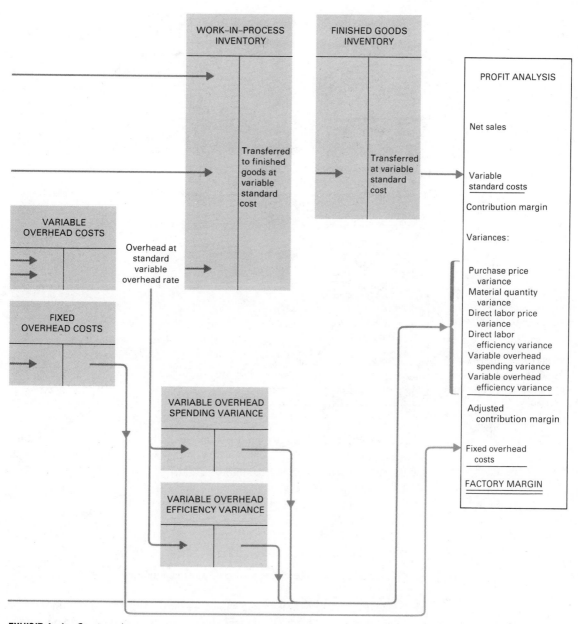

EXHIBIT 6–1 Continued

```
                    BOOKCASE 10A—LARGE
                    STANDARD COST CARD

    Direct materials
       100 feet @ $.30                              $30.00
    Direct labor
       8 hours @ $4.00                               32.00
    Variable overhead
       8 hours @ $1.50                               12.00
    Total variable standard cost                    $74.00
```

```
                    BOOKCASE 11A—SMALL
                    STANDARD COST CARD

    Direct materials
       50 feet @ $.30                               $15.00
    Direct labor
       5 hours @ $4.00                               20.00
    Variable overhead
       5 hours @ $1.50                                7.50
    Total variable standard cost                    $42.50
```

EXHIBIT 6–2
Variable standard cost cards for Forddon Furniture Company

cards in Exhibit 6–2 for its two products before the beginning of the accounting period. These standards represent the best estimates of what production costs should be during the coming accounting period.

In addition to the variable standard costs per product for material and labor, management also prepared the following flexible budgets:

Total overhead = $9,600 per month + $1.50 per direct labor hour

Total selling expenses = $2,400 per month + $2.00 per unit sold

Total administrative expenses = $3,000 per month

The standard variable overhead rate shown on the standard cost cards in Exhibit 6–2 was taken directly from the flexible budget for overhead at $1.50 per direct labor hour. This results in variable overhead costs of $12.00 for Bookcase 10A and $7.50 for Bookcase 11A. Because fixed overhead, selling expenses, and administrative expenses are treated as period costs under variable costing, they are not included on the standard cost cards, which show only the product costs. However, budgets would be prepared and actual costs would be controlled by comparing them with the budget at the end of the accounting period. This role of the Performance Budget was discussed in the last chapter and will be illustrated again later.

Plans called for production of 575 Style 10A bookcases at 8 hours each, for a total of 4,600 direct labor hours; and 1,000 Style 11A bookcases at 5 hours each, for a total of 5,000 direct labor hours. Thus, the total of 9,600 direct labor hours was planned. This level was considered as being within the relevant range of activity.

During January, actual production was started on 550 Style 10A bookcases and 1,200 Style 11A bookcases. (Actual production differed from planned production because of unexpected shifts in sales demand.) Two batches of raw material were purchased. The first batch was 70,000 feet at a price of $.27 per foot. The second batch was 50,000 feet at $.32 per foot. During the month 118,000 feet of direct materials were issued to the factory. Production employees spent 10,400 direct labor hours on the bookcases, at $4.10 per hour. Actual overhead incurred was $24,400, of which $9,000 was fixed and $15,400 was variable. At the end of the accounting period, 50 of the Style 10A bookcases were incomplete and remained in the factory. These 50 units had all materials issued and 40% of the direct labor and variable overhead needed to complete the 50 units (or 20 equivalent units for direct labor and variable overhead; 50 equivalent units of material). The completed bookcases (500 of 10A and 1,200 of 11A) were placed in the finished goods storeroom. Customers purchased 450 of the 10A bookcases at $125 each and 1,100 of the 11A bookcases at $60 each. Actual selling expenses were $2,000 fixed and $2,800 variable. The actual administrative expenses were $3,500. There were no beginning inventories in the Work-in-Process Inventory or Finished Goods Inventory.

MATERIALS PURCHASES

The following two journal entries record the purchases of materials.[1]

Raw Materials Inventory $21,000		
Materials Price Variance	$ 2,100	
Accounts Payable		$18,900

Raw Materials Inventory $15,000		
Material Price Variable .... $ 1,000		
Accounts Payable		$16,000

By recording the Raw Materials Inventory at standard price (70,000 × $.30 = $21,000), there are no accounting complications such as LIFO, FIFO, or average inventory costing, because all materials will be carried at their standard cost. The credit to Accounts Payable must, of course, be recorded at the actual price suppliers are paid (70,000 × $.27 = $18,900).

---

[1]We will omit explanations of all journal entries in this chapter.

The **material price variance** is the difference between the actual price and the standard price, times the actual quantity of materials purchased. Perhaps a more accurate title would be the *material purchased price variance*. The material price variance may be expressed in formula form.

$$\begin{matrix} \text{Material} \\ \text{price} \\ \text{variance} \end{matrix} = \left[\begin{matrix} \text{Standard price} \\ \text{per unit of} \\ \text{material} \end{matrix} - \begin{matrix} \text{Actual price} \\ \text{per unit of} \\ \text{material} \end{matrix} \right] \begin{matrix} \text{Actual quantity} \\ \times \text{ of materials} \\ \text{purchased} \end{matrix}$$

When actual costs exceed standard costs, the variance is unfavorable. Thus, a Material Price Variance account with a debit balance is unfavorable (**U**). With a credit balance it is favorable (**F**).

In the Forddon Company the material price variance is computed as

First purchase:

$$\begin{matrix} \text{Material} \\ \text{price} \\ \text{variance} \end{matrix} = [\$.30 - \$.27] \times 70,000 \text{ feet}$$

$$= \$2,100 \text{ } \mathbf{F}$$

Second purchase:

$$\begin{matrix} \text{Material} \\ \text{price} \\ \text{variance} \end{matrix} = [\$.30 - \$.32] \times 50,000 \text{ feet}$$

$$= \$(1,000) \text{ } \mathbf{U}$$

The total material price variance is favorable in the amount of $1,100.

Ideally, the material price variance should be isolated at the time the purchase invoice is recorded. It is then possible to sum all the invoices on a particular day by raw material class, by supplier, or by purchasing agent. Purchasing management can receive daily reports on the price variance for the previous day's purchases.

Responsibility for analyzing the price variance lies with the purchasing officers. Because purchases are made continuously, it is important to report the variances regularly. There may be many causal factors for the price variance. A sudden change in the production volume can force the purchasing agent to buy uneconomic quantities, inflation can force the prices upward, material shortages can modify the supplier's pricing structure, or the purchasing department may simply fail to find the most desirable supplier. Obviously, the responsibility for some of these factors, such as the sudden change in production schedule, rests with someone other than the purchasing agent. It would be naive to assign automatically all results directly to the purchasing officer without a detailed analysis. It is generally true, however, that the causes rest with the purchasing agent and that it is his or her responsibility to explain unusual circumstances.

ISSUE OF MATERIALS

The following journal entry records the issue of raw materials to the factory.

Work-in-Process Inventory $34,500
Material Quantity Variance............ $ 900
    Raw Materials Inventory........................... $35,400

Each unit of product in the Work-in-Process Inventory is costed at the cost shown on the standard cost card. Because materials for 550 large bookcases and 1,200 small bookcases were issued to production, the Work-in-Process Inventory should be charged for (550 × $30) + (1,200 × $15), or $34,500. The Raw Materials Inventory must be credited for the actual quantity issued, costed at the standard material price. Because 118,000 feet were actually used and the Raw Materials Inventory is costed at standard cost ($.30), the credit to the inventory is $35,400.

The **material quantity variance,** sometimes called the **material usage variance,** measures how well the physical resources were utilized. It is computed by multiplying the standard cost per unit of raw materials by the difference between the actual materials used and the amount of materials that should have been used to produce the actual units. Accountants often call the actual units produced times the standard quantity per unit the **standard quantity allowed.** This is the quantity that should have been used for the actual production. In formula form the material quantity variance is

$$\begin{matrix} \text{Material} \\ \text{quantity} \\ \text{variance} \end{matrix} = \left[\left(\begin{matrix} \text{Actual} \\ \text{units} \\ \text{produced} \end{matrix} \times \begin{matrix} \text{Standard} \\ \text{quantity} \\ \text{per unit} \end{matrix} \right) - \begin{matrix} \text{Actual quantity} \\ \text{of} \\ \text{materials used} \end{matrix} \right]$$

$$\begin{matrix} \text{Standard price} \\ \times \text{ per unit of} \\ \text{raw materials} \end{matrix}$$

In the Forddon Company the material quantity variance is computed as

$$\begin{matrix} \text{Material} \\ \text{quantity} \\ \text{variance} \end{matrix} = [(550 \times 100) + (1,200 \times 50) - 118,000] \times \$.30$$

$$= [55,000 + 60,000 - 118,000] \times \$.30$$

$$= \$(900) \text{ U}$$

The company used 3,000 feet of materials in excess of standard; the result is an unfavorable material quantity variance of $900.

The material quantity variance can be isolated any time output is measured (in some cases on a daily basis), by department, by worker, or by responsibility center.

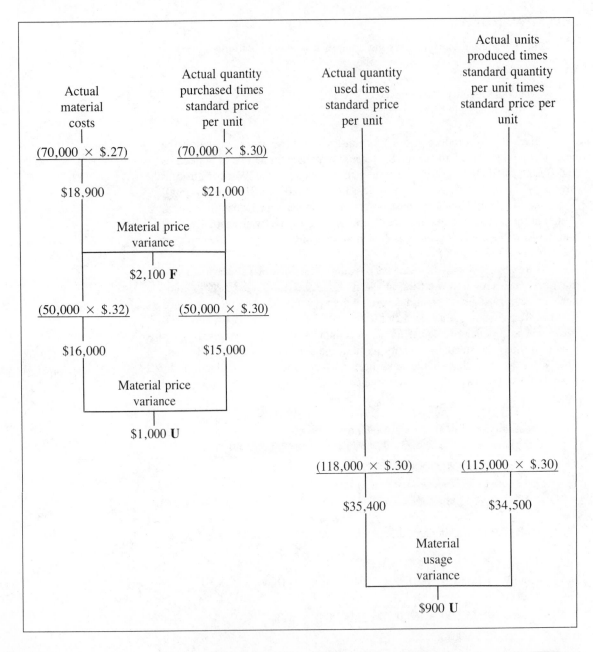

There can be many reasons for a material quantity variance. Excess usage may be the result of carelessness by the workers using the material, improper machine adjustment, or the substitution of substandard material. Also, employees could be taking materials home or stockpiling them throughout the factory for later use. Another possible cause is a modification of quality control standards during a period. Less-than-standard usage could result from the substitution of materials of higher quality than the standard, improvements in the production process, or extra care by the workers in performing their jobs.

Examination of some of the causal factors for the material quantity variance indicates that overall responsibility for the variance lies with the production personnel. As with all variances, this premise should not be accepted without further investigation. For example, assume that a close examination showed the principal cause of a favorable material quantity variance to be the substitution of above-standard materials. This higher quality material should result in less waste than was anticipated when the standard quantity was set, and could account for a favorable quantity variance. It could also help account for an unfavorable material price variance because above-standard materials would probably cost more. Both variances would have been unavoidable if the materials specified in developing the standard costs were not available, and the purchasing agent bought the only material available.

The calculation of the two variances for material can be summarized in the schedule on page 194. A careful comparison of this schedule with the previous formulas will show they are the same concept, stated in a different format.

Occasionally, firms will carry their Raw Materials Inventory at actual prices. In these cases the price variance is determined on raw materials issued, rather than on materials purchased. To use a different example, assume that the Porter Company had a standard cost for materials of 6 pounds at $5.00 per pound. The total material costs per unit of finished goods was therefore $30.00. Also assume that in producing 150 units they used 880 pounds which were carried in the Raw Materials Inventory at their actual cost of $4.80 per pound. The material variances would be as shown in the following schedule:

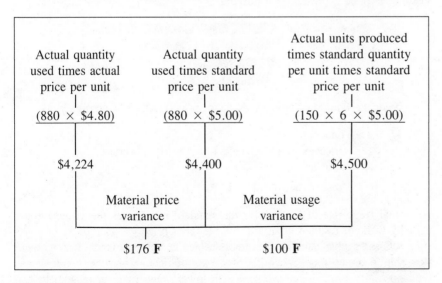

The material price variance in this case is really a materials issued price variance. This definition and calculation approach is inferior to a materials purchased price variance because the price variance is a function of purchasing, not of issuing raw materials. In addition, from a motivation standpoint rapid feedback is important. Waiting until the materials are issued will be too late for any corrective actions that could be undertaken.

DIRECT LABOR PURCHASED AND CONSUMED

The following journal entry records the direct labor.

Work-in-Process Inventory $40,640
Labor Price Variance....................$ 1,040
Labor Efficiency Variance..............$ 960
   Accrued Payroll.................................... $42,640

The debit to Work-in-Process Inventory is for the actual units produced times standard hours per unit times the standard wage rate per hour. During the month the company worked on 550 of the Style 10A bookcases, completing the equivalent of 520 (500 units finished plus 50 units 40% complete). The production of 520 of the 10A style *should* consume 4,160 labor hours (520 units × 8 hours), and the 1,200 Style 11A bookcases should consume 6,000 hours (1,200 units × 5 hours). Thus, the debit to Work-in-Process Inventory would be 10,160 standard hours times the $4.00 standard wage rate. The credit to Accrued Payroll is for the actual wages paid (10,400 × $4.10).

The **labor price variance** parallels the material price variance. Often called the **wage rate variance,** it is the difference between the standard wage rate and the actual wage, multiplied by the actual hours worked. The labor price variance may be expressed as a formula.

$$\text{Labor price variance} = \left[\begin{array}{cc} \text{Standard wage} & \text{Actual wage rate} \\ \text{rate per hour} & \text{per hour} \end{array} \right] \times \begin{array}{c} \text{Actual hours} \\ \text{worked} \end{array}$$

For the Forddon Company the labor price variance is computed as

$$\text{Labor price variance} = [\$4.00 - \$4.10] \times 10,400 \text{ hours}$$

$$= \$(1,040) \text{ U}$$

An actual wage rate of $.10 above the standard rate, times the 10,400 hours actually worked, resulted in an unfavorable labor price variance of $1,040.

One possible cause of a favorable wage rate variance is that management was able to obtain a better worker mix than predicted when the standard was developed. By hiring more workers with lower wage rates, management can affect the wage rate variance. If these workers are less skilled than the skill level planned in the standard wage rate, their employment could have an unfavorable effect on both the material quantity variance and the labor efficiency variance. Unskilled workers probably waste more material and time than do skilled workers. Also, a labor-mix problem may arise because of failures in production control to schedule the workers' activities properly.

Just as the labor price variance parallels the material price variance, the **labor efficiency variance** is built upon the same theory as the material quantity variance. As with materials, the actual units produced times the standard hours per unit is called the **standard quantity allowed,** or **standard hours allowed.** The efficiency variance is the difference between the hours workers should have consumed in actual production and the actual hours worked, multiplied by the standard hourly wage rate. This variance may be expressed in formula form.

$$\text{Labor efficiency variance} = \left[\left(\begin{array}{c}\text{Actual} \\ \text{units} \\ \text{produced}\end{array} \times \begin{array}{c}\text{Standard} \\ \text{hours} \\ \text{per unit}\end{array}\right) - \begin{array}{c}\text{Actual} \\ \text{hours} \\ \text{worked}\end{array}\right] \times \begin{array}{c}\text{Standard} \\ \text{wage} \\ \text{rate}\end{array}$$

For the Forddon Company the labor efficiency variance is computed as

$$\text{Labor efficiency variance} = [(520 \times 8) + (1,200 \times 5) - 10,400 \text{ hours}] \times \$4.00$$

$$= [4,160 + 6,000 - 10,400] \times \$4.00$$

$$= \$(960) \textbf{ U}$$

Bookcase 10A required 4,160 standard hours (520 × 8), and Bookcase 11A required 6,000 (1,200 × 5). The excess of actual hours (10,400) over the standard hours allowed (10,160), times the standard wage rate resulted in an unfavorable labor efficiency variance of $960.

If actual hours worked had been identified by product, the labor efficiency variance could be computed for each product. For example, if 4,500 of the actual labor hours were spent on Product 10A, the labor efficiency variance for Product 10A would be $1,360 unfavorable [(4,160 − 4,500) × $4.00]. The labor efficiency variance for Product 11A would be $400 favorable [(6,000 − 5,900) × $4.00]. A detailed analysis of this type can facilitate management's decisions about production plans and selling prices by product line.

This variance is of prime significance to the production managers. It measures how well they use their workers' time. Many causes of the variance stem from the work itself. Poor production planning may have created idle time, machine breakdowns could have occurred, changes in planned volumes could have affected the learning-curve estimates, blueprints and designs could have had errors, or failures to receive raw materials on time could have created worker inactivity. The individual worker and group supervisor should be aware of the labor efficiency variances, in hours or units of output, on a daily basis. The *real* control takes place at this point. The statement of the variance in dollar terms at the end of the month is less valuable to the supervisor than is the variance stated in hours; typically the supervisor's planning and controlling activities are in hours.

The calculation of the two variances for labor can be summarized into the following schedule.

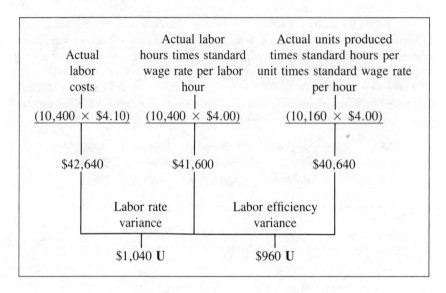

INCURRENCE OF ACTUAL OVERHEAD COSTS

The following journal entry records the actual overhead costs.

Variable Overhead Control $15,400
Fixed Overhead Control .... $ 9,000
　　Various Accounts $24,400

The Variable Overhead Control and Fixed Overhead Control accounts will have subsidiary ledgers where the details are classified. Some firms have a *natural* classification of factory overhead in their subsidiary ledgers. They record overhead detail by the nature of the invoice. Separate records are kept for indirect materials, indirect labor, maintenance, heat-light-power, insurance, depreciation of factory buildings, depreciation of factory machinery, and so forth. Other firms prefer a *functional* classification of costs in the subsidiary ledger. In these firms the costs are recorded by the function they perform. Examples of functional classifications are departments, cost centers, and factory operations such as materials handling and storage, purchasing, production engineering, and quality control.

　　Many accounts would be credited to record actual overhead. Raw Materials Inventory would be credited for indirect materials; Accrued Payroll, for indirect labor; Accumulated Depreciation, for depreciation charges; Prepaid Expenses, for such things as prepaid insurance; and Payables, for invoices to be paid.

APPLICATION OF VARIABLE OVERHEAD
TO WORK-IN-PROCESS INVENTORY

The following journal entry records the application of variable overhead to the units produced.

Work-in-Process Inventory $15,240
    Variable Overhead Applied $15,240

Work-in-Process Inventory is charged for the units produced times the standard hours allowed per unit times the standard *variable* overhead hourly rate (10,160 hours × $1.50). The 10,160 hours are the same 10,160 hours used in the charge to Work-in-Process Inventory for standard labor. The Variable Overhead Applied account accumulates the amount of variable overhead charged to Work-in-Process Inventory.

DETERMINATION AND ISOLATION OF VARIABLE OVERHEAD VARIANCES

The difference between Variable Overhead Applied and Variable Overhead Control is Under- or Overapplied Variable Overhead, which can be separated into the variable overhead efficiency variance and the variable overhead spending variance.

When the volume base of the flexible budget is direct labor hours, it is implied that every hour the workers save or waste has a direct impact upon variable overhead expenditures. Because variable costs should change with changes in volume, and volume is measured by direct labor hours, a savings in labor hours also results in a savings of variable overhead costs. Labor hours saved means variable overhead dollars saved, and labor hours wasted means variable overhead dollars wasted. The **variable overhead efficiency variance** measures the cost impact upon variable overhead caused by the labor efficiency. This may be expressed as a formula.

$$\begin{matrix} \text{Variable} \\ \text{overhead} \\ \text{efficiency} \\ \text{variance} \end{matrix} = \left[\left(\begin{matrix} \text{Actual} \\ \text{units} \\ \text{produced} \end{matrix} \times \begin{matrix} \text{Standard} \\ \text{labor hours} \\ \text{per unit} \end{matrix} \right) - \begin{matrix} \text{Actual} \\ \text{labor hours} \\ \text{worked} \end{matrix} \right]$$
$$\times \begin{matrix} \text{Standard variable} \\ \text{overhead rate} \\ \text{per hour} \end{matrix}$$

For the Forddon Company the variable overhead efficiency variance would be

$$\text{Variable overhead efficiency variance} = (10{,}160 \text{ hours} - 10{,}400 \text{ hours}) \times \$1.50$$

$$= \$(360) \ \mathbf{U}$$

This variance is unfavorable because the actual hours exceeded the standard hours per unit times actual production. The company wasted $360 of variable overhead because the workers were not efficient. Note that the variable overhead efficiency variance is equal to the labor efficiency variance in hours times the standard variable overhead rate (240 hours × $1.50).

If the company does not use direct labor hours as a volume base for determining the flexible budget, the variable overhead efficiency variance will not be directly related to the labor efficiency variance. If the company uses machine hours as a basis of measuring cost variability the following formula would express the efficiency variance.

$$\text{Variable overhead efficiency variance} = \left[\left(\begin{array}{l} \text{Actual} \\ \text{units} \\ \text{produced} \end{array} \times \begin{array}{l} \text{Standard} \\ \text{machine hours} \\ \text{per unit} \end{array} \right) - \begin{array}{l} \text{Actual} \\ \text{machine hours} \\ \text{used} \end{array} \right]$$

$$\times \begin{array}{l} \text{Standard variable} \\ \text{overhead rate} \\ \text{per machine hour} \end{array}$$

The theory of this variance is the same as that of the variance based on labor hours, but the causal factors are different. Causes for an unfavorable variable overhead efficiency variance based on machine hours could include improper maintenance schedules, unscheduled and random machine breakdowns, or human failures in the use of the machines.

As stated earlier, the best method of establishing overhead standards begins with developing a flexible budget. The flexible budget in a standard cost setting states the cost behavior patterns for overhead that the company *should* experience if operations are efficient. The **variable overhead spending variance** is the difference between the actual variable overhead costs incurred and the amount that the flexible budget indicates should be spent on variable overhead costs for the actual volume worked. It is the difference between actual costs and the flexible budget for variable costs times actual hours worked. (As you will recall from Chapter 5, the flexible budget for variable costs times the actual hours worked was called the Performance Budget.) In formula form the variable overhead spending variance is

$$\begin{matrix} \text{Variable} \\ \text{overhead} \\ \text{spending variance} \end{matrix} = \begin{pmatrix} \begin{matrix} \text{Standard variable} \\ \text{rate per hour} \\ \text{from flexible budget} \end{matrix} \times \begin{matrix} \text{Actual} \\ \text{hours} \\ \text{worked} \end{matrix} \end{pmatrix} - \begin{matrix} \text{Actual} \\ \text{variable} \\ \text{overhead costs} \end{matrix}$$

For the Forddon Furniture Company the variable overhead spending variance would be

$$\begin{matrix} \text{Variable} \\ \text{overhead spending} \\ \text{variance} \end{matrix} = [\$1.50 \times 10,400 \text{ hours}] - \$15,400$$

$$= \$200 \text{ F}$$

A comparison of the formula above to determine the variable overhead spending variance with the formulas to compute the material or the labor price variances shows parallel computations. This can be seen if the formula above is expressed as

$$\begin{matrix} \text{Variable overhead} \\ \text{spending variance} \end{matrix} = \begin{bmatrix} \begin{matrix} \text{Standard} \\ \text{variable} \\ \text{overhead} \\ \text{rate} \end{matrix} - \begin{matrix} \text{Actual} \\ \text{variable} \\ \text{overhead} \\ \text{rate} \end{matrix} \end{bmatrix} \times \begin{matrix} \text{Actual} \\ \text{hours} \\ \text{worked} \end{matrix}$$

Remember that the actual units times the standard hours per unit equals the standard quantity (hours) allowed for the units actually produced.

The calculation of the two variances for variable overhead can be summarized into the following schedule.

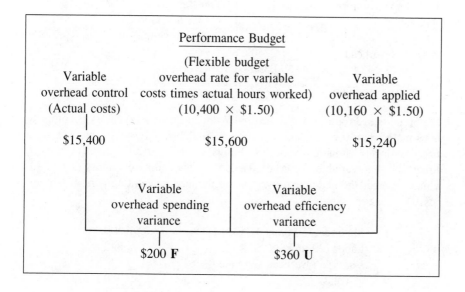

To isolate these variances within the accounting system, the following entry is made.

Variable Overhead Applied..................	$15,240	
Variable Overhead Efficiency Variance.......	$ 360	
Variable Overhead Spending Variance..............		$ 200
Variable Overhead Control.........................		$15,400

This entry closes the Variable Overhead Applied and the Variable Overhead Control accounts, transferring the differences between these accounts into two variance accounts. The algebraic sum of the two variances is $160 unfavorable, which is the amount of underapplied variable overhead.

COMPLETION AND TRANSFER TO FINISHED GOODS INVENTORY

The following journal entry transfers the goods from Work-in-Process Inventory to the Finished Goods Inventory.

Finished Goods Inventory	$88,000	
Work-in-Process Inventory...........................		$88,000

The amount of the transfer was determined as [(500 × $74) + (1,200 × $42.50)], or $88,000. The Work-in-Process Inventory account, after posting, would be as shown in the following T-account.

Work-in-Process Inventory

Beginning Inventory	$ 0	Transferred to	
Materials	34,500	Finished Goods	$88,000
Labor	40,640	Ending Inventory	2,380
Variable Overhead	15,240		
	$90,380		$90,380
Beginning Inventory	$ 2,380		

The 50 units of Product 10A in the final Work-in-Process Inventory is complete as to materials (50 equivalent units of material) but only 40% complete as to direct labor and variable overhead (50 units × 40%, or 20 equivalent units of direct labor and variable overhead). The cost of the ending inventory of $2,380, which becomes the beginning inventory of the next accounting period, is composed of the following:

Materials (50 units × $30)	$1,500
Labor (20 units × $32)	640
Variable Overhead (20 units × $12)	240
Total	$2,380

SALES AND COST OF GOODS SOLD RECOGNITION

The entry to record the sales for the period would be

Cash (or Accounts Receivable)............ $122,250
    Sales...$122,250

There were 450 Style 10A bookcases sold at $125 each and 1,100 Style 11A bookcases sold at $60 each.

The following journal entry records the transfer from Finished Goods Inventory to Cost of Goods Sold.

Cost of Goods Sold $80,050
    Finished Goods Inventory.......................... $80,050

Because the Finished Goods Inventory is carried at variable standard cost, the transfer to Cost of Goods Sold will be at variable standard cost [(450 × $74) + (1,100 × $42.50)]. The Finished Goods Inventory account, after posting, would be

Finished Goods Inventory

Beginning Inventory	$ 0	Units Sold	$80,050
Units Completed	88,000	Ending Inventory	7,950
	$88,000		$88,000
Beginning Inventory	$ 7,950		

The final Finished Goods Inventory, based on the physical count, can be reconciled as

Style 10A   50 × $74.00 = $3,700
Style 11A   100 × $42.50 = 4,250
Total ending inventory $7,950

RECORDING SELLING AND ADMINISTRATIVE EXPENSES

The following summary entry records the selling and administrative expenses.

Variable Selling Expense Control $2,800
Fixed Selling Expense Control $2,000
Administrative Expense Control $3,500
    Various Accounts $8,300

At this point managerial reports for the period costs can be prepared. These reports should contrast the planned level of expenditures with the actual performance. The following tabulation shows a performance report for the Ford-don Company for selling and administrative expenses.

The original budget (page 190) showed that the variable selling expenses should be $2.00 times the actual units sold. The company sold 450 Style 10A bookcases and 1,100 Style 11A bookcases for a total of 1,550 units. Thus, variable selling expenses in the Performance Budget are (1,550 × $2.00), or $3,100. The Performance Budget for the fixed costs also came from the original flexible budget equations.

	Performance Budget Allowances	Actual Expenditures	Spending Variance
Variable expenses:			
Selling expenses	$ 3,100	$ 2,800	$300 **F**
Fixed expenses:			
Overhead	$ 9,600	$ 9,000	$600 **F**
Selling expenses	2,400	2,000	400 **F**
Administrative expenses	3,000	3,500	(500) **U**
Total fixed expenses	15,000	14,500	500 **F**
Total period costs	$18,100	$17,300	$800 **F**

DISPOSITION OF VARIANCES

The following entry closes the standard cost variances to Cost of Goods Sold.

Cost of Goods Sold (or Income Summary) $1,960
Variable Overhead Spending Variance .... $ 200
Material Price Variance $1,100
    Material Quantity Variance .... $ 900
    Labor Price Variance $1,040
    Labor Efficiency Variance .... $ 960
    Variable Overhead Efficiency Variance .... $ 360

    In the entry above we closed the variance accounts to Cost of Goods Sold. This treats the variances as a period cost; only the standard costs are treated as product costs. An alternative treatment would be to prorate the variances to the appropriate inventory accounts. This would, via an after-the-fact allocation, treat the variances as product costs. The proration would convert the inventory values from standard costs to actual costs.

    We have adopted the closing of the variances to Cost of Goods Sold for two reasons. First, the motivation for proration is primarily a financial account-ing issue of inventory valuation and income measurement. From a management point of view, this proration can become a negative motivator and negate the time and energy spent in developing the standards and the variances. Second, and more theoretical, is that it would include in the inventory dollars spent for both efficiencies and inefficiencies.

THE FORDDON FURNITURE COMPANY
CONTRIBUTION MARGIN INCOME STATEMENT
For the Month of January 19X7

Sales		$122,250	100%
Less: Standard variable cost of goods sold		80,050	65%
Standard contribution from production		$ 42,200	35%
Adjustments for variances:			
Material price variance	$1,100		
Material quantity variance	(900)		
Labor price variance	(1,040)		
Labor efficiency variance	(960)		
Variable overhead spending variance	200		
Variable overhead efficiency variance	(360)	(1,960)	
Adjusted contribution margin from production		$ 40,240	
Variable selling costs		2,800	
Contribution margin from operations		$ 37,440	
Less fixed costs:			
Fixed overhead expense	$9,000		
Fixed selling expenses	2,000		
Administrative expenses	3,500		
Total fixed costs		14,500	
Income		$ 22,940	

EXHIBIT 6–3
Income statement using
variable standard costing

Generally, most firms close the variances, or prorate them if that is their method of choice, only at the end of the fiscal year. This is because many factors will change throughout the year. These variations will cause short-term variances that will "wash out" over a longer time period. We have closed the variance accounts in our example only for illustrative purposes.

PREPARATION OF INCOME STATEMENT

Exhibit 6–3 shows the income statement prepared with variable standard costs. This income statement is constructed in the format of the contribution margin approach with the variances from standard costs treated as period costs.

SUMMARY OF STANDARD COST VARIANCES

The previous discussion in this chapter has shown how the standard cost variances are calculated as a part of the ongoing, recording system. This approach of explanation was chosen because it parallels how the variances would be measured in an actual firm. However, there are times, particularly for management analysis, where the calculation of the variances will not be presented in journal entry form. Exhibit 6–4 shows an analysis of all of the variances of the Forddon Furniture Company without journal entries.

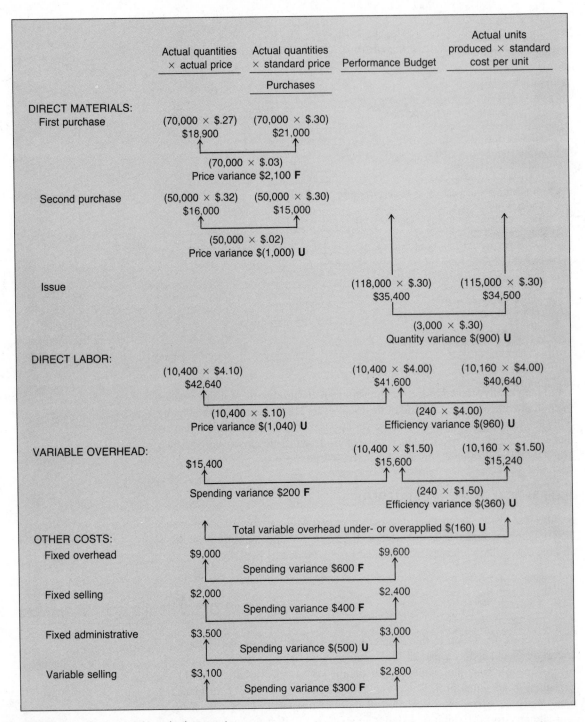

EXHIBIT 6—4 Summary of standard cost variances

SELECTION OF A STANDARD COST SYSTEM

A standard cost system, particularly when coupled with a flexible budget, is one of the most sophisticated planning and control systems available to management. The strength of the system rests upon (1) the magnitude of preplanning and thought involved in the development and installation of the standard system, and (2) the reporting of meaningful and timely variances that focus management's actions. The role of the system in inventory valuation and income measurement, while useful, is only a secondary goal of standard costing.

A standard cost system is not an end in itself, nor will it prove satisfactory for all firms. To develop standards a firm must have a reasonably solid experience base with a stable product or service line. Without experience and stability it would be difficult to develop standards that would be useful benchmarks. Further, the development of standards can be expensive. If management does not believe that there will be sufficient savings from production efficiencies gained to offset the development costs, the installation would be uneconomical. If management is happy with the current efficiencies there is no need to install a standard cost system.

The ability to develop meaningful variances implies that the firm and its environment are stable. Because a meaningful variance is one that focuses management's attentions, the greater the potential number of explanations concerning the cause of a variance, the less informative the variance. The more specific the causal factors are, the more useful the variance is in directing attention. Firms with unstable product lines, changing production facilities, flexible management philosophies and organizational structures, or volatile external environments are not good candidates for standard costing. There are simply too many factors affecting the variance interpretations.

SUMMARY

Standard cost systems are intended to aid management in the planning and control of costs. Standard costs are predeterminations of what costs *should* be if production is efficient. Standards must be established for each material, labor, and variable overhead cost. They are set by examining production processes, material usage patterns, work measurement and time studies, learning curves, and the development of a flexible budget for overhead.

There are numerous approaches to the setting of standards. The most useful in planning and controlling costs are normal standards, sometimes called *currently attainable standards*. These costs are achievable. They provide realistic benchmarks for workers' activities and represent reasonable goals for performance.

The value of a standard cost system is predicated upon the ability to extract meaningful variances by developing standard costs for one unit of product. Then, by comparing actual activity with standards, it is possible to assess performance. There are two types of variances applicable to all variable costs: the price variance and the quantity variance. The price (rate) variance is

$$(\text{Standard price} - \text{Actual price}) \times \text{Actual quantity}$$

The quantity (efficiency) variance is

$$(\text{Standard quantity allowed} - \text{Actual quantity}) \times \text{Standard price}$$

These variances act as direction finders. They indicate when actual performance differs from standard performance but do not give the causal factors for these differences. In this sense, the variances could be looked upon as the starting point of investigation, rather than as the terminal point. Management must use the variances as attention-directing devices, and then follow up with a more detailed analysis of the causes and their effects.

To achieve the maximum benefits from standard costs, they should be blended into the accounting system. In this way standard costs become both planning and control vehicles and inventory costing values.

APPENDIX 6-1

LEARNING CURVES

In industries with a high proportion of hand-work labor, the learning curve has been useful in estimating labor time. The learning curve, which shows that workers have a constant rate of improvement, is a mathematical expression of the well-known adage, "Practice makes perfect." Everyone, at some point, has performed a repetitive task over a long period of time. With each repetition one becomes more proficient and requires less time. Machinists, as a result of their accumulated skills, know how to lay out their work and choose their tools in an efficient way. Accrued skills and familiarity, orderly work layout and tooling, and better selection of suitable designs and materials are sources of improvement with experience.

The airframe industries, beginning in the 1930s, found that this improvement was regular and predictable. In general terms, empirical studies have shown that the improvement was a constant percentage over doubled quantities.

A learning curve indicates that the *rate* of improvement is constant.[1] It does not imply that all production activities have the same rate of improvement. For most aircraft fabrication and assembly-line labor, the *average* improvement rate for all labor used on an airplane during World War II was about 80%. However, it was found that a welder improves at a different rate than a riveter. The quantification of the learning-curve rate for any given activity can only be found empirically.

If direct labor is subject to a 90% cumulative learning curve, this means that the *average* time for two units is 90% of the time required for one unit. For example, if the first unit required 2,000 direct labor hours and a 90% cumulative learning curve is used, then the *average* for two units is predicted to be 1,800 hours (2,000 × .90); this would *total* 3,600 hours for the two units. Because this is an average, the marginal hours for the second unit would be 1,600 hours [(1,800 × 2) − 2,000]. At four units the *average* would be 1,620 (1,800 × .90), or a *total* of 6,480 hours (1,620 × 4). It would take a *total* of 2,880 hours (6,480 − 3,600) to produce the third and fourth units.

To provide a second example, Exhibit A6–1 shows the projected *average* labor hours plotted on graph paper with a 69% learning curve where the first unit of a new product took 100 hours. The *average* labor hours for two units is estimated at 69 hours. This would *total* 138 hours for the two units. At four units the *average* would be approximately 48 hours. This would be a *total* of 192 hours for the four units. At eight units the *average* would be 33 hours per unit. This would be a *total* of 264 hours for the eight units. By the sixteenth unit the *average* unit would take 23 hours; this would *total* 368 hours.

Not only will the learning-curve phenomenon affect direct labor, it will also affect variable overhead. Remember that variable overhead, when measured on a labor hour basis, is considered to increase or decrease as a function of labor time. Thus labor savings will also save variable overhead costs.

In an industry with a large production volume, the learning curve becomes less significant over time. Exhibit A6–1 shows why. At first the curve slopes downward rapidly; then it decreases slowly. Firms with a large volume of repetitive operations move quickly down the learning curve, soon they are operating at a volume where the curve is relatively flat. The learning curve is still operative, but the results are not as spectacular.

---

[1]In mathematical notation the learning curve is

$$y = aX^b$$

where

y = *Average* number of labor hours for X units.

a = Number of hours required for first unit.

X = Cumulative number of units produced.

b = Factor of learning determined by dividing the log of the learning rate (i.e., 80%) by the log of 2.

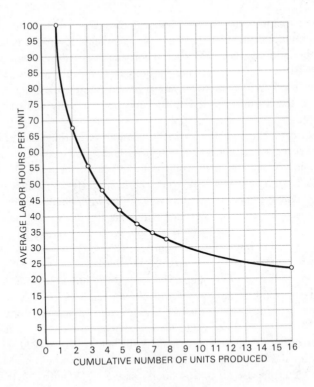

EXHIBIT A6–1
Illustration of learning curve

In some production activities the learning curve is not useful. For instance, in an automated production line, the speed of the line, not the workers' individual learning capabilities, determines their time. Some firms segregate production tasks into many small uncomplicated activities. Employees learn the simple tasks rapidly, and the firm soon reaches the relatively flat portion of the curve.

The learning-curve phenomenon will have an effect on many aspects of accounting. To illustrate these affects, let's assume that a firm begins producing a new product line on January 1 that is subject to the learning curve. Impacts will include

Budgeting/planning—Because units produced in January will take more labor hours than units produced in the following December, this will have to be reflected in the labor budgets. This could also have an impact upon personnel hiring and layoff policies.

Standard cost setting—The establishment of standard costs, particularly for direct labor and variable overhead, will have to reflect the learning curve. For example, assume the firm will produce 16 units of the new product. If the firm uses the labor hours of the first unit to establish the standard, then all subsequent activities, and hence variances, will appear favorable. If the firm uses the average labor hours at the sixteenth unit, then all variances prior to that unit will be unfavorable.

Performance evaluation—Without taking the learning curve into account, it can appear that management is doing a good job of operational cost control because costs are decreasing over time. Yet, given the knowledge of the learning curve, this is an expected result. Successful performance evaluation should include all known variables.

Decision making—Coupled to performance evaluation is decision making. The learning curve could have a significant impact upon how management makes decisions. As one example, it could affect decisions about employee stability. High turnover or massively interrupted production runs could mean ''starting over'' again on the learning curve, which would waste labor costs. A second example of the impact of learning curves on decision making is in the area of product pricing.

Inventory valuation—Where a firm uses historical costing, any products produced in January would appear to cost more than products produced in the following December. This would affect inventory valuation, income measurement, and overhead rates, all of which management would have to consider.

PROBLEMS AND CASES

6-1 *(Material Variances)*. The Industrial Banding Company produces banding materials for industry. The following data apply to the production of wide bands in their Upland plant for the month of January.

Standard material cost per roll of wide banding	100 ft at $.60 per foot
Actual cost of materials purchased (120,000 feet)	$84,000
Units produced	1,050 units
Inventory of raw materials:	
Beginning inventory	none
Ending inventory	10,000 ft

REQUIRED:

A. Compute the material price variance.

B. Compute the material usage variance.

C. Prepare journal entries to record the raw material transactions for the Upland plant.

6-2 *(Labor Variances)*. The following data apply to labor costs for the Sideland plant of the Industrial Banding Company for the month of February.

Standard direct labor hours per roll of wide banding	.5 hours
Standard wage rate per hour	$6.00 per hour
Actual wages paid	$11,000
Actual direct labor hours	2,000 hours
Standard variable overhead application rate	$4.00 per hour
Number of units produced	4,400 units

REQUIRED:

A. Compute the labor rate variance.

B. Compute the labor efficiency variance.

C. Compute the variable overhead efficiency variance.

D. Prepare the journal entries to record the labor transactions for the month.

6-3 *(Variable Overhead Variances).* The Industrial Banding Company uses a standard variable costing system. Data for the month of February follow for their Lowland plant, which manufactures industrial staplers.

Flexible budget on which the overhead standard is based:

$600 per month plus $1.50 per direct labor hour

Standard direct labor hours per unit	.2 hours
Number of units produced	1,000 units
Actual overhead for the month	$1,000, of which $650 was fixed
Actual direct labor hours during February	220 hours

REQUIRED:

A. Compute the variable overhead spending variance.

B. Compute the variable overhead efficiency variance.

C. Compute the labor efficiency variance in hours.

D. Prepare the journal entries for overhead for the month.

E. Did the firm control the fixed overhead costs?

6-4 *(Setting Labor Standards).* The Alton Company is going to expand its Punch Press Department. It is about to purchase three new punch presses from Equipment Manufacturers, Inc. Equipment studies indicate that for Alton's intended use, the output rate for one press should be 1,000 pieces per hour. Alton has very similar presses now in operation. At the present time, production from these presses averages 600 pieces per hour.

A study of the Alton experience shows that the average is derived from the following individual outputs.

Worker	Daily Output
L. Jones	750
J. Green	750
R. Smith	600
H. Brown	500
R. Alters	550
G. Hoag	450
Total	3600
Average	600

Alton management also plans to institute a standard cost accounting system in the very near future. The company engineers are supporting a standard based on 1,000 pieces per hour, the accounting department is arguing for 750 pieces per hour, and the department supervisor is arguing for 600 pieces per hour.

REQUIRED:

A. What arguments would each proponent be likely to use to support his or her case?

B. Which alternative best reconciles the needs of cost control and the motivation of improved performance? Explain.

(CMA adapted)

6-5 *(Causes of Variance)*. For each of the following independent events indicate which variances would be affected and whether the effect is favorable or unfavorable.

1. The material standard was based on a test run of 100 units. Demand exceeded expectation and the number of units produced during June was much greater than the number planned.

2. The purchasing agent bought substandard material at a large savings. Because of the lower quality of material, more scrap will be produced and an additional employee must be hired to assist in the cutting operation.

3. Several rush orders were completed during the month within the standard time allotted; however, a large amount of overtime was required.

4. The wage rate increases with the cost-of-living index. The rate of inflation is lower than what was predicted at this point in time.

5. The plant supervisor hired some temporary, unskilled production-line workers to substitute for skilled workers who were on temporary assignment at a new out-of-state plant.

6. Production control failed to schedule a new job and had to notify the customer that delivery would have to be postponed until next month.

7. To ensure an on-time completion of an important order, the plant manager hired an outside firm to clean the plant; the cleanup is usually done by the regular workers at the end of the day and is included in the labor standards. Because of this action, no overtime work was needed.

8. A power outage hit the plant for 3 hours during the mid-day shift.

9. The manager of Department A transferred to Department B, 100 units with a subcomponent that was inadequately tightened. The workers in Department B tightened the subcomponent as they performed their normal duties on the units.

10. A new quality control inspector was unusually severe. His rejections required extra rework on the units.

6-6 (Calculate Variances from Incomplete Data). The following data are available for the Belair Company.

Standard labor hours allowed	42,000 hours
Actual labor hours used	40,000 hours
Standard labor rate per hour	$6.30
Labor wage rate variance	$8,400 favorable

REQUIRED:

Using the above data, determine the following.

A. Total direct labor payroll.

B. Direct labor efficiency variance.

C. Prepare the journal entry for labor.

6-7 (Calculate Variances From Incomplete Data). The following data are available for the Macon Company.

Units of product manufactured	500 units
Direct labor:	
Standrd hours per unit	3 hours
Standard wage rate per hour	$7.00
Actual labor hours	1,470 hours
Actual total labor cost	$10,143
Variable overhead:	
Standard variable overhead per hour	$4.60
Actual variable overhead incurred	$ 6,800

REQUIRED:

Using the above data, compute the following.

A. The labor rate variance.

B. The labor efficiency variance.

C. The variable overhead spending variance.

D. The variable overhead efficiency variance.

E. Labor costs charged to Work-in-Process.

F. Variable overhead applied to Work-in-Process.

G. Variable overhead over- or underapplied.

6-8 *(Material and Labor Variances in a Hospital)*. The West Valley Community Health Center has established standards for some routine activities including certain lab tests. The standards for performing a particular lab test are as follows:

Lab technician	.2 hours @ $8.00	= $1.60
Materials	2 cc @ $1.00	= $2.00

During 19X7, 3,000 tests were performed. The tests used 650 hours and 5,800 cubic centimeters of material. Actual costs were

Lab technician	$5,850
Material	$8,700

REQUIRED:

A. Compute the price (rate) variances and the efficiency (usage) variances for both the technicians and the material. Indicate whether the variances were favorable or unfavorable.

B. The lab technicians maintained the records of their time by type of tests performed. There are no independent checks on their time. Overall, the tests show a small unfavorable technician efficiency variance. None of the tests shows a large favorable or large unfavorable variance for the year. The health center is trying to decide whether to hire another lab technician or contract outside for some of the tests. How useful will the technician efficiency variance by type of tests be for this decision? Explain.

6-9 *(Labor and Overhead Variances)*. The Perky Company uses a standard variable cost system in its factory. The flexible budget, which serves as a standard for the Assembly Department, which assembles electric coffee pots, is

	BUDGET ALLOWANCES	
	Fixed Cost per Month	Variable Cost per Direct Labor Hour
Direct labor	—	$5.00
Overhead		
Inspection	$1,800	$ .05
Rework labor	—	$ .25
Supervision	$3,000	—
Labor fringe benefits	$1,000	$ .30
Payroll taxes	$ 500	$ .40
Supplies	—	$ .50
Other	$1,700	$ .10

The standard labor hours for the assembly of one coffee pot is .5 hr. During the month of June the department assembled 14,000 coffee pots. Actual direct labor hours totaled 7,100. Actual departmental costs for the month were

Direct labor	$36,210
Inspection	1,900
Rework labor	2,125
Supervision	3,300
Labor fringe benefits	2,970
Payroll taxes	3,900
Supplies	3,900
Other	2,100
	$56,405

REQUIRED:

A. Prepare a standard cost card for labor and variable overhead in the Assembly Department.

B. Calculate the labor rate variance, the labor efficiency variance, and the overhead efficiency variance.

C. Prepare a Performance Budget report that shows the total overhead spending variance, in total and by each cost item.

6-10 (*Calculation of Variances*). The B. Turner Company manufactures a linkage for automobile overdrives. The standard cost for this part is

Material:	
Shaft (1 @ $30.00)	$30.00
Ballbearing unit (4 @ $5.00 each)	20.00
Labor (3 hours @ $10.00)	30.00
Variable overhead (4 machine hours @ $2.00)	8.00
Total Standard Cost per Unit	$88.00

During October actual production was 90 units, although the management had originally planned to produce 100 units. Actual data for October were

> Material:
>> Purchases:
>>> 100 shafts at $32.00 each
>>> 450 ballbearing units at $4.80 each
>> Issues:
>>> 94 shafts
>>> 380 ballbearing units
> Labor:
>> 110 hours at $9.00
>> 190 hours at $11.00
> Variable overhead incurred was $775
> Actual machine hours totaled 410

REQUIRED:

Prepare a schedule of the standard cost variances.

6-11 *(Prepare a Schedule of Variances with Process Costing Data).* The Riser Company uses a variable standard cost system. The standard cost per unit is as shown here.

STANDARD COST CARD

Materials:		
Q (5 pounds at $2.00)	$10.00	
R (1 unit at $2.00)	2.00	$12.00
Labor:		
2.5 hours at $6.00 per hour		15.00
Variable Overhead:		
2.5 hours at $4.00 per hour		10.00
Total Standard Cost per unit		$37.00

The Riser Company began the month of June 19X8 with a beginning inventory of 400 units in process. These 400 units had 75% of the two materials and 25% of the conversion costs added. During the month 9,000 units were completed and transferred to finished goods. There were 500 units in the June 30, 19X8 ending inventory of Work-in-Process. These units had 80% of their materials and 60% of the conversion costs added.

Actual data for the month were

1. 45,000 pounds of material Q were purchased and issued at a total cost of $99,000.

2. 9,200 units of material R were purchased and issued at a total cost of $19,320.
3. 24,000 direct labor hours were used at a total cost of $139,200.
4. Actual variable overhead incurred totaled $98,500.

REQUIRED:

Prepare a schedule showing all material, labor, and variable overhead variances. (Note: calculate the material price variances on materials issued.)

6-12 *(Computation of Variances).* The Dearborn Company manufactures Product X in standard batches of 100 units. A variable standard cost system is used. The standard costs for one batch of X follow.

Raw materials (60 pounds @ $.45)	$ 27.00
Direct labor (36 hours @ $4.00)	144.00
Variable overhead (36 hours @ $2.75)	99.00
Total standard cost per unit	$270.00

The overhead rate was based on normal output of 240 batches. The flexible budget for overhead is

Budgeted overhead per month = $15,120 + $2.75 per direct labor hour

Production for April amounted to 210 batches. There were no beginning or ending inventories. Actual data for April are

Raw materials used	13,000 pounds
Cost of raw materials used	$ 6,110
Direct labor cost	$31,600
Actual overhead (of which $14,544 is fixed)	$35,344
Average actual variable overhead rate per hour	$ 2.60

REQUIRED:

Prepare a schedule that contains a detailed explanation of the variances between actual costs and standard costs. Indicate whether they are favorable or unfavorable. (The number of actual direct labor hours is not stated in the problem but can be computed from the data. Remember that variable overhead is applied on the basis of direct labor hours.)

(CPA adapted)

6-13 *(Standard Variable Costing—Journal Entries and Income Statement).* Avery Company produces a single product and uses a standard cost system. Cost and revenue data for each unit are shown in the schedule on page 219. These per unit data were based on producing and selling 10,000 units.

Material: 3 quarts of Compound R @ $3.20 = $9.60
           2 ounces of Compound C @ $4.40 =   8.80 $18.40

Direct labor:
  2 hours @ $5.80   11.60
Overhead: Applied on the basis of direct labor (40% fixed)   8.00
General and Selling (75% fixed)   12.80
  Total cost $50.80
Profit   9.20
Selling price $60.00

All inventories are maintained at standard variable cost. Variances are closed to cost of goods sold.
    Transactions for the month of April follow.

1. During April, purchases consisted of 7,000 gallons of Compound R for $12 per gallon, 1,200 pounds of Compound C at a cost of $70 per pound, and $8,000 of factory supplies.

2. During April, 9,000 units were completed and sent to finished goods. Because of its highly perishable nature during production, no work-in-process inventory is carried from one day's production to the next. During April, 6,850 gallons of Compound R and 1,100 pounds of Compound C were used in production.

3. Hourly wage rates were 5% above the standard rate. Direct labor cost was $103,530.

4. Factory overhead for the month was $74,800, of which $30,000 was fixed.

5. Selling and administrative expenses for the month were $125,000, of which $24,000 was variable.

6. During April, 8,000 units were sold at the standard selling price.

REQUIRED:

A. Assuming standard variable costing, prepare journal entries to record the transactions for April.

B. Prepare an income statement using the contribution margin approach.

6-14 *(Standard Process Costing).* The Strong Scent Company produces a liquid product used in perfume. A standard variable costing system is used with process costing. Standard material and variable conversion costs for a 1-centigram vial are as follows:

Direct materials   (10 packets @ $6.00) = $60.00
Variable labor   (2 hours @ $5.00) =   10.00
Variable overhead   (2 hours @ $2.50) =   5.00
   Total standard cost per unit $75.00

Material is added only at the beginning of the process, and conversion costs are added uniformly throughout the process. At the beginning of the month, there were 200 vials in process complete as to materials but only 60% complete as to conversion costs. During the month, material was added to start 500 vials of product; 400 vials were finished and sent to finished goods; and 300 vials were left in the ending inventory 40% finished as to conversion costs.

Actual costs for the month were

Direct materials	5,200 packets @	$6.20
Variable labor	750 hours @	$4.90
Variable overhead		$2,300

REQUIRED:

A. What is the total cost of the units in the beginning Work-in-Process Inventory?

B. What is the number of equivalent units (vials) for material? For conversion costs?

C. What is the cost of the 300 units in ending inventory of Work-in-Process?

D. Prepare journal entries for the month setting forth all variances. Assume that the beginning and ending balances of Raw Materials Inventory are zero.

6-15 *(Journal Entries and Income Statement).* The Spindle Factory produces a line of mohair sweaters for distribution to wholesalers. Standards for their costs are

Direct material: 5 skeins @ 4 ounces	$7.50
Direct labor: 2 hours @ $4.00	$8.00
Overhead: $24,300 + $2.10 per direct labor hour	
Selling expenses: $15,300 + $1.00 per unit sold	
Administrative expenses: $21,986 + $0 per unit sold	

Normal capacity is 9,000 units, or 18,000 direct labor hours per month. There were no beginning inventories in the Raw Materials, Work-in-Process, or Finished Goods inventories.

Actual data for the month were

Sales: 9,200 units at $30 per unit

Production: Materials were issued for 9,500 units started; labor and overhead were added for 9,400 units; 9,300 units were completed and transferred to Finished Goods Inventory

Raw materials:
  Purchases: 2,000 boxes of yarn (24 skeins per box) at $37.20 per box
  Issues: 1,990 boxes of yarn

Direct labor: 19,850 actual hours at $4.10 per hour

Overhead:
   Variable $42,985
   Fixed $26,320
Selling expenses:
   Variable $ 9,300
   Fixed $15,345
Administrative expenses: $23,500

REQUIRED:

A. Prepare journal entries for the Spindle Factory, assuming that the firm uses variable standard costing.

B. Prepare an income statement for the month. Treat all variances as period costs.

6-16 *(Job Order/Standard Cost System Variances).* Ross Shirts, Inc. manufactures short- and long-sleeved men's shirts for large stores. Ross produces a single quality shirt in lots to each customer's order and attaches the store's label to each. The standard variable costs for a dozen long-sleeved shirts are

Direct materials (24 yards at $.75)	$18.00
Direct labor (3 hours at $7.45)	22.35
Variable overhead (3 hours at $6.00)	18.00
Total cost per dozen	$58.35

During October, Ross Shirts worked on three orders for long-sleeved shirts. Job cost records for the month disclose the following:

Lot	Units in Lot	Material Used	Hours Worked
30	1,000 dozen	24,100 yards	2,980
31	1,700 dozen	40,440 yards	5,130
32	1,200 dozen	28,825 yards	2,890

The following information is also available.

1. Ross purchased 95,000 yards of material during the month at a cost of $72,000.

2. Direct labor costs incurred amounted to $82,500 during October.

3. There was no Work-in-Process at October 1. During October, Lots 30 and 31 were completed. All material was issued for Lot 32 and it was 80% completed as to labor and overhead on October 31.

4. Actual variable overhead costs incurred were $63,684.

REQUIRED:

A. Compute the materials price variance for October and indicate whether it is favorable or unfavorable.

B. For each production lot and for the company as a whole compute the total amount of each of the following variances and indicate whether the variance is favorable or unfavorable; (1) material usage variance; (2) labor efficiency variance; (3) variable overhead efficiency variance.

C. Compute for the company as a whole the labor rate variance and variable overhead spending variance.

(CPA adapted)

6-17 *(Comprehensive Variance Analysis).* The Maple Furniture Company uses a variable standard cost system in accounting for its production costs. The standard cost of a unit of furniture follows.

Lumber (100 feet at $200 per 1,000 feet)	$20.00
Direct labor (4 hours at $5.00 per hour)	20.00
Variable overhead (30% of standard direct labor)	6.00
Total unit cost	$46.00

Standard variable overhead was determined from the following overhead costs at different levels of activity.

Direct Labor Hours	Overhead
5,200	$10,800
4,800	$10,200
4,400	$ 9,600
4,000 (normal capacity)	$ 9,000
3,600	$ 8,400

The actual unit costs for one month were as follows:

Lumber used (110 feet at $180 per 1,000 feet)	$19.80
Direct labor (4¼ hours at $5.20 per hour)	22.10
Variable overhead ($7,500 ÷ 1,200 units)	6.25
Total actual unit cost	$48.15
Actual fixed overhead	$3,060

REQUIRED:

A. From the overhead data, develop the linear equation for the flexible budget.

B. Determine the variable overhead rate per direct labor hour.

C. Compute the following variances and indicate whether they were favorable or unfavorable. (Assume that beginning and ending inventories are zero.)

  1. Material price variance.

  2. Material usage variance.

  3. Labor rate variance.

  4. Labor efficiency variance.

5. Variable overhead efficiency variance.

6. Variable overhead spending variance.

D. Prepare journal entries for the data above.

(CPA adapted)

6-18 *(Standard Cost Variances in a Service Concern).* The Montana Company, a cable television company, operates in a rural area. As a service organization they are not concerned with inventory costing. However, their president asked the accountant to develop standard costs to make their end-of-the-month reports more meaningful. Using a detailed study of material and labor reports, plus regression analysis, the accountant developed the following standards and flexible budgets.

New installations:
  Materials:
    Decoder box (1 at $30.00) $30.00
    Cable (100 feet at $.10)   10.00
    Wire splitters (2 at $1.00)   2.00 $42.00
  Labor:
    On-site time (1 hour at $8.00) $ 8.00
    Travel time (1 hour at $8.00)   8.00   16.00
  Total prime costs of installation $58.00

Repair shop:
  Materials (1 package components) $ 5.00
  Labor (1 hour at $10.00)   10.00
  Total prime costs of repair $15.00

The overhead analysis resulted in the following flexible budgets, determined on a monthly basis.

Truck expense	$1,200 + $ .50 (per installation hour)
Labor benefits	$ 0 + $1.50 (per direct labor hour)
Utilities	$ 500 + $ .30 (per direct labor hour)
Indirect materials	$ 0 + $4.00 (per installation made)
Rent	$3,000 + $ 0
Supervision	$1,500 + $ 0

The standards for labor were based on the following analysis.

Installation: the four employees in the installation department averaged 160 hours per month each. In a typical month each installer would average 80 new installations.

Repairs: the two employees in the repair department also averaged 160 hours per month each. In a typical month each employee would complete 160 repairs.

The actual data for July were

New installations		380
Repairs completed		340
Decoder boxes	(390 units)	$12,090.00
Cable	(40,000 feet)	$ 3,600.00
Splitters	(720 each)	$ 684.00
Components	(325 packages)	$ 1,543.75
Installers' wages	(680 hours)	$ 5,576.00
Repair wages	(320 hours)	$ 3,400.00

Overhead costs:	
Truck expense	$ 1,450
Labor benefits	1,650
Utilities	875
Indirect materials	1,480
Rent	3,000
Supervision	1,600
Total overhead	$10,055

REQUIRED:

A. Compute material and labor variances for both the installation and repair departments.

B. Prepare a cost report for overhead, using a Performance Budget approach, that sets forth all spending variances.

C. At this time the company does not apply variable overhead to their installation and repair functions. If they were to decide to develop variable overhead rates for these two activities, what overhead rate would you recommend?

6-19 *(Appendix: Learning Curves and the Establishment of Standard Costs).* Howard Trevor, president of the Bounty Boatbuilding Company, had been unhappy for some time with his Cost Accounting Department. He was convinced that the accounting for labor costs was inaccurate. The labor efficiency variance did not seem to follow a predictable pattern, and he was hesitant to rely on the data for either worker control or product pricing. Mr. Trevor felt that he had to develop the ability to control labor hours on boatbuilding before he could undertake a new swimming pool project he had been planning.

Bounty Boatbuilding Company manufactured large, expensive fiberglass sailboats. For a specific model year the marine architect would design the hull and running gear and build a small model; this was completed one year in advance. About nine months before production was to begin, a set of fiberglass molds was prepared and a single prototype was cast. After testing the prototype the molds were adjusted and production begun. The production volume per model averaged between 30 and 60 units depending on customer acceptance.

Before continuing his work on the new project of building precast fiber-glass swimming pools, Mr. Trevor attended an executive seminar that focused on methods of controlling production labor. Mr. Clark Brando presented many new ideas to Mr. Trevor. Most interesting was the concept of the learning curve.

Mr. Trevor felt certain that the learning curve described by Mr. Brando could account for the problems he was having with the labor efficiency variance. In a private conversation with Mr. Brando he learned that a 69% curve would be reasonable in the boatbuilding industry. However, Mr. Brando questioned the 69% curve in the swimming pool project. Mr. Trevor determined to take the concept of the learning curve into account in planning the swimming pool project. He felt that if the learning curve was empirically shown here, he would then apply it to the boatbuilding as well. Early in 19X7 the first pool was completed at the following costs.

Material	$ 500
Direct labor (240 hours @ $4.00)	$ 960
Variable overhead (applied at $1.00 per direct labor hour)	$ 240
Forms (molds and forms that have a 100-pool life)	$1,000

Mr. Trevor plans to produce a total of 16 pools during the year. Research by the trade association for the swimming pool industry found a learning curve of 75% for the production of fiberglass pools.

REQUIRED:

A. Which of the costs for the first pool are subject to an improvement in learning?

B. What is the cost of the second pool produced?

C. Calculate the total cost of pools 9 through 16.

D. How would you set standard costs for the pool division?

E. How could the learning curve account for the problems in the labor efficiency variance?

6-20 (Appendix: Learning Curves). The Kelly Company plans to manufacture a product called Electrocal, which requires a substantial amount of direct labor on each unit. Based on the company's experience with other products that required similar amounts of direct labor, management believes that there is a learning factor in the production process used to manufacture Electrocal.

Each unit of Electrocal requires 50 square feet of direct material at a cost of $30 per square foot for a total material cost of $1,500. The standard direct labor rate is $25 per direct labor hour. Variable manufacturing overhead is assigned to products at a rate of $40 per direct labor hour. The company adds a markup of 30% on variable manufacturing cost in determining an initial bid price for all products.

Data on the production of the first two lots (16 units) of Electrocal is as follows:

1. The first lot of eight units required a total of 3,200 direct labor hours.
2. The second lot of eight units required a total of 2,240 direct labor hours.

Based on prior production experience, Kelly anticipates that there will be no significant improvement in production time after the first 32 units. Therefore, a standard for direct labor hours will be established based on the average hours per unit for units 17–32.

REQUIRED:

A. What is the basic premise of the learning curve?
B. Based on the data presented for the first 16 units, what learning rate appears to be applicable to the direct labor required to produce Electrocal? Support your answer with appropriate calculations.
C. Calculate the standard for direct labor hours that Kelly Company should establish for each unit of Electrocal.
D. After the first 32 units have been manufactured, Kelly Company was asked to submit a bid on an additional 96 units. What price should Kelly bid on this order of 96 units? Explain your answer.
E. Knowledge of the learning-curve phenomenon can be a valuable management tool. Explain how management can apply the learning curve in the planning and controlling of business operations.

(CMA adapted)

6-21 *(Case Problem on Dual Standards).* Harden Company has experienced increased production costs. The primary area of concern identified by management is direct labor. The company is considering adopting a standard cost system to help control labor and other costs. Useful historical data are not available because detailed production records have not been maintained.

Harden Company has retained Finch & Associates, an engineering consulting firm, to establish labor standards. After a complete study of the work process, the engineers recommended a labor standard of one unit of production every 30 minutes or 16 units per day for each worker. Finch further advised that Harden's wage rates were below the prevailing rate of $3.00 per hour.

Harden's production vice-president thought that this labor standard was too tight and the employees would be unable to attain it. From his experience with the labor force, he believed a labor standard of 40 minutes per unit or 12 units per day for each worker would be more reasonable.

The president of Harden Company believed the standard should be set at a high level to motivate the workers, but he also recognized the standard should be set at a level to provide adequate information for control and reasonable cost comparisons. After much discussion, management decided to use a dual standard. The labor standard recommended by the engineering firm of one unit every 30 minutes would be employed in the plant as a motivation device, and a cost standard of 40 minutes per unit would be used in reporting. Management also concluded that the workers would not be informed of the cost standard used for reporting purposes. The production vice-president conducted several sessions prior to implementation in the plant, informing the workers of the new standard cost system and answering questions. The new standards were not related to incentive pay but were introduced at the time wages were increased to $3.00 per hour.

The new standard cost system was implemented on January 1, 19X4. At the end of six months of operation, the following statistics on labor performance were presented to top management. (**U** designates an unfavorable variance; **F**, a favorable variance.)

	January	February	March	April	May	June
Production (units)	5,100	5,000	4,700	4,500	4,300	4,400
Direct labor hours	3,000	2,900	2,900	3,000	3,000	3,100
Variance from labor standard	$1,350 **U**	$1,200 **U**	$1,650 **U**	$2,250 **U**	$2,250 **U**	$2,700 **U**
Variance from cost standard	$1,200 **F**	$1,300 **F**	$ 700 **F**	$ 0	$ 400 **U**	$ 500 **U**

Raw material quality, labor mix, and plant facilities and conditions have not changed to any great extent during the six-month period.

REQUIRED:

A. Discuss the impact of different types of standards on motivation, and specifically discuss the effect on motivation in Harden Company's plant of adopting the labor standard recommended by the engineering firm.

B. Evaluate Harden Company's decision to employ dual standards in its standard cost system.

(CMA adapted)

6-22 *(Comprehensive Standard Variable Cost Problem).* Mr. Beal, the president of Beal Boats, a producer of small fiberglass boats, has asked you for assistance. Mr. Beal described his concern in the following conversation.

> When my daughter Sally was home last month she made a study of our costs and prepared the profit chart in Exhibit 1. She said that this chart shows what my profit should be at different levels of sales. I think she has done a great job; from this chart I can tell what my profits ought to be if we sell more boats or lose an order. She also suggested that my bookkeeper prepare a new kind of income statement that would agree with the chart. It has something to do with expensing fixed overhead costs rather than putting them in the inventory like we have been doing. Today my bookkeeper gave the new income statement for March (Exhibit 2), and the profit is about one-third of what the profit chart says it ought

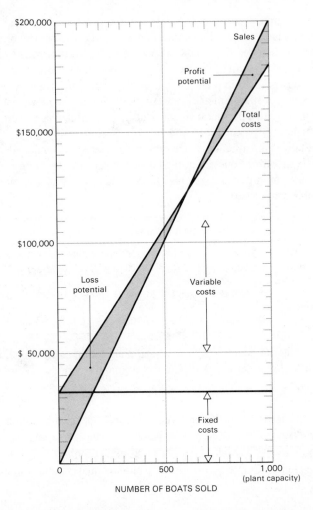

EXHIBIT 1

to be. I know that we cut the price on one special order, but that should account for only about $2,000. We got a good buy on some substandard material, but the supplier's salesperson said it would take only a little more material and a little more labor to use the substandard material. He assured me that we would save money on the deal. I haven't checked with the factory manager yet, but the sales manager assures me that he spent about what he should have.

Sally won't be home for a couple of months, and I can't wait that long to find out what is wrong. Can you tell me if something is wrong with the income statement or the profit chart? Here's a copy of Sally's notes on how the profit chart was prepared (Exhibit 3). Oh yeah, it's our policy to maintain no inventory of Work-in-Process or Finished Goods.''

REQUIRED:

Prepare a report showing why profits are not as large as they should be.

BEAL'S BOATS
ACTUAL INCOME STATEMENT
(Variable costing format)
Month of March

Sales (1,000 boats)		$198,000
Variable costs:		
Raw material purchased	$52,640	
Less: Ending inventory	2,000	
Cost of raw materials used	$50,640	
Direct labor	61,200	
Variable overhead	24,000	
Selling commissions	19,800	155,640
Contribution margin		$ 42,360
Fixed costs:		
Overhead	$23,000	
Selling and administration	13,500	36,500
Income		$ 5,860

Additional data:

Boats produced	1,000
Boats sold	1,000, regular selling price $200
Direct labor	12,000 labor hours

Materials	Purchases	Beginning Inventory	Ending Inventory
Compound R	70,000 pounds @ $.50	0	4,000 pounds
Finish	980 gallons @ $18	0	0

EXHIBIT 2

Dear Pop:

As you know, two materials are required to produce the boat, 60 pounds of Compound R and 1 gallon of finish. The regular market prices are $.60 per pound and $18.00 per gallon, respectively. On the average, a boat should be built and finished in 10 hours of direct labor with an average wage rate of $5.00 per hour. Variable overhead is directly related to direct labor hours.

A sales commission of 10% of sales is paid to the sales force. A month of high actvity and a month of low activity were selected to develop the cost behavior patterns in the profit chart. The particular months were chosen because everyone agreed that costs were under control in those months. Cost data for the two months were

	Month of Low Activity	Month of High Activity
Number of units sold	600	1,000
Number of units produced	600	1,000
Overhead	$34,000	$44,000
Selling and administrative expenses (excluding sales commissions)	$13,000	$13,000

Love,
Sal

EXHIBIT 3

part **3**

ABSORPTION COSTING SYSTEMS AND COST ALLOCATIONS

chapter **7**

OVERHEAD AND ABSORPTION COSTING

As stated in Chapter 4, there are two principal systems of product costing—absorption and variable. The operational difference between these two systems is in the handling of fixed production costs. Variable costing excludes fixed overhead from the product costs, while absorption costing includes it. In general, management accountants believe the variable costing data are useful for management planning and control. At the same time, absorption costing, according to Generally Accepted Accounting Principles, is required for external financial reports.

This difference in preferred data presentations between management and financial accounting can be cumbersome. Because of the pervasive requirements of financial reporting, many firms do not use variable costing; rather, they use absorption costing both internally and externally. These firms are foregoing some of the benefits of variable costing in planning and control while simultaneously enjoying ease in external reporting. Other firms seek the benefits of using variable costing for internal reporting but must then incur the cost of converting to absorption costing for external reports.

This book focuses on management planning and control, so variable costing was used in Chapters 5 and 6 illustrations. This, in effect, is only one-half the picture; in this chapter we will complete the picture. This chapter on absorption costing has three sections. The first section examines some issues underlying the development of an overhead rate that includes fixed costs. The second section illustrates a standard absorption costing system and compares it with a variable costing system. The final section shows how a firm could convert a variable costing format to an absorption costing format for external reports.

ISSUES IN DEVELOPING OVERHEAD RATES

An overhead rate is an apportionment of the indirect costs of production to the products using an activity measure. There are three issues important to the development of an absorption costing overhead rate: (1) What is an acceptable *measure* of production activity? (2) When should overhead be applied to the products? And (3) What is an acceptable *level* of the production activity?

PRODUCTION BASES FOR OVERHEAD RATES

The production base is a common denominator—a way to equate all of the units produced. If a firm produces only one product, such as a 12-ounce bottle of soft drink, the overhead rate can be determined quite simply by dividing the dollars of overhead by the number of bottles produced. This automatically results in an overhead cost per unit of product.

In firms where different items are produced, the production base must serve as a common denominator among products. Where the firm produces dissimilar products, the validity of the overhead rate rests upon the determination of a cause-and-effect relationship between the dollars spent for overhead and the base used to allocate the dollars to the product.

Firms can be separated into two categories: those that are highly automated and those that are labor intensive. In highly automated firms the overhead costs are composed primarily of equipment costs such as power, maintenance, and depreciation charges. A measure of the time the machines are used to produce the product is a good basis for allocating overhead. These firms would typically use some form of machine-hour basis for applying overhead.

In firms that are labor intensive the majority of overhead dollars is composed of labor-oriented costs. In labor-oriented firms, the best common denominator among products is the amount of labor time or labor dollars spent on each product. The overhead rate in these firms is based upon direct labor hours or direct labor dollars. Of these, direct labor hours are more widely used. Most overhead costs are more closely related to the time workers spend in production than to the amount of pay workers receive. Only if labor wage rates are the same throughout the production process, or if higher-paid skills require proportionately less time, will the direct labor hour basis and the direct labor dollar basis of applying overhead yield approximately the same results. When this is not the case, the overhead rate based upon direct labor hours will probably describe more precisely a cause-and-effect relationship.

Where firms have dissimilar departments, they may use departmental rates. One department could use an overhead rate with a labor base while another department uses an overhead rate with a machine-hour basis. This will be discussed in the next chapter.

TIMING OF OVERHEAD RATES

The second question involves the problem of *when* the overhead rate is calculated and when the overhead costs are applied to the product. A **historical overhead rate** is applied to Work-in-Process *after* the production period is completed. The historical overhead rate is determined by dividing the actual overhead costs by the actual measure of production volume. Because all actual overhead costs are charged to Work-in-Process Inventory with historical rates, there will be no under- or overapplied overhead.

The use of a historical overhead rate has distinct drawbacks. First, the unit costs of production cannot be calculated on a timely basis because overhead cannot be charged to Work-in-Process Inventory until all production for the period has been completed and measured. Second, there are problems of seasonality. Some of the overhead costs are fixed and do not change with changes in volume. Thus, when there are seasonal fluctuations in volume, the overhead rate will fluctuate because a fixed cost is constant in total dollar amount but varies per unit as the volume changes. Third, with a historical overhead rate, it is often difficult to ensure that overhead costs are being incurred efficiently because of a lack of a comparison benchmark.

To overcome the deficiencies in the historical overhead rate, many firms adopt a **predetermined overhead rate.** Before the beginning of the accounting period the firm estimates the overhead and the volume base and computes a predetermined rate by dividing the estimated dollars of overhead by the estimated production base.

LEVELS OF PRODUCTION ACTIVITY

The product costs via the fixed overhead rate can be affected by the choice of the predetermined activity level for the denominator. The higher the proportion of fixed costs to variable costs in overhead, the more sensitive the choice of the denominator level. It is the presence of fixed costs interacting with production output that creates fluctuations in the total overhead rate, as shown below.

As the volume measure of production output increases or decreases, the fixed overhead rate will change. Remember from Chapter 2 that a fixed cost per unit varies inversely to increases in volume. To show this, let's calculate a fixed overhead rate for the firm that has a monthly flexible overhead budget of $y_c = \$36,000 + \$1.00(x)$, where x represents direct labor hours. The overhead rate with absorption costing would be computed as shown in the accompanying tabulation.

	Period 1	Period 2	Period 3
Production output in terms of direct labor hours	18,000	24,000	12,000
Overhead:			
Fixed costs	$36,000	$36,000	$36,000
Variable costs	18,000	24,000	12,000
Total overhead costs	$54,000	$60,000	$48,000
Overhead rate per direct labor hour			
Fixed overhead rate	$ 2.00	$ 1.50	$ 3.00
Variable overhead rate	1.00	1.00	1.00
Total overhead rate	$ 3.00	$ 2.50	$ 4.00

This illustration shows that the total overhead rate fluctuates because of the interaction of production volume with fixed costs. The variable rate of $1.00 per hour remains constant during the three periods. With variable costing the variable overhead rate applied to the products would be $1.00 in each period; with absorption costing the overhead rate would be either $3.00, $2.50, or $4.00, depending on the period. The $3.00, $2.50, or $4.00 could be described as an *average* total overhead cost per unit of production during the time period.

The production output depends on available plant volume and customer demand for the product. Using either plant volume or sales demands as their starting point, accountants typically use one of three possible volume philosophies.

1. *Practical capacity*—This capacity is the maximum output capability of the existing plant over a long period of time. As the maximum capacity that can be achieved over an extended period of time, given the existing management policies of workweek, shifts, and employee mix, the fixed overhead rate will be the minimum unit cost that the firm can achieve. In the language of the standard coster, it would be an *ideal* standard.

2. *Average or normal volume*—This volume is that which is needed to meet average sales expectancies over a relatively long period of time. This estimate allows the averaging of seasonal and some cyclical variations in volume.[1] In the language of the standard coster this would be an *average* standard.

3. *Expected or budgeted volume*—This volume is the planned or anticipated level of activity for the coming accounting period. It corresponds to the *expected* standard.

The predetermined overhead rate overcomes some of the averaging and lack of timeliness problems that result with use of a historical overhead rate. One additional step is necesary to make it a *standard* overhead rate. The cost estimates used in the numerator must represent what costs should be if the firm adequately controls costs. The flexible budget and the analysis that underlies it are applicable here. A "tight" flexible budget would serve as an excellent tool for estimating standard costs. For the volume estimate, the rate would be a standard rate if the base was a measure of the production activity that *should* be used to achieve the planned output.

STANDARD ABSORPTION COSTING ILLUSTRATED

The following section illustrates standard absorption costing using the Grant Company. The discussion below differs from the presentation in Chapter 6. In this chapter we do *not* use journal entries as a mode of explanation. However, the possible journal entries for the Grant Company using both absorption and variable costing are summarized in Exhibit 7–1 on pages 240–241.

---

[1]Seasonal variations are variations in output or customer demand within a fiscal or calendar year. Cyclical variations are variations in output or customer demand occurring over an economic business cycle.

For purposes of demonstrating standard absorption costing, assume that the Grant Company developed the following standard costs for its single product.

Materials (5 pounds @ $3.00)		$15.00
Direct labor (8 hours @ $5.00)		40.00
Overhead:		
Variable (8 hours @ $2.50)	$20.00	
Fixed (8 hours @ $1.50)	12.00	32.00
Standard cost per unit		$87.00

The Grant Company based the predetermined standard overhead rate on a forecasted normal volume of 1,000 units per month, or 8,000 direct labor hours. Actual data for the month of April were

Actual units completed and transferred	1,000 units
Beginning inventory of Work-in-Process	None
Beginning inventory of Finished Goods	None
Ending inventory of Work-in-Process 50% complete as to materials and conversion costs	200 units
Material purchases (5,700 pounds)	$16,530
Material issues	5,600 pounds
Direct labor (9,000 hours)	$46,800
Variable overhead	$21,000
Fixed overhead	$11,500
Fixed selling expenses	$ 7,500
Variable selling expenses	$ 9,500
Administrative expenses	$10,000
Sales (950 units)	$130 per unit

The first step in the solution is to determine the equivalent units manufactured during the accounting period. These were

	Materials	Labor and Overhead
Transferred out	1,000	1,000
Final inventory:		
Materials (200 × 50%)	100	
Labor and overhead (200 × 50%)		100
Equivalent units	1,100	1,100

In this particular instance both materials and conversion costs had the same equivalent units.

MATERIALS, LABOR, AND VARIABLE OVERHEAD

There are no accounting differences between absorption and variable costing, nor differences in the determination of variances for materials, labor, and variable overhead. However, as a method of review, the calculation of these variances is presented below.

MATERIALS PRICE VARIANCE

The Materials Price Variance is $570 favorable because the actual price of $2.90 is less than the standard price of $3.00. This is determined by taking the difference between the standard price per unit of raw materials and the actual price per unit of raw materials times the actual quantity purchased:

$$\$570 \textbf{ F} = [\$3.00 - (\$16,530 \div 5,700)] \times 5,700$$

MATERIAL QUANTITY VARIANCE

The Material Quantity Variance is $300 unfavorable because more materials were actually used than the standard cost system allowed. This is determined as the difference between the standard quantity allowed (1,100 × 5) and the actual quantity issued (5,600) times the standard price per unit ($3.00).

$$\$300 \textbf{ U} = [(1,100 \times 5) - 5,600] \times \$3.00$$

LABOR PRICE (RATE) VARIANCE

The Labor Price Variance is $1,800 unfavorable because the actual wage rate per hour exceeded the standard wage rate per hour. This is determined as the difference between the standard wage rate per hour ($5.00) and the actual wage rate per hour ($5.20 = $46,800 ÷ 9,000 hours) times the actual hours used (9,000).

$$\$1,800 \textbf{ U} = [\$5.00 - \$5.20] \times 9,000$$

LABOR EFFICIENCY VARIANCE

The Labor Efficiency Variance is $1,000 unfavorable because the 9,000 actual hours exceeded the standard hours allowed of 8,800. The variance is the difference between the standard hours allowed (1,100 × 8) and the actual hours (9,000) times the standard wage rate per hour ($5.00).

$$\$1,000 \textbf{ U} = [(1,100 \times 8) - 9,000] \times \$5.00$$

Type of Entry	Entries for Standard Absorption Costing		Entries for Standard Variable Costing
Materials Purchases	Raw Materials Inventory Materials Price Variance Accounts Payable	$17,100 $ 570 $ 16,530	Same
Issue of Materials	Work-in-Process Inventory Material Quantity Variance Raw Materials Inventory	$ 16,500 $ 300 $ 16,800	Same
Direct Labor Purchased and Consumed	Work-in-Process Inventory Labor Price Variance Labor Efficiency Variance Accrued Payroll	$ 44,000 $ 1,800 $ 1,000 $ 46,800	Same
Incurrence of Actual Overhead Costs	Variable Overhead Control Fixed Overhead Control Various Accounts	$ 21,000 $ 11,500 $ 32,500	Same
Application of Variable Overhead to Work-in-Process Inventory	Work-in-Process Inventory Variable Overhead Applied	$ 22,000 $ 22,000	Same
Determination and Isolation of Variable Overhead Variances	Variable Overhead Applied Variable Overhead Efficiency Variance Variable Overhead Spending Variance Variable Overhead Control	$ 22,000 $ 500 $ 1,500 $ 21,000	Same
Application of Fixed Overhead to Work-in-Process Inventory	Work-in-Process Inventory Fixed Overhead Applied	$ 13,200 $ 13,200	No Entry

	Standard Variable Costing	Standard Absorption Costing

Completion and Transfer to Finished Goods Inventory	Finished Goods Inventory $ 87,000
	  Work-in-Process Inventory $ 87,000
		Finished Goods Inventory $ 75,000
		  Work-in-Process Inventory $ 75,000

Determination of Fixed Overhead Variances	Fixed Overhead Applied $ 13,200
	  Fixed Overhead Spending Variance $ 500
	  Fixed Overhead Volume Variance $ 1,200
	  Fixed Overhead Control $ 11,500
		No Entry

Sales and Cost of Goods Sold Recognition	Cash $123,500
	  Sales $123,500
	Cost of Goods Sold $ 82,650
	  Finished Goods Inventory $ 82,650
		Cash $123,500
		  Sales $123,500
		Cost of Goods Sold $ 71,250
		  Finished Goods Inventory $ 71,250

Disposition of Variances	Variable Overhead Spending Variance $ 1,500
	Material Price Variance $ 570
	Fixed Overhead Spending Variance $ 500
	Fixed Overhead Volume Variance $ 1,200
	  Cost of Goods Sold $ 170
	  Material Quantity Variance $ 300
	  Labor Price Variance $ 1,800
	  Labor Efficiency Variance $ 1,000
	  Variable Overhead Efficiency Variance $ 500
		Variable Overhead Spending Variance $ 1,500
		Material Price Variance $ 570
		  Cost of Goods Sold $ 1,530
		  Material Quantity Variance $ 300
		  Labor Price Variance $ 1,800
		  Labor Efficiency Variance $ 1,000
		  Variable Overhead Efficiency Variance $ 500

Selling and Administrative Expenses	Fixed Selling Expense Control $ 7,500 Variable Selling Expense Control $ 9,500 Administrative Expense Control $ 10,000 Various Accounts $ 27,000	Same

EXHIBIT 7–2 Comparative journal entries for standard variable costing and standard absorption costing

VARIABLE OVERHEAD SPENDING AND EFFICIENCY VARIANCES

The difference between Variable Overhead Control ($21,000) and Variable Overhead Applied ($22,000) shows that variable overhead is overapplied by $1,000. This overapplied overhead can be separated into two variances: the Variable Overhead Spending Variance and the Variable Overhead Efficiency Variance.

The calculation of the Variable Overhead Spending Variance and the Variable Overhead Efficiency Variance can be summarized into the following schedule.

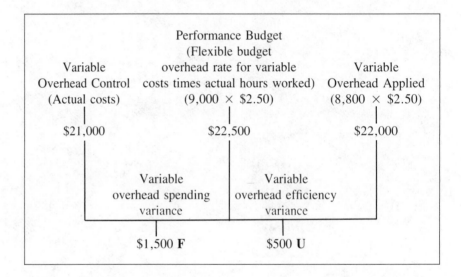

The Variable Overhead Spending Variance is $1,500 favorable. This indicates that actual rate of expenditure was less than the allowed rate of expenditure. The Variable Overhead Efficiency Variance is unfavorable. The actual hours (9,000) exceeded the standard hours allowed (8,800) by 200 hours. For each inefficient hour the company had a planned variable overhead expenditure of $2.50 per hour.

FIXED OVERHEAD APPLICATION TO WORK-IN-PROCESS

The fixed overhead rate for the Grant Company is shown on the standard cost card as $1.50 per direct labor hour. Because the fixed overhead rate is determined by dividing the flexible budget allowance for fixed costs by the predetermined normal volume, it is possible to reconstruct the flexible budget. The normal volume of the Grant Company was 1,000 units per month, and each unit had a standard labor hour allowance of 8 hours; thus the normal hours were 8,000. Further, because the fixed overhead rate was $1.50 this implies that the flexible budget allowance was $12,000. Therefore, the overall flexible budget for overhead is $y_c = \$12,000 + \$2.50$ per direct labor hour.

The amount of fixed overhead applied to Work-in-Process is $13,200. This is determined by multiplying the actual equivalent units produced (1,100) times the standard hours per unit (8 hours) times the fixed overhead rate per direct labor hour ($1.50). Similar to variable overhead, an applied account is used to accumulate the amount of overhead charged to Work-in-Process. (To see the journal entries, refer to Exhibit 7–1.)

DETERMINATION AND ISOLATION OF FIXED OVERHEAD VARIANCES

The actual fixed overhead costs were $11,500; fixed overhead applied was $13,200. Fixed overhead was overapplied by $1,700. The overapplied fixed overhead can be divided into two variances: a spending variance and a volume variance.

First, we can see that the Grant Company originally planned to spend $12,000 for fixed overhead. It actually spent $11,500. The difference of $500 between the planned level of expenditure and the actual level is the fixed **overhead spending variance.** Expressed in formula form:

$$\text{Fixed overhead spending variance} = \left(\begin{array}{c}\text{Fixed costs from}\\\text{standard flexible budget}\end{array}\right) - \left(\begin{array}{c}\text{Actual fixed}\\\text{overhead costs}\end{array}\right)$$

For the Grant Company this variance is:

$$\text{Fixed overhead spending variance} = (\$12,000 - \$11,500) = \$500 \textbf{ F}$$

Second, because the Grant Company actually produced more than the number of units planned, the fixed overhead costs were overapplied. If only the production planned for the period was produced, the Grant Company would have had 8,000 standard direct labor hours. Instead, actual production allowed standard direct labor hours at 8,800, or 800 hours above plan. The 800 extra hours times the fixed overhead application rate of $1.50 per standard direct labor hour resulted in a favorable volume variance of $1,200 (800 × $1.50), as shown in the following computation.

$$\text{Fixed overhead volume variance} = \left(\begin{array}{c}\text{Standard}\\\text{fixed}\\\text{overhead}\\\text{rate}\end{array} \times \begin{array}{c}\text{Standard}\\\text{direct}\\\text{labor}\\\text{hours}\end{array}\right) - \begin{array}{c}\text{Fixed costs}\\\text{from standard}\\\text{flexible budget}\end{array}$$

$$= (\$1.50 \times 8,800) - \$12,000$$

$$= \$13,200 - \$12,000$$

$$= \$1,200 \textbf{ F}$$

The volume variance is favorable because the company applied more fixed costs than it had planned.

The **fixed overhead volume variance** results from the application of fixed overhead costs to the products through a predetermined overhead rate. Unless the planned number of hours is exactly equal to the standard hours allowed during the period, a volume variance will occur. The volume variance is favorable (overabsorbed) if more hours are allowed (and therefore more fixed overhead applied) than planned. If the volume used to apply fixed overhead is less than the standard normal hours, the volume variance is unfavorable (underabsorbed).

The volume variance can be illustrated through the graph in Exhibit 7–2. The Grant Company budgeted fixed overhead at $12,000 per month. Because production was planned at 8,000 standard normal hours for the month, the standard fixed overhead rate was $1.50 ($12,000 ÷ 8,000 hours) per standard direct labor hour.

In our example the $12,000 of fixed overhead costs are assumed to remain constant over the entire production range. At the same time, the fixed overhead costs assume the characteristics of a variable cost when they are applied to Work-in-Process through the overhead rate. The application of fixed overhead is represented by a straight line from the zero cost and activity point through $12,000 of cost at the 8,000-hour level. Short of the 8,000-hour level, an unfavorable volume variance results when an insufficient amount of fixed overhead costs is applied to the products. Beyond the 8,000-hour level, more fixed overhead costs are applied than budgeted.

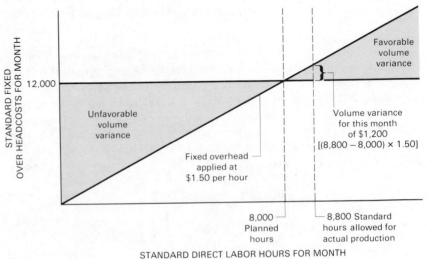

EXHIBIT 7–2   Volume variance

The calculation of the two fixed overhead variances can be summarized into the following schedule.

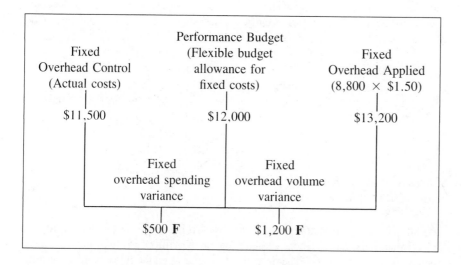

COMPLETION AND TRANSFER TO FINISHED GOODS INVENTORY

Under standard absorption costing $87,000 is transferred from Work-in-Process Inventory to the Finished Goods Inventory. The amount of the transfer is determined by multiplying the number of units completed and transferred to Finished Goods Inventory times the standard cost from the standard cost cards (1,000 units × $87).

The final Work-in-Process Inventory consists of the cost of 200 units 50% complete as to materials, direct labor, variable overhead, and fixed overhead. The cost of the ending inventory of $8,700 is composed of the following:

Materials (100 units × $15)	$1,500
Labor (100 units × $40)	4,000
Variable overhead (100 units × $20)	2,000
Fixed overhead (100 units × $12)	1,200
Total Ending Inventory	$8,700

The Work-in-Process Inventory under absorption costing is larger than the Work-in-Process Inventory would be under standard variable costs, because it has absorbed $1,200 of fixed overhead.

SALES AND COST OF GOODS SOLD RECOGNITION

The value of the 950 units sold and transferred from Finished Goods Inventory to Cost of Goods Sold under standard absorption costing is $82,650. Because the Finished Goods Inventory is carried at full standard cost, the transfer to Cost of Goods Sold will be at $87 per unit. The cost of the units transferred under standard absorption costing will exceed the cost under standard variable costing by $11,400, the amount of fixed overhead included in the standard cost.

The cost of the Finished Goods Inventory under standard absorption costing exceeds the cost under standard variable costing by $600 [(50 units × $12.00)], owing to the inclusion of fixed overhead.

A COMPARISON OF STANDARD ABSORPTION AND STANDARD VARIABLE COSTING

As shown by the comparative journal entries in Exhibit 7–1, the accounting for direct materials, direct labor, variable overhead, selling, and administrative expenses would not change. The only difference between the two cost flow systems is that fixed overhead has been applied to the products with absorption costing; of course, this also affects the values of the inventories and the cost of goods sold.

There are three major differences between the income statements under standard absorption costing in Exhibit 7–3 and standard variable costing in Exhibit 7–4. First, under standard absorption costing unadjusted Cost of Goods Sold is $82,650, whereas under standard variable costing it is $71,250. The $11,400 difference is due to the inclusion of fixed costs. Second, the additional variances computed under standard absorption costing, Fixed Overhead Spending Variance and Fixed Overhead Volume Variance, are included in the adjustments to Cost of Goods Sold. Finally, because the fixed overhead costs are included in the product costs under standard absorption costing, they are not shown separately as period costs as under standard variable costing.

The difference in income between standard absorption costing ($14,020 in Exhibit 7–3) and standard variable costing ($12,220 in Exhibit 7–4) is $1,800. This is accounted for by the fixed overhead costs in the ending inventories under standard absorption costing. This is true in this example because there were no beginning inventories. All fixed costs were matched with the revenue of the

THE GRANT COMPANY
ABSORPTION COSTING INCOME STATEMENT
For the Month of April, 19X7

Sales		$123,500
Less Standard cost of goods sold		82,650
Gross margin		$ 40,850
Adjustments for variances:		
Material price variance	$ 570	
Material quantity variance	(300)	
Labor price variance	(1,800)	
Labor efficiency variance	(1,000)	
Variable overhead spending variance	1,500	
Variable overhead efficiency variance	(500)	
Fixed overhead spending variance	500	
Fixed overhead volume variance	1,200	170
Adjusted gross margin		$41,020
Less:		
Fixed selling expenses	$ 7,500	
Variable selling expenses	9,500	
Administrative expenses	10,000	27,000
Income		$ 14,020

EXHIBIT 7–3
Income statement using standard absorption costing

THE GRANT COMPANY
CONTRIBUTION MARGIN INCOME STATEMENT
For the Month of April, 19X7

Sales		$123,500
Less: Standard of variable cost of goods sold		71,250
Standard contribution from production		$ 52,250
Adjustments for variances:		
Material price variance	$ 570	
Material quantity variance	(300)	
Labor price variance	(1,800)	
Labor efficiency variance	(1,000)	
Variable overhead spending variance	1,500	
Variable overhead efficiency variance	(500)	(1,530)
Adjusted contribution margin from production		$ 50,720
Variable selling costs		9,500
Contribution margin from operations		$ 41,220
Less fixed costs:		
Fixed overhead expense	$11,500	
Fixed selling expenses	7,500	
Administrative expenses	10,000	
Total fixed costs		29,000
Income		$ 12,220

EXHIBIT 7–4
Income statement using variable standard costing

period under standard variable costing. These differences can be reconciled as follows:

Work-in-Process Inventory:		
Absorption costing	$8,700	
Variable costing	7,500	$1,200
Finished Goods Inventory:		
Absorption costing	$4,350	
Variable costing	3,750	600
		$1,800

CONVERSION FROM VARIABLE TO ABSORPTION COSTING

When a firm uses variable costing internally it is necessary for external reporting purposes to convert the financial statements to absorption costing by removing the fixed overhead costs from the variable costing income statement and apportioning them between the inventories and cost of goods sold. The accounting records do not have to be changed; the ledger accounts and job cost sheets can remain on variable costing. The conversion involves restating the inventories and cost of goods sold amounts only on the financial statements prepared for creditors, stockholders, and other external users.

In this chapter we have one example to demonstrate the principles of the conversion process. There are two other examples in the Appendix. One shows the conversion of the historical job cost system of the Roving Jack Company, the illustration in Chapter 5. The other example shows the conversion of a standard cost system using the Forddon Company illustration from Chapter 6.

The conversion from variable to absorption costing requires that the Cost of Goods Sold and the inventories of Work-in-Process and Finished Goods be adjusted to include the fixed costs. To illustrate this, assume that the Polk Company had the variable costing income statement shown in Exhibit 7–5. Also assume that the accountant determined, from last year's conversion data and this year's fixed overhead rate, that the following fixed costs were applicable to the inventories.

	Beginning Inventory	Ending Inventory
Work-in-Process	$15	$20
Finished Goods	$30	$40

Using these data, the recognition of the fixed costs can be accomplished in a schedule as shown in Exhibit 7–6.

POLK COMPANY
CONTRIBUTION MARGIN INCOME STATEMENT

Sales (100 units)			$2,000
Variable cost of sales:			
Work-in-Process Beginning Inventory		$ 200	
Current production costs:			
Materials	$400		
Labor	700		
Variable overhead	500	1,600	
Subtotal		$1,800	
Work-in-Process Ending Inventory		300	
Cost of Goods Manufactured		$1,500	
Finished Goods Beginning Inventory		500	
Cost of Goods available for sale		$2,000	
Finished Goods ending inventory		600	
Variable Cost of Goods Sold			1,400
Contribution margin from production			$ 600
Less: Variable selling expenses			100
Contribution margin from operations			$ 500
Less: Fixed costs:			
Overhead		$ 300	
Selling expenses		150	450
Income			$ 50

EXHIBIT 7–5
Polk Company income statement using variable costing

Cost of Goods Sold under variable costing		$1,400
Add: Fixed costs of prior period applicable to beginning inventories of:		
Work-in-Process	$15	
Finished Goods	30	45
Add: Fixed costs of production for current accounting period		300
Subtotal		$1,745
Less: Fixed costs of current period applicable to ending inventories of:		
Work-in-Process	$20	
Finished Goods	40	60
Cost of Goods Sold under absorption costing		$1,685

EXHIBIT 7–6
Conversion from variable to absorption costing for the Polk Company

The adjusted cost of goods of $1,685 can then be used to prepare an absorption osting income statement. An abbreviated statements would be as follows:

POLK COMPANY
INCOME STATEMENT UNDER ABSORPTION COSTING

Sales (100 units)		$2,000
Cost of Goods Sold (absorption)		1,685
Gross margin		$ 315
Less selling expenses:		
Variable	$100	
Fixed	150	250
Income		$ 65

From this example we can see that the absorption costing income is $15 greater than the variable costing income. This is because using absorption costing the ending inventories were valued at $15 more ($60 − $45). This $15, a period cost in variable costing, is a product cost in absorption costing.

SUMMARY

The overhead rate, overhead dollars divided by some measure of production activity, is the accountant's method of allocating overhead costs to the product. The application of overhead to products requires the accountant to select a measure such as units of output, machine hours, direct labor hours, or direct labor dollars, that best describes a cause-and-effect relationship between the overhead cost and the production activity.

There are two types of overhead rates. The first is a historical overhead rate, where actual overhead cost is applied to the Work-in-Process Inventory after the production for the period is completed. There is no under- or over-applied overhead with historical overhead rates because actual overhead is applied using an actual activity measure. The second is a predetermined overhead rate that requires the accountant to estimate both overhead costs and production output before actual production begins.

The selection of the predetermined overhead volume measure is important because the fixed costs in overhead will vary per unit of output with changes in output. Overhead rates may be based on three different volume measures: first, practical capacity, the maximum volume sustainable in the long run; second, normal volume, the volume necessary to meet sales demand in the long run; and third, expected or budgeted volume, the volume planned for the coming accounting period.

Standard absorption costing differs from standard variable costing in that the fixed production costs are applied to Work-in-Process. The application of the fixed overhead results in the possibility of a volume variance.

In firms where variable costing is used internally, it is necessary to convert the financial statements to absorption costing.

CONVERSION FROM VARIABLE TO ABSORPTION COSTING

EXAMPLE 1—CONVERSION IN A HISTORICAL COST SYSTEM USING THE CHAPTER 5 ILLUSTRATION

In this section the conversion of the Roving Jack Company's statements from variable to absorption costing is shown. This company was the extended illustration in Chapter 5. The Variable Costing Cost of Goods Sold shown in Exhibit A7–1 was taken from Exhibit 5–5.

The first step in the conversion is to determine the amount of fixed costs from the prior period applicable to the beginning inventories. This would adjust

Cost of Goods Sold under variable costing (including overhead variance)		$11,209
Add: Fixed costs of prior period applicable to beginning inventories of:		
Work-in-Process	$ 585	
Finished Goods	0	585
Add: Fixed costs of production for current accounting period		3,900
Subtotal		$15,694
Less: Fixed cost at current period applicable to ending inventories of:		
Work-in-Process	$1,500	
Finished Goods	1,398	2,898
Cost of Goods Sold under absorption costing (including overhead variance)		$12,796

EXHIBIT A7–1
Conversion from variable to absorption costing for the Roving Jack Company

the beginning inventories to absorption costing. At the beginning of the month the inventories (under variable costing) were

Work-in-Process Inventory:		Total Variable	Direct Labor
	Job	Costs	Hours
	101	$2,820	210
	102	2,137	170
	103	1,585	70
		$6,542	450
Finished Goods Inventory:		None	

To complete the conversion of the beginning inventories the accountant had to refer to September data (not shown in the chapter) to obtain the direct labor hours shown for each job above and the fixed overhead rate for the month of September. Assume that during September actual fixed overhead costs were $4,030 and that 3,100 direct labor hours were worked. A fixed overhead rate of $1.30 per hour ($4,030 ÷ 3,100 hours) is applicable to the beginning inventory under absorption costing. The beginning Work-in-Process Inventory would be increased in the financial statements by $585 (450 hours × $1.30). This makes the beginning inventory value for Work-in-Process Inventory $7,127 ($6,542 + $585). There were no finished units on hand so the remaining fixed overhead costs of September were applicable to September's Cost of Goods Sold.

The second step is to add the current period's fixed costs of production. These costs are to be treated as product costs, not period costs, under absorption costing.

The third step in the conversion is to deduct the fixed costs applicable to the ending inventories, because under absorption costing they are held in the inventories until the product is sold. At the end of the current month of October the Work-in-Process and Finished Goods inventories, under variable costing consisted of

Work-in-Process Inventory	(Job 104)	$10,550
Finished Goods Inventory	(Job 101)	$ 8,470

During October the actual fixed costs were $3,900 and the actual labor hours were 2,600. The fixed overhead rate for the month was $1.50 ($3,900 ÷ 2,600 hours). The hours of direct labor in each inventory and the overhead to be added to each inventory are

Inventory	Direct labor hours	×	Fixed overhead rate	=	Applicable fixed overhead
Work-in-Process (Job 104)	1,000 (October)		$1.50		$1,500
Finished Goods (Job 101)	210 (September)		$1.30		$ 273
	750 (October)		$1.50		1,125
					1,398
Total fixed costs added to ending inventories					$2,898

The ending inventories in the financial statements for October must be increased by $2,898.

Income under absorption costing is $2,313 larger than it is under variable costing. This difference in income results from increasing the beginning inventory (and therefore increasing cost of goods sold) by $585 and increasing the ending inventory (and therefore decreasing cost of goods sold) by $2,898.

EXAMPLE 2—CONVERSION IN A STANDARD COST SYSTEM USING THE CHAPTER 6 ILLUSTRATION

In this section we will illustrate the conversion of a standard variable costing system to a standard absorption costing system. Exhibit A7–2 shows this conversion for the Forddon Furniture Company, the extended example in Chapter 6.

Cost of Goods Sold under variable costing (including all variances)		$82,010
Add: Fixed costs of prior period applicable to beginning inventories:		
Work-in-Process	$ 0	
Finished Goods	0	0
Add: Fixed costs of production for the current accounting period		9,000
Subtotal		$91,010
Less: Fixed costs of current period applicable to ending inventories:		
Work-in-Process	$160	
Finished Goods	900	1,060
Cost of Goods Sold under absorption costing (including all variances)		$89,950

EXHIBIT A7–2
Conversion from standard variable to standard absorption costing for the Forddon Furniture Company

The Cost of Goods Sold at standard variable cost is taken from Exhibit 6–3. In this exhibit the Cost of Goods Sold before standard cost variances was $80,050; the sum of the variances from standard was $1,960 unfavorable. This gives the adjusted variable Cost of Goods Sold of $82,010.

The first step in the conversion is to add any applicable fixed costs from the prior period to the beginning inventory. Because the beginning inventories were zero there are no adjustments.

The second step in the conversion is to add the actual fixed costs of production for the current period. This amount was $9,000, as shown in Exhibit 6–3.

The third step is to deduct the fixed costs associated with the ending inventories of Work-in-Process and Finished Goods. This requires two pieces of data: a fixed overhead rate and the quantity of units, expressed in terms of direct labor hours, in the ending inventories.

In the Forddon illustration the flexible budget for overhead was $y_c = \$9,600 + \$1.50$ per direct labor hour. The planned production volume for the period was 9,600 direct labor hours. The standard fixed overhead rate would be $1.00 per direct labor hour ($9,600 ÷ 9,600 hours). This overhead rate would be used to cost the inventory at standard, not at historical cost.

The actual units in the ending inventories are shown below (see illustration from Chapter 6 for the original data).

Work-in-Process:
    Style 10A (20 equivalent units × 8 hours)   160 hours
Finished Goods:
    Style 10A (50 units × 8 hours)   400
    Style 11A (100 units × 5 hours)   500
Total direct labor hours in ending inventories   1,060 hours

With the fixed overhead rate of $1.00 per hour the adjustment is $1,060. This results in an adjusted Cost of Goods Sold under absorption costing of $89,950 including all standard cost variances.

The income from absorption costing will be $1,060 larger than the income from variable costing. Exhibit 6–3 shows that variable costing income is $22,940; thus absorption costing income would be reported at $24,000.

7-1 *(Predetermined Rates at Different Volume Levels)*. Given:

Production levels (in direct labor hours)	9,000	12,000	6,000
Overhead costs:			
Fixed overhead	$72,000	$ 72,000	$72,000
Variable overhead	27,000	36,000	18,000
Total overhead costs	$99,000	$108,000	$90,000
Overhead rate per direct labor hour:			
Fixed overhead rate	_____	_____	_____
Variable overhead rate	_____	_____	_____
Total overhead rate	_____	_____	_____

REQUIRED:

A. Fill in the blanks above.

B. What is the flexible budget for overhead?

C. If actual production is 10,000 direct labor hours, how much overhead would be applied, assuming they base their predetermined overhead rate on 12,000 direct labor hours?

7-2 *(Various Production Bases for Overhead Rates)*. The Blue Candle Company is attempting to develop overhead rates for the coming year. The accountant has estimated the following operating levels in the plant (in direct labor hours).

Practical capacity	60,000
Average or normal capacity	40,000
Expected (budgeted) capacity	30,000

Assume that the estimated overhead costs for the coming year are

Fixed overhead	$120,000
Variable overhead	$2.00 per direct labor hour

REQUIRED:

A. Determine the overhead rates for each potential level of operations.

B. Discuss the implications of each activity level. What activity level would you choose? Why?

7-3   *(Calculation of Overhead Rates).* The Masenholder Company produces a line of sterling-silver napkin rings. At the beginning of the year the accountant had developed the following data for use in predetermining the overhead rate.

Fixed overhead	$54,000
Variable overhead	$36,000
Budgeted activity level	12,000 direct labor hours

By the end of the year the following information was available.

Actual fixed overhead	$58,500
Actual variable overhead	$32,000
Actual activity level	12,000 direct labor hours
Standard hours allowed	10,500 direct labor hours

REQUIRED:

A. Determine the predetermined standard overhead rate.

B. Using the predetermined standard overhead rate from part *A*, determine the overhead applied. Was the company over- or underapplied? By how much?

C. Calculate the actual (historical) overhead rate.

7-4   *(Computing Labor and Overhead Variances with Absorption Costing).* Joan Waters operates a small business with wide seasonal fluctuations. Budgeted overhead is $12,000 per month plus $2.00 per direct labor hour at the normal volume of 1,000 units. The standard labor cost per unit of production is 3 hours at $5.00 per hour. During June, 800 units were produced, which required 2,500 direct labor hours at a total labor cost of $12,000. Actual overhead amounted to $17,200, of which $5,500 was variable.

REQUIRED:

Compute the following variances:

A. Labor efficiency variance.

B. Variable overhead efficiency variance.

C. Variable overhead spending variance.

D. Fixed overhead spending variance.

E. Fixed overhead volume variance.

7-5   *(Determine Overhead Variances).* The following data are available for the Auburn Company.

Budgeted fixed overhead costs	$7,800
Actual fixed overhead incurred	$8,000
Normal volume	12,000 hours
Standard hours allowed	13,000 hours
Actual hours worked	12,500 hours

REQUIRED:

Using the above data, calculate

A. The fixed overhead rate per hour.

B. Fixed overhead applied to Work-in-Process.

C. Fixed overhead over- or underapplied.

D. Fixed overhead spending variance.

E. Fixed overhead volume variance.

7-6   *(Overhead Data from Incomplete Data).* The Hartley Company had the following data.

Actual total overhead incurred	$134,000
Flexible budget for overhead	$90,000 + $.60 (*DLH*)
Total overhead rate (fixed and variable)	$2.10
Spending variance	$8,000 **U**
Volume variance	$7,500 **F**

REQUIRED:

Using the above data, calculate the following:

A. The normal (denominator) volume.

B. The actual labor hours used.

C. The standard hours allowed for the actual production.

D. The overhead efficiency variance.

7-7   *(Calculation of Overhead Variances).* The Jordan Company had the following data from its standard cost system.

Budgeted fixed overhead	$75,000
Fixed overhead rate per hour	$3
Variable overhead rate per hour	$5
Actual units produced *times* standard hours per unit	23,500
Actual fixed overhead incurred	$76,000
Actual variable overhead incurred	$120,000
Actual labor hours	24,000

REQUIRED:

Using the above data, determine the following:

A. Factory overhead applied, assuming absorption costing.

B. The fixed overhead spending variance.

C. The variable overhead spending variance.

D. The fixed overhead volume variance.

E. The variable overhead efficiency variance.

7-8 *(Overhead Rates in a Job Cost System)*. The Albert Company uses a job cost system to determine the cost of its products. A predetermined overhead rate is used to apply overhead to individual jobs. The rate is based on direct labor hours in Department A and machine hours in Department B. The following production and cost estimates were made at the start of the year.

	Department A	Department B
Direct materials	$300,000	$100,000
Direct labor	$480,000	$ 80,000
Variable overhead	$240,000	$200,000
Fixed overhead	$240,000	$160,000
Machine hours	40,000	80,000
Direct labor hours	160,000	10,000

REQUIRED:

A. What are the predetermined overhead rates for both Departments A and B under absorption costing?

B. Assume that costs and production data for Job 19 were as follows:

	Department A	Department B
Direct materials	$30	$20
Direct labor	$40	$15
Direct labor hours	14	4
Machine hours	2	5

How much overhead should be charged to Job 19 under absorption costing?

C. What is the total cost for Job 19? What is the variable cost for Job 19?

7-9 *(Overhead Variances for Performance Assessment)*. The factory manager of the Bell Chimes Company was severely criticized by the vice-president of operations for overspending at a time when sales (and production) had dropped unexpectedly. The vice-president had studied the cost reports of every responsibility center for excessive costs. In the factory cost report he found the following data:

	Actual	Budget	Variance
OVERHEAD COSTS September 19X6			
Direct labor hours	24,000	30,000	6,000
Actual overhead	$80,000	$90,000	$10,000 **F**
Overhead applied	72,000	90,000	18,000 **U**
Underapplied overhead	$ 8,000	0	$ 8,000 **U**

The factory manager was confused. Labor hours were exactly at standard, and he was certain that he had controlled the overhead costs to the best of his ability. He reviewed the previous cost reports and noticed that the budgeted amounts had been the same since January 1, 19X6. He came to you for assistance.

You found that the predetermined overhead rate would have been $4 if the expected level of production for the year had been 240,000 hours.

REQUIRED:

A. Compute the overhead variances for September 19X6.

B. Prepare a report to the vice-president of operations explaining the cause of the "overspending." Explain fully, using your analysis from part A.

7-10 *(Predetermined Overhead Rates).* The Raintree Manufacturing Company uses a standard absorption costing system. Overhead is applied on a machine-hour basis in Department A and a direct labor hour basis in Department B. The firm made the following projections at the beginning of the year.

	Department A	Department B
Direct labor cost	$ 2,400	$40,000
Fixed overhead	$30,000	$12,500
Variable overhead	$ 6,000	$25,000
Standard direct labor hours	100	5,000
Standard machine hours	250	1,250

REQUIRED:

A. Compute the standard overhead rate for each department.

B. The cost sheet for Job 125 shows costs and activity levels as follows:

	Department A	Department B
Standard direct materials	$18	$32
Standard direct labor	$24	$16
Direct labor hours allowed	1	2
Machine hours allowed	2	1

1. How much overhead should be applied to Job 125?

2. What is the total cost of Job 125?

C. At the end of the year the actual data were as follows:

	Department A	Department B
Direct labor cost	$ 3,200	$42,000
Fixed overhead	$32,000	$12,000
Variable overhead	$10,000	$24,000
Direct labor hours allowed	120	4,800
Machine hours allowed	300	1,100

Determine the amount of under- or overapplied overhead by department, and indicate if it was overapplied or underapplied.

7-11 *(Analysis of Overhead Variances—Different Costing Methods).* Hot Air Stove Company estimated the following overhead costs for 19X8.

Variable overhead:	
Indirect labor	$ 4,500
Factory supplies	2,700
Fixed overhead:	
Heat and light	800
Factory depreciation	5,200
Factory administration	8,400
	$21,600

The Hot Air Stove Company planned to produce 600 units using a total of 1,800 standard direct labor hours. Cost behavior studies have shown that changes in variable overhead costs relate closely to changes in direct labor hours.

REQUIRED:

A. Calculate the standard overhead rate based upon direct labor hours for
  1. Standard absorption costing.
  2. Standard variable costing.

B. Assume that actual production for 19X3 was 500 units requiring 1,600 hours. Calculate overhead costs applied under
  1. Standard absorption costing.
  2. Standard variable costing.

C. Assume that actual production in 19X3 was 500 units requiring 1,600 hours and actual overhead costs were

Indirect labor	$4,000
Factory supplies	$2,200
Heat and light	$ 850
Factory depreciation	$5,200
Factory administration	$8,500

  1. Determine the amount of under- or overapplied overhead under absorption costing.

2. Compute the overhead variances under standard absorption costing and prepare a report to the factory manager indicating how well she controlled her factory overhead costs during 19X3.

3. Compute the variances under standard variable costing and prepare a report to the factory manager indicating how well she controlled her overhead costs during 19X3.

7-12 *(Contrast of Overhead Rates in Absorption and Variable Costing).* The Andrews Company had the following overhead cost and volume experiences:

Month	Direct Labor Hours	Total Overhead Costs
January	10,000	$33,950
February	12,000	$37,350
March	11,000	$35,750
April	11,500	$36,450

The Andrews Company, in developing its standard cost system, planned a volume for May of 11,300 direct labor hours. This volume should have resulted in 2,825 units produced. During May actual production was 2,750 units; these units required 10,800 direct labor hours and a total overhead cost incurred of $34,900, of which $17,200 was fixed.

REQUIRED:

Using the above data determine the following:

A. The flexible budget for overhead using the high-low method.

B. The standard overhead rate assuming variable costing.

C. The standard overhead rate assuming absorption costing.

D. The total overhead applied to Work-in-Process assuming variable costing.

E. The total overhead applied to Work-in-Process assuming absorption costing.

F. The following variances assuming absorption costing:

1. The overhead spending variances.

2. The variable overhead efficiency variance.

3. The fixed overhead volume variance.

7-13 *(Job Costing Using Machine-Hour-Based Overhead Rate).* The Do-Little Company manufactures scratch pads using a standard, absorption job order system. It assigns overhead to the jobs using machine hours allowed as the application base. The standard absorption overhead rate is $10.00 per machine hour, which was based on a flexible budget of $y_c = \$7,800 + \$3.50$ (per machine hour).

The August 1, 19X9 inventories, at standard costs, consisted of the following:

Raw Materials and Supplies	$3,700
Work-in-Process (Job 203)	$1,200
Finished Goods (Job 202)	$4,300

During the month of August the following jobs were in the factory.

Job	Standard Materials	Standard Labor	Actual Machine Hours	Standard Machine Hours Allowed
203	$ 800	$ 500	150	160
204	1,100	1,400	500	480
205	900	1,200	450	460

Overhead costs incurred during August were

Factory maintenance (fixed)	$ 2,600
Factory heat and power (variable)	1,800
Factory supplies (variable)	1,775
Depreciation of equipment (fixed)	5,925
Total overhead costs	$12,100

Job 202 was shipped early in the month; the customer was billed $6,800. Job 203 was shipped late in the month; the customer was billed $5,800. Job 204 was completed and transferred to finished goods but was not sold.

REQUIRED:

A. Prepare a schedule of overhead variances for all of the above data.

B. Determine Cost of Goods Sold and the balances of Finished Goods Inventory and Work-in-Process Inventory.

7-14 *(Development of Overhead Rates).* The North Plains Company has decided to develop a predetermined overhead rate for application of overhead to their products. The company uses a standard absorption costing system. The plant engineer gathered the following production data (in direct labor hours), all of which are within the relevant range.

Plant capacity	36,000
Normal (average) level of production	24,000
Expected level of production for 19X8	20,000
Hours required for one unit of production	10

The cost accountant, in a study of overhead costs, believed that the two most representative volume–cost years were as follows:

	Volume	Overhead Costs
19X4	30,000 direct labor hours	$147,000
19X7	21,000 direct labor hours	$124,500

REQUIRED:

A. Compute the predetermined overhead rate at each of the following levels:

   1. Plant capacity.

   2. Normal (average) level of production.

   3. Expected level of production for 19X8.

B. Assuming that during 19X8 the company produced 2,500 units, worked 26,000 actual hours, and incurred overhead costs of $138,500 (of which $75,000 is fixed), compute the volume variance using each of the overhead rates developed in part A.

C. Using the data in part B, compute the fixed and variable overhead spending variances and the variable overhead efficiency variance.

7-15 *(Comparison of Variable and Absorption Costing).* Pierce Corporation produces medical equipment. During the month only one job was started and was in process (Job 1252). The data pertaining to the month were

Standard direct materials and labor	$40,680
Actual variable overhead incurred	$12,300
Actual fixed overhead incurred	$13,700
Actual administrative and selling expenses	$ 5,250
Standard direct labor hours allowed	3,950

Pierce's flexible budget for factory overhead is $12,000 + $3.00 (per direct labor hour).

REQUIRED:

A. 1. If Pierce uses an absorption costing system and applies overhead to Work-in-Process upon an expected activity level of 4,000 direct labor hours, determine the balance in the account "Work-in-Process—Job 1252" at the end of the month.

   2. If Job 1252 was finished during the month and was sold for $74,950, what was the income for the month? Prepare an income statement that explicitly recognizes over- or underapplied overhead.

B. 1. If Pierce uses variable costing, what is the balance in the "Work-in-Process—Job 1252" account at the end of the month, assuming that the job remains unsold and overhead is applied on an expected activity level of 3,000 direct labor hours?

   2. What is the income for the month if Job 1252 was finished during the month and sold for $74,950? Prepare an income statement that explicitly recognizes over- or underapplied overhead.

7-16 *(Comparison of Income Using Alternative Volume Levels)*. The Mossy Company has sales of $500,000 in both May and June (100,000 units at $5.00 per unit). The following production costs apply to each of the two months.

Fixed costs per month $300,000
Variable costs per unit $ 1.10

Production for May was 100,000 units. Production for June was 300,000 units, the output at 100% of practical capacity. The May 1 Finished Goods Inventory was zero.

REQUIRED:

A. Compute the cost of ending inventory at the end of June, assuming that the company uses standard absorption costing to cost the inventory. Also assume that the standard overhead rate is determined on the basis of expected capacity. In the month of May the overhead rate was based on 100,000 units; in the month of June the overhead rate was based on 300,000 units.

B. Compute the unit cost of production during the month of May, assuming that the company used absorption costing with a standard overhead rate based upon "practical" capacity of 300,000 units.

C. Compute the contribution margin of the Mossy Company.

D. Compute the income for the month of May, assuming that the company used variable costing.

E. Compute the income for the month of June, assuming that the company used absorption costing with a "normal" standard overhead rate based upon a normal activity level of 200,000 units.

7-17 *(Variances with Standard Absorption Costing)*. The Old Paint Glue Factory produces a glue product for home use. The company has developed standards for its manufacturing costs. The standard cost card for one case of glue follows.

```
                STANDARD COST CARD
                     ONE CASE
──────────────────────────────────────────────
Material:
   Material H (2 liters @ $4.00)        $ 8.00
   Containers (10 @ $.10)                 1.00
Direct labor (.5 hours @ $8.00)          4.00
Variable overhead (.5 hours @ $2.00)     1.00
Fixed overhead (.5 hours @ $4.00)        2.00
Total standard cost                     $16.00
```

The overhead standards are based on the flexible budget of $y_c = \$16,000 + \$2.00$ per direct labor hour.

At the beginning of the month, inventories consisted of 1,000 liters of raw material H and 400 completed cases in the finished goods. Containers are purchased as they are used. During the month, 6,000 cases of glue were produced and transferred to finished goods. The beginning and ending Work-in-Process inventories are zero.

Transactions for the month are listed below.

1. Purchased the following materials on account:

Material H:	20,000 liters @ $3.80	$76,000
Containers:	62,000 @ $.09	5,580
		$81,580

2. Materials issued to production during the month:

Material H:	13,600 liters
Containers:	62,000 containers

3. Direct labor for the month was 2,800 hours @ $8.10 per hour.

4. Actual overhead incurred during June was $6,500 for variable overhead and $18,000 for fixed overhead.

5. Sales for the month were 6,200 cases at $24 per case.

6. Actual selling and administrative costs were $30,000, of which $8,000 were variable.

REQUIRED:

A. Prepare a schedule of variances for June (assume standard absorption costing).

B. Prepare an income statement.

C. How did actual production compare with the production used to determine the standard overhead rate?

7-18 *(Absorption and Variable Costing and Review of C-V-P).* Flear Company has a maximum productive capacity of 210,000 units per year. Normal volume is 180,000 units per year. Fixed overhead is $360,000 per year, and variable production costs are $11 per unit. Variable selling expenses are $3.00 per unit, and fixed selling expenses are $242,000 per year. The unit sales price is $20.

During 19X1 the company produced 160,000 units and sold 150,000. The beginning inventory consisted of 10,000 units. Cost of the beginning inventory was $130,000 under absorption costing ($11 variable and $2.00 fixed cost per unit) and $110,000 under variable costing ($11 variable cost per unit).

REQUIRED:

A. What is the breakeven point expressed in dollar sales?

B. How many units must be sold to earn an income of $60,000 per year?

C. How many units must be sold to earn an income of 10% on sales?

D. Assuming that the predetermined fixed overhead rate of $2.00 per unit was based upon normal volume, compute the cost of production under absorption costing in 19X1. Compute the volume variance under absorption costing.

E. Compute the cost of production under variable costing in 19X1. Why is there no volume variance under variable costing?

F. Assuming that the volume variance under absorption costing is added to Cost of Goods Sold, prepare income statements for 19X1 under

1. Absorption costing.
2. Variable costing.

G. Briefly account for the difference in income between the two income statements.

(CPA adapted)

7-19 *(Variances with Standard Absorption Costing)*. The Terry Company manufactures a commercial solvent that is used for industrial maintenance. This solvent is sold by the drum and generally has a stable selling price. Due to a decrease in demand for this product, Terry produced and sold 60,000 drums in December 19X6, which is three-fourths of normal volume.

The following information is available regarding Terry's operations for the month of December:

1. Standard costs per drum of product manufactured were as follows:

Materials:	
10 gallons of raw material	$20
1 empty drum	1
Total materials	$21
Direct labor:	
1 hour	$ 7
Factory overhead (fixed):	
Per direct labor hour	$ 4
Factory overhead (variable):	
Per direct labor hour	$ 6

2. Costs incurred during December 19X6 were as follows:

Raw materials:
  600,000 gallons were purchased at a cost of $1,150,000.
  700,000 gallons were used.
Empty drums:
  85,000 drums were purchased at a cost of $85,000.
  60,000 drums were used.
Direct labor:
  65,000 hours were worked at a cost of $470,000.
Factory overhead:

Depreciation of building and machinery (fixed)	$230,000
Supervision and indirect labor (semivariable)	360,000
Other factory overhead (variable)	76,500
Total factory overhead	$666,500

3. The flexible budget for supervision and indirect labor is $90,000 + $4.50 per direct labor hour.

REQUIRED:

Prepare a schedule of variances for December 19X6, assuming that the firm uses absorption costing. (Hint: develop a spending variance for each cost in overhead; do not develop a variable or fixed spending variance.)

(CPA adapted)

7-20 *(Journal Entries and Income Statement).*

REQUIRED:

Using the data of the Spindle Factory found in problem 6-15, prepare all journal entries and an income statement, assuming they use standard absorption costing.

7-21 *(Conversion from Variable to Absorption).* The vice-president for sales of Huber Corporation has received the income statement for November 19X9. The statement has been prepared on the variable costing basis and is reproduced below. The firm has just adopted a variable costing system for internal reporting purposes.

HUBER CORPORATION
INCOME STATEMENT
For the Month of November 19X9
($000 omitted)

Sales		$2,400
Less: Variable standard cost of goods sold		1,200
Manufacturing margin		$1,200
Less: Fixed manufacturing costs at budget	$600	
Fixed manufacturing cost spending variance	0	600
Gross margin		$ 600
Less: Fixed selling and administrative costs		400
Income before taxes		$ 200

The controller attached the following notes to the statements.

1. The unit sales price for November averaged $24.
2. The standard unit manufacturing costs for the month were

Variable cost	$12
Fixed cost	4
Total cost	$16

The unit rate for fixed manufacturing costs is the standard overhead rate based upon a normal monthly production of 150,000 units.

3. Production for November was 45,000 units in excess of sales.

4. The inventory at November 30 consisted of 80,000 units.

REQUIRED:

A. The vice president for sales is not comfortable with the variable costing basis and wonders what the income would have been under the absorption cost basis.

1. Present the November income statement on an absorption cost basis.

2. Reconcile and explain the difference between the variable costing and the absorption costing income figures.

B. Explain the features associated with variable costing income measurement that should be attractive to the vice-president for sales.

(CMA adapted)

7-22 *(Journal Entries from Income Statement).* The following income statement is for the Arnold Company for 19X6.

Sales (200,000 units)		$2,000,000
Cost of Goods Sold:		
Materials	$300,000	
Direct labor	400,000	
Factory overhead	600,000	1,300,000
Gross margin at standard		$ 700,000
Less: Standard variances		
Material price and usage variance	$ 12,000 U	
Direct labor rate and efficiency		
variances	18,000 F	
Variable overhead spending	4,000 U	
Variable overhead efficiency	8,000 F	
Fixed overhead budget	7,000 F	
Other underapplied overhead	20,000 U	3,000 U
Adjusted gross margin		$ 697,000
Selling and administrative expenses		600,000
Income before taxes		$ 97,000

Other data include the following:

a. There were no beginning inventories.

b. Fixed overhead is absorbed at $2.00 per unit; normal volume is 250,000 units.

c. The standard direct labor rate is $4.00 per hour.

d. Variable overhead is applied at the rate of $2.00 per direct labor hour.

e. Actual direct labor hours were 116,000.

f. The standard price for materials is $.50 per pound.

g. Material purchases were 800,000 lb at $3,000 over standard price.

h. One-third of the selling and administrative costs were variable selling expenses.

REQUIRED:

A. Prepare all journal entries for the period assuming absorption costing.

B. Prepare a variable costing income statement.

7-23 *(Comprehensive Absorption Costing Flows with Journal Entries).* On January 1, 19X6 the Charleston Company had no beginning inventory of Finished Goods but had the following Work-in-Process Inventory.

Job	Materials	Labor	Variable Overhead	Fixed Overhead	Total
203	$11,800	$12,500	$2,000	$1,500	$27,800
204	$ 500	700	500	400	2,100
Total beginning inventory					$29,900

From its inception the Charleston Company had made a study of its fixed and variable costs at the beginning of each year. The development of the flexible budgets was used in their budgeting process, in the development of their absorption costing overhead rate applied on direct labor hours, and in their cost control. To calculate the overhead rate for product costing, the controller developed the following budgeted costs, based on the estimated volume of 14,000 direct labor hours per month.

Variable:		
Indirect materials	$4,900	
Indirect labor	6,300	
Utilities	4,200	$15,400
Fixed (per month)		
Depreciation	$7,200	
Supervision	5,400	12,600
Total budgeted overhead		$28,000

During January the company incurred the following costs and labor hours that were directly traceable to the jobs:

Job	Materials	Labor	Labor Hours
203	$ 2,300	$ 3,500	750
204	4,900	15,200	3,500
205	5,900	17,200	4,100
206	8,100	24,000	4,300
207	800	2,100	350
January Total	$22,000	$62,000	13,000

Actual overhead costs incurred in January were

Indirect materials	$ 4,700
Indirect labor	6,100
Utilities	4,100
Depreciation	7,200
Supervision	5,600
Total actual overhead	$27,700

During January the factory completed Jobs 203, 204, 205, and 206 and transferred them to finished goods. Jobs 203, 204, and 205 were sold during the month. Job 203 sold for $49,065, Job 204 sold for $39,400, and Job 205 sold for $42,750.

In addition to the production costs, the Charleston Company incurred selling expenses of $17,600. Of these $8,400 were fixed selling costs; the remainder were considered variable costs. (Hint: This is **not** a standard cost system. Overhead is applied on the basis of actual direct hours.

REQUIRED:

A. Using the above data prepare the following journal entries:

  1. The purchase of raw materials. (Assume that the Raw Materials Inventory increased $2,500 in January and that both direct and indirect materials are kept in the Raw Materials Inventory.)
  2. The issue of direct materials to Work-in-Process.
  3. The issue of indirect materials.
  4. The purchase and consumption of labor, both direct and indirect.
  5. The incurrence of other factory overhead.
  6. The application of overhead to Work-in-Process.
  7. The transfer from Work-in-Process Inventory to Finished Goods Inventory.
  8. The Cost of Goods Sold.
  9. The closing of the Factory Overhead Applied and Factory Overhead Control accounts to Over- or Underapplied Overhead.
  10. The incurrence of selling expenses.
  11. The monthly sales.

B. Prepare in good form an income statement.

C. The president of the company was pleased because actual overhead of $27,700 was less than the budgeted overhead of $28,000. Show whether this is a correct or incorrect perception by preparing an overhead cost report using a Performance Budget approach.

D. Determine the ending inventory values for Work-in-Process and Finished Goods by preparing T-accounts of these two accounts.

7-24 *(Cost-Volume-Profit Relationships Under Absorption Costing).*

Background

In mid-April, Mr. Peter Lewis, a product manager of Borden Corporation, returned from a sales convention. As soon as possible, he met with the division controller, Ms. Joanne Scott, to report on a presentation in which the chief financial officer of a competitor strongly recommended the breakeven chart for analyzing product profitability.

Profitability was very much on Mr. Lewis' mind. The profit of his product was lagging behind expectations, and he was considering several alternatives. The address at the convention impressed him that breakeven analysis could possibly help him better understand the effects of these alternatives.

Ms. Scott indicated that she would have a breakeven chart ready for Mr. Lewis' product in a few days.

Breakeven Chart

Upon becoming division controller a year ago, Ms. Scott had extended and refined the absorption or full-cost system for determining the cost of the division's various products.

Under the absorption costing system, selling and administrative expenses were treated as period expenses, that is, viewed as an expense of the period incurred rather than as a cost of the product. All manufacturing costs, both variable and fixed, however, were treated as product costs. As a product is produced, its variable and fixed manufacturing costs follow the product into inventory. When the product is sold, the manufacturing costs leave inventory and become the expense Cost of Goods Sold.

Assigning variable manufacturing costs to the product is a relatively simple matter. Basically, this is done using the variable cost per unit of product. Such information is readily available from engineering specifications for the product, labor time studies, and overhead budgets.

Fixed manufacturing costs create problems of assignment, however, because they remain the same in total over a relatively wide range of output. Thus, the fixed costs per unit vary with the rate of output. In the system installed by Ms. Scott, the fixed manufacturing costs were spread over the product's "normal" capacity and assigned to the product in this way.

To illustrate, the fixed manufacturing overhead ("burden") for Mr. Lewis' product is budgeted at $50,000 a month for the current year. The practical maximum production capacity for the product is 10,000 units a month, and the normal or average monthly capacity that Mr. Lewis would like to attain is 8,000 units a month. Thus, each unit produced is assigned a fixed overhead cost of $6.25 based on normal capacity. If the output of the month is less than the normal of 8,000 units, the fixed manufacturing costs of the idle capacity become the "volume variance." This variance is charged to expense in the month it occurs.

From the product cost and other financial records of the division, Ms. Scott prepared the breakeven chart reproduced as Exhibit 1 for Mr. Lewis.

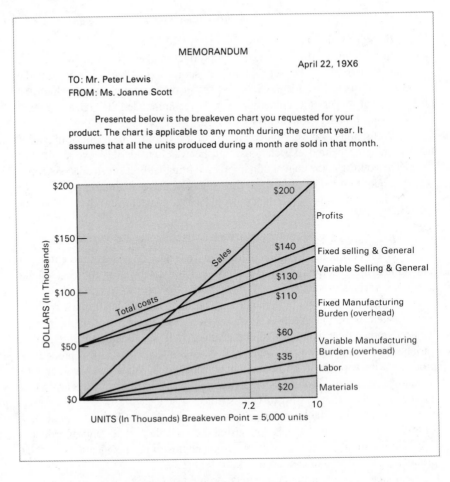

MEMORANDUM

April 22, 19X6

TO: Mr. Peter Lewis
FROM: Ms. Joanne Scott

Presented below is the breakeven chart you requested for your product. The chart is applicable to any month during the current year. It assumes that all the units produced during a month are sold in that month.

EXHIBIT 1

Alternatives Under Consideration

A problem that Mr. Lewis faced was that the product's sales volume was not consistently exceeding 8,000 units in each month. For May, for example, the expected volume was 7,200 units. From Ms. Scott's breakeven chart, Mr. Lewis estimated that the net profit before income taxes would be "around $25,000." Particularly in view of the product's unsatisfactory performance in January–March, and probably again in April, Mr. Lewis felt that this estimate was unsatisfactory.

Mr. Lewis and his associates were seriously studying several alternatives for stimulating profitability.

1. One possibility was to combine aggressively a lower selling price and increased promotion activity in order to stimulate demand. It was estimated that a 4% reduction in price and an increase in promotion expenditures of $3,000 would lead to a 15% increase in volume.

2. In February, Mr. Lewis read an article in a trade journal in which a
    product manager for another firm described a successful experiment
    with a sales compensation scheme designed to stimulate volume.
    Mr. Lewis estimated that a similar scheme structured along the fol-
    lowing lines would increase the volume of his product per month by
    as much as 20%.

    a. For every unit sold in excess of 90% of the volume expected for
        the month, the sales staff would earn additional commissions of
        $5.00. Volume in excess of 110% of the expected monthly vol-
        ume would bring additional commissions of $7.50 per unit.

    b. With the intensified selling effort that should result, product
        advertising could be reduced by $2,000 a month.

3. Mr. Lewis' marketing assistant was skeptical of both the above al-
    ternatives. She stated:

    > I hate to see us cut the price because of our long-standing repu-
    > tation for high quality. These commission plans sound good.
    > However, I fear that once we start this plan, we'll have trouble
    > stopping it even after it loses effectiveness. Our salespeople will
    > become used to these additional commissions, and we'll lose
    > goodwill if later we ever try to eliminate them.

    The assistant proposed instead that advertising expenditures be in-
    creased. She felt that a minimum increase of $8,000 a month would
    be necessary to have any impact. At this level of advertising, she
    thought monthly volume could increase as much as 20%, the same
    as Mr. Lewis estimated under the sales commission plan.

4. The most dramatic alternative was a proposal to add another product
    to the existing line. About a month ago, Mr. Lewis had been ap-
    proached by a Midwest chain of retail stores to manufacture a vari-
    ation of the main product under the chain's private label. The chain
    would guarantee purchase of 4,000 units a month at a price of
    $12.50. The use of lower-grade materials would reduce the mate-
    rial cost by $.50 per unit. Variable selling costs would be avoided
    on the new product, but administrative costs would increase
    $1.00 a unit. As total output approached around 10,000 units, vari-
    able labor and burden costs would rise about $.75 a unit, while
    supervisory costs would increase about $2,000. By renting new
    equipment for $144,000 per year, the monthly productive capacity
    could be increased by about 3,000 units. Mr. Lewis felt certain
    that Borden's home office would approve this expenditure "if it
    could be justified."

Actual Results In May

A combination of procrastination plus the complex nature of the contem-
plated alternatives eventually caused Mr. Lewis to make no changes for the

EXHIBIT 2

> **BORDEN CORPORATION**
> **LEWIS PRODUCT**
> **INCOME STATEMENT FOR MAY**
>
> | | | |
> |---|---:|---:|
> | Sales (7,200 units) | | $144,000 |
> | Expenses: | | |
> | Standard Cost of Goods Sold | | |
> | (@ $12.25 per unit)* | $88,200 | |
> | Unfavorable Manufactured Variances: | | |
> | Volume | 2,500 | |
> | Spending | 2,800 | |
> | Selling and general | 22,000 | 115,500 |
> | Profit before income tax | | $ 28,500 |
>
> *Based on the unit variable manufacturing costs implicit in the breakeven chart on Exhibit 1 and on a unit fixed manufacturing cost of $6.25.

month of May. As previously noted, he therefore expected a volume of 7,200 units and a profit of about $25,000 for the month.

Indeed, the actual sales volume achieved in May was 7,200 units. However, Mr. Lewis was pleasantly surprised to learn from the income statement that the before-tax profit for the month was $28,500. Exhibit 2 contains the report of the results for May. Mr. Lewis asked Ms. Scott to interpret the causes of the unexpected improvement in profits in May.

REQUIRED:

A. What assumptions underlie Ms. Scott's breakeven chart in addition to those she identifies?

B. What is the precise amount of profit indicated by the breakeven chart at 7,200 units? Verify Ms. Scott's calculation of the breakeven point as 5,000 units.

C. With respect to the four alternatives,

1. Estimate the profit and breakeven points under each one for May.

2. Differentiate among the alternatives according to

a. The variables in the product's cost-volume-profit structure that each one emphasizes or manipulates.

b. The relative riskiness of each one in the event of estimation errors.

D. Reconcile the profit found in the answer to part B with the profit for May shown on Exhibit 2. Give the amount of each item that accounts for the difference. Based on this analysis, should Mr. Lewis be encouraged by the results?

7-25 *(Analysis of Defective Standard Cost System).* Edwin Nixon founded Institutional Furniture 15 years ago after a successful career in secondary education where he had responsibility for selecting school equipment. The first few years were difficult, but the company gained experience and finally won three large contracts.

For the 10 years until 19X2, the company maintained a steady growth rate. Then in the spring of 19X2 the company began experiencing a profit decline. One of the first actions management took was to install a standard cost system, which was fully operational by the end of 19X3. The standard cost system, including the updating of the standard cost cards, was manually operated until June 19X4 when the company began using a computer service bureau. The major reason for turning to a computerized system was the ability to update standard cost cards on the 276 product-line items on a day-to-day basis.

The standard cost system adopted was an "Actual-In, Standard-Out" system. Standards are applied to production costs only; the marketing, administrative, and product development costs are accounted for on an actual cost basis. The philosophy of setting the standards can best be described as "expected actual." That is, if all went as planned, the actual costs and standard costs would be identical and all variances would be zero.

During the first two years the standard cost system appeared to operate smoothly. The problem of declining profits seemed under control when the earnings per share increased. The variance balances were becoming progressively larger each period, but the variances were matched against revenue without managerial comment.

When Mr. Nixon received the financial statements for the 12 months ended December 31, 19X4, he was completely shocked. The income statement, shown in Exhibit 1, showed a total unfavorable variance of $164,011. Mr. Nixon was at a loss to understand the problem but because the final net profit figure was satisfactory he took no action except to ask for monthly reports. (See Exhibit 2 for the December 19X5 monthly report.)

After December 31, 19X5, the auditors informed Mr. Nixon that in order to certify the financial statements it would be necessary to reduce the book inventories by $266,669 (see Exhibit 3 for the auditor's schedule). This reduced after-tax profits for the calendar year even further below the $11,380 reported on the unaudited statement (see Exhibit 1). This inventory write-down, coupled with the low net income, resulted in the rejection of a substantial bank loan requested for capital equipment procurement. Mr. Nixon was crestfallen and totally unable to determine the reasons for the loss or its magnitude. As a first step he called for monthly inventories in the future; he also called upon a management consulting firm to (1) identify what had caused the loss and (2) recommend changes in the plant operations and accounting system that would correct the problem.

INSTITUTIONAL FURNITURE
UNAUDITED INCOME STATEMENTS
For the 12 Months Ended December 31

	19X4	19X5
Net sales	$5,370,786	$5,786,581
Standard cost of sales	4,340,552	4,640,218
Standard gross profit	$1,030,234	$1,146,363
Over/Under* Absorbed overhead	255,510	9,133
Gain/Loss* variances	164,011*	226,231*
Gross profit	$1,121,733	$ 929,265
Marketing expense	$ 390,523	$ 435,562
Administrative expense	269,989	342,027
Product development and field installation expenses	152,661	156,416
Total expenses	813,173	934,005
Net operating profit	$ 308,560	$ 4,740*
Other income	31,363	24,662
Net profit before taxes and bonuses	$ 339,923	$ 19,922
Provisions for bonuses	39,355	5,533
Net profit before taxes	$ 300,568	$ 14,589
Federal income tax	144,165	3,209
Net profit after taxes	$ 156,403	$ 11,380

*Indicates loss or unfavorable variance

EXHIBIT 1

The factory is divided into two production areas. In the first area lumber and core are prepared, covered with plastic or birch veneer, and cut to form the parts necessary for assembly. These parts are stored in a large area under the supervision of the wood parts controller, who keeps a cardex quantity record and locator file of all parts in his area. As necessary, parts are withdrawn and taken to the second area where they are assembled, finished, and packed for shipment. All work in the factory is cycled every two weeks, and no work is begun without written orders from production control. For products within the 276-standard product line the production control personnel add a small percentage to the quantity needed for production to ensure an adequate quantity. If spoilage is not as large as the percentage allowed, the overage is stored in the wood parts controller's area.

All raw materials are issued to the Work-in-Process Inventory when purchased; that is, there are no Raw Material Inventory accounts. To facilitate accounting control there are eight raw material subclassifications in the Work-

INSTITUTIONAL FURNITURE
STATEMENT OF GAIN OR LOSS*
CAUSED BY VARIANCES
For Period Ended Dec. 31, 19X5

	Current Month This Year	Year to Date This Year
Purchase variance		
Veneer	$ 60	$ 3,137
Plastic	434	2,465
Hardware	1,079	734*
Miscellaneous	1,019	12,477
Lumber	355	10,693
Core stock and hi gard overlay	51*	8,076
Colorlith	—	—
Subcontract	157*	15,424*
Total gain/loss*	$ 2,739	$ 20,690
Average labor		
Rate variance		
Cutting	$ 23	$ 2,445*
Veneer	231*	2,885*
Plastic	67	280
Machine and sand	549	1,449
Assembly	211*	5,123*
Finishing	317*	7,329*
Packing	139*	3,208*
Modification	670	5,481
Hi gard	—	2,015*
Total gain/loss*	411	15,795*
All other variances		
Veneer	$ 21,311*	$ 23,807*
Plastic	8,091*	4,181*
Hardware	2,678	58,871
Miscellaneous	18,814*	8,931
Lumber	36,163*	51,963*
Core stock and hi gard overlay	49,072*	25,365*
Process labor	62,052*	102,921*
Process overhead	95,542*	189,228*
Finished goods other	13,995	32,101*
Finished goods—burden rate change	8,513	128,060
Colorlith	2,578	2,578
Total gain/loss*	263,281*	231,126*
Total gain or loss* due to variance	$260,131*	$226,231*

*Indicates loss variance

EXHIBIT 2

SMITH AND SMITH, CPAs
SCHEDULE OF INVENTORY REDUCTION
FOR INSTITUTIONAL FURNITURE
Dec. 31, 19X5

	Physical Inventory 12-31-X5	Book Inventory 12-31-X5	Auditor's Adjustment to Books 12-31-X5
Veneer	$ 90,199.99	$ 111,293.20	$ (21,093.21)
Plastic	20,903.01	29,356.15	(8,453.14)
Hardware	134,992.77	137,226.95	(2,234.16)
Glue	3,561.78	9,696.86	(6,135.08)
Finish	6,991.88	13,020.64	(6,028.76)
Packing	23,120.68	33,113.23	(9,992.55)
Lumber	81,598.43	116,252.59	(34,654.16)
Core	192,620.14	244,502.96	(51,882.82)
Labor	90,662.18	148,109.82	(57,447.64)
Overhead	139,619.74	228,110.77	(88,491.03)
Finished goods	816,092.61	798,926.74	17,165.87
Colorlith	50,797.51	48,219.69	2,577.82
	$1,651,160.74	$1,917,829.60	$266,668.86

EXHIBIT 3

in-Process Inventory. All raw materials are costed in the Work-in-Process Inventory at standard cost. Purchases are recorded with the following entry:

Work-in-Process (e.g., lumber)	$AQ \times SP$	
Purchase Variance	$(SP - AP)AQ$	
Accounts Payable		$AQ \times AP$

(AQ is the actual quantity purchased, AP the actual price paid per unit of raw material, and SP the predetermined standard price per unit.)

The purchasing agent, whenever cognizant of a price change, notifies the production control manager, the accounting department, and the industrial design department of the impending price change. The standard costs are then changed in the next available computer run to reflect the new prices.

Lumber, a basic material, is purchased in large quantities from three principal suppliers. Only one supplier provides certified lumber. Daily reports are prepared by the lead cutter showing the board feet of lumber bundles opened and board feet of usable lumber obtained. In past years the yield of "clear or better" lumber has run about 57%. Beginning in 19X5, the company instituted a policy of purchasing "Grade 1 or better" instead of "clear or better" (about $161 per 1,000 bd ft). After the shift the yield dropped to 55–56%.

The yield is the direct responsibility of the lead cutting man. As the boards pass his area all uanacceptable parts are cut out and thrown onto a conveyor belt that leads to the "hog"—a machine that grinds the materials into sawdust. The sawdust is sold at current market prices; the proceeds are not significant. The lumber, after cutting, is then bonded into suitable panel sizes for veneering.

The veneer is held by the company on consignment. The company has entered into an agreement with a broker to store veneer for both themselves and the broker. The veneer is sent directly to Institutional Furniture by the broker's suppliers. When veneer shipments are received the veneer supervisor checks the marked bundles against the master packing list. Whenever a bundle is used by Institutional Furniture, the supervisor indicates the specific bundle on the master packing list. Monthly, these master packing lists and a list of usage are sent to the broker, who then bills the company. When one of the broker's other customers needs veneer, the broker comes to the factory and makes a withdrawal. No formal records of these external withdrawals are made becuase all accounting and responsibility lies with the broker. All parties think this is an excellent arrangement because the company has a constant supply of veneer available in a tight market, because there is no working capital invested in veneer inventory, and because the supervisor can choose the best bundles for company use. At the same time the broker has free storage space.

The core materials are used in places where the bonded lumber panels are inappropriate: doors, drawer bottoms, under plastic on table tops, and unexposed backing. The core, purchased from four suppliers, is received directly by the department where physical counts are made and recorded on the incoming packing slips. The core is stored in the factory and used as needed. The price of core has been dropping consistently from $128 to $112, and finally to $103 per 1,000 bd ft on the last invoice.

Hardware and plastic are purchased on an annual purchase order based on last year's usage. Shipments against the annual purchase order are requested whenever the storeroom reports a shortage. All receipts come directly to the storeroom where a cardex file is maintained on a periodic inventory basis. Hardware is issued to the factory without paperwork upon request of a supervisor; furthermore, there are no records of the hardware at the workbenches. Once a year all hardware throughout the plant is collected, returned to the storeroom, counted, and reentered on the cardex records. Plastic is issued in full-roll quantities upon supervisor requests.

There are nine departments for labor cost accumulation. Each department is charged monthly for its labor costs by the following entry:

Work-in-Process (department)	$AH \times SP$
Labor Price Variance	$(SP - AP)\,AH$
Payroll Payable	$AH \times AP$

(AH is the actual hours worked; AP the actual hourly wage paid the workers; and SP the average standard hourly wage of the specific department.)

Overhead is applied to the Work-in-Process Inventory on the basis of a predetermined rate. Currently the application rate is 154% of labor cost.

When the goods have been manufactured and packed into cartons the production control forms are completed. These forms notify production control of the completion of the jobs and also serve as an accounting document. The slips are accumulated by product on a spread sheet in the accounting department. Each product total is then multiplied by the standard cost of the item. The sum of the standard costs for the items packed is then debited to Finished Goods and credited to Work-in-Process. When the items are billed to the customers, they are charged to Cost of Goods Sold, and the Finished Goods Inventory is credited for the standard cost of the items billed.

There are at least three types of unusual transactions that do not follow the same accounting procedures.

1. *Modifications*. Last year the company made about $556,000 in sales of modified units. The modification could be major (replacement of doors with drawers) or minor (changing a color). Since these items are not in the normal product line, there are no standard costs. All actual costs are charged to Work-in-Process. To relieve the Work-in-Process Inventory and charge the Finished Goods Inventory, the company uses a predetermined formula. This formula is (*AQ* packed × Selling price quoted by sales personnel) × 78%. The relief of the inventory subaccounts for raw materials is also done by formula: 10% veneer, 15% hardware, etc.

2. *Sales on a bid basis*. Some jobs are accepted on a bid basis. There is no standard cost card for these products. Work-in-process is charged for the actual costs incurred. The relief to the inventory is for the original bid cost prepared by the sales force. At least one extra unit of each type is manufactured. Any production overruns on the bid items are shipped to the purchaser without inventory relief because they are not counted on the packing slips.

3. *Spoilage and rework*. The company has a particular problem with ''falldown''—products that do not pass an inspection point. When feasible the company reworks these items to obtain a usable product. The product is returned to the responsible department and left for rework. This rework is not rescheduled by the production control area. The department is expected to find a way to integrate this extra effort into its normal workday. If the existing part cannot be repaired, a replacement is drawn from the wood parts controller. The defective part goes directly to the hog. If the piece cannot be reworked, it is isolated into a separate area for a warehouse sale of ''seconds'' once per year. No records have been kept on the rework quantities.

REQUIRED:

A. Discuss the standard cost system used by International Furniture. What strengths and weaknesses do you see? How would you modify the system to overcome the weaknesses you perceive?

B. Comment on the inventory control system. Does it facilitate the control aspects of the standard cost system?

chapter **8**

THE ALLOCATION OF INDIRECT COSTS

Throughout the accounting process, revenues and costs are being classified, segregated, and traced to specific focal points, such as products and services, departments, and responsibility centers. Some costs are capable of being traced and logically associated with a specific focal point. These are **direct costs.** Others, **indirect costs,** are not logically assignable to a focal point without some type of allocation process. In this chapter we will look at the problems of assigning, or allocating, indirect costs. First, we will look at how accountants allocate indirect costs for inventory valuation. Included in this section are issues of departmental overhead rates and accounting for multiple products. In the second section of this chapter we will look at how the allocation of indirect costs can be used for management decisions such as product-line emphasis, accounting for services, and responsibility center control.

INDIRECT COSTS AND INVENTORY VALUATION

One of the thorniest problems that the accountant faces is the allocation of indirect (sometimes called **common** or **joint**) costs. A principal motivation of this allocation is inventory valuation and the matching of costs with revenue for income measurement. Two inventory valuation issues are important: overhead and multiple products.

OVERHEAD AND DEPARTMENTAL RATES

In earlier chapters we discussed direct and indirect materials and direct and indirect labor. Direct materials and direct labor were defined as those that the accountant could trace to a specific unit of product without allocation; indirect materials and indirect labor were those that the accountant could not or did not trace to specific units of product. These indirect costs of material and labor were combined with other indirect costs such as depreciation, maintenance, utilities, and supervision into the account, Overhead Control. Thus factory overhead was composed of costs that could not be directly traced to units of product.

The factory overhead rate is the accountant's method of attaching these indirect costs to the products for inventory valuation. The illustrations in the previous chapters have used a **plant-wide** overhead rate. That is, the total overhead costs of the firm have been applied to all products throughout the firm using a single overhead rate.

In many firms the plant-wide rate is too crude a measure of product cost. Where a firm is organized into production departments, with departments differing in size, function or purpose, and activity or volume base, the plant-wide rate may be too broad an average. Where these departmental structures exist it is possible to develop departmental overhead rates.

In the factory there are two broad classes of departments. **Producing departments** actually work on the product. They modify and convert the raw materials, by adding labor and overhead, into a finished product. Examples of producing departments are machining, fabricating, painting, plating, stamping, and assembly departments. Departments that support the producing departments but do not work directly on the final product are called **service or support departments.** Their purpose is to make the producing departments more efficient and effective. Examples of service departments include toolrooms, storerooms, timekeeping, cafeterias, maintenance, production scheduling, personnel, medical services, power-generating plants, and materials handling.

In the development of an overhead rate all overhead costs must be related to the products in the producing departments—the only departments that come in contact with the products. Therefore, service department costs must be allocated to the producing departments in order for the producing departments' overhead rates to include all production costs.

The determination of departmental overhead rates requires a four-step sequence of apportioning costs. First, all direct departmental costs are *traced* to individual producing or service departments. Then, all indirect departmental costs are *allocated* to the individual departments. Next, the costs of service departments are *allocated* to the producing departments. Finally, the producing departments' fully allocated costs are *applied* to the products via the overhead rate.

For a complete illustration of the development of departmental overhead rates, let's assume that the Strident Company has two producing departments, fabrication and assembly, and two service departments, maintenance and medical services. The various parts going into the final products are machined in the Fabrication Department and assembled in the Assembly Department. Overhead costs in the overhead control subsidiary ledger are indirect labor, employee fringe benefits, indirect materials, depreciation of machinery, depreciation of building, factory supervision, and telephone expense. Because of the nature of the production activities, management uses machine hours in the Fabrication Department and direct labor hours in the Assembly Department to apply overhead to the Work-in-Process Inventory. Statistical data necessary to allocate the indirect costs were gathered by the company and are shown in Exhibit 8–1.

The clearest way to see the allocation of the costs to the producing departments is through a worksheet. When the worksheet is completed, *all* overhead costs will be allocated to the two producing departments for the computation of departmental overhead rates. Through the departmental overhead rates, each unit of product will receive a share of overhead. Accountants use three different techniques to complete the worksheet—the direct method, the step method, and the reciprocal method. The direct and step methods are illustrated in the next sections; the reciprocal method is shown in the Appendix to this chapter.

Departmental Statistics	Total	SERVICE DEPARTMENTS		PRODUCING DEPARTMENTS	
		Maintenance	Medical	Fabrication	Assembly
Machine hours	6,000	None	None	4,000	2,000
Total labor hours	8,000	1,500	500	2,000	4,000
Value of equipment	$120,000	$10,000	$20,000	$50,000	$40,000
Square feet occupied	50,000	8,000	2,000	20,000	20,000
Number of telephones	35	7	8	10	10
Maintenance hours used	2,900	100	50	1,750	1,000
Number of employees	97	10	7	30	50

EXHIBIT 8–1   Departmental statistics of the Strident Company

DIRECT METHOD

The direct method is illustrated in worksheet form in Exhibit 8–2. The logic of this worksheet development is shown below.

Step 1. All departmentally direct costs are *traced* to individual producing or service departments. Indirect labor, employee fringe benefits, and indirect materials were traced to the two service and producing departments when the costs were originally recorded.

Step 2. Costs that are indirect to the service or producing departments must be *allocated* or *apportioned* to them before service department costs are reallocated to the producing departments. The Strident Company cannot trace depreciation of machinery, depreciation of building, factory supervision, and telephone expense directly to any departments. Therefore, these costs must be apportioned. This requires an allocation base. The most important criterion in choosing an allocation base is a cause-and-effect relationship. To find a cause-and-effect relationship, the accountant should ask, "Why do these costs rise and fall?" One way to ask this question is by using an analytical method such as regression analysis to test for significant relationships. In this way the cost allocation is made so that the costs are allocated relative to their causal factor.

Using the criterion of cause and effect, the following allocations were made. Depreciation of machinery was apportioned on the basis of machinery value. Because the Maintenance Department had $10,000 in equipment, out of a total equipment base of $120,000, it received $400 [($10,000 ÷ $120,000) × $4,800] as its share. In a similar manner, building depreciation was apportioned on the basis of square feet occupied, factory supervision on the basis of direct labor hours, and telephone expense on the number of instruments.

The total overhead costs of operating each of the four departments can now be determined. The sum of the direct and indirect costs of operating the

THE STRIDENT COMPANY
DEPARTMENTAL COST WORKSHEET
For June 19X4

Step	Cost	Allocation Base	Total	SERVICE DEPTS. Maintenance	SERVICE DEPTS. Medical	PRODUCING DEPTS. Fabrication	PRODUCING DEPTS. Assembly
1	Indirect labor	Traced directly	$28,500	$2,000	$1,500	$10,000	$15,000
1	Employee fringe benefits	Traced directly	12,900	500	300	5,000	7,100
1	Supplies/indirect materials	Traced directly	6,700	1,000	700	3,000	2,000
2	Depreciation of machinery	Value of machinery	4,800	400	800	2,000	1,600
2	Depreciation of building	Square feet occupied	6,000	960	240	2,400	2,400
2	Factory supervision	Total labor hours	3,200	600	200	800	1,600
2	Telephone expense	Number of phones	700	140	160	200	200
	Total overhead costs		$62,800	$5,600	$3,900	$23,400	$29,900
3	Distribute Maintenace Department costs	Maintenance hours used by production departments		($5,600)	—	3,564	2,036
3	Distribute Medical Department costs	Number of employees in production departments			($3,900)	1,463	2,437
	Total overhead costs					$28,427	$34,373
	Basis of overhead rate					4,000 machine hours	4,000 labor hours
4	Departmental overhead rate					$7.11 per machine hour	$8.59 per labor hour

EXHIBIT 8–2 Direct method—Worksheet for the departmental allocation of costs of the Strident Company

Maintenance Department is $5,600; Medical Service, $3,900; Fabrication, $23,400; and Assembly, $29,900.

Step 3. The next step is the *allocation* of the service department costs to the producing departments. In the direct method costs of the service departments are allocated only to the producing departments.

The Maintenance Department costs are allocated directly to the two producing departments on the basis of the maintenance hours used by the producing departments. The Fabrication Department used 1,750 hours of maintenance time out of a total of 2,750 hours used by production departments resulting in an allocation of $3,564 [(1,750 ÷ 2,750) × $5,600]. Excluded from the allocation base are the 100 hours used by the Maintenance Department to maintain its own equipment and the 50 hours of maintenace used by the Medical Department.

The Medical Services Department costs are allocated to the producing departments on the basis of the number of employees in the respective departments. The Assembly Department receives $2,437 of medical service costs [(50 ÷ 80) × $3,900]. Only the 80 employees in the two producing departments are used for the allocation.

Step 4. The final step involves the computation of departmental overhead rates so the fully allocated costs can be *applied* to the products. The total, fully allocated costs of the Fabrication Department are $28,427. Because the department used 4,000 machine hours, the overhead rate is $7.11 per machine hour ($28,427 ÷ 4,000 machine hours). The overhead rate for the Assembly Department is $8.59 per direct labor hour ($34,373 ÷ 4,000 direct labor hours).

STEP METHOD

Exhibit 8–3 shows the same data for the Strident Company using the step method of allocating service departments' costs. In the worksheet in Exhibit 8–3, Steps 1 and 2 are the same as in the direct method. The difference between the two methods lies at Step 3. In the step method, recognition is given to the fact that the service departments provide services to *all* departments, not just the producing departments. The method chosen by the Strident Company was to allocate maintenance department costs first on the basis of maintenance hours used by other departments. The Maintenance Department serviced the Medical Department as well as the two producing departments. Thus, the Medical Department received an allocated share of maintenance costs. After the allocation of Maintenance Department costs was completed, Medical Department costs were allocated to the producing departments. This particular sequence was chosen because the Maintenance Department provided relatively more service to the Medical Department than the Medical Department provided to the Maintenance Department. As a general rule, the sequence should begin with the department that renders the greatest service to the greatest number of departments and continue stepwise to the departments giving the least service to other departments.

The Maintenance Department costs in Exhibit 8–3 were allocated on the basis of maintenance hours used. The Fabrication Department used 1,750 hours of maintenance time, resulting in an allocation of $3,500 [(1,750 ÷ 2,800) × $5,600]. Notice that the allocation is based on 2,800 hours. Excluded are the 100 hours used by the Maintenance Department to take care of its own equipment. If these hours were included in the allocation base, the Maintenance

THE STRIDENT COMPANY
DEPARTMENTAL COST WORKSHEET
For June 19X4

Step	Cost	Allocation Base	Total	SERVICE DEPTS. Maintenance	SERVICE DEPTS. Medical	PRODUCING DEPTS. Fabrication	PRODUCING DEPTS. Assembly
1	Indirect labor	Direct	$28,500	$2,000	$1,500	$10,000	$15,000
1	Employee fringe benefits	Direct	12,900	500	300	5,000	7,100
1	Supplies/indirect materials	Direct	6,700	1,000	700	3,000	2,000
2	Depreciation of machinery	Value of machinery	4,800	400	800	2,000	1,600
2	Depreciation of building	Square feet occupied	6,000	960	240	2,400	2,400
2	Factory supervision	Total labor hours	3,200	600	200	800	1,600
2	Telephone expense	Number of phones	700	140	160	200	200
	Total overhead costs		$62,800	$5,600	$3,900	$23,400	$29,900
3	Distribute Maintenance Department	Maintenance hours used		($5,600)	100	3,500	2,000
	Subtotal				$4,000	$26,900	$31,900
3	Distribute Medical Department	Number of employees			($4,000)	1,500	2,500
	Total overhead costs					$28,400	$34,400
	Basis of overhead rate					4,000 machine hours	4,000 labor hours
4	Departmental overhead rate					$7.10 per machine hour	$8.60 per labor hour

EXHIBIT 8–3   Step method—worksheet for the departmental allocation of costs of the Strident Company

Department would be apportioned some of its own costs. These would have to be reallocated, and the reallocations would continue indefinitely.

The Medical Services Department costs were allocated on the basis of the number of employees. The Assembly Department received $2,500 of medical services costs [(50 ÷ 80) × $4,000]. Only 80 employees were used in the allocation, not the full 97; once the costs of a service department are allocated to the producing departments, no subsequent service department costs are reallocated to it.

RECIPROCAL METHOD

It should be noted that the step method, unlike the direct method, gives recognition to the fact that the service departments service each other. However, this recognition is not totally satisfactory. In the Strident Company the Medical Department also provided services to the Maintenance Department, although the step allocation procedure does not take this into account.

The reciprocal method recognizes that each service department may interact with all other service departments. By the use of simultaneous equations the total interplay between the departments is taken into account. In this way the reciprocal method provdes a more comprehensive allocation scheme than either the direct or step methods. In our example we have only two service departments, which allows the use of simultaneous equations. A worksheet showing the reciprocal cost allocation for the Strident Company is shown in the Appendix to this chapter. This solution format would be unworkable if there were more than a few service departments. For larger firms the reciprocal method would require the use of matrix algebra and a computer.

OTHER ISSUES INVOLVING DEPARTMENTAL RATES

Before we leave the allocation of indirect costs to departments, three other areas should be discussed. First, the Strident Company could have chosen to use a single, **plant-wide (blanket)** overhead rate for the entire company. If a plant-wide rate had been used, the allocation of indirect costs and service department costs would not have been necessary. The single rate would have been computed by dividing total overhead by some activity base. For the Strident Company, a plant-wide rate based on machine hours would have been $10.47 per machine hour ($62,800 ÷ 6,000 machine hours). Whether a firm will prefer the plant-wide rate or a departmental rate will depend on (1) the perceived accuracy and precision of the overhead rates in inventory valuation and (2) the cost of developing the rates (information economics). There is no "perfect" or clearly superior way of applying overhead; the method chosen will always be a function of the use made of the data.

Second, the illustration of the Strident Company involved a manufacturing concern. The same principles can be applied to service and governmental entities as well. For example, most hospitals use a departmental cost allocation worksheet to determine their costs per service rendered—data they find useful in pricing decisions and cost reimbursements from governmental agencies and insurance companies. In a hospital the "producing or revenue" departments could include medical wards, surgical wards, radiology departments, and outpatient care. Supporting or service departments could include housekeeping departments, laundries, pharmacies, and laboratories. We will examine service concerns later in this chapter.

Third, the motive underlying the development of departmental overhead rates is inventory valuation, and ultimately income determination. These are financial accounting issues. There is a serious question of how useful this information is to management in planning, controlling, and assessing operating performance. The allocation of costs to departments opens to examination the area of responsibility accounting. This will be covered later in this chapter and again in Chapter 13.

INDIRECT COSTS AND MULTIPLE PRODUCTS

In many industries the production process consists of taking a single material input and producing more than one final product. In the petroleum industry a barrel of crude oil is refined into fuel oil, premium gasoline, regular gasoline, and many other types of petroleum products. The meat-packing industry produces hamburger, roasts, steaks, and many other products from a single steer. In the lumber industry a single log produces many different products. These production processes are called **joint processes.**

The costs of the barrel of crude oil, the steer, or the log are **joint costs**—costs that are incurred to process a single raw material into more than one manufactured product. At the time joint costs are introduced into the production process, it is impossible to identify one finished product from another. Joint costs represent the costs of a single material, a single production process, or a series of production processes that simultaneously produce two or more finished products.

For inventory valuation purposes these joint costs, which are indirect costs, must be apportioned to the separate products. Without this cost assignment the matching of costs with revenue for individual products would be impossible. For such joint cost problems, accountants typically use one of two allocation techniques. One is to apportion the joint costs on a quantity basis such as number of units produced, labor hours, or a specific industry measure such as ton-miles. The second allocation technique uses the relative sales value of the various products to apportion joint costs.

To illustrate these methods let's assume the following data.

	Product A	Product B
Selling price per unit	$ 6	$ 15
Variable costs per unit	$ 4	$ 7
Labor hours per unit	1	3
Units produced	15,000	10,000
Joint costs of production	$120,000	

QUANTITY METHOD

The joint costs represent costs incurred that are applicable to both products. The labor hours used per unit of product and the quantity of each product manufactured are possible quantitative bases of allocating the joint costs. The method chosen should be simple, easy to measure, and relate the "cause" (activity base used to apportion) with the "effect" (cost).

The joint costs could be allocated on the basis of total labor hours as shown below.

	Total Labor Hours	Ratio	Joint Costs
Product A (15,000 × 1)	15,000	15/45	$ 40,000
Product B (10,000 × 3)	30,000	30/45	80,000
Total	45,000	45/45	$120,000

An allocation based on the number of units produced would assign joint costs in the following manner:

	Total Units Produced	Ratio	Joint Costs
Product A	15,000	15/25	$ 72,000
Product B	10,000	10/25	48,000
Total	25,000	25/25	$120,000

When costs are allocated on a quantity basis the cost per unit of quantity is the same. For example, when the cost of a steer is divided between steak and hamburger on a poundage basis, the cost per pound of the two products is the same. This bothers many people because steak sells for more per pound than does hamburger. Thus, the quantity basis should be used only where the selling prices of the products are similar.

RELATIVE SALES-VALUE METHOD

Where the production process results in products with widely differing selling prices, the most common technique of allocating joint costs is the relative sales-value basis. Using the relative sales-value basis, the allocation of joint costs in this example would be

	Total Units Produced	Selling Price per Unit	Sales Value	Ratio	Joint Costs
Product A	15,000	$ 6	$ 90,000	90/240	$ 45,000
Product B	10,000	$15	150,000	150/240	75,000
Total	25,000		$240,000	240/240	$120,000

Notice that the effect of this allocation is to provide a constant gross margin percentage for each product at the point of split-off. This fact makes the relative sales-value method unsuitable for management decisions, although it is useful in inventory costing. Gross margins by product, after the allocation of the joint cost, are

	Product A		Product B	
Sales value	$90,000	100%	$150,000	100%
Less apportioned joint cost	45,000	50%	75,000	50%
Gross margin	$45,000	50%	$ 75,000	50%

The same amount of total joint costs will be allocated to the products, regardless of which allocation procedure is used. However, different allocation techniques may generate widely differing unit costs. To summarize the above example, the full inventoriable cost of Product A for each of the three methods is

	ALLOCATION BASES		
	Direct Labor Hours	Number of Units Produced	Relative Sales Value
Direct variable costs per unit	$4.00	$4.00	$4.00
Joint costs per unit, as allocated	2.67*	4.80†	3.00‡
Total cost per unit of Product A	$6.67	$8.80	$7.00

*$40,000 ÷ 15,000 units.
†$72,000 ÷ 15,000 units.
‡$45,000 ÷ 15,000 units.

INVENTORY VALUATION AND DECISION MAKING

A word of caution is necessary. Although allocating the joint costs may be necessary for inventory costing, it can be misleading for managerial decision making. Any method of allocating joint costs is arbitrary and does not reflect the incremental effect of decisions. First, there is a danger that the unit cost after the allocation will be treated as a variable or incremental cost. This would, of course, not be true if the joint cost included some fixed costs. Second, and more important, is that the joint cost is nonrelevant in all decisions relating to what products should be produced in the joint process or subsequent to the incurrence of the joint costs.

To illustrate this point, assume that the Insect Control Chemical Company produces three products: D, E, and F. Raw material X enters the process

Department 1 of the factory. Department 1 separates Material X into Products D, E, and F. During the past year $260,000 of Material X was issued to Department 1. Other costs of operating Department 1 were $140,000. Department 1 output was 100,000 pounds of Product D, 50,000 pounds of Product E, and 200,000 pounds of Product F. The end of the production process in Department 1 is called the **split-off point,** where a single raw material yields two or more different products. Each product has a ready market at this point of split-off. At the point of split-off, Product D sells for $2.00 per pound, Product E for $4.00 per pound, and Product F for $.50 per pound.

After the split-off, Product D could be processed further in Department 2, with the additional cost of $200,000. After the additional processing Product D would sell for $4.50 per pound. After the split-off, Product E could be processed further in Department 3 for $60,000 additional costs. After this additional processing, Product E would sell for $5.00 per pound. Product F is not suitable for further processing and must be sold at the point of split-off. These production possibilities can be shown diagrammatically:

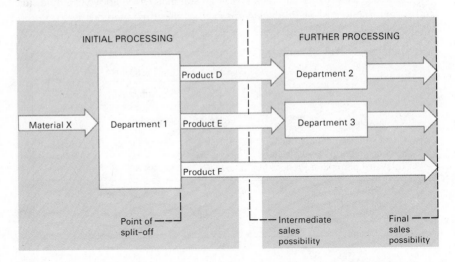

A summary of the costs and revenues is:

Product	Joint Costs	Sales Value at Split-off	Additional Processing Costs	Sales Value after Further Processing	Net Benefit from Further Processing
D	Not relevant	$200,000	$200,000	$450,000	$50,000
E		200,000	60,000	250,000	(10,000)
F		100,000	—	100,000	None
Total	$400,000	$500,000	$260,000	$800,000	

What action should management take? Whether to produce Products D and E further should depend on the added contribution margin generated by further production. In this example, because Product D generates $250,000 of additional revenue and only $200,000 of additional costs, it should be produced further. Product E, however, generates $60,000 of additional costs and only $50,000 of additional revenue and should not be produced further. Using the optimum strategy, the company would generate the following income:

Sales ($450,00 + $200,000 + $100,000)	$750,000
Separable costs of additional processing	200,000
Separable margin	$550,000
Joint costs ($260,000 + $140,000)	400,000
Income	$150,000

The joint costs ($400,000) are not relevant to the sell-or-process decision; they will not change because of subsequent decisions. In any incremental analysis, joint costs such as these are not relevant. Costs incurred before the point of split-off are common to all products and cannot be treated as incremental costs of the individual products, even if allocated. Of course, a firm would not incur the joint cost in the first place unless they believed the sum of all revenues would exceed the sums of all costs.

It may seem inadequate to talk about incremental income for the products rather than net income. To speak of "net" income by product line requires the allocation of joint costs to the various products. Incremental income, on the other hand, is the contribution of the individual products to the firm's joint costs and income. The allocation of joint costs, regardless of how they are allocated, will not change the income of the firm over time and can mislead the decision maker into believing that the allocated joint costs are relevant in measuring incremental income.

Thus there is an accounting paradox. Joint costs are irrelevant for incremental production decisions because the joint costs do not change as a result of the decision to sell or process further. Yet for inventory costing and income-determination purposes, the financial accountant must allocate joint costs to the products.

INDIRECT COSTS AND MANAGEMENT DECISION MAKING

In the previous section we looked at how indirect costs are allocated for inventory valuation: a financial accounting topic. In this section we will look at three areas where the allocation of indirect costs can be expanded: (1) the allocation of selling and administrative expenses for product-line decisions, (2) the allocation of indirect costs for pricing and control in service concerns, and (3) the role of indirect-cost allocation in management performance assessment.

PRODUCT-LINE PROFITABILITY

There are at least two motives underlying the need to allocate all costs of the firm to product or service lines. First, if a firm is to optimize profit it must ensure that each product is contributing to the firm's well-being. Second, there are product and service pricing situations where the contract price provides for the reimbursement of all costs, including selling and administrative, plus an agreed-upon element of profit. Examples of this type of contract include some reimbursments to hospitals and certain governmental purchasing contracts in the national defense area.

Product-line profitability asks the question, "What is the full cost of producing and selling each product?" The costing systems that we have studied so far deal only with the costs of producing the product. To answer the full cost of producing and selling a product the accountant must now allocate indirect administrative and indirect marketing costs to the various products. Some marketing costs, such as sales commissions, freight, and sales staff selling a single product may be traceable to specific products. The large majority of marketing and administrative costs, however, are indirect costs to product lines and must be allocated on some equitable basis.

To illustrate the allocation of administrative and marketing costs, assume the following income statement for the ABC Company.

ABC COMPANY
INCOME STATEMENT
For the Year Ended December 31, 19X2

Sales		$600,000
Expenses:		
Cost of sales	$400,000	
Advertising	40,000	
Freight out	31,000	
Sales commissions	30,000	
Salaries	77,500	578,500
Income		$ 21,500

The ABC Company wants an income statement that presents income by product for each of its three products. Administrative and marketing costs are to be classified into order-getting costs (costs incurred to make the sale), order-filling costs (costs to fill the order after the sale is made), and administrative costs. The following data were gathered by the controller to develop the product-line income statement.

Sales. The sales journal showed the following:

Product A	$300,000	50%
Product B	180,000	30%
Product C	120,000	20%
Total	$600,000	100%

Cost of Sales. The inventory records showed the following:

Product A	$220,000	55%
Product B	120,000	30%
Product C	60,000	15%
Total	$400,000	100%

Advertising ($40,000). Half of the advertising can be traced directly to Product A. The balance relates to all products and is to be allocated on the basis of sales.

Freight Out ($31,000). Freight out relates to the number of units shipped.

Sales Commissions ($30,000). The salespeople receive a 5% commission on sales in addition to salaries.

Salaries ($77,500). Salaries include the following: (1) sales salaries ($36,000), three salespeople at $12,000 each (two salespeople sell Product A and the third allocated equally between Product B and C); (2) warehouse salaries ($15,500), the cost is for filling orders and relates to the number of units shipped; and (3) administrative salaries ($26,000), costs that are best related to the cost of sales for each product.

ALLOCATING SALES AND COST OF SALES TO PRODUCT LINES

Sales and Cost of Sales. The first step is to reclassify cost of sales by product line. Assume that the accounting records showed the following:

		PRODUCT		
	Total	A	B	C
Number of units sold		10,000	9,000	12,000
Sales	$600,000	$300,000	$180,000	$120,000
Cost of sales	400,000	220,000	120,000	60,000
Gross margin	$200,000	$ 80,000	$ 60,000	$ 60,000

ALLOCATING ORDER-GETTING COSTS TO PRODUCT LINES

Order-getting costs are the costs to make the sale. In our example they include advertising, sales commissions, and sales salaries.

	PRODUCTS		
	A	B	C
Advertising $40,000			
Related to Product A	$20,000		
Balance on basis of sales			
(50%, 30%, and 20%)	10,000	$ 6,000	$ 4,000
Sales commissions $30,000			
(5% of sales)	15,000	9,000	6,000
Sales salaries $36,000			
Product A sales salaries	24,000		
Product B and C sales salaries			
(50% to each)		6,000	6,000
Total order-getting costs	$69,000	$21,000	$16,000

ALLOCATING ORDER-FILLING COSTS TO PRODUCT LINES

Order-filling costs are the costs incurred to fill the orders after the sale is made. These costs usually relate to the number of products and distances they are shipped. In our example, order-filling costs include freight out and warehouse salaries.

	A	B	C
Freight out $31,000			
($1 per unit shipped, $31,000/31,000			
units)	$10,000	$ 9,000	$12,000
Warehouse salaries $15,500			
($.50 per unit shipped, $15,500/31,000			
units)	5,000	4,500	6,000
Total	$15,000	$13,500	$18,000

ALLOCATING ADMINISTRATIVE COSTS TO PRODUCT LINES

Administrative costs relate to the general administration of the company. There is no direct relation with any particular product as there often is with some marketing costs. Two bases are commonly used to allocate administrative costs: sales and some measure of total costs. Generally, some measure of total costs reflects the effort of management better than total sales. In this example, we allocated administrative salaries on the basis of cost of sales, which is a very widely used basis.

	A	B	C
Administrative salaries $26,000			
(based on cost of sales, 55%,			
30%, 15%)	$14,300	$ 7,800	$ 3,900

The resulting income statement by product line is presented in Exhibit 8–4. Product A shows a loss of $18,300, while Products B and C show incomes of $17,700 and $22,100, respectively. Now that the manager knows this information, what should be done? Should Product A be dropped? These questions are considered in Chapters 9 and 10, which are concerned with short-range pricing and production decisions. To the extent that the price of a product may be based on the full cost of a product (including marketing and administrative costs) plus a profit, the data in Exhibit 8–4 are relevant. However, care must be used in making decisions with information that contains allocated costs.

ABC COMPANY
INCOME STATEMENT BY PRODUCT LINE
For the Year Ended December 31, 19X2

PRODUCT LINE

	A	B	C
Sales	$300,000	$180,000	$120,000
Identifiable Costs			
Cost of Goods Sold	$220,000	120,000	$ 60,000
Advertising	20,000	—	—
Sales commissions	15,000	9,000	6,000
Sales salaries	24,000	—	—
Total identifiable costs	279,000	129,000	66,000
Product-line contribution	$ 21,000	$ 51,000	$ 54,000
Allocated costs			
Advertising	$ 10,000	$ 6,000	$ 4,000
Sales salaries	—	6,000	6,000
Freight out	10,000	9,000	12,000
Warehouse salaries	5,000	4,500	6,000
Administrative salaries	14,300	7,800	3,900
Total allocated costs	39,300	33,300	31,900
Income (loss)	$ (18,300)	$ 17,700	$ 22,100

EXHIBIT 8–4
Income statement by
product line

SERVICE-LINE PROFITABILITY

The examples in the first part of this chapter have been in a manufacturing setting with resultant problems of inventory valuation. However, approximately one-half of the economic activity in the United States is involved in the delivery of services or specific programs of activity. In this section we will examine cost allocations for service concerns.

THE NATURE OF SERVICE CONCERNS

There are many types of service concerns. At one extreme are governmental entities that provide services that private businesses cannot or will not provide—national defense, parks, legal systems, public safety, and highways, for example. At the other extreme are privately held, profit-motivated organizations delivering services—accounting firms, medical clinics, and computer data services, for example. In between these two extremes are a myriad of organizations: some public, some private; some not-for-profit, some with a profit motive; some large, some small.

While the wide range of organizations makes a summary description of their accounting practices difficult, they do face similar decisions regarding pricing, volume, service–program mix, and cost control of their services. Without inventories to cost, accounting for services and programs can be simpler because there is no need to distinguish between product or period costs; all costs are period costs. However, the issues of direct and indirect costs and controllable and noncontrollable costs are very important to these organizations.

Many service concerns develop a program approach for management planning and control. A **program** is a focal point of activity that concentrates on the output of the organization, rather than specific inputs. The program approach focuses on the output services instead of the more traditional approach of concentrating on the organizational structure and inputs.

ALLOCATING COSTS IN A SERVICE CONCERN

To illustrate the costing of a service concern, we will use a not-for-profit medical center—the Sports Injury Clinic. The clinic needs cost information for three general purposes. First, the clinic needs a measure of the full cost of providing services to set fees and support insurance reimbursement requests. Second, the clinic needs costs and revenues related to the department (responsibility center) responsible for the activities. This allows the individual managers to control costs by controlling their activities. Third, the clinic needs to attach costs to the departments to ascertain an appropriate product mix.

The measurement of the full cost of services requires a series of four steps.

Step 1. Identify the individual departments.
Step 2. Classify revenues and costs by departments.

Step 3. Allocate the cost of support departments to service delivery departments.

Step 4. Determine the cost of each procedure or service.

Step 1—Identify the Individual Departments. The ability to control costs depends on how clearly the departments are identified and responsibilities for revenues and costs defined. The Sports Injury Clinic, our example, has two major service delivery departments. The first, Medical–Surgical, diagnoses injuries, prescribes treatment, performs surgery as needed, and monitors the patient's medical care. The second, Physical Therapy, monitors the rehabilitative exercise programs.

There are two support departments in the Sports Injury Clinic. The Administration Department maintains the client files, provides records for the fee reimbursements, and manages the personnel. The Occupancy Department is a cost pool that includes building costs and repairs and maintenance.

The list below summarizes these departments.

Support Departments	*Service Delivery Departments*
Administration	Medical–Surgical
Occupancy	Physical Therapy

Step 2—Classify Revenues and Costs by Departments. Exhibit 8–5 presents the total of direct costs that were traceable to each department. In our example we have classified the costs as fixed and variable. In our previous examples in this chapter involving manufacturing concerns, we have not used

	SUPPORT		SERVICE DELIVERY		
	Administration	Occupancy	Medical–Surgical	Physical Therapy	Total
Direct costs (traced to departments):					
Variable	$10,000	$ 0	$ 20,000	$10,000	$ 40,000
Fixed	40,000	30,000	80,000	10,000	160,000
Total	$50,000	$30,000	$100,000	$20,000	$200,000
Allocation bases:					
Patient visits:					
Number of visits			6,000	4,000	10,000
Percentage			60%	40%	100%
Revenue production			90%	10%	100%
Square footage	30%	10%	20%	40%	100%
Personnel count	40%	10%	40%	10%	100%

EXHIBIT 8–5 Data for cost allocation for Sports Injury Clinic

this classification; rather, we simply listed the costs by type such as salaries and utilities. Either of these two approaches to cost classifications could be used in either production or service concerns. We have used the fixed and variable dichotomy to illustrate a different approach.

Exhibit 8–5 also summarizes the statistical data for use as allocation bases. As a part of their day-to-day data collection the clinic accumulates these statistics. For example, the square footage occupancies of the four departments are 30% for Administration, 10% for Occupancy, 20% for Medical–Surgical, and 40% for Physical Therapy. A personnel count shows 40% in Administration, 10% in Occupancy, 40% in Medical–Surgical, and 10% in Physical Therapy.

Exhibit 8–6 illustrates the development of the worksheet to determine the full cost of services. As a first step in developing the worksheet we have entered all direct costs to the departments. In our example we have maintained the distinctions between fixed and variable costs.

Step 3—Allocate the Cost of Support Departments to Service Delivery Departments.

There are two issues to be considered in allocating the support departments to the service delivery departments. The first involves the bases of allocation that should be used. The second involves the method of allocation that is appropriate.

Ideally the basis for allocating a cost will bear a relationship to its use. Occupancy cost, for example, could be allocated on the basis of square footage because there appears to be a cause-and-effect relationship. The proper allocation

	SUPPORT		SERVICE DELIVERY		
	Administration	Occupancy	Medical–Surgical	Physical Therapy	Total
Direct costs (traced to departments):					
Variable	$10,000	$ 0	$ 20,000	$10,000	$ 40,000
Fixed	40,000	30,000	80,000	10,000	160,000
Total	$50,000	$30,000	$100,000	$20,000	$200,000
Allocate fixed occupancy (2)	9,900	(30,000)	6,600	13,500	0
Allocate variable administration (1)	(10,000)		6,000	4,000	0
Allocate fixed administration (3)	(49,900)	0	39,920	9,980	0
	$ 0	$ 0	$152,520	$47,480	$200,000
Cost per patient visit			$ 25.42	$ 11.87	
Allocation bases:					
(1) Patient visits			60%	40%	100%
(2) Square footage (omit occupancy)	33%		22%	45%	100%
(3) Personnel (omit administration and occupancy)			80%	20%	100%

EXHIBIT 8–6 Illustration of cost allocations for Sports Injury Clinic

depends on the activity that "drives" the cost. Some of the costs of the Administration Department involve patient records; these costs are best related to number of visits. Other administration costs will relate to the number of personnel. Still others, such as the chief administrator's salary, will have no direct relationship to any activity.

We have assumed in our example that the variable administration costs are allocated on the basis of patient visits. Fixed administration costs are allocated on the basis of personnel count. Occupancy costs are allocated on the basis of square footage.

The step method of allocation was chosen. We could, of course, have used the direct or reciprocal methods instead. We chose the step because it does give recognition to the fact that the occupancy costs are relevant to both the Administration Department and the two service delivery departments. A direct allocation would have ignored this.

In Exhibit 8–6 the variable and fixed costs are allocated separately. This allows the perservation of the variable–fixed relationships. Obviously the order of support department allocation will affect the amount of costs allocated to a particular department. Generally the costs of a support department that benefits most other departments but draws least from other departments should be allocated first. Based on this criterion, we chose the following order of allocation; (1) fixed occupancy and (2) variable and fixed administration.

Note the revision to the allocation bases required in the step method. Occupancy costs were allocated to administration (33%), medical–surgical (22%), and physical therapy (45%). In computing these percentages, the square footage devoted to the Occupancy Department itself was ignored. Further, the fixed administration costs were allocated to the Medical–Surgical and Physical Therapy departments, ignoring the use of administration by occupancy.

The determination of the method of allocation, the order of allocation, and the bases of allocations are policy issues. To a large extent they are philosophical issues with no right or wrong answers.

Step 4—Determine the Cost of Each Procedure or Service. The last step in measuring the full cost of services involves determining the unit cost for each type of service or procedure. In this example, the average cost per patient visit was determined for each department. The cost per patient visit for the Medical–Surgical Department was $25.42. The cost per patient visit to physical therapy was $11.87 per visit. If we assume that the direct costs included payments to physicians, this cost could be used in setting fees for patients or third-party reimbursements.

This example assumes that patient visits were fairly uniform in duration. If they are not uniform some adjustment for different-length visits must be made. For example, one patient visit could be a routine examination of a sprained ankle, whereas another visit could involve in-office surgery that requires significant time. In these cases the Sports Injury Clinic faces many of the same problems in costing as the manufacturing firm with multiple products.

RESPONSIBILITY ACCOUNTING AND INDIRECT-COST ALLOCATION

TRADITIONAL RESPONSIBILITY REPORTING

The underlying assumption supporting the concept of responsibility accounting is that the performance of managers should be evaluated by how well they managed those resources over which they had control. For example, in the previous illustration of the Strident Company (Exhibits 8–2 and 8–3) the manager of the Fabrication Department was responsible for only $20,000 of controllable costs. (This assumes that the depreciation of machinery, while based on the values of machinery, is the responsibility of the department manager.) However, at the level of the vice-president of production, $62,800 of costs were controllable. The departmental overhead allocations do not stress which costs are controllable by an individual manager and which are not controllable. For this reason a report similar to the format shown in Exhibit 8–7 should be used by management in the planning and control process. This style of report shows that the manager of the Fabrication Department is not responsible for the costs of other departments. As can be seen, responsibility accounting changes the perspective of the control from an organizational standpoint to a personal or individual one.

Exhibit 8–7 has three underlying assumptions. The first assumption is that costs (and revenues) can be organized by levels of management within the firm. The second assumption is that costs (and revenues) traced to a specific level of management are controllable at that level. Finally, the third assumption is that appropriately descriptive accounting data can be generated as a basis for evaluating actual performance.

In an earlier section of this chapter, indirect costs (the majority noncontrollable) were allocated first to departments and then through an overhead rate to products for inventory valuation purposes. The traditional model of responsibility accounting states that this allocation, while useful for inventory valuation, is dysfunctional in assessing management performance. In the traditional model of performance evaluation managers should not be given responsibility for costs (or revenues) beyond their control.

One concern (caution) must be noted when using responsibility accounting as the basis of a management control system. The choice of the performance measure will substantially influence the behavior of the managers. Managers will concentrate their energies in those areas where their performance is measured in an objective (numerical) way and where their actions will clearly affect the results. That is, if the performance measure is "cost minimization," then manages will seek to minimize costs. There are many examples where the resulting "cost minimization" was not in the long-run best interests of the firm; examples include deferring maintenance, postponing research and development, or reducing staff to the point where an adequate service level is not available. As a result of this behavioral influence, a clear statement of controllable costs (and revenue), coupled with a clear understanding of the organizational goals, is critical to the traditional responsibility accounting model.

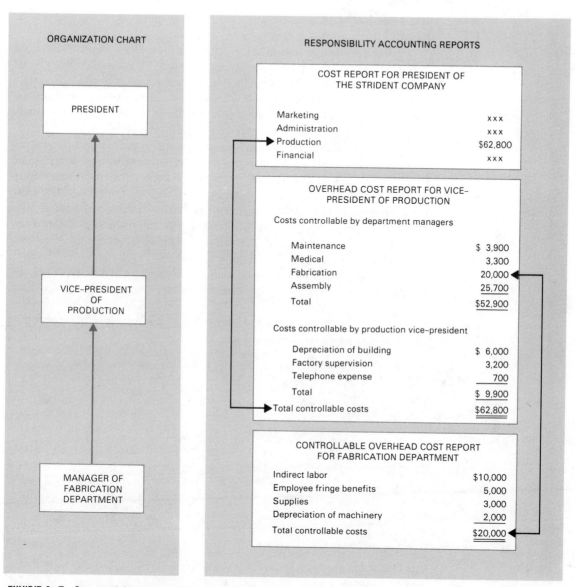

EXHIBIT 8–7 Responsibility reports of the Strident Company

ALLOCATIONS AND MANAGERIAL MOTIVATION

Alternatives to the traditional model have been proposed. Typically the goal in any system design is to devise an accounting information system, as well as a reward structure, that motivates managers to act in the best interests of the organization. One suggestion to accomplish this goal congruency has been a proposal to deemphasize controllable costs, proposing instead that control system design be focused on *who bore the risk, rather than who exerted the control*.

There is another question of whether controllability is best expressed via "the costs expended" or "the resources consumed." If controllability is based on the costs expended, then the allocation of indirect costs would be inappropriate for management evaluation. If, however, controllability is based on resources consumed, then the allocation of indirect costs would be not only appropriate, but essential for management evaluation.

To illustrate the differences between "costs expended" and "resources consumed," let's use a computer processing department as an example. The Computer Processing Department, a service department, has the responsibility of supporting the two producing departments—fabrication and assembly. Data for the Computer Processing Department are shown in the top of Exhibit 8–8. The department has annual costs of $60,000; $40,000 of these costs are fixed while $20,000 are variable. The measure of variability is "computer processing unit minutes," called CPU by the company.

The Computer Department has an annual capacity of 180,000 CPU. To accomplish their basic processing requirements the Fabrication and Assembly

---

COMPUTER PROCESSING DEPARTMENT

Fixed Costs (depreciation, rentals, supervisors)		$40,000
Variable Costs (utilities, supplies, programming)		20,000
Total Annual Costs		$60,000
Annual Computer Usage Available		180,000 CPU
Annual Basic Usage:		
Fabrication	50,000 CPU	
Assembly	30,000 CPU	80,000 CPU
Annual Uncommitted Usage		100,000 CPU
METHOD 1—Capacity to Serve Allocation:		
Fabrication [(50,000 ÷ 80,000) × $60,000]		$37,500
Assembly [(30,000 ÷ 80,000) × $60,000]		22,500
		$60,000
METHOD 2—Dual Capacity and Usage Allocation:		
Fabrication		
Fixed [(50,000 ÷ 80,000) × $40,000]		$25,000 +
Variable ($20,000 ÷ 100,000 CPU)		$.20 per CPU
Assembly		
Fixed [(30,000 ÷ 80,000) × $40,000]		$15,000 +
Variable ($20,000 ÷ 100,000 CPU)		$.20 per CPU
METHOD 3—Usage Allocation:		
Fabrication $.333 per CPU used		
Assembly $.333 per CPU used		
($60,000 ÷ 180,000 = $.333)		

EXHIBIT 8–8 Alternative cost allocation methods

departments are allocated 50,000 and 30,000 CPUs, respectively. The remaining 100,000 CPUs are available to the two producing departments for special studies, unusual programs, seasonal variations, and expected growth.

The expenditure of this $60,000 is certainly not controllable by the managers of the two producing departments in the traditional sense. Three different allocation procedures are shown in Exhibit 8–8. Each procedure alters the controllability of the Computer Data-Processing Department costs, at least as far as the managers of the Fabrication and Assembly departments are concerned.

Method 1—Capacity to Serve Allocation. The first procedure would allocate the $60,000 total costs to the producing departments using a rate based on the Computer Department's basic utilization capacity. For example, $37,500 [(50,000 ÷ 80,000) × $60,000)] is allocated to the Fabrication Department. If both departments were totally free to use the computer capacity as they wished (without a basic usage requirement), a 50 : 50 allocation could be supported. Using the Capacity to Serve allocation method, the costs assigned would be noncontrollable by the producing departments. The allocated costs would be the same whether or not the managers used the computer services. Therefore, one strong behavioral motivation of the producing department managers would be to use as many of these resources as possible. There are no incremental (controllable) costs of usage; neither the costs nor the consumption of the resources are controlled.

Method 2—Dual Capacity and Usage Allocation. The second allocation method would use two stages to allocate the $60,000. The first stage is a charge for providing the available capacity. In our example $40,000 of the costs are fixed; this implies these costs are incurred to provide the available capacity. Because the producing departments have basic usage requirements, these fixed costs have been divided on the ratio of the basic CPU capacity. In one sense this is a "retainer fee" that permits the producing departments to use 50,000 and 30,000 CPUs of services, respectively. Anything in excess of this level of use is charged at the rate of $.20 per CPU ($20,000 ÷ 100,000 CPU). With this allocation procedure the cost of computer processing becomes controllable by producing departments once they exceed their basic CPU allowance. As a result of this allocation, the producing departments would use the services freely until the basic allowance is consumed; beyond that point usage would probably be monitored to minimize the incremental charge.

Method 3—Usage Allocation. The third allocation procedure makes all of the Computer Department's costs controllable from the producing department's viewpoint. The service from the Computer Department, including the basic usage requirement, is "sold" to the producing departments at the rate of $.333 per CPU ($60,000 ÷ 180,000 CPU). If a producing department does not use the computer service there is no charge. One behavioral implication of this allocation procedure is that the producing departments will use the computer services as little as possible to minimize departmental charges. This could result in actions to reduce the basic usage, as well as discretionary usage. 'If this happens the Computer Department could have excess idle capacity; depending on management action at this point, there could be a spiraling increase in costs per CPU caused by the spiraling decrease in CPU usage.

Of course this is a very simplistic example, but it does point out that often "control" is an illusion created by the accounting data. At no time in our example did the producing department managers have any direct control over the expenditure of resources by the Computer Department. However, it might be noted that using the third allocation procedure, the producing managers will be the most affected by both the consumption of the computer resources and the "charge" for the use. That "charge" per CPU could increase if the Computer Department costs increased or if the volume of services demanded decreased.

A good accounting system should provide incentives for efficient and effective performance by managers of both the service and the producing departments. This would include a method of ensuring prudent use of the service departments' resources by the producing departments, the consumer. It would be too simplistic to adopt the traditional view and say that all cost allocations will automatically lead to bad management accounting.

By "charging" the consumers for the usage of a service department's output, the demand can be rationed. Further, producing department managers can more easily compare externally supplied prices and quality with that supplied internally. This can promote interdepartmental communication, which, in the long run, can be beneficial to the firm.

Each allocation procedure has costs and benefits. Some of these allocation methods are required for reports external to the firm; others have economic consequences; still others have behavioral implications. Which method should be chosen in a particular circumstance will depend on the motives for making the allocation.

SUMMARY

The distinction between direct and indirect costs is a critical distinction in determining the cost of something. A direct cost can be traced to the focal point of costing. An indirect cost cannot be traced. We must first define the focal point of our costing—a time period, as in financial accounting; a department, as in cost control; or a product or service, as in determining a unit cost for inventory valuation or pricing—before we can identify whether a cost is direct or indirect.

In firms that have a departmental organization, it is often necessary to calculate departmental overhead rates. This process requires the apportionment of indirect costs to the departments and the allocation of service department costs to producing departments. Separate overhead rates are then calculated for each producing department. The departmentalization of overhead costs is useful in determining departmental overhead rates, but it does not identify controllable and noncontrollable costs. For this reason, many firms recast their costs for management reports into a responsibility accounting format that identifies costs with the responsibility centers exercising control over them.

Steps in determining the full cost of a product or service include (1) identifying the departments for cost control, (2) tracing direct costs to departments, (3) allocating the cost of service departments to producing departments, and (4) determining the unit cost of the product or service.

There are different theories as to the behavioral implications of allocating service department costs to the producing departments. Many of these differences rest on what constitutes a "controllable" cost, how that cost is measured, and at what point in the organization the "control" is exercised.

APPENDIX

RECIPROCAL ALLOCATIONS

As stated in the chapter, the direct method and the step method do not fully recognize the interactions between the service departments. In this sense they are approximations based upon simplifying assumptions. The recognition of the reciprocal services through the algebraic method of simultaneous equations overcomes these simplifying assumptions. As a result this method is the most theoretically sound.

The example of the Strident Company in Exhibits 8–1, 8–2, and 8–3 had two service departments and two producing departments. This will require two simultaneous equations. The construction of these equations requires a recasting of the data in Exhibit 8–1 as shown below:

Departmental Statistics	Total	SERVICE DEPTS. Maintenance	SERVICE DEPTS. Medical	PRODUCING DEPTS. Fabrication	PRODUCING DEPTS. Assembly
Maintenance hours used	2,900	100	50	1,750	1,000
Percentage	100%	—	.018	.625	.357
Number of employees	97	10	7	30	50
Percentage	100%	.111	—	.333	.556

These data show the percentages of services rendered to the other departments. Using these percentages, the simultaneous equations are

Let M = total costs, after reallocations, of Maintenance Department

Let N = total costs, after reallocations, of Medical Department

$$M = \$5,600 + .111(N)$$
$$N = \$3,900 + .018(M)$$

THE STRIDENT COMPANY
DEPARTMENTAL COST WORKSHEET
For 19X4

				SERVICE DEPTS.		PRODUCING DEPTS.	
Step	Cost	Allocation Base	Total	Maintenance	Medical	Fabrication	Assembly
1	Indirect labor	Direct	$28,500	$2,000	$1,500	$10,000	$15,000
1	Employee fringe benefits	Direct	12,900	500	300	5,000	7,100
1	Supplies/indirect materials	Direct	6,700	1,000	700	3,000	2,000
2	Depreciation of machinery	Value of machinery	4,800	400	800	2,000	1,600
2	Depreciation of building	Square feet occupied	6,000	960	240	2,400	2,400
2	Factory supervision	Total labor hours	3,200	600	200	800	1,600
2	Telephone expense	Number of phones	700	140	160	200	200
	Total overhead costs		$62,800	$5,600	$3,900	$23,400	$29,900
3	Distribute Maintenance Department	Maintenance hours used		(6,045)	109	3,778	2,158
3	Distribute Medical Department	Number of employees		445	(4,009)	1,335	2,229
	Total overhead costs			$ 0	$ 0	$28,513	$34,287
	Basis of overhead rate					4,000 machine hours	4,000 labor hours
4	Departmental overhead rate					$7.13 per machine hour	$8.57 per labor hour

EXHIBIT A8–1   Reciprocal departments—Worksheet for the departmental allocation of costs of the Strident Company

Substituting,

$$M = \$5,600 + .111(\$3,900 + .018M)$$
$$.998M = \$6,033$$
$$M = \$6,045$$

and

$$N = \$3,900 + .018(\$6,045)$$
$$N = \$4,009$$

These amounts represent the total costs of the two service departments assuming each is charged for the benefits received from other service departments. These amounts are then allocated using the percentages shown above. This allocation is shown in Exhibit A8–1.

A close examination of Exhibits 8–2, 8–3, and A8–1 will show that, while the dollar amounts charged to the two producing departments are different, they are not significantly different. This is because the dollar amounts of the two service departments are relatively small, and their usage of other service department services is also relatively small. This may not always be the case in practice. When a firm uses the simpler methods of step or direct allocation, these results should be tested occasionally with the simultaneous equation method to ensure the simpler methods are providing reasonable approximations.

It should also be noted that the manual calculation of simultaneous equations with a large number of service and producing departments would be unduly cumbersome. The use of computers and matrix algebra can facilitate these calculations.

PROBLEMS AND CASES

8-1 *(Joint Cost Allocation).* BMI is an educational institution with two programs: remedial mathematics and remedial reading. The manager would like to know the cost of each program. Program and cost data are:

	Math	*Reading*
Hours of service delivered	4,000	6,000
Student fee per hour	$8.00	$5.00

Faculty salaries, including fringe benefits, were $47,500 and building costs were $8,300.

REQUIRED:

A. Determine the amount of joint costs to be assigned to each program using the number of units produced.

B. Determine the amount of joint costs to be assigned to each program using the relative sales-value method.

8-2 *(Direct Method Allocation).* The Darien Company provided you with the following departmental information and requested your assistance in determining the total costs of the three producing departments.

Department	Direct Costs	Square Feet	Maintenance Hours
Occupancy	$ 3,000	—	—
Maintenance	8,000	1,000	—
Producing 1	20,000	4,000	200
Producing 2	10,000	2,000	180
Producing 3	30,000	3,000	120
	$71,000	10,000	500

The company uses the direct method.

REQUIRED:

A. Allocate occupancy costs to the production departments.

B. Allocate maintenance costs to the production departments.

C. Determine the total costs of each production department that will be used in establishing overhead rates.

8-3 *(Direct Method of Allocation).* The Gordon Company, a sheltered workshop for disabled persons, is developing accounting data to price its services more effectively. The workshop specializes in the restoration of antique furniture. One department is involved in stripping and refinishing furniture; the other specializes in recaning chairs and couches. Both activities require highly skilled individuals, and Gordon's employees have a reputation of high-quality work. There are three support departments—Accounting, Maintenance, and Medical—in addition to the two producing departments of Refinishing and Recaning. Allocation bases are, number of employees for Accounting Department costs, square feet for the Maintenance Department costs, and number of employees treated for medical costs.

The following data were accumulated for your use in determining the total overhead costs to be used for costing.

	Support			Producing	
	Accounting	Maintenance	Medical	Refinishing	Recaning
Direct costs	$5,000	$15,000	$10,000	$60,000	$45,000
Number of employees	15	45	5	250	200
Square feet	1,500	500	1,500	7,500	4,500
Employees treated	0	10	1	60	30

REQUIRED:

A. Allocate the service department costs to the producing departments using the direct method.

B. What do you think of the allocation bases chosen by the Gordon Company? Suggest other allocation bases.

8-4 *(Step Method of Allocation)*. Refer to the information in problem 8-3. Assume that the Gordon Company uses the step method and allocates the service department costs in the following order: Accounting, Maintenance, and Medical.

REQUIRED:

A. Allocate the service department costs to the producing departments using the step method.

B. What do you think of the order of allocation used by the Gordon Company? Explain.

C. Reverse the order of allocation. How much did it change the total costs in the recaning department?

8-5 *(Direct Method of Allocation)*. The Carlson Corporation has four departments. The costs of the service departments (Administration and Housekeeping) are allocated to the production departments (Manufacturing and Painting) at the end of each period. Administration costs are allocated on the basis of number of employees and housekeeping on square feet. Data for the current period are as follows:

	Administration	Housekeeping	Manufacturing	Painting
Direct costs	$20,000	$5,000	$85,000	$65,000
Number of employees	15	25	400	100
Square feet	2,500	250	5,000	2,500
Direct labor hours	—	—	9,604	2,826
Machine hours	—	—	6,200	—

Manufacturing overhead is applied by machine hours.
Painting overhead is applied by direct labor hours.

REQUIRED:

A. Use the direct method of allocation to allocate the service department costs to the production departments.

B. Determine the overhead application rates for manufacturing and painting.

8-6 *(Step Method of Allocation).* Refer to the data for the Carlson Corporation in Problem 8-5. Assume that the step method is used with housekeeping costs allocated first.

REQUIRED:

Determine the departmental overhead application rates.

8-7 *(Appendix: Reciprocal Method of Allocation).* Refer to the data for the Carlson Corporation in problem 8-5. Assume that the reciprocal method of allocation is used. The number of employees and square-feet data are expressed below in percentage form.

	Administration	Housekeeping	Manufacturing	Painting
Number of employees	—	4.76%	76.19%	19.05%
Square feet	25.00%	—	50.00%	25.00%

REQUIRED:

Determine the departmental overhead application rates.

8-8 *(Joint Cost Allocation).* Fizzle, Inc., produces glues for many purposes. The products are produced in batches by adding three materials in a cooking process. At the end of the cooking process each product can be sold. Only Slime can be produced further.

Data for one batch are as follows:

Labor costs: $50,000
Material costs: 500 pounds of Material X @ $20 per pound
                   300 pounds of Material Y @ $40 per pound
                   200 pounds of Material Z @ $90 per pound
Production output:
Goop   400 pounds at a sales value of $80 per pound
Sticky-stuff   250 pounds at a sales value of $275 per pound
Slime   350 pounds at a sales value of $175 per pound

Slime can be converted to 300 pounds of GotCha selling for $250 per pound by spending another $10,000.

REQUIRED:

A. Allocate the joint costs to the three products using

1. Quantity of output.

2. Relative sales value.

B. Should Slime be processed further or sold at split-off? Explain.

8-9 *(Allocation of Service Department Costs).* Cannery Row Clinic, a not-for-profit medical clinic serving the low-income population of Pampas, needs cost data to justify its grant from the state. During the budgetary allocation process last year they received a grant of $20,000; this was based on 2,000 forecasted patient visits at an average rate of $10 per visit.

At a recent board of directors meeting the granting agency has decided to change the funding formula. No longer will grants be made on an "average" visit. The clinic is now required to determine the historical costs for the past year, by type of service provided, and then use these data in their grant request.

The director of the clinic prepared the following data relative to the clinic.

There are two service departments, Occupancy and Administration, and two revenue producing departments, Medical Services and Radiology. Data for these four departments for the last year are

	Occupancy	Administration	Medical	Radiology
Direct costs	$3,000	$3,800	$12,000	$2,500
Number of patient visits			1,500	600
Square footage		2,000	3,000	1,000
Number of personnel	1	2	6	2

Grantor rules require that occupancy be allocated on the basis of square feet occupied by a department and administration on the basis of number of personnel.

The only variable costs are supplies, amounting to $1.00 per patient visit for medical visits and $2.00 for radiology visits.

REQUIRED:

Prepare a grant request for the coming year assuming that cost behavior patterns will remain unchanged and that forecasted patient visits are 1,800 medical and 650 radiology. Show the allocation of the service department costs to the revenue producing departments and explain why you chose the particular method of allocation.

8-10 *(Effect of Dropping a Department on Allocated Costs).* The Western General Hospital currently employs its own janitorial staff, which incurs the following costs per year.

Labor	$100,000
Supplies	40,000
Overhead	130,000
	$270,000

The hospital employees are asking for a 25% wage increase and it appears that an increase of at least 20% will be necessary. An outside contractor has approached the hospital and offered a three-year contract to do the job for $200,000 per year. Overhead includes depreciation of $20,000, allocated administrative and other fixed costs of $100,000, and variable indirect costs of $10,000.

REQUIRED:

A. Should the Western General Hospital accept the offer? Show your analysis.

B. If a 25% wage increase is granted to the hospital employees, what is the highest contract price the hospital could pay the outside contractor without increasing total hospital costs? Explain fully.

C. What impact will it have on other departments if the hospital accepts the offer?

8-11 *(Allocated Costs and Dropping a Department).* A hospital performs a certain lab test with the following average costs per test.

Lab technician	$1.50
Supplies	1.00
Overhead	2.50
	$5.00

An outside lab has offered to do the tests for $3.00 each. If the center accepts the offer, it will release the appropriate technician and sell the lab equipment at its book value. Lab overhead is composed of depreciation of lab equipment calculated on a straight-line basis, amounting to $.20 per test, an apportioned share of administrative costs, and variable overhead equal to 50% of the salary of the lab technician.

REQUIRED:

A. Prepare an analysis to show whether the center should do the test itself or accept the offer.

B. How much of the administrative cost will other departments have to bear if the lab is dropped?

C. Why might the hospital reject the outside contract?

8-12 *(Sell or Process Further Decision).* From a particular joint process, McCormick Company produces three products: X, Y, and Z. Each product may be sold at the point of split-off or processed further. Additional processing requires no special facilities, and production costs of further processing are entirely variable and traceable to the products involved. In 19X3 all three products were processed beyond split-off. Joint production costs for the year were $60,000. Sales values and costs needed to evaluate McCormick's 19X3 production policy follow.

Product	Units Produced	Sales Values at Split-off	Sales Values	Added Cost
			ADDITIONAL COSTS AND SALES VALUES IF PROCESSED FURTHER	
X	6,000	$25,000	$32,000	$9,000
Y	4,000	$41,000	$45,000	$7,000
Z	2,000	$24,000	$42,000	$8,000

Joint costs are allocated to the products in proportion to the relative physical volume of output for income statement purposes.

REQUIRED:

A. Prepare a production schedule that will maximize firm profits.

B. Prepare an Income Statement at the maximum profit level.

C. Do you agree with the method chosen for allocating joint costs to the inventory? Why or why not?

D. What is the ending inventory values assuming 1,000 units of Y and 500 units of Z are on hand at the end of 19X3?

(CPA adapted)

8-13 *(Overhead Costs and Pricing Decisions).* The Douglas Company produces two products for which the following cost and production data are estimated.

	Product A	Product B
Units produced and sold	20,000	40,000
Direct materials cost, per unit	$4	$ 9
Direct labor costs, per unit	$6	$15
Direct labor hours, per unit	2 hours	5 hours
Variable overhead, per unit	$2	$ 6
Fixed overhead, per month	$360,000	

The Douglas Company prices are set by adding a 30% markup to the full production cost.

REQUIRED:

A. Compute the selling prices of the two products, assuming that the fixed costs are allocated to the products on the basis of total labor hours.

B. Assume that the Douglas Company uses absorption costing with an overhead rate based on 240,000 direct labor hours to account for its products. The maximum capacity of the plant is 250,000 direct labor hours per month. The government would like to buy 1,000 units of Product B with slight modifications. The government would reimburse all normal costs of production plus a fixed fee of $2,500. The 1,000 units could be produced using the excess capacity, although the required modifications would cost the firm $1,000 for additional setup time on the machines. Prepare a schedule showing the profit the Douglas Company would earn on this special order, assuming other sales would be unaffected.

8-14 *(Cost Allocations to Product Lines)*. In its production process the Wilbur Company incurs joint costs of $48,000. The following data concerning possible allocation bases were compiled.

	Variable Production Costs	Labor Hours	Machine Hours	Units Produced	Selling Price
Product A	$45	3	1	1,200	$ 55
Product B	$90	5	4	1,500	$110

REQUIRED:

A. What is the full cost for each product under each of the following allocation bases?

1. Variable production costs.

2. Labor hours.

3. Machine hours.

4. Units produced.

5. Relative sales-value method.

B. Which allocation base do you prefer? Why?

8-15 *(Step Method, Variable and Fixed Costs)*. The Shirley J. Company has prepared a budget showing the following departmental costs and statistical data:

	OVERHEAD		Total Direct Costs*	Square Feet	Kilowatt-Hours	Direct Labor Hours
	Variable	Fixed				
Factory supervision	$ 0	$18,000	—	—	—	—
Occupancy	0	20,000	$ 20,000	—	—	—
Power and light	10,000	6,000	16,000	20,000	—	—
Machining	6,000	18,000	124,000	30,000	10,000	10,000
Finishing	20,000	30,000	200,000	50,000	8,000	20,000
	$36,000	$92,000	$360,000	100,000	18,000	30,000

*Includes direct material and direct labor.

The company allocates the service departments to the producing departments using the step method. Compute separate fixed and variable overhead rates.

REQUIRED:

A. Allocate the costs of the service departments using the step method. The sequence and bases can be determined from the data above. Maintain the distinction between fixed and variable costs.

B. Compute the variable and fixed overhead rates for each production department.

8-16 *(Allocation of Indirect Departmental Costs).* The Bennett Corporation is a manufacturing concern with three separate production departments. The following statistics have been kept concerning these departments.

	Department 1	Department 2	Department 3
Direct labor hours	40,000	25,000	22,000
Number of employees	450	220	240
Factory floorspace (square feet)	12,000	6,000	4,000
Machine hours worked	3,000	8,000	5,000

The firm is trying to determine the most appropriate base with which to allocate the following costs.

Factory maintenance	$24,200
Depreciation of factory building	$33,000
Employee cafeteria	$24,300
Depreciation of machinery	$32,000
Supervisory salaries	$65,520

REQUIRED:

A. What method of allocation would you recommend for each indirect cost? Why?

B. Does the order of allocation matter in this situation (i.e., depreciation of building allocated before factory maintenance, etc.)? Why or why not?

C. Prepare a schedule that shows your allocations and the total costs charged to each of the three producing departments. Round to the nearest whole percentage.

D. Would your allocation for factory maintenance change if you discovered that it was incurred almost entirely in servicing the factory building? How?

8-17 *(Dual Allocation Rates).* Hackensack University installed a WATS line to minimize their long-distance telephone expense. The controller has been asked by the board of regents to devise an allocation process to charge the cost of the WATS line to the three colleges within the university. A staffperson in the controller's office developed the following data after the first year of WATS operation.

Service	School of Business	School of Education	School of Engineering
Budgeted volume: 132,000 minutes	30%	30%	40%
Actual volume: 105,600 minutes	30%	20%	50%
Number of phones: 80 instruments	30	20	30
Number of faculty: 75 professors	20	30	25

The actual costs for the first year were

WATS line (fixed)	$ 66,000
All other long-distance phone service (variable)	198,000
Total long-distance phone expense	$264,000

There have been numerous complaints concerning the WATS line. The most common theme is that the line is always busy, forcing many individuals to dial long distance directly instead of using the WATS line. As a result, long-distance charges were much higher than originally planned. There has been some pressure to install a second WATS line.

REQUIRED:

A. Allocate the cost of long-distance phone service
   1. Based on the Capacity to Serve.
   2. Based on the Dual Capacity and Usage.
   3. Based on Usage only.
B. Which allocation procedure would you choose? Why?
C. What would you recommend to the board of regents to address the complaints, as well as control costs?

8-18 *(Decisions to Close Plant).* You have been engaged to assist management of the Stenger Corporation in arriving at certain decisions. The Stenger Corporation has its home office in Philadelphia and leases factory buildings in Rhode Island, Georgia, and Illinois. The same single product is manufactured in all three factories. The following information is available regarding 19X4 operations.

	Total	Rhode Island	Illinois	Georgia
Sales	$900,000	$200,000	$400,000	$300,000
Fixed costs:				
Factory	$180,000	$ 50,000	$ 55,000	$ 75,000
Administration	59,000	16,000	21,000	22,000
Variable costs	500,000	100,000	220,000	180,000
Allocated home office				
expense	63,000	14,000	28,000	21,000
Total	802,000	180,000	324,000	298,000
Profit from operations	$ 98,000	$ 20,000	$ 76,000	$ 2,000

Home office expense is allocated to the plants on the basis of units sold. The sales price per unit is $10.

The management of Stenger Corporation is displeased with the poor performance of the Georgia factory. The lease on the Georgia factory expires at the end of 19X5. If the lease is renewed, the annual rental will increase by $15,000. If the Georgia factory is shut down, proceeds from the sale of equipment will just cover termination expenses.

If the Georgia factory is shut down, Stenger Corporation will continue to serve the customers of the Georgia factory by one of the following methods:

1. Expand the Rhode Island factory. This would increase fixed expenses of the Rhode Island factory by 15%. In addition, shipping expenses of $2.00 per unit will be incurred on the increased production.

2. Enter into a contract with a competitor who will serve the customers of the Georgia factory. The competitor will pay Stenger Corporation a commission of $1.60 per unit.

REQUIRED:

A. What will the incomes of Stenger Corporation be under each alternative?

B. Prepare a recommendation to the management of Stenger Corporation.

(CPA adapted)

8-19 *(Departmentalization of Costs: Multiple Choice).* The Parker Manufacturing Company has two production departments (Fabrication and Assembly) and three service departments (General Factory Administration, Factory Maintenance, and Factory Cafeteria). The following is a summary of costs and other data for each department prior to allocation of service department costs for the year ended June 30, 19X3.

The costs of the general factory administration department, factory maintenance department, and factory cafeteria are allocated on the basis of direct labor hours, square footage occupied, and number of employees, respectively.

	Fabrication	Assembly	General Factory Administration	Factory Maintenance	Factory Cafeteria
Direct labor costs	$1,950,000	$2,050,000	$90,000	$82,100	$87,000
Direct material costs	$3,130,000	$ 950,000	—	$65,000	$91,000
Manufacturing overhead costs	$1,650,000	$1,850,000	$70,000	$56,100	$62,000
Direct labor hours	562,500	437,500	31,000	27,000	42,000
Number of employees	280	200	12	8	20
Square footage occupied	88,000	72,000	1,750	2,000	4,800

REQUIRED:

Round all final calculations to the nearest dollar.

1. Assuming that Parker elects to distribute service department costs directly to production departments without inter-service department cost allocation, the amount of Factory Maintenance Department costs that would be allocated to the Fabrication Department would be
   a. $0
   b. $111,760
   c. $106,091
   d. $91,440

2. Assuming the same method of allocation as in item 1, the amount of General Factory Administration Department costs allocated to the Assembly Department would be
   a. $0
   b. $63,636
   c. $70,000
   d. $90,000

3. Assume that Parker elects to distribute service department costs to other service departments (starting with the service department with the greatest total costs) as well as the production departments. (Note: Once a service department's costs have been reallocated, no subsequent service department costs are recirculated back to it.) The amount of Factory Cafeteria Department costs allocated to the Factory Maintenance Department would be
   a. $0
   b. $96,000
   c. $3,840
   d. $6,124

4. Assuming the same method of allocation as in item 3, the amount of Factory Maintenance Department costs allocated to the Factory Cafeteria would be
   a. $0
   b. $5,787
   c. $5,856
   d. $148,910

(CPA adapted)

8-20 *(Overhead Allocation and Cost Control)*. The Kelly Company, founded 20 years ago, has achieved a moderate degree of success. The company manufactures and sells pottery items. All manufacturing takes place in one plant that has four departments. Each manufacturing department produces only one product. The four products of Kelly Company are plaques, cups, vases, and plates. Sam Kelly, the president and founder, credits the company's success to the well-designed quality products and to an effective cost control system. The system was installed early in the firm's existence to improve cost control and to serve as a basis for planning.

The company establishes standard costs for material and labor with the participation of plant management. Each year the plant manager, the department heads, and the time study engineers are invited by top management to recommend changes in the standards for the next year. Top management reviews these recommendations and the records of actual performance for the current year before setting the new standards. As a general rule, tight standards representing very efficient performance are established. Top management does this so that no inefficiency or slack will be included in cost goals. The plant manager and department heads are charged with cost control responsibility, and the variances from standard costs are used to measure their performance in carrying out this charge.

No standards are set for factory overhead because the management believes it is too difficult to predict and relate overhead to output. The actual factory overhead for the departments and the plant is accumulated in one "pool." The actual overhead is then allocated to the departments on the basis of departmental output. The schedule below is a three-year summary of overhead allocation among the departments.

	19X5		19X6		19X7	
Department	Units Produced	Allocated* Overhead	Units Produced	Allocated* Overhead	Units Produced	Allocated* Overhead
Plaques	300,000	$120,000	330,000	$126,000	180,000	$ 60,000
Cups	250,000	100,000	270,000	103,091	360,000	120,000
Vases	200,000	80,000	220,000	84,000	300,000	100,000
Plates	250,000	100,000	280,000	106,909	360,000	120,000
Totals	1,000,000	$400,000	1,100,000	$420,000	1,200,000	$400,000

*Dollar amounts are rounded to the nearest dollar.

The company's executives are convinced that more effective cost control can be obtained than is currently being realized from the standard cost system. A review of cost performance for recent years disclosed several factors that led them to this conclusion. The factors disclosed were:

1. Unfavorable variances were the norm rather than the exception, although the size of the variances was quite uniform.

2. Department managers took steps that, while benefiting their own departments, were detrimental to overall company performance.

3. Employee motivation, especially among first-line supervisors, appeared to be low.

REQUIRED:

A. What are the probable effects, if any, on the motivation of the plant managers and department heads from
   1. The participative standard cost system?
   2. The use of "tight" standards?
   Explain the reasons for your conclusions.
B. What effect, if any, will the practice of applying actual overhead costs on the basis of actual units produced have on the motivation of department heads to control overhead costs? Explain your answer.

(CMA adapted)

8-21 *(Allocation of Overhead to Product Lines).* The Herbert Manufacturing Company is a manufacturer of custom-designed restaurant and kitchen furniture. Herbert Manufacturing uses a job order cost accounting system. Actual overhead costs incurred during the month are applied to the products on the basis of actual direct labor hours required to produce the products. The overhead consists primarily of supervision, employee benefits, maintenance costs, property taxes, and depreciation.

Herbert Manufacturing recently won a contract to manufacture the furniture for a new fast-food chain that is expanding rapidly in the area. In general, this furniture is durable but of a lower quality than Herbert Manufacturing normally manufactures. To produce this new line, Herbert Manufacturing must purchase more molded plastic parts for the furniture than for its current line. Through innovative industrial engineering, an efficient manufacturing process for this new furniture has been developed that requires only a minimum capital investment. Management is very optimistic about the profit improvement the new product line will bring.

At the end of October, the start-up month for the new line, the controller has prepared a separate income statement for the new product line. On a consolidated basis the gross profit percentage was normal; however, the profitability for the new line was less than expected.

At the end of November the results were somewhat improved. Consolidated profits were good, but the reported profitability for the new product line was less than expected. John Herbert, president of the corporation, is concerned that knowledgeable stockholders will criticize his decision to add this lower-quality line at a time when profitability appeared to be increasing with their standard product line.

The results as published for the first nine months, for October and for November, are presented below.

HERBERT MANUFACTURING COMPANY
(000 omitted)

	Fast-Food Furniture	Custom Furniture	Consolidated
Nine months			
Year-to-date, 19X8			
Gross sales	—	$8,100	$8,100
Direct material	—	$2,025	$2,025
Direct labor:			
Forming	—	758	758
Finishing	—	1,314	1,314
Assembly	—	558	558
Overhead	—	1,779	1,779
Cost of sales	—	6,434	6,434
Gross profit	—	$1,666	$1,666
Gross profit percentage	—	20.6%	20.6%
October 1978			
Gross sales	$400	$ 900	$1,300
Direct material	$200	$ 225	$ 425
Direct labor:			
Forming	17	82	99
Finishing	40	142	182
Assembly	33	60	93
Overhead	60	180	240
Cost of sales	350	689	1,039
Gross profit	$ 50	$ 211	$ 261
Gross profit percentage	12.5%	23.4%	20.1%
November 19X8			
Gross sales	$800	$ 800	$1,600
Direct material	$400	$ 200	$ 600
Direct labor:			
Forming	31	72	103
Finishing	70	125	195
Assembly	58	53	111
Overhead	98	147	245
Cost of sales	657	597	1,254
Gross profit	$143	$ 203	$ 346
Gross profit percentage	17.9%	25.4%	21.6%

Mr. Jameson, cost accounting manager, has stated that the overhead allocation based only on direct labor hours is no longer appropriate. On the basis of a recently completed study of the overhead accounts, Mr. Jameson feels that only the supervision and employee benefits should be allocated on the basis of direct labor hours, and the balance of the overhead should be allocated on a machine hour basis. In his judgment the increase in the profitability of the custom design furniture is due to a misallocation of overhead in the present system.

The actual direct labor hours and machine hours for the past two months are shown below.

	Fast-Food Furniture	Custom Furniture
Machine Hours:		
October:		
Forming	660	10,700
Finishing	660	7,780
Assembly	—	—
	1,320	18,480
November:		
Forming	1,280	9,640
Finishing	1,280	7,400
Assembly	—	—
	2,560	17,040
Direct Labor Hours:		
October:		
Forming	1,900	9,300
Finishing	3,350	12,000
Assembly	4,750	8,700
	10,000	30,000
November:		
Forming	3,400	8,250
Finishing	5,800	10,400
Assembly	8,300	7,600
	17,500	26,250

The actual overhead costs for the past two months were:

	October	November
Supervision	$ 13,000	$ 13,000
Employee benefits	95,000	109,500
Maintenance	50,000	48,000
Depreciation	42,000	42,000
Property taxes	8,000	8,000
All other	32,000	24,500
Total	$240,000	$245,000

REQUIRED:

A. Based on Mr. Jameson's recommendation, reallocate the overhead for October and November using direct labor hours as the allocation base for supervision and employee benefits. Use machine hours as the base for the remaining overhead costs.

B. Support or criticize Mr. Jameson's conclusion that the increase in custom design profitability is due to a misallocation of overhead. Use the data developed in part A to support your analysis.

C. Mr. Jameson has also recommended that consideration be given to using predetermined overhead absorption rates calculated on an annual basis rather than allocating actual cost over actual volume each month. He stated that this is particularly applicable now that the company has two distinct product lines. Discuss the advantages of predetermined overhead rates.

(CMA adapted)

8-22 *(Allocation of Marketing Costs to Products).* The Scent Company sells men's toiletries to retail stores throughout the United States. For planning and control purposes the Scent Company is organized into twelve geographic regions with two to six territories within each region. One sales representative is assigned to each territory and has exclusive rights to all sales made in that territory. Merchandise is shipped from the manufacturing plant to the 12 regional warehouses, and the sales in each territory are shipped from the regional warehouse. National headquarters allocates a specific amount at the beginning of the year for regional advertising.

The net sales for the Scent Company for the year ended September 30, 19X4, totaled $10 million. Costs incurred by national headquarters for national administration, advertising, and warehousing are summarized as follows:

National administration	$250,000
National advertising	125,000
National warehousing	175,000
	$550,000

The results of operations for the South Atlantic Region for the year ended September 30, 19X4, are as follows:

SCENT COMPANY
STATEMENT OF OPERATIONS FOR SOUTH ATLANTIC REGION
For the Year Ended September 30, 19X4

Net sales		$900,000
Costs and expenses:		
Advertising fees	$ 54,700	
Bad-debt expense	3,600	
Cost of sales	460,000	
Freight-out	22,600	
Insurance	10,000	
Salaries and employee benefits	81,600	
Sales commissions	36,000	
Supplies	12,000	
Travel and entertainment	14,100	
Wages and employee benefits	36,000	
Warehouse depreciation	8,000	
Warehouse operating costs	15,000	
Total costs and expenses		753,600
Territory contribution		$146,400

The South Atlantic Region consists of two territories—Green and Purple. The salaries and employee benefits consist of the following items:

Region vice-president	$24,000
Regional marketing manager	15,000
Regional warehouse manager	13,400
Sales personnel (one for each territory with all receiving the same salary base)	15,600
Employee benefits (20%)	13,600
	$81,600

The sales personnel receives a base salary plus a 4% commission on all items sold in their territory. Bad-debt expense has averaged .4% of net sales in the past. Travel and entertainment costs are incurred by the sales personnel calling upon their customers. Freight-out is a function of the quantity of goods shipped and the distance shipped. Thirty percent of the insurance is expended for protection of the inventory while it is in the regional warehouse, and the remainder is incurred for the protection of the warehouse. Supplies are used in the warehouse for packing the merchandise that is shipped. Wages relate to the hourly-paid employees who fill orders in the warehouse. The warehouse operating costs account contains such costs as heat, light, and maintenance.

The following cost analyses and statistics by territory for the current year are representative of past experience and are representative of expected future operations.

	Green	Purple	Total
Sales	$300,000	$600,000	$900,000
Cost of sales	$184,000	$276,000	$460,000
Advertising fees	$ 21,800	$ 32,900	$ 54,700
Travel and entertainment	$ 6,300	$ 7,800	$ 14,100
Freight-out	$ 9,000	$ 13,600	$ 22,600
Units sold	150,000	350,000	500,000
Pounds shipped	210,000	390,000	600,000
Salespeople miles traveled	21,600	38,400	60,000

REQUIRED:

A. The top management of Scent Company wants the regional vice-presidents to present their operating data in a more meaningful manner. Therefore, management has requested the regions to separate their operating costs into the fixed and variable components of order-getting (e.g., sales commissions), order-filling (e.g., freight-out), and administration. Prepare a schedule that presents the costs for the region by territory with the costs separated into variable and fixed categories by order-getting, order-filling, and administrative functions.

B. Suppose the top management of Scent Company is considering splitting the Purple Territory into two separate territories (Red and Blue). From the data that have been presented, identify what data would be relevant to this decision (either for or against) and indicate what other data you would collect to aid top management in its decision.

C. If Scent Company keeps its records in accordance with the classification required in part A, can standards and flexible budgets be employed by the company in planning and controlling marketing costs? Give reasons for your answer.

(CMA adapted)

8-23 *(Profit Plan and Cost Allocations in a Hospital).* The administrator of Appletown Hospital has asked you to prepare an operating budget (Profit Plan) for the next year ending June 30, 19X2, and presented you with a number of service projections for the year. The following are estimated room requirements for inpatients by type of service.

Type of Patient	Total Patients Expected	Average Number of Days in Hospital	PERCENTAGE OF REGULAR PATIENTS SELECTING TYPES OF SERVICE		
			Private	Semiprivate	Ward
Medical	2,100	7	10%	60%	30%
Surgical	2,400	10	15%	75%	10%

Daily rentals per patient are $80 for a private room, $70 for a semiprivate room, and $50 for a ward.

Operating room charges are based on man-minutes (number of minutes the operating room is in use multiplied by number of personnel assisting in the operation). The per-man-minute charges are $.26 for inpatients and $.44 for outpatients. Studies for the current year show that operations are divided by type as follows:

Type of Operation	Number of Operations	Average Number of Minutes per Operation	Average Number of Personnel Required
A	800	30	4
B	700	45	5
C	300	90	6
D	200	120	8
	2,000		
Outpatient	180	20	3

The following is a budget of direct costs for the year ending June 30, 19X2, by departments.

Service departments:	
Maintenance of plant	$ 100,000
Operation of plant	55,000
Administration	195,000
All others	384,000
Revenue-producing departments:	
Operating room	136,880
All others	1,400,000
Total direct costs	$2,270,880

All service department costs are to be allocated to the revenue producing departments. The following information is provided for cost-allocation purposes.

	Square Feet	Salaries
General services:		
Maintenance of plant	12,000	$ 80,000
Operation of plant	28,000	50,000
Administration	10,000	110,000
All others	36,250	205,000
Revenue-producing departments:		
Operating room	17,500	30,000
All others	86,250	605,000
	190,000	$1,080,000

Bases of allocations:
   Maintenance of plant—salaries
   Operation of plant—square feet
   Administration—salaries
   All others—8% to operating room
               92% to other revenue-producing services

REQUIRED:

Prepare schedules showing the computation of

A. The number of patient days (number of patients multiplied by average stay in hospital) expected by type of patients (medical or surgical) and type of room service (private, semiprivate, or ward).

B. Expected gross revenue from room service.

C. The total number of man-minutes expected for operating-room services for inpatients and outpatients. For inpatients, show the breakdown of total operating-room man-minutes by type of operation.

D. Expected gross revenue from operating-room services.

E. Cost per man-minute for operating-room services, assuming that the step-down method of cost allocation is used. (Costs of the general services departments are allocated first to the general services departments that they serve and then to the revenue-producing departments.)

F. Operating budget (Profit Plan) showing the budget for each revenue-producing center and the entire hospital.

(CPA adapted)

8-24 *(Departmentalization of Costs for Decision Making).* Thrift-Shops, Inc., operates a chain of three food stores in a state that recently enacted legislation permitting municipalities within the state to levy an income tax on corporations operating within their respective municipal limits. The legislation establishes a uniform tax rate, which the municipalities may levy, and regulations that provide that the tax is to be computed on income derived within the taxing municipality after a reasonable and consistent allocation of generation overhead expenses. General overhead expenses have not been allocated to individual stores previously and include warehouse, general office, advertising, and delivery expenses.

Each of the municipalities in which Thrift-Shops, Inc., operates a store has levied the corporate income tax as provided by state legislation, and management is considering two plans for allocating general overhead expenses to the stores. The 19X9 operating results before general overhead and taxes for each store were as shown on the following page.

Additional information includes the following:

1. One-fifth of the warehouse space is used to house the central office, and depreciation on this space is included in other central office expenses. Warehouse operating expenses vary with quantity of merchandise sold.

2. Delivery expenses vary with distance and number of deliveries. The distances from the warehouse to each store and the number of deliveries made in 19X9 are illustrated in the following tabulation.

Store	Miles	Number of Deliveries
Ashville	120	140
Burns	200	64
Clinton	100	104

3. All advertising is prepared by the central office and is distributed in the areas in which stores are located.

4. As each store was opened, the fixed portion of central office salaries increased $7,000 and other central office expenses increased $2,500. Basic fixed central office salaries amount to $10,000 and basic fixed other central office expenses amount to $12,000. The remainder of

central office salaries and the remainder of other central office expenses vary with sales.

	STORE			
	Ashville	Burns	Clinton	Total
Sales (net)	$416,000	$353,600	$270,400	$1,040,000
Less: Cost of sales	215,700	183,300	140,200	539,200
Gross margin	$200,300	$170,300	$130,200	$ 500,800
Less local operating expenses:				
Fixed	$ 60,800	$ 48,750	$ 50,200	$ 159,750
Variable	54,700	64,220	27,448	146,368
Total	115,500	112,970	77,648	306,118
Income before general overhead and taxes	$ 84,800	$ 57,330	$ 52,552	$ 194,682

General overhead expenses were as follows:

Warehousing and delivery expenses:

Warehouse depreciation.............................	$ 20,000	
Warehouse operation	30,000	
Delivery expenses	40,000	$ 90,000

Central office expenses:

Advertising...	$ 18,000	
Central office salaries	37,000	
Other central office expenses	28,000	83,000
Total general overhead...........................		$ 173,000

REQUIRED:

A. For each of the following plans for allocating general overhead expenses, compute the income of each store that would be subject to the municipal levy on corporation income.

Plan 1. Allocate all general overhead expenses on the basis of sales volume.

Plan 2. First, allocate central office salaries and other central office expenses evenly to warehouse operations and each store. Second, allocate the resulting warehouse operations expenses, warehouse depreciation, and advertising to each store on the basis of sales volume. Third, allocate delivery expenses to each store on the basis of delivery miles times number of deliveries.

B. Management has decided to expand one of the three stores to increase sales by $50,000. The expansion will increase local fixed operating expenses by $7,500 and require 10 additional deliveries from the warehouse. Determine which store management should select for expansion to maximize corporate profits.

(CPA adapted)

8-25 *(Cost Determination and Reimbursement in Not-for-Profit Setting).* Midtown Mental Health Center served a large population in the core area of a major city. Midtown was funded primarily by one source—a parent agency that advanced funds to the center on a monthly basis. Jill Day, the assistant director of Midtown, consulted with her staff of professionals around the middle of each month to get their input on the following month's projected demand for services. This estimate was the basis for budgeting professional staff hours and determining the financial needs for the following month. For budgeting purposes, total costs were estimated to be twice the direct labor cost. Overhead, the difference between total cost and direct labor cost, was made up of costs such as rent on the small building, telephone, office supplies, and supplies for the children's workshop. Because direct labor cost represented the largest portion of the agency's budget, Jill reasoned that it would be the best barometer for predicting financial need.

The staff knew the community well and over the years no major differences occurred between predicted and actual demand. As the center became more visible to the community the demand for services rose, but this increase was almost always expected. This good forecasting meant that the regular staff's overtime was cut to a minimum and that part-time and volunteer staff could be scheduled well in advance.

Historically, another benefit of good forecasting was Midtown's ability to arrange for funds needed for the month to be deposited to their account at the beginning of the month. The plan by which the parent agency reimbursed Midtown was based on direct service payroll cost as forecasted. Some time ago, it was determined that the average wage rate for members of the professional staff was $7.00 per hour. Jill would multiply forecasted direct labor hours by the $7.00 figure to arrive at forecasted total direct service payroll cost and forward this before the twenty-fifth of the month. The parent agency would then forward an amount equal to 200% of this direct labor cost to Midtown by the first of the following month. Midtown provided no-fee services primarily to low-income and occupationally disabled individuals. Occasionally small donations were received from clients, but these were used to buy coffee and rolls for the waiting area at the agency.

This procedure had worked well for years. However, during each of the preceding four months Jill had to request additional funds during the month to meet current expenses, even though the actual demand was in line with projections. The parent agency, though able to meet these four requests for additional funds, wanted Jill to develop a new and more effective procedure for estimating financial requirements. Jill's first step, a review of the cost report for the past four months and a comparison with the prior year, showed a startling change in performance results (see Exhibit 1).

Jill believed that the agency's problem was rising costs and the inability of the present forecasting system to take these into account. Unfortunately, the available cost data told her little about the cost relationships for individual services. Midtown's operating costs were categorized into the nine accounts shown in Exhibit 1. Individual client cost records were not used, and the cost of services provided on a per-client basis was never calculated.

Detailed data existed on only direct professional hours spent with clients and supplies used during certain group and family therapy sessions. Each professional was requested to fill in the amount of time spent with each client and the supplies used on that client's records.

Jill's first step was to establish some overall cost relationships. Professional staff, for example, fell into three different pay grades, with the following regular hourly wage rates.

Social Worker II	$9.00
Social Worker I	$7.00
Clerical and aides	$4.00

MIDTOWN MENTAL HEALTH CENTER
COMPARATIVE COST DATA AND BUDGET REQUISITIONS

	Average Monthly Costs Based on Four Months	
	Previous Year	Current Year
A. Comparative Cost Data		
Direct service payroll	$23,400	$27,200
Fringe benefits	17,550	20,400
Overtime wages	2,340	5,440
Overtime fringe benefits	1,755	4,080
Rent	200	200
Utilities	340	360
Children's workshop supplies	170	180
Other supplies	50	50
Equipment depreciation	100	100
Total	$45,905	$58,010
B. Budget Requisition for Reimbursement from Parent Agency		
1. Estimated direct professional hours	3,400	3,600
2. Budgeted reimbursement (1) × $7 × 200%	$47,600	$50,400
C. Number of Professional Staff on Payroll		
SW II	5	8
SW I	8	8
Clerical and aides	4	2

EXHIBIT 1

These rates applied to a regular workweek of 40 hours. For work in excess of this number of hours, employees were paid an overtime premium of 50% on top of their regularly hourly rate. During the current year the center was expected to generate 3,500 hours of professional service per month.

In addition to their wages, employees also received various kinds of benefits, including vacation pay, health insurance, and an opportunity to participate in the retirement plan. The cost of these benefits to Midtown Mental Health amounted to about 75% of its total payroll.

Rent was minimal and did not vary at all. Utilities and children's workshop supplies expenses tended to vary with the volume of service. Most other expenses remained more or less fixed per month.

In addition to the above Jill also collected information on a recently completed case. The length of the agency's relationship with the client in this case was three and one-half weeks. The direct service time spent with the client was as follows:

	Type of Service	Level of Staffperson	Hours
Week 1	Intake	Aide	1.50
	Adult Counseling	SW I	2.00
	Family Session	SW II	1.50
Week 2	Child Therapy	SW II	1.75
	Family Session	SW II	3.00
Week 3	Adult Counseling	SW I	2.50
	Family Session	SW I	1.50
Week 4	Family Session	SW II	2.75
			16.50

REQUIRED:

A. Analyze the reasons for recent operating deficits.

B. Using all available information, determine the actual cost of serving the recent client.

C. Evaluate the validity of budget rate for reimbursement currently in use.

D. Develop an updated forecasting model.

E. Discuss steps Jill could take to ensure efficient operations.

(Prepared by Ronald G. Rauch under the direction of Professor Kavasseri V. Ramanathan)

part **4**

THE USE OF DATA IN MAKING DECISIONS

chapter **9**

REVENUE AND PRICING DECISIONS

One of the most important operating decisions management must make is establishing the selling prices for its products and services. In the long run the firm's prices must be sufficient to cover all costs and leave a profit margin adequate to reward the investors for the use of their funds. In this chapter we will look at how accounting and economic data can be used by management to make pricing decisions. We will study pricing from three different perspectives. First, we will examine pricing where there is an established marketplace. The economic theory of pricing, as shown by supply and demand curves, is relevant here. Second, we will examine pricing decisions where prices are determined by costs plus a profit margin. Third, we will look at the role of the contribution margin approach in pricing decisions.

OPEN-MARKET PRICING

A large segment of microeconomic theory is devoted to pricing. Economic theory assumes that there is a known, open, and free marketplace for the goods and services being offered for sale. There are two key elements in assessing the market structure. The first concerns the number of buyers and sellers in the marketplace. Typically, the larger the number of buyers and sellers, the more competitive the market.

Second, the market structure is influenced by the extent to which the product is standardized. If other products are reasonable substitutes for the ones offered for sale, there will be increased competition. For example, in the transportation industry a plane, a bus, and a railroad may be in competition to provide service between two points. The more easily one mode of transportation can be substituted for another, the greater the competition. Also, the nature of the product can determine the market structure. For example, with a highly perishable product, such as fresh strawberries, it is impossible to compete in many geographic markets without incurring large transportation and distribution costs.

THE ECONOMIC THEORY OF PRICE

The basic factors in economic theory are the supply of the product and the demand for it. The quantity of the product that customers will buy over a period of time depends on the price. The higher the price, the fewer the units of product customers will be willing to buy; the lower the price, the more units of product they will buy. A typical demand curve (*dd*) is shown in Exhibit 9–1. The **demand curve** relates the market prices and the quantity of the product the *customers* want to buy. The demand curve slopes downward and to the right, showing that when the price is increased, customers will be willing to buy a smaller quantity, and when prices are lowered, customers will buy a larger quantity.

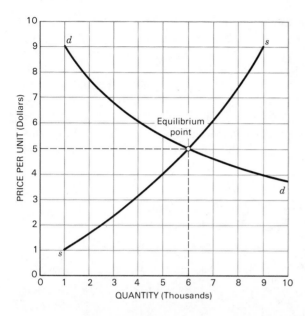

The **supply curve** relates the market prices and the quantity of product that the *suppliers* or *producers* are willing to supply. As shown in Exhibit 9–1, the supply curve (*ss*) rises upward to the right. At a higher price the supplier will increase output. However, as production increases, the supplier ultimately faces diminishing returns on the productive facilities. **Diminishing returns** recognizes that as the use of production facilities increases, it takes more productive energy per unit to produce one additional unit. Workers become tired and less efficient, machines break down more often, factories become crowded, and premium prices must be paid to get material and labor.

How do supply and demand interact to determine the market price? The demand schedule shows us the quantities demanded by the customers combined with the prices they are willing to pay. We can then say, "If customers demand so much, the price will be thus and so." The supply schedule shows us how much the producers are willing to produce at various prices. We can then say, "If so much product is available, the price is thus and so, and the producers will provide so much product." However, neither schedule alone tells what the price will be or how much will be produced by the suppliers or purchased by the customers.

The market price will be determined at the intersection point of the supply and demand curves. At this **equilibrium point** the amount the producers will provide equals the amount the customers demand, and the market is cleared. This point is shown on Exhibit 9–1 where the equilibrium price is $5.00 and the equilibrium quantity is 6,000 units. If the market price were to increase, to $9.00 for example, the quantity supplied would increase to 9,000 units. The increased price would cause the quantity demanded to decrease to 1,000 units.

At $9.00 the quantity supplied would exceed the quantity demanded. Excess supply would cause the price demanded to decrease. The impact of the excess oil supplies in 1986 provide an excellent example of the resulting decrease in price. At a point lower than the equilibrium price, say, $4.00 per unit, the quantity demanded would exceed the quantity supplied, and the buyers would "bid" the price up.

The previous discussion has assumed that the changes taking place were in the quantity supplied or the quantity demanded. The difference in the quantity demanded is shown in the graph on the left. The movement is along a single demand curve.

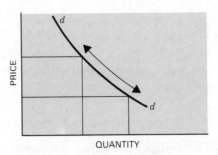
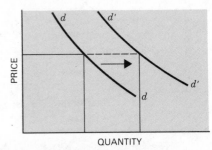

It is also possible that the demand or supply curve might shift. For example, the graph on the right shows a difference in the customer demand that is independent of price differences. The demand curve could shift because of changes in consumer tastes, consumer income, or the prices of related products that could be substituted. In the same way, the supply curve could shift because of changes in the factors of production or the cost of the inputs.

The way in which a change in price affects the demand is called **price elasticity.** If a small decrease in price creates a large increase in quantity sold, the demand is called *elastic*. If a substantial decrease in price is required to increase quantity sold, demand is called *inelastic*. The raising or lowering of the price of an inelastic product would have little or no effect on the amount of product sold. Whether a product has elastic or inelastic demand characteristics can be vital to decisions regarding price changes. While a manager may be able to see broad stages of price elasticity, it is often difficult to perceive it accurately.

The scope of the demand curve for a particular firm depends on its market structure—that is, the degree of competition in the market for the product. There are four broad classes of market structures: pure competition, pure monopoly, monopolistic competition, and oligopoly.

PURE COMPETITION

In a purely competitive market there are a large number of buyers and sellers; each firm's transactions are so small in relation to the total market that they do not affect the price of its product or service.[1] The price is determined in the marketplace. The firm can sell as much as it wishes if it sells at the market price. More importantly, it cannot sell *any* product at a higher price. The firm's demand curve is horizontal. The price is constant and the average revenue and the marginal revenue are equal. A purely competitive firm (1) can sell nothing above the equilibrium price, (2) can sell all it produces at exactly that price, and (3) would have no reason to lower its price below the existing market price. Management's decision in a purely competitive market is to select the output (volume) level, given the price, that maximizes the firm's profits.

PURE MONOPOLY

In a pure monopoly there is only one producer. The demand curve of the monopolist will slope downward to the right. For profit maximization the firm should operate at the output level where its marginal cost equals the marginal revenue. This point will simultaneously determine the optimum price and output level. The monopolistic firm can determine either the price or the quantity, but not both. Given one, the other is determined automatically by the market.

MONOPOLISTIC COMPETITION

It is very rare to find pure competition or pure monopoly. Most firms have some competition, though not pure competition. In the monopolistic competitive market structure the customers believe that there are differences between the products of different firms. These firms have a number of competitors producing substitutable products. Nevertheless, they have some control over their pricing policies. These firms face downward-sloping demand curves, in contrast to the horizontal demand curve in a purely competitive market.

If a firm is successful in differentiating its product from the products of other firms, it will have greater flexibility in pricing and output decisions. A firm with strong product differentiation and loyal customers has greater control over its prices.

OLIGOPOLY

In an oligopoly there are a few large sellers, each with a large share of the market. These firms interact. The revenue of a given seller depends on the reactions of competitors to changes in its selling prices. An action taken by one firm will cause a reaction by others. If an oligopolistic seller raises prices and competitors raise theirs, or if the firm lowers its prices and they lower theirs,

---

[1]Other assumptions of pure competition include perfect homogeneity of the products, free entry and exits to the market, and perfect information about price, cost, and quality by the buyers and sellers in the market.

its demand curve will have the same general shape as the demand curve for the whole market. In the oligopoly marketplace, the optimal price and output decision depends on how competing firms react.

PRICING: AN ART OR A SCIENCE?

Economic theory provides a straightforward approach to establishing price and volume for pure monopoly, pure competition, and monopolistic competition. Under an oligopolistic market, the approach is more complex and often impossible to specify, since firms can interact in many ways. Because of this complexity, price leadership by the dominant firm, or firms, is common, and stable prices develop. Also, oligopolistic firms actively engage in nonprice competition such as service improvement, style differences, and advertising.

While the theoretical pricing model developed by the economists is sound, it is difficult to apply directly in practice. First, it assumes that the firm's demand curve is known. Generally management does not have available data that are accurate and reliable enough to give more than a rough picture of the demand curve. Therefore, while firms may consider the shape of the demand curve, they may not be able to do so in an exacting way.

Second, economics assumes that firms are profit maximizers. Many legal and societal goals and constraints influence management's desire for profits. Certainly stability, growth, and security are important to managers, and these can be obtained short of total profit maximization.

Third, many factors besides price affect a firm's demand function. For example, there is a necessary interaction between marketing and distribution policies, promotional and advertising policies, sales staff deployment, customer services offered, and the types of products sold. All these factors have a heavy influence on the amount of product that can be sold at a specific price.

In a very real sense pricing is an art rather than a science. Economics provides a sound theoretical background that may be difficult to apply in practice. These difficulties in determining the demand functions have led many managements to adopt a trial-and-error (**heuristic**) approach to pricing.

FULL COST-BASED PRICING

One method of heuristically establishing price is to calculate the cost of the product and then add a markup for income. This method has been called **cost-based pricing, cost-plus pricing,** or **average cost pricing.** Each term implies that an addition for income is made to some suitable cost base. This approach is based on the fact that in the long run the firm must recover *all* of its costs plus a normal profit margin if it is to remain in business. Full cost-based pricing is applicable both to standard or new products offered in the open market and to specially designed, nonstandard products.

PRICING STANDARD PRODUCTS

To illustrate how a firm might price standard or new products, let's assume that a firm has budgeted production of 150,000 units requiring the following costs. Management would also like to earn a 15% rate of return on the stockholders' equity of $1,000,000. The **target price,** that is, the price management will seek in the marketplace, will be determined as follows:

	Total	Per Unit
Direct materials	$ 150,000	$1.00
Direct labor	250,000	1.67
Variable overhead	125,000	.83
Fixed overhead	75,000	.50
Fixed selling and administrative	300,000	2.00
Total cost	$ 900,000	$6.00
Desired income (15% × $1,000,000)	150,000	1.00
Target revenue (price)	$1,050,000	$7.00

If the marketplace accepts the price of $7.00, the firm will recover all of its costs and earn the desired rate of return on stockholders' equity at a volume of 150,000 units. If the price is too high, relative to the competition, then the sales volume will be less than budgeted and the firm will fail in achieving its goals. If the price is too low, relative to the competition, actual volume should exceed the planned volume and the firm will become a price leader. Of course, in a competitive marketplace the firm would be foregoing available profits. In this way, the target price represents the first step in a heuristic approach to setting the selling price.

In the illustration above, the target price was based on the *total* cost of the firm. As we illustrated in Chapters 5, 6, and 7 on product costing, firms typically do not use cost accounting systems that measure *total* cost per unit of product. Rather, firms measure product costs on either an absorption or variable costing basis. Both of these systems record only designated production costs as product costs; neither system treats the selling and administrative costs as product costs. Thus, in order to develop target prices using these product costs, management must apply a markup percentage to the production costs that includes an allowance for the period costs and the desired rate of return. For example, let's assume that through past experience management has determined that a markup of 75% of the product cost measured through absorption costing will provide a reasonable target price. The determination of the target price of $7.00 would be

	Total	Per Unit
Direct material	$ 150,000	$1.00
Direct labor	250,000	1.67
Variable overhead	125,000	.83
Fixed overhead	75,000	.50
Total cost	$ 600,000	$4.00
Markup (75% of cost)	450,000	3.00
Target revenue (price)	$1,050,000	$7.00

Given the same market, the firm would have to use a markup of 100% of cost if the product costs were determined by variable costing. In this case the target price would be determined as follows:

	Total	Per Unit
Direct material	$ 150,000	$1.00
Direct labor	250,000	1.67
Variable overhead	125,000	.83
Total cost	$ 525,000	$3.50
Markup (100% of cost)	525,000	3.50
Target revenue (price)	$1,050,000	$7.00

The selection of an absorption or variable costing system is not the pivotal issue in establishing the target price. The important issues are the determination of the markup percentage *relative* to the measured product cost, and the acceptance by the marketplace of the target price. The optimum resolution of the pricing dilemma depends on management's insight into what the market will accept and the relationship of this price to the product cost. If management believes that the firm is in a strong position, they may adjust the markup percentage upward; if they sense a weakening of their market position, they may adjust the markup percentage downward.

Cost-based pricing cannot be considered as a rigid, deterministic formula. It is simply one way of determining the target price on the first trial in a trial-and-error approach. If, as we stated before, the target price is unacceptable to the buyers in the market, the firm will have no choice but to adjust the selling price or to change their product line.

It is also incorrect to assume that a firm will use the same markup percentage for all products in its product line. The markup will vary according to competition, industry custom, and customer acceptance. The percentage markup will also vary according to the company goals of creating an interaction between profit margin and inventory turnover. Many firms have found that a slightly lower profit margin is more than offset by increased volume. Since the basic goal is a satisfactory profit, and profit is a function of both profit margin and turnover, the firm may adopt a range of markup strategies.

PRICING NONSTANDARD PRODUCTS

Where there is demand for a product that does not currently exist, such as the space program's space shuttle, competition goes beyond pricing issues. Here, competition is based on scientific and technical competence, management skills, and past experience, not on price alone. In these situations price is determined by negotiation and contract commitments.

Although a large number of different contract types are available, two broad classes are typical:

1. In a **fixed-price contract** both parties agree to a price that remains unchanged for the life of the contract. A fixed-price contract requires past experience with the product or relatively low risk for both the buyer and seller.

2. In a **cost-reimbursable contract** the seller is reimbursed all reasonable (allowable) costs incurred in fulfilling the contract plus an agreed-upon fee. The buyer assumes a large portion of the risk, because the seller will be reimbursed for all allowable costs. The seller should not suffer a loss, but could fail to make an acceptable rate of return on productive assets.

Three broad types of cost-reimbursable contracts have been widely used. In the **cost-plus-percentage contract** (CPP), the fee is a percentage of the actual costs incurred. If the contract is cost-plus-10%, and the supplier incurred costs of $100,000, the supplier would earn profits of $10,000 on the contract and $110,000 would be the price to the buyer. If the costs were $200,000, the fee would be $20,000 and the total price, $220,000. This contract is potentially dangerous for the buyer because the supplier can indiscriminately incur costs to increase the fee. It was used for government contracting during wartime but it is not widely used today.

In the **cost-plus-fixed-fee contract** (CPFF) the buyer and the seller negotiate a fee based on budgeted costs. Suppose, for example, that both the supplier and the buyer believe that costs of $500,000 are reasonable to design and manufacture a space shuttle component, and that a fee of 15% of this cost, or $75,000, is fair and adequate. The contract would be for $575,000. If, because of cost overruns, the actual costs were $600,000, the buyer would reimburse the supplier $675,000—the original fee of $75,000 plus all costs allowed in the contract. The actual profit return, based on cost, is 12.5% ($75,000 ÷ $600,000) rather than the planned 15%. Because the extra costs probably consumed company capacity, the lower return on costs may mean that the overall rate of return for the seller will fall below an acceptable rate to maintain the investment.

An **incentive contract** can be used to encourage a supplier to conserve costs. For example, an incentive contract may call for cost-plus-fixed-fee if the company meets or exceeds the original budgeted costs and include a preagreed way for the buyer and seller to share in cost savings when costs are below budget. Assume that a firm has an incentive contract that calls for sharing with the buyer all cost savings in a 50:50 ratio. The original contract was for $500,000 costs and a $75,000 fee. If the firm incurs allowable costs of $460,000 to complete the job, it will be reimbursed $555,000 ($460,000 costs + $75,000 fee + ½ of $40,000 savings). The firm's profit percentage would be raised to 20.7% ($95,000 ÷ $460,000), considerably higher than the 15% originally planned. If the seller is unsuccessful in reducing costs and actual costs are $600,000, the seller would receive $675,000 ($600,000 costs + $75,000 fee), and the return would fall to 12.5% ($75,000 ÷ $600,000).

In those situations where the price is determined by a contractual cost-based formula, cost accounting plays a vital role. Because the contract calls for the reimbursement of all allowable costs, both the buyer and the seller have a stake in how costs are defined, measured, and accumulated.

Between 1970 and 1980 the Cost Accounting Standards Board (CASB) was charged with assisting governmental agencies as buyers of goods and services in understanding and negotiating cost-based prices. To accomplish this task, the board issued standards of cost accounting to which government suppliers must conform. These cost standards are to ensure that the government pays a fair price for the goods it buys on a cost-based contract. It must be recognized that the intent of the CASB was *not* to develop cost data for managerial decision making, but to simplify the pricing and auditing problems of the U.S. government. This function has now been transferred to the General Accounting Office (GAO).

ISSUES IN DETERMINING FULL COSTS

At least two problems plague the determination of full cost. First, fixed costs per unit are a function of the production volume. In a pricing situation this is troublesome. Second, in a multiproduct setting there are problems in allocating joint costs to product lines.

PROBLEMS IN APPORTIONING FIXED COSTS

The proper treatment of the fixed costs presents a problem. The determination of a total cost per unit requires that fixed costs be apportioned over a specific number of units. The fixed overhead costs in the previous example were $75,000, and the fixed selling and administrative expenses were $300,000. At a production and sales output of 150,000 units, the fixed costs per unit are $2.50

($375,000 ÷ 150,000 units). If the company's volume increased to 300,000 units, the per-unit fixed cost would drop to $1.25 ($375,000 ÷ 300,000 units). The per-unit fixed cost would increase to $5.00 ($375,000 ÷ 75,000 units) if the volume dropped to 75,000 units. Unlike the fixed costs, the variable costs will remain at $3.50 per unit at all levels.

Assuming that the firm has a policy of adding to its total cost a 10% profit margin, it could have the following prices, depending on its volume decision.

Number of units	75,000	100,000	150,000	300,000
Variable costs per unit	$3.50	$3.50	$3.50	$3.50
Fixed costs per unit	5.00	3.75	2.50	1.25
Total costs per unit	$8.50	$7.25	$6.00	$4.75
10% Markup on cost	.85	.73	.60	.48
Selling price	$9.35	$7.98	$6.60	$5.23

When the decision maker selects 150,000 units as the most likely sales volume, the income per unit is expected to be $.60. Let's assume that on the basis of this budget a selling price of $6.60 is established and, because of an unexpected market penetration, actual sales were 200,000 units. The actual income and the budgeted income are shown in Exhibit 9–2. As shown in Exhibit 9–2, the "total" fixed costs do not change. The increase in income is totally attributable to the increased contribution margin resulting from the sale of 50,000 units more than planned.

	BUDGETED (150,000 UNITS)		ACTUAL (200,000 UNITS)	
	Amount	Per Unit	Amount	Per Unit
Sales	$990,000	$6.60	$1,320,000	$6.60
Variable costs	525,000	3.50	700,000	3.50
Contribution margin	$465,000	$3.10	$ 620,000	$3.10
Fixed costs	375,000	2.50	375,000	1.88
Income	$ 90,000	$0.60	$ 245,000	$1.22

EXHIBIT 9–2
Effects of volume changes
on income

PROBLEMS IN APPORTIONING JOINT COSTS

There is also a major problem with firms that have multiple products. A price based on full cost assumes that there is a satisfactory way to allocate all manufacturing costs and, in some cases, selling and administrative costs among the several products. Joint costs are not inherently traceable to individual products or product lines, and some method must be used to apportion them. Factory overhead is one of the most common joint costs that pose continual problems.

Overhead rates should be viewed as the accountants' attempt to allocate joint costs.

Nearly all the examples in this text have been based on a simple setting with one, two, or three products. In these examples the measure of volume typically has been direct labor, with both variable and fixed overhead applied on a direct labor basis. The "real world," however, is very complex, with hundreds or even thousands of products. Yet conventional accounting systems often apply costs to products using plant-wide overhead rates or overhead rates from a limited number of departments.

The tremendous growth of overhead costs and the decline in labor cost as a percentage of total costs have often led to misleading product costs. In new manufacturing facilities today, direct labor is often less than 10% of total manufacturing costs. This can result in overhead rates of 1,000% to 2,000%. In these settings direct labor is a very poor measure of volume. In addition, with the exception of material costs, it may be very difficult to measure fixed and variable costs in the conventional manner.

An example of misleading product costs is presented by Johnson and Kaplan.[2] Their example involved a company with thousands of products priced to generate a 40% to 45% profit margin with conventional application of overhead based on direct labor. However, when the overhead was analyzed and applied on bases other than direct labor hours, 77% of the products were found to be unprofitable. In their example over three-fourths of the products were candidates for repricing, replacing, redesigning, or changing them in some way to make them profitable. The real concern was that the company believed their costs and developed pricing strategies from them.

Based on their study, Johnson and Kaplan recommended that firms develop considerably more sophisticated methods of apportioning joint costs to product lines. Their analysis of overhead involved a study of the transactions or events that "drive" the costs in the support departments. They concluded that costs relating to the procurement, handling, and storage of raw materials should be applied on the basis of the material used rather than direct labor. Setup costs should be related to the number of setups. Some costs such as power, repairs and maintenance, and depreciation of machinery should be applied using machine hours. Other costs such as worker fringe benefits, employee cafeterias, and personnel support should be applied using labor hours. By identifying costs that relate to specific "drivers" or transactions, and accumulating them into specific cost pools, it would be possible to develop overhead rates that are specific, rather than general, in nature. The same form of analysis could also be used in studying selling, general and administrative expenses.

As overhead grows in magnitude and direct labor shrinks in volume because of automation, the problem will become more prevalent. Over the years

---

[2]H. Thomas Johnson and Robert B. Kaplan, *Relevance Lost, the Rise and Fall of Management Accounting* (Boston: Harvard University Press, 1987), p. 240.

accountants have developed both plant-wide and departmental overhead rates for both financial reporting requirements and facilitation of management decisions. These overhead apportionments may no longer be adequate for management.

The Johnson and Kaplan example highlights some important trends in manufacturing that impact pricing decisions. First, simple cost plus pricing procedures depend on the ability to apportion overhead in an economically feasible manner (information economics). The trend toward the use of multiple overhead rates such as purchasing rates, material rates, labor rates, and machine-hour rates, dramatically increases the cost of gathering data and developing the necessary rates to implement cost-plus pricing procedures. The computer and its high-speed processing can be a powerful ally making this approach economically feasible.

Second, the type of capacity and technological changes have implications for pricing. Increased automation and installation of cost-saving equipment is resulting in the phasing out of older facilities. In these older facilities labor usage reflected production levels. However, as the newer technologies are installed, labor can tend to behave more like a fixed cost than a variable cost. This would make questions of volume much more critical in developing cost-plus data.

STRENGTHS AND WEAKNESSES OF FULL COST-BASED PRICES

Although the cost-based pricing formula is simple, it does not agree with economic theory, because it ignores the relationships between demand and price and between price and volume. The price determined by full cost plus a markup may be so high that there are no customers. If so, some of the volume potential of the firm will be idle. There is a circularity problem. Volume is used to determine price in the full cost-based pricing formula, yet the number of units the company sells, and therefore the firm's volume, may depend on price.

Nevertheless, pricing policies based on full cost are widely used. Why? Certainly, a principal reason is the inability of the decision maker to quantify the demand curve. This inability to apply economic theory leads the business manager to apply intuitive judgment coupled with trial-and-error methods. Many decision makers begin with a full-cost approach and then, on the basis of buyers' reaction, adjust the price. In this way the full cost-based price represents a first approximation—a target price whose markup must be adjusted to meet the actual marketplace.

Another reason for the adoption of full cost-based prices is the belief that they represent a "floor" or "safe" price that will prevent losses. This safety factor is more illusory than real. Although the per-unit sales price will cover the per-unit full cost, losses may still be incurred if the sales volume is not achieved.

Perhaps the most convincing reason for the use of cost-based prices is that the costs of a particular firm are comparable with costs of other firms in the industry. One firm's costs are reasonable estimates of its competitors' costs, and hence its prices are likely to be comparable to those of its competitors. If most companies use similar facilities to perform similar activities, they will have similar full costs and, thus, similar prices if they produce at about the same volume level.

CONTRIBUTION MARGIN-BASED PRICING

In addition to serving as a potential cost base for establishing the price of new or standard products, the contribution margin approach is also useful in a number of other pricing decisions. Because it does not require an expected volume to allocate the fixed costs, the answer is not a function of the volume chosen. The contribution margin approach uses the incremental view that the only costs relevant to pricing decisions are those costs that would be avoided if the sales order were not accepted. Among those situations where contribution margin approaches are useful are

1. Pricing policies recognizing price–volume interactions.
   A. Evaluating proposals to increase profits by increasing volume.
   B. Deciding how far to go in meeting competitive prices.
2. Product-line contribution.
   A. Identifying the most profitable product.
   B. Identifying products needing attention for profit improvement.
   C. Improving sales mix.
3. Pricing special orders.
   A. One-time-only orders.
   B. Distress pricing.

PRICING AND VOLUME INTERACTIONS

As shown in Chapter 3, the contribution margin approach leads directly into the study of cost, volume, profit, and revenue interactions. To illustrate how the contribution margin can be used in price and volume decisions, assume that a firm has the following cost structure:

Variable production costs	$6 per unit
Variable selling costs	$3 per unit
Fixed production costs	$24,000 per unit
Fixed selling costs	$12,000 per year

Management is considering a target price of $15 with the goal of a profit of $9,000 for the year. What volume must the firm achieve? Using the analysis shown in Chapter 3, we can see that the necessary volume to achieve this profit is 7,500 units.

$$\text{Volume necessary to achieve a profit of \$9,000 with a \$15 selling price} = \frac{\$36,000 + \$9,000}{\$15 - (\$6 + \$3)} = 7,500 \text{ units}$$

If the target price was unacceptable in the marketplace and the firm had to lower the price to $12, the necessary volume would double to 15,000 units.

$$\text{Volume necessary to achieve a profit of \$9,000 with a \$12 selling price} = \frac{\$36,000 + \$9,000}{\$12 - (\$6 + \$3)} = 15,000 \text{ units}$$

Now, let's assume that the firm's target price becomes $12 as a result of management's assessment of the price the market will accept. Accordingly, management plans a production level of 15,000 units, which they believe is achievable. On a per-unit basis they can now establish ceiling and floor prices.

Variable costs		$ 9.00 Floor price
Fixed costs ($36,000 ÷ 15,000)	$2.40	
Profit ($9,000 ÷ 15,000)	$ .60	3.00
Target price		$12.00 Ceiling price

The firm has a market-based ceiling price, which is the maximum price within the marketplace that the firm can achieve. This ceiling price represents the goal of the firm in pricing policy. In distressful situations the firm should reduce its price no lower than the floor of $9.00, which is the variable cost per unit. Below $9.00 the firm would be paying the customer to take the goods; at any price above $9.00 the firm would recover some of the fixed costs. Stated another way, the minimum price they would charge is the price that would result in a contribution margin of zero.

PRODUCT-LINE CONTRIBUTIONS

The contribution margin approach allows an examination of the way in which each class of products contributes toward the recovery of fixed costs and profit contribution. Exhibit 9–3 shows a contribution margin income statement by product line.

	PRODUCT A (10 Units)	PRODUCT B (20 Units)	PRODUCT C (50 Units)	TOTAL
Sales	$3,000	$4,000	$5,000	$12,000
Variable production costs	2,500	2,400	2,500	7,400
Contribution margin from production	$ 500	$1,600	$2,500	$ 4,600
Variable nonproduction costs	500	600	1,000	2,100
Contribution margin	$ 0	$1,000	$1,500	$ 2,500
Separable (identifiable) fixed costs	300	400	300	1,000
Product margin	$ (300)	$ 600	$1,200	$ 1,500
Apportioned fixed costs	200	400	400	1,000
Income (loss)	$ (500)	$ 200	$ 800	$ 500

EXHIBIT 9–3   Contribution margin income statements by product line

Because the fixed costs do not change with changes in volume, the important data are those that show the product that contributes most to the company's profits. Product A has a zero contribution margin; Product B has a contribution margin of $50 per unit and a contribution margin ratio of 25% ($1,000 ÷ $4,000); Product C has a contribution margin of $30 per unit and a contribution margin ratio of 30% ($1,500 ÷ $5,000). Product A is not contributing to company profits. Both Products B and C are profitable, although Product B returns the highest contribution margin per unit.

This exhibit also shows another important point. Certain fixed costs, shown on the statement as **identifiable or separable fixed costs,** have been specifically identified with the product line. Other fixed costs, shown on the statement as **apportioned fixed costs,** have been allocated. The separable fixed costs are fixed costs that would be avoided if the product line were dropped. Sometimes they are called **avoidable fixed costs.** Where there are separable fixed costs, a better measure of the product line's contribution is the **product margin,** determined after deducting separable fixed costs from the product's contribution margin.

Where the company is already committed to the separable fixed costs or to retention of the product line, the fixed costs directly associated with the product line are not relevant, and the decision maker should look to the contribution margin of the product. In those instances where the company is not yet committed to the product line or the separable fixed costs, the product margin after separable costs is more appropriate for the decision maker. The apportioned fixed costs would not be relevant in either case.

If there is unused capacity, the firm can realize additional profits by increasing the sales of products with a positive contribution margin (Products B and C). Profits also may be increased by decreasing the sales of any products with a negative or zero contribution margin (Product A). Which product in

Exhibit 9–3 should the company emphasize? Because of the identifiable fixed costs and zero contribution margin, Product A should be eliminated. While Product C has the highest contribution margin ratio (30%), Product B has the highest unit contribution margin ($50). Because they currently sell more than twice as many units of C (at $100 per unit) as B (at $200 per unit), it may well be that the opportunities for additional dollar sales may be greater with C, which has a greater contribution ratio and therefore may be the best product to push. The firm should produce and sell in such a way as to maximize the *total contribution margin in dollars*—not the contribution margin ratio. With this type of product-line analysis the firm can achieve a better product mix and an increased profitability of their product lines.

PRICING SPECIAL ORDERS

To illustrate how special-order pricing decisions can be made with a contribution margin approach, let's assume that the C. M. Manufacturing Company has excess productive capacity. Normal plant capacity is 150,000 units per year; current operations are 100,000 units per year. The current production of 100,000 units is sold in the regular markets for $2.00 each. Variable costs are $1.20 per unit and annual fixed costs are $60,000. The following income statement is based on current production and sales.

C. M. MANUFACTURING COMPANY
CONTRIBUTION MARGIN INCOME STATEMENT
For the Year Ended December 31, 19X6

Sales (100,000 × $2.00)	$200,000
Variable costs (100,000 × $1.20)	120,000
Contribution margin (100,000 × $.80)	$ 80,000
Fixed costs	60,000
Income	$ 20,000

The firm's full cost is [$1.20 + ($60,000 ÷ 100,000 units)], or $1.80 per unit. Now assume that it receives an offer from a foreign buyer to manufacture and sell an additional 20,000 units at $1.50. Should it accept the order? The price of $1.50 is below the full cost of $1.80 but above the $1.20 variable cost. If the additional order does not affect the regular market price of $2.00, only the variable costs are relevant to the decision. The additional order would increase income. The following income statement assumes that the special order was accepted.

C. M. MANUFACTURING COMPANY
CONTRIBUTION MARGIN INCOME STATEMENT
For the Year Ended December 31, 19X6

	Regular	Special	Total
Sales: Regular (100,000 × $2.00	$200,000		
Special (20,000 × $1.50)		$30,000	$230,000
Variable costs			
Regular (100,000 × $1.20	120,000		
Special (20,000 × $1.20)		24,000	144,000
Contribution margin	$ 80,000	$ 6,000	$ 86,000
Fixed costs			60,000
Income			$ 26,000

The special order increased the income by $6,000. The unit contribution margin on the special order is $.30 ($1.50 − $1.20) and the total contribution margin on the additional order is $6,000 ($.30 × 20,000 units).

What would happen to the firm if the special order affected its current market? Assuming that the demand curve was such that *all* products had to be offered at the special-order price, the income statement would then show a loss.

C. M. MANUFACTURING COMPANY
CONTRIBUTION MARGIN INCOME STATEMENT
For the Year Ended December 31, 19X6

Sales (120,000 × $1.50)	$180,000
Variable costs (120,000 × $1.20)	144,000
Contribution margin (120,000 × $.30)	$ 26,000
Fixed costs	60,000
Loss	$ (24,000)

If the special order infiltrates the regular market, it could jeopardize the firm's profit structure. If special-order pricing dominates, the lower price will increase demand but could, at the same time, reduce income. This possible effect has caused many people to reject variable cost-based pricing for both long-run and short-run decisions in favor of full cost-based prices. Obviously, before any decision is made to sell a regular product at a special price, serious consideration must be given to the potential effect of this decision on regular sales.

The contribution margin approach holds that the short-run objective of a pricing decision is to maximize the firm's total contribution margin. If the contribution margin is maximized, income will be maximized. It accepts the view that any unit providing a positive contribution margin will enhance the firm's profit picture. To illustrate this view further, let's assume that a firm has the following cost and revenue structure.

Normal selling price at 100% of normal capacity of	
100,000 units	$5.00 per unit
Variable production costs	$3.00 per unit
Variable selling costs	$1.00 per unit
Fixed production costs	$30,000 per year
Fixed selling costs	$20,000 per year

It has received an offer to sell 10,000 units per year for the next five years to a special buyer at a special price of $3.50. Once the contract is consummated, the buyer will take delivery of the goods at the factory; no variable selling costs will be required on these 10,000 units. Should the firm accept the offer? Comparative income statements are shown in Exhibit 9–4. According to these income statements, the answer is no. To accept the order would reduce profits by $5,000. What is the minimum price acceptable for this order to maintain current profits? For this decision the fixed costs are not relevant; they do not change as a result of the decision. To maintain the current profit rate there must be an average contribution margin of $1.00 per unit, the current contribution margin. In order for the remaining 90,000 units to achieve this contribution margin, the 10,000-unit special order must also achieve a contribution margin of $1.00. The variable production costs of $3.00 will be the only relevant costs for the special order. The minimum price would be $4.00 ($3.00 variable cost + $1.00 contribution margin). At a price of $4.00 or above, the special order would be acceptable; below $4.00 it would be unacceptable.

	Without Special Order		With Special Order	
Sales	(100,000 × $5.00)	$500,000	(90,000 × $5.00)	$450,000
			(10,000 × $3.50)	35,000
		$500,000		$485,000
Variable costs:				
Production	(100,000 × $3.00)	$300,000	(100,000 × $3.00)	$300,000
Selling	(100,000 × $1.00)	100,000	(90,000 × $1.00)	90,000
		400,000		390,000
Contribution margin	(100,000 × $1.00)	$100,000		$ 95,000
Fixed costs:				
Production	$30,000		$30,000	
Selling	20,000		20,000	
Total		50,000		50,000
Income		$ 50,000		$ 45,000

EXHIBIT 9–4 Effects of special order on income

To carry the contribution margin approach one step further, let's assume that the company has an excess inventory of 500 units that it cannot sell in its normal market because of a style change. What is the minimum price it can accept for these units and be better off than it would be if it scrapped them? A full cost-based approach might respond $4.50 [($300,000 + $100,000 + $30,000 + $20,000) ÷ 100,000 units]. A deeper analysis shows that the fixed costs remain unchanged. Further, the variable costs to produce the products are not relevant because the units have already been produced. The only relevant cost is the variable selling cost. If the firm could sell the 500 units for $1.10 the firm would be $50 [($1.10 − $1.00) × 500 units] better off than if it did not sell them. If it sold the units for $.80 each, it would lose an additional $.20 per unit ($1.00 − $.80).

To carry this illustration one more step, let's assume that the 500 excess units are a seasonal product that is still in style. The firm has the choice of carrying the items in the inventory for six months at a carrying cost of $300 or selling them now for $2.50 each and replacing them later. It is estimated that in six months the variable production costs will have risen to $3.50 because of a new labor contract. The relevant benefits and costs are the revenue potential, the carrying costs they would forego if they sold the units now, and the replacement costs.

	Sell Now; Replace Later	Hold in Inventory
Revenue	$ 1,250	
Replacement Costs	(1,750)	
Carrying Costs		$(300)
Net Cost	$ (500)	$(300)

The firm would incur $200 more in costs if it were to sell now and replace the units later. Here, as in the previous illustrations, the only relevant costs are the future differential costs.

A word of warning about the role of the contribution margin approach in pricing special orders seems appropriate at this point. A firm would have no need to accept a lower price for its product if it could sell all it wished at the normal price. For a firm to accept less than the normal price, it must be facing some adverse condition such as idle capacity, a marketplace where there is a strong price competition, or a distressful situation, such as a rapid style change.

If a firm were constantly to reduce its selling prices to just above the variable costs, the volume would have to increase to cover the fixed costs and contribute to profit. There is always the danger that the use of the contribution margin could lead to short-run underpricing and that, as a result, the long-run financial health of the firm would be jeopardized.

PRICING STRATEGIES

There are really two prices that are relevant from management's perspective. The first is a "target" price, which can be a number of combinations of product costs plus a markup to cover all other costs of the organization including a return to the investors. The second price is the "market" price—that is, the price that the product is actually generating in the marketplace. Management needs to compare the "market" price with the possible "target" prices to determine a pricing strategy.

The target price, as shown in the left-hand portion of the model, is divided into four segments. The ideal target price would be in segment 1, which is the sum of all costs plus a profit. At this price, the firm would earn a satisfactory profit.

	TARGET PRICES	MARKET PRICES
Segment 4	Variable costs of production and sales	Lower
+		
Segment 3	Fixed costs of production	
+		
Segment 2	Fixed costs of sales and administration	
+		
Segment 1	Normal profit markup	Higher

The market price, as shown in the right-hand portion of the model, is determined by supply and demand and other economic conditions and may fluctuate over the life of the product.

In general, pricing **significantly** above the "target" price in segment 1 in the model (even if the market will bear the cost) creates an open invitation to competition. While profits could be increased in the short run, the firm would be selling their long-run market share to obtain these profits. As a result, the firm must continually introduce new products to replace those that would face intensive price competition.

However, pricing **slightly** above the "target" price in segment 1 can be done by an organization protected by patents, capital plant requirements, or other barriers to competition. It is an attractive strategy if there is a slow product decline or a stable environment. Under these conditions profits are substantial in both the short and the long run.

Pricing **below** the "target" price in segment 1 is not usually in the long-run best interests of the firm but may be necessary in the short run because of market conditions. Deviations from the "target" price should be analyzed to determine causal factors. Acceptable temporary reasons might include competitive conditions, growth strategies, excessive productive capacity, or low-demand conditions.

Specific analysis of "target" prices below segment 1 should compare the "market" price to the comparable step on the "target" price model—an analysis that seeks to discern trends that will affect management strategies. As an example, assume the "market" price of a product is in segment 1 of the "target" price. If the market price is moving toward segment 2, the product may be subject to increased competition, changes in technology, or similar pressures. This movement could be considered an early-warning sign of more intensive competition to come. If, on the other hand, the market price has entered segment 1 by moving up from segment 2, this could be a signal of an improving market. Examples of causal factors for this upward movement would include a successful cost reduction program or a successful advertising campaign.

Next, assume that the "market" price is in segment 2. This should cause management concern, in that it could indicate predatory pricing conditions, market overcapacity, significant cost advantages by competitors, and, certainly, the need for a better profit margin. Note that some of the causal factors could be temporary such as an oversupply of the product. Other factors, such as a cost advantage by competitors, may require major investment of resources by the firm to rectify the situation—a long-run solution.

Of greater concern to management in both the long run and the short run is if the "market" price is in segment 3. Selling at this price will produce a loss on the product. Caution is warranted, however, to ensure that this loss is not due to some inappropriate allocation procedure. The firm must avoid the cost trap related to volume and overhead applications. Even at this "market" price the product may be contributing to covering the fixed costs of the firm, but the question management now must ask is, "Can the capacity be used in some better way?"

When the "market" price is in segment 4 the firm is in an intolerable situation. Questions should be raised concerning dropping the product line. It is a survival pricing condition used only in the short run to weather a severe crisis. The firm is selling the product below its variable cost. As stated earlier, the variable cost of production represents a floor. If the firm views this "market" price as relatively stable the only choice is abandonment of the product line.

In summary, management strategies should be related to the firm's objectives. While short-run variations may occur, the economic laws of supply and demand will apply in the long run. Further, most products face some kind of an elastic demand curve; that is, if prices are increased the volume will decrease and if prices are decreased the volume will increase. From the firm's perspective it is desirable to have the "market" price somewhere near the desired "target" price. While many organizations have growth goals resulting in a tendency to decrease prices to increase volume, care must be taken because this strategy does not necessarily lead to increased profits. Certainly, a valuable skill for rational decision makers is the ability to balance long-run and short-run considerations.

PRICE DISCRIMINATION

Because of their size, cost structure, large customer base, or favorable market position, some firms can price their products low enough to drive competitors out of business. However, Congress has passed a number of antitrust laws in order to protect and encourage wholesome competition. In 1914 passage of the Clayton Act created the Federal Trade Commission (FTC), an administrative and semijudicial agency empowered to restrict unfair methods of competition and deceptive practices by competitors.

In 1936 the Clayton Act was amended by the Robinson–Patman Act. Among the principal subsections of this law are those relating to unfair price discrimination. When a seller is charged by a buyer with discriminating in price between customers, the seller must show that the different prices were the result of cost differentials. However, a seller can justify the lower price by showing that it was made to meet an equally low offer by a competitor. If a firm is considered to have discriminated in price, the FTC can issue an order for it to stop selling at that price.

Because the Robinson–Patman Act deals with price differences to buyers of the same product, it is relevant only to standard products. In a case where the nature of a contract between a buyer and seller allows the seller to effect a cost savings that is shared with the buyer, price discrimination would not exist. Discrimination can exist only where the *same* products and services are provided to different buyers at different prices.

Although prices differ between buyers, price discrimination may not exist. In defense of charges brought under the Robinson–Patman Act, the comparison of cost differences is potentially important. Although it is not the only defense,[3] it is a crucial one; the seller may justify actual differences in price by showing that costs were different. Cost differences are readily justified when the price depends on the quantity of an individual order or shipment. In these instances the differences in cost must be shown to result from the quantity sold or the method of selling. For example, simply showing that there are differences in the costs of shipping carload lots, as opposed to partial carload lots, may be all that is necessary to justify differences in costs and, hence, prices between orders of two different sizes.

Generally, the cost differences are more readily traced to selling and distribution costs than to production costs. Where the goods are produced for warehouse stock, the costs of manufacturing goods for specific customers are indistinguishable. In these cases, production costs are not relevant because they are not differential costs. However, whether a particular product was identified

---

[3]Other defenses could include proving that the price differences were not discriminatory; that in consideration of discounts, allowances, and rebates, the prices were similar; that all business was intrastate; that the goods were not of similar grade or quality; or that the customers had different functional status, such as retailer and wholesaler.

with a particular customer before it was manufactured or afterward, differences in costs of distribution may be attributed to differences in quantities sold, shipping methods, or modes of selling. Here the Robinson–Patman Act has a positive impact on management accounting because it has made it necessary that accountants strive to understand and evaluate the firm's distribution costs.

It would be misleading to imply that all firms must constantly be on the defense against price discrimination charges. Most pricing and cost decisions lie outside the scope of the Robinson–Patman Act. A charge of unfair price discrimination must be brought by an injured party stating that the seller discriminated in price between different purchases of goods of like grade and quality in an attempt to lessen competition. Although cost defenses under the Robinson–Patman Act do happen, they are not an everyday event for most firms.

SUMMARY

In economic theory the price and output quantity where the market is in equilibrium is at the intersection of the demand curve and the supply curve. This is true whether the market structure is pure competition, pure monopoly, monopolistic competition, or oligopoly. Market structures affect the shape and slope of the demand curve but do not change the underlying principle that the intersection of the supply and demand curves determines the equilibrium price and output.

While theoretically sound, economic pricing theory is difficult to apply in practice. Because the exact shape of the demand curve is very difficult to measure, many firms rely on full cost-based prices, although they are less sound theoretically. This approach can best be thought of as a first estimate of price. The actual obtainable price is found by trial and error.

The contribution margin approach offers some insights into the pricing dilemma. In special-order and distress pricing situations, the contribution margin offers a decision attitude that is more relevant than full cost-based prices. Nevertheless, in the long run all revenue must cover all costs and provide an adequate income to give the investors a reasonable return on their investment. It is not enough to use only full cost or only the contribution margin in pricing decisions. The decision maker should choose the best approach for specific circumstances.

In today's complicated business world there are many influences besides demand that determine price. Governmental and political factors operate to stop unfair price discrimination, in part because the U.S. economic system is based on the assumption that price competition is desirable. Another cause of the political and legal constraints is the need to protect the consumer from unfair pricing practices.

9-1 *(Full-Cost Pricing).* The Slugger Company manufactures baseball bats that have variable costs of $10 per unit. The fixed costs related to the manufacturing of the bats are $60,000 per year. All selling and administrative costs are fixed at $40,000 per year. Management computes the selling price by adding a 10% markup to the full cost.

REQUIRED:

A. What selling price per unit must be charged if 50,000 bats are produced and sold?

B. What selling price per unit must be charged if 25,000 bats are produced and sold?

9-2 *(Maximum Cost to Meet Market Price).* The Blo-Dri Company is considering manufacturing a new line of hair dryers. In order to be competitive, market research has determined the hair dryers would have to be priced at $10. Management requires a 15% return on investment from any new endeavor. It would take an investment in productive assets and working capital of $250,000 to produce 15,000 hair dryers per year, and the fixed production costs would be $60,000.

REQUIRED:

A. What is the maximum variable cost per unit the company may incur to meet these requirements?

B. Assuming the variable cost in part A, what would be the markup on product cost if the company used contribution margin-based pricing?

9-3 *(Volume Needed to Generate Income).* The ABC Company produces a plastic plumbing component that wholesales for $5.00 per unit. Their fixed costs per year are expected to be $300,000 and variable costs are estimated to be $3.00 per unit.

REQUIRED:

A. How many parts must ABC sell to generate operating income of $25,000?

B. Assuming the company used full cost-based pricing and planned the production and profit in part A, what would be the markup on product costs?

C. Assume instead that the company used the contribution margin-based pricing, what would be their markup on product cost?

9-4   *(Market-based Price).* The Leisure and Sporting Goods Division of AMG Corporation made a thorough market study for a new lawn dart game. Data concerning units demanded at various prices for the new product follow:

Price	Quantity Demanded (Units)
$12.00	200,000
$11.00	400,000
$10.00	1,000,000
$ 9.00	2,000,000
$ 8.50	3,000,000
$ 8.00	5,000,000
$ 7.50	7,000,000

Plant capacity available for this product is limited to 3 million units. Because the life of the product is expected to be short, the company will not increase capacity. Fixed costs for the product are projected at $2 million per year and variable costs are estimated to be $7.00 per unit.

REQUIRED:

A. Determine the optimum price and volume that will maximize income.

B. The company is considering a national promotional campaign that will cost $2 million. The campaign should result in the following revised demand schedule:

Price	Quantity Demanded (Units)
$12.00	300,000
$11.00	600,000
$10.00	1,400,000
$ 9.00	3,000,000
$ 8.50	5,000,000
$ 8.00	8,000,000

What recommendations would you make to management?

9-5   *(Volume/Price to Achieve a Desired Profit).* Ski Wear Company has the following costs for their glove line:

Variable production costs	$4.50 per unit
Variable selling costs	$1.50 per unit
Fixed production costs	$20,000 per month
Fixed general and selling costs	$10,000 per month

Management would like to achieve a $6,000 profit per month from the sale of gloves. The company is currently considering a selling price of $10 per pair.

REQUIRED:

A. How many pair will they have to produce and sell in order to cover costs and achieve the desired profit?

B. Assume the firm cannot produce more than 7,500 pair of gloves. What price should they set to achieve the same profit?

9-6 *(Special-Order Pricing)*. The Riff-Raff Shoe Company produces high-fashion shoes. For one particular shoe, variable production costs per pair were $6.50 and variable selling costs were $1.75. There are identifiable fixed production costs of $34,000 and fixed selling costs of $25,000. At the selling price of $13 per pair, the firm has been able to sell the entire 20,000 pairs it can produce with available capacity. Riff-Raff has been requested to supply a one-time-only order of 10,000 pairs of shoes to the Nickel Department Store chain at a price of $10 per pair. Management estimates that the variable costs of selling these 10,000 pairs will be cut to $.75 per pair and that the fixed identifiable selling costs will be $20,000 instead of $25,000.

REQUIRED:

A. Should management accept this order? Why or why not? Support your conclusions.

B. Assume that fashions have changed to the point where one style of shoe, currently produced and in the inventory, is no longer marketable. Given the costs above, what is the least amount management should ask for these 3,000 pairs of shoes? Why? Will the firm make a profit or sustain a loss? What will be the amount of the profit or loss?

C. Given the original cost data, what is the quantity of shoes that must be sold to break even?

9-7 *(Special Order)*. The East Company plant, with a capacity of 50,000 units, is currently operating at 30,000 units. The product produced in this plant has a selling price of $5.00 per unit. Standard variable costs are $3.00 per unit and the fixed costs are $1.00 at full capacity. Management has received an offer for an additional 10,000 units at $4.50 per unit.

REQUIRED:

A. What is the unit contribution margin of the special order?

B. What is the total contribution margin generated by the special order?

C. Prepare a contribution margin income statement assuming the firm accepts the special order.

9-8   *(Pricing at Different Volumes)*. The Merry Melody Company is planning to add a line of children's recorders. They have calculated that direct material would be $3.00 per unit, direct labor would be $2.00 per unit, variable overhead would be $1.75 per unit, and the fixed overhead would be $20,000. Management requires a 20% markup on total manufacturing costs.

REQUIRED:

A. Compute the selling price for three production levels: 10,000 recorders, 15,000 recorders, and 20,000 recorders.

B. Why does the selling price change based on the number of units produced?

C. Assume the firm chose to manufacture 15,000 recorders and priced them according to part A. What is their income if they actually produce and sell 17,000 recorders?

D. What is their income if they produce 15,000 as planned but sell only 13,000 recorders?

9-9   *(Pricing a Special Order)*. The E-Z Chair Company has the capacity in their chair plant to produce 20,000 chairs per year. Currently they are producing 16,000 chairs at a selling price of $200 per chair. The cost to produce each chair is:

Materials	$80
Variable conversion cost	50
Fixed overhead	40
Total costs	$170

The company has received an offer to produce and sell 2,000 chairs for $165 each. The unusual selling and administrative costs associated with this order would be $10,000. The president prepared the following analysis to determine whether to accept the offer:

Selling price per chair		$165
Costs per chair:		
Production costs	$170	
Selling and administrative costs	5	175
Loss per chair		$ 10

REQUIRED:

Because you are the salesperson who worked to get the special order, the president asks you to justify why he should lose $10 per unit on this order.

9-10   *(Pricing a Special Order)*. E. Berg and Sons build custom-made pleasure boats ranging in price from $10,000 to $250,000. For the past 30 years, the senior Mr. Berg has determined the selling price of each boat by estimating the costs of material and labor, prorating a portion of estimated total overhead, and adding 20% to these estimated costs.

For example, a recent price quotation was determined as follows:

Direct materials	$ 5,000
Direct labor	8,000
Overhead (25% of labor)	2,000
Total estimated costs	$15,000
Plus 20%	3,000
Selling price	$18,000

If the customer rejected the price and business was slack, Mr. Berg would often reduce his markup to as little as 5% over estimated costs. Thus, average markup for the year is estimated at 15%.

Ed Berg, Jr. has just completed a course on pricing and believes the firm could use some of the techniques discussed in the course. The course emphasized the contribution margin approach to pricing and Ed feels such an approach would be helpful in determining the selling prices of their custom-made boats.

At the beginning of each year the overhead rate is established by dividing total estimated overhead by estimated direct labor cost. This year's total overhead, which includes selling and administrative expenses, was estimated at $150,000, of which $90,000 is fixed and the remainder is variable. Direct labor was estimated at $600,000 for the year.

REQUIRED:

A. Assume the customer in the example rejected the $18,000 quotation and also rejected a $15,750 quotation (5% markup) during a slack period. The customer countered with a $15,000 offer.

1. What is the difference in income for the year between accepting or rejecting the customer's offer?

2. What is the minimum selling price Ed Berg, Jr. could have quoted without reducing or increasing income?

B. What advantages does the contribution margin approach to pricing have over the approach used by the senior Mr. Berg?

C. What pitfalls are there, if any, to contribution margin pricing?

(CMA adapted)

9-11 *(Government Contract—Incentive Versus Fixed Fee).* The Uff Da Company has been in a bidding competition to supply to the government a special sled with the ability to traverse all terrains and to perform many specialized jobs in the snow. It was agreed upon by management and the government negotiators that the cost of designing and manufacturing five prototypes for experimental purposes should be $750,000. They agreed upon a fee of 12% of cost to be included in the contract price.

REQUIRED:

A. Determine income and the income as a percentage of costs, assuming a cost overrun of $150,000 on a cost-plus-fixed-fee contract.

B. Determine income and the income as a percentage of costs, assuming a cost incentive contract with a 50:50 ratio and actual costs that were 15% below budgeted costs.

C. Which contract in part A or B would you prefer if you were the management of the Uff Da Company? If you were a government negotiator? Why?

9-12 *(Government Contract—Incentive).* Star Treking Products, Inc., is developing a backpack for the government that would enable individuals to cross rivers and small lake surfaces without boats or bridges. The company is working under a cost-plus-fixed-fee contract that includes a cost incentive provision with a 50:50 ratio. The contract also contains a clause for noncompletion that assesses a penalty of 5% of total cost per month if the delivery date is not met.

Up to this point, actual costs are 20% below the estimated costs of $300,000. However, there have been developmental problems that could postpone the completion date several months. An accelerated work program would finish the job on time, thus avoiding the penalty for late delivery, but it would result in a 20% overrun on costs. If the completion date is not accelerated, but the job is finished one month late (which is best current estimate), costs will exceed the original budget by 10%. The original profit was a fixed fee based on 15% of estimated costs.

REQUIRED:

A. What are your recommendations to management? You should be concerned with the recommendations that will reduce costs and maximize the return to the company.

B. Would your answer differ if you were the government negotiator charged with administering this contract?

9-13 *(Computation of Incremental Income. Note: Knowledge of Probabilities Required).* The Norway Company wants to determine the best sales price for a new popcorn popper with a variable cost of $4.10 per unit. The sales manager has estimated probabilities of achieving annual sales levels for various selling prices, as shown in the following chart.

Sales Level	Selling Price			
(Units)	$4	$5	$6	$7
20,000	—	—	20%	80%
30,000	—	10%	40%	20%
40,000	50%	50%	20%	—
50,000	50%	40%	20%	—

The division's current profit rate is 5% on annual sales of $1,200,000; an investment of $400,000 is needed to finance the new sales.

REQUIRED:

A. Prepare a schedule computing the expected incremental income for each of the sales prices proposed for the new product. The schedule should include the expected sales levels in units (weighted according to the sales manager's estimated probabilities), the expected total monetary sales, expected variable costs, and the expected incremental income.

B. What price should be charged to maximize income? Explain.

C. Assuming that fixed costs of $8,600 are allocated to the new product, and interest rate on the money borrowed to finance the product is 10%, prepare an income statement for the new product.

(CPA adapted)

9-14 *(Cost-based Pricing).* Knotty Pine Woodworking Company came to you for assistance when the bookkeeper presented the income statement showing a large loss for the second year of operations. The loss of $70,000 was expected for the first year when the company operated at a low level. However, the management of Knotty Pine Woodworking was shocked to discover a loss of $160,000 for the second year.

The president of the company could not understand how they could be operating at near-capacity and losing money. The company was consistently short of cash, a common problem when operations are expanding.

From your preliminary examination you found very poor accounting records, but you are satisfied that the data in the financial statements are correct and that there is no significant fraud. The company manufactures a line of kitchen cabinets. Because of the lack of detailed records, it is impossible to develop data about the cost of the product beyond the limited data for 19X0 and 19X1. The selling price was set by the president to undersell competition. Condensed income statements are presented below.

KNOTTY PINE WOODWORKING
INCOME STATEMENT
19X0 and 19X1

	19X0	*19X1*
Sales ($40 each)	$100,000	$ 400,000
Operating expenses:		
Beginning inventory of materials	$ 0	$ 20,000
Operating expense	190,000	570,000
Total	$190,000	$ 590,000
Ending inventory of materials	20,000	30,000
Expenses for year	170,000	560,000
Loss	$ (70,000)	$(160,000)
Other data:		
Units produced	2,500 units	10,000 units
Units sold	2,500 units	10,000 units
Assets invested in business	$100,000	$100,000
Capacity in units	12,000	12,000

REQUIRED:

A. Why did the company lose $160,000 in the second year?

B. Reconstruct the company data using the contribution margin format.

C. What price must be set to earn a profit of 8% of sales, assuming cost relationships remain constant?

D. What price must be set to earn a contribution margin ratio of 30%?

E. What price must be set to earn 15% on the assets invested in the business?

9-15 *(Pricing and Cost Analysis in an International Setting).* Bill Cool, the general manager of the International Division of the Far Flung Drug Company, finds himself faced with an extremely difficult competitive situation in Argentina. A Japanese competitor is underpricing him on his major product (''superpill'') in the Argentine market, and he is faced with total loss of all Argentine sales for this product.

Bill's problem as he sees it is a matter of meeting his competitor's price. Superpill and the Japanese competitive product are basically equal from the point of view of quality and performance. Delivery and credit terms are also similar. The basic financial facts are as follows:

Prices
Superpill	$1.00 per gross
Japanese pill	$ .60 per gross

Annual volume
5,000,000 gross plus an estimated 5% annual growth factor

Manufacturing cost
(including transportation) $ .70 per gross

In this situation Bill felt that he could not afford to meet the competitive price of $.60, because his division would then show a loss of $.10 per unit. He then remembered, somewhat vaguely, a discussion he got involved in while attending an executive development program. The discussion revolved around the idea that manufacturing costs are best thought of as consisting of two separate components, fixed and variable. The fixed costs were then described as a ''kind of handicap'' that a company tried to overcome by generating a sufficient profit contribution, that is, the difference between sales and variable costs.

Bill wondered if these concepts might be applicable to his situation. As the result of a cable to his company's main office in Atlanta, Bill found that the accounting staff of Far Flung Drugs did not separate variable and fixed costs in their cost accounting system. However, they turned Bill's question over to a cost analyst who estimated that $.30 of the $.70 per-unit manufacturing cost represented fixed costs.

Based on the above information, Bill calculated variable costs per gross as $.40 and a profit contribution of $.20 per gross if the competitive price was met. With these facts in hand Bill went to Atlanta to discuss his problem with the headquarters pricing policy staff.

In Atlanta, all agreed that the company's other products were covering the fixed costs, and that capacity was available for the foreseeable future to produce sufficient amounts of superpill. All also agreed that the competitive price had to be met and could be met without any adverse effects and with a $.20 per-gross profit contribution. Thus, Bill Cool went home satisfied that he could retain his Argentine superpill business at a price that would be profitable to Far Flung Drugs.

A few months later Bill noticed that reports concerning the profitability of South American sales were getting worse and worse. He couldn't understand this because everything seemed to be going well from a volume and cost point of view.

Bill decided that he had to uncover the causes of his poor showing, so he started to take apart the profit report for South America. To his surprise he found that the headquarters accounting staff were charging his Argentine sales of superpill with a manufacturing cost of $.70 rather than $.40. His anticipated profit contribution of $.20 per gross was in effect turned into a loss of $.10 per gross. An expected annual profit contribution of $1 million ($.20 × 5,000,000 gross) was being turned into a loss of $500,000 ($.10 × 5,000,000 gross) by a group of accountants.

Bill then tried to explain his poor South American showing to the company's executive committee at a special meeting called by the executive committee. They couldn't understand his explanation because that they were as concerned as the accountants with the "full cost" of manufacturing. Bill left the meeting, muttering to himself, "I make a sound and profitable decision and the accounting department makes me look like a bum. I guess they and the executive committee are really telling me to give up the Argentine market for superpill."

REQUIRED:

A. Assuming that superpill is a profitable product at the $.60 price, how would you adjust the profit report for South American sales to conform with Bill Cool's sound decision?

B. Was Bill Cool's decision really sound; that is, was there something wrong with the analysis that preceded Bill's decision?

(Prepared by William L. Ferrara)

9-16 *(Comprehensive Pricing)*. Beloxie Enterprises was formed in 19X0 by Mr. Dodson to produce and market a new kind of glue called Silly Glue. Facilities with a capacity of 1 million units per year were leased at the beginning of 19X0 and the following projection of costs was developed.

| Production: | $.15 per unit produced plus $100,000 per year |
| Selling and administration: | $.05 per unit sold plus $50,000 per year |

The marketing consultant reported that at a price of $.40 per unit the company would sell all it could produce. However, Mr. Dodson, the inventor of Silly

Glue, believed that the product was worth more than $.40 and set a price of $.50.

During 19X0 the company produced at capacity, incurring costs exactly as projected, but sold only 500,000 units. Mr. Dodson was delighted when his accountant presented him with the following income statement showing an income of $50,000 for 19X0.

BELOXIE ENTERPRISES
INCOME STATMEENT
19X0

Sales (500,000 units @ $.50)		$250,000
Cost of goods sold:		
Production costs (1,000,000 units)	$250,000	
Less: Inventory (500,00 units @ $.25)	125,000	125,000
Gross margin		$125,000
Selling and administrative expenses		75,000
Income		$ 50,000

Mr. Dodson examined his costs at 500,000 units and concluded that he would have to raise his price to $.60 in order to cover costs and generate his target profit of $50,000 per year. So far, he had achieved his profit objective in spite of what the consultant had said. He was, however, facing serious cash flow problems and had accumulated a large inventory.

During 19X1, Mr. Dodson sold only 300,000 units at the $.60 selling price. He had reduced production to 300,000 and therefore did not build inventory further. Mr. Dodson was pleased to see an income of $40,000 for the year, as shown below. Because of the decline in sales, he had expected a lower profit. Again, costs were exactly as projected.

BELOXIE ENTERPRISES
INCOME STATEMENT
19X1

Sales (300,000 units @ $.60)		$180,000
Cost of goods sold:		
Beginning inventory (500,000 units @ $.25)	$125,000	
Current production costs (300,000 units @ $.4833)	145,000	
Total available	$270,000	
Ending inventory @ FIFO (200,000 @ $.25, 300,000 units @ $.4833)	195,000*	75,000
Gross margin		$105,000
Selling and administrative expenses		65,000
Income		$ 40,000

*Rounding error in unit cost.

At the beginning of 19X2, Mr. Dodson again examined his costs. At the 300,000-unit level of production his unit cost to produce was slightly over $.48, and selling and administrative costs were approximately $.22. At a selling price of $.60 he was losing approximately $.10 on each unit.

Mr. Dodson began planning a new alternative for 19X2. If the price was raised to $.75 per unit, the consultant's report indicated he would sell approximately 200,000 units, which would also be the production budget. By producing and selling less than 300,000 units in 19X2 he would be able to reduce fixed overhead by $20,000 and fixed selling and administrative costs by $15,000. At the same time, a chain of department stores wants to buy 300,000 units of Silly glue per year at $.30 per unit. There will be no variable selling expenses for these units.

REQUIRED:

A. Assuming that Beloxie Enterprises adopts only the first alternative and raises the price to $.75 per unit in 19X2, prepare a profit plan for 19X2 that is consistent with the accounting methods employed in the income statements for 19X0 and 19X1. Comment on the amount of the resulting profit or loss.

B. What would be the impact if the special order is accepted? Mr. Dodson questions the wisdom of accepting an order at $.30 per unit when his lowest possible total unit cost would be $.35 at full capacity. What other factors would affect his decision?

C. Assuming the cost structure in years 19X0 and 19X1, what is the breakeven point in units if the selling price is $.50? If it is $.60? How does this compare with the income statements for 19X0 and 19X1?

D. Recast the income statements using variable costing and the contribution margin approach. Comment on the results when compared with the income statements for 19X1 and 19X2 prepared by the accountant.

E. Develop a demand curve (just determine the amounts at different prices, do not plot a curve) showing units demanded at $.40, $.50, $.60, and $.75. Using this information and the cost structure of the company, develop a pricing strategy for Beloxie Enterprise for the year 19X2. You should consider the special order in your strategy by assuming it will not affect regular sales.

F. On the basis of your pricing strategy in part E, prepare a Profit Plan using variable costing and the contribution margin approach for 19X2.

9-17 *(Pricing a Special Order).* Jenco Inc. manufactures a combination fertilizer/weedkiller under the name Fertikil. This is the only product Jenco produces at the present time. Fertikil is sold nationwide through normal marketing channels to retail nurseries and garden stores.

Taylor Nursery plans to sell a similar fertilizer/weedkiller compound through its regional nursery chain under its own private label. Taylor has asked Jenco to submit a bid for a 25,000-pound order of the private-brand compound.

Although the chemical composition of the Taylor compound differs from Fertikil, the manufacturing process is very similar.

The Taylor compound would be produced in 1,000-pound lots. Each lot would require 60 direct labor hours and the following chemicals:

Chemicals	Quantity in Pounds
CW-3	400
JX-6	300
MZ-8	200
BE-7	100

The first three chemicals (CW-3, JX-6, MZ-8) are all used in the production of Fertikil. BE-7 was used in a compound that Jenco has discontinued. This chemical was not sold or discarded because it does not deteriorate and there have been adequate storage facilities. Jenco could sell BE-7 at the prevailing market price less $.10 per pound selling/handling expenses.

Jenco also has on hand a chemical called CN-5, which was manufactured for use in another product that is no longer produced. CN-5, which cannot be used in Fertikil, can be substituted for CW-3 on a one-for-one basis without affecting the quality of the Taylor compound. The quantity of CN-5 in inventory has a salvage value of $500.

Inventory and cost data for the chemicals that can be used to produce the Taylor compound are as shown below.

Raw Material	Pounds in Inventory	Actual Price per Pound When Purchased	Current Market Price per Pound
CW-3	22,000	$ .80	$ .90
JX-6	5,000	$ .55	$ .60
MZ-8	8,000	$1.40	$1.60
BE-7	4,000	$ .60	$ .65
CN-5	5,500	$ .75	(salvage)

The current direct labor rate is $7.00 per hour. The manufacturing overhead rate is established at the beginning of the year and is applied consistently throughout the year using direct labor hours (DLH) as the base. The predetermined overhead rate for the current year, based on a two-shift capacity of 400,000 total DLH with no overtime, is as follows:

Variable manufacturing overhead	$2.25 per DLH
Fixed manufacturing overhead	3.75 per DLH
Combined rate	$6.00 per DLH

Jenco's production manager reports that the present equipment and facilities are adequate to manufacture the Taylor compound. However, Jenco is within 800 hours of its two-shift capacity this month before it must schedule overtime. If need be, the Taylor compound coud be produced on regular time by shifting a portion of Fertikil production to overtime. Jenco's rate for overtime hours is one-and-one-half the regular pay rate or $10.50 per hour. There is no allowance for any overtime premium in the manufacturing overhead rate.

Jenco's standard markup policy for new products is 25% of full manufacturing cost.

REQUIRED:

A. Assume Jenco Inc. has decided to submit a bid for a 25,000-pound order of Taylor's new compound. The order must be delivered by the end of the current month. Taylor has indicated that this is a one-time order that will not be repeated. Calculate the lowest price Jenco should bid for the order and not reduce its income.

B. Without prejudice to your answer to part A, assume that Taylor Nursery plans to place regular orders for 25,000-pound lots of the new compound during the coming year. Jenco expects the demand for Fertikil to remain strong again in the coming year. Therefore, the recurring orders from Taylor will put Jenco over its two-shift capacity. However, production can be scheduled so that 60% of each Taylor order can be completed during regular hours or Fertikil production could be shifted temporarily to overtime so that the Taylor orders could be produced on regular time. Jenco's production manager has estimated that the prices of all chemicals will stabilize at the current market rates for the coming year and that all other manufacturing costs are expected to be maintained at the same rates or amounts.

Calculate the price Jenco Inc. should quote Taylor Nursery for each 25,000-pound lot of the new compound assuming that there will be recurring orders during the coming year.

(CMA adapted)

9-18 *(Product Pricing in Sales Regions).* The Justa Corporation produces and sells three products. The three products, A, B, and C, are sold in both a local market and in a regional market. At the end of the first quarter of the current year, the following income statement, showing income by market, was prepared.

	Total	Local	Regional
Sales	$1,300,000	$1,000,000	$300,000
Cost of Goods Sold	1,010,000	775,000	235,000
Gross margin	$ 290,000	$ 225,000	$ 65,000
Selling expenses	$ 105,000	$ 60,000	$ 45,000
Administrative expenses	52,000	40,000	12,000
Total expenses	157,000	100,000	57,000
Income	$ 133,000	$ 125,000	$ 8,000

Management has expressed special concern with the regional market because of the extremely poor return on sales. This market was entered a year ago because of excess capacity. It was originally believed that the return on sales would improve with time, but after a year no noticeable improvement can be seen from the results as reported in the quarterly income statement.

In attempting to decide whether to eliminate the regional market, the following information was gathered.

The selling expenses in the income statement are for local and regional sales offices and include both variable and fixed costs. If a market is dropped, the sales office will be closed. All administrative expenses are fixed for the period.

SALES BY PRODUCTS

	PRODUCTS		
	A	B	C
Sales	$500,000	$400,000	$400,000
Variable manufacturing expenses as a percentage of sales	60%	70%	60%
Variable selling expenses as a percentage of sales	3%	2%	2%

SALES BY MARKET FOR EACH PRODUCT

Product	Local	Regional
A	$400,000	$100,000
B	$300,000	$100,000
C	$300,000	$100,000

Cost of Goods Sold in the income statement includes both variable costs and fixed costs. Administrative costs and fixed manufacturing costs were allocated to the two markets to develop a full-cost income statement.

REQUIRED:

A. Prepare a quarterly income statement showing contribution margins by region.

B. Assuming that there are no alternative uses for the Justa Corporation's present capacity, would you recommend dropping the regional market? Why or why not?

C. Prepare a quarterly income statement showing contribution margins by products.

D. It is believed that a new product can be ready for sale next year if the Justa Corporation decides to go ahead with continued research. The new product can be produced by simply converting equipment used at present in producing Product C. This conversion will increase fixed costs by $10,000 per quarter. What must be the minimum contribution margin per quarter for the new product to make the changeover financially feasible?

(CMA adapted)

9-19 *(Choosing from Three Pricing Alternatives).* Auer Company had received an order for a piece of special machinery from Jay Company. Just as Auer Company completed the machine, Jay Company declared bankruptcy, defaulted on the order, and forfeited the 10% deposit paid on the selling price of $72,500.

Auer's manufacturing manager identified the costs already incurred in the production of the special machinery for Jay as follows:

Direct materials used		$16,600
Direct labor incurred		21,400
Overhead applied:		
Manufacturing:		
Variable	$10,700	
Fixed	5,350	16,050
Fixed selling and administrative		5,405
Total cost		$59,455

Another company, Kaytell Corporation, would be interested in buying the special machinery if it is reworked to Kaytell's specifications. Auer offered to sell the reworked special machinery to Kaytell as a special order for a net price of $68,400. Kaytell has agreed to pay the net price when it takes delivery in two months. The additional identifiable costs to rework the machinery to the specifications of Kaytell are as follows:

Direct materials	$ 6,200
Direct labor	4,200
	$10,400

A second alternative available to Auer is to convert the special machinery to the standard model. The standard model lists for $62,500. The additional identifiable costs to convert the special machinery to the standard model are:

Direct materials	$ 2,850
Direct labor	3,300
	$ 6,150

A third alternative for the Auer Company is to sell, as a special order, the machine as is (e.g., without modification) for a net price of $52,000. However, the potential buyer of the unmodified machine does not want it for 60 days. The buyer offers a $7,000 down payment with final payment upon delivery.

The following additional information is available regarding Auer's operations:

1. Sales commission rate on sales of standard models is 2% while the sales commission rate on special orders is 3%. All sales commissions are calculated on net sales price (i.e., list price less cash discount, if any).

2. Normal credit terms for sales of standard models are 2/10, net/30. Customers take the discounts except in rare instances. Credit terms for special orders are negotiated with the customer.

3. The application rates for manufacturing overhead and the fixed selling and administrative costs are as follows:

Manufacturing:
    Variable   50% of direct-labor cost
    Fixed   25% of direct-labor cost
Selling and administrative:
    Fixed   10% of the total of direct material, direct labor, and manufacturing overhead costs

4. Normal time required for rework is one month.

5. A surcharge of 5% of the sales price is placed on all customer requests for minor modifications of standard models.

6. Auer normally sells a sufficient number of standard models for the company to operate at a volume in excess of the breakeven point.

Auer does not consider the time value of money in analyses of special orders and projects whenever the time period is less than one year because the effect is not significant.

REQUIRED:

A. Determine the dollar contribution each of the three alternatives will add to the Auer Company's before-tax profits.

B. If Kaytell makes Auer a counteroffer, what is the lowest price Auer Company should accept for the reworked machinery from Kaytell? Explain your answer.

C. Discuss the influence fixed factory overhead cost should have on the sales prices quoted by Auer Company for special orders when

    1. A firm is operating at or below the breakeven point.

    2. A firm's special orders constitute efficient utilization of unused capacity above the breakeven volume.

(CMA adapted)

9-20 *(Choosing a Pricing Strategy)*. Stac Industries is a multiproduct company with several manufacturing plants. The Clinton plant manufactures and distributes two household cleaning and polishing compounds—regular and heavy duty—under the Cleen-Brite label. The forecasted operating results for the first six months of 19X0 when 100,000 cases of each compound are expected to be manufactured and sold are presented in the following statement.

CLEEN-BRITE COMPOUNDS—CLINTON PLANT
FORECASTED RESULTS OF OPERATIONS
For the Six-month Period Ending June 30, 19X0
($000 omitted)

	Regular	Heavy Duty	Total
Sales	$2,000	$3,000	$5,000
Cost of sales	1,600	1,900	3,500
Gross profit	$ 400	$1,100	$1,500
Selling and administrative expenses			
Variable	$ 400	$ 700	$1,100
Fixed*	240	360	600
Total selling and administrative expenses	640	1,060	1,700
Income (loss) before taxes	$ (240)	$ 40	$ (200)

*The fixed selling and administrative expenses are allocated between the two products on the basis of dollar sales volume on the internal reports.

The regular compound sold for $20 a case and the heavy-duty compound sold for $30 a case during the first six months of 19X0. The manufacturing costs by case of product are presented in the following schedule. Each product is manufactured on a separate production line. Annual normal manufacturing capacity is 200,000 cases of each product. However, the plant is capable of producing 250,000 cases of regular compound and 350,000 cases of heavy-duty compound annually.

	Cost per Case	
	Regular	Heavy Duty
Raw materials	$ 7.00	$ 8.00
Direct labor	4.00	4.00
Variable manufacturing overhead	1.00	2.00
Fixed manufacturing overhead*	4.00	5.00
Total manufacturing cost	$16.00	$19.00
Variable selling and administrative costs	$ 4.00	$ 7.00

*Depreciation charges are 50% of the fixed manufacturing overhead of each line.

The schedule below reflects the concensus of top management regarding the price–volume alternatives for the Cleen-Brite products for the last six months of 19X0. These are essentially the same alternatives management had during the first six months of 19X0.

REGULAR COMPOUND		HEAVY-DUTY COMPOUND	
Alternative Prices (per Case)	Sales Volume (in Cases)	Alternative Prices (per Case)	Sales Volume (in Cases)
$18	120,000	$25	175,000
20	100,000	27	140,000
21	90,000	30	100,000
22	80,000	32	55,000
23	50,000	35	35,000

Top management believes the loss for the first six months reflects a tight profit margin caused by intense competition. Management also believes that many companies will be forced out of this market by next year and profits should improve.

REQUIRED:

A. What unit selling price should Stac Industries select for each of the Cleen-Brite compounds (regular and heavy duty) for the remaining six months of 19X0? Support your selection with appropriate calculations.

B. Without prejudice to your answer to part A, assume the optimum price–volume alternatives for the last six months were a selling price of $23 and volume level of 50,000 cases for the regular compound and a selling price of $35 and volume of 35,000 cases for the heavy-duty compound.

  1. Should Stac Industries consider closing down its operations until 19X1 in order to minimize its losses? Support your answer with appropriate calculations.

  2. Identify and discuss the qualitative factors that should be considered in deciding whether the Clinton plant should be closed down during the last six months of 19X0.

9-21 *(Pricing a Special Order).* Framar, Inc. manufactures automation machinery according to customer specifications. The company is relatively new and has grown each year. Framar operated at about 75% of practical capacity during the 19X7–X8 fiscal year. The operating results for the most recent fiscal year are presented below.

FRAMAR, INC.
INCOME STATEMENT
For the Year Ended September 30, 19X8
(000 omitted)

Sales		$25,000
Less: sales commissions		2,500
Net sales		$22,500
Expenses:		
Direct material		$ 6,000
Direct labor		7,500
Manufacturing overhead—variable:		
Supplies	$ 625	
Indirect labor	1,500	
Power	125	2,250
Manufacturing overhead—fixed:		
Supervision	$ 500	
Depreciation	1,000	1,500
Corporate administration		750
Total expenses		18,000
Net income before taxes		$ 4,500
Income taxes (40%)		1,800
Net income		$ 2,700

Most of the management personnel had worked for firms in this type of business before joining Framar, but none of the top management had been responsible for overall corporate operations or for final decisions on prices. Nevertheless, the company has been successful.

The top management of Framar wants to have a more organized and formal pricing system to prepare quotes for potential customers. Therefore, it has developed the pricing formula presented on page 380. The formula is based on the company's operating results achieved during the 19X7–X8 fiscal year. The relationships used in the formula are expected to continue during the 19X8–X9 year. The company expects to operate at 75% of practical capacity during the current 19X8–X9 fiscal year.

APA, Inc. has asked Framar to submit a bid on some custom-designed machinery. Framar used the new formula to develop a price and submitted a bid of $165,000 to APA, Inc. The calculations to arrive at the bid price are given next to the following pricing formula.

PRICING FORMULA

Details of Formula		APA Bid Calculations
Estimated direct material cost	$XX	$ 29,200
Estimated direct labor cost	XX	56,000
Estimated manufacturing overhead calculated at 50% of direct labor	XX	28,000
Estimate corporate overhead calculated at 10% of direct labor	XX	5,600
Estimated total costs excluding sales commissions	$XX	$118,800
Add 25% for profits and taxes	XX	29,700
Suggested price (with profits) before sales commissions	$XX	$148,500
Suggested total price equal suggested price divided by .9 to adjust for 10% sales commission	$XX	$165,000

REQUIRED:

A. Calculate the impact the order from APA, Inc. would have on Framar, Inc.'s net income after taxes if Framar's bid of $165,000 were accepted by APA.

B. Assume APA, Inc. has rejected Framar's price but has stated it is willing to pay $127,000 for the machinery. Should Framar, Inc. manufacture the machinery for the counteroffer of $127,000? Explain your answer.

C. Calculate the lowest price Framar, Inc. can quote on this machinery without reducing its net income after taxes if it should manufacture the machinery.

D. Explain how the profit performance in 19X8–X9 would be affected if Framar, Inc. accepted all of its work at prices similar to the $127,000 counteroffer of APA, Inc. described in part B.

(CMA adapted)

9-22 *(Selection of Marketing Strategy)*. The Calco Corporation has been a major producer and distributor of molded and assembled plastic products for industrial use in its region for the past 20 years. Annual sales have averaged $60 million for the past 4 years. Several times during this 20-year period the company has considered entering the consumer products market with items that could be manufactured in its facilities. Each time the product idea was sold to another company because Calco had no experience in the consumer markets, and its facilities were at or near full capacity.

Late last year the Product Engineering Department presented a proposal to produce a plastic storage unit that was designed especially for the consumer market. The product was very well suited for the company's manufacturing process. No costly modification of machinery or molds would be required, nor would operations in the Assembly Department have to be changed in any way. In addition, there was an adequate amount of manufacturing capacity available due to the recent expansion of facilities and a leveling of the sales growth in its industrial product lines.

The Calco management was receptive to this proposal. Although they had rejected consumer products in prior years, the arguments for the product were more persuasive this year: there was excess capacity, the products fit very well into the manufacturing process, and Calco's industrial markets appeared to be maturing. Therefore, entering the consumer market would give the company added opportunity to expand its sales.

The management is considering two alternatives for marketing the product. The first is to add this responsibility to Calco's current Marketing Department. The other alternative is to acquire a small new company named Jasco, Inc. Jasco was started by some former employees of a firm that specialized in marketing plastic products for the consumer market when they lost their jobs as a result of a merger. Jasco has not yet started operations.

Calco has never used independent distributors. Consequently, the management would prefer to acquire a distributor rather than merely enter into a contract for distribution of the product. The founders of Jasco are receptive to such an approach. In fact, Calco could acquire Jasco complete with personnel for a very nominal sum.

The manufacturing costs will be the same for either marketing alternative. The Product Engineering Department has prepared the following estimates of the unit manufacturing costs for the new storage unit.

Direct materials	$14.00
Direct labor	3.50
Manufacturing overhead	10.00
Total	$27.50

The total overhead rate for all of Calco's manufacturing activities is $20.00 per hour. The rate is composed of $5.00 per hour for supplies, employee benefits, power, etc.; and $15.00 per hour for supervision, depreciation, insurance, taxes, etc.

Calco's Marketing Department has used their experience in the sale of industrial products to develop a proposal for the distribution of the new consumer product. The Marketing Department would be reorganized so that several positions that were scheduled for elimination now would be assigned to the new product. The Marketing Department's forecast of the annual financial results for its proposal to market the new storage units appears on page 382.

Sales (100,000 units @ $45.00)	$4,500,000
Costs:	
Cost of units sold (100,000 units @ $27.50)	$2,750,000
Marketing costs	
Positions that were to be eliminated	600,000
Sales commissions (5% of sales)	225,000
Advertising program	400,000
Promotion program	200,000
Share of current Marketing Department's management costs	100,000
Total costs	4,275,000
Net income before taxes	$ 225,000

The Jasco founders also prepared a forecast of the annual financial results based on their experience in marketing consumer products. The forecast presented below was based on the assumption that Jasco would become part of Calco and be responsible for marketing the new storage unit in the consumer market.

Sales (120,000 units @ $50.00)	$6,000,000
Costs:	
Cost of units sold (120,000 units @ $27.50)	$3,300,000
Marketing costs:	
Personnel—sales	660,000
Personnel—sales management	200,000
Commissions (10%)	600,000
Advertising program	800,000
Promotion program	200,000
Office rental (the annual rental of a long-term lease	
already signed by Jasco)	50,000
Total costs	5,810,000
Net income before taxes	$ 190,000

REQUIRED:

A. Discuss the factors that Calco Corporation should consider before it enters into the consumer products market.

B. Revise the forecasts of annual financial results prepared by Calco's Marketing Department and Jasco's founders so that the forecasts present the appropriate financial data to be used to make a decision as to which alternative to select should Calco Corporation decide to enter the consumer market.

C. If Calco Corporation should decide to enter the consumer products market, it will have to evaluate the two marketing proposals.

   1. Compare the reliability of the proposals presented by Calco's Marketing Department and Jasco's founders.

2. Identify the nonquantitative factors Calco's management should consider when choosing between the two alternatives.

Would any of the items discussed be important enough to warrant selection of one alternative over the other regardless of the estimated financial effect in profits? Explain your answer.

(CMA adapted)

9-23 *(Pricing on Inaccurate Costs).* Hitech Company produces three products: Hitech, Lotech, and Brednbutr. Prices were established to yield a profit of approximately 20% on sales. Increased competition has reduced the sales of Lotech in recent years, so that the company has not been able to maintain the desired profit rate. The president, however, is pleased to see sales increasing in the new Hitech line. A product-line income statement for Hitech Company is presented in Exhibit 1.

The controller recently attended a seminar where a case almost identical to her company was presented. In that case it was demonstrated that while many companies were showing a satisfactory return on their products, the costing system was providing inaccurate product costs. As a result, companies were overpricing some products and underpricing other products, losing out on sales that were actually profitable by overpricing and making less profit on products that were underpriced. The seminar leader showed how costs could be related to cost "drivers" and transactions and, therefore, could produce more accurate costs.

The controller was concerned that her use of a single plant-wide overhead rate might be distorting costs and therefore the pricing of the three products.

	Hitech	Brednbutr	Lotech	Total
Sales	$300,000	$160,000	$100,000	$560,000
Production costs:				
Material	$100,000	$ 30,000	$ 10,000	$140,000
Direct labor	25,000	20,000	20,000	65,000
Overhead	50,000	40,000	40,000	130,000
Total	175,000	90,000	70,000	335,000
Gross margin	$125,000	$ 70,000	$ 30,000	$225,000
General and selling costs	60,000	32,000	20,000	112,000
Income	$ 65,000	$ 38,000	$10,000	$113,000
Income as percentage of sales	22%	24%	10%	20%
Additional data:				
Units sold	100,000	20,000	10,000	
Selling price	$3.00	$8.00	$10.00	
Overhead rate (percentage of direct labor)	200%	200%	200%	200%
General and selling (percentage of sales)	20%	20%	20%	20%

EXHIBIT 1   Product-line income statement, 19X9

When she expressed her concerns to the president, he pointed out that as long as the company was earning about 20% on sales he was happy with overall performance. He was disappointed that sales of Lotech were decreasing; with its low profit on sales it just might be time to consider phasing out Lotech in favor of more Hitech production.

After her discussion with the president, the controller decided to examine both the overhead and general and selling accounts. She was satisfied that costing for material and labor was sufficiently accurate. The company had been using one plantwide rate to allocate overhead to products based on direct labor cost. General and selling costs had been allocated to products on the basis of sales dollars. Production of the products, Lotech and Brednbutr, were in older, labor-intensive facilities, while production of Hitech was in largely automated facilities.

The analysis showed that overhead tended to fall into three categories. Material-related costs included procurement, handling, and storage of raw materials and work-in-process. These costs varied among the products and should be applied on the basis of material cost. Labor-related costs included fringe benefits and personnel costs. These costs were approximately 60% of direct labor. Finally, machine-related costs varied widely among the products and should be applied on the basis of machine hours.

The controller traced about one-half the general and selling costs to product lines. She found that Hitech accounted for the majority of the product-related general and selling expenses. The other one-half of general and selling expenses were common costs with no direct relationship to any product. She decided to continue to allocate those costs on the basis of sales.

The results of her study are presented in Exhibit 2. She has come to you to review her work and for assistance in analyzing the revised product-line income statement.

	Hitech	Brednbutr	Lotech	Total
Units sold	100,000	20,000	10,000	
Selling price	$3.00	$8.00	$10.00	
Production costs:				
Material cost	$100,000	$30,000	$10,000	$140,000
Labor cost	$ 25,000	$20,000	$20,000	$ 65,000
Total overhead				$130,000
Total general and selling				$112,000
New cost application rates:				
Material-related overhead rate	15%	3.33%	10%	
Labor-related overhead rate	60%	60%	60%	
Machine-related overhead	$6.00	$2.00	$1.00	
Machine hours	10,000	5,000	4,000	
Product-related general and selling	$ 30,000	$20,000	$ 6,000	
Common general and selling rate (percentage of sales)	10%	10%	10%	10%

EXHIBIT 2   Revised data for product-line income statement, 19X9

REQUIRED:

A. Using the revised data in Exhibit 2, prepare a revised product-line income statement showing income by product and profit as a percentage of sales. Do you agree with the president's observation that it was time to consider phasing Lotech out and expanding production of Hitech?

B. Does your revised product-line income statement help to explain why sales of Lotech were declining and sales of Hitech were increasing? Explain.

C. What price must be charged for each product to generate 20% profit on sales for each product? In view of the statements about the firm's competitive position, do these prices seem reasonable? Explain.

9-24 *(Cost and Pricing Strategies. Note: Problem Requires the Use of Probabilities).* Bob Cooler, controller of Amex Company, is in the process of preparing an income budget for next year. On the basis of the best estimates available, the following statement was prepared by his staff.

Sales (100,000 units @ $10)		$1,000,000
Variable costs:		
Manufacturing ($5 per unit)	$500,000	
Marketing ($.50 per unit)	50,000	550,000
Marginal contribution		$ 450,000
Fixed costs:		
Manufacturing	$200,000	
Marketing	50,000	
Administrative	100,000	350,000
Net income before tax		$ 100,000
Taxes		50,000
Net income after tax		$ 50,000

For many years Bob had wondered whether he and his staff were giving management the kind of budgeted income statement most useful to them. This was not a new issue to Bob. Only five years ago he had converted all income budgets into a variable costing format in order to take advantage of the built-in breakeven and cost-volume-profit data. However, this didn't seem to satisfy management completely, even though they were quite pleased with the variable costing philosophy.

Recently, Bob had been discussing variable costing with a group of controllers from other companies. Bob found that many of them were no longer using the term fixed costs, because they believed they had found too many possible misconceptions arising from the use of the term. The main misconception was the idea that fixed costs implied to many report users "a homogeneous mass of unchangeable costs." As a replacement for fixed costs the general consensus was that two new terms were to be used: *committed* and *managed*. These two new terms were to help draw attention to two distinct subdivisions of fixed costs.

Before Bob left the discussion, he asked for and received the following definitions:

> *Fixed costs.* Those costs that would not vary with activity within certain ranges of activity.
>
> *Committed costs.* Those fixed costs to which a company is committed, usually long in advance of the particular year to which they apply. Essentially these are long-run commitments, for example, depreciation, property taxes, and basic minimum staff levels (salary, fringe benefits, etc.).
>
> *Managed costs.* Those fixed costs to which a company commits itself for short periods of time. Thus, managed costs can be modified in the short run. Two examples of managed costs are advertising and sales promotion as well as research and development.

Bob realized that the two categories of fixed costs had to be considered in the light of individual company circumstances. Since the basic distinction between the two cost categories relates to short-run versus long-run commitments and not to specific elements of cost, one can expect similar kinds of costs to involve long-run commitments in some companies and short-run commitments in other companies. With these thoughts in mind, Bob directed his staff to reexamine the above income budget. His directive stated that "the income budget should be reformulated so as to include the distinction between managed and committed fixed costs." He also made it clear that short-term commitments were to be defined as those commitments that could be modified during the budget year, while long-term commitments were to be defined as those commitments that could *not* be modified during the budget year.

Within two weeks the new income budget was prepared and delivered to the controller. It was as follows:

Sales (100,000 units @ $10)		$1,000,000
Variable costs:		
Manufacturing ($5 per unit)	$500,000	
Marketing ($.50 per unit)	50,000	550,000
Marginal contribution		$ 450,000
Managed costs:		
Manufacturing	$ 20,000	
Marketing	10,000	
Administrative	40,000	70,000
Short-run margin		$ 380,000
Committed costs:		
Manufacturing	$180,000	
Marketing	40,000	
Administrative	60,000	280,000
Net income before tax		$ 100,000
Tax—50%		50,000
Net income after tax		$ 50,000

The controller was quite pleased with the new income budget. He especially liked the added information provided on "short-run margin" which was an immediate by-product of distinguishing between managed and committed fixed costs. To him the short-run margin pointed out the real contribution to earnings that could be attributed to anticipated results for next year. Bob also liked the inference that committed costs were something on the order of a handicap that had to be covered by a short-run margin before a net profit could be realized. Because Bob was so pleased with the new income budget, he submitted it to management in preparation for an executive committee budget review session to be held in two weeks.

During the next two weeks Bob heard nothing from the management or the executive committee and, for this reason, he felt quite good. Unfortunately, however, no news was not good news in this case, as Bob found out when he entered the executive committee session to discuss the proposed income budget.

The company president first asked Bob about the reliability of the estimates. It seemed that the president had recently attended a seminar on quantitative methods in business management at a leading eastern university, where he was introduced to the notion of expected value. Thus, the president pursued his original question by stating that it seemed to him that the budget represented a series of estimates that were expected averages. Bob stated that this was true. The president pressed Bob further by asking him if he or his staff could estimate a range around which one might predict each of the expected averages would vary.

Bob thought a moment and replied that he was quite certain about the estimates of committed costs because they represented commitments already made by the executive committee. He stated that he was not quite as certain about managed costs, because commitments for them were not all made and those commitments already made could be modified, if necessary, during the year. These managed costs represented R & D of $40,000 included under administration, advertising and promotion of $10,000 included under marketing, and $20,000 of manufacturing costs that could be dispensed with if volume of activity was substantially below 100,000 units.

Before Bob could continue, the marketing vice-president stated that volume of activity could differ substantially from the 100,000-unit projection. The estimate of the market research staff was that a pessimistic view of sales volume is 80,000 units, given a $10 price and $10,000 of promotion and advertising. Given the same price and promotion, the highest volume to be expected would be about 110,000 units. The president and manufacturing vice-president then added that if volume decreased to 80,000 units, managed manufacturing costs would be decreased by $10,000 and certain R & D projects costing $15,000 would be delayed until some future year. If volume increased to 110,000 units, $10,000 would be added to managed manufacturing costs.

At this point in the meeting Bob was a bit flustered, even though he was quite elated about the kind of information generated by the discussion. He noticed that only two items in the income statement hadn't been considered— these were the variable costs. He quickly realized that the marketing cost of

$.50 per unit was a sales commission fixed by a compensation agreement with sales personnel. The only other cost to be considered was manufacturing variable cost, which he knew had varied in prior years between $4.80 and $5.10 per unit. He informed the executive committee of these facts. They then directed him to prepare budgeted income data incorporating as much as possible of the above data for a presentation to be made next week.

REQUIRED:

A. Prepare the data requested by the executive committee.

B. Assume all facts as given in the case except that the mean value of variable manufacturing cost is $5.00 with a standard deviation of $.20 per unit. Determine the range within which net income will fall 68% of the time for the average, pessimistic, and optimistic volume levels.

C. Assume that sales volume and variable manufacturing costs were stated in the following terms:

Volume	Probability
80,000 units	.3
100,000 units	.5
110,000 units	.2

Variable Manufacturing Cost	Probability
$5.10	.2
5.00	.6
4.80	.2

Prepare a budgeted income statement given the above and other facts in the case.

D. Assume that the Amex Company desires to prepare an analysis for two alternative pricing situations that can be compared to the analysis of part *C* in order to determine which price would be most appropriate. All facts are as given except for variable manufacturing costs as given in part *C* and the two pricing alternatives below.

Price No. 1—$8 per Unit

Volume	Probability
100,000 units	.2
110,000 units	.5
130,000 units	.3

Price No. 2—$10 per Unit

This price is the same as the price in the case; however, due to an increase of $10,000 in advertising and promotion, volume estimates will change as follows:

Volume	Probability
90,000 units	.2
110,000 units	.4
120,000 units	.4

(Prepared by William L. Ferrara)

9-25 *(Pricing in a Public Marina)*. The Port of Fogbank is a not-for-profit small-craft marina located on the New England coast. The port contains approximately 550 sport and commercial boats of various sizes. One of the most difficult and controversial issues at Fogbank Public Port has been the determination of fair and equitable charges for its services. The greatest problems have centered upon the areas of moorage and utility pricing.

Moorage

Moorage is the fee assessed to a particular vessel for the right to secure to port docks and facilities. It is the functional equivalent of rent on an apartment or office space and is paid by most users on a lease basis for six months or a year.

Problems

There are several important issues involved with the conflict over moorage pricing. Some of the more pertinent problems are described below.

Demand Far Exceeds Supply. At the present time, the public ports do not have one unused dock available. In fact, every port has a waiting list of enough boats to replace 50% of the current fleet if the space existed. Most ports now even charge a fee just for the privilege of being on the waiting list. No one is exactly sure of the demand, however, because many vessels are on more than one waiting list. At the current turnover rates, the wait could be as long as three or four years before a new registrant would receive a dock for his or her boat.

Commercial Subsidy. Moorage rates on commercial vessels are lower than those for equivalently sized pleasure boats. One reason for this is that revenue dollars from commercial fishing vessels are a major boost to the local economy. Some economists have estimated that each dollar turns over approximately seven times for items such as fuel, supplies, crew salaries, and repairs. The revenues from commercial fishermen are therefore seen as quite important to the community and are to be attracted through lower moorage rates. A large fishing vessel (75 feet) may gross nearly half a million dollars during a successful season.

Commercial Versus Sport Vessels. Fogbank's facilities are used by both recreational and commercial vessels. There are some significant differences, however, in the expectations by each group regarding port services and facilities. Commercial operators need rugged, practical docks and facilities; the recreational user desires aesthetically pleasing and convenient facilities. Both groups want low cost, although the pleasure boat owner is somewhat more willing to accept higher prices. Pleasure boat operators do not wish to pay for hoists, lift trucks, and fish-cleaning equipment, while the fishermen have little use for small dock carts, personalized nameplates, and brightly painted surroundings.

Commission Approval Required. All rate changes must be approved by Fogbank's five-member port commission. The commissioners are elected officials representing the community. There has been some criticism that unrealistically low rates have been maintained to facilitate reelection. Some critics have even suggested that economic pricing has become much too complex for the commission to accomplish, and the function should therefore be turned over to an economic consulting firm.

Maintenance and Replacement. Two factors that the Fogbank management feels must be included in a moorage fee are provisions for maintenance and replacement. Recent environmental legislation has made it all but impossible for new marinas to be developed in the area. Also, routine wear and tear must be planned for in the master budgeting process. For these reasons, the management strongly feels that current moorage pricing should reflect the future demands. Moorage lessees, however, disagree. "Why should I pay for facilities I'll never use?" is a common response. The pleasure boat owner claims that the large commercial vessels do all of the damage with their boats going in and out all the time. The commercial operator counters by saying that they are competent professionals—it's the Sunday sailor who drives his craft into the light poles and pilings. Port management recognizes that a problem exists in planning for future maintenance and replacement, yet it is unclear just how this may fairly and effectively be accomplished. Exhibit 1 is included to show the current construction costs of port facilities.

Private Enterprise. The criticism of unfair competition has been leveled by private ports and marinas. They believe that Fogbank's moorage rates are unfairly low due to tax subsidies and government assistance. The rates are approximately 60% lower than those of the private installations. The commission has been ignoring the complaints, however, because there is so much excess demand. Private marinas and yacht clubs usually have far fewer commercial fishing vessels, but much more modern facilities.

Moorage Assessment Options

Several different methods are currently in practice in the Northeast for assessing moorage fees. Fogbank uses the linear footage method. Several other assessment methods, described below, are in use at other ports.

```
                    FOGBANK PUBLIC PORT
            CURRENT AVERAGE CONSTRUCTION COSTS
                FOR A PORT WITH 100 VESSELS

1. Construction cost per berth for dock and walking @ $75 per
   foot. Assume one hundred 36-foot berths = 3,600 linear feet:     $270,000

2. Total land frontage required = 230 feet @ $1,000 per foot:        230,000

3. Parking: Assume one stall per two slips with an average cost
   per stall of $1,200:                                               60,000

4. Lighting: Assume 20 high-pressure sodium lighting fixtures @
   $1,200 each:                                                       24,000

5. Restroom facilities: Minimum of $10,000                           10,000

6. Water connections                                                  8,000

7. Fencing and security                                               6,000

8. Office (minimum)                                                   35,000

9. Bulkheads @ $70 per foot                                           16,100
   Total                                                            $659,100

Costs exclusive of permits, design charges, tidelands leases, legal and accounting
fees. Also not included are dredging and mobilization costs of construction
crews.

The current cost of municipal financing is approximately 8%. Any major project of
this nature is assumed to have an estimated life of 15 years.
```

EXHIBIT 1

Linear Footage. The most commonly applied method is to bill each vessel on its overall length (e.g., the total distance from bow to stern). Fogbank's current rates under this method are $.60 and $.85 for commercial and sport boats, respectively. The rate is per linear foot per month. A variation of this method is to compare the length of the vessel with the length of the dock that it occupies. If the vessel is longer than the dock, then the rate applies to the boat. If the dock is longer than the boat, then the rate would apply to the dock instead.

Square Footage. A much less frequently used method is to assess moorage fees on the total amount of water space required by a vessel. Owners of smaller boats feel this process would tend to compensate for some of the inequities in the ''sport versus commercial'' rivalry because the commercial craft have much broader beams. As with the linear footage plans, the rate could apply to the vessel or slip, whichever is greatest.

Flat Rate. One method of moorage assessment in other harbors has been to charge all port tenants one standard fee for the use of the facilities. The principal reason for this practice is the simplicity of administration. This technique has not gained widespread acceptance because of the obvious disregard of vessel size. As a result, the use has been limited almost exclusively to smaller boat harbors where there is greater consistency of vessel size.

Expense Recovery Basis. While all of the above methods examine the issue of *how* to allocate charges, they do not deal with *what* the rates should be. One method for determining rates is an expense recovery scheme whereby total anticipated operating costs are divided by the total linear footage, square footage, or number of vessels. This computation then determines what the rate will be for the coming fiscal year per measurement unit (e.g., per linear foot, square foot, or per vessel). (See Exhibit 2.)

Estimation. Following a preliminary investigation, it appears that rates are based on some increase over the previous year's rate. The rate is additionally checked to make sure that it is one that will not be criticized too heavily by the tenants. The rate must be approved by the commission before it is implemented in the billing process.

Utilities

In addition to moorage fees, or included therein, are the ancillary charges for items such as garbage, water, electricity, and sewage service. While a few ports use individual metering devices for each vessel's electrical consumption, the Port of Fogbank does not. Also, it is impossible to assess accurately the individual utilization of water and garbage services.

For the recreational boater the assumption is that consumption is heavily dependent on the season (i.e., more activity during the summer months), whereas commercial vessels tend to have a more uniform demand pattern throughout the year. It is also believed that the commercial vessels require more of the utility services than the pleasure boats, but this has not been substantiated.

FOGBANK PUBLIC PORT
VESSEL DISTRIBUTION BY SIZE*

Vessel Length Interval Midpoint	Average Width	Number of Vessels		Square Feet		Linear Feet	
		Sport	Commercial	Sport	Commercial	Sport	Commercial
25 –	10	196	84	49,000	21,000	4,900	2,100
33	12	70	47	27,720	18,612	2,310	1,551
41.5	14	25	25	14,525	14,525	1,037.5	1,037.5
50	15	10	15	7,500	11,250	500	750
60	16	4	16	3,840	15,360	240	960
70+	18	0	18	0	22,680	0	1,260
Totals		305	205	102,585	103,427	8,987.5	7,658.5
Percentage Total Vessel distribution by size*		59.8	40.2	49.8	50.2	54.0	46.0

*Current port population (September 1, 19X7). Full-time lessees only.

EXHIBIT 2

FOGBANK PUBLIC PORT
UTILITY CHARGES: 19X7

	Electricity	Water/Sewage
January	$ 645.00	$ 130.00
February	720.00	145.00
March	680.00	170.00
April	760.00	253.00
May	832.00	157.00
June	550.00	221.00
July	392.00	96.00
August	599.00	140.00
September	360.00	195.00
October	380.00	210.00
November	360.00	150.00
December	476.00	140.00
Total	$6,754.00	$2,007.00
Grand Total*	$8,761.00	

*For a port with approximately 500 sport and commercial vessels.

The above utility charges are exclusive of lighting, office utilities, and other miscellaneous charges not directly traceable to the dock facilities. The complete port utility bill for the year was $14,400.

EXHIBIT 3

Along with the issues of pricing, Fogbank has been experiencing some discouraging problems down on the docks. For example, lightbulbs are being stolen from the fixtures, water is left running, and some firefighting equipment has been taken. In one case, there had been several complaints by the fishermen about the lack of security, so key-lock gates were installed at all of the ramps leading to the docks. Within weeks all of the gates had been pulled from their hinges by tenants who had forgotten their keys. While only a few vessel operators and their crews are responsible, everyone bears the cost of replacement and repairs. After many of these incidents the port's management was reluctant to provide pleasant, modern equipment, fearful that it will once again be stolen or vandalized. As a result, there are many complaints that port management is careless in maintaining the utility services and, therefore, should not be charging so much. Exhibit 3 has been included to show the utility charges for the 19X7 calendar year. Exhibit 4 on page 394 shows an operations and activities summary for the port's fiscal year, July 1, 19X7–June 30, 19X8.

REQUIRED:

A. Prepare a table showing moorage collections for both sport and commercial vessels based on the linear footage method. Fogbank's current rates are $.85 and $.60 per foot per month for sport and commercial boats, respectively.

   1. What are the average collections per month per vessel (sport, commercial, overall for the port)?

```
┌─────────────────────────────────────────────────────────────────┐
│                                                                   │
│                     FOGBANK PUBLIC PORT                           │
│             OPERATIONS AND ACTIVITIES SUMMARY 19X7                │
│                                                                   │
│     Resources                                                     │
│        Moorage income              $160,400.00*                   │
│        Utilities                      6,400.00                    │
│        Taxes                         12,500.00                    │
│        Interest                       5,400.00                    │
│        Parking fees                  12,725.00                    │
│        Miscellaneous                  4,600.00                    │
│                                                     $202,025.00   │
│     Expenses                                                      │
│        Personnel services                                         │
│           Salaries                 $ 80,288.00                    │
│           Payroll taxes and insurance  13,257.00                  │
│           Repair materials           44,680.00                    │
│           Utilities                  14,400.00                    │
│           Legal and accounting       16,300.00                    │
│           Engineering services        2,500.00                    │
│           Miscellaneous supplies      3,700.00                    │
│                                                      175,125.00   │
│        Capital outlay                                             │
│           Automobile               $  6,500.00                    │
│           Office equipment            1,250.00                    │
│           Land and improvements       2,800.00                    │
│                                                       10,550.00   │
│        Other expenditures                                         │
│           Bond redemption          $  6,000.00                    │
│           Other bonds                 4,750.00                    │
│           Contingencies               5,600.00                    │
│                                                       16,350.00   │
│     Net Operating Gain or Loss                      $     0.00    │
│                                                                   │
│     *All figures have been rounded to the nearest whole dollar.   │
└─────────────────────────────────────────────────────────────────┘
```

EXHIBIT 4

2. What is the overall rate per month per linear foot?

3. What is the average rate per square foot per month?

B. Prepare a table showing the square footage distribution of revenue in each length category (i.e., in *each* length class, compute an equivalent square footage moorage rate). Discuss the findings from this process.

C. Under the present pricing system, how much are the commercial fishing vessels being subsidized, if at all?

D. What are some guidelines for determining the actual moorage rates?

E. What are some suggestions for equitably assessing utility rates? Should the practice of a flat fee all year be continued, or does a seasonal rate structure appear more appropriate? What is suggested by the fact that utility and equipment services are being stolen and vandalized?

(Prepared by David E. Isett under the direction of Kavasseri V. Ramanathan)

chapter **10**

RELEVANT COSTS AND PRODUCTION DECISIONS

In this chapter we explore how the decision maker uses accounting data to make production volume decisions. The topics in this chapter focus on how best to use existing productive capacity. Questions asked include: ''How many units should the firm produce?'' ''Should it produce more of Product X than Product Y, or more of Product Y than Product X?'' ''Should a product be dropped?''

CRITERIA FOR DECISION DATA

Each decision made by management is unique. Different decisions call for different data. To be relevant, data must exhibit the characteristics of **differentiality** and **futurity.** Past benefits and costs are the results of a prior decision that cannot be changed. Past costs are generally irrelevant because no future decision can change what has already happened. The role of the past in decision making lies in what can be learned from it. Further, a benefit or cost that is identical in all the available alternatives does not affect the choice and, therefore, is not relevant to the decision.

Crucial to any measure of differential data is the **opportunity cost,** the foregone income that would have been earned had another alternative been chosen. In examining the possible income that a firm could earn or costs that a firm could save in the selection of one alternative over another, we are viewing these as opportunity costs. The term *opportunity cost* is not often used, but it is implied. When the contribution margin is used to measure the impact of production output decisions it is being treated as an opportunity cost.

THE CONTRIBUTION MARGIN AND PRODUCTION DECISIONS

Chapters 2 and 3 explained the role of fixed and variable costs in determining the contribution margin and in assessing cost-volume-profit interactions. In Chapter 9 we showed how the contribution margin facilitates pricing decisions. Now let's turn our attention to how the contribution margin can be used in making production output decisions. The benefit of the contribution margin is that it measures the combined effect of changes in revenue and variable costs, allowing a direct measure of the impact of output variations. Typically, fixed costs do not change and therefore are not relevant to production decisions as long as the firm stays within the relevant range of activity.

The decisions examined in this chapter using the contribution margin are whether to add a new product, sell a product or process it further, make or buy component parts, drop a product line, or manufacture the optimum product combination.

ADDING A NEW PRODUCT

Assume that Product A of the Sultan Company has not achieved the customer acceptance expected and that the company has excess productive capacity. In its search for new products to produce with existing facilities, the Sultan Company narrowed its study to two: Product B and Product C. The following tabulation shows estimated selling prices and costs directly associated with these new products.

	Product B	Product C
Selling price per unit	$20 per unit	$2.50 per unit
Costs:		
Direct materials	$10 per unit	$ .80 per unit
Direct labor	$ 3 per unit	$ .45 per unit
Variable overhead	$ 1 per unit	$ .15 per unit
Variable selling costs	$ 2 per unit	$ .50 per unit
Identifiable fixed selling costs	$6,000 per year	$10,000 per year

The current fixed overhead of $15,000 per year and nontraceable fixed selling costs of $5,000 per year would not be affected and are not relevant. The Sultan Company has sufficient excess capacity to produce 4,000 units of Product B or 30,000 units of Product C. Market studies indicate that these units may be sold at the planned market prices.

Which product should be added? Projected income statements show the contribution margin and product margin for the two new products.

	PRODUCT B		PRODUCT C	
Number of units	4,000		30,000	
	Per Unit	Amount	Per Unit	Amount
Sales	$20.00	$80,000	$2.50	$75,000
Direct materials	$10.00	$40,000	$ .80	$24,000
Direct labor	3.00	12,000	.45	13,500
Variable overhead	1.00	4,000	.15	4,500
Variable selling costs	2.00	8,000	.50	15,000
Total variable costs	16.00	64,000	1.90	57,000
Contribution margin	$ 4.00	$16,000	$ .60	$18,000
Identifiable fixed selling costs		6,000		10,000
Product margin		$10,000		$ 8,000

After subtracting the directly identifiable fixed selling costs from the contribution margin, the result is the **product margin,** the amount that income should increase by producing and selling the product. Product B, with a product margin of $10,000, should be produced and sold. The $8,000 contribution margin from Product C foregone by selecting Product B is an example of an opportunity cost.

SELL OR PROCESS FURTHER

The Sultan Company currently manufactures only Product A, which is sold to other firms that process it further. During normal operations 10,000 units of Product A are produced per year; they sell for $10 each. The following costs are incurred to produce and sell these 10,000 units.

| | PRODUCT A | |
	Per Unit	Total
Direct materials	$2.00	$20,000
Direct labor	3.00	30,000
Variable overhead costs	1.00	10,000
Variable selling costs	.25	2,500
Fixed overhead costs	1.50	15,000
Fixed selling costs	.50	5,000
Total unit cost	$8.25	$82,500

Assume that the Sultan Company has excess capacity. They could use this capacity to process Product A further or to produce Product B. After additional processing, Product A could be sold for $14 per unit. The following are estimates of the *additional* costs of processing 10,000 units of Product A further.

Direct labor	$1.25 per unit
Variable overhead costs	$ .75 per unit
Variable selling costs	$ .50 per unit
Fixed overhead costs	$8,000 per year
Fixed selling costs	$5,000 per year

The tabulation on page 399 shows the contribution margin and the product margin of Product A, both with and without the additional processing. The contribution margin would increase by $15,000 and the product margin by $2,000 if the Sultan Company decided to process the product further.

The original per-unit cost included fixed overhead costs of $1.50 and fixed selling expenses of $.50. These were calculated by dividing the total fixed costs of overhead and selling expenses by the number of units normally produced and sold. Therefore, the fixed overhead is $15,000 ($1.50 × 10,000 units) and the fixed selling expenses are $5,000 ($.50 × 10,000 units). The decision to process further does not change this fixed cost structure; these fixed costs are nonrelevant. The practice of stating fixed costs on a per-unit basis is potentially misleading and should be avoided in making differential decisions.

	WITHOUT FURTHER PROCESSING		PRODUCT A WITH FURTHER PROCESSING		DIFFERENCE FROM PROCESSING FURTHER	
	Per Unit	Total	Per Unit	Total	Per Unit	Total
Sales	$10.00	$100,000	$14.00	$140,000	$4.00	$40,000
Variable costs:						
Direct material	$ 2.00	$ 20,000	$ 2.00	$ 20,000	—	—
Direct labor	3.00	30,000	4.25	42,500	$1.25	$12,500
Variable overhead	1.00	10,000	1.75	17,500	.75	7,500
Variable selling costs	.25	2,500	.75	7,500	.50	5,000
Total variable costs	6.25	62,500	8.75	87,500	2.50	25,000
Contribution margin	$ 3.75	$ 37,500	$ 5.25	$ 52,500	$1.50	$15,000
Identifiable fixed costs		—		13,000		13,000
Product margin		$ 37,500		$ 39,500		$ 2,000

The Sultan Company has considered two different uses for its excess capacity. One alternative was to add a new product. Of the two products considered, Product B would make the greatest contribution to income. Another desirable choice was to process Product A further. Which of the two alternatives should be chosen?

The income statements show that the new product will contribute $10,000 toward income, whereas processing Product A further will contribute only $2,000 toward income. The excess capacity should be used to produce Product B. The choice of Product B, rather than processing Product A further, is another example of an opportunity cost.

MAKE OR BUY COMPONENT PARTS

Another important production decision is whether to make or buy component parts. This decision can involve both quantitative and qualitative factors. Nonquantitative factors to consider include quality differences, dependability of supply, possible unemployment of workers because of shutdown, and the inability to change our minds and resume production without significant costs. Because of these factors, many firms, to ensure their flow of finished products, control the total production flow from extraction or manufacture of the raw materials to the completion of the final product. This control, called vertical integration, creates an operation much less dependent on suppliers and allows the firm to earn profits from manufacturing its subcomponents. However, the manufacture of subcomponents requires that skilled labor and productive facilities be available.

The economic effects of the make-or-buy decision are best seen through the contribution margin approach of measuring incremental income. The purchase price of the parts plus other incremental costs of procurement, such as ordering and receiving, can be compared with the additional costs of producing the part. As long as the incremental costs of making the part are less than the costs of buying it, the firm should manufacture the part. When the incremental manufacturing costs exceed the purchase costs, the part should be purchased from the supplier.

To illustrate, assume that a firm has prepared the following cost estimate for the manufacture of a subcomponent—a motor casting—based on an annual production of 5,000 parts.

	Per Unit	Total
Direct materials	$ 5	$ 25,000
Direct labor	8	40,000
Variable overhead	4	20,000
Fixed overhead (37.5% of direct-labor cost)	3	15,000
Total cost per motor casting	$20	$100,000

A supplier has offered to provide the motor casting at a price of $16.50; the firm estimates that costs of ordering, receiving, and inspecting each part will be $1.50. The key to the decision lies in the examination of those costs that will change between the alternatives. Assuming that the productive capacity will be idle if not used to manufacture the part, the incremental analysis is as follows.

	PER UNIT		TOTAL OF 5,000 UNITS	
	Make	Buy	Make	Buy
Direct material	$ 5	—	$25,000	—
Direct labor	8	—	40,000	—
Variable overhead	4	—	20,000	—
Purchase price plus ordering, receiving, and inspection costs	—	$18	—	$90,000
Total relevant costs	$17	$18	$85,000	$90,000

In this case the company should make the product rather than purchase it from the supplier. The variable costs to produce the part are $17; the purchase costs are $18 ($16.50 + $1.50). The fixed overhead is not relevant to the decision.

Let's carry the illustration one step further. Assume that management can choose to make the motor casting or buy it from the supplier, using the excess capacity to make 5,000 pump housings. Cost and revenue estimates for the pump housing follow.

Pump Housing		
Selling price		$ 25.00
Direct material	$ 8.00	
Direct labor	10.00	
Variable overhead	4.00	
Fixed overhead (37.5% of direct labor cost)	3.75	
Total costs		25.75
Loss per unit		$(.75)

At first glance it would seem unprofitable to produce the pump housing; total costs exceed total revenue by $.75 per unit. Closer examination shows that the variable costs per unit of producing the pump housing are $22 ($8 + $10 + $4), and the contribution margin per unit is $3.00 ($25 − $22), or a total of $15,000 ($3 × 5,000). If the motor castings are sold for $26, the total contribution margin for producing and selling motor castings will be $45,000 [($26 − $17) × 5,000 units]. However, if motor castings are purchased and the pump housing produced, the total contribution margin will increase to $55,000.

	Motor Castings		Pump Housings		Total
Sales	$26	$130,000	$25	$125,000	$255,000
Variable costs	18	90,000	22	110,000	200,000
Contribution margin	$ 8	$ 40,000	$ 3	$ 15,000	$ 55,000

Management's optimum decision would be to produce the pump housing and buy the motor casting. The fixed costs of the factory are not relevant to the make-or-buy decision, although they must be covered before the firm makes a profit.

The previous discussion assumed that the firm did not need additional plant facilities to produce the unit. If the plant had to be enlarged or new equipment purchased, the firm would need to make a long-range capacity decision. The savings from producing the part would have to be compared to the additional investment to ensure an adequate rate of return on the investment. In this situation the make-or-buy alternatives would be an integral input to the capital investment decision shown in Chapter 11.

DROPPING A PRODUCT LINE

Assume that the Wagner Company manufactures and sells three products: G, H, and I. Income statements for the three products and for the total firm are shown in Exhibit 10–1. Management is considering dropping Product G because it is apparently not contributing to the income of the firm. Recasting the product income statements into a contribution margin format allows an examination of the products according to their respective incremental contribution margins. As shown in the recasted income statements in Exhibit 10–2, the joint costs are common to all products and hence are irrelevant to the decision.

From Exhibit 10–2 the role of the three products in contributing to income is clearer. Product G has a positive product margin to help cover the joint

	THE WAGNER COMPANY INCOME STATEMENT For the Year Ended December 31, 19X7			
	Product G	Product H	Product I	Total
Sales	$100,000	$300,000	$200,000	$600,000
Variable costs	60,000	210,000	150,000	420,000
Contribution margin	$ 40,000	$ 90,000	$ 50,000	$180,000
Fixed costs:				
Identifiable to products	$ 30,000	$ 30,000	$ 20,000	$ 80,000
Joint costs allocated on sales basis	10,000	30,000	20,000	60,000
Total fixed costs	40,000	60,000	40,000	140,000
Income	$ 0	$ 30,000	$ 10,000	$ 40,000

EXHIBIT 10–1　Income statements by product line with apportioned joint costs

	THE WAGNER COMPANY INCOME STATEMENT For the Year Ended December 31, 19X7			
	Product G	Product H	Product I	Total
Sales	$100,000	$300,000	$200,000	$600,000
Variable costs	60,000	210,000	150,000	420,000
Contribution margin	$ 40,000	$ 90,000	$ 50,000	$180,000
Fixed costs identifiable to products	30,000	30,000	20,000	80,000
Product margin	$ 10,000	$ 60,000	$ 30,000	$100,000
Joint costs				60,000
Income				$ 40,000

EXHIBIT 10–2　Income statements by product line

costs, although it is not as large as the product margins of the other two products. If Product G were discontinued, the income would decline.

A customer offered to purchase 2,000 units of Product J at $30 per unit if the Wagner Company would produce them. To produce Product J, the variable costs are estimated at $24,000; the fixed costs specifically identifiable with Product J are $20,000. Because the plant has no idle capacity, one of the existing products would have to be dropped. Would this be profitable? Let's look at the product margin of Product J.

Sales (2,000 × $30)	$60,000
Variable costs (2,000 × $12)	24,000
Contribution margin (2,000 × $18)	$36,000
Identifiable fixed costs	20,000
Product margin before joint costs	$16,000

If Product J can be produced in the void left by dropping Product G, it would be economically sound to do so. If, on the other hand, the production of Product J would require the productive time, space, and energy devoted to either Product H or Product I, it would be an unwise choice.

Suppose that management was considering producing one-third more of Product H instead of accepting the offer to produce Product J. The productive facilities used for Product G could be used for this increase. The identifiable fixed costs currently associated with Product G would be associated with the additional units of Product H. The product margin of the incremental quantity of Product H follows.

Sales	$100,000
Variable costs	70,000
Contribution margin	$ 30,000
Identifiable joint costs	30,000
Product margin before joint costs	$ 0

Given these three alternatives, the decision hierarchy should be to produce Product J and, if this is not possible, to produce Product G. Producing an additional one-third of Product H would not be profitable.

MANUFACTURING THE OPTIMUM PRODUCT COMBINATION

In assessing production decisions, management must decide how best to allocate the firm's limited production resources. If facilities are not limited, management can produce all it wants of any product. In previous examples we have assumed that the firm was not faced with resource limitations. However, all resources are limited in some way. The maximum amount of resources that can be committed to production is a restriction or **constraint.**

TWO OR MORE PRODUCTS WITH ONLY ONE CONSTRAINT

Assume that a company produces two products, K and L, with the following contribution margins per unit.

	Product K		Product L	
Sales	$6.00	100%	$20.00	100%
Variable costs	4.00	67%	16.00	80%
Contribution margin	$2.00	33%	$ 4.00	20%

The annual fixed costs of production are $36,000, which remain unchanged regardless of the combination of products produced. If there are no production constraints, the product with the highest contribution margin per unit should be produced until demand is satisfied. In our illustration the firm should emphasize Product L, which has a contribution margin per unit of $4.00. The decision rule can be stated simply: "Choose the product with the highest contribution margin per unit until the demand is satisfied; then choose the product with the next highest contribution margin per unit." This decision will maximize income.

Where demand for the product is greater than the production capabilities of the firm, and the production is subject to a single constraint, the firm should maximize the total contribution margin per unit of constraint. To illustrate, let's assume that the firm has a production constraint of 100,000 machine hours; the machine capacity is the scarce resource. Further, assume that Product K requires two machine hours to produce and Product L requires five machine hours. One way to express this constraint is to determine the contribution margin per machine hour.

	Product K	Product L
Selling price	$6.00	$20.00
Variable costs	4.00	16.00
Contribution margin	$2.00	$ 4.00
Divided by machine hours required per unit	2	5
Contribution margin per machine hour	$1.00	$ .80

Because Product K returns the highest contribution margin per machine hour, it is the preferred product. The firm should limit its production to Product K as long as the market demand and cost structure are unchanged.

TWO OR MORE PRODUCTS AND TWO OR MORE CONSTRAINTS

Where there is only one limiting factor, the contribution margin per unit of the limiting factor will determine the most profitable use of the resources. This is true even with a large number of products. However, in all but the most simple of production settings there are many limiting factors and many products, and a more powerful model is needed. Where there are two or more products and two or more limiting factors, a mathematical technique called **linear programming** provides a solution that maximizes profits or minimizes costs. Linear programming is the standard technique for determining how materials, labor, and productive facilities can be used to provide the most favorable output.

Because the linear programming solution becomes progressively more difficult to solve as the number of outputs or limiting factors is increased, ultimately a computer must be used. The inputs to the linear programming model include

1. The output to be achieved, called the **objective function.** This will generally be a maximization of the contribution margin or a minimization of costs.
2. The limiting factors or **constraints.** The major limitations are imposed by demand for the product, material availability, labor or machine time, and other facilities constraints.

GRAPHIC SOLUTION

Linear programming can be demonstrated graphically when there are only two products and a limited number of constraints. A graphic illustration is a good way to visualize the decision process taking place in linear programming. A graphic solution shows what combinations of the two products are feasible to produce. Then, from these feasible combinations the most profitable one is chosen.

For this illustration, assume that the Kee Lamp Company produces two models of designer lamps, a floor lamp and a table lamp. Because of her innovative and artistic designs, the lamps by Beverly Kee have become popular. Production involves two processes: fabrication in Department A (where parts are machined) and assembly in Department B (where parts are assembled and finished). The table lamp uses a wood piece that is purchased from a local furniture manufacturer.

Objective Function. Given a profit motive, Beverly Kee should produce the number and combination of lamps that will maximize the contribution margin. She has determined that the contribution margin of each floor lamp is $30 and each table lamp is $50.

Constraints. All limitations on production and sales of lamps must be identified. Beverly Kee has identified four constraints:

1. Demand—At the present selling prices the market will accept 21 floor lamps and all the table lamps produced per month.
2. Productive time, fabrication—The Fabrication Department has only 72 hours of productive time available per month. Fabrication of each floor lamp requires 3 hours and each table lamp requires 4.5 hours.
3. Productive time, assembly—The Assembly Department has only 66 hours of productive time available per month. Assembly of each floor lamp requires 2 hours and each table lamp requires 6 hours.
4. Supply—The local furniture factory is only able to supply 20 units of raw material per month.

The graph in Exhibit 10–3 shows the number of floor lamps that can be produced and sold on the horizontal scale and the number of table lamps on the vertical scale.

The next step is to plot the constraints in relationship to the products. In Exhibit 10–3 there are four constraint lines. These lines were determined as follows:

Demand—The market will accept only 21 floor lamps. This market limitation is shown as a vertical line from the floor lamp axis at the 21-lamp level.

Fabrication—With 72 hours of production time available, the Fabrication Department can produce either 24 floor lamps (72 ÷ 3) or 16 table lamps (72 ÷ 4.5); these points have been plotted and connected by a line. Along that line are the possible combinations of the product mix that will not exceed 72 hours.

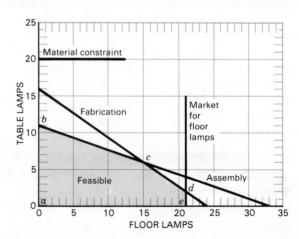

EXHIBIT 10-3 Graphic plot of constraints

Assembly—With 66 hours of production time available, the Assembly Department can produce either 11 table lamps (66 ÷ 6) or 33 floor lamps (66 ÷ 2); these points have been plotted and connected by a line. Along that line are the possible combinations of the product mix that will not exceed 66 hours.

Supply—Material is available for 20 table lamps per month. This constraint is plotted as a horizontal line on the table lamp axis at the 20 level.

When the constraints are plotted, the area below and to the left of the lines show the feasible combinations of lamps. From the graph it can be seen that more floor lamps can be produced than sold and that the material supply constraint for table lamps is not relevant. The shaded area represents *all* possible combinations. The next step is to choose the most profitable, from these many possibilities.

Solution. Beverly Kee's objective function is to maximize the contribution margin. Therefore, the combination of lamps that will produce the greatest contribution margin must be determined. Maximization of the contribution margin will occur only at one of the intersecting points in Exhibit 10–3. The intersecting points are labeled on the graph. The total contribution margin at each labeled intersecting point on the graph are:

a.   0 floor lamps × $30 contribution margin = $ 0
     0 table lamps × $50 contribution margin =   0
                                                $ 0

b.   0 floor lamps × $30 contribution margin = $ 0
    11 table lamps × $50 contribution margin =   550
                                                $550

c. 15 floor lamps × $30 contribution margin = $450
     6 table lamps × $50 contribution margin =   300
                                                $750

d. 21 floor lamps × $30 contribution margin = $630
     2 table lamps × $50 contribution margin =   100
                                                $730

e. 21 floor lamps × $30 contribution margin = $630
     0 table lamps × $50 contribution margin =   0
                                                $630

The optimal solution is to produce and sell 15 floor lamps and 6 table lamps for a total contribution margin of $750.

MORE COMPLEX SOLUTIONS

In most firms there are more than two products, several departments, and many constraints. Visualize a company with 15 products manufactured in various combinations through 20 departments. The graphic method would be completely inadequate. A computer would be required, using a procedure called the simplex method. Using matrix algebra, the simplex method works toward the optimal solution by repeating the computational routine over and over until the best solution is reached. The management accountant's role should be to determine the inputs to the model and interpret the results.

PLANNING INVENTORIES

Firms hold inventories for two basic reasons: transactions and contingencies. The firm must hold a minimum amount of inventory to satisfy production and sales demands. If the rate of usage and delivery dates could be predicted with certainty, the firm would need to hold only the minimum inventory level necessary for the known transactions. However, business activity is not certain and provision must be made for contingencies, as well as for expected transactions.

Exhibit 10–4 shows the fluctuations of the level of a Raw Material Inventory item over a period of time. A similar illustration could be prepared for a Finished Goods Inventory item as well. The cycle begins when goods are

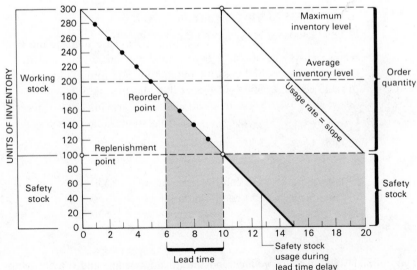

EXHIBIT 10–4   Illustration of inventory model

received at the **replenishment point.** In our example, 200 units are delivered on Day 0, when the inventory balance is 100 units. This brings the inventory level to 300, the maximum level the inventory will reach. As goods are withdrawn from the inventory, at the rate of 20 units per day, the balance of inventory on hand declines until it reaches 180 units. This level is the **reorder point,** the point at which an order must be placed to provide a **lead time** of 4 days to ensure delivery when needed. If delivery is on time, the next **replenishment point** is reached at Day 10. If delivery is delayed for any reason, the company has five days of safety stock.

In Exhibit 10–4 the inventory can be viewed as composed of two components—**working stock** (200 units) and **safety stock** (100 units). If actual events correspond identically to the planned events, the average inventory balance will be 200 units. Because usage is assumed to be constant each day, the average balance of working stock will be one-half of the working stock. Of course, the safety stock will not be touched if the usage rate and lead time are as planned. Thus, the average balance of safety stock will be 100 units. The average inventory on hand will be the sum of the average working stock and average safety stock, or 200 units.

The important decisions in inventory planning are the quantity to order each time an order is placed and the amount of the safety stock. The objectives of inventory planning should be to ensure that the organization maintains an optimal balance of inventory that will minimize total costs of having an inventory.

ECONOMIC PURCHASE ORDER QUANTITIES

A decision model has been developed to determine the optimum quantity of materials to be purchased at one time. Each time a purchase is made the firm incurs **purchasing costs**—additional clerical, handling, processing, and transportation costs. To minimize the costs of purchasing, the firm could order its entire annual needs at one time. However, if they did this, they would have a large average inventory of working stock and increased **carrying costs**—storage-space costs, insurance, property taxes, losses from spoilage and obsolescence, and foregone return on money invested in inventory.

The optimum amount to purchase at any one time is the quantity that would minimize the total costs of purchasing and carrying the inventory. To illustrate, let's assume that Part 23 has an annual usage of 900 units at a cost of $3.00 per unit. The cost of processing each order is $10 and the cost of carrying one unit in inventory for a year is $.60 (20% of inventory cost). The usage is assumed to be uniform throughout the year. Exhibit 10–5 shows the total of ordering and carrying costs at several order sizes. The column with the lowest total cost shows the approximate economic order quantity.

				Order Size				
Order size in units	20	60	150	180	225	300	450	900
Average inventory in units (Order size ÷ 2)	10	30	75	90	113	150	225	450
Number of purchases (Annual use ÷ order size)	45	15	6	5	4	3	2	1
Annual ordering cost (Orders × $10)	$450	$150	$60	$50	$40	$30	$20	$10
Annual carrying cost (Avg inventory × $.60)	6	18	45	54	68	90	135	270
Total cost for year	$456	$168	$105	$104	$108	$120	$155	$280
				Lowest Cost				

EXHIBIT 10–5   Costs of different order sizes

The optimum quantity can be determined by the formula

$$EOQ = \sqrt{\frac{2AB}{C}}$$

where

EOQ = Economic order quantity.
A = Annual usage in units.
B = Cost of placing one order.
C = Annual cost of carrying one unit in inventory for one year.

$$EOQ = \sqrt{\frac{2(900)(\$10)}{\$.60}} = \sqrt{\frac{\$18,000}{\$.60}} = 173 \text{ units}$$

A graphic solution of economic order quantity is presented in Exhibit 10–6. In this illustration, order quantity in units is plotted on the horizontal axis and dollars of cost are plotted on the vertical axis. Note that both the graph (Exhibit 10–6) and the table (Exhibit 10–5) show a wide range where a difference in order quantity will cause only a small difference in total costs. Management should be aware of this effect on costs when it is necessary to deviate from the exact economic order quantity; for example, where purchases must be made in standard quantities.

The same logic would apply to determining the size of production runs. Where products are produced in batches, the firm must incur a **setup** cost each time a batch is produced. These setup costs include the additional costs of

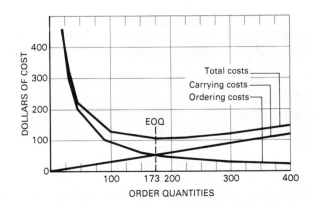

EXHIBIT 10—6
Economic order
quantity graph

preparing and realigning the machines; installing dies, jigs, and templates; necessary paperwork to prepare the production run; and reorienting the workers to their jobs. By substituting setup costs for procurement costs, the formula will provide the optimum quantity that should be produced on each production run.

The EOQ formula was built upon the assumption of continual, uniform usage. Where this is not true, more sophisticated models are appropriate. Next, the *EOQ* formula deals only with the working stock; it does not facilitate the decision about safety stock levels. Finally, the quality of the *EOQ* answer is dependent on accurate and relevant ordering and carrying costs. Allocated fixed costs can distort the measure of these costs.

SAFETY STOCK QUANTITIES

Economic order quantities dealt with "how much" to order. In dealing with safety stock, the problem is "when" to buy, or the reorder point. This can be determined by calculating the lead time (the time between placing an order and receiving the delivery) and the usage rate. If usage and delivery are certain, there is no need for safety stock. The safety stock provides for uncertainties in usage rate and lead times.

There are many methods of determining safety stock levels. One intuitive rule is to have a larger safety stock if there is high-quantity usage, long lead times, or infrequent ordering schedules. Smaller safety stocks can be maintained when there is low usage, short lead time, or frequent ordering. The best theoretical approach is to develop a formula, similar to the *EOQ* formula, that balances the costs of carrying the safety stock with the costs of being out of stock.

JUST-IN-TIME

The traditional batch processing "pushes" production through the manufacturing operation, often building up large Raw Material or Work-in-Process inventories. In the late 1970s and early 1980s, Japanese manufacturers developed just-in-time inventory and production processes that dramatically shortened the production cycle, minimized inventories, improved quality, and reduced manufacturing costs.

Just-in-time (J-I-T) is a "demand-pull" manufacturing system. By realigning the manufacturing process into a continuous flow, by reducing setup times, and by producing only what is needed when it is needed, both working stock and safety stock inventory can be nearly eliminated and manufacturing costs reduced dramatically. J-I-T is much more than a way to reduce inventories and improve return on assets; it is a revolutionary change in the manufacturing process.

The following are the actions required for J-I-T implementation and benefits realized by the implementation.

1. The first step is to rearrange the manufacturing process from clusters of like machines to a grouping that allows a continuous flow. This will substantially reduce setup times. In one firm, cycle time was reduced from 8 days to 2 hours. Examples of reduced setup time from 8 hours to 12 minutes have been reported.

2. The next step is to begin with the final product demand and then produce only what is needed, when it is needed, and in the quantity needed. A "demand-pull" system has reduced the Work-in-Process Inventory by as much as 90%.

3. To create materials flow, the next step is to contract on a long-term basis with a limited number of suppliers (ideally only one per part) to deliver what is needed, when it is needed. For practical purposes, delivery is made straight to the production process, nearly eliminating Raw Materials Inventory. One manufacturer found that over 60% of the plant was used to store raw materials and work-in-process. Implementing J-I-T was like doubling the size of the factory.

4. To ensure a smooth flow, no defective components are passed on to the next process. One benefit of the shortened cycle times and the continuous process is that it allows more concentration on quality. With small production quantities and no defective components coming into a process, problems of quality are detected and corrected quickly. Quality control is built into the process.

5. With J-I-T paperwork is greatly reduced. With a limited number of suppliers committed to quality, the Accounts Payable process is simplified. Further, by consolidating a number of isolated processes into a continuous-flow process, the number of transfers in the accounting records is reduced. One high-tech firm indicated a reduction from tens of thousands of transfers per month to less than 60.

6. Also, accounting records are simplified. In place of recording Raw Materials and Work-in-Process inventories, only one In-Process Inventory is needed.

Where J-I-T has been implemented, it has had a revolutionary impact on processing time, on quality, and on costs. The inventory models examined earlier in this chapter change dramatically when inventories are virtually eliminated.

One word of caution is warranted. Labor conditions in the United States are substantially different from those in Japan. Many times in this country labor unrest and/or contract negotiations are coupled with a labor strike. There are several recent examples where the J-I-T procedures had been implemented and a minor strike by a minor supplier had major consequences. There was no safety stock to provide a cushion when things did not go as planned.

SUMMARY

The accountant has a role to play in management's production decisions by providing data on relevant costs. Relevant costs are future costs—estimates of what the decision maker believes *will* happen. They are also differential costs. To be relevant, a future cost must differ among alternatives. For this reason, many fixed costs are not relevant to production decisions. All historical costs are nonrelevant. Joint costs are also nonrelevant for all decisions subsequent to their incurrence.

The contribution margin plays a vital role in short-range production decisions as an estimate of incremental future revenue. To obtain the maximum profit from an existing plant, the decision should be to maximize the total contribution margin of the firm. All decisions on whether to make or buy a component part, to add or drop a product, or to sell a product or process it further hinge on an analysis of differential contribution margins.

Where there are multiproduct and plant production constraints, linear programming facilitates choosing an optimum product mix. It recognizes the constraints of the departments to determine which outputs are feasible. The objective function, to maximize the product contribution margins, enables management to select the product mix that will maximize total contribution margin. Another important decision area is the appropriate inventory levels. The economic order quantity determines the working stock by purchasing quantities that minimize the procurement and carrying costs. Safety stock is determined by when the order is placed. A new manufacturing and inventory system, just-in-time, provides materials when needed, in the amount needed. Just-in-time, as an inventory control system can practically eliminate inventory levels, including safety stock.

PROBLEMS AND CASES

10-1 *(Make-or-Buy Decision)*. The following costs pertain to a motor that is part of the final product of Happy Trails Company.

Direct materials	$ 5.00
Direct labor	12.00
Factory overhead	50.00
Total cost per motor	$67.00

Sixty percent of the overhead is not affected by a make-or-buy decision.

REQUIRED:

If Happy Trails can buy the motor elsewhere for $40, should they do so? Explain.

10-2 *(Economic Purchase Order Quantities)*. An equipment dealership sells 600 new machines evenly throughout the year. The cost of carrying one machine in inventory for a year is $180. The purchase order cost per order is $540.

REQUIRED:

Calculate the economic order quantity.

10-3 *(Graph of Inventory Model)*. Quickee Print Shop is studying its use of reproduction paper. The following information was developed from past data.

Annual usage (in boxes)	20,000
Economic order quantity (in boxes)	1,600
Normal lead time (in working days)	10
Maximum expected lead time (in working days)	15
Working days per year	250

REQUIRED:

Prepare a graph similar to Exhibit 10–4. Label the following: *EOQ*, reorder point, safety stock level, replenishment point, maximum inventory level, and average inventory level.

10-4 *(Contribution Margin with Constraints)*. Three different grades of carpet are produced at the Southland Carpet plant. The excessive demand for the carpets has resulted in a backlog of orders. The direct labor rate is $4.00 per hour, and there are only 800 labor hours available each week. The cost and sales revenue associated with each grade are:

	Grade 1	Grade 2	Grade 3
Selling price per yard	$40	$32	$25
Production expenses:			
Direct materials	$ 8	$14	$15
Direct labor	$16	$ 8	$ 4
Variable overhead	$ 4	$ 2	$ 1
Fixed overhead	$ 4	$ 2	$ 1

REQUIRED:

A. What is the contribution margin per hour of labor that will be obtained on each grade of product?

B. Considering the time constraint, which grade of carpet should the company work on next week? Show calculations.

10-5 *(Reorder Point, Safety Stock)*. The following relate to a component purchased by the Shumate Corporation.

Annual usage (in units)	12,500
Normal lead time (in working days)	25
Maximum lead time (in working days)	30
Working days per year	250
Assume constant use.	

REQUIRED:

Determine the following: reorder point; safety stock.

10-6 *(Sell or Process Further)*. The Hawk Manufacturing Company produces three different products from a joint process. Each of these products can be processed further or sold at the split-off point. Joint processing costs to the split-off point total $50,000. No special facilities are required if the products are processed further. For each product, the additional processing costs (all variable), the sales value after further processing, and the sales value at split-off are shown below.

Product	Additional Processing Costs	Finished Sales Value	Sales Value at Split-off
1	$10,000	$30,000	$17,500
2	$15,000	$45,000	$35,000
3	$12,500	$40,000	$27,000

REQUIRED:

A. Assuming the products are produced in equal amounts, which of the products should be sold at the split-off point and which should be further processed? Show calculations.

B. Given the optimum production schedule, what is the profit of Hawk Manufacturing Company?

10-7 *(Make-or-Buy Decision)*. The Johnson Shoe Company manufactures a variety of running shoes in their athletic shoe line. They have always manufactured all the components of their specially designed shoe. An outside supplier has offered to provide the outer sole to the Johnson Shoe Company at a cost of $4.50 per shoe. The accountant for Johnson Shoe Company gathered the following information showing their cost to produce the soles internally:

	Per Sale	*Per Year*
Direct materials	$1.50	$ 30,000
Direct labor	1.25	25,000
Variable overhead	.75	15,000
Fixed overhead, direct	.80	16,000
Fixed overhead, common and allocated	1.25	25,000
Total cost	$5.55	$111,000

The direct fixed overhead is composed of one-half supervisory salaries and one-half depreciation of special equipment that has no resale value.

REQUIRED:

A. Assume there are no alternative uses for the facilities. Would it be beneficial to Johnson to accept the outside supplier's offer? Why?

B. Assume that a new product could be developed at the facilities if Johnson were to accept the outside offer. What would be the minimum product margin the new product would have to generate in order for this alternative to be chosen?

10-8 *(Adding a Product)*. The Rubber Bumper Company is searching for new products to replace unprofitable products and to utilize idle capacity. Capacity is measured by labor hours. The standard wage rate is $6.00 per hour.

One new product, a modified case for eyeglasses, will have the following revenue and cost characteristics.

Revenue		$10.00
Costs:		
Direct materials	$3.80	
Direct labor	1.20	
Variable overhead	1.80	
Fixed overhead (150% of direct labor)	1.80	
Fixed selling and administrative (10% of sales)	1.00	9.60
Income		$ .40

REQUIRED:

A. Should the new product be added to utilize idle capacity? Explain.

B. Should the new product be added to replace a product that is currently show-ing a loss of $1.00 per unit but is generating a contribution margin of $10 per labor hour? Explain.

10-9 *(Product-Line Contributions).* The Hepa Filter Company has three major product lines: air filters, oil filters, and gas filters. The gas filter line showed a loss last year, and management is considering dropping the line. The following revenue and cost information relate to last year's sales. The depreciation is related to special equipment and has no resale value. If a product line is dis-continued, one-half the supervisory labor would be transferred to another part of the company and one-half would be terminated.

	Gas	Air	Oil	Total
Sales	$ 90,000	$140,000	$260,000	$490,000
Less: Variable expenses	50,000	40,000	110,000	200,000
Contribution margin	$ 40,000	$100,000	$150,000	$290,000
Less: Fixed expenses				
Supervision	$ 15,000	$ 25,000	$ 60,000	$100,000
Traceable advertising	14,000	15,000	2,000	31,000
Heat, lighting	1,000	1,000	1,000	3,000
General administration	13,000	18,000	30,000	61,000
Rent	9,000	12,000	20,000	41,000
Depreciation	4,000	5,000	6,000	15,000
Total fixed	56,000	76,000	119,000	251,000
Income (loss)	$(16,000)	$ 24,000	$ 31,000	$ 39,000

REQUIRED:

Calculate the increase or decrease in overall company income if the gas filter line is dropped. Explain why the line should be discontinued or kept.

10-10 *(Discontinuance of a Line).* The Vita-Rich Dairy produces three types of cheese: Mozzarella, Cheddar, and Swiss. Sales of Swiss cheese have been declining; further, Swiss cheese showed a loss on last month's income statement. Management is considering discontinuing the Swiss cheese line and has provided you with the following information.

1. The utility bill will be reduced by $100 per month if Swiss cheese is eliminated.

2. The supervisor will be transferred to the Cheddar Department. His salary is $2,000 per month.

3. All vats and equipment would be transferred from the Swiss Department equally between Cheddar and Mozzarella. One-third of the insurance and property taxes in the Swiss Department relate to the vats and equipment; the remaining is related to inventories.

4. Besides the supervisor, there is one employee in each of the five production phases of Swiss cheese. The two employees in curding and milling will be transferred to the Mozzarella Department. Those in matting, salting, and shaping will be terminated. The salaries are as follows: curder, $1,250 per month; miller, $1,025 per month; matter, $1,175 per month; salter, $1,375 per month; shaper, $1,175 per month.

5. The maintenance expense and general and administrative (G & A) expenses are allocated on a percentage of sales.

VITA-RICH DAIRY
INCOME STATEMENT
For the Month Ended January 31, 19X7

	Swiss	Mozzarella	Cheddar	Total
Sales	$45,000	$80,000	$110,000	$235,000
Variable expenses	24,000	37,000	54,000	115,000
Contribution margin	$21,000	$43,000	$ 56,000	$120,000
Fixed expenses:				
Salaries	$ 8,000	$ 8,500	$ 9,200	$ 25,700
Utilities	850	1,200	1,000	3,050
General advertising	1,750	1,750	1,750	5,250
Direct advertising	2,700	4,000	3,000	9,700
Building rent	4,800	7,200	6,200	18,200
Depreciation of vats				
and equipment	4,300	5,900	8,000	18,200
Insurance	650	1,000	1,050	2,700
Property taxes	250	325	350	925
Maintenance expense	836	1,496	2,068	4,400
G & A Expense	903	1,615	2,232	4,750
Total fixed expenses	25,039	32,986	34,850	92,875
Income or (loss)	$ (4,039)	$10,014	$ 21,150	$ 27,125

REQUIRED:

Assume that there is no other use for the space now being occupied by the Swiss Cheese Department and that the discontinuance of that department would have no effect on the other cheese products. Would it be beneficial to eliminate the Swiss cheese line? Support your answer with computations.

10-11 (*Linear Programming*). Girth, Inc. makes two kinds of men's suede leather belts, with the following revenue and costs for each product.

	Belt A	Belt B
Selling price per unit	$19.50	$5.75
Direct material	$ 5.00	$1.00
Direct labor	6.00	3.00
Variable overhead	1.50	.75
Fixed overhead	2.00	1.00
Allocated general and selling expense	1.00	.30
Income per belt (loss)	$ 4.00	$ (.30)

Girth, Inc. is able to sell all the belts it can make. Constraints are

1. Belt A requires a fancy buckle, of which only 400 are available per day.
2. Girth, Inc. has the capacity to make 1,000 units of B per day. Each A belt requires twice as much manufacturing time as a B belt.
3. Belt B requires a plain buckle, of which 700 are available per day.
4. Only enough suede is available to produce 800 belts per day.

REQUIRED:

A. Prepare a graph, labeling each of the constraints by using their corresponding numbers.

B. From the graph determine how many units of Belt A and Belt B should be produced to maximize daily sales.

C. From the graph, determine how many units of Belt A and Belt B should be produced to maximize income.

D. The supplier of fancy buckles (for Belt A) informs Girth, Inc. that it cannot supply more than 100 fancy buckles a day. Other facts remain the same.

1. Reflect this new information on the graph.

2. Determine the number of each of the two belts that should be produced to maximize income.

(CMA adapted)

10-12 (*Discontinuing a Product*). The management of the Myers Company are not satisfied with the profit of Product B. The most recent income statement follows:

	Total	Product A	Product B
Sales	$264,000	$120,000	$144,000
Cost of Goods sold	190,000	55,000	135,000
Gross margin	$ 74,000	$ 65,000	$ 9,000
Operating expenses	56,500	25,000	31,500
Income	$ 17,500	$ 40,000	($22,500)
Units sold		10,000	18,000
Selling price per unit		$12.00	$8.00
Variable cost of goods sold per unit		$5.25	$7.10
Variable operating expenses per unit		$1.00	$1.20
Labor hours per unit		1.0	0.5
Wage rate per hour		$8.00	$8.00

REQUIRED:

A. What will be the effect on income if Product B is dropped and sales of A are unaffected? Explain.

B. What will be the effect on income of dropping Product B if dropping Product B also results in losing sales of 1,000 units of Product A? Explain.

C. What will be the effect on income if the capacity used to produce Product B is instead used to produce Product A? Assume the capacity is expressed in labor hours and there are no market limitations. Explain.

10-13 *(Production with Scarce Resources)*. The Exotic Products Company produces a number of products from a rare material in a process requiring highly skilled employees. Because a number of material shortages are possible, planning is difficult.

For the next quarter three products are to be produced with the following *per-unit* revenue, cost, and production characteristics.

	Products		
	Unival	Doxem	Trion
Selling price	$5,120	$1,780	$1,986
Direct material	$ 200	$ 400	$ 150
Direct labor	2,400	600	720
Variable overhead (30% of labor)	720	180	216
Fixed overhead (50% of labor)	1,200	300	360
Total costs	4,520	1,480	1,446
Income	$ 600	$ 300	$ 540
Units of material (kilograms)	20	40	15
Hours of labor	200	50	60
Machine hours	30	50	150
Power consumption (kilowatt-hours)	40	10	18
Projected demand (units)	2,400	800	1,600

REQUIRED:

A. How many units of each product should be produced if there are no shortages of resources?

B. How many units of each product should be produced if only 80,000 kilograms of material are available?

C. How many units of each product should be produced if only 100,000 hours of direct labor are available?

D. How many units of each product should be produced if only 60,000 machine hours are available?

E. How many units of each product should be produced if only 81,600 kilowatt-hours of power are available?

10-14 (*Optimizing Production*). The management of the Ramaglia Company are not satisfied with the profit of Product N. The most recent income statement follows:

	Total	Product M	Product N	Product O
Sales	$36,600	$12,000	$15,000	$9,600
Cost of Goods Sold	21,100	6,100	9,000	6,000
Gross margin	$15,500	$ 5,900	$ 6,000	$3,600
Operating expenses	10,840	2,200	6,000	2,640
Income	$ 4,660	$ 3,700	$ 0	$ 960
Units sold		1,000	1,500	1,200
Selling price per unit		$12.00	$10.00	$8.00
Variable cost of goods sold per unit		$6.00	$3.00	$4.00
Variable operating expenses per unit		$2.00	$1.00	$2.00
Labor hours per unit		0.5	0.2	0.4

REQUIRED:

Each of the following proposals is independent of the other proposals. Assume that labor is the measure of productive capacity in each case.

A. Part of the plant in which Product N is produced can be converted easily to the production of Product M. Assume that capacity is measured in labor hours. If half the capacity devoted to Product N is devoted to the production of Product M, what is the effect on income?

B. If the Ramaglia Company has excess capacity and more units of each product could be sold, production of which product should be expanded first? (Assume that labor is the only constraint.)

C. Assume that 1,200 hours of labor are available, no more than 2,000 units of Product N can be sold, and the market is unlimited for Products M and O. What production will maximize profits?

10-15 *(Comprehensive—Dropping and Adding Products)*. The Horton Door Company has produced five different products for many years. During 19X0, Mr. Horton, the president, contracted with a computerized accounting service bureau to maintain the accounting records and prepare departmental statements. At the end of 19X0, Mr. Horton received the following income statement by product lines.

HORTON DOOR COMPANY
INCOME STATEMENT
Year 19X0

PRODUCTS

	1	2	3	4	5	Total
Sales	$100,000	$100,000	$100,000	$100,000	$100,000	$500,000
Expenses	70,000	80,000	85,000	95,000	150,000	480,000*
Income (loss)	$ 30,000	$ 20,000	$ 15,000	$ 5,000	$ (50,000)	$ 20,000

*Fixed costs of $200,000 are allocated to the products on the basis of sales.

The long-term market for the company's products is limited. The company cannot expect future sales of its products to exceed the sales in year 19X0. In an attempt to improve profits and strengthen the company, Mr. Horton decided to drop Product 5, which showed a loss of $50,000 in 19X0.

Mr. Horton was pleased with the following income statement for 19X1. Profits for the company increased to $30,000 after dropping Product 5 but Product 4 showed a loss of $5,000.

HORTON DOOR COMPANY
INCOME STATEMENT
Year 19X1

PRODUCTS

	1	2	3	4	Total
Sales	$100,000	$100,000	$100,000	$100,000	$400,000
Expenses	80,000	90,000	95,000	105,000	370,000*
Income (loss)	$ 20,000	$ 10,000	$ 5,000	$ (5,000)	$ 30,000

*Fixed costs of $200,000 are allocated to the products on the basis of sales.

At the beginning of 19X2, Mr. Horton decided to drop Product 4. Mr. Horton was surprised to see a $15,000 loss for 19X2 with losses shown for both

Products 2 and 3. He was assured by his managers that cost behavior patterns had not changed. The income statement for 19X2 follows.

HORTON DOOR COMPANY
INCOME STATEMENT
Year 19X2

PRODUCTS

	1	2	3	Total
Sales	$100,000	$100,000	$100,000	$300,000
Expenses	96,666	106,667	111,667	315,000
Income (loss)	$ 3,334	$ (6,667)	$ (11,667)	$ (15,000)

REQUIRED:

A. Explain fully why profits increased when Product 5 was dropped but decreased when Product 4 was dropped.

B. Explain why Products 2 and 3 now show a loss.

C. Three alternatives have been proposed for the Horton Door Company. Only one of the three can be accepted.

  1. Drop Products 2 and 3 and sublease a portion of the facilities for $100,000 per year.

  2. Maintain Products 1, 2, and 3 and add a new Product 6. Sales of the new product will be $200,000, variable costs $100,000, and identifiable fixed costs $30,000.

  3. Maintain Products 2 and 3 and change Product 1 by adding identifiable fixed costs of $20,000 per year. The new Product 1 will have double the current sales and variable costs.

  Prepare an income statement by product for each alternative and indicate which alternative should be accepted.

10-16 (*Alternative Uses of Idle Capacity*). Query's Quarry produces a line of building blocks that it markets through building materials stores for $.20 each. Currently, 1 million blocks are produced each year using only 60% of plant capacity. Standard costs per block were

Direct materials	$.060
Direct labor	.015
Variable overhead	.020
Variable selling	.025
Fixed overhead	.030
Fixed selling	.010
	$.160

Management would like to use the excess capacity and has three possibilities. Only one of the three may be selected.

1. The company could produce additional units of the regular block and ship the additional production out of the present market area, which is saturated. Management estimates that the company could market 600,000 blocks this way. Additional freight charges would be $.025 per block and fixed overhead would increase by $100,000 per year. There would be no other changes in the cost structure.

2. The company could process the regular block further, making it into a decorative block. Management believes the company could sell 300,000 decorative blocks at a price of $.35 each, in addition to current sales of 1 million regular blocks. The following estimates are for the additional costs of processing 300,000 blocks further.

Direct material	$.005
Direct labor	.065
Variable overhead	.030
Variable selling	.010
Fixed overhead	.005
Fixed selling	.015
	$.130

3. The company could produce and market a new product, X-Brick, to cover walls behind wood-burning stoves. The product would be sold in a package of bricks. The capacity could be used to produce 60,000 units (packages) per year at a price of $10 per unit with the following unit cost estimates:

Direct materials	$2.00
Direct labor	2.50
Variable overhead	1.50
Variable selling	1.00
	$7.00

The new X-Brick would require additional fixed overhead of $60,000 and fixed selling cost of $40,000.

REQUIRED:

A. Prepare a profit plan setting forth the contribution margin and income for current production of 1 million blocks (assuming no changes).

B. Prepare a profit plan for each of the three alternatives. Your profit plan should show *only* the incremental effect of each alternative setting forth the product margin.

C. Which alternative should be selected? What will be the total income of the company if that alternative is selected? How much does it exceed the next best alternative?

10-17 *(Make-or-Buy Decisions).* The Vernom Corporation, which produces and sells to wholesalers a highly successful line of summer lotions and insect repellents, has decided to diversify in order to stabilize sales throughout the year. A natural area for the company to consider is the production of winter lotions and creams to prevent dry and chapped skin.

After considerable research, a winter products line has been developed. However, because of the conservative nature of the company management, Vernom's president has decided to introduce only one of the new products for this coming winter. If the product is a success, further expansion in future years will be initiated.

The product selected (called Chap-off) is a lip balm that will be sold in a lipstick-type tube. The product will be sold to wholesalers in boxes of 24 tubes for $8.00 per box. Because of available capacity, no additional fixed charges will be incurred to produce the product. However, a $100,000 fixed charge will be absorbed by the product to allocate a fair share of the company's present fixed costs to the new product.

Using the estimated sales and production of 100,000 boxes of Chap-off as the standard volume, the accounting department has developed the following costs.

Direct labor	$2.00 per box
Direct materials	3.00 per box
Total overhead	1.50 per box
Total	$6.50 per box

Vernom has approached a cosmetics manufacturer to discuss the possibility of purchasing the tubes for the Chap-off. The purchase price of the empty tubes from the cosmetics manufacturer would be $.90 per 24 tubes. If the Vernom Corporation accepts the purchase proposal, it is estimated that direct labor and variable overhead costs would be reduced by 10% and direct material costs would be reduced by 20%.

REQUIRED:

A. Should the Vernom Corporation make or buy the tubes? Show calculations to support your answer.

B. What would be the minimum purchase price acceptable to the Vernom Corporation for the tubes? Support your answer with an appropriate explanation.

C. Instead of sales of 100,000 boxes, revised estimates show sales volume at 125,000 boxes. At this new volume additional equipment, at an annual rental of $10,000, must be acquired to manufacture the tubes. However, this incremental cost would be the only additional fixed cost required even if sales increased to 300,000 boxes. (The 300,000 level is the goal for third year of production.) Under these circumstances, should the Vernom Corporation make or buy the tubes? Show calculations to support your answer.

D. The company has the option of making and buying at the same time. What would be your answer to part C if this alternative were considered? Show calculations to support your answer.

E. What nonquantifiable factors should the Vernom Corporation consider in determining whether to make or buy the lipstick tubes?

(CMA adapted)

10-18 *(Make-or-Buy Decision).* The Xyon Company has purchased 80,000 pumps annually from Kobec Inc. The price has increased each year and reached $68 per unit last year. Because the purchase price has increased significantly, Xyon management has asked that an estimate be made of the costs to manufacture it in its own facilities. Xyon's products consist of stamping and castings. The company has little experience with products requiring assembly.

The engineering, manufacturing, and accounting departments have prepared a report for management that included the estimate shown below for an assembly run of 10,000 units. Additional production employees would be hired to manufacture the subassembly. However, no additional equipment, space, or supervision would be needed.

The report states that the total costs for 10,000 units are estimated at $957,000 or $95.70 a unit. The current purchase price is $68 a unit so the report recommends a continued purchase of the product.

Components (outside purchases)	$120,000
Assembly labor*	300,000
Factory overhead†	450,000
General and administrative overhead‡	87,000
Total costs	$957,000

*Assembly labor consists of hourly production workers.

†Factory overhead is applied to products on a direct-labor dollar basis. Variable overhead costs vary closely with direct-labor dollars.

Fixed overhead	50% of direct-labor dollars
Variable overhead	100% of direct-labor dollars
Factory overhead rate	150% of direct-labor dollars

‡General and administrative overhead are applied at 10% of the total cost of material (or components), assembly labor, and factory overhead.

REQUIRED:

A. Was the analysis prepared by the engineering, manufacturing, and accounting departments of Xyon Company and the recommendation to continue purchasing the pumps that followed from the analysis correct? Explain your answer and include any supportive calculations you consider necessary.

B. Assume that Xyon Company could experience labor cost improvements on the pump assembly consistent with an 80% learning curve. An assembly run of 10,000 units represents the initial lot or batch for measurement purposes. Should Xyon produce the 80,000 pumps in this situation? Explain your answer.

(CMA adapted)

10-19 *(Economic Setup Cost Estimation).* Pointer Furniture Company manufactures and sells office furniture. In order to compete effectively in different quality and price markets it produces several brands of office furniture. The manufacturing operation is organized by the item produced rather than by the furniture line. Thus, the desks for all brands are manufactured on the same production line. For efficiency and quality control reasons the desks are manufactured in batches. For example, 10 high-quality desks might be manufactured during the first two weeks in October and 50 units of a lower-quality desk during the last two weeks. Because each model has its own unique manufacturing requirement, the change from one model to another requires the factory's equipment to be adjusted.

The management of Pointer wants to determine the most economical production run for each of the items in its product lines. The manager of the cost accounting department is going to adapt the economic order quantity (*EOQ*) inventory model for this analysis.

One of the cost parameters that must be determined before the model can be employed is the setup cost incurred when there is a change to a different furniture model. The cost accounting department has been asked to determine the setup cost for the desk (Model JE 40) in its junior executive line as an example.

The Equipment Maintenance Department is responsible for the changeover adjustments on production lines in addition to the preventive and regular maintenance of all the production equipment. The equipment maintenance staff has a 40-hour workweek; the size of the staff is changed only if there is a change in the workload that is expected to persist for an extended period of time. The Equipment Maintenance Department had 10 employees last year, and they each averaged 2,000 hours for the year. They are paid $9.00 an hour, and employee benefits average 20% of wage costs. The other departmental costs, which include such items as supervision, depreciation, and insurance, total $50,000 per year.

Two men from the Equipment Maintenance Department are required to make the change on the desk line for Model JE 40. They spend an estimated 5 hours in setting up the equipment as follows:

Machinery changes	3 hours
Testing	1 hour
Machine readjustments	1 hour
Total	5 hours

The desk production line on which Model JE 40 is manufactured is operated by five workers. During the changeover these workers assist the maintenance workers when needed and operate the line during the test run. However, they are idle for approximately 40% of the time required for the changeover.

The production workers are paid a basic wage rate of $7.50 an hour. Two overhead bases are used to apply the indirect costs of this production line because some of the costs vary in proportion to direct labor hours while others vary with machine hours. The overhead rates applicable for the current year are as follows:

	Based on Direct Labor Hours	Based on Machine Hours
Variable	$2.75	$ 5.00
Fixed	2.25	15.00
	$5.00	$20.00

These department overhead rates are based on an expected activity of 10,000 direct labor hours and 1,500 machine hours for the current year. This department is not scheduled to operate at full capacity because production capability currently exceeds sales potential at this time.

The estimated cost of the direct materials used in the test run totals $200. Salvage material from the test run should total $50.

REQUIRED:

A. Prepare an estimate of Pointer Furniture Company's setup cost for desk Model JE 40 for use in the economic production run model. For each cost item identified in the problem, justify the amount and the reason for including the cost item in your estimate. Explain the reason for excluding any cost item from your estimate.

B. Identify the cost items that would be included in an estimate of Pointer Furniture Company's cost of carrying the desks in inventory

(CMA adapted)

10-20 *(Discontinuing a Product).* Olat Corpration produces three gauges. These gauges measure density, permeability, and thickness and are known as D-gauges, P-gauges, and T-gauges, respectively. For many years the company has been profitable and has operated at capacity. However, in the last two years prices on all gauges were reduced and selling expenses increased to meet competition and keep the plant operating at full capacity. Third-quarter results, as shown below, are representative of recent experiences.

OLAT CORPORATION
INCOME STATEMENT
THIRD QUARTER 19X3
($000 omitted)

	D-Gauge	P-Gauge	T-Gauge	Total
Sales	$900	$1,600	$ 900	$3,400
Costs of Goods Sold	770	1,048	950	2,768
Gross margin	$130	$ 552	$ (50)	$ 632
Selling and administrative expenses	185	370	135	690
Income before income taxes	$ (55)	$ 182	$(185)	$ (58)

Mel Carlo, president, is very concerned about the results of the pricing, selling, and production policies. After reviewing the third-quarter results he announced that he would ask his management staff to consider a course of action that includes the following three suggestions.

1. Discontinue the T-gauge line immediately. T-Gauges would not be returned to the line of products unless the problems with the gauge can be identified and resolved.

2. Increase quarterly sales promotion by $100,000 on the P-gauge product line in order to increase sales volume 15%.

3. Cut production on the D-gauge line by 50%, a quantity sufficient to meet the demand of customers who purchase P-gauges. In addition, the traceable advertising and promotion for this line would be cut to $20,000 each quarter.

George Sperry, controller, suggested that a more careful study of the financial relationships be made to determine the possible effect on the company's operating results as a consequence of the president's proposed course of action. The president agreed, and JoAnn Brower, assistant controller, was given the assignment to prepare an analysis. In order to prepare the analysis, she gathered the following information.

1. All three gauges are manufactured with common equipment and facilities.

2. The quartery general selling and administrative expense of $170,000 are allocated to the three gauge lines in proportion to their dollar sales volume.

3. Special selling expenses (primarily advertising, promotion, and shipping) are incurred for each gauge as follows.

	Quarterly Advertising and Promotion	Shipping Expense
D-gauge	$100,000	$ 4 per unit
P-gauge	$210,000	$10 per unit
T-gauge	$ 40,000	$10 per unit

4. The unit manufacturing costs for the three products are as follows:

	D-Gauge	P-Gauge	T-Gauge
Raw material	$17	$ 31	$ 50
Direct labor	20	40	60
Variable manufacturing overhead	30	45	60
Fixed manufacturing overhead	10	15	20
	$77	$131	$190

5. The unit sales prices for the three products are as follows:

D-gauge	$ 90
P-gauge	$200
T-gauge	$180

6. The company is manufacturing at capacity and is selling all the gauges it produces.

REQUIRED:

A. JoAnn Brower has suggested that the Olat Corporation's product-line income statement as presented for the third quarter of 19X3 is not suitable for analyzing proposals and making decisions such as the ones suggested by Mel Carlo.

1. Explain why the product-line income statement as presented is not suitable for analysis and decision making.

2. Describe an alternative income statement format that would be more suitable for analysis and decision making, and exlain why it is better.

B. Use the operating data presented for Olat Corporation and assume that President Mel Carlo's proposed course of action had been implemented at the beginning of the third quarter of 19X3. Then evaluate the president's proposed course of action by specifically responding to the following points.

1. Are each of the three suggestions cost effective? Your discussion should be supported by a differential analysis that shows the net impact on income before taxes for each of the three suggestions.

2. Was the president correct in eliminating the T-gauge line? Explain your answer.

3. Was the president correct in promoting the P-gauge line rather than the D-gauge line? Explain your answer.

4. Does the proposed course of action make effective use of Olat's capacity? Explain your answer.

C. Are there any nonquantitative factors that Olat Corporation should consider before it considers dropping the T-gauge line? Explain your answer.

(CMA adapted)

10-21 *(Sell or Process Further)*. Talor Chemical Company is a highly diversified chemical processing company. The company manufactures swimming pool chemicals, chemicals for metal-processing companies, specialized chemical compounds for other companies, and a full line of pesticides and insecticides.

Currently, the Noorwood plant is producing two derivatives, RNA-1 and RNA-2, from the chemical compound VDB developed by Talor's research labs. Each week 1,200,000 pounds of VDB are processed at a cost of $246,000 into 800,000 pounds of RNA-1 and 400,000 pounds of RNA-2. The proportion of these two outputs is fixed and cannot be altered because this is a joint process. RNA-1 has no market value until it is converted into a product with the trade name Fastkil. The cost to process RNA-1 into Fastkil is $240,000. Fastkil wholesales at $50 per 100 pounds.

RNA-2 is sold as is for $80 per 100 pounds. However, Talor has discovered that RNA-2 can be converted into two new products through further processing. The further processing would require the addition of 400,000 pounds of compound LST to the 400,000 pounds of RNA-2. The joint process would yield 400,000 pounds each of DMZ-3 and Pestrol—the two new products. The additional raw material and related processing costs of this joint process would be $120,000. DMZ-3 and Pestrol would each be sold for $57.50 per 100 pounds. Talor management has decided not to process RNA-2 further based on the following analysis. Talor uses the physical method to allocate the common costs arising from joint processing.

		PROCESS FURTHER		
	RNA-2	DMZ-3	Pestrol	Total
Production in pounds	400,000	400,000	400,000	
Revenue	$320,000	$230,000	$230,000	$460,000
Costs:				
VDB costs	$ 82,000	$ 61,500	$ 61,500	$123,000
Additional raw materials (LST) and processing of RNA-2	—	60,000	60,000	120,000
Total costs	82,000	121,500	121,500	243,000
Weekly gross profit	$238,000	$108,500	$108,500	$217,000

A new staff accountant who was to review the analysis above commented that it should be revised and stated, "Product costing of products such as these should be done on a net relative sales value basis, not a physical volume basis."

REQUIRED:

A. Discuss whether the use of the net relative sales value method would provide data more relevant for the decision to market DMZ-3 and Pestrol.

B. Critique the Talor Company's analysis and make any revisions that are necessary. Your critique and analysis should indicate

1. Whether Talor Chemical Company made the correct decision.

2. The gross savings (loss) per week of Talor's decision not to process RNA-2 further, if different from the company prepared analysis.

(CMA adapted)

10-22 *(Economic Order Quantity)*. SaPane Company is a regional distributor of automobile window glass. With the introduction of the new subcompact car models and the expected high level of consumer demand, management recognizes a need to determine the total inventory cost associated with maintaining an optimal supply of replacement windshields for the new subcompact cars introduced by each of the three major manufacturers. SaPane is expecting a daily demand for 36 windshields. The purchase price of each windshield is $50.

Other costs associated with ordering and maintaining an inventory of these windshields are as follows:

1. The historical ordering costs incurred in the Purchase Order Department for placing and processing orders is shown below:

Year	Orders Placed and Processed	Total Ordering Costs
1978	20	$12,300
1979	55	$12,475
1980	100	$12,700

Management expects the ordering costs to increase 16% over the amounts and rates experienced the last three years.

2. The windshield manufacturer charges SaPane a $75 shipping fee per order.

3. A clerk in the Receiving Department receives, inspects, and secures the windshields as they arrive from the manufacturer. This activity requires eight hours per order received. This clerk has no other responsibilities and is paid at the rate of $9 per hour. Related variable overhead costs in this department are applied at the rate of $2.50 per hour.

4. Additional warehouse space will have to be rented to store the new windshields. Space can be rented as needed in a public warehouse at an estimated cost of $2,500 per year plus $5.35 per windshield.

5. Breakage cost is estimated to be 6% of the average inventory value.

6. Taxes and fire insurance on the inventory are $1.15 per windshield.

7. The desired rate of return on the investment in inventory is 21% of the purchase price.

Six working days are required from the time the order is placed with the manufacturer until it is received. SaPane uses a 300-day work year when making economic order quantity computations. The economic order quantity formula is

$$EOQ = \sqrt{\frac{2\ (\text{Annual demand})(\text{Ordering cost})}{\text{Storage cost}}}$$

REQUIRED:

A. Calculate the following values for SaPane Company.

1. The value for ordering cost that should be used in the EOQ formula.

2. The value for storage cost that should be used in the EOQ formula.

3. The economic order quantity.

4. The minimum annual relevant cost at the economic order quantity point.

5. The reorder point in units.

B. Without prejudice to your answer to part A, assume that the economic order quantity is 400 units, the storage cost is $28 per unit, and the stockout cost is $12 per unit. SaPane wants to determine the proper level of safety stock in order to minimize its relevant costs. Using the following probability schedule for excess demand during the reorder period, determine the proper amount of safety stock.

Number of Units Short Due to Excess Demand During Reorder Period	Probability of Occurrence
60	.12
120	.05
180	.02

(CMA adapted)

10-23 *(Linear Programming)*. Excelsion Corporation manufactures and sells two kinds of containers—paperboard and plastic. The company produced and sold 100,000 paperboard containers and 75,000 plastic containers during the month of April. A total of 4,000 and 6,000 direct labor hours were used in producing the paperboard and plastic containers, respectively.

The company has not been able to maintain an inventory of either product, due to the high demand; this situation is expected to continue in the future. Workers can be shifted from the production of paperboard to plastic containers and vice versa, but additional labor is not available in the community. In addition, there will be a shortage of plastic material used in the manufacture of the plastic container in the coming months due to a labor strike at the facilities of a key supplier. Management has estimated there will be only enough raw material to produce 60,000 plastic containers during June.

The income statement for Excelsion Corporation for the month of April is shown below. The costs presented in the statement are representative of prior periods and are expected to continue at the same rates or levels in the future.

EXCELSION CORPORATION
INCOME STATEMENT
For the Month Ended April 30, 19X8

	Paperboard Containers	Plastic Containers
Sales	$220,800	$222,900
Less: Returns and allowances	$ 6,360	$ 7,200
Discounts	2,440	3,450
	8,800	10,650
Net sales	$212,000	$212,250
Cost of sales:		
Raw material cost	$123,000	$120,750
Direct labor	26,000	28,500
Indirect labor (variable with		
direct labor hours)	4,000	4,500
Depreciation—machinery	14,000	12,250
Depreciation—building	10,000	10,000
Cost of sales	177,000	176,000
Gross margin	$ 35,000	$ 36,250
Selling and general expenses:		
General expenses—variable	$ 8,000	$ 7,500
General expenses—fixed	1,000	1,000
Commissions	11,000	15,750
Total operating expenses	20,000	24,250
Income before tax	$ 15,000	$ 12,000
Income taxes (40%)	6,000	4,800
Net income	$ 9,000	$ 7,200

REQUIRED:

A. The management of Excelsion Corporation plans to use linear programming to determine the optimal mix of paperboard and plastic containers for the month of June to achieve maximum profits. Using data presented in the April income statement, formulate and label the

1. Objective function.

2. Constraint functions.

B. Identify the underlying assumptions of linear programming.

C. What contribution would the management accountant normally make to a team established to develop the linear programming model and apply it to a decision problem?

(CMA adapted)

10-24 *(Make-or-Buy Decision).* The Liquid Chemical Company sells a range of high-grade products that, because of their chemical properties, call for careful packing. The company has always made a feature of the special properties of the containers used. They had a special patent lining made from a material known as GHL and operated a department specially to maintain their containers in good condition and to make new ones to replace those that were past repair.

Mr. Walsh, the general manager, had for some time suspected that the firm might save money and get equally good service by buying the containers outside. After careful inquiries, he approached a firm specializing in container production, Packages, Inc., and obtained quotations from them. At the same time he asked Mr. Dyer, the controller, to let him have an up-to-date statement of the cost of operating the Container Department.

Within a few days, the quotation from Packages came in. They were prepared to supply all the new containers required—at that time running at the rate of 3,000 a year—for $60,000 per annum, the contract to run for a term of five years certain and thereafter to be renewable from year to year. If the number of containers required increased, the contract price would be increased proportionately. Additionally, and irrespective of whether the above contract was concluded or not, Packages undertook to carry out purely maintenance work on containers, short of replacement, for a sum of $17,500 per annum on the same contract terms.

Mr. Walsh compared these figures with the cost figures prepared by Mr. Dyer covering a year's operations of the Container Department, as follows:

Materials		$20,000
Labor		35,000
Departmental overheads:		
Manager's salary	$8,000	
Rent	1,500	
Depreciation of machinery	6,000	
Maintenance of machinery	1,350	
Other expenses	6,300	23,150
		$78,150
Proportion of general administrative overheads		6,750
Total cost of department for year		$84,900

Walsh's conclusion was that no time should be lost in closing down the department, and in entering into the contracts offered by Packages. However, he felt bound to give the manager of the department, Mr. Duffy, an opportunity to question this conclusion before he acted on it. He therefore called him in and put the facts before him, at the same time making it clear that Duffy's own position was not in jeopardy, for even if his department were closed down, there was another managerial position shortly becoming vacant to which he could be moved without loss of pay or prospects.

Mr. Duffy looked thoughtful, and asked for time to think the matter over. The next morning he asked to speak to Mr. Walsh again, and said he thought there were a number of considerations that ought to be borne in mind before this department was closed down. "For instance," he said, "What will you do with the machinery? It cost $48,000 four years ago, but you'd be lucky if you got $8,000 for it now, even though it's good for another four years at least. And then there's the stock of GHL we bought a year ago. That cost us $30,000, and at the rate we're using it now, it'll last us another three years or so. We used up about a quarter of it last year. Dyer's figure of $20,000 for materials probably includes about $7,500 for GHL. But it'll be tricky stuff to handle if we don't use it up. We bought well—$150 a ton we paid for it—and you couldn't buy it today for less than $180. But you wouldn't have more than $120 a ton left if you sold it, after you'd covered all the handling expenses."

Walsh thought that Dyer ought to be present during this discussion. He called him in and put Duffy's points to him. "I don't much like all this conjecture," Dyer said. "I think my figures are pretty conclusive. Besides, if we are going to have all this talk about 'what will happen if,' don't forget the problem of space we're faced with. We're paying $2,750 a year in rent for a warehouse a couple of miles away. If we closed Duffy's department, we'd have all the warehouse space we need without renting."

"That's a good point," said Walsh. Although I must say, I'm a bit worried about the men if we close the department. I don't think we can find room for any of them elsewhere in the firm. I could see whether Packages can take any of them. But some of them are getting on. There's Walters and Hines, for example. They've been with us since they left school 40 years ago. I'd feel bound to give them a small pension—$1,000 a year each, say."

Duffy showed some relief at this. "But I still don't like Dyer's figures," he said. "What about this $6,750 for general administrative overheads? You surely don't expect to fire anyone in the general office if I'm closed down, do you?"

"Probably not," said Dyer, "but someone has to pay for these costs. We can't ignore them when we look at an individual department, because if we do that with each department in turn, we shall finish up by convincing ourselves that general managers, accountants, typists, stationery, and the like don't have to be paid for. And they do, believe me."

"Well, I think we've thrashed this out pretty fully," said Walsh, "but I've been turning over in my mind the possibility of perhaps keeping on the maintenance work ourselves. What are your views on that, Duffy?"

"I don't know," said Duffy, "but it's worth looking into. We shouldn't need any machinery for that, and I could hand the supervision over to a supervisor. You'd save $2,000 a year there, say. You'd only need about one-fifth of the men, but you could keep on the oldest. You wouldn't save any space, so I suppose the rent would be the same. I shouldn't think the other expenses would be more than $2,600 a year."

"What about materials?" asked Walsh.

"We use about 10% of the total on maintenance," Duffy replied.

"Well, I've told Packages that I'd let them know my decision within a week," said Walsh. "I'll let you know what I decide to do before I write to them."

(Prepared by Professor David Solomons)

10-25 *(Pricing Strategy)*. The Microcomputer Division of Time Unlimited, Inc., manufactures and sells two models of computers. The smallest one, the RAM-64, has 64K internal memory, two double-density 5¼-inch floppy disk drives with 197K bytes each, a detachable full typewriter keyboard, and a 12-inch video display of 80 columns × 24 rows with scrolling capability. In addition, it includes as standard software a profit plan, a household budget program, a word-processing system, and two computer games of the customer's choice. It can be used either as a home computer or in a small business where the data-processing needs are not extensive. The other model, the RAM-128, is larger than the RAM-64 and has greater capacity including two 8-inch double-sided double-density disk drives holding over 700K bytes. In addition to the software package offered with the RAM-64, a complete accounting program and a sophisticated statistical analysis package are included as part of the standard software. However, it still is classified as a microcomputer. The RAM-128 is purchased by businesses that want a small computer with the additional data-processing capabilities that the smaller model does not offer. Time Unlimited, Inc.'s prices are higher than their competitors because the RAM computers offer processing and programming features not available from competitors, as well as a superior warranty and service program. Time Unlimited usually announces any price changes after the competition has posted theirs for the year.

Late in 19X1, the Computer Division managers held a meeting where the following discussion took place. In attendance were

Jon Patric, marketing manager

Andrea Suzanne, chief accountant

Ross Edwards, vice-president of the computer division

Jim Mathews, production manager

Jon Patric: In a few months we are going to raise the price of the RAM-64 from $1,800 to $2,000 per unit while our competition will be raising their prices from $1,700 to $1,850 per unit. In addition, the price of the RAM-128 will go from $13,500 to $15,000 per unit. By contrast, our competition is planning on raising their prices from $12,500 to $14,000. We project that our microcomputer sales division should sell at least 40,000 units of the RAM-64 at $1,800 per unit; at $2,000 per unit we should sell at least 20,000 units. Our market studies also indicate that at \$13,500 per unit we should sell at least 4,000 units of RAM-128 while at \$15,000 per unit we project sales of at least 2,000 units. I'm very concerned about this decrease in our volume of sales and question the advisability of raising our prices at this time.

Andrea Suzanne: The reason we are increasing the prices of the RAM-64 and RAM-128, Jon, is due to the fact that labor and material prices have gone up about 12% over the past year. Our increase in price just reflects the cost of inflation. I have finished compiling some current data (Exhibit 1) through June of 19X1 if anyone is interested. One idea to decrease cost would be to cut the 10% sales commission to 7% or 8%. That's all our competitors are paying their sales staff. Also, our service warranty costs have increased from 4% to approximately 7% of sales. We really need to know the cause of this increase.

ESTIMATED COST OF RAM-64 AT DIFFERENT PRODUCTION VOLUMES THROUGH JUNE 19X1

Volume	10,000 Units	20,000 Units	30,000 Units	40,000 Units	50,000 Units
Raw materials	$ 144	$ 144	$ 144	$ 144	$ 144
Purchased parts	160	160	160	160	155
Direct labor	510	500	490	485	490
Departmental overhead					
Direct*	35	34	32	33	33
Equipment depreciation	144	72	48	36	29
Indirect[†]	235	120	80	60	48
General overhead[‡]	127	125	120	122	123
Production costs	$1,355	$1,155	$1,074	$1,040	$1,022
Marketing and administration[§]	677	578	537	520	511
Total costs	$2,032	$1,733	$1,611	$1,560	$1,533

ESTIMATED COST OF RAM-128 AT DIFFERENT PRODUCTION VOLUMES THROUGH JUNE 19X1

Volume	1,000 Units	2,000 Units	3,000 Units	4,000 Units	5,000 Units
Raw materials	$ 1,450	$ 1,450	$ 1,450	$ 1,450	$ 1,450
Purchased parts	1,740	1,740	1,740	1,730	1,720
Direct labor	4,600	4,500	4,350	4,400	4,500
Departmental overhead					
Direct*	400	380	373	365	370
Equipment depreciation	870	435	290	218	174
Indirect[†]	1,305	652	435	326	261
General overhead[‡]	1,110	1,100	1,087	1,095	1,100
Production costs	$11,475	$10,257	$ 9,725	$ 9,584	$ 9,575
Marketing and administration[§]	5,738	5,129	4,858	4,793	4,788
Total costs	$17,213	$15,385	$14,583	$14,377	$14,363

*Power, supplies, repairs.
[†]Supervision, interest, rent, property taxes.
[‡]Allocated on the basis of 25% of direct labor.
[§]Allocated on the basis of 50% of production costs.

EXHIBIT 1   Time Unlimited, Inc.

Income Statement for Year Ending December 31, 19X0 (000's)			
	RAM-64	RAM-128	Total
Gross sales	$54,000	$40,500	$94,500
Expenses:			
Raw materials	$ 3,880	$ 3,915	$ 7,795
Purchased parts	4,320	4,698	9,018
Direct labor	12,960	11,745	24,705
Direct overhead	864	980	1,844
Equipment depreciation	1,440	870	2,310
Indirect overhead	2,160	1,174	3,334
General overhead	3,240	2,935	6,175
Marketing and administration	14,364	13,114	27,478
Total expenses	43,228	39,431	82,659
Income	$10,772	$ 1,069	$11,841

Sold In 19X0: 30,000 units of RAM-64
　　　　　　　 3,000 units of RAM-128

EXHIBIT 2
Time Unlimited, Inc.

Ross Edwards: Jon, if we kept both models at the current price, would the competition keep their prices at the current level or would they still raise their prices? We really need to know this. Also, it seems from the attached income statement (Exhibit 2) that the RAM-128 line is not as profitable as the RAM-64 line. Perhaps we should be concentrating our marketing efforts on the RAM-64. It also seems to me we should seriously consider Andrea's suggestion on reducing sales commissions.

Jon Patric: Our competition would probably raise their prices even if we kept ours the same, though perhaps not as much as originally planned, Ross, We are currently in a strong market position (Exhibit 3) and I would not like to see this market share lost. In response to Andrea's suggestion, I am certain that a decrease in the level of commissions would seriously affect our market share because of decreased salespeople's motivation.

Jim Mathews: From a product-line evaluation standpoint, we are not making much money on the RAM-128. Maybe we should drop it and produce only the RAM-64 or develop another model. I realize we cannot transfer all of the equipment that is used in manufacturing the RAM-128 to the manufacture of the RAM-64, but we can transfer the labor that is used to produce the RAM-128 to produce the RAM-64. However, your question on increasing warranty costs, Andrea, is harder to answer. Up through 19X0 we have always considered 4% of the sales price of both the micros a reasonable estimate of our costs of servicing the computers under the one-year warranty and this proved accurate in the past. But with the increase in parts and labor costs as well as some small problems in this year's production process, it's not surprising that warranty costs have increased. In fact, I'm rather surprised the increase wasn't more. It is important, given our current marketing strategy, that we maintain the highest possible reputation in this area. At least that's what Jon is always telling me.

RAM-64: PRICES AND SALES				
	SALES VOLUME		PRICE (PER UNIT)	
Selling Year	Industry Totals	Time Unlimited	Competition's Average Price	Time Unlimited
19W8	40,000	5,000	$ 5,000	$ 6,000
19W9	75,000	10,000	$ 2,500	$ 2,700
19X0	150,000	30,000	$ 1,700	$ 1,800
19X1	200,000	—	$ 1,850	$ —

RAM-128: PRICES AND SALES				
	SALES VOLUME		PRICE (PER UNIT)	
Selling Year	Industry Totals	Time Unlimited	Competition's Average Price	Time Unlimited
19W8	7,500	500	$20,000	$23,000
19W9	15,000	1,500	$15,000	$16,500
19X0	25,000	3,000	$12,500	$13,500
19X1	35,000	—	$14,000	—

EXHIBIT 3
Time Unlimited, Inc.

Andrea Suzanne: To get back to the idea of dropping the RAM-128 line, we really may want to give that further consideration. Our records show that the nontransferable RAM-128 equipment has a book value of $4,350,000. We should be able to sell this equipment for around $2,000,000. This would give us a good cash inflow, enough perhaps to develop a new product line.

Jim Mathews: Great idea, Andrea. Our current plant capacity is 50,000 units of the RAM-64 and 5,000 units of the RAM-128. With the cash from the sale of the RAM-128 equipment we could expand our plant capacity to 70,000 units of the RAM-64. It would cost about $3 million for an additional building and equipment, give or take a little.

Ross Edwards: Well, I can see from our discussion that there are several options open to us. I do have an additional concern. After reviewing the data brought in by Andrea, I'm not exactly sure how much it is costing us to produce and sell either of our models. We really need this piece of information. And while you are thinking about that, please keep one important point in mind. Our divisional goal is an income of 12% of sales, so we should consider that when seeking solutions to the questions that were brought up in today's meeting. It is reasonably urgent that we come up with a suitable analysis as soon as possible. We are almost through the year now and must make some decisions for the coming year. I'll see you back here in one week.

REQUIRED:

A. Evaluate the suggestions offered at the meeting.

B. Recommend a strategy to management.

chapter **11**

LONG-RANGE DECISIONS

APPENDIX: THE CONCEPT OF PRESENT VALUE
TIME VALUE OF MONEY
FUTURE AND PRESENT VALUE
DEVELOPMENT OF PRESENT-VALUE FACTORS
COMPUTATION OF PRESENT VALUE
COMPUTATION OF PRESENT VALUE OF AN ANNUITY
USE OF PRESENT-VALUE TABLES

In Chapter 1, management decisions were divided into long-range capacity decisions and short-range operating decisions. Long-range decisions have two unique characteristics. First, they involve change in the productive or service potential of the firm. Once a change has been initiated, it may be difficult and costly to reverse the decision. Second, there is typically a long span of time before benefits from a long-range investment are fully realized. During this period of time the company has incurred a cost for the use of the capital. This cost, referred to as the time value of money, must be included in the analysis before making any investment decision.

As we have stressed throughout this text, all decisions, both long-run and short-run, derive from the firm goals—the overall guidelines that determine the character and direction of the firm. As shown in Exhibit 11–1, these goals are the starting point of long-run decisions, decisions that affect the firm's operations for years to come. A decision to build a new production facility commits a firm to a production method, a geographic territory, and a scope of operations for an extended time period. Failure to make satisfactory long-run decisions means that the firm most likely will fail to achieve its goals.

Next the firm must take action to obtain the resources and the facilities. As shown in Exhibit 11–1, the decisions to take these actions should be based on long-range forecasts of the needs of the firm. In this way the goals of the firm are coordinated with the economic environment in which the firm exists. The long-run decisions that commit the firm and require the use of resources over an extended future time period, are

1. Obtaining new facilities or expanding existing facilities. This choice concerns which of the available facilities should be obtained and for what purpose they should be used. This decision is based on estimates as to which facility will give the largest return on the required investment. Examples include buying new machinery, building a new office building, leasing or purchasing additional salespersons'

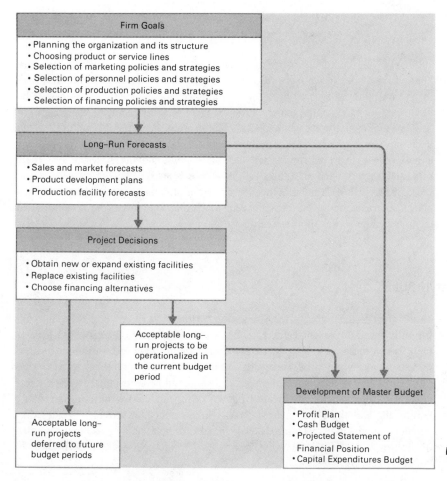

Firm Goals

- Planning the organization and its structure
- Choosing product or service lines
- Selection of marketing policies and strategies
- Selection of personnel policies and strategies
- Selection of production policies and strategies
- Selection of financing policies and strategies

Long-Run Forecasts

- Sales and market forecasts
- Product development plans
- Production facility forecasts

Project Decisions

- Obtain new or expand existing facilities
- Replace existing facilities
- Choose financing alternatives

Acceptable long-run projects to be operationalized in the current budget period

Acceptable long-run projects deferred to future budget periods

Development of Master Budget

- Profit Plan
- Cash Budget
- Projected Statement of Financial Position
- Capital Expenditures Budget

EXHIBIT 11–1 Long-range planning flow

automobiles, purchasing a subsidiary company, or adding a new production line.

2. Replacing existing facilities. Here the decision concerns substituting new facilities for existing facilities. This decision is based on estimates that the savings from the new equipment, when compared with the old equipment, will offset the costs of the new equipment. Examples include replacing a manual bookkeeping system with a computer system, buying a new computer model to replace an older model, replacing 2-ton delivery trucks with 5-ton trucks, or replacing an inefficient lathe with one that is numerically controlled.

3. Choosing financial alternatives. This choice involves selecting modes of obtaining resources. One example is whether to lease or purchase an asset. Here the question is whether the resources in-

vested in the purchase alternative would earn an adequate return when contrasted with resources that would be committed in leasing.

Long-range decisions relate to specific projects. The decision rules are applied on a specific case-by-case basis. However, as shown in Exhibit 11–1, in any one budgetary period the acquisitions scheduled for that period will be integrated into the capital expenditures budget. This allows management to co-ordinate the capital expenditure plans with current operational plans. Once the decision has been implemented and the resources have been acquired, it becomes a part of the overall firm capacity. At this point the investments lose their separate identity, and the short-range decisions to maximize the use of the facilities become paramount. Once the decisions are operationalized the revenues and costs traceable to the long-run decisions commingle with the revenues and costs traceable to the short-range decisions.

LONG-RANGE DECISION RULE

The critical factor in a long-range decision is time. The time factor is recognized formally through present-value calculations. In long-range decisions an invest-ment is favorable if the benefits from the investment, adjusted for the time value of money, are equal to or greater than its costs, also adjusted for the time value of money. Any investment that provides discounted benefits equal to discounted costs will earn exactly the desired rate of return and will contribute to main-taining the wealth of the enterprise. Any investment that provides greater dis-counted benefits than discounted costs will contribute to an increase in the wealth of the firm. The basic assumption of any long-range decision is that the firm is trying to maximize its wealth.

MEASUREMENT OF BENEFITS AND COSTS

For analyzing decisions involving long periods of time, the investor is concerned with the timing of when cash is invested and when cash is received. When cash is invested it is not available for other uses, and when cash is recovered it is available for reinvestment elsewhere.

The cash inflows from an investment must be sufficient to recover the initial investment and to provide a satisfactory return to the investor. For ex-ample, consider an investment for $12,010, that will produce cash inflows of $5,000 each year for three years. The asset will be worn out and have no further value at the end of the three years. During the entire lifetime of the investment, cash flows will be: $12,010 outflow at the beginning of the first year and $5,000 inflow at the end of each of the next three years.

Period	(1) Investment at Beginning of Year	(2) Cash Received	(3) Return on Investment 12% (1) × 12%	(4) Recovery of Investment (2) − (3)	(5) Investment at End of Year (1) − (4)
Year 1	$12,010	$5,000	$1,441	$ 3,559	$8,451
Year 2	8,451	5,000	1,014	3,986	4,465
Year 3	4,465	5,000	535	4,465	0
Totals			$2,990	$12,010	

EXHIBIT 11–2
Demonstration of return on investment

Exhibit 11–2 shows that the firm actually earns a return of 12% on the investment and also recovers the entire investment. (Later in this chapter we will show how the actual return of 12% is determined.) In the first year the return on investment is $1,441 ($12,010 × 12% = $1,441) and recovery of the investment is $3,559 ($5,000 − $1,441 = $3,559). In Years 2 and 3, the dollar amount of return declines because a portion of the investment has been recovered and the amount still invested in the project, on which the earnings are based, is smaller. In each of the three years the firm earns 12% on the investment balance at the beginning of the year.

Due to the importance of the time value of money, the timing and magnitude of cash flows are important to any long-range decision. For example, assume that the total cash inflows in our example remained at $15,000 but that the timing changed to $6,000 in Year 1, $5,000 in Year 2, and $4,000 in Year 3. This is a better investment because the firm has recovered $1,000 two years earlier. The additional $1,000 recovered in Year 1 may be invested in some other project.

For proper analysis of an investment the relevant information includes:

1. A method to recognize the time value of money.
2. Measurement of cash inflows.
3. Measurement of cash outflows.
4. A measure of the time value of money—that is, a rate-of-return measure.

RECOGNIZING THE TIME VALUE OF MONEY USING PRESENT VALUE ANALYSIS

The time value of money in long-range decisions is formally recognized by discounting all cash flows to their present value. Investors would rather have a dollar now than at a future date. This is true for two reasons: First, a dollar received today may be invested, resulting in some larger amount a year from now. The investor who will receive a dollar a year from now will have only one dollar. The difference between these amounts is the time value of money. Second, any delay involves uncertainty. The old adage, "a bird in hand is worth two in the bush," refers to both time value of money and a lack of certainty.

Different cash flows are compared by discounting them to their present values. The Chapter 11 appendix presents an expanded discussion of the concept of present value. A review of this appendix will provide the necessary background for present-value calculations.

MEASUREMENT OF CASH OUTFLOWS

In any investment decision the relevant cash outflows are the *incremental cash outflows* that are directly traceable to the investment. In most decisions there are substantial cash outflows. An investment in a new building would involve an initial outlay for its purchase or construction. In the case of construction, the initial outlay may be spread over several years. In addition, all cash outflows related to the building subsequent to acquisition must be identified. For a building such outflows would include maintenance, repairs, property taxes, and similar cash outflows directly related to the building over its useful life.

All additional resources required for the higher level of activity must be considered in the decision. In most cases, additional productive facilities also require additional working capital to support the increased level of activity. It will be necessary for the firm to have larger amounts of raw materials, work-in-process, and finished goods; increased sales will necessitate additional Accounts Receivable and inventory balances as well as wages and other production costs. The amount of working capital needed to support a plant can often be greater than the cost of the plant facilities. Although the entire amount of working capital should be recovered by the end of the venture, there is a cost associated with the resources invested in the working capital.

When an investment decision involves any nonmonetary resource currently owned by the firm, such as a building or equipment, the relevant "cost" is the opportunity cost of the asset, not the book value in the accounting records. For example, assume that a division manager is deciding whether to sell an idle plant or use it to produce a new product. If the plant is retained, the investment amount relevant to the decision is the sales price foregone, not the undepreciated cost shown in the accounting records.

MEASUREMENT OF CASH INFLOWS

Like cash outflows, the relevant cash inflows are the *incremental cash inflows* to be received in the future and directly related to the decision. In most long-range decisions the cash inflows are spread over the life of the investment. A new plant generates cash inflows in the form of increased contribution margin (increased sales less increased variable costs).

The distinction between revenue, expense, or asset transactions is not carried over into cash flows. A cash inflow directly attributable to the investment, regardless of the reason, should be considered. Therefore, a dollar of cost saved is equivalent to a dollar of revenue received from the sale of product and should be considered cash inflow. For example, if a new labor-saving machine is installed, the cash inflow should include the savings in expenses, such as labor and fringe benefits, that require cash. There is also no distinction between cash inflow from revenue during the life of an investment and cash inflow from the sale or salvage of the productive asset at the end of the project. Therefore, when the plant is discontinued and the working capital may be used for other purposes, the reduction of working capital should be considered a cash inflow. There may be differential tax effects, but that is a separate issue.

MEASUREMENT OF THE RATE OF RETURN

There are many possible rate-of-return measures that a firm could use as a discount rate.[1] One possible measure is to use an opportunity cost by asking, "What is the return available for the funds in the next best alternative?" For example, this opportunity cost could be the return available on another potential project, the return available from short-term investments, or the return from investing in long-term bonds. These discount rates may or may not ensure the firm will maintain its wealth. Most firms make long-term investments in order to maintain or add to the wealth of the firm; thus they try to use a rate-of-return measure that will accomplish this goal. As a result many firms use some measure of the cost of their own capital; if they earn the cost of obtaining and maintaining their capital they will achieve the goal of wealth maintenance. If they earn in excess of this cost, they will have added to the wealth of the firm.

The liability and owners' equity section of the statement of financial position list the sources and the magnitude of the firm's capital. This information, along with the specific cost of each source of capital, allows the firm to estimate its "average" cost of capital. The weighted-average cost of this capital should be the minimum rate of return required across the aggregate of all long-range decisions.

However, the use of a single discount rate for all investment projects may not be appropriate where the projects have different degrees of risk. Some firms deal with this issue by ranking the projects by risk classes and adjusting the discount rate accordingly. For example, high-risk projects would be assessed using a higher rate of return than moderate-risk projects, and moderate-risk projects would be assessed using a higher rate of return than low-risk projects.

[1]The rate of return, or discount rate, has also been called the minimum rate, the hurdle rate, the required rate, and the cutoff rate.

The combination of all projects considered should provide a rate of return adequate to compensate for the average risk level of the proposed projects.

The illustrations of the techniques of investment analysis in this section will assume a weighted-average cost of capital without regard to risk. Then, later in the chapter we will look specifically at adjustments for risk and other factors affecting long-term investment decisions.

ILLUSTRATION OF TECHNIQUES THAT SATISFY THE LONG-RANGE DECISION RULE

Three techniques satisfy the long-run decision rule, in that they measure discounted cash benefits and cash costs.

1. Net present value.
2. Discounted benefit–cost ratio or profitability index.
3. Adjusted rate of return or internal rate of return.

These three techniques vary only in the way the decision criteria are stated. The first two, net present value and discounted benefit–cost ratio, apply a desired or predefined discount rate to cash flows. This permits a measurement of the alternatives by their net present values or the ratio of discounted benefits to discounted costs. The third method, the adjusted rate of return, computes the rate of return actually earned from each investment opportunity.

The following example will be used to illustrate these techniques. The Arbuckle Company is considering the purchase of a piece of equipment that will increase efficiency and reduce cash operating costs. The new equipment will require an investment of $12,010 at the beginning of the project and will produce cash savings of $5,000 per year for the next three years. Assume the applicable cost of capital is 10% and all cash inflows occur at the end of the period.

NET PRESENT VALUE

The net present value of the project is the difference between the present values of all future cash inflows and the present value of all future cash outflows. All future cash inflows and outflows are discounted to their present values by the use of a predetermined discount rate. When the net present value is zero (discounted cash inflows are equal to discounted cash outflows), the investment will earn the predefined rate of return. If the net present value is positive (discounted cash inflows exceed discounted cash outflows), the investment will earn a rate of return greater than the predefined rate of return. If the present value is negative (the discounted cash inflows are less than the discounted cash outflows), the investment will earn a rate of return less than the predefined rate of return.

The steps in calculating the net present value of an investment are

1. Determine all incremental cash flows relevant to the investment. A time line showing the amount and timing of each cash flow helps the understanding of a complex problem. Show cash outflows as negative amounts.
2. Find the present value of each cash flow. Use the appropriate present value factors from Appendix A or B at the end of this book. In many complex problems it will be easier to sum the cash flows by year and apply the present value factor to the net cash flow by year.
3. Sum the present values to arrive at the net present value.

Exhibit 11–3 shows a positive net present value of $420. A positive net present value indicates that the discounted cash inflows are greater than the discounted cash outflows. The investment is earning more than the desired 10% rate of return and should be accepted.

Two approaches to compute the present values were used in Exhibit 11–3. In the first part of the exhibit, the present-value factors for single cash

Investment project: original investment $12,010, cash operating savings $5,000 per year. Project life 3 years. Desired rate of return 10%.

	Cash Flow Time Line				Present Value Factor	Present Value
	Year					
	0	1	2	3		
Illustration Using Appendix A Table—Present Value of $1						
Cash outflow:						
Initial investment	($12,010)				1.000	($12,010)
Cash inflows:						
Year 1		$5,000			0.909	$ 4,545
Year 2			$5,000		0.826	4,130
Year 3				$5,000	0.751	3,755
Total cash inflows						12,430
Net present value						$ 420
Illustration Using Appendix B Table—Present Value of an Annuity of $1						
Cash outflows:						
Initial investment	($12,010)				1.000	($12,010)
Cash inflows:						
Annual savings		$5,000	$5,000	$5,000	2.486	12,430
Net present value						$ 420

EXHIBIT 11–3 Illustration of net present value

flows were used. In the lower part of the exhibit, the present-value factor for an annuity was used. Because the present-value factor for an annuity of $1 is the aggregation of present-value factors for single amounts (.909 + .826 + .751 = 2.486), use of either table will achieve the same results. However, the annuity table may be used only if the cash flows are identical over time.

DISCOUNTED BENEFIT–COST RATIO

The discounted benefit–cost ratio is the ratio of discounted cash inflows to discounted cash outflows. The technique is identical to the net present-value method through the first two steps. However, instead of netting the discounted cash inflows and discounted cash outflows and arriving at a net present value, the ratio of discounted cash inflows to discounted cash outflows is computed.

A ratio of 1.00 indicates that the discounted cash inflows are exactly equal to the discounted cash outflows, and that the actual rate of return is equal to the desired rate of return. Therefore, any discounted benefit–cost ratio of 1.00 or greater indicates a favorable investment project.

Using the data from Exhibit 11–3, the discounted cash inflows are $12,430 and the discounted cash outflows are $12,010. The discounted benefit–cost ratio is 1.035, indicating that the long-run decision rule is satisfied and the investment should be accepted.

ADJUSTED RATE OF RETURN (INTERNAL RATE OF RETURN)

The adjusted rate of return determines the actual rate of return of an investment opportunity. This method determines the rate necessary to make the discounted cash inflows equal to the discounted cash outflows.

The approach used to compute net present value is used to compute the adjusted rate of return. The adjusted rate of return is determined by computing a series of net present values with different rates of return until a net present value of zero is reached. For example, try a rate of return of 10%; if this results in a positive net present value use a higher rate of return until a net present value of zero is reached. If a negative net present value is achieved, try a lower rate of return until the net present value equals zero.

The net present value of our example in Exhibit 11–3 is a positive $420. This indicates that the actual adjusted rate of return is above 10%. As a second attempt, let us use a rate of return of 12%. The net present value at 12% is

Present value of cash outflows:	
($12,010) × 1.000	($12,010)
Present value of cash inflows:	
$5,000 × 2.402 (Appendix B)	12,010
Net present value	$ 0

If cash inflows over the life of the investment are uneven, this trial-and-error approach must be followed. However, if an initial cash outflow is followed by a series of equal cash inflows, a simpler approach may be used to determine the adjusted rate of return. In this case, (1) determine the present-value annuity factor to equate discounted cash outflows with discounted cash inflows, and (2) find that present-value factor (or the nearest to it) in the Appendix B present-value annuity table. The calculation is as follows:

Determine the present-value annuity factor that equates discounted cash inflows with discounted cash outflows.

$$\text{Initial investment} = \text{Annual cash inflow} \times \text{Present value annuity factor (pvf)}$$

$$
\begin{aligned}
\$12,010 &= \$5,000 \times \text{pfv} \\
\text{pvf} &= \$12,010/\$5,000 \\
\text{pvf} &= 2.402
\end{aligned}
$$

Find the nearest present-value annuity factor in the three-year row of the Appendix B present value table.

The present value annuity factor in the three-year row and 12% column of the present-value table in Appendix B is 2.402, indicating an adjusted rate of return of exactly 12%.

These illustrations were constructed to provide a rate of exactly 12%. If the net present value is not exactly zero, or if the present-value factor falls between two columns in the present-value table, it will be necessary to interpolate. Interpolation is explained in the appendix, where the concepts and calculations of present value are explained.

In practice, business calculators or canned computer programs are available for such calculations. Spreadsheets for microcomputers (particularly Lotus 1-2-3) are powerful tools that allow the solving of complex investment problems including computations of the adjusted rate of return. However, it is the authors' belief that the student should understand the underlying calculations before relying solely on these modern tools.

STRENGTHS AND WEAKNESSES OF INVESTMENT ANALYSIS TECHNIQUES

Exhibit 11–4 presents strengths and weaknesses of the three investment analysis models that satisfy the long-range decision rule. Net present value is the conceptually superior model and, used appropriately, will provide a proper decision recommendation.

Strengths	Weaknesses
Net present value:	
1. Conceptually superior method— basis for the long-run decision rule because it considers the time value of money.	1. Does not provide the actual rate of return.
2. May be applied in all settings— including uneven cash flows, and major cash outflows during the life of the project.	2. Difficult to compare projects with large size differences.
3. The decision criterion accepts only those projects that meet the desired rate of return.	3. Difficult to compare projects with unequal lives.
4. An easy method to use.	
Discounted Benefit–Cost Ratio:	
1. Based on the net present value method, it has most of its strengths.	1. Does not provide the actual rate of return.
2. Basic method in public sector— allows benefits and costs to be incorporated easily.	
3. Provides a basis to compare investment alternatives, including differing sizes.	
Adjusted Rate of Return:	
1. Considers the time value of money.	1. May generate two rates of return when large cash outflows occur during the life of the project.
2. Determines the actual rate of return for a project.	2. Assumes that as investment is recovered, cash will be invested at same rate.
3. Easy-to-understand decision criterion.	3. Computations become complex with uneven cash flows.
4. Provides a basis to compare investment alternatives, including differing sizes.	

EXHIBIT 11–4
Strengths and weaknesses of investment analysis techniques

IMPACT OF INCOME TAXES ON LONG-RANGE DECISIONS

The previous sections in this chapter stressed that the relevant cash flows in long-range decisions are the future incremental cash inflows and outflows directly attributable to the investment. Income taxes are cash disbursements, generally with a significant impact on the timing and amount of cash flows from long-lived assets. The tax code is complex; many provisions were enacted by Congress to encourage investment in productive assets. The Internal Revenue Code of 1986 removed or changed a number of provisions that had an impact on long-range decisions. Over the next few years we can expect additional changes. Because of the compexity of the tax laws and their state of flux, this discussion is limited to the effect of depreciation on after-tax cash flows. To deal with the many specific rules within the tax code would be far beyond the scope of this book. However, the principles underlying the illustrations can be applied to other tax code provisions as they evolve.

AFTER-TAX CASH FLOWS

Exhibit 11–5 illustrates the effect of taxes on cash flows in an investment project. The first column presents revenue and expense projections for the first year of the investment project. The second column shows a direct measurement of the cash flows for the first year of the project. In this example, sales result in cash inflows of $100,000, operating expenses result in cash outflows of $60,000, and income taxes at a 40% tax rate result in cash outflows of $4,000. The project is expected to generate $36,000 of cash in the first year. This part of the example computes income taxes as a single cash outflow for the year.

Instead of computing and presenting income taxes as a single amount, the incremental effect of taxes on each cash flow may be calculated. The incremental cost of a tax-deductible item is not the cash paid for the item; rather, it is the amount of payment after considering the reduction in income taxes resulting from the payment. The $60,000 of operating expenses have an after-tax cost of only $36,000 [$60,000 − ($60,000 × 40%)]. Revenue of $100,000 will have an after-tax benefit of only $60,000 [$100,000 − ($100,000 × 40%)]. When using the incremental measurement procedure it is easier to multiply the net cash inflow or outflow by the complement of the tax rate (100% − the tax rate). Using a tax rate of 40%, the complement of the tax rate is 60% (100% − 40%).

	Annual Revenue and Expense Projections	DIRECT MEASUREMENT METHOD	INCREMENTAL MEASUREMENT METHOD	
		Cash Flows	After-Tax Effect	After-Tax Cash Flows
Sales	$100,000	$100,000	60%	$60,000
Cash operating expenses	(60,000)	(60,000)	60%	(36,000)
Depreciation	(30,000)		40%	12,000
Net income before income taxes	$ 10,000	$ 40,000		
Income taxes (40%)	(4,000)	(4,000)		
Net income	$ 6,000			
Net cash flow		$ 36,000		$36,000

EXHIBIT 11–5   Illustration of after-tax cash flows (first year of project)

EFFECT OF DEPRECIATION

The effect of depreciation on after-tax cash flows is more difficult to explain. In computing taxable income for financial accounting purposes, the cost of a long-lived asset is amortized over the life of the asset. Cash is paid when the asset is purchased, but that cost is expensed through depreciation over the life of the asset. Therefore, depreciation does not represent a cash outflow; rather it is a noncash deduction for tax purposes. As such, depreciation will reduce the cash outflow for income taxes.

In the second column of Exhibit 11–5, where taxes are shown as a direct cash outflow, no cash flow is shown for depreciation. However, the amount of income taxes paid reflects the tax rate applied to the taxable income shown in column one. Depreciation was deducted in the calculation of the income for the year.

In the fourth column of the exhibit, where the incremental after-tax cash flows are shown for each item, the deduction of $30,000 for depreciation reduces income taxes by $12,000 ($30,000 × 40%). The reduction of income taxes, as well as the reduction of any expense, is treated as a cash inflow.

Either the direct or the incremental measurement approach will give the same annual cash flows for the project. The choice of which method to use depends on the complexity of the project and personal preference.

ACCELERATED COST RECOVERY SYSTEM (ACRS)

There were major changes in the Internal Revenue Code in 1986 that relate to investment in long-lived assets. These changes repealed the investment credit and capital gains provisions, and revised the Accelerated Cost Recovery System. When enacted in 1981, ACRS replaced the concept of useful life of an asset with arbitrary "recovery periods." A recovery period is the number of years over which the cost of an asset is to be amortized. The 1986 code revision replaced "recovery periods" with a schedule of allowable declining-balance depreciation percentages for eight property classes. The 1986 ACRS classes, the type of assets in each class, and the depreciation methods are presented in Exhibit 11–6.

ACRS depreciation schedules for the 3, 5, 7, and 10-year assets are based on double-declining-balance depreciation. The 15- and 20-year ACRS depreciation schedules use the 150%-declining-balance method. Schedules for the 27.5- and 31.5-year assets are based on straight-line depreciation. Optionally, a firm may choose to use straight-line depreciation rather than declining-balance depreciation.

Declining-balance depreciation is computed by taking either 200% or 150% (depending on the asset class) times the annual straight-line rate and multiplying this rate times the remaining undepreciated balance. Because the

Class	Type of Asset	Depreciation Method*
3-year	Specific industries—special tools; road tractor units	200% Declining-balance (DB)
5-year	Automobiles; trucks; research equipment; computers; selected industries— equipment	200% DB
7-year	Office furniture; railroad cars; most machinery and equipment	200% DB
10-year	Water transport equipment; selected industries— equipment	200% DB
15-year	Land improvements; selected industries—equipment	150% DB
20-year	Farm buildings; power- generating and distribution equipment	150% DB
27.5-year	Residential rental property	Straight-line
31.5-year	Nonresidential rental property	Straight-line

*Straight-line depreciation may be used as an optional method.

EXHIBIT 11—6
Asset classes in accelerated cost recovery system (ACRS)

declining-balance method will not depreciate the asset fully, the taxpayer may change to the straight-line method when the straight-line method provides more depreciation than the declining-balance method over the remainder of the life of the asset.

For the 5-year asset class, the annual declining-balance depreciation rate is 40%, determined as follows:

$$(100\% \div \text{life}) \times \text{Declining-balance percentage}$$
$$(100\% \div 5) \times 200\% = 40\%$$

Assuming a $30,000 cost, depreciation for the 5 years with the double-declining-balance method is computed as follows:

Year 1 $30,000 × 40% = $12,000

Year 2   ($30,000 − $12,000) × 40% = $7,200

Year 3   ($30,000 − $12,000 − $7,200) × 40% = $4,320

Year 4 and 5   ($30,000 − $12,000 − $7,200 − $4,320) ÷ 2 = $3,240
(Years 4 and 5 switch to the straight-line method. The double-declining-balance method will produce only $2,592 of depreciation in the fourth year.)

For the 20-year class, the annual depreciation rate is 7.5%, determined as follows:

$$(100\% \div \text{life}) \times \text{Declining-balance percentage}$$
$$(100\% \div 20) \times 150\% = 7.5\%$$

Exhibit 11–7 presents the cost recovery percentages over the life of the property classes using declining-balance depreciation. For the 5-year class the rates are 40.0% in the first year, 24.0% in the second year, 14.4% in the third year, and 10.8% in the fourth and fifth years. The year of switching to straight-line depreciation for each class is also shown in Exhibit 11–7.

This presentation of ACRS depreciation is subtantially simplified. One of the more complex provisions of the tax code allows only a half-year of depreciation in the year of acquisition. The code assumes that, "on the aver-

Period	Declining Balance (DB) 200%				Declining Balance 150%	
	3-Year Class	5-Year Class	7-Year Class	10-Year Class	15-Year Class	20-Year Class
Rate*	66.67%	40.00%	28.57%	20.00%	10.00%	7.50%
1	66.7%	40.0%	28.6%	20.0%	10.0%	7.5%
2	22.2%	24.0%	20.4%	16.0%	9.0%	6.9%
3	11.1%[†]	14.4%	14.6%	12.8%	8.1%	6.4%
4		10.8%[†]	10.4%	10.2%	7.3%	5.9%
5		10.8%	8.7%[†]	8.2%	6.6%	5.5%
6			8.7%	6.6%	5.9%	5.1%
7			8.7%	6.6%[†]	5.9%[†]	4.7%
8				6.6%	5.9%	4.5%[†]
9				6.6%	5.9%	4.5%
10				6.6%	5.9%	4.5%
11					5.9%	4.5%
12					5.9%	4.5%
13					5.9%	4.5%
14					5.9%	4.5%
15					5.9%	4.5%
16						4.5%
17						4.5%
18						4.5%
19						4.5%
20						4.5%
Total	100.0%	100.0%	100.0%	100.0%	100.0%	100.0%

EXHIBIT 11–7
ACRS Cost recovery percentages by property class

*Annual rate for 200% DB = (100% ÷ life) × 2
Annual rate for 150% DB = (100% ÷ life) × 1.5
[†]Conversion to straight-line method.

age,'' assets are placed in service in the middle of the year. To simplify the computations in this chapter we will assume a full year of depreciation in the year of acquisition.

ILLUSTRATION OF THE IMPACT OF INCOME TAXES ON LONG-RANGE DECISIONS

The illustration of the net-present-value method in Exhibit 11–2 ignored income taxes. Before considering the impact of income taxes a positive net present value of $420 was calculated and acceptance of the project was recommended. What impact will income taxes have on the decision? Exhibit 11–8 presents the same investment proposal but includes an income tax rate of 40% and ACRS declining-balance depreciation.

After considering income taxes, in Exhibit 11–8, the investment project now shows a negative net present value and should be rejected. From a positive net present value of $420 in Exhibit 11–2, the net present value drops in Exhibit 11–8 to a negative $358 using double-declining-balance depreciation, and a negative $572 using straight-line depreciation. Compare the net present values produced by the different depreciation methods. By taking a larger amount of depreciation in the early years with double-declining-balance depreciation, and thereby postponing income taxes, the net present value is $214 ($572 − $358) higher than with straight-line depreciation. Any advancement of cash inflows or postponment of cash outflows will increase the net present value of the investment proposal.

In Year 1, assuming the firm uses double-declining-balance depreciation, there is a loss of $3,011 ($5,000 − $8,011). If the firm has income, in addition to this investment, the loss in Year 1 will shield that income from taxes. If the firm has no additional income then a carryback may be possible. Depending on the tax law, the firm's previous tax rates, and the firm's prior years' net incomes, it is possible that such a ''carryback'' would generate a tax refund. If all of the conditions were in place, the firm would receive a refund of $1,204 ($3,011 × 40%). The determination of the after-tax cash flows in Exhibit 11–8 makes the assumption of income from other sources or a refund (as do most present-value calculations). This refund of $1,204 plus the cash inflows from savings of $5,000 totals the $6,204 shown as the total annual cash flows in Year 1.

To examine tax consequences in a different setting let's assume that the Wilson Company is for sale. It is estimated that the Wilson Company will have a $3 million operating loss for the year. Two companies, the Collin Company and the Davies Company, are considering purchasing the Wilson Company because of the tax benefits of the $3 million operating loss. The Collin Company estimates it will have an operating profit of $500,000. The Davies Company predicts an operating profit of $3 million. If the Collin Company purchases the Wilson Company, it may be able to take advantage of only $500,000 of the tax shield. Using a 40% tax rate this represents a cash inflow

Investment project: Original investment $12,010, cash operating savings $5,000 per year, Project life 3 years. Desired rate of return 10%. Income tax rate 40%. Double-declining balance depreciation.

	Tax Effect	Cash Flow Time Line				Present Value Factor	Present Value
		Year					
		0	1	2	3		
Before-tax cash flows:							
Cash outflow:							
Initial investment		($12,010)					
Cash inflows:							
Annual savings			$5,000	$5,000	$5,000		
Depreciation (no cash flow)							
(200% declining balance)							
Year 1 (66.7%)			$8,011*				
Year 2 (22.2%)				$2,666			
Year 3 (11.1%)					$1,333		
Straight-line							
(33.3% per year)			$4,004	$4,003	$4,003		
Net present value—after taxes:							
(200% declining balance)							
Cash outflows:							
Initial investment	0%	($12,010)				1.000	($12,010)
Cash inflows:							
Annual savings	60%		$3,000†	$3,000	$3,000		
Depreciation	40%		3,204‡	1,066	533		
Total annual cash flows:							
Year 1			$6,204			0.909	5,640
Year 2				$4,066		0.826	3,359
Year 3					$3,533	0.751	2,653
Net present value							($ 358)
Net present value—after taxes:							
(Straight-line depreciation)							
Cash outflows:							
Initial investment	0%	($12,010)				1.000	($12,010)
Cash inflows:							
Annual savings	60%		$3,000	$3,000	$3,000	2.486	7,458
Depreciation	40%		$1,602§	$1,601	$1,601	2.486	3,980
Net present value							($ 572)

*$12,010 × 66.7%
†$5,000 × 60%
‡$8,011 × 40%
§$4,004 × 40%

EXHIBIT 11—8   Illustration of net present value—after taxes

of $200,000 ($500,000 × 40%) in the first year. The balance of the benefits will have to be postponed until later years. The Davies Company, however, will be able to take full advantage of the loss in the year of purchase. Again, using a 40% tax rate, this represents a $1,200,000 cash inflow ($3,000,000 × 40%) in the year of purchase.

The above example is a simplistic explanation of a very complex tax situation. There are many issues such as tax carrybacks and the source of the $3 million loss for the Wilson Company, which may affect the estimations of cash flows. This does illustrate, however, how strong an influence the tax law can have on investment decisions.

RISK AND UNCERTAINTY

The decision maker rarely can project all cash flows with certainty. Actual cash flows seldom occur exactly as projected. To the extent that one lacks information to determine the probability of alternative outcomes, the decision maker faces **uncertainty,** which increases the riskiness of any decision. A lack of information may be brought into manageable proportions by a search for more complete data or by avoiding the alternatives that carry the possibility of large losses.

The search for better information becomes a question of information economics. Information has a cost. Additional data should be sought only to the point where their benefits exceed the cost of obtaining them. Each long-range decision is unique. With the exception of a few recurring long-range decisions, there may be very little relevant information in the accounting data bank. Data must be drawn from sources outside the company, often at a high cost.

Increased **risk** may result from conditions over which the firm has no control. For example, a local service firm that contracts with a professional sports team to provide souvenirs and novelties faces the risk that the team may move. The novelty firm has no control over whether the owners will choose to move the team. Even if the team stays, management will be uncertain about how many T-shirts, baseball caps, or other novelties will be sold.

Three methods of adjusting for risk are commonly used in practice.

1. Requirement of a higher-than-normal rate of return.
2. Requirement of a shorter-than-normal payback period, the period needed to recover the original cost (payback period is described later in this chapter).
3. Adjustment of estimated cash flows by use of probability estimates.

The first method involves the use of a higher desired rate of return for more risky projects. To illustrate, let's assume three classes of risk: high, moderate, and low. By applying higher required rates of return to the moderate- and high-risk classes, the investment decision process places less weight on distant cash inflows as the degree of risk increases. For example, a firm may require a 10% rate of return for low-risk projects, an 18% rate for moderate-risk projects, and a 24% rate for high-risk projects. Therefore, a high-risk project would necessitate larger cash inflows earlier in the life of the investment to meet the required rate of return.

The second method of compensating for risk is to consider only the cash inflows in the early life of the project. Commonly, the short payback period, which is the time in years necessary for the cash inflows to repay the original investment, is used in combination with the net-present-value method. The net-present-value method determines whether an investment will earn at least a desired rate of return; the payback period places a limit on acceptable risk. For example, the novelty firm may be reasonably certain that the professional sports team will remain for two years; it would take at least that long to negotiate and accomplish a move. The firm may choose to accept investment projects with a net present value at the desired rate of return and a maximum payback of two years.

In the third method, the consideration of risk and uncertainty involves estimating the probabilities of different cash flows. One way is to make three estimates of future cash flows for each investment opportunity: an optimistic estimate, a most likely estimate, and a pessimistic estimate. By assigning subjective probabilities to each of these predictions, the decision maker can decide whether the risk of loss is too great to accept the investment, regardless of the most probable favorable return.

For example, assume that the decision maker expects an optimistic outcome 2 out of 10 times and therefore assigns a probability of .2 to the optimistic cash flow projections. The most likely projections are expected to occur 5 out of 10 times and a probability of .5 is assigned to the most likely cash flow projections. Finally, the pessimistic outcome is expected to occur 3 times out of 10 and a probability of .3 is assigned to the pessimistic projections. Let's assume that the following after-tax cash flows were projected:

	Optimistic	Most Likely	Pessimistic
First year	$ 1,200	$1,200	$1,200
Second year	$ 9,500	$7,000	$2,000
Third year	$13,500	$6,000	$1,000

The cash projections to be used in investment analysis would be computed as follows:

First year ($1,200 × .2) + ($1,200 × .5) + ($1,200 × .3) = $1,200
Second year ($9,500 × .2) + ($7,000 × .5) + ($2,000 × .3) = $6,000
Third year ($13,500 × .2) + ($6,000 × .5) + ($1,000 × .3) = $6,000

By assigning subjective probabilities to the estimates, we have a good picture of the risk facing the company in this investment. Are the probable cash flows worth the risk of a 30% chance that the investment will lose money? Management would pay considerable attention to this question if such a loss would cause the company to fail.

THE IMPACT OF INFLATION ON LONG-RANGE DECISIONS

Most of our decision models were developed during periods of relatively low inflation. In projecting cash flows for an investment there is a tendency to project the first year's or the average year's cash flows and use this amount as the cash flow for each year of the project's life. In a period of high inflation this will seriously understate future cash flows. Most firms still ignore inflation or have difficulty in adjusting their decision models to cope with inflation.

The process of adjustment for inflation can be relatively simple. In predicting each cash flow, the inflationary trend should be included. If a particular revenue or expense item is expected to move at about the rate of inflation in the economy, projected rates of change in a general price level index will be appropriate. Where other revenue or expense items are expected to move at a level above or below the general level of inflation, a higher or lower adjustment should be used. Some costs, such as depreciation (important because of its impact on taxes) and fixed costs established by long-term contracts may not be subject to price level changes.

In the discussion on the measurement of the rate of return, we concluded that the discount rate used for long-range decisions should be based on the weighted-average cost of capital. The cost of capital for a firm will reflect the market rate used by investors. This rate has three components: a return for the use of money similar to rent (the real interest rate), a component for the degree of risk in the firm, and a component for expected inflation. Therefore, as long as the desired rate of return reflects the market rate used by investors, no adjustment in the discount rate is necessary.

While the discount rate need not be adjusted, it is necessary to consider the inflation rate in the cash inflow and cash outflow predictions. As an illustration, assume that the Ross Company is considering an investment with the following projection of revenues and costs.

	Production at Current Price Levels	Inflationary Expectations
Investment (3-year life)	$6,000	
Annual revenue	$5,000	10% inflation
Annual material expenses	$1,000	15% inflation
Annual other variable expenses	$1,000	12% inflation
Tax rate 40%		
Discount rate 14%		

	Cash Flow	Present Value (14%)
Investment	$(6,000)	× 1,000 = $(6,000)
Annual cash flows:		
Revenue	$ 5,000	
Materials	(1,000)	
Other variable costs	(1,000)	
Taxes	(400)*	
Net annual cash inflows	$ 2,600	× 2.322 = 6,037
Positive net present value		$ 37

*Revenue	$5,000	
Expenses	(2,000)	
Depreciation	(2,000)	(6,000/3)
Net income before taxes	$1,000	
Tax at 40%	$ 400	

EXHIBIT 11–9
Net present value of after-tax cash flows before inflationary adjustment

Before considering the impact of inflation, the investment cost is $6,000, generating annual after-tax cash inflows of $2,600 (assuming straight-line depreciation), which produces a positive net present value of $37. This is shown in Exhibit 11–9.

The inflation adjustments include inflating the revenues by 10%, the

		YEAR			
	0	1	2	3	Present Value
Investment	$(6,000)				× 1.000 = $(6,000)
Revenue		$5,500	$6,050	$6,650	
Material		(1,150)	(1,320)	(1,520)	
Other variable costs		(1,120)	(1,250)	(1,400)	
Taxes*		(492)	(592)	(692)	
Annual cash inflows:					
Year 1		$2,738			× .877 = 2,401
Year 2			$2,888		× .769 = 2,221
Year 3				$3,038	× .675 = 2,051
Positive net present value					$ 673

*Computation of taxes:				
Revenue		$5,500	$6,050	$6,650
Expenses		(2,270)	(2,570)	(2,920)
Depreciation (6,000 ÷ 3)		(2,000)	(2,000)	(2,000)
Net income before taxes		$1,230	$1,480	$1,730
Tax at 40%		$ 492	$ 592	$ 692

EXHIBIT 11–10   Net present value of after-tax cash flows with inflationary adjustments

materials by 15%, and other variable costs by 12%. Because depreciation is based on original cost, no adjustment is required.

Year	REVENUE			MATERIALS			OTHER VARIABLE COSTS		
	Unadjusted	10% Inflation	Adjusted	Unadjusted	15% Inflation	Adjusted	Unadjusted	12% Inflation	Adjusted
1	$5,000	1.10	$5,500	$1,000	1.15	$1,150	$1,000	1.12	$1,120
2	$5,000	1.21	$6,050	$1,000	1.32	$1,320	$1,000	1.25	$1,250
3	$5,000	1.33	$6,650	$1,000	1.52	$1,520	$1,000	1.40	$1,400

Using these adjusted cash flows, the investment still requires a cash outflow of $6,000 but the cash inflows become $2,738 in the first year, $2,888 in the second, and $3,038 in the third, producing a positive net present value of $673. Computation of the net present value is shown in Exhibit 11–10.

CAPITAL RATIONING AND COMPARISONS OF ALTERNATIVES

PROBLEMS OF CAPITAL RATIONING

The techniques of net present value, discounted benefit–cost ratio, and adjusted rate of return are acceptable methods of deciding whether a specific project is economically appropriate. Given the assumptions implicit in the cost of capital, a zero net present value and benefit–cost ratio equal to 1 will maintain the firm's wealth. When there are excess resources in the capital resource pool, the firm should invest in any project that is economically acceptable, as long as the project is consistent with firm goals.

When the resources in the pool are not adequate to invest in all available favorable projects, the decision maker must select a way of ranking the projects. The goal, with capital rationing, is to select those projects that will add the largest value to the firm. To illustrate this problem, let's assume that a firm has five projects that are acceptable. Each of these projects is independent of the other and *not* mutually exclusive. Mutually exclusive means that when one project is accepted, the other is automatically rejected. Data for the five projects are shown below.

Project	Initial Investment	Net Present Value	Benefit–Cost Ratio
A	$20,000	$1,662	1.08
B	$ 9,000	$1,553	1.17
D	$10,000	$ 776	1.08
E	$24,000	$1,125	1.05
F	$ 7,000	$1,300	1.19

If the firm has $70,000 to invest, all five projects are feasible and should be accepted. If the firm has only $10,000 to invest, Project B would return the largest net present value. Project B, with a net present value of $1,553, is preferable to Project F with a net present value of $1,300, even though the benefit–cost ratio for Project F is higher. This is true because Project B consumes more of the $10,000 resource pool than does Project F. Thus, while one dollar of investment in Project F yields a higher benefit–cost ratio than one dollar of investment in Project B, there are not as many dollars of investment in Project F. This, of course, assumes that the opportunity cost of the uninvested resource pool is zero.

Now, let's assume that there is $20,000 in the resource pool. By a trial-and-error method, we can determine that in addition to the individual Projects A, B, D, and F, the following combinations of projects are available:

Projects	Total Investment	Total Net Present Value
B and D	$19,000	$2,329
B and F	$16,000	$2,853
D and F	$17,000	$2,076

The combination of Projects B and F returns the highest combined net present value ($2,853) with the lowest investment ($16,000).

From this example we can see that the net present value is a useful measure in capital rationing situations. If the original investment requirements of each project were identical, we could rank the projects by their individual excess net present value without worrying about possible combinations. Where there is capital rationing, the net present values must be considered in total over the feasible projects. In our illustration, Project A has the highest net present value for any of the five projects; yet with capital rationing situations it will not always be among the accepted proposals.

It should also be noted that under each of the capital rationing illustrations, idle resources remained in the investment pool. Firms would not typically leave these dollars idle or consider their opportunity cost zero. As a minimum, the firm should seek secure, short-term investments such as treasury bills. Idle resources result in lower return on the stockholders' equity, an unfavorable situation.

PROBLEMS OF COMPARISON

Two problems in comparing investment alternatives should be discussed. The first concerns unequal lives; the second, reinvestment of cash as it is recovered. These problems relate only to the methods that use discounted cash flow techniques.

When the productive lives of investment opportunities differ widely, it may be necessary to set a life span common to all investments being considered. One way is to use the shortest life as the time period for analysis. Investment opportunities with longer lives would be treated as if they were terminated early; a salvage value is used to measure the value at termination. A second way assumes replacement of the short-lived assets and uses the longest life as the time period for analysis. For example, a firm is considering which truck to purchase for making deliveries. One truck has a three-year life and the other, six years. Both will provide the necessary service, but the second truck requires a larger initial investment. We may base the investment on a time frame of three years, treating the resale value of the six-year truck as a cash inflow at the end of the first three years. Another method would be to consider the replacement of the three-year truck with another three-year truck, making the lives equal at six years. However, caution should be used. Inflationary conditions should be considered, particularly when using the "longest" investment life alternative.

Inherent in discounted cash flow analysis is the assumption that as cash is recovered from an investment, it will be reinvested at the rate originally planned. In the net-present-value and discounted benefit–cost ratio methods, the assumed rate of reinvestment is the predefined rate of return. Because we will not accept an investment below the predefined rate, this is a reasonable assumption. However, in the adjusted rate-of-return method, when there is capital rationing because of a shortage of funds, it is assumed that cash will be reinvested at the actual rate of return of the project. If a project with a high rate of return returns cash soon and few investment projects are available when the cash is recovered, the project may be less desirable. If the timing of cash flows differs widely among investment projects, the adjusted rate-of-return method may lead to inadequate decisions. The firm may not be able to reinvest at the actual rate achieved by the investment being considered.

TECHNIQUES THAT DO NOT CONSIDER THE TIME VALUE OF MONEY

Discounted cash flow is a relatively recent concept. It is only in the last three decades or so that it has been widely taught in business schools and used extensively in practice. Two techniques of investment analysis are widely used in industry that do not satisfy the long-range decision rule requiring adjustment for the time value of money—the payback period and unadjusted rate-of-return methods. A discussion of these methods follows.

PAYBACK PERIOD

Payback period is a simple technique that asks the question, "How long does it take to recover the initial investment?" Investment opportunities are ranked according to the time, in years, required to recover the initial investment.

Investment project: Original investment $12,010, cash operating savings $5,000 per year. Project life 3 years. Income tax rate 40%.

(Data drawn from Exhibit 11–8)

AFTER-TAX PAYBACK PERIOD:
(Assuming straight-line depreciation)

Initial investment   ($12,010)
Annual cash inflows $ 4,601

Payback period = $12,010 ÷ $4,601 = 2.61 years

AFTER-TAX PAYBACK PERIOD:
(Assuming double-declining-balance depreciation)

		Amount Recovered
Initial investment	($12,010)	
Cash inflows:		
Year 1	$ 6,204	$ 6,204
Year 2	4,066	4,066
Year 3	3,533 Year of recovery	1,740
		$12,010

Payback period = 2 + ($1,740 ÷ $3,533) = 2.49 years

EXHIBIT 11–11
Illustration of payback period

Exhibit 11–11 presents the computation of the payback period for our continuing example. First, where the annual cash inflows are equal, the payback period is determined by dividing the original investment by the annual cash inflows. Using straight-line depreciation for tax computations, the payback period is 2.61 years. Second, when the annual cash inflows are unequal, cash inflows are summed in chronological order until the point is reached when cash inflows equal the original investment. Because the double-declining-balance method of depreciation resulted in larger cash inflows in Year 1, the payback period is shorter, at 2.49 years. To evaluate the decision by the payback method, a decision criterion must be set, such as 2 years.

Although the payback period is very simple to compute, it has serious shortcomings because it does not consider the life or relative profitability beyond the payback period. The two investments shown on page 467 would have the same payback period. Investment Y is clearly the better investment and would be ranked above Investment X by all other techniques of investment analysis.

The payback method is a very conservative technique. In a high-risk situation, for example, where threat of nationalization of foreign investments exists, the benefits of the projected long life of the investment might never be enjoyed. In such cases, an investment with a short payback period and low rate of return may be preferable to an investment with a higher rate of return but a longer payback period. Payback period can serve as a supplement to other methods. For example, one way to compensate for risk is to set a maximum payback period and use this period as a constraint in conjunction with the net-present-value or adjusted rate-of-return methods.

Investment	Initial Investment	Annual Cash Inflow	Productive Life	Payback Period
X	$10,000	$5,000	3 years	2 years
Y	$10,000	$5,000	10 years	2 years

UNADJUSTED OR ACCOUNTING RATE OF RETURN

An **unadjusted or accounting rate of return** (not adjusted for the time value of money) is widely used. It is simple to compute and, because it is consistent with the accounting measurements of income, can be computed from the accounting records. This method divides the average income from the investment as measured by the accounting concept of income, by the initial investment.[2] The income calculation amortizes the initial investment over the life of the project.

Using the data from Exhibit 11–8, the unadjusted rate of return for our continuing example is 4.98%. The computation follows:

Annual income:	
Annual cash savings	$ 5,000
Annual depreciation (straight-line $12,010 ÷ 3 years)	4,003
Annual income before taxes	$ 997
Income taxes (40%)	399
Average annual income after taxes	$ 598
Initial investment	$12,010

Unadjusted rate of return:
Average annual income ÷ initial investment =
$598 ÷ $12,010 = 4.98%.

To evaluate an unadjusted rate of return of 4.98%, management must have established a target rate of return.

With the unadjusted rate-of-return method, a dollar of revenue received or cost paid late in the life of the investment will have the same impact as a

---

[2]The investment figure may be measured in several ways. Two of the most common measures are initial investment and average investment. We have chosen the initial investment for simplicity of calculation.

dollar received or paid initially. This effect can lead to improper decisions. For example, assume the following investment alternatives and ignore income taxes.

	Investment M	Investment N
Initial investment	$10,000	$10,000
Net cash inflows:		
Year 1	$ 7,000	$ 1,000
Year 2	$ 4,000	$ 4,000
Year 3	$ 1,000	$ 7,000
Salvage value	$ 0	$ 0
Net present value (10% rate)	$ 418	$ (530)
Adjusted rate of return	13.2%	7.6%
Payback period	1.75 years	2.71 years
Unadjusted rate of return	6.7%	6.7%

Clearly, Investment M is superior to Investment N, using either the net-present-value or adjusted rate-of-return method. However, both investments have the same unadjusted rate of return. However, as long as accounting rate-of-return performance measures (discussed in Chapter 14) are used, some managers will continue to use accounting rate-of-return measures for long-run decisions.

LONG-RANGE DECISIONS IN THE PUBLIC SECTOR

Many enterprises in the public sector face the same long-range decisions as private enterprise. For example, government-owned utilities and transportation systems face the same long-range decisions as investor-owned utilities and transportation companies. The tremendous growth in economic activity by government and other not-for-profit organizations has led to a search for systematic methods of analyzing public expenditures. Decision making in the public sector has been highly qualitative. Often it has been influenced more by political expediency and funds available than by economic efficiency. Measures of economic efficiency must be used to ensure that decisions are economically sound, as well as politically expedient.

Every decision should have at its core the relationship between benefits and costs of the particular project. In the private sector the primary goal of long-range decisions is the maximization of the wealth of the enterprise. In the public sector the concept is much broader; the goal of **benefit–cost analysis** is to maximize the welfare of society. We are asking, "Will society be better off by engaging in a particular act?" In place of cash inflows to the organization, the public sector is concerned with social benefits. In place of cost, the public sector is concerned with social cost or social value foregone. Given these "reframed" views of benefits and costs, the method of analysis should follow the investment

decision rules in this chapter. There is, however, substantial difficulty in identifying and measuring social benefits and social costs in terms of cash flows.

SUMMARY

The critical factor in any long-range decision is time. The time factor raises two
problems. First, because all resources have a cost, the time value of money
must be reflected when there is a long period of time between investment and
a full realization of the benefits. The practice of discounting all benefits and
costs to their present value is an adjustment for the time value of money.

Second, cash flows provide the relevant measures of costs and benefits
for long-range decisions. Accounting's measurement of net income includes
allocations of cost in order to match cost with revenue. This distorts the decision
information such as cash flows.

The most significant practical problem in long-range decision making is
the development of estimates of future cash flows relevant to each alternative.
One major problem in developing these estimates is income taxes. Also, during
a period of high inflation, failure to adjust future cash flows for changing prices
may seriously understate or overstate the value of an investment.

Five investment analysis techniques were introduced. Only the first
three—net present value, discounted benefit–cost ratio, and adjusted rate-of-
return techniques—consider the time value of money. The net present value and
discounted benefit–cost ratio methods use a predefined rate of return and base
the decision criterion on whether this desired rate of return was achieved. The
adjusted rate-of-return method determines the actual rate of return earned by the
investment. The payback period method measures how long it takes to recover
the initial investment. The unadjusted rate-of-return method computes the return
achieved by dividing the average accounting income from the investment by the
initial investment.

APPENDIX

THE CONCEPT OF PRESENT VALUE

TIME VALUE OF MONEY

Because a dollar in hand today can be invested to earn a return, it has a greater
value than a dollar to be received at any time in the future. For example, $100
invested in a savings account at 6% interest will grow to $106 at the end of one

year and will double in slightly under 12 years if the interest is not withdrawn and allowed to compound. The difference between a dollar invested now and the dollar received at some future time is the **time value of money.** This difference is the rate of return you must receive to be indifferent about receiving a dollar today or waiting until some future point in time to receive the dollar. The person who receives the dollar today will have $1.06 one year from now. The person who receives the dollar one year from now will have only the dollar.

FUTURE AND PRESENT VALUE

Assume that a firm invests $1,000 for a period of three years and that the investment pays a 10% return compounded at the end of each year. Compounding means that interest is left in the account and added to the investment. The growth of the investment is presented in Exhibit A11–1. The value to which $1,000 will grow at the end of the three years at 10% compounded annually is its *future value,* $1,331. If you are satisfied with a 10% rate of return on your investment, you should be indifferent toward receiving $1,000 now, $1,100 one year from now, $1,210 two years from now, or $1,331 three years from now. Each amount is the future value of $1,000. The future value is the amount to which a given investment will grow at the end of a given period of time, compounded at a given annual rate of interest.

In a long-range decision we want to compare a series of cash inflows and a series of cash outflows at different times over the life of the investment to determine whether a satisfactory rate of return is achieved. We could compare the future values of each alternative at some future point in time. However, because the decision is being made now (in the present period), almost everyone states the cash flows in the present value of the investment. Present value is the amount that must be invested now to reach a given amount at a given point of time in the future. Present value is what a given future flow of cash is worth today. This is the amount you should pay for the future stream of cash if you are to earn your desired rate of return. In our illustration, the present value of $1,331 to be received three years from now is $1,000. Accordingly, the present

EXHIBIT A11–1
Future value—$1,000 compounded at 10% annually

Year	Investment at Beginning of Period	Interest at 10% for Period	Investment at End of Period	Formula $I(1 + r)^n$
0 (Now)			$1,000	I
1	$1,000	$100	$1,100	$I(1 + r)$
2	$1,100	$110	$1,210	$I(1 + r)(1 + r)$
3	$1,210	$121	$1,331	$I(1 + r)(1 + r)(1 + r)$

value of $1,210 to be received two years from now is $1,000, and $1,100 to be received a year from now is also $1,000.

DEVELOPMENT OF PRESENT-VALUE FACTORS

To be useful we must develop either a set of present-value factors for $1.00 or an equation that may be applied to any cash flow or stream of cash flows to measure their present value. Such a set of values would allow us to determine the present value of any amount at any future date for any rate of interest.

Continuing the illustration begun in Exhibit A11–1, we may determine the present value of $1.00 by dividing the present value of our $1,000 investment by its future value. This computation in Exhibit A11–2 provides the present value of $1.00 to be received now and at the end of one, two, and three years. We now have the following present-value table.

Period	Present Value Factor (10%)
1	.909
2	.826
3	.751

A similar table could be prepared for any discount rate and any future point in time.

Period	Investment* at End of Period (Future Value) at 10%	Present Value Future Value	General Formula
0 (Now)	$1,000	$\dfrac{\$1,000}{\$1,000} = 1.000$	$\dfrac{I}{I}$
1	$1,100	$\dfrac{\$1,000}{\$1,100} = .909$	$\dfrac{I}{I(1 + r)}$
2	$1,210	$\dfrac{\$1,000}{\$1,210} = .826$	$\dfrac{I}{I(1 + r)^2}$
3	$1,331	$\dfrac{\$1,000}{\$1,331} = .751$	$\dfrac{I}{I(1 + r)^3}$

*Developed in Exhibit A11-1.

EXHIBIT A11–2
Development of present-value factors

COMPUTATION OF PRESENT VALUE

To apply these present-value factors, let us assume that we have the choice of receiving $6,000 over a period of three years in one of the following two streams.

Received at End of Year	Cash Flow Stream A	Cash Flow Stream B
1	$2,000	$3,000
2	$2,000	$2,000
3	$2,000	$1,000

Which stream of cash flows is best? We should accept the çash flow stream with the highest present value. Assume that we are satisfied to earn 10% on our investment.

PRESENT VALUE OF CASH FLOW STREAM A (10%)				PRESENT VALUE OF CASH FLOW STREAM B (10%)			
Year	Cash Flow	× Present-Value Factor	= Present Value	Year	Cash Flow	× Present-Value Factor	= Present Value
1	$2,000	.909	$1,818	1	$3,000	.909	$2,727
2	$2,000	.826	1,652	2	$2,000	.826	1,652
3	$2,000	.751	1,502	3	$1,000	.751	751
			$4,972				$5,130

Clearly, cash flow stream B has a higher present value, $5,130, compared with the present value $4,972, for cash flow stream A.

If you are satisfied to earn 10% on your investment, you should be willing to pay $5,130 for stream B of cash flows but only $4,972 for stream A. This is the key point in long-range decisions. The value of any investment to the firm is its present value. Let us demonstrate that a payment of $4,792 for stream A will allow us to earn 10% on our investment *and* recover our original investment.

Year	Investment at Beginning of Year	Cash Received at End of Year	PART OF CASH RECEIPT		Investment at End of Year
			10% Income	Recovery of Principal	
1	$4,972	$2,000	$ 497	$1,503	$3,469
2	$3,469	2,000	347	1,653	$1,816
3	$1,816	2,000	182	1,818	$ (2)*
		$6,000	$1,026	$4,974*	

*Rounding error of $2.00.

Allowing for a rounding error of $2.00, by investing $4,972 and receiving $2,000 each year, we will earn exactly 10% on our investment and recover the entire investment.

COMPUTATION OF PRESENT VALUE OF AN ANNUITY

Refer again to the computation of the present value of stream A. Each present-value factor was multiplied by $2,000. We could have summed the present-value factors (.909 + .826 + .751) and multiplied the sum times $2,000. A stream of equal payments at equal intervals of time is called an **annuity.** We may simplify the calculation of the present value of an annuity by developing a set of present-value factors for the present value of an annuity of $1.00. This may be done simply by cumulating the present-value factors in our present-value-of-$1.00 table (Appendix A, end of book).

Year	Present Value of $1.00	Present Value of an Annuity of $1.00
1	.909	.909
2	.826	1.735 (.909 + .826)
3	.751	2.486 (.909 + .826 + .751)

The present value of an annuity of $2,000 for three years is $4,972 ($2,000 × 2.486), the same present value we computed earlier.

USE OF PRESENT-VALUE TABLES

More complete present-value tables (and the equations underlying them) are presented in Appendixes A and B at the end of the book. If a given interest rate is not presented in the table, interpolation between two present-value factors can be made. Interpolation involves the estimation of a present-value factor for a rate or time period between two factors in the table. For example, what is the present-value factor applicable to a sum to be received three years from now with interest computed at 9%? The table in Appendix A shows present-value factors for 8% in three years (.794) and 10% in three years (.751) but does not include the factor for 9%. You want a factor that is approximately halfway between .751 and .794. The amount may be computed as [.751 + (½ × (.794 − .751))], or .7725. This amount differs slightly from the amount calculated by the formula, .7722, because the present-value formula is not linear. However, for most purposes, interpolation is sufficiently accurate.

PROBLEMS AND CASES

11-1 *(Use of Present-Value Tables).* Determine the present value of each of the following cash flows. (Ignore income taxes.)

A. $1,000 to be received at the end of 5 years at 16%.

B. $4,000 to be received at the end of each year for 6 years at 12%.

C. $10,000 to be received at the end of 20 years at 20%.

D. $5,280 to be received at the end of each year for 7 years at 8%.

E. $3,000 to be received at the end of each year beginning in Year 3 and ending in Year 6 at 10%.

11-2 *(Determine Original Investment from Cash Flows).* Gratias Company acquired an asset with a three-year life for $15,000 that produced the following cost savings:

Year	Cash Savings
1	$8,000
2	$6,000
3	$4,000

Ignore income taxes.

REQUIRED:

A. Assuming a desired rate of return of 12%, what is the net present value of the investment?

B. If the investment project achieved a net present value of $800 with a desired rate of return of 12%, what was the amount of the original investment?

11-3 *(Choice of Cash Flows).* You have just won the state lottery. You are offered the choice of receiving $373,450 today or $50,000 per year for the next 20 years. (Ignore income taxes.)

A. Without using present-value tables, what is your intuitive feeling of which alternative you should accept?

B. Assuming you are satisfied with a 10% return on investment, which alternative should you accept?

C. What rate of return did the state use in setting up the choices?

11-4 *(Present Value—Cash Flows).* Consider each of the following cases independently.

A. Hiram Able is about ready to retire. He may take his retirement pay in a single payment of $200,000 or an annuity of $17,436.79 for 20 years. What rate of interest is the pension plan earning during the 20 years?

B. Your aunt has promised to give you a new car when you graduate in three years. The car will cost $8,000. How much must your aunt place in her credit union now, if it earns 6% compounded annually, to pay for the car in three years?

C. On your return to your alma mater for the 20-year reunion of your graduation class, you and several members of your class who have been unusually successful decide to contribute an accounting chair that will provide $20,000 per year for 20 years. With pledges from other members of your class, you go to the trust department of your bank to create a trust that will fund the chair. The bank's trust officer will guarantee an 8% return on the trust. Payments will be made at the end of each of the next 20 years. You may assume that there will be no taxes on the trust or the donors. How much must you and your classmates deposit with your banker to provide for the chair?

11-5 *(Complete the Blanks, Net Present Value).* Determine the amount for each blank.

	A	B	C	D
Original investment	$10,000	$12,000	$20,000	_____
Annual cash inflows (end of year)	$ 2,000	$ 4,000	_____	$3,000
Life of investment	5 years	6 years	10 years	3 years
Desired rate of return	10%	_____	6%	20%
Net present value	_____	$ 4,444	$ 0	$3,000

11-6 *(Payback and the Accounting Rate of Return).* The Copy Cat Company operates eight "storefront" branches where they provide speedy photocopy and blueprint reproductions. Top management is now considering opening a ninth branch. They estimate the branch will have the following revenue and expense patterns:

Revenue per year		$35,000
Rent ($600 per month)		$ 7,200
Operating supplies/maintenance		$ 7,000
Salaries		$12,000
Depreciation:		
Photocopy machine cost	$19,200	
Estimated life	4 years	$ 4,800

REQUIRED:

A. Determine the unadjusted (accounting) rate of return.

B. Determine the payback period.

11-7 *(Present Value of After-Tax Cash Flows)*. Determine the present value of the after-tax cash flows for each of the following situations. The tax rate is 40%. (Show a cash outflow in parentheses.)

A. $6,000 from sale of an asset with a book value of $6,000 at the end of its five-year life, assuming a 12% rate of return.

B. $4,000 payment for maintenance at the end of each of the next four years, assuming an 8% rate of return.

C. Recovery of $10,000 of working capital at the end of a seven-year project, assuming a 16% rate of return.

D. Second-year depreciation for a five-year asset (ACRS), costing $100,000, assuming a 10% rate of return.

E. Cost savings of $3,000 at the beginning of Years 2 through 6, assuming a 14% rate of return.

11-8 *(Before- and After-tax Present Values)*.

A. Compute the net present value of each of the following investments and indicate which should be accepted. Assume a 12% cost of capital and no shortage of funds. (Ignore taxes.)

| | Initial | Cash Inflows by Year | | |
Investment	Investment	1	2	3
F	$15,000	$9,000	$9,000	$2,000
G	$ 9,000	$3,750	$3,750	$3,750
H	$ 6,750	$4,500	$ 0	$4,500

B. Assuming a 30% tax rate and straight-line depreciation, compute the net present value of the investments and indicate which should be accepted. What was the impact of income taxes on your decision?

11-9 *(Present Value, Unadjusted Rate of Return, and Inflation)*. The Black Ink Company is considering a project that requires an investment of $4,275 and produces the following cash inflows.

Year	Cash Flow
1	$1,000
2	$2,000
3	$3,000

Ignore income taxes, assume a 12% required rate of return, and assume no salvage value.

REQUIRED:

A. Compute the net present value of the investment.

B. What is the approximate adjusted rate of return on the investment?

C. What is the approximate unadjusted rate of return on this investment assuming a three year life and straight-line depreciation?

D. Compute the net present value of this investment assuming the cash flows in part A must be adjusted for inflation of 6% compounded annually. Assume the 12% rate of return includes an appropriate inflation factor.

11-10 *(Present Value of Additional Income).* Julie received an MBA from Stamvard University and accepted a position in the controller's department at Special Foods. She was pleased to find Sam, an undergraduate classmate from State U, who had accepted a position with Special Foods immediately upon graduation.

In comparing financial positions, Julie's starting salary was equal to Sam's salary, even though he had been with the company for two years. During the two years Sam had saved $10,000 including the increased equity in the home he had purchased when he started to work for Special Foods. Julie, on the other hand, was $10,000 in debt. Sam indicated that although they were in approximately equal positions in the company (in terms of income), he had avoided the $20,000 investment that Julie had made to graduate from Stamvard. Julie countered that her MBA should provide her with an annuity in the form of added income that should be worth more than the $20,000 investment. She estimated her salary would average about $4,000 per year more than Sam's and she expected to work for the company at least 25 years.

REQUIRED:

A. Assuming that Julie has a desired rate of return of 14%, what is the average minimum additional income she would have to earn to be financially equal to Sam?

B. Assume that Julie's income will exceed Sam's income by the following amounts:

> Next 5 years   —$0 per year
> Following 10 years—$2,000 per year
> Following 10 years—$8,000

How does the value of Julie's annuity compare with Sam's investment? Explain.

11-11 *(Five Approaches to Capital Investment Project).* Hazman Company plans to replace an old piece of equipment that is obsolete and is expected to be unreliable under the stress of daily operations. The equipment is fully depreciated, and no salvage value can be realized upon its disposal.

One piece of equipment being considered would provide annual cash savings of $7,000 before income taxes. The equipment would cost $18,000 and have an estimated useful life of five years with no salvage value.

Hazman uses the straight-line depreciation method on all equipment for both book and tax purposes. The company is subject to a 40% tax rate. Hazman has an after-tax cost of capital of 14%.

REQUIRED:

A. Calculate for Hazman Company's proposed investment in new equipment the after-tax

1. Payback period.

2. Accounting rate of return.

3. Net present value.

4. Profitability (present value) index.

5. Internal rate of return.

Assume all operating revenues and expenses occur at the end of the year.

B. Identify and discuss the issues Hazman Company should consider when deciding which of the five decision models identified in part A it should employ to compare and evaluate alternative capital investment projects.

C. What would be the effect on the net present value of using ACRS depreciation assuming a five-year asset class?

(CMA adapted)

11-12 *(Capital Rationing).* The Scrooge Company has budgeted $100,000 for capital expenditures in 19X1. The following investment proposals have been submitted to the investment committee for approval.

Proposal	Original Investment	Life of Project	Payback Period	Adjusted Rate of Return
A	$30,000	3	2	20%
B	$10,000	6	3	12%
C	$50,000	8	5	13%
D	$20,000	2	1	25%
E	$20,000	5	4	8%
F	$10,000	4	3	16%
G	$30,000	10	5	14%

The company's cost of capital is 10%.

REQUIRED:

Which proposals should be accepted? Explain. Discuss the impact of risk and these investments.

11-13 *(Fill in the Blanks: Net Present Value and Adjusted Rate of Return).* Complete the blanks in the following table. (Ignore income taxes.)

	A	B	C	D
Initial investment	$14,420	____	$10,000	$4,644
Annual cash inflow (end of year)	____	$2,981	____	$2,000
Life of investment	5 years	10 years	6 years	____
Desired rate of return	____	12%	6%	____
Net present value	$ 744	____	$ 2,642	($432)
Adjusted rate of return	12%	8%	____	14%

11-14 *(Purchase Versus Lease).* Valley Clinic has always leased its equipment from the manufacturer. A new piece of X-ray equipment was ordered before the new administrator was hired. When asked to sign the lease contract, she questioned the terms of the lease and asked for purchase terms. The equipment manufacturer provided the following comparative data.

	Purchase	*Lease*
Life of equipment	5 years	5 years
Original cost	$48,000	—
Annual maintenance, insurance, property taxes	$ 3,000	
Repairs in second year	$ 5,000	
Annual rental		$32,275
Salvage value	$10,000	

The clinic uses straight-line depreciation assuming no salvage value, a 14% required rate of return, and is subject to a tax rate of 40%.

REQUIRED:

A. Evaluate the contract for the administrator and prepare a recommendation, supported by proper analysis, as to whether she should purchase or lease the equipment.

B. What would be the impact on your decision if ACRS depreciation with a five-year asset class is used?

11-15 *(Purchase Versus Leasing).* The Downtown Data Corporation sells computer services to its clients. As a part of a feasibility study to acquire a new computer, the company developed the following data.

1. The purchase price of the computer is $130,000. Maintenance, property taxes, and insurance will be $20,000 per year. Because of technology changes and expected growth of the service, the company expects to replace the computer at the end of five years. The resale value at that time will be about $10,000. The company will use ACRS depreciation.

2. The equipment supplier will rent the same equipment to Downtown Data for $52,180 per year plus 10% of the annual billings from the use of the equipment. The rental price includes maintenance.

3. The estimated billings for the service bureau will be $100,000 the first year, $200,000 the second year, and $300,000 thereafter.

4. Annual operating costs whether leased or purchased will be $60,000 with a programming and start-up cost of $20,000 in the first year.

5. The income tax rate is 30%.

6. The company expects a rate of return of 16% on long-range investments.

REQUIRED:

Determine whether the equipment should be acquired and, if so, whether it should be purchased or rented.

11-16 *(Present-Value Analysis of Pollution Control Equipment)*. The Hillsdale Smelter is required to reduce the level of pollutants it discharges into the air. Emission control must take place in two stages, with the first stage requiring a 50% reduction of pollutants for the next five years. Equipment that will meet stage 1 standards is available at a cost of $399,000. This equipment will have a salvage value of approximately $24,000 when replaced by stage 2 equipment at the end of five years. During the first stage, recovered materials may be sold at a contribution margin of $100,000 per year.

The company pays taxes at a 40% rate and expects to take advantage of the tax incentive of ACRS depreciation.

The company's weighted-average cost of capital is 12%. This rate is used as the desired rate of return for projects of moderate risk. The City of Hillsdale is concerned that the company may close the smelter. The city council wants to provide some incentive to make the investment economically feasible.

REQUIRED:

Prepare an analysis of this project. What kind of incentive, if one is needed, would you recommend to the Hillsdale City Council?

11-17 *(Long-Range Decisions for Hospital)*. The board of trustees of Rose General Hospital, a not-for-profit hospital, is considering replacement of certain X-ray equipment. Although the old equipment would function for several years, the new equipment will reduce operating costs by $8,000 per year. The new equipment will cost $52,000 and have a 10-year life with no salvage value. The administrator believes that the salvage value of the present equipment will just cover the cost of removal.

The hospital has operated at a small loss for several years with approximately two-thirds of the new facilities financed through issuance of long-term debt and one-third through grants and contributions. Because of the 9% interest rate on the long-term debt, the administration has set a desired rate of return of 10%.

REQUIRED:

A. Should the hospital acquire the new X-ray equipment? Explain.

B. A new clinic, organized to provide limited care to the residents of a low-income neighborhood, has offered to purchase the old X-ray equipment for $3,000. How does this affect your decision in part A?

C. Assume that it is now three years since the new X-ray equipment was acquired, and a much superior X-ray unit has become available that is smaller and much more efficient. The new equipment will cost $70,000 and will reduce the annual costs by $15,000. Its useful life will be seven years with no salvage value. Because of the advanced technology, the old X-ray equipment has no salvage value. Should the new equipment be acquired? When the proposal was presented to the hospital board, one member of the board thinks it is a mistake to replace good equipment "every three years." He wants to know why the mistake was made and to be sure that the hospital administrator will not make the same mistake again. How would you answer this board member?

11-18 *(Cash Flows and Present Value in a Sports Team Setting).*

Part A

You are preparing an analysis for a group of investors who wish to purchase a professional football team. Two franchises are available: (1) a franchise in the United States Football League, a strong and profitable league, for $20 million and (2) a franchise in the new International Football League for $2 million. The investors have raised the entire $20 million. If the franchise in the IFL is purchased, the money saved can be utilized to pay bonuses over the next five years to attract stars from the USFL. If this course of action is followed, it is believed that the two leagues would be equal in quality and value by the end of the fifth year. Assume that the funds may be invested at 12% until needed for the bonuses.

REQUIRED:

If the bonuses are paid in equal amounts at the end of each of the next five years, what is the maximum annual bonus that may be paid to recruit USFL players? Ignore taxes.

Part B

The Leadville Leadfoots, a professional football team that has been in last place for several years, plans to build a team that will be in the playoffs in three years. The team has drafted a Heisman Trophy winner, Steamroller Jones, and is about to begin contract negotiations. The team will play 18 games during the season.

Attendance has been very poor for the past several years. If Steamroller joins the team, ticket sales should increase by at least 20,000 tickets per game. The manager believes that Steamroller will have an impact upon ticket sales for 10 years or less. A study of cost-volume-revenue relationships shows that the contribution margin's effect on cash flow for each additional ticket sold is $8.00.

REQUIRED:

A. Prepare a projection of incremental cash flows that should result if Steamroller signs with the Leadfoots.

B. Assuming a 14% rate of return for all investments, what is the value of Steamroller to the team if he plays for 10 years?

11-19 *(Net Present Value, Payback, and Risk).* Worldwide Exploration has the option of selecting only one of three projects available to them. Each of the three projects cost an "up-front" fee of $90,000 for core-drilling rights and extraction rights fees. However, the projects differ in their projected net positive cash flows (revenues less expenses). The projected positive cash flows are

	Project A	Project B	Project C
Year 1	$30,000	$50,000	$20,000
Year 2	$30,000	$40,000	$30,000
Year 3	$30,000	$30,000	$40,000
Year 4	$30,000	$20,000	$50,000
Year 5	$30,000	$10,000	$30,000

Each of these projects also differ in their riskiness:

Project A is located in the U.S. National Forest reserve. The typical U.S. Bureau of Interior contract is a fixed term contract for five years or more.

Project B is located on government land in a friendly South American country, although there have been massive street riots recently demanding the leadership institute land reform policies.

Project C is located on private land in northern Canada. The owner of the land is willing to sign a two-year lease at this time with an option for a three-year renewal. The renewal option is dependent on the passage of a "homestead" tax exclusion by the Canadian Parliament.

REQUIRED:

A. Compute the excess net present value of each project. Given this information, which project would you choose? Why?

B. Compute the payback period for each project. Using only the payback period, which project would you choose? Why?

C. Given the firm's expectations of risk, net present value, and payback period, which project would you choose? Why?

11-20 *(Impact of Shopping Center on Municipality).* The town of Bath, located near an urban area, has been asked to grant a permit for a new shopping center. As the only member of the town council with a knowledge of capital budgeting, you have been asked to develop an analysis of the economic impact on the resources of the town.

Your investigation revealed the following direct benefits and costs to the town over a 20-year period.

A. Incremental Direct Benefits

1. Sales tax on construction: $20,000 per year for first four years.

2. Sales tax from shopping center sales: $100,000 per year beginning in Year 5.

3. Increase in property taxes: $200,000 per year beginning in Year 5.

4. Business licenses and permits: $20,000 per year beginning in Year 4.

5. Added taxes to the city from new residents attracted because of the shopping center: $30,000 per year beginning in Year 5.

B. Incremental Direct Costs

1. Added police protection: $40,000 per year beginning in Year 1 with an additional $40,000 per year beginning in Year 4.

2. Added street maintenance: $30,000 per year beginning in Year 1.

3. Fire protection: $20,000 per year beginning in Year 1.

4. Other city government: $30,000 per year beginning in Year 1.

REQUIRED:

A. Assuming a 6% cost of capital, compute the discounted benefit–cost ratio for this decision. On the basis of this criterion, should the town council approve the permit?

B. Assume that opponents of the shopping center are arguing that 6% is too low and that the appropriate discount rate is 12%. Recompute the discounted benefit–cost ratio using 12%. How does the higher rate affect your recommendation in part *A*?

C. Discuss the measures of social costs and social benefits requested by the town council. Explain any changes you would like to see.

11-21 *(Machine Replacement Decision).* The WRL Company makes cookies for its chain of snack food stores. WRL Company purchased a special cookie cutting machine; this machine has been utilized for three years. WRL Company is considering the purchase of a newer, more efficient machine. If purchased, the new machine would be acquired on January 2, 19X1. WRL Company expects to sell 300,000 dozen cookies in each of the next four years. The selling price of the cookies is expected to average $.50 per dozen.

WRL Company has two options: (1) continue to operate the old machine, or (2) sell the old machine and purchase the new machine. No trade-in was offered by the seller of the new machine.

	Old Machine	New Machine
Original cost of machine at acquisition	$80,000	$120,000
Salvage value at the end of useful life for depreciation purposes	$10,000	$ 20,000
Useful life from date of acquisition	7 years	3 years
Expected annual cash operating expenses:		
Variable cost per dozen	$.20	$.14
Total fixed costs	$15,000	$ 14,000
Depreciation method used for tax purposes:	Straight-line	ACRS 200% double-declining-balance depreciation
Estimated cash value of machines:		
January 2, 19X1	$40,000	$120,000
December 31, 19X4	$ 7,000	$ 20,000

WRL Company is subject to an overall income tax rate of 40%. Assume that all operating revenues and expenses occur at the end of the year. Assume that any gain or loss on the sale of machinery is treated as an ordinary tax item and will affect the taxes paid by WRL Company at the end of the year in which it occurred.

WRL Company requires an after-tax return of 16% on capital projects.

REQUIRED:

A. Use the net-present-value method to determine whether WRL Company should retain the old machine or acquire the new machine.

B. Instead of your answer to part A, assume that the quantitative differences are so slight between the two alternatives that WRL Company is indifferent to the two proposals. Identify and discuss the nonquantitative factors that are important to this decision that WRL Company should consider.

(CMA adapted)

11-22 *(Net-Present-Value Analysis with Inflation Adjustment).* Catix Corporation is a divisionalized company, and each division has the authority to make capital expenditures up to $200,000 without approval of the corporate headquarters. The corporate controller has determined that the cost of capital for Catix Corporation is 12%. This rate does not include an allowance for inflation, which is expected to occur at an average rate of 8% over the next five years. Catix pays income taxes at the rate of 40%.

The Electronics Division of Catix is considering the purchase of an automated assembly and soldering machine for use in the manufacture of its printed circuit boards. The machine would be placed in service in early 19X1. The divisional controller estimates that if the machine is purchased, two positions will be eliminated yielding a cost savings for wages and employee benefits. However, the machine would require additional supplies, and more power would be required to operate the machine. The cost savings and additional costs in current 19X0 prices are as follows:

Wages and employee benefits of the two positions eliminated ($25,000 each)	$50,000
Cost of additional supplies	$ 3,000
Cost of additional power	$10,000

The new machine would be purchased and installed at the end of 19X0 at a net cost of $80,000. If purchased, the machine would be depreciated on a straight-line basis for both book and tax purposes. The machine will become technologically obsolete in four years and will have no salvage value at that time.

The Electronics Division compensates for inflation in capital expenditure analyses by adjusting the expected cash flows by an estimated price level index. The adjusted after-tax cash flows are then discounted using the appropriate discount rate. The estimated year-end index values for each of the next five years are presented below.

Year	Year-End Price Index
19X0	1.00
19X1	1.08
19X2	1.17
19X3	1.26
19X4	1.36
19X5	1.47

The Plastics Division of Catix compensates for inflation in capital expenditure analysis by adding the anticipated inflation rate to the cost of capital and then using the inflation adjusted cost of capital to discount the project cash flows. The Plastics Division recently rejected a project with cash flows and economic life similar to those associated with the machine under consideration by the Electronics Division. The Plastics Division's analysis of the rejected project was as follows:

Net pretax cost savings	$37,000
Less incremental depreciation expenses	20,000
Increase in taxable income	$17,000
Increase in income taxes (40%)	6,800
Increase in after-tax income	$10,200
Add back noncash expense (depreciation)	20,000
Net after-tax annual cash inflow (unadjusted for inflation)	$30,200
Present value of net cash inflows using the sum of the cost of capital (12%) and the inflation rate (8%) or a minimum required return of 20%	$77,916
Investment required	(80,000)
Net present value	$ (2,084)

All operating revenues and expenditures occur at the end of the year.

REQUIRED:

A. Prepare an analysis of the automated assembly and soldering machine for the Electronics Division. Explain any necessary assumptions.

B. Evaluate and contrast the methods used by the Plastics Division and the Electronics Division to consider inflation adjustments in their long-range decisions.

C. What recommendations can you make to the management of the two divisions concerning inflation adjustments?

(CMA adapted)

11-23 *(Present-Value Analysis—Make or Buy).* Lamb Company manufactures several lines of machine products. One unique part, a valve stem, requires specialized tools that need to be replaced. Management has decided that the only alternative to replacing these tools is to acquire the valve stem from an outside source. A supplier is willing to provide the valve stem at a unit sales price of $20 if at least 70,000 units are ordered annually.

Lamb's average usage of valve stems over the past three years has been 80,000 units each year. Expectations are that this volume will remain constant over the next five years. Cost records indicate that unit manufacturing costs for the last several years have been as follows.

Direct material	$ 3.80
Direct labor	3.70
Variable overhead	1.70
Fixed overhead‡	4.50
Total unit cost	$13.70

If the specialized tools are purchased, they will cost $2,500,000 and will have a disposal value of $100,000 after their expected economic life of five years. Straight-line depreciation is used for book purposes, but ACRS is used for tax purposes. The specialized tools are considered three-year properties for ACRS purposes. The company has a 40% marginal tax rate, and management requires a 12% after-tax return on investment.

The sales representative for the manufacturer of the new tools stated, "The new tools will allow direct labor and variable overhead to be reduced by $1.60 per unit." Data from another manufacturer using identical tools and experiencing similar operating conditions, except that annual production generally averages 110,000 units, confirms the direct labor and variable overhead savings. However, the manufacturer indicates that it experienced an increase in raw material cost due to the higher quality of material that had to be used with the new tools. The manufacturer indicated that its costs have been as follows:

---

‡Depreciation accounts for two-thirds of the fixed overhead. The balance is for other fixed overhead costs of the factory that require cash expenditures.

Direct material	$ 4.50
Direct labor	3.00
Variable overhead	.80
Fixed overhead	5.00
Total unit cost	$13.30

REQUIRED:

A. Present a discounted cash flow analysis covering the economic life of the new specialized tools to determine whether Lamb Company should replace the old tools or purchase the valve stem from an outside supplier. Give consideration to tax implications.

B. Identify additional factors Lamb Company should consider before a decision is made to replace the tools or purchase the valve stem from an outside supplier.

(CMA adapted)

11-24 *(Present-Value Analysis—New Market)*. U.S. Metal Corporation introduced in mid-19X2 a major product line to a new marketing area in southwestern Ohio. Public acceptance of the product line has exceeded original expectations. U.S. Metal's management believes this level of demand will continue through December 19X8.

The company had planned to serve the area directly from its Chicago plant where the customers would obtain the product f.o.b. Chicago. However, the high demand cannot be handled effectively in this manner. The management has identified two alternatives that could be initiated in January 19X3.

1. Continue to manufacture the product in Chicago but establish a warehouse 300 miles away in Dayton, Ohio, to distribute the product.

2. Provide a manufacturing, warehousing, and distribution facility in the Dayton area. This facility would not be operational until January 19X5. Consequently, a temporary warehouse would still have to be used during the first two years of the project.

Customers would obtain the product f.o.b. Dayton under both alternatives.

Bill Minnick, Controller, has agreed to prepare an analysis to compare the two alternatives. He gathered the following facts for analysis.

1. The Chicago plant has sufficient capacity to manufacture the additional product volume expected to be demanded in the new marketing area. Only maintenance and insurance costs are expected to increase at the Chicago plant as a result of the additional manufacturing volume. These costs are expected to be $20,000 higher than normal in 19X3 and can be expected to increase by $3,000 annually as long as the product line is manufactured in Chicago.

2. U.S. Metal can lease sufficient warehouse space in Dayton for $24,000 annually. A lease agreement can be arranged for this

amount for any period from two to six years. The annual lease payment would be due on December 31 for the following year.

3. Warehousing personnel would be hired to manage and operate the warehouse. The annual initial warehousing cost, excluding the lease payment, is estimated at $50,000. This amount is expected to increase by 10% annually.

4. Five truckloads of product per day, 250 days per year, would be shipped from Chicago to the Dayton warehouse by common carrier as long as the product is manufactured in Chicago. Each truckload would average 30,000 pounds. One common carrier has quoted U.S. Metal a freight rate of $1.00 per hundred-weight for a 30,000-pound truckload ($300) plus a 20% fuel surcharge applied on the total freight charge for the one-way trip between Chicago and Dayton. The fuel surcharge is expected to continue at the same percentage through 19X8 but the freight rate per hundred-weight for a 30,000-pound truckload is expected to increase each year as presented below.

19X4	1.10
19X5	1.25
19X6	1.40
19X7	1.50
19X8	1.60

5. A building suitable for manufacturing, warehousing, and distributing the product line can be obtained in Dayton for $50,000 annually on a 20-year lease. The lease would be signed December 31, 19X2, so that the equipment installation could be started on January 1, 19X3. The lease payments would be remitted on December 31 for the following year.

6. The Dayton warehousing operations and personnel would be transferred from the original leased warehouse to the combined facility in January 19X5. Because all functions would be in the same facility, annual warehousing personnel costs would be 10% lower than the cost of maintaining a separate warehouse as described in the first alternative.

7. The estimated total cost of the manufacturing equipment for the Dayton plant is $1.2 million. The equipment would be acquired and paid for as follows:

December 19X2	$ 510,000
December 19X3	450,000
December 19X4	240,000
	$1,200,000

The equipment would be fully operational in January 19X5.

8. The new equipment at the Dayton plant would be capable of manufacturing the product line at the same rate and costs, exclusive of maintenance and insurance, experienced at the Chicago plant. Annual maintenance and insurance costs for the Dayton equipment are expected to be $70,000 for the first year the equipment is operational and increase $5,000 annually thereafter during the life of the project.

9. The new equipment would have a 20-year estimated economic life with no estimated salvage value at the end of 20 years. The company would use the Accelerated Cost Recovery System (ACRS) to write off the cost of the new manufacturing equipment for tax purposes. Once the equipment is placed in service, the new equipment would be written off over five years according to the ACRS recovery schedule.

10. If the market for the product line lasts only through 19X8 as forecasted, the company could use the plant and equipment for other products. However, Minnick estimates U.S. Metal could sell the Dayton equipment in December 19X8 for $900,000 if the equipment is no longer needed. The building could be sublet for $50,000 per year for the remaining term of the lease when it is no longer needed.

11. U.S. Metal is subject to a 40% tax rate on operating income. Assume that taxes are paid in the year in which the transactions occur.

REQUIRED:

Calculate the after-tax cash flows for the period 19X2 through 19X8 by year for each of the two alternatives being considered by U.S. Metal Corporation, assuming that U.S. Metal will use discounted cash flow techniques in its decision process. (Discounted cash flow calculations are not required.)

(CMA adapted)

11-25 *(Present Value—Pricing Products).* Wardl Industries is a manufacturer of standard and custom-design bottling equipment. Early in December 19X3 Lyan Company asked Wardl to quote a price for a custom-designed bottling machine to be delivered on April 1, 19X4. Lyan intends to make a decision on the purchase of such a machine by January 1, so Wardl would have the entire first quarter of 19X4 to build the equipment.

Wardl's standard pricing policy for custom-designed equipment is 50% markup on full cost. Lyan's specifications for the equipment have been reviewed by Wardl's Engineering and Cost Accounting departments, and they made the following estimates for raw materials and direct labor hours (DLH).

Raw materials	$256,000
Direct labor (11,000 DLH at $15)	165,000

Manufacturing overhead is applied on the basis of direct labor hours. Wardl normally plans to run its plant 15,000 direct labor hours per month and assigns overhead on the basis of 180,000 direct labor hours per year. The overhead application rate for 19X4 of $9.00 per DLH is based on the following budgeted manufacturing overhead costs for 19X4.

Variable manufacturing overhead	$ 972,000
Fixed manufacturing overhead	648,000
Total manufacturing overhead	$1,620,000

The Wardl production schedule calls for 12,000 direct labor hours per month during the first quarter. If Wardl is awarded the contract for the Lyan equipment, production of one of its standard products would have to be reduced. This is necessary because production levels can only be increased to 15,000 direct labor hours each month on short notice. Furthermore, Wardl's employees are unwilling to work overtime.

Sales of the standard product equal to the reduced production would be lost, but there would be no permanent loss of future sales or customers. The standard product whose production schedule would be reduced has a unit sales price of $12,000 and the following cost structure.

Raw materials	$2,500
Direct labor (250 DLH at $15)	3,750
Overhead (250 DLH at $ 9)	2,250
Total cost	$8,500

Lyan needs the custom-designed equipment to increase its bottle-making capacity so that it will not have to buy bottles from an outside supplier. Lyan Company requires 5 million bottles annually. Its present equipment has a maximum capacity of 4,500,000 bottles with a directly traceable cash outlay cost of $.15 per bottle. Thus, Lyan has had to purchase 500,000 from a supplier at $.40 each. The new equipment would allow Lyan to manufacture its entire annual demand for bottles and experience a raw material cost savings of $.01 for each bottle manufactured.

Wardl estimates that Lyan's annual bottle demand will continue to be 5 million bottles over the next five years, the estimated economic life of the special-purpose equipment. Wardl further estimates that Lyan has an after-tax cost of capital of 10% and is subject to a 40% marginal income tax rate, the same rates as Wardl.

REQUIRED:

A. Wardl Industries plans to submit a bid to Lyan Company for the manufacture of the special-purpose bottling equipment.

   1. Calculate the bid Wardl would submit if it follows its standard pricing policy for special-purpose equipment.

2. Calculate the minimum bid Wardl would be willing to submit on the Lyan equipment that would result in the same profits as planned for the first quarter of 19X4.

B. Wardl Industries wants to estimate the maximum price Lyan Company would be willing to pay for the special-purpose bottling equipment.

1. Calculate the present value of the after-tax savings in directly traceable cash outlays that Lyan could expect to realize from the new special-purpose bottling equipment.

2. Identify the other factors Wardl would have to incorporate in its estimate of the maximum price Lyan would be willing to pay for the equipment.

3. Describe how the cost savings (part B, 1) and the other factors (part B, 2) would be combined to calculate the estimate of the maximum price Lyan would be willing to pay for the equipment.

(CMA Adapted)

part 5
PLANNING AND CONTROL SYSTEMS FOR DECISION IMPLEMENTATION

BUDGETING: A SYSTEMATIC APPROACH TO PLANNING

A decision involves change. Each decision can be treated as a unique, independent activity, but this approach can be dangerous. In practice, every decision affects other areas of the operation. A pricing decision will affect the production volume; the production volume in Department A will affect the production volume of Department B; raw material purchases will affect not only the cost of production, but also the cash flow of the firm.

Management has the responsibility of coordinating its plans into an integrated whole. Without coordination the individual managers may actually work at cross purposes; what seems to be a good decision from one department's point of view can be a bad decision from the standpoint of the total firm. One way to provide coordination is through the budget—a summary of the planned results of individual departmental decisions, expressed in financial terms. This chapter presents an overview of the budgeting process for the firm as a whole. In the next chapter we will focus on profit planning through responsibility centers.

THE PLANNING PROCESS

The purpose of business planning is to reduce uncertainty about the future and, through coordination of plans, increase the chances of achieving the goals and objectives of the organization. Within a planning system is the basic assumption that management can plan its activities and, through these plans, manipulate or control the relevant variables that determine the destiny of the firm. Among the variables subject to control are employee quality and quantity, capital sources, product lines, production methods, and the cost structure of the firm. Other external variables affect the operations of the firm but are not subject to manipulation by management. Management can, however, anticipate the direction and magnitude of these variables to maximize their favorable consequences or minimize their unfavorable consequences. Examples of external variables not subject to control are population changes, national economic growth, competitive activities of other firms, and governmental action.

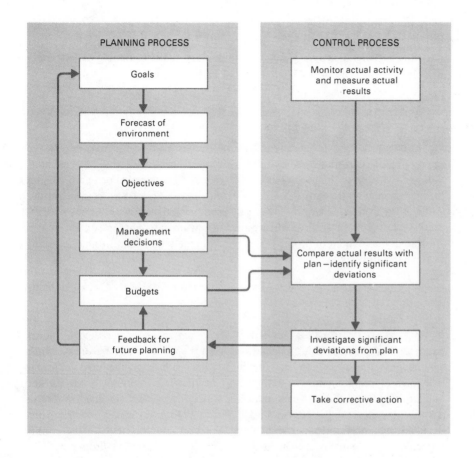

PLANNING PROCESS

Goals

Forecast of
environment

Objectives

Management
decisions

Budgets

Feedback for
future planning

CONTROL PROCESS

Monitor actual activity
and measure actual
results

Compare actual results with
plan—identify significant
deviations

Investigate significant
deviations from plan

Take corrective action

EXHIBIT 12–1
Planning and control
process

As stated in Chapter 1, the planning process begins with the establishment of the firm's goals. The action management takes to achieve these goals leads to decisions and, in turn, to the development of the budget. An illustration of the planning process and its interrelationship with the control process is presented in Exhibit 12–1. The budget is not only an expression of management's plans but also a basis of comparison with actual results in the control process.

GOALS

Goals are statements of the desired position of the firm in the future. They are directional and motivational in nature and are seldom quantified. Generally, they are statements about the desired direction the relevant variables should take in determining the long-range destiny of the firm. A primary goal is survival of the firm. Survival, however, is dependent on earning satisfactory profits. Thus, a fundamental goal is often stated as ''an adequate profit to sustain the investment in the long run.'' Subgoals of this profit goal may include desired product lines, competitive position, and organizational structure. Other goals may be less profit-oriented, such as goals of community service, technological advancement, or political influence.

OBJECTIVES

Objectives provide a quantitative and time framework for the goals within the environmental constraints. They are specific performance targets and calendar dates by which desired accomplishments should be attained. For example, the profit *goal* may be to earn satisfactory profits across time so as to increase the value of the firm to the stockholders. The profit *objective,* however, may specify a 20% rate of return on investment, a 6% profit on sales, or, in some cases, a specific dollar amount of profit. Objectives provide targets that, if attained, will achieve the firm's goals.

BUDGETS

In a business enterprise a **budget** is the formal statement of management's goals and objectives expressed in financial terms for a specific future period of time. The budget permeates every level of activity, integrating revenue plans, expense plans, asset requirements, and financing needs. The comprehensive master budget includes and unifies each manager's activities. This coordinating role is a major, if not *the* major, function of the budget. In most firms there are many decision makers; failure to bring their plans into congruence with the firm's objectives can result in each manager marching to a different drummer. The budget may be thought of as the network that ties the decisions of the subsystems into a firm-wide system.

THE CONTROL PROCESS

One of the basic functions of budgeting is to provide a benchmark for controlling actual performance. In Exhibit 12–1, the control process involves a number of steps. First, the accounting system monitors actual performance in financial terms.

Second, actual performance is compared with the plan and any significant deviations from the plan are identified. The principle of **management by exception** suggests that as long as operations conform with the plan, the activity is under control and no intervention is required. Only exceptional or significant variances require management action. Where possible, control limits that represent the range of normal deviations from plan should be developed for each variable measured.

Third, there must be a feedback mechanism, through reports to management, to inform operating management of deviations from plans. Ideally, feedback is made as soon as possible after the activity is performed.

Fourth, action may be required. Where there is a deviation from the plan, corrective action should be taken to bring all future activities in line with the plan. Action may involve enforcing existing policies, retraining employees, or changing the manufacturing process. If the deviation is a result of a plan that is unrealistic or incorrect, the plan may have to be revised.

MASTER BUDGET

The **master budget** is expressed in financial terms and sets out management's plans for the operations and resources of the firm for a given period of time. The term *budget* alone usually refers to the master budget, a network of many component schedules or subbudgets. Exhibit 12–2 presents an illustration of

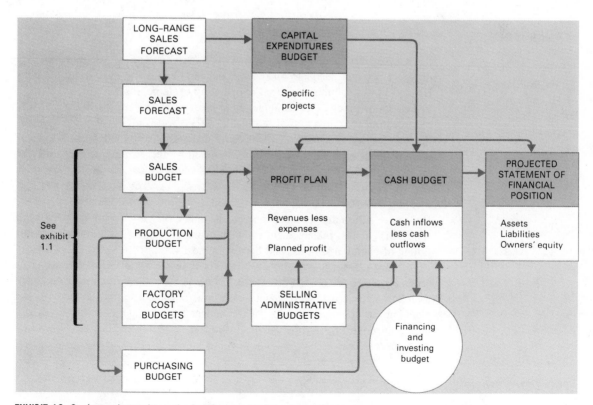

EXHIBIT 12–2   Interrelationships of subcomponents of master budget

interrelationships of the subcomponents of a master budget. The master budget is usually presented in four parts: a *Profit Plan* for operations, a *Cash Budget*, a *Projected Statement of Financial Position*, and a *Capital Expenditures Budget*. Supporting schedules or budgets are prepared for all the necessary inputs; these include sales forecasts, sales budgets, production budgets, budget for the purchases of material and the costs of the various areas of responsibility. The supporting schedules should present data in as much detail and from as many different dimensions as management considers useful and economically feasible.

PROFIT PLAN

The **Profit Plan** is the operating plan detailing revenue, expenses, and the resulting income for a specific period of time. The format is usually a projected income statement. The Profit Plan reflects the results of the short-range decision models. It is the firm's optimal plan in light of management's expectations of the future. It is a **Static Budget** because only one level of sales activity is expected.

CASH BUDGET

A company cannot undertake the activities necessary to carry out short-range decisions without adequate financial resources. Cash is the focal point of short-term resource planning because the operating cycle begins with the investment of cash in the purchase or manufacture of inventories and ends with the recovery of cash from the collection of receivables. The Cash Budget is the most important tool in managing short-term resources. Advance knowledge of cash needs allows the firm to provide for optimal liquidity and to find the best way of financing the business. The **Cash Budget** converts all planned actions into cash inflows and cash outflows so management can visualize its plans in terms of their cash impact. As implied in Exhibit 12–2 the development of the Cash Budget is substantially dependent on the other budgets. With knowledge of future cash status, management can plan expense payments, credit policies, the timing of capital additions, and borrowing needs.

The critical use of the Cash Budget is in the control process, which is implemented *in advance* of the events. There is little value in comparing actual cash flow transactions with planned cash flow transactions after the fact. In cash planning the continual revision of the budget for short periods of time *before the event* provides control.

PROJECTED STATEMENT OF FINANCIAL POSITION

The **Projected Statement of Financial Position** is a formal statement of the resources of the firm and their sources at the *end* of the budget period. The interrelationships of profit planning are presented in Exhibit 12–2. The projected balances of the assets and liabilities for the Projected Statement of Financial Position are the results of the many decisions made in the development of the Profit Plan, Cash Budget, and Capital Expenditures Budget.

CAPITAL EXPENDITURES BUDGET

The **Capital Expenditures Budget** is a formal list of all approved plans for the procurement or disposition of productive assets. The budgeting process for capital expenditures differs from that of the profit plan and other parts of the master plan. As shown in Exhibit 12–2, the need for capital expenditure projects is based on long-term sales and product forecasts. Capital expenditures are approved by *individual project* throughout the year as the need and opportunity arise. Planning for resource needs, however, requires an estimation of the timing and amount of cash flows for capital expenditures. How to develop the Capital Expenditures Budget was discussed in Chapter 11.

DEVELOPMENT OF A MASTER BUDGET

This section is devoted to a step-by-step development of a master budget for the Warren Company, on a quarterly basis. To keep our illustration simple, the Warren Company produces a single product in a single process. To illustrate the planning process, the example in this chapter starts with the basic goals of the Warren Company, develops key forecasts and cost behavior patterns that provide the basis for setting objectives, and develops the Profit Plan, Cash Budget, and Projected Statement of Financial Position. Finally the control process is demonstrated by comparing the actual results for the Warren Company with the Profit Plan.

BASIC GOALS

Management had previously spent considerable thought on establishing the firm's long-run goals. Their fundamental goal was to earn a minimum profit that would ensure maintenance of the firm's value. To achieve this profit they had decided that they did not want to expand into new markets, that little research and development expense was justified, and that promotion and advertising were needed because their markets were weakening.

SETTING OBJECTIVES

Objectives are the specific performance targets from which the master budget is developed. Objectives are developed by forecasting the environment and setting specific targets for future periods. Four key forecasts are necessary for establishing objectives: (1) the sales forecast, (2) cost behavior patterns and flexible budget equations, (3) product costs, which are best stated as standard costs, and (4) required inventory levels.

PROJECTED PROFIT PLAN
STEP 1—DEVELOPMENT OF THE SALES FORECAST

Sales for a particular company depend on many factors. Too often the price factor is overemphasized. Nonprice factors, such as customer service and promotion, may have a greater impact on sales volume than price. In order to plan its sales, a firm must have knowledge of the market in which it operates. Ideally, it knows the impact of each relevant variable on product sales, including the effect of price, customer service, and promotion. It is more likely, however, that a firm has only partial information and must turn to additional market research to supply the needed market data.

There are two approaches to sales forecasting. One, which we will term a *macro* approach, develops a model to forecast total sales. The other projects sales by product, customer, territory, or salesperson, and then groups these individual estimates into an overall sales forecast. We will call this a *micro* approach.

MACRO APPROACH

Where a firm is fortunate enough to have both a picture of its demand curve and a knowledge of its own cost structure, the optimum sales level may be determined by economic analysis. In Chapter 9 we examined the economic approach to pricing. Unfortunately, a demand curve is difficult, if not impossible, to determine in practice. Seldom will a firm have reliable knowledge of more than a very small segment of the demand curve. Market research is one way to develop information about the market so that a picture of demand may be drawn.

One method used in estimating total sales is the development of a mathematical model that describes the relationship between relevant variables and company sales. Simple regression analysis may be used to measure the relationship between sales of the firm (the dependent variable) and some relevant variable on which sales depend (the independent variable). Ideally, changes in the independent variable will lead (precede) changes in company sales. For example, for a company selling a product used in home construction, the number of residential building permits issued in the market area may be closely related to potential sales. If there is a good relationship between sales and building permits issued, and permits lead sales, then regression analysis will provide an estimate of the *next* period's sales based on housing starts in *this* period. Seldom, however, does one find such a clear relationship.

Where sales are influenced by more than one variable, multiple regression provides a mathematical statement of the relationship between sales and several variables. Instead of using only building permits, as in our earlier example, the firm might also use consumer disposable income and the availability of mortgage money in a multiple regression model.

Another approach to forecasting total sales is market-share analysis. By applying a company's expected share of the market to economic forecasts of an entire market or industry, a projection of that firm's sales is obtained.

MICRO APPROACH

A company's sales force is a potential source of information about future sales. Salespeople can vary from order-takers with very little knowledge of the market to technical specialists who may have a better knowledge of customer needs than the customers themselves. A salesperson with good customer relationships and a knowledge of the market can often project sales with a high degree of accuracy. Total sales projections for the company can be constructed by compiling the salespeople's projections of sales by product line or territory.

In some industry settings it is also possible to ask the customers about their purchasing plans. This method would be most feasible where the number of customers is small and the customer and the supplier have an ongoing positive relationship. One instance of this interaction is the situation where the customer and supplier share in the design or construction of the product.

If at all possible, the sales forecast should be based on more than one projection. A projection of total sales, through regression analysis or share of the market, for instance, should be compared with a composite estimate such as an aggregate of the sales staff's forecasts. If the projections differ significantly, further investigation may be needed.

Assume the Warren Company used both macro and micro sales forecasting techniques to develop the following sales forecast for 19X1:

Quarter	Sales Forecast
1	1,000 units
2	1,500 units
3	2,000 units
4	1,800 units
Total for 19X1	6,300 units

STEP 2—DEVELOPMENT OF COST BEHAVIOR PATTERNS

The knowledge of how costs change with volume is very important for accurate profit planning. Chapter 2 developed the methodology of separating costs into their fixed and variable components and developing a flexible budget equation.

	Variable	Fixed
Production costs:		
Direct materials—variable (per unit of raw material)	$2.00	
Direct labor—variable (per direct labor hour)	$6.00	
Overhead:		
Variable costs (per direct labor hour)	$3.00	
Fixed costs (per quarter)		$15,000
Depreciation (per quarter)		10,000
Total fixed production costs per quarter		$25,000
Selling and administrative costs:		
Variable selling (per unit sold)	$5.00	
Fixed selling and administrative:		
Advertising (per quarter)		$14,000
Salaries (per quarter)		12,000
Total fixed selling and administrative costs (per quarter)		$26,000
Planned discretionary sales promotion:		
Payable in Quarter 1		$15,000
Payable in Quarter 3		8,000
Total discretionary costs per year		$23,000

EXHIBIT 12–3
Cost behavior patterns,
Warren Company

Assume that the Warren Company applied the techniques in Chapter 2 and determined the cost behavior patterns in Exhibit 12–3. This exhibit presents the cost behavior of all costs of the company. It includes production costs as well as selling and administrative costs. These data will become the starting point for the development of standard costs for direct materials, direct labor, and variable overhead in the next step. These behavior patterns also become the cost objectives for fixed factory overhead costs and selling and administrative costs.

STEP 3—DEVELOPMENT OF PRODUCT COSTS

The Warren Company uses variable standard costing to measure its product costs. Standard costs are predeterminations of what costs should be if production is efficient. They are set by examining production processes, material usage patterns, time and motion studies, and learning curves, and by developing flexible budgets for overhead. The process of standard development and the use of cost standards in evaluating cost efficiency were presented in Chapter 6.

Assume that the Warren Company developed standards that represent realistic benchmarks for production activities and represent reasonable goals for performance. Those standards for direct materials, direct labor, and variable overhead for the production of one unit are presented in Exhibit 12–4. These standard costs become a part of the cost objectives of the Warren Company.

Material (4 pounds at $2.00)	$ 8.00
Direct labor (6 hours at $6.00)	36.00
Variable overhead (6 hours at $3.00)	18.00
Total variable cost per unit	$62.00

EXHIBIT 12–4
Standard cost card,
Warren Company
(one unit)

STEP 4—DEVELOPMENT OF COMPANY OBJECTIVES

On the basis of their long-run goals and their assessment of the environment for the next two years, the management of Warren Company prepared the objectives shown in Exhibit 12–5. Some of the objectives relate to relationships the company hopes to achieve and maintain over a two-year period. Other objectives relate to specific targets for 19X1. Each objective, however, provides a target of how much it should be and when it is to be achieved. The objectives will be

Profit objectives:
Achieve a net income after tax of
   1. 12% of reported owners' equity at the beginning of the year.
   2. 8% of net sales.

Marketing objectives:
   1. Increase dollar sales of the company by 10%.
   2. Conduct sales promotions in Quarters 1 and 3 costing $15,000 and $8,000, respectively.

Cost objectives:
   1. Incur variable manufacturing costs of $62 per unit manufactured.
   2. Incur variable selling costs of $5 per unit sold.
   3. Incur fixed costs of manufacturing of $25,000 per quarter, or $100,000 per year.
   4. Incur fixed costs of selling of $26,000 per quarter, or $104,000 per year.

Inventory objectives:
   1. Maintain finished goods inventory at 40% of next quarter's sales.
   2. Maintain raw material inventory of 50% of next quarter's usage.

Financing objectives:
   1. Use line of credit at bank to maintain $10,000 minimum cash balance.
   2. Collect 50% of receivables in quarter of sale, balance in following quarter.
   3. Pay all accounts payable in quarter following purchase.
   4. Pay all labor, overhead, selling, and administrative costs in quarter incurred.
   5. Pay dividends of $10,000 per quarter.

Personnel objectives:
Move toward a stable work force with no more than 10% turnover through layoffs.

Capital additions objectives:
Obtain new factory equipment of $50,000 in Quarter 4.

EXHIBIT 12–5
Objectives for 19X1,
Warren Company

communicated down through the company and will become the basis for development of the master budget.

STEP 5—DEVELOPMENT OF SALES BUDGET

Where productive capacity of a company is limited, a company may not be able to produce at the level of the sales forecast. In this case the combination of products that generates the largest total contribution margin should be produced. We will assume that the Warren Company has adequate productive capacity to meet the sales forecast; thus, the sales forecast becomes the sales budget. If production capacity were limited, it would act as a constraint.

Using the sales forecast and a budgeted average selling price of $120 per unit, the budgeted sales, by quarter, are shown in Exhibit 12–6.

	WARREN COMPANY SALES BUDGET For the Year Ended December 31, 19X1				
	QUARTER				
	1	2	3	4	Year
Sales forecast (units)	1,000	1,500	2,000	1,800	6,300
Selling price	$120.00	$120.00	$120.00	$120.00	$120.00
Total sales	$120,000	$180,000	$240,000	$216,000	$756,000

EXHIBIT 12–6 Sales budget, Warren Company

STEP 6—DEVELOPMENT OF PRODUCTION BUDGET

The production budget expresses management's plans for production volume. It provides the activity base for planning the variable production cost levels and any discretionary fixed production costs. The computation of budgeted production is as follows:

> Budgeted sales in units *plus*
> Desired ending inventory of finished units *less*
> Beginning inventory of finished units *equals*
> Required production in units.

The production budget is shown in Exhibit 12–7. The ending inventory figures come from the objectives for the Warren Company that established the desired ending inventory levels at 40% of the sales of the following period. The beginning inventory in Quarter 1 would come from the physical inventory at the close of last period. In our example we have assumed that this inventory is 500 units;

WARREN COMPANY
PRODUCTION BUDGET
For the Year Ended December 31, 19X1

	QUARTER				
	1	2	3	4	Year
Budgeted sales (units)	1,000	1,500	2,000	1,800	6,300
Add: Required ending inventory of finished goods*	600	800	720	440	440
Total units needed	1,600	2,300	2,720	2,240	6,740
Less: Beginning inventory of finished goods†	500	600	800	720	500
Budgeted production	1,100	1,700	1,920	1,520	6,240

*Ending inventory is 40% of next quarter's sales. Quarter 4 ending inventory of 440 assumes budgeted sales in Quarter 1, 19X2 will be 10% greater than budgeted sales in Quarter 1, 19X1.

†Beginning inventory is prior quarter's ending inventory. Quarter 1 beginning inventory is assumed to be 500 finished units.

EXHIBIT 12–7 Production budget, Warren Company

the company's ending inventory of last period does not meet with their ending inventory objectives, which will, of course, affect the production levels in Quarter 1.

STEP 7—DEVELOPMENT OF THE RAW MATERIALS PURCHASES BUDGET

The raw materials purchases budget in Exhibit 12–8 shows both the amount of materials required for production and the dollar amount that must be purchased. Computation is as follows:

Required production in units *times*   (Exhibit 12–7)
Standard material quantity per unit *equals*   (Exhibit 12–4)
Materials required for production *plus*
Desired ending inventory of raw materials *less*   (Exhibit 12–5)
Beginning inventory of raw materials *equals*
Required purchases of raw materials.

In Exhibit 12–8 the ending inventory levels have been set using the company's objectives of 50% of the next quarter's usage. The beginning inventory in Quarter 1 will come from the physical inventory at the end of the previous accounting period. In our illustration we have assumed this level to be 2,000 units, which may or may not meet the current year's inventory requirements.

The quantities of raw materials to be purchased are then converted into dollars of purchases using the cost behavior patterns for material from Exhibit 12–3.

WARREN COMPANY
RAW MATERIALS PURCHASES BUDGET
For the Year Ended December 31, 19X1

	QUARTER				
	1	2	3	4	Year
Budgeted production (units)	1,100	1,700	1,920	1,520	6,240
Materials per finished unit (pounds)	4	4	4	4	4
Raw material needed for production (pounds)	4,400	6,800	7,680	6,080	24,960
Add: Required ending inventory*	3,400	3,840	3,040	2,420	2,420
Total needs	7,800	10,640	10,720	8,500	27,380
Less: Beginning inventory†	2,000	3,400	3,840	3,040	2,000
Required purchases of raw materials (pounds)	5,800	7,240	6,880	5,460	25,380
Material cost per pound	$2.00	$2.00	$2.00	$2.00	$2.00
Required purchases	$11,600	$14,480	$13,760	$10,920	$50,760

*Ending inventory is 50% of next quarter's usage. Quarter 4 ending inventory assumes raw material needed for production in Quarter 1, 19X2 will be 10% greater than raw material needed in Quarter 1, 19X1.
†Beginning inventory is prior quarter's ending inventory. Quarter 1 beginning inventory is assumed to be 2,000 pounds.

EXHIBIT 12–8   Raw materials purchases budget, Warren Company

STEP 8—FACTORY COST BUDGET

The Factory Cost Budget (Exhibit 12–9) (sometimes called the Cost of Goods Manufactured Budget) is prepared by applying the cost objectives for the factory to the production levels set in the production budget. Raw material costs are determined by applying the standard material cost to the material requirements developed in Exhibit 12–8. Direct labor requirements are developed by multiplying the standard labor hours required per unit times the production levels from the production budget. The amount of direct labor required lets the company plan labor needs for the year. Because of the seasonal nature of the sales for the Warren Company, the objectives for low inventory and low labor turnover cannot both be met. Assuming the company will continue with its past policy of minimizing inventory levels, direct labor hours will vary from 6,600 in Quarter 1 to 11,520 in Quarter 3. Budgeted direct labor cost and budgeted variable overhead cost are determined by applying the standard costs to the direct-labor hours required. The flexible budget for fixed overhead completes the Factory Cost Budget.

The Factory Cost Budget could be separated into three separate budgets: a direct material budget, a direct labor budget, and a factory overhead budget. This would be necessary if the firm had more than one product, different classes of labor, or other types of complexities.

WARREN COMPANY
FACTORY COST BUDGET
For the Year Ended December 31, 19X1

	QUARTER				
	1	2	3	4	Year
Required production	1,100	1,700	1,920	1,520	6,240
Raw materials:					
Raw material needed for production (lb)	4,400	6,800	7,680	6,080	24,960
Standard cost per pound	$2.00	$2.00	$2.00	$2.00	$2.00
Budgeted material cost	$ 8,800	$ 13,600	$ 15,360	$ 12,160	$ 49,920
Direct labor:					
Total hours required	6,600	10,200	11,520	9,120	37,440
Standard direct labor cost per hour	$6.00	$6.00	$6.00	$6.00	$6.00
Budgeted direct labor cost	39,600	61,200	69,120	54,720	224,640
Variable overhead:					
Total hours required	6,600	10,200	11,520	9,120	37,440
Standard variable overhead per direct labor hour	$3.00	$3.00	$3.00	$3.00	$3.00
Budgeted variable overhead	19,800	30,600	34,560	27,360	112,320
Total variable factory costs	$68,200	$105,400	$119,040	$ 94,240	$386,880
Fixed overhead:					
Budgeted fixed overhead	$15,000	$ 15,000	$ 15,000	$ 15,000	$ 60,000
Factory depreciation	10,000	10,000	10,000	10,000	40,000
Total budgeted fixed overhead	25,000	25,000	25,000	25,000	100,000
Budgeted factory costs	$93,200	$130,400	$144,040	$119,240	$486,880

EXHIBIT 12–9   Warren Company

STEP 9—SELLING AND ADMINISTRATIVE EXPENSE BUDGET

The Selling and Administrative Expense Budget is prepared by applying the flexible budgets for selling and administrative expenses to volume levels from the sales budget. Exhibit 12–10 on page 510 presents the Selling and Administrative Expense Budget for the Warren Company.

STEP 10—PROFIT PLAN

Because the primary goal of the company is to earn a satisfactory profit, the Profit Plan is the key part of the master budget. It represents the combination of all operating plans as profitability measures. Further, actual performance for the year will be compared to the Profit Plan.

The Profit Plan in Exhibit 12–11 was developed using the budgets in Exhibits 12–6 through 12–10. The standard variable cost of sales was developed by multiplying the units sold by the variable costs of manufacturing of $62.

WARREN COMPANY
SELLING AND ADMINISTRATIVE EXPENSE BUDGET
For the Year Ended December 31, 19X1

	QUARTER				
	1	2	3	4	Year
Budgeted sales (units)	1,000	1,500	2,000	1,800	6,300
Variable selling expenses per unit	$5.00	$5.00	$5.00	$5.00	$5.00
Budgeted variable selling expenses	$ 5,000	$ 7,500	$10,000	$ 9,000	$ 31,500
Fixed selling and administrative expenses:					
Advertising	14,000	14,000	14,000	14,000	56,000
Salaries	12,000	12,000	12,000	12,000	48,000
Discretionary sales promotion	15,000	–0–	8,000	–0–	23,000
Total selling and administrative expenses	$46,000	$33,500	$44,000	$35,000	$158,500

EXHIBIT 12–10   Selling and Administrative Expenses Budget, Warren Company

The estimated income taxes were based on 40% of the income of $106,000, or $42,400. Management was aware that the net income in Exhibit 12–11 was based on variable costing, not on absorption costing, which would be required for the final tax return. Because they budgeted greater sales (6,300 units) than production (6,240 units), they knew that the income under variable costing would be higher than income under absorption costing. The before-tax income difference would be approximately $960 [60-unit inventory decrease times the fixed rate per unit of $16 rounded ($100,000 ÷ 6,240 units)], and the estimated taxes would be approximately $384 to $385 overstated. Management decided to take a conservative approach in estimating taxes; therefore, they used the variable costing income in their budgetary process.

One other item on the Profit Plan requires further explanation. Interest expenses of $600 and $300 are shown for Quarter 3 and Quarter 4, respectively. These amounts were not available on the first iteration of the Profit Plan. It was not until the Cash Budget was prepared (see section below) that it became apparent that it would be necessary to borrow $20,000 in Quarter 2 with repayments scheduled for Quarters 3 and 4. Once this added expense was known, it was necessary to revise the Profit Plan.

PROJECTED CASH BUDGET

The Cash Budget should be an active, day-to-day part of a cash management program. There are two aspects of cash planning. The first involves the timing of cash flows. To maintain liquidity the firm must plan for the sources of cash

WARREN COMPANY
PROFIT PLAN
For the Year Ended December 31, 19X1

	QUARTER				
	1	2	3	4	Year
Sales	$120,000	$180,000	$240,000	$216,000	$756,000
Less: Variable costs:					
Standard variable cost of sales	$ 62,000	$ 93,000	$124,000	$111,600	$390,600
Variable selling	5,000	7,500	10,000	9,000	31,500
Total variable costs	67,000	100,500	134,000	120,600	422,100
Contribution margin	$ 53,000	$ 79,500	$106,000	$ 95,400	$333,900
Fixed costs:					
Overhead	$ 15,000	$ 15,000	$ 15,000	$ 15,000	60,000
Depreciation	10,000	10,000	10,000	10,000	40,000
Advertising	14,000	14,000	14,000	14,000	56,000
Salaries	12,000	12,000	12,000	12,000	48,000
Interest*	0	0	600	300	900
Sales promotions	15,000	0	8,000	0	23,000
Total fixed costs	66,000	51,000	59,600	51,300	227,900
Budgeted income before taxes	($ 13,000)	$ 28,500	$ 46,400	$ 44,100	$106,000
Estimated income taxes†	10,600	10,600	10,600	10,600	42,400
Budgeted income after taxes	($ 23,600)	$ 17,900	$ 35,800	$ 33,500	$ 63,600

*Refer to the Cash Budget in Exhibit 12–12.
†Taxes estimated at 40% of annual net income before taxes, paid in four equal installments.

EXHIBIT 12–11 Profit Plan, Warren Company

necessary to meet cash requirements during a given period of time. The second aspect of cash planning involves maintaining a proper cash balance. An organization needs cash for transaction and precautionary purposes, but an excessive amount of cash reduces profitability. Too little cash subjects the firm to additional costs and increases the risk of insolvency. The Cash Budget identifies when cash flows will occur and allows the firm to time investments, borrowings, capital expenditures, and other discretionary payments, such as dividends, so as to optimize the cash balance.

The Cash Budget in Exhibit 12–12 on page 512 separates cash flows from operations from other cash flows. Unless the owners are willing to invest additional funds, operations must ultimately provide the necessary cash flows to maintain the firm. The amounts on the Cash Budget were determined as follows:

Cash Collected from Customers. The company estimates it will collect 50% of the sales in the quarter the sales were made and the balance in the

WARREN COMPANY
CASH BUDGET
For the Year Ended December 31, 19X1

	QUARTER				
	1	2	3	4	Year
Cash flows from operations:					
Sources:					
Collection from customers	$150,000	$150,000	$210,000	$228,000	$738,000
Uses:					
Payment of expenses:					
Purchases of materials	$ 10,000	$ 11,600	$ 14,480	$ 13,760	$ 49,840
Direct labor and overhead	74,400	106,800	118,680	97,080	396,960
Selling and administrative					
expenses	46,000	33,500	44,000	35,000	158,500
Estimated income taxes	10,600	10,600	10,600	10,600	42,400
Total	141,000	162,500	187,760	156,440	647,700
Net cash flow from operations	$ 9,000	($ 12,500)	$ 22,240	$ 71,560	$ 90,300
Other cash flows:					
Current borrowing		20,000			20,000
Repay current borrowing			(10,000)	(10,000)	(20,000)
Interest on loan			(600)	(300)	(900)
Dividends	(10,000)	(10,000)	(10,000)	(10,000)	(40,000)
Capital additions				(50,000)	(50,000)
Net change in cash	($ 1,000)	($ 2,500)	$ 1,640	$ 1,260	($ 600)
Beginning cash balance	15,000	14,000	11,500	13,140	15,000
Ending cash balance	$ 14,000	$ 11,500	$ 13,140	$ 14,400	$ 14,400

EXHIBIT 12–12   Cash Budget, Warren Company

following quarter (see Exhibit 12–5). The beginning balance of Accounts Receivable, taken from last year's accounts, was $90,000.

	QUARTER				
	1	2	3	4	Year
Sales (Exhibit 12–6)	$120,000	$180,000	$240,000	$216,000	$756,000
Expected cash collections:					
Accounts Receivable, 1-1-X1	$ 90,000				$ 90,000
First-quarter sales	60,000	$ 60,000			120,000
Second-quarter sales		90,000	$ 90,000		180,000
Third-quarter sales			120,00	$120,000	240,000
Fourth-quarter sales				108,000	108,000
Total cash collections*	$150,000	$150,000	$210,000	$228,000	$738,000

*50% collected in quarter of sale, balance in quarter following sale.

Cash Payments for Purchases of Materials. It is the company policy to pay for all purchases in the period following the purchase (see Exhibit 12–5). The beginning balance of Accounts Payable, taken from last year's accounts, was $10,000.

	QUARTER				
	1	2	3	4	Year
Purchases (Exhibit 12–8)	$11,600	$14,480	$13,760	$10,920	$50,760
Expected cash payments:					
Accounts Payable, 1-1-X1	$10,000				$10,000
Quarter 1 purchases		$11,600			11,600
Quarter 2 purchases			$14,480		14,480
Quarter 3 purchases				$13,760	13,760
Total cash payments*	$10,000	$11,600	$14,480	$13,760	$49,840

*Payments for purchases are made in the period following purchase.

Cash Payments for Direct Labor, Overhead, and Selling and Administrative Expenses. It is the company's policy to pay these expenses in the period they are incurred.

	QUARTER				
	1	2	3	4	Year
Cash payments for direct labor and overhead (Exhibit 12–9)					
Direct labor	$39,600	$ 61,200	$ 69,120	$54,720	$224,640
Variable overhead	19,800	30,600	34,560	27,360	112,320
Fixed overhead	15,000	15,000	15,000	15,000	60,000
Total	$74,400	$106,800	$118,680	$97,080	$396,960

Payment is made in quarter costs are incurred.
Depreciation is a noncash expense.

	QUARTER				
	1	2	3	4	Year
Cash payments for selling and administrative expenses (Exhibit 12–10)	$46,000	$ 33,500	$ 44,000	$35,000	$158,500

Payment is made in quarter cost is incurred.

The estimated income taxes were determined from the Profit Plan. Other cash flows came from the dividend objective, the capital expenditures objective, and the borrowing activities needed to meet the minimum cash balance of $10,000 (see Exhibit 12–5).

PROJECTED STATEMENT OF FINANCIAL POSITION

The master budget is completed with the preparation of the Projected Statement of Financial Position, which shows the consequences of planned operating actions on the financial resources of the firm. Planning and control of the various financial resources are interwoven through the various planning steps in developing the Profit Plan, Cash Budget, and Capital Expenditures Budget. The Projected Statement of Financial Position consolidates the results.

The Projected Statement of Financial Position for the Warren Company is presented in Exhibit 12–13, along with the statement of financial position for

WARREN COMPANY
STATEMENT OF FINANCIAL POSITION
ACTUAL AND PROJECTED

	ACTUAL December 31, 19X0	PROJECTED December 31, 19X1
ASSETS		
Current assets:		
Cash	$ 15,000	$ 14,400
Accounts Receivable	90,000	108,000
Finished Goods Inventory	31,000	27,280
Raw Materials Inventory	4,000	4,840
Total current assets	$140,000	$154,520
Plant, property, and equipment:		
Land	$ 40,000	$ 40,000
Buildings and equipment	300,000	350,000
Accumulated depreciation	(110,000)	(150,000)
Total plant, property, and equipment	230,000	240,000
TOTAL ASSETS	$370,000	$394,520
LIABILITIES AND STOCKHOLDERS' EQUITY		
Current liabilities:		
Accounts Payable	$ 10,000	$ 10,920
Stockholders' equity:		
Common Stock	$300,000	$300,000
Retained Earnings	60,000	83,600
Total stockholders' equity	360,000	383,600
Total liabilities and stockholders' equity	$370,000	$394,520

EXHIBIT 12–13
Projected Statement of Financial Position

the previous year. The source of each amount in the Projected Statement of Financial Position is explained by reference to the exhibits and schedules.

Cash, $14,400 is the ending cash balance from the Cash Budget (Exhibit 12–12).

Accounts Receivable, $108,000, represents one-half the sales of the last quarter.

Inventory of Finished Goods, $27,280, is determined from the production budget (Exhibit 12–7). Ending inventory was planned at the level of 40% of the next quarter's sales, assuming a 10% increase in budgeted sales as noted. The unit costs were taken from the standard cost card (Exhibit 12–4).

$$440 \text{ units} \times \$62 \text{ standard cost} = \$27,280$$

Materials inventory, was determined from the purchases budget (Exhibit 12–8), where estimated ending inventory was projected at 50% of the following quarter's usage, assuming a 10% increase over the first quarter's needs.

$$2,420 \text{ pounds} \times \$2 \text{ per pound} = \$4,840$$

Land is unchanged from the beginning statement of financial position.

Building and equipment, $350,000, includes the total of the beginning balance from the beginning statement of financial position and the $50,000 of capital expenditures made during the year.

Beginning balance	$300,000
Capital expenditures	50,000
Ending balance	$350,000

Accumulated depreciations, $150,000, includes the beginning balance of $110,000, and the sum of depreciation from Exhibit 12–3 amounting to $40,000 for the year.

Accounts Payable, $10,920, represents the last quarter's purchases from Exhibit 12–8.

Common stock, $300,000, remained unchanged from the beginning amount.

Retained earnings, $83,600, represents the beginning balance of retained earnings plus the net income from the profit plan (Exhibit 12–11) less the dividends paid in the Cash Budget (Exhibit 12–12).

Beginning balance (assumed)	$60,000
Plus net income	63,600
Less dividends	40,000
Ending balance	$83,600

COMPARISON OF MASTER BUDGET WITH CORPORATE OBJECTIVES

The Profit Plan is the focal point of the master budget. It shows the profit that management can expect to earn, given the resources and facilities committed. Is the planned profit of $63,600 enough? Earlier we presented a set of company objectives (Exhibit 12–5) developed by the Warren Company. A comparison of these objectives and the Profit Plan is presented in Exhibit 12–14. The Profit Plan met or exceeded all company objectives with two exceptions. The first involves a conflict in objectives. In a highly seasonal market the company cannot hold inventories at a percentage of the next quarter's sales *and* maintain a stable work force. If a stable work force is to be achieved, the company must build inventories in periods of low sales activity. The second unmet objective involves the ability to meet budgeted fixed costs. Because of the need to borrow cash, the firm had to incur interest expense.

ILLUSTRATION OF THE CONTROL PROCESS

The control process begins after the planning process is completed and as the decisions are being implemented. The accounting system performs a monitoring role by accumulating actual performance data, comparing the actual results with the plans, and communicating the results to management.

The depth of detail in reporting should vary depending on the needs of the particular manager. When the need for greater detail is important to pinpoint areas needing management action, the analysis should be carried further. Expansion of the analysis should continue until the cost of additional detail is not justified by the benefits of obtaining further information.

In this chapter we have taken a firm-wide view. The next chapter will describe how a budgeted system can be designed as a responsibility reporting system tailored to individual managers. A summary of actual results for the first quarter of 19X1 for the Warren Company is presented in Exhibit 12–15.

Exhibit 12–16 shows a performance report for the first quarter of the Warren Company. The first column (1) shows the Profit Plan taken from Exhibit 12–11. The second column (2) shows the Performance Budget. The planned level of activity is seldom achieved exactly. When the actual level of performance differs from planned performance, a **Performance Budget** can be prepared after the fact to show what revenues and costs should have been at the actual level of activity. The Performance Budget is the flexible budget adjusted to the actual volume of 1,200 units. By comparing the actual results with the Performance Budget, management can then focus on price and efficiency variances. A comparison of the actual results with the Profit Plan does not have this focus because the Profit Plan is based on the budgeted 1,000 units while actual results are based on 1,200 units. While many firms use the ''profit plan to actual

Objectives	Master Budget Projections
Profit objectives:	
Achieve a net income after tax of	
1. 12% of reported owners' equity at the beginning of the year.	17.67% ($63,600 ÷ $360,000)
2. 8% of net sales.	8.4% ($63,600 ÷ $756,000)
Marketing objectives:	
1. Increase dollar sales of the company by 10%.	Management is satisfied with sales volume increase.
2. Conduct sales promotions in Quarters 1 and 3 costing $15,000 and $8,000, respectively.	Objective served as basis of cost budgets.
Cost objectives:	
1. Incur variable manufacturing costs of $62 per unit manufactured.	Objective served as basis of cost budgets.
2. Incur variable selling costs of $5 per unit sold.	Objective served as basis of cost budgets.
3. Incur fixed costs of manufacturing of $25,000 per quarter; or $100,000 per year.	Objective served as basis of cost budgets.
4. Incur fixed costs of selling of $26,000 per quarter, or $104,000 per year.	Unable to achieve budget because of need to borrow, which added $900 interest.
Inventory objectives:	
1. Maintain finished-goods inventory at 40% of next quarter's sales.	Objective served as basis of budgets.
2. Maintain raw material inventory of 50% of next quarter's usage.	Objective served as basis of budgets.
Financing objectives:	
1. Use line of credit at bank to maintain $10,000 minimum cash balance.	Was necessary to borrow $20,000 against credit line.
2. Collect 50% of receivables in quarter of sale, balance in following quarter.	Objective served as basis of budgets.
3. Pay all accounts payable in quarter following purchase.	Objective served as basis of budgets.
4. Pay all labor, overhead, selling and administrative costs in quarter incurred.	Objective served as basis of budgets.
5. Pay dividends of $10,000 per quarter.	Objective served as basis of budgets.
Personnel objectives:	
Move toward a stable work force with no more than 10% turnover through layoffs.	Unable to achieve; labor and inventory budgets in conflict.
Capital additions objectives:	
Obtain new factory equipment of $50,000 in Quarter 4.	Objective served as basis for budgets.

EXHIBIT 12–14
Objectives for 19X1 compared to master budget

WARREN COMPANY
ACTUAL RESULTS
Quarter 1, 19X1

Actual sales	1200 units	$150,000
Standard variable Costs of Goods Sold for units sold		$ 74,400
Actual variances from standard		($250)
Variable selling costs		$ 6,120
Fixed costs:		
Overhead		$ 15,500
Depreciation		$ 10,000
Advertising		$ 14,400
Salaries		$ 12,000
Other		$ 15,000
Actual income before taxes		$ 2,330
Actual production	1200 units	
Actual production data to determine variances:		
Materials purchased	6,500 pounds @ $2.10 per pound	
Materials used	4,900 pounds	
Direct labor	7,000 hours @ $6.10 per hour	
Variable overhead		$ 21,500

EXHIBIT 12–15
Actual results for
Quarter 1, 19X1

comparison'' (called a Static Budget analysis), we will use the Performance Budget comparison in this chapter because it is a superior analysis.

In the Performance Budget (column 2), selling prices, standard product costs, and variable selling costs per unit are multiplied by the actual sales volume of 1,200 units. Fixed costs in the Performance Budget are the same as in the Profit Plan, because fixed costs do not change with volume changes.

One analysis is to compare the Profit Plan with the Performance Budget (see column 4). The Profit Plan, reflecting planned activity, shows a loss of $13,000. The Performance Budget, reflecting a higher level of activity, shows a loss potential of $2,400. Because of the higher level of activity in the Performance Budget, the revenue increased by $24,000 and the variable costs increased by $13,400. In summary, there is a potential $10,600 profit increase over the planned profit because of increased activity.

Another way to determine the change in potential profit due to changes in volume is to focus on the contribution margin. The contribution margin per unit is $53 (selling price $120 less variable costs of $62 + $5). The sale of 200 additional units should produce additional contribution margin, and therefore additional profit, of $10,600 (200 × $53).

A final analysis available is the comparison of the Performance Budget with the actual results, which is shown in column 5. An increase in the sales price increased profit by $6,000. At the same time, actual costs were above the

WARREN COMPANY
PERFORMANCE REPORT
Quarter 1, 19X1

	(1)	(2)	(3)	(4)	(5)
					(2–3)
				(1–2)	Price
				Sales	Spending
	Profit	Performance		Activity	Efficiency
	Plan	Budget	Actual	Variance	Variances
Units	1,000	1,200	1,200	200	—
Sales	$120,000	$144,000	$150,000	$24,000	$6,000 F
Standard variable cost of sales	62,000	74,400	74,400	(12,400)	0
Standard contribution margin from					
manufacturing	$ 58,000	$ 69,600	$ 75,600	$11,600	$6,000 F
Variances from standard:					
Material price variance			($650)		($650) U
Material usage variance			(200)		(200) U
Labor rate variance			(700)		(700) U
Labor efficiency variance			1,200		1,200 F
Variable overhead spending variance			(500)		(500) U
Variable overhead efficiency variance			600		600 F
Total variances			(250)		(250) U
Adjusted contribution margin from					
manufacturing	$ 58,000	$ 69,600	$ 75,350	$11,600	$5,750
Variable selling expenses	5,000	6,000	6,120	(1,000)	(120) U
Contribution margin	$ 53,000	$ 63,600	$ 69,230	$10,600	$5,630 F
Fixed costs:					
Overhead	$ 15,000	$ 15,000	$ 15,500	$ 0	($500) U
Depreciation	10,000	10,000	10,000	0	0
Advertising	14,000	14,000	14,400	0	(400) U
Salaries	12,000	12,000	12,000	0	0
Other	15,000	15,000	15,000	0	0
Total fixed costs	66,000	66,000	66,900	0	(900)
Income (loss) before taxes	($ 13,000)	($ 2,400)	$ 2,330	$10,600	$4,730

EXHIBIT 12–16   Performance report

Performance Budget. First, there were variances from standard costs. These variances, which total $250 unfavorable, were determined as follows:

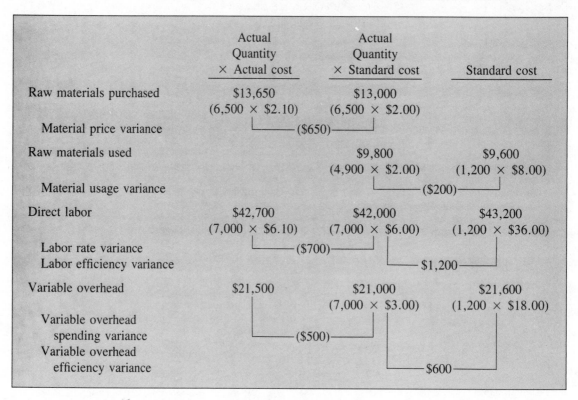

	Actual Quantity × Actual cost	Actual Quantity × Standard cost	Standard cost
Raw materials purchased	$13,650 (6,500 × $2.10)	$13,000 (6,500 × $2.00)	
Material price variance	└──── ($650) ────┘		
Raw materials used		$9,800 (4,900 × $2.00)	$9,600 (1,200 × $8.00)
Material usage variance		└──── ($200) ────┘	
Direct labor	$42,700 (7,000 × $6.10)	$42,000 (7,000 × $6.00)	$43,200 (1,200 × $36.00)
Labor rate variance	└──── ($700) ────┘		
Labor efficiency variance		└──── $1,200 ────┘	
Variable overhead	$21,500	$21,000 (7,000 × $3.00)	$21,600 (1,200 × $18.00)
Variable overhead spending variance	└──── ($500) ────┘		
Variable overhead efficiency variance		└──── $600 ────┘	

In addition to the production variances, there were also variances for variable selling expenses ($120, unfavorable), fixed overhead ($500, unfavorable), and advertising ($400, unfavorable). All of these variances totaled $1,270, unfavorable. In sum, because of price, spending and efficiency variances there should be a potential profit increase of $4,730.

REPORTS TO TOP MANAGEMENT

Reports to top management should do three things: first, for control they should explain the difference between the profit in the Profit Plan and actual profit, drawing attention to significant problem areas; second, they should show the aggregate date used in financial reports; and third, they should provide feedback about the achievement of goals and objectives.

One way to show why planned and actual profit differ is a summary report called the Report on Profit Plan. The report shows only variances from the Profit Plan. To be effective, the differences should be grouped by functional areas or by responsibility centers (manufacturing, marketing, and administration). The Report on Profit Plan for the Warren Company (Exhibit 12–17) shows

```
                        WARREN COMPANY
                    REPORT ON PROFIT PLAN
                        Quarter 1, 19X1

PLANNED PROFIT                                            ($13,000)
Variances from plan due to marketing:
    Sales activity variance                 $10,600
    Sales price variance                      6,000
    Variance in variable selling costs         (120)
    Variance in advertising costs              (400)
        Total                                             16,080
Variances due to manufacturing:
    Variances in variable production costs   ($250)
    Variance in fixed overhead                (500)
        Total                                               (750)
ACTUAL PROFIT                                            $ 2,330
```

EXHIBIT 12–17
Report on Profit Plan

favorable variances from plan due to marketing of $16,080 and unfavorable variances due to manufacturing of $750. There were no variances in administrative costs.

As a final step, top management needs a comparison of the actual results with the original objectives. Overall, it can be said that the firm achieved its objectives in the first quarter. Because of the seasonal pattern of sales, a loss was expected in the first quarter with profits for the remainder of the year. Instead, a small profit was shown in the first quarter.

Because production equaled sales, there were no increases in inventories as planned (Exhibit 12–7). On the other hand, the material inventory requirement was exceeded. The planned material inventory increase was 1,400 pounds (Exhibit 12–7). The Warren Company actually increased the material inventory levels by 1,600 pounds (Exhibit 12–15). Finally, while the Warren Company did fairly well in meeting their overall production cost objectives ($250, unfavorable), a review shows that the spending variances were $1,850 unfavorable while the efficiency variances were $1,600 favorable.

SUMMARY

To achieve its long-run goals and objectives, management must plan and control actual operations. The budget serves as a focus of the planning process, as an integrative tool for the many plans, and as a reference for control. By comparing actual results with plans on a timely basis, management can ensure that actual performance is congruent with the plans.

The master budget is composed of four separate subcomponents. The profit plan is the operating plan detailing revenues, expenses, and income in the form of a projected income statement. The projected statement of financial position includes the planned asset, liability, and equity levels. The cash budget shows the effects of management's plans on cash inflows and outflows. The capital expenditures budget details planned procurements and disposals of the major production assets.

The differences between actual profit and planned profit can be analyzed at a number of levels. Static analysis consists of comparing the actual results with the planning budget. More appropriate for managerial control is the comparison of the actual results with the Performance Budget. The Performance Budget is the flexible budget with standard costs adjusted to the actual volume.

PROBLEMS AND CASES

12-1 *(Sales Forecast).* The Horace Company is a small steel company selling to the construction industry in a limited geographic area. The sales manager has developed a model to predict sales based on building permits issued. She has developed the following regression equation:

Sales in thousands of dollars $= 92.5 + 20.946$ (construction permits in millions of dollars)

She subscribes to a data service for the construction industry that has predicted construction permits to be $980,000,000).

REQUIRED:

What is the sales forecast produced by the sales manager's model?

12-2 *(Sales Forecast—Demand Curve).* Gregor Company undertook a thorough research of the market for the company's single product. Data concerning demand for the company's product is as follows:

Price	Quantity Demanded (Units)
$5.00	100,000
$4.00	300,000
$3.00	600,000
$2.50	1,100,000
$2.00	2,000,000
$1.50	3,400,000
$1.00	5,000,000

Plant capacity is 3 million units. Fixed costs are $1 million; variable costs are $1.00 per unit.

REQUIRED:

A. Determine the optimum level of production and sales.

B. Prepare a Profit Plan for the company at the optimum level using a contribution margin approach.

C. What assumptions are inherent in this approach to developing a Profit Plan?

12-3 *(Sales Forecast).* The management of the Bright Light Company is attempting to develop a forecast of the company's sales for 19X8. The following estimates were derived independently.

Trend-line estimate (projection of past sales trend)	$8,200,000
Composite of estimates from sales staff	$7,900,000
Sales manager's planned sales quota	$8,500,000

Share of the market (share of the market for lights has been 12%. The total market for lights has been estimated at $66,600,000 by the State University business research department.)

Simple regression of sales with disposable income: (Regression equation: $y_s = \$1,600,000 + .02(x)$, where (x) is disposable income in the market area. Standard error: $100,000. Disposable income in the market area was estimated by the Department of Commerce at $320,000,000.)

The sales staff expect their estimates to be used as sales quotas and the sales manager expects his estimate to be a maximum for bonus purposes.

REQUIRED:

Prepare a sales forecast from the five projections. Explain how you considered or weighted the various projections.

12-4 *(Schedule of Cash Collections).* The Haslip Company is in the process of preparing a Cash Budget for the second quarter. The sales budget for the second quarter follows:

	Sales in Units
April	10,000
May	12,000
June	13,000

The selling price is $10 per unit. Accounts Receivable at March 31 include $24,000 from February and $45,000 from March that are expected to be collected. The established pattern of collections for the Haslip Company is as follows:

Collections in month of sale	50%
Collections in month after sale	25%
Collections in second month after sale	20%
Uncollectible	5%
	100%

REQUIRED:

A. Prepare a schedule of cash collections by month for the second quarter. Assume the firm uses an allowance for bad-debt procedure.

B. Assuming the collection pattern, how many units were sold in February? In March?

12-5 *(Production Budget).* Carlton Company prepared a sales budget for the first half of 19X9 as follows:

	Sales in Units
January	20,000
February	25,000
March	40,000
April	30,000
May	30,000
June	25,000

A production budget must be prepared for the first quarter. The January 1 inventory included 5,000 finished units. Mr. Carlton has recently set a finished-goods inventory objective of 25% of the next month's sales.

REQUIRED:

Prepare a production budget for the first quarter showing production by month and for the quarter.

12-6 *(Raw Material Purchases Budget, Cash Payments Schedule).* The purchasing manager for the Gabriel Company is preparing a raw materials purchases budget from the following production budget prepared by the production manager.

	Budgeted Production in Units
July	30,000
August	40,000
September	50,000
October	60,000
November	50,000
December	50,000

Each unit requires 5 pounds of Compound P costing $3.00 per pound. A price increase to $3.20 is expected for purchases in September and later. The production manager believes that the inventory level of 10,000 pounds of Compound P on June 30 is too low. She wants to increase the inventory level to 20% of the next month's production requirements. June 30 Accounts Payable included $225,000 from June purchases of Compound P. Fifty percent of purchases are paid in the month of purchase, with the balance paid in the following month.

REQUIRED:

A. Prepare a raw materials purchases budget showing purchases of Compound P by month and in total for the third quarter.

B. Show the amount of cash paid each month for purchases of Compound P.

C. How many units of Compound P were purchased in June?

12-7 *(Factory Cost Budget, Cash Payments Schedule).* The standard cost card for the Joshua Company follows:

```
┌─────────────────────────────────────────────┐
│            STANDARD COST CARD                │
│                ONE UNIT                      │
│                                              │
│   Raw materials (10 pieces at $1)      $10   │
│   Direct labor (.5 hours at $12)         6   │
│   Variable overhead (.5 hours at $4)     2   │
│   Fixed overhead* (.5 hours at $20)     10   │
│                                        ────   │
│                                        $28   │
│                                        ════   │
│                                              │
│   *25% of fixed overhead is depreciation.    │
└─────────────────────────────────────────────┘
```

The annual Profit Plan was based on an average production and sales level of 10,000 units per month. Labor and fixed overhead are paid in the month they are incurred; variable overhead is paid in the month after it is incurred.

	Scheduled Production in Units
August and September (planned and actual)	8,000
October	9,000
November	10,000
December	11,000

REQUIRED:

A. Prepare a Factory Cost Budget showing budgeted labor and overhead costs by month for the factory.

B. Prepare a schedule of cash payments for labor and overhead by month.

12-8 *(Sales Budget, Production Budget)*. The Wicker Works produces a line of three straw products: a hamper, a chest, and a large basket. The company does not have a formal budgetary system. Management has described its planning and control system as "experience and good judgment."

Sales during the current year were $700,000. The sales manager believes that sales will increase by about 10% each year, and projects sales at $770,000 for the coming year. The production manager is planning to increase production by about 10%. Planned production by product would be

Hamper	12,000 units
Chest	500 units
Basket	42,000 units

The controller compiled the following information.

	LAST YEAR'S SALES		ENDING INVENTORY
	Amount	Unit Price	
Hamper	$360,000	$20	1,500 units
Chest	60,000	$25	3,000 units
Basket	280,000	$ 7	3,000 units
	$700,000		

In addition, the controller found that with the exception of the last quarter, when sales were about 40% of the annual total, sales were fairly uniform throughout the year. The controller believes that the inventory policy should require an ending level of one-half of the next quarter's sales.

REQUIRED:

A. Prepare a sales budget and production budget by quarter and in total for the year.

B. Write a brief recommendation to top management detailing your reasons for recommending implementation of the budget process for all departments.

C. If you could have any two specific pieces of additional information to help persuade management to adopt a budgeting system, what would you request? Why?

12-9 *(Accuracy of Accounting Information)*. Arnie Jenson, president of Green River Woodworking, has just received a request for an additional 700 special-order kitchen cabinets from Ramsey Construction. After reviewing Job 52, a recently completed job for the same type of cabinet, he accepted the order. Data from Job 52 follow.

	Standard	Actual	Efficiency Variance
		JOB 52	
Sales	$15,000	$15,000	
Variable costs:			
Material	$ 2,000	$ 1,950	$ 50
Labor	8,000	8,400	(400)
Variable overhead*	2,000	2,100	(100)
Total variable costs	12,000	12,450	$(450)
Contribution margin	$ 3,000	$ 2,550	
Identifiable fixed costs	2,000	1,050	
Product margin	$ 1,000	$ 1,500	

*Applied on the basis of labor hours. Standard rate is $8.00 per hour.

Arnie was not concerned about the $400 variance in labor because Job 52 was a new job. He reasoned that performance should improve on the second job.

While walking through the factory on the way to his office, he overheard Ollie Ajax, the group leader for special cabinet construction, talking to another group leader. ". . . those work tickets on Job 52," Ajax was saying.

The other man answered, "You mean you plugged the labor hours too?"

"Of course," replied Ajax, "Johnson [the foreman] hits the roof if the variances are over 50 hours on any job. We just keep them under 50 hours and everyone is happy. Saves having to explain to the boss and get chewed out. Why, I bet we were at least 30% over standard on that Ramsey job. There is no way we can make standard on that type of job. We loaded the hours on other jobs."

REQUIRED:

A. Assuming the 30% estimate of labor variance on Job 52, correct the report that was presented to Mr. Jenson.

B. Were any costs other than labor affected?

C. How would the additional information have affected his decision?

D. What suggestions do you have concerning the control system and reporting to management?

12-10 (Develop a Profit Plan). Kitti and Fred Maltby had just started a business called "Homeowner Surrogate." Their business was based on the belief that many families in their community were professional, dual-income families who, due to time constraints, needed a variety of household chores performed. Kitti and Fred's company currently offered services such as housecleaning, painting, and shopping. They felt that their motto, "Leave the details to us," and their guarantee of customer satisfaction would attract a large number of clients.

To ensure that they had adequate resources, they decided during the Christmas holidays to plan their financial activities for the coming year. A survey of their existing and potential clients indicated that the most popular service would be housecleaning, followed by painting, and then shopping. They had the policy of billing their clients for all actual materials used. This allowed them to simplify their revenue forecasts.

Housecleaning	3,000 hours at $8 per hour
Painting	1,500 hours at $10 per hour
Shopping	800 hours at $25 per hour

In estimating their expenses they assumed an average wage rate, including all benefits, of $7 per hour for their helpers. In addition, the following expenses seemed reasonable, given their experiences.

Insurance	$2,500 per year
Depreciation on car	$1,100 per year
Telephone expense	$ 600 per year
Supplies	$ 500 per year + $2.00 per hour for housecleaning and painting
Gas and oil	$ 200 per year + $1.00 per billable hour

While they knew that many of these estimates were averages, Kitti and Fred felt that this would give them a good indication of what they could expect during the coming year.

REQUIRED:

A. Develop a Profit Plan.

B. Compute the level of activity at which the company will break even.

C. If they hold the service mix and volume constant, by how much must their prices increase to earn a before-tax profit of $12,000?

12-11 *(Comprehensive Master Budget).* Two women who had been working in pottery as a hobby received so many requests for stoneware dishes that they decided to produce the sets commercially. They formed a company, withdrew their savings, refinanced their homes, purchased equipment, rented an old barn, and started business as The Crockery Barn. They need additional financing from the bank and came to you for assistance in financial planning. Upon formation, the company has the following assets:

Cash	$ 2,000
Equipment	$20,000

The women expect to sell 500 sets of dishes at $100 per set during the first six months. They believe an inventory of 20 finished sets is needed to fill rush orders. Because of drying time required, there will always be 20 half-finished sets in production. Costs (except depreciation and interest) for the first six months should be

Production	$10,000 plus $50 per set produced
Selling and administration	$5,000 plus $10 per set sold

Purchases and sales will be on account, with average balances of $20,000 for Accounts Receivable and $4,000 for Accounts Payable. Other payments will be made in the month the costs are incurred. A minimum cash balance of $2,000 is necessary.

The bank is willing to grant a two-year loan of up to $25,000 with 10% interest payable at maturity. Equipment is to be depreciated by the straight-line method over an estimated useful life of five years.

REQUIRED:

A. Prepare a master budget for the first six months of operations. Your master budget should include a Profit Plan, a Cash Budget, and Projected Statement of Financial Position. The contribution margin approach is to be used.

B. Compute the breakeven point and margin of safety. Do not consider interest expense in your calculations.

12-12 *(Continuation of Problem 12-11—Reports to Management)*. At the end of the first six months of operations The Crockery Barn asked you to continue your financial consultation.

Orders for the first six months exceeded expectations and the women actually sold 600 sets of dishes at an average price of $110. Inventory levels were maintained at 20 finished sets and 20 half-finished sets.

Actual costs were as follows:

Production:	
Variable	$ 60 per set
Fixed	$11,000
Selling and administration:	
Variable	$ 8 per set
Fixed	$ 5,500
Interest expense	$ 700
Depreciation of equipment	$ 2,000

REQUIRED:

A. Prepare an income statement showing Profit Plan, Performance Budget, actual results, and variances.

B. Prepare a report on profit plan that explains the difference between planned income in problem 12-11 and actual income.

C. Comment on the performance of The Crockery Barn.

12-13 *(Simple Master Budget)*. Mike Gibson decided, after 10 years of working for others, to open his own company—Qualified Yard Maintenance Service. He surveyed many potential customers and felt that he would be able to bill the following hours at $10 per hour in 19X7.

Winter quarter	100 h
Spring quarter	600 h
Summer quarter	800 h
Fall quarter	300 h

Based on his sales forecasting, he incorporated with a capital investment of $5,000. His first decision was to buy a used truck with an estimated useful life of three years and no salvage value for $2,400 cash. He then purchased, for cash, his lawnmowers, trimmers, and edgers for $1,200, which he knew would last two years before needing replacement. Based on his past experiences, he estimated he would use an average of $3.00 per working hour in chemicals, fertilizers, and supplies. He predicted his other expenses would be

Gas/oil for truck: $100 in the winter quarter; $300 in the spring quarter; $500 in the summer quarter; and $200 in the fall quarter.

Dumping fees: $125 per quarter.

Truck maintenance: $300 in the winter quarter.

Newspaper advertising: $100 per quarter.

Telephone expense: $90 per quarter.

Liability insurance: $400 in the winter quarter; $200 in the spring quarter.

Licenses and city taxes: $135 in the winter quarter.

All expenses, with the exception of depreciation expenses, would be paid in cash in the quarter they were incurred. Clients would be billed on a monthly basis. Mike expected to receive 100% of his billings. However, he expected to receive 75% in the quarter billed and 25% the following quarter.

REQUIRED:

A. Prepare a Profit Plan for each quarter and for the year. (Assume there are no income taxes.)

B. Prepare a Cash Budget by quarter.

C. Prepare a Statement of Financial Position as of December 31, 19X7.

12-14 *(Cash Budget)*. Prime Time Court Club (PTCC) has been in business for five years. The club has experienced cash flow problems each year, especially in the summer when court use is quite low and new membership sales are insignificant. Temporary loans have been obtained from the local bank to cover the summer shortages. Additional permanent capital has also been invested by the owners.

The owners and the bank have decided some action needs to be taken at this time to improve PTCC's net cash flow position. They would like to review a quarterly Cash Budget based on a revised fee structure that hopefully would increase club revenues. The purpose of the Cash Budget would be to anticipate better both the timing and amounts of the probable cash flow of the club and to determine if the club can survive.

John Harper, club manager, recommended that the membership dues be increased and that the hourly court time fees be replaced with a monthly charge for unlimited court use. He believes that this plan will increase membership and that the cash flow and timing problem should be reduced. The proposed fee schedule, which is consistent with rates at other clubs, is presented below. In his opinion, the proportions of the different membership categories should not change, but the total number of members will increase by 10%. Court use will also increase an estimated 20% as a result of this new program. The pattern of use throughout the year is not expected to change.

The present fee structure, the distribution among membership categories, and the projected 19X3 operating data including membership status, court usage, and estimated operating costs are presented on page 532. The projected operating data presented in the table were based on the present fee structure before Harper's proposed fee schedule was recommended.

REQUIRED:

A. Construct a quarterly Cash Budget for one year for PTCC, assuming the new fee structure is adopted and John Harper's estimates of increases in membership and court use occur. Assume the transition from the old to the new fee structure is immediate and complete when preparing the budget.

B. Will John Harper's proposal solve the summer cash shortfall problem? Explain your answer.

C. Will John Harper's proposal support a conclusion that the club can become profitable and survive in the long run? Explain your answer.

(CMA adapted)

PROPOSED FEE SCHEDULE		
Membership Category	*Annual Membership Fees*	*Monthly Court Charges*
Individual	$ 75	$10
Youth	45	8
Family	150	18

```
┌─────────────────────────────────────────────────────┐
│              PRESENT FEE STRUCTURE                    │
│                                                       │
│            Annual membership dues                     │
│    Individual                              $ 45       │
│    Youth                                     30       │
│    Family                                   100       │
│                                                       │
│                 Court time fees                       │
│    Prime                              $10 per hour    │
│    Regular                             $6 per hour    │
│                                                       │
│            MEMBERSHIP DISTRIBUTION                    │
│                                                       │
│    Individual                              50%        │
│    Youth                                    20        │
│    Family                                   30        │
│                                            100%       │
└─────────────────────────────────────────────────────┘
```

PROJECTED OPERATING DATA

Quarter	Membership Renewal or New Memberships	Court Time in Hours		Costs	
		Prime	Regular	Fixed Costs*	Variable Costs
1	600	5,500	6,000	$ 56,500	$ 57,500
2	200	2,000	4,000	56,500	30,000
3	200	1,000	2,000	56,500	15,000
4	600	5,500	6,000	56,500	57,500
	1,600			$226,000	$160,000

*Includes a quarterly depreciation charge of $12,500.

12-15 *(Cash Budget; Statement of Financial Position).* You have just been elected treasurer of the Farmville Racquet Club for the year 19X1. The accounting records are limited to a checkbook and a desk drawer full of invoices and receipts. The board of governors has asked you to prepare a financial plan for the next year. Disturbed by the decline in cash during the past year, the board must consider a dues increase. The present cash balance is $3,000; the board wants a cash balance of $5,000 by year-end.

An examination of the records produced the following information. There are 200 members who have paid dues of $50 per year and $3.00 per hour for use of the tennis courts. The club owns four courts, each of which is used an average of five hours per day for approximately 300 days per year.

In addition to the $3,000 in the bank, club assets consist of receivables from members of $2,000, half of which apply to members who have moved away and should be written off, and land and tennis courts worth $50,000. The club owes $600 for maintenance performed in 19X0.

For managing the club, a tennis pro is paid one-third of the court fees billed. The pro also gives lessons and sells equipment. Cash payments last year, in addition to the payment to the tennis pro, were: maintenance $12,000, utilities $3,000, property taxes $2,000, new playing surface $10,000, and miscellaneous $1,000. During 19X1, taxes and utilities are expected to increase by 50%, new surfaces will cost $6,000, and miscellaneous expenses will be $1,000. Maintenance costs and the contract with the pro are expected to remain unchanged. At the end of the year, 5% of 19X1 court fees are expected to be outstanding; an unpaid maintenance expense should be $1,000.

The board does not want you to consider depreciation.

REQUIRED:

A. Prepare a Statement of Financial Position at the beginning of 19X1.

B. Prepare a Cash Budget for 19X1 that will achieve the cash flow objectives of the board. How much will dues have to be increased?

C. Assuming that dues are increased, prepare a Projected Statement of Financial Position at December 31, 19X1.

D. What recommendations can you make to the board of directors?

12-16 *(Cash Budget; Profit Plan).* Joy Ely graduated three years ago from State University with a major in accounting. Since graduation she has been working for a large CPA firm in Urbanville. She has had excellent training and challenging assignments from the CPA firm, but wants to live in a smaller city. One of the CPAs in her hometown wants to retire at the end of June and will sell his practice.

For the past few years he has withdrawn about $20,000 per year. Joy may purchase the practice for $20,000, payable 25% down and one-fourth at the end of each of the next three years without interest. His billings to clients last year, by quarter, were: January through March, $18,000; April through June, $9,000; July through September, $6,000; and October through December, $9,000. Of a quarter's billings, 5% are uncollectible and 20% of the balance are collected in the next quarter. Because of the change in ownership, Ms. Ely can expect her billings to be only half the previous billings for the first quarter she owns the practice (July through September), two-thirds in the next quarter, and from then on equal to the previous owner's billings. She expects his pattern of cash collections to continue.

Office rent, telephone expense, and secretarial expense will be $600 per month. Part-time help will be used after business increases and will cost $500 during October through December, $1,800 during January through March, and $800 during April through June. Automobile expenses will be $40 per month plus 2% of billings to clients. The state recently enacted continuing education requirements. Joy will spend $400 in the first quarter and $800 in the second quarter she owns the business to meet these requirements. Other expenses will be 8% of billings. Two-thirds of automobile and other expenses will be paid in the month of the expense; one-third in the month following the expense. The remaining expenses will be paid in the month the expense is incurred.

The $20,000 purchase price includes $2,000 of equipment, $2,000 of accounts receivable, and $16,000 for the clients' files. The equipment is old and is to be depreciated over two years; the amount allocated to clients' files will be amortized over four years.

Joy has accumulated $6,000 in savings and will invest the entire amount in the practice. She believes she must withdraw at least $600 per month for personal living expenses for the first year.

REQUIRED:

A. Assuming that Joy Ely purchases the accounting practice on July 1, prepare a Profit Plan by quarter for the first year she owns the business.

B. Prepare a Cash Budget by quarter for the first year.

C. How much revenue is needed each quarter to break even?

12-17 *(Profit Plan and Cash Budget for Health Center)*. Mesa County Health Association is a nonprofit health association organized to provide health care for a low-income rural population. Medical service will be provided to all residents of the county regardless of their ability to pay. About 30% of the patients who come to the health center are financially able to pay for medical services. The balance of the costs of the health center will be covered by a federal grant. The executive committee of the health center has asked you to prepare a budget to support the grant request.

Mesa County Health Association serves a rural county with about 18,000 residents, of whom 40% are expected to become patients of the health center. Each patient is expected to average five visits per year. Assume that the visits are spread evenly throughout the year.

Physicians will be employed by the health center. Each physician can see 500 patients per month. One nurse is required for each 300 patient visits per month. The average physician's salary is $4,000 per month and nurses receive $1,000 per month. Physicians may be hired on a half-time basis if necessary. All other employees will be full-time employees.

Operating costs of the health center include the following:

Medical supplies	$3.00 per patient visit
Lab and X-ray technicians	$3,000 per month
Rent	$12,000 per year
Administration	$3,800 per month plus $.50 per visit
Other expenses	$1,000 per month plus $.20 per visit

The physicians and "other expenses" are paid in the month following the month in which the expense is incurred. The remainder of the expenses are paid in the month the expense is incurred. The grant will be received in equal monthly installments. Assume a two-month delay in payment by the patients who are paying their own bills.

All facilities except an X-ray unit costing $4,800 will be leased. The equipment will be depreciated on a straight-line basis over four years.

The health center has a beginning cash balance of $15,000. A local grant was received from the community to provide working capital and purchase the X-ray equipment.

REQUIRED:

A. Determine the projected expenses for the year. What billing rate will be required to cover all costs?

B. Prepare a Profit Plan for the year.

C. Prepare a Cash Budget for the year.

12-18 (*Sales Budget and Profit Plan Using Expected Values*). Telmatt Industries designs and manufactures toys. Past experience indicates that the product life cycle of a toy is three years. Promotional advertising produces large sales in the early years, but there is a substantial sales decline in the final year of a toy's life.

Consumer demand for new toys placed on the market tends to fall into three classes. About 30% of the new toys sell well above expectations, 60% sell as anticipated, and 10% have poor consumer acceptance.

The management of Telmatt Industries has decided to produce a new toy. The following sales projections were made after carefully evaluating consumer demand for the new toy.

Consumer Demand for New Toy	Chance of Occurring	ESTIMATED SALES		
		Year 19X7	Year 19X8	Year 19X9
Above average	30%	$1,200,000	$2,500,000	$600,000
Average	60%	$ 700,000	$1,700,000	$400,000
Below average	10%	$ 200,000	$ 900,000	$150,000

Variable production costs are estimated at 30% of sales. Fixed production expenses, excluding depreciation, related to the new toy are estimated at $50,000 per year. New machinery costing $860,000 will be installed by January 1, 19X7, to produce the new toy. The new machinery will be depreciated by the sum-of-the-years'-digits method. There is no other use anticipated for the equipment. It will be sold at the end of the third year at its salvage value, expected to be $110,000. A vacant portion of the plant that has no other prospect for use will ·be used to produce the toy. Rent expense apportioned to this space is $20,000 per year.

Advertising and promotional expenses are expected to be $100,000 the first year, $150,000 the second year, and $50,000 the third year. Assume that state and federal taxes will total 60% of income.

REQUIRED:

A. Prepare a sales budget for this new toy in each of the three years, taking into account the probability of above-average, average, and below-average sales occurring.

B. Prepare a Profit Plan for the new toy for each of the three years of its life.

(CPA adapted)

12-19 *(Review of Breakeven Analysis; Analysis of Performance).* At the end of 19X3, the following income statement was prepared for The Window Dresser, a custom drapery shop.

THE WINDOW DRESSER
INCOME STATEMENT
For the Year 19X3

Sales (6,500 yards)		$104,000
Cost of Goods Sold		63,700
Gross margin		$ 40,300
Operating expenses:		
Salaries and commissions	$25,000	
Depreciation	6,000	
Supplies	5,600	
Utilities	700	
Advertising	4,200	41,500
Loss		$ (1,200)

Ms. Drugge, the owner of the shop, does not believe that her shop should have shown a loss for the year. Although a downturn in the economy of the area resulted in fewer sales than planned, she believes that The Window Dresser should still be above breakeven. She believed that she had increased her selling prices to more than enough to offset the increases in the cost of fabric.

At the beginning of 19X3, Ms. Drugge developed the following planning data.

Sales	10,000 yards @ $15	
Cost of fabric	$9.00 per yard (60% of sales)	
Operating expenses:		

	Fixed	*Variable (% of sales)*
Salaries	$10,000	12%
Depreciation	$ 6,000	—
Supplies	—	5%
Utilities	$ 800	—
Advertising	$ 1,200	3%

REQUIRED:

A. On the basis of the planning data, what was Ms. Drugge's breakeven point in dollars of sales?

B. Considering only the changes in the cost of fabric and her selling price, what is the new breakeven point?

C. Prepare a report to Ms. Drugge explaining the performance for the period.

12-20 *(Comprehensive Planning and Control with Master Budget).* Parkland Doctors' Clinic serves a suburban community of about 24,000 population, of which 25% are expected to become patients of the clinic. Each patient is expected to average five visits per year. You may assume that patient visits occur evenly throughout the year. Normally, about 5% of the billings of $17 per patient visit are not collected. Accounts Receivable at the end of the year is expected to be equal to an average month's net billings.

Each doctor can serve about 600 patient visits per month. A half-time consulting physician is available if the patient load requires less than a full-time doctor. (For example, if 3,750 patient visits require 6¼ doctors, one half-time and six full-time doctors would be hired.) One nurse is required for each 500 patient visits per month. The average individual doctor's salary is $4,000 per month; a nurse's average salary is $1,000 per month. Doctors are paid in the following month; all other personnel are paid in the month service is performed.

Operating costs for the clinic include

Administrative salaries	$5,000 per month
Lab and X-ray technicians	$4,000 per month
Medical supplies	$1.50 per patient visit
Rent	$24,000 per year
Medical and financial records	$1,000 per month plus $.25 per patient visit
Other operating costs	$500 per month plus $.15 per patient visit

Medical supplies are purchased monthly on 30-day terms. The medical and financial records are maintained by a computer service bureau. Payment is made in the month following service. All other operating costs are paid in the month of service.

The statement of financial position at the end of 19X1 follows.

PARKLAND DOCTORS' CLINIC
STATEMENT OF FINANCIAL POSITION
December 31, 19X1

Assets		Equities	
Cash	$10,000	Accounts payable	$12,500
Accounts Receivable (net)	25,000	Salaries payable	4,000
Supplies	2,000	Owners' equity	20,500
	$37,000		$37,000

REQUIRED:

A. Prepare a Profit Plan for 19X2.

B. Prepare a Cash Budget for 19X2. Assume a desired minimum cash balance of $5,000. A line of credit is available if needed. (Ignore interest expense.)

C. Prepare a Projected Statement of Financial Position at the end of 19X2.

12-21 *(Continuation of Problem 12–20—Reporting to Management)*. During 19X2 the following actual events were recorded for the Parkland Doctors' Clinic.

1. Patient visits amounted to 28,000 in 19X2. The billing rate through the year was $17 per patient visit. The collection rate was better than anticipated. Only 3% of 19X2 billings were considered uncollectible.

2. Costs for 19X2:

Doctors' salaries	$200,000
(December salaries $14,000)	
Nurses salaries	$ 62,000
Administrative salaries	$ 60,000
Lab and X-ray technicians' salaries	$ 45,000
Medical supplies	$ 39,200
Rent	$ 24,000
Medical and financial records	$ 19,000
Other costs	$ 11,000

3. Other information:
   During the last month of 19X2 there were 2,000 patient visits. Supplies of $2,800 were purchased, and the bill for medical and financial records was $1,500. The inventory of supplies at the end of 19X2 was $2,000.

REQUIRED:

A. Prepare an income statement for 19X2 for the Parkland Doctors' Clinic. Your income statement should compare actual results with plans in problem 12-20 and identify variances.

B. Prepare a cash flow statement for the year.

C. Prepare a Statement of Financial Position at the end of 19X2.

12-22 *(Profit Plan, Cash Budget, Projected Statement of Financial Position)*. Exotic Imports, Inc. was organized to import unusual gift items. The Statement of Financial Position on April 1, 19X0, the date the company was organized, follows.

```
                        EXOTIC IMPORTS, INC.
                  STATEMENT OF FINANCIAL POSITION
                           April 1, 19X0

               Assets                          Equities

   Cash                    $ 30,000    Capital stock    $100,000
   Land                      20,000
   Buildings and equipment   50,000
                           $100,000                     $100,000
```

Sales for the first six months are expected to be as follows:

April	$ 40,000	July	$200,000
May	$ 60,000	August	$250,000
June	$120,000	September	$100,000

The owners are worried about the cash position of the company for the first three months of operations. They believe that cash flows will be favorable after June. The company plans to borrow any amount needed to carry it through the first quarter as soon as a minimum cash balance of $10,000 is reached. A line of credit has been arranged at the bank requiring interest of 1% per month on the money borrowed. Interest will be paid at the time the loan is repaid.

The contribution margin ratio on sales is expected to be 60%. The company plans to carry an inventory equal to expected sales for the next two months. Purchases are paid in the following month.

Variable selling expenses are expected to equal 20% of sales. Fixed selling and administrative expenses are expected to be $30,000 per month, including $1,000 of depreciation. Eighty percent of the expenses will be paid in the month of expense; the balance will be paid in the following month.

Sixty percent of sales are expected to be cash sales. The balance of sales will be credit card sales with 25% collected in the month of sale and 75% in the following month.

REQUIRED:

A. Prepare a Profit Plan by month for the first three months of operations.

B. Prepare a Cash Budget by month for the first three months of operations. How much does the company have to borrow to maintain a minimum cash balance of $10,000? How soon?

C. Prepare a Projected Statement of Financial Position at June 30, 19X0.

D. Compute the breakeven point in sales dollars, ignoring any interest cost. Does it appear that the problems of liquidity will be solved and that the firm will be profitable after June?

12-23 *(Cash Budget Under Differing Conditions)*. The Wooden Mouse, Inc. is a specialty gift shop in a popular ski area. For the past two years, skiing has been poor and, as a result, several speciality shops have failed. The Wooden Mouse has serious cash flow problems and needs help in planning cash flows for the coming season. Snow for the 19X3 ski season is expected to be normal, so the following sales may be expected:

December	$20,000
January	$50,000
February	$60,000
March	$30,000
April	$20,000
May to November	$10,000 per month

The inventory policy is to maintain an inventory equal to the next two months' sales. The beginning inventory is $12,000, the minimum amount required if a poor season is predicted.

Purchases are subject to 5/10, n/60 terms. (A 5% discount is allowed on payments within 10 days of the purchase; the balance is due within 60 days.) All purchases are made in the first half of the month. No purchases were made during October; purchases during November were $5,000. Because of the cash shortage, no discounts have been taken for two years.

Fifty percent of the sales are for cash; the balance are on credit cards with a 5% service charge. One-half of the credit sales are collected in the month of sale; one-half are collected in the month following the sale. Sales in November were $10,000.

The company has a 60% gross margin rate, operating expenses are $9,000 per month (including $1,000 of depreciation) plus 20% of sales. Seventy-five percent of the expenses are paid in the month the expense is incurred; the balance is paid in the following month.

A line of credit for $45,000 was arranged at the bank; $8,000 was drawn against the line of credit in November. Interest is 1% per month on the unpaid loan balance and is payable on April 1. The loan principle is to be reduced as soon as cash is available but must be paid in full by April. All loan transactions (except interest) must be in even thousand-dollar amounts. The company must maintain a minimum cash balance of $2,000, which is the December 1 balance. Because the shop will operate at a loss for the remainder of the year, the owner wants a cash balance of $15,000 on May 1. Ignore income taxes.

REQUIRED:

A. Prepare a Cash Budget, by month, for the 19X3 ski season (December–April). Assume that discounts will be taken.

B. Will the owner of Wooden Mouse, Inc. be able to accomplish the cash and loan payment objectives during the 19X3 ski season? If cash requirements exceed the line of credit during a particular month, what can the firm do to improve cash inflows or reduce or postpone cash outflows? Explain, but do not recast the Cash Budget.

C. Using the data for the Wooden Mouse, Inc., assume that the long-run weather forecast is for little snow and, therefore, poor skiing. Sales for the company are projected as follows if the weather is bad for skiing:

December	$10,000
January	$20,000
February	$25,000
March	$20,000
April	$10,000
May to November	$10,000 per month

Prepare a new Cash Budget. What are your recommendations for the owners of Wooden Mouse, Inc.?

12-24 *(Profit Plans to Compare Alternatives).* Ric Roberts had started in the restaurant business as a dishwasher when he was in high school. During his years in college he continued to work in all facets of the food industry and at graduation acquired his first, small neighborhood restaurant. He operated this restaurant for the next three years, developing and sharpening the management tools he would need in the future. His long-range plans were to build a chain of quality restaurants, franchised throughout the United States, focusing on family activities and wholesome, moderately priced food.

In 19X2 rising rates of mortgage defaults and foreclosures across the country were creating a miniboom for sharp-eyed real estate investors who knew how to rescue distressed properties. This condition was particularly prevalent in the Pacific Northwest, where the economic climate produced by the decline in the housing, construction, and forest product industries provided many investment opportunities. The poor economic climate had a severe effect on the restaurant industry. Declining margins and decreased sales because of decreased disposable income resulted in a significant number of closings.

In the Fall of 19X3, Ric sold his profitable restaurant property in the midwest for $175,000 and migrated to the Pacific Northwest, forming Home Place, Inc. During 19X4 Home Place, Inc. acquired its first restaurant in Washington State and remodeled it according to the plan for a quality family restaurant. Ric had chosen a location outside the metropolitan area in a small "bedroom" community.

Toward the end of 19X4 an opportunity arose to lease a second restaurant building that would require $200,000 in lease-hold improvements before it could be opened for business. This building was located in Everett, a small city of 56,000 and offered an excellent opportunity to expand into new territory.

A review of the partial balance sheet (Exhibit 1) data clearly showed the need for additional working capital and a meeting with the bank. The next day

11-30-X4					
	HOME PLACE, INC.				
	WORKING CAPITAL STATEMENT				
	Months of September, October, and November, 19X4				
	September		October		November
Current assets:					
Cash	$46,709		$39,481		$ 8,631
Food	11,238		14,175		15,735
Supplies	2,127		2,363		2,622
Total current assets		$60,074		$56,019	$ 26,988
Current liabilities					
Accounts Payable		(23,365)		(31,538)	(38,357)
Net working capital		$36,709		$24,481	$(11,369)

EXHIBIT 1

the following conversation took place between Ric Roberts and Mark Michaels of Interstate First Bank.

Ric: "I know the business is in a bit of a cash bind, but as my banker you must realize that the restaurant industry has not done well because of the slow economic recovery. I have just taken a look at the monthly reports from the restaurant in Bothell. After reading the first three months' operating statements (Exhibit 2), I am encouraged. As you can see, the restaurant shows a small profit after only three months. Unfortunately, the cash flow is weaker than I had planned. Originally I had planned a growth rate of 15% per month for the first year of operations and 12% per annum for the next four years. Actual sales are currently growing at an acceptable rate of about 11% per month; obviously even though this rate is lower than planned growth rate it is relatively strong. I now believe that the rate will be 11% per month until September or October of next year and then will smooth to about 8% per annum for the foreseeable future.

Mark: Ric, I hate to dampen your optimism, but our economists believe the current economic conditions are going to continue for some time. Unemployment exceeds 12% in the state; interest rates, while decreasing somewhat, are still high; and even if people had some disposable income, they are holding it back until things improve. So far you have gone against the trend, but if you lease the second restaurant the pressure for additional liquid assets will be quite real. You want a loan to increase working capital and to pay for the lease-hold improvements in Everett but, to put it on the line, where are you going to get the cash flow to make the loan payments?

Ric: As far as the restaurant in Bothell is concerned, I have done some research and am considering adding a cocktail lounge to help achieve a profit level that

11-30-X4

HOME PLACE, INC.
BOTHELL INCOME STATEMENT
For Months of September, October, November, 19X4

	SEPTEMBER		OCTOBER		NOVEMBER	
	Amount	Percentage	Amount	Percentage	Amount	Percentage
Net sales	$36,450	100.0	$40,500	100.0	$45,000	100.0
Operating expenses:						
Food	$14,580	40.0	$14,985	37.0	$15,750	35.0
Labor*	12,029	33.0	11,745	29.0	11,700	26.0
Utilities†	1,458	4.0	2,025	5.0	2,200	5.0
Supplies	2,552	7.0	1,418	3.5	1,575	3.5
Building‡	10,206	28.0	10,125	25.0	10,125	22.5
Total expenses	40,825	105.0	40,298	99.5	41,350	92.0
Gross margin	$ (4,375)		$ 202		$ 3,650	
Selling expenses	2,190	6.0	2,430	6.0	2,700	6.0
Operating income	$ (6,565)		$ (2,228)		$ 950	

*Including wages, social security payments, vacation and sick leave benefits, and medical costs.
†Assume expense for power, light, and heat is directly proportional to the number of operating hours. Current operating hours per day are 10.
‡Including property and equipment lease payments, property taxes, property insurance, and building services. No changes in the total costs are expected for the next 10 months.

EXHIBIT 2

would be equal to or surpass that which was originally budgeted. This particular restaurant is located downtown and is the most accessible one in the area. Further, it has been open for only three months and business is continuing to grow. Currently it is operating 10 hours per day from 11 A.M. to 9 P.M., six days a week. I really believe that adding a cocktail lounge would be one opportunity we could explore at this time. If done in a tasteful manner it should not destroy our image of a family restaurant.

I have done some market studies on restaurants with lounges. I estimate from my research that during the first six months of operating the lounge there would be a 50% chance of averaging $17,500 revenue per month, a 20% chance of averaging $20,000 revenue per month, and a 30% chance of averaging only $5,000 revenue per month from the cocktail lounge alone. After the first six months I would expect a planned growth in lounge sales of 6% per annum.

Based on past experiences, I estimate that an additional $3,450 of labor expenses would be incurred for handling up to $20,000 of lounge revenue and another extra $1,725 if revenue were $20,000 or more. Currently the building and the majority of the equipment are leased under a five-year contract with monthly lease payments of $5,500. Additional lounge equipment could be leased from the same firm for $1,200 per month plus 2% of total lounge sales. The lounge business appears to be very attractive financially. Liquor costs would run about 20% of sales compared to 35% for food. Supplies and selling expenses should bear the same relationship to lounge sales that they bear to food sales. Utilities should increase by about $400 per month, because we would extend our business hours to 2 A.M.

However, I am a little concerned. My overall plan was to build a franchise of family-oriented restaurants. If I add the cocktail lounge, I estimate a loss of 20% of my family restaurant sales because my overall clientele will change and some people will not like that. This really concerns me.

Mark: I'm not disagreeing with your forecast of increased sales or your estimates of expenses, but I will really need to see the impact on your operating income. Further, if you lease that restaurant building in Everett, regardless of how good a deal, your liquid assets will be in a very precarious position. As it is right now your asset structure cannot withstand the additional, even if temporary, drain for the remodel/opening of a second restaurant. Frankly, at this point the bank's position is quite negative about lending any more resources. Show me how you plan to solve your cash flow problems in the restaurant you are now operating. When you have that data, then come and talk to us about your Everett plans.

Needless to say, the meeting had not gone as Ric had planned. The move to the Northwest had been an attempt to take advantage of the weak economy and the bargains that condition produced. In truth the bargains had been numerous and the choices between them had been difficult. There were many more bargains than Ric had resources. His own capital could not support a second restaurant without help from the bank. He decided he had no choice but to comply with Mark's suggestion for further support data and another meeting.

REQUIRED:

A. Prepare projected income statements and a statement of projected cash flows for each month from December 19X4 through July 19X5. Assume that the cost patterns of the Bothell restaurant in the month of November 19X4 will be representative of cost patterns for the next eight months.

B. Prepare an analysis, including supporting financial data, of the suggestion to add a cocktail lounge. Limit your analysis to six months. Assume that the lounge would begin operations on February 1, 19X5.

C. Using the data developed above, what recommendations would you make to Ric? What other information would you like to have?

chapter **13**

RESPONSIBILITY ACCOUNTING AND BUDGETARY CONTROL

This chapter expands the study of the budgeting system by looking at responsibility accounting. The planning and control system, with an overview of the budgetary process, was examined in the previous chapter. We now use the concept of responsibility accounting to show how both departmental budgets and reports are developed and integrated into a responsibility reporting system.

RESPONSIBILITY ACCOUNTING

Effective planning and control systems are structured around the implicit or explicit areas of responsibility within the organization. Responsibility areas may be departments (drilling or maintenance department), product lines (pickles or mustard), territories (West or South), or any other type of identifiable unit or combination of units. The specific types of responsibility areas depend on the nature of the firm and its activities.

Ideally, the budgetary system, as well as the accounting system, is tailored to the relevant organization level and the particular individual involved. Budgetary reports should include the specific revenues and expenses over which the manager has control, called **controllable** revenues and expenses. A cost or benefit is controllable by an individual if it is directly affected by that person's decisions, regardless of how the cost or benefit is actually accounted for within the data system. For example, if a salesperson accepts a rush order that requires exceptional production costs, such as additional setups and overtime, the cost report for the marketing unit should bear the additional production costs. The production department has no control over the delivery date that gave rise to the additional costs. Care must be taken, however; excessive zeal is pinpointing responsibility may lead to interdepartmental conflict that is more detrimental to the company than lack of control over the particular cost. Where control is shared, the assignment of responsibility must be decided by the superior who is responsible for the common activity. One overriding principle is that arbitrary allocations of costs should not enter into a responsibility cost system.

We are using the term **responsibility center** in a broad sense. It could be as small as an individual machine or as large as the Chevrolet Division of General Motors. It could be a sales department in a department store, a service department, a specific production line, a warehouse unit, a group of salespeople, or a tax section in the accounting department. Size is not the criterion for development of a responsibility center. The important criteria are (1) that a subdivision relevant to operating performance is separable and identifiable, and (2) that there are relevant measures of performance.

Accountants usually classify responsibility centers into three classes: cost centers, profit or contribution centers, and investment centers. Each of the three has different characteristics in regard to the financial data available for performance assessment.

COST CENTERS

A **cost center** is a responsibility center where costs (expenses) are the principal planning and control data. Performance is assessed by comparing the actual expenses with the Performance Budget, which shows the expenses the center should have incurred, given their actual activity. Any variances between actual and budgeted expenses are the primary focus of management assessment. In firms where the budgetary process is underdeveloped, the control data may consist of a comparison of current expenses with past expenses.

It is difficult to assess the effectiveness and efficiency of a cost center, even with a budget, because the financial impact of decisions is measured only by costs. There is no corresponding *financial* measure of what the cost center accomplished. If not done carefully, the analysis of a cost center may lead to the assumption that "the best cost center is the one that spends the least." This attitude ignores benefits contributed by the cost center to the overall firm.

Because no financial benefits are traced to cost centers, most firms mix financial and nonfinancial data in performance assessment. The effort of the department is measured in financial terms (costs), whereas the benefits are measured in nonfinancial terms (number of units produced, number of customers waited on, or number of invoices processed, for example). It is impossible to determine whether the efficiency of the cost center is acceptable without relating the financial and nonfinancial data. Comparison with the budget will tell whether actual performance conformed with planned expenditures, but it will not tell whether this performance was effective.

PROFIT OR CONTRIBUTION CENTERS

In a **profit center,** or **contribution center,** both cost and revenue data are measurable in financial terms, which provides greater scope in assessing performance. The profit center is more sophisticated, in terms of management planning and control potential, then a cost center. Because outputs as well as inputs may be measured in a profit center, its ability to earn a "satisfactory profit" may be assessed.

Because the manager should be held accountable for the controllable revenues and costs, the allocation of indirect costs should be avoided. The inclusion of an allocated portion of service department costs will only confuse the issue. Accordingly, many firms prefer to think in terms of contribution centers rather than profit centers. In a contribution center the department's controllable costs are deducted from its controllable revenue. The resulting departmental margin is the department's contribution to the firm's joint costs and, ultimately, income.

Implicit to the profit center concept is the assumption that a manager's economic decisions affect the profits of the division. Thus, there can be an effective assignment of responsibility for both costs and revenues. Second, it is assumed that an increase in the profit center's income or departmental margin will act to increase the income of the firm. Without this implied relationship, a manager could optimize a division's income to the detriment of the firm's income. Third, and very important, is the assumption that the profit center's activities are not significantly dependent on the actions of the other divisions. It must have some autonomy.

INVESTMENT CENTERS

In an **investment center,** performance is measured not only by income, but also by relating this income to the asset investment. The investment center concept makes it possible to assess the efficiency of investment utilization; the rate of return on investment may be used in performance evaluation. Investment centers are treated as individual businesses where the manager is responsible for all activities—costs, revenues, and investments. We will examine investment centers in the next chapter.

RESPONSIBILITY ACCOUNTING AND THE PLANNING PROCESS

The planning process has both a downward and an upward flow of information. Before the budget can be developed by the responsibility centers, direction through goals and objectives must come downward from the top. Top management sets the broad direction of the firm through goals and the development of specific objectives. With these goals and objectives as guidelines, the operating budgets are developed by the responsibility center with an upward flow of data.

This planning process is illustrated in Exhibit 13–1. In this exhibit the downward flow of information begins with goals. It draws upon the environment for forecasts of economic, competitive, regulatory, and other external influences, setting specific targets for objectives. Finally, management makes the necessary decisions to put the planning process in force. Four levels of responsibility are presented in this illustration. The number of levels within an organization will depend on the style of management and the way the company is organized. Typically the lowest level of responsibility, involving group leaders or individual employees, has little direct involvement in the budget or the accounting reports. In the factory and administrative departments, with responsibility for costs, the departmental reports project the resources needed to achieve the objectives set by higher levels of management. In the marketing departments, with responsibility for both revenue and costs, the budget will focus on contribution or profit generated. Departmental budgets are compiled into functional area budgets for

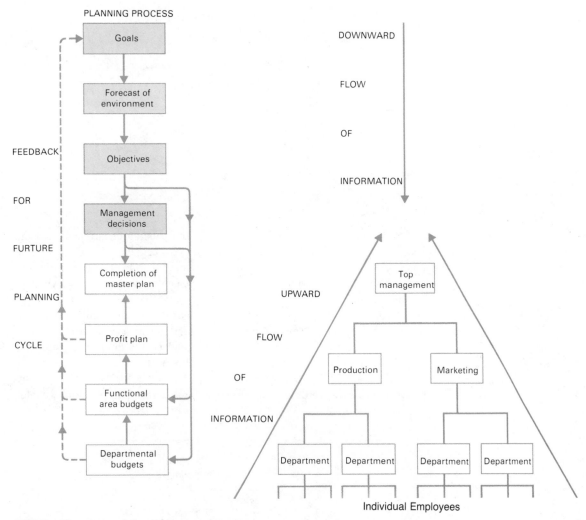

EXHIBIT 13-1 Flow of information in the planning process

the factory and marketing areas. Finally, the functional area budgets are compiled into the Profit Plan. As a final step in the planning process the goals and objectives implicit in the profit plan are tested through the completion of the other components of the master budget.

To show how responsibility center budgets are developed and integrated into a Profit Plan, we will use the Karl Company. The Karl Company has the following organizational structure.

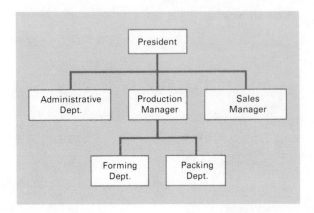

The production areas, including the forming and packing departments and the production manager's administrative areas, are cost centers. The administrative department is also a cost center. The marketing department is a contribution center. The firm as a whole is an investment center; there are no divisional investment centers.

The Karl Company produces two sizes of plastic terrariums: a 1-gallon size, which they term "small" and a 5-gallon size, which they term "large." The terrariums differ only in the size of the molds used in the forming process. After molding the products are packaged for shipment.

Background data necessary to develop the budget for the Karl Company are the standard cost cards and the cost behavior patterns by responsibility center

EXHIBIT 13–2
Background cost data for
the Karl Company

STANDARD COST CARD SMALL TERRARIUM			
	Forming Department	Packing Department	Total
Direct Material:			
Plastic—1 pound	$ .40		$ .40
Carton—1 gallon		$.30	.30
			$ .70
Direct Labor:			
.1 hours @ $5.00	.50		$ .50
.1 hours @ $3.00		.30	.30
			.80
Variable Overhead:			
.1 hours @ $4.00	.40		$ .40
.1 hours @ $1.00		.10	.10
			.50
Total Variable Cost	$1.30	$.70	$2.00

STANDARD COST CARD
LARGE TERRARIUM

	Forming Department	Packing Department	Total
Direct Material:			
Plastic—3 pounds	$1.20		$1.20
Carton—5 gallon		$ .60	.60
			$1.80
Direct Labor:			
.2 hours @ $5.00	1.00		$1.00
.1 hours @ $3.00		.30	.30
			1.30
Variable Overhead:			
.2 hours @ $4.00	.80		$ .80
.1 hours @ $1.00		.10	.10
			.90
Total Variable Cost	$3.00	$1.00	$4.00

OVERHEAD COSTS

FACTORY RESPONSIBILITY CENTERS

	Forming	Packing	Factory Management	Total
Variable rate (per labor hour)	$4.00	$1.00	None	
Fixed (per year)				
Depreciation	$32,000	$ 4,000	$ 4,000	$ 40,000
Other fixed production costs	12,000	8,000	40,000	60,000
Total	$44,000	$12,000	$44,000	$100,000

MARKETING COSTS:
Variable (per unit sold) $.50 for small terrarium
    $.80 for large terrarium

Fixed (per year):	
Depreciation	$ 24,000
Other fixed marketing costs	56,000
Total	$ 80,000

ADMINISTRATIVE COSTS:

Fixed (per year):	
Depreciation	$ 4,000
Other fixed administrative costs	36,000
Total	$ 40,000

EXHIBIT 13–2
Con't.

	QUARTER				Total for Year
	1	2	3	4	
Budgeted Sales in Units:					
Small	8,000	16,000	48,000	8,000	80,000
Large	8,000	6,000	20,000	6,000	40,000
Budgeted Sales in Dollars:					
Small	$ 40,000	$ 80,000	$240,000	$40,000	$400,000
Large	64,000	48,000	160,000	48,000	320,000
Total Sales	$104,000	$128,000	$400,000	$88,000	$720,000
Budgeted Production in Units:					
Small	10,000	32,000	28,000	8,000	78,000
Large	6,000	13,000	13,000	7,000	39,000

EXHIBIT 13–3   Data from sales and production budgets for the Karl Company

in Exhibit 13–2, and data from the sales and production budgets in Exhibit 13–3. Because a discussion of goals, objectives, and the downward flow of information were illustrated in the previous chapter, they are omitted here.

DEVELOPMENT OF DEPARTMENTAL BUDGETS BY RESPONSIBILITY AREA

With responsibility reporting, each departmental report includes only those revenues and costs over which the manager has control. In the Karl Company each revenue or cost has been related to the lowest level of management with the authority to influence or change it.

Factory departments, and the factory as a whole, are cost centers with responsibility only for costs. Exhibits 13–4 and 13–5 present the departmental budgets for the Forming and Packing departments, respectively. Development of the departmental budgets for the factory started with the required production levels from the production budget (Exhibit 13–3). The material, direct labor, and variable overhead costs are developed by applying the production levels from the production budget to the standard cost cards in Exhibit 13–2. Fixed overhead also comes from the cost behavior patterns in Exhibit 13–2.

As the upward flow of information continues, the departmental budgets for the factory are compiled into the Factory Cost Budget in Exhibit 13–6. Note that the costs for the Forming and Packing departments are shown as one-line entries in the Factory Cost Budget. Focus is on responsibility for costs. Therefore, costs controllable by subordinate departments are separated from costs directly controllable by the factory manager. A summary of factory costs is shown at the bottom of the Factory Cost Budget.

	QUARTER				Total for Year
	1	2	3	4	
Material	$11,200	$28,400	$26,800	$11,600	$ 78,000
Direct labor	11,000	29,000	27,000	11,000	78,000
Variable overhead	8,800	23,200	21,600	8,800	62,400
Total variable costs	$31,000	$80,600	$75,400	$31,400	$218,400
Departmental fixed costs:					
Depreciation	$ 8,000	$ 8,000	$ 8,000	$ 8,000	$ 32,000
Other fixed production costs	3,000	3,000	3,000	3,000	12,000
Total fixed costs	11,000	11,000	11,000	11,000	44,000
Total department cost	$42,000	$91,600	$86,400	$42,400	$262,400
Physical data:					
Production:					
Small	10,000	32,000	28,000	8,000	78,000
Large	6,000	13,000	13,000	7,000	39,000
Material (pounds)	28,000	71,000	67,000	29,000	195,000
Direct labor hours	2,200*	5,800	5,400	2,200	15,600

*For example, (1,000 small × .1) + (6,000 large × .2)

EXHIBIT 13—4   Cost Budget for Forming Department

	QUARTER				Total for Year
	1	2	3	4	
Material	$ 6,600	$17,400	$16,200	$ 6,600	$ 46,800
Direct labor	4,800	13,500	12,300	4,500	35,100
Variable overhead	1,600	4,500	4,100	1,500	11,700
Total variable costs	$13,000	$35,400	$32,600	$12,600	$ 93,600
Departmental fixed costs:					
Depreciation	$ 1,000	$ 1,000	$ 1,000	$ 1,000	$ 4,000
Other fixed production costs	2,000	2,000	2,000	2,000	8,000
Total fixed costs	3,000	3,000	3,000	3,000	12,000
Total department cost	$16,000	$38,400	$35,600	$15,600	$105,600
Physical data:					
Production:					
Small	10,000	32,000	28,000	8,000	78,000
Large	6,000	13,000	13,000	7,000	39,000
Material:					
1-gallon size	10,000	32,000	28,000	8,000	78,000
5-gallon size	6,000	13,000	13,000	7,000	39,000
Direct labor hours	1,600	4,500	4,100	1,500	11,700

EXHIBIT 13—5   Cost Budget for Packing Department

	QUARTER				Total for Year
	1	2	3	4	
Costs controllable by subordinate department:					
Forming Department	$42,000	$ 91,600	$ 86,400	$42,400	$262,400
Packing Department	16,000	38,400	35,600	15,600	105,600
Total	$58,000	$130,000	$122,000	$58,000	$368,000
Costs controllable by factory manager directly:					
Depreciation	$ 1,000	$ 1,000	$ 1,000	$ 1,000	$ 4,000
Other fixed production costs	10,000	10,000	10,000	10,000	40,000
Total	11,000	11,000	11,000	11,000	44,000
Total factory costs	$69,000	$141,000	$133,000	$69,000	$412,000
Summary of costs					
Material	$17,800	$ 45,800	$ 43,000	$18,200	$124,800
Direct labor	16,800	42,500	39,300	15,500	113,100
Variable overhead	10,400	27,700	25,700	10,300	74,100
Total variable costs	$44,000	$116,000	$108,000	$44,000	$312,000
Fixed costs	25,000	25,000	25,000	25,000	100,000
Total factory costs	$69,000	$141,000	$133,000	$69,000	$412,000

EXHIBIT 13–6 Cost Budget for factory manager

The marketing area, as contrasted with the factory, is a profit or contribution center. The manager has responsibility for both revenues and costs. Marketing responsibility begins with product-line budgets that show product contribution, that is, the amount each product contributes toward common company costs and company income. Product contribution is computed by deducting the standard variable production costs, variable marketing costs, and any fixed marketing costs incurred for the particular product from its sales. These product-line budgets are combined into a contribution budget for the Marketing Department in Exhibit 13–7. The Marketing Department's controllable fixed costs are deducted from the product contribution margin to determine the marketing contribution to firm profits.

COMPILATION OF DEPARTMENTAL BUDGETS INTO THE PROFIT PLAN

The first level of budget compilation was illustrated in Exhibit 13–6 where factory department cost budgets were compiled into the Factory Cost Budget and in Exhibit 13–7 where product-line budgets were compiled into the Marketing Area Budget. Because a responsibility accounting system groups accounting data by responsibility area, other possible aggregations, such as by type of cost, are lost; these data must be presented as supplementary information.

	QUARTER				Total for Year
	1	2	3	4	
Product: Small terrarium					
Sales	$40,000	$80,000	$240,000	$40,000	$400,000
Variable production costs	16,000	32,000	96,000	16,000	160,000
Contribution margin from production	$24,000	$48,000	$144,000	$24,000	$240,000
Variable selling costs	4,000	8,000	24,000	4,000	40,000
Contribution margin from operations	$20,000	$40,000	$120,000	$20,000	$200,000
Product: Large terrarium					
Sales	$64,000	$48,000	$160,000	$48,000	$320,000
Variable production costs	32,000	24,000	80,000	24,000	160,000
Contribution margin from production	$32,000	$24,000	$ 80,000	$24,000	$160,000
Variable selling costs	6,400	4,800	16,000	4,800	32,000
Contribution margin from operations	25,600	19,200	64,000	19,200	128,000
Total contribution margin	$45,600	$59,200	$184,000	$39,200	$328,000
Less: Fixed marketing costs					
Depreciation	$ 6,000	$ 6,000	$ 6,000	$ 6,000	$ 24,000
Other fixed marketing costs	14,000	14,000	14,000	14,000	56,000
Total fixed costs	20,000	20,000	20,000	20,000	80,000
Marketing contribution	$25,600	$39,200	$164,000	$19,200	$248,000

EXHIBIT 13–7   Contribution margin budget for Marketing Department

A summary by type of cost is illustrated at the bottom of the Factory Cost Report (Exhibit 13–6).

The Profit Plan by quarter is presented in Exhibit 13–8. Alternative forms of the Profit Plan, such as by product line, could also be presented. The data on the Profit Plan in Exhibit 13–8 are a compilation from the previous responsibility center budgets, although they have been regrouped. There is one item that requires additional comment. The total budgeted costs of production were $69,000 (see Exhibit 13–6) in the fourth quarter. However, the total production costs on the Profit Plan in the fourth quarter are $65,000 (cost of sales of $40,000 plus fixed production costs of $25,000). The $4,000 difference is the budgeted increase in the Finished Goods Inventory of 1,000 large terrariums at $4.00 each. The difference between the planned sales and planned production is shown in Exhibit 13–3. Compilation of the various responsibility center budgets into an overall profit plan for the Karl Company may give the impression that this aggregation is simply a mechanical task. Responsibility center budgets represent the goals of individual managers. Ultimately these goals must be related to company goals and goal congruence achieved. Actually, the process is an iterative cycle, which may involve several tries at each level of compilation before

| | QUARTER | | | | Total |
	1	2	3	4	for Year
Sales	$104,000	$128,000	$400,000	$ 88,000	$720,000
Variable costs:					
Cost of sales	$ 48,000	$ 56,000	$176,000	$ 40,000	$320,000
Marketing	10,400	12,800	40,000	8,800	72,000
Total variable costs	58,400	68,800	216,000	48,800	392,000
Contribution margin	$ 45,600	$ 59,200	$184,000	$ 39,200	$328,000
Fixed costs:					
Production	$ 25,000	$ 25,000	$ 25,000	$ 25,000	$100,000
Marketing	20,000	20,000	20,000	20,000	80,000
Administration	10,000	10,000	10,000	10,000	40,000
Total fixed costs	55,000	55,000	55,000	55,000	220,000
Income before taxes	$ (9,400)	$ 4,200	$129,000	$(15,800)	$108,000
Income taxes (50%)					54,000
Net income after taxes					$ 54,000

EXHIBIT 13–8   Profit Plan, by quarter

the goals and operating budgets are congruent and budgets are perceived as fair and attainable by the managers.

RESPONSIBILITY ACCOUNTING AND THE CONTROL PROCESS

Accounting's role is to provide information relevant to user needs. To be relevant to the needs of management, a reporting system must reflect the factors over which each manager has control and must identify the areas that need management attention. Responsibility accounting and management by exception are ways of stressing relevant data.

The reporting function of accounting requires the feedback of information to management so that performance can be evaluated and, if necessary, actions altered. The reporting function also provides a base of information about the activities over which an individual manager has responsibility. This data base can then serve as feedback for future planning cycles.

Exhibit 13–9 shows the actual data for the Karl Company for the fourth quarter. These data are then combined with the Profit Plan data and the Performance Budget into a series of responsibility reports. Exhibit 13–10 illustrates how three of these reports provide an upward flow within the Karl Company's responsibility system.

At the lowest levels in the organization, emphasis is almost exclusively on nonfinancial information. Group leaders and individual employees are measured in nonfinancial terms: How many hours must they work? How many

KARL COMPANY
ACTUAL DATA
Fourth Quarter

Raw material purchases:	
Plastic: 45,000 pounds at $.42	$ 18,900
1-gallon boxes: 6,000 at $.35	$ 2,100
5-gallon boxes: 15,000 at $.58	$ 8,700
Production:	
Small: 6,000 units	
Large: 12,000 units	
Sales:	
Small: 6,000 units at $5.00	$ 30,000
Large: 12,000 units at $10.00	$120,000
Forming department variable costs:	
Plastic used: 41,000 pounds at $.40	$ 16,400
Direct labor: 2,800 hr at $5.15	$ 14,420
Variable overhead	$ 11,000
Packing Department variable costs:	
1-gallon boxes used: 6,000 at $.30	$ 1,800
5-gallon boxes used: 13,000 at $.60	$ 7,800
Direct labor: 1,900 hours at $3.20	$ 6,080
Variable overhead	$ 1,800
Marketing Department variable costs:	
Variable selling expenses	$ 14,600

Fixed costs:

	Depreciation	Other	Total
Forming Department	$8,000	$ 3,300	$11,300
Packing Department	$1,000	$ 1,800	$ 2,800
Factory administration	$1,000	$ 9,000	$10,000
Marketing	$6,000	$16,000	$22,000
Administration	$1,000	$ 8,000	$ 9,000

EXHIBIT 13–9
Actual data for fourth quarter

units must they produce? How much scrap is allowed? Salespeople are interested in quantity sold, number of calls, number of customers, and other data related to the selling effort. The individual employee is not involved with accounting reports. Here information needs are met by nonfinancial data, and performance is evaluated in nonfinancial terms when actual results are compared with the standards. The time frame of information at this level is very short. Most information is concerned with day-by-day activities. This is shown at the bottom of Exhibit 13–10.

At the department manager level there is concern over costs. This is illustrated by the Forming Department manager's report in Exhibit 13–11. The department is identified as a cost center, and costs for which the manager is responsible are accumulated for the department. However, the department man-

KARL COMPANY
Fourth Quarter

		Profit Plan	Performance Budget	Actual	Activity Variance	Price, Spending, Efficiency Variances
PRESIDENT: Monthly report summarizing all data. Emphasis is on deviations from plan. On exception basis, president may receive any information.	Revenue	$88,000	$126,000	$150,000	$38,000	$24,000 F
	Factory costs	65,000	85,000	84,300	(20,000)	700 F
	Marketing costs	28,800	32,600	36,600	(3,800)	(4,000) U
	Administration	10,000	10,000	9,000	0	1,000 F
	Income (loss) (Exhibit 13–8)	($15,800)	($1,600)	$ 20,100	$14,200	$21,700 F

		Performance Budget	Actual	Price, Spending, Efficiency Variances
FACTORY MANAGER (See Exhibit 13–12): Monthly report showing revenues and costs by department. Summary nonfinancial data weekly and monthly.	Forming Department	$54,800	$53,120	$1,680 F
	Packing Department	19,200	20,280	(1,080) U
	Unfavorable material price variance	0	900	(900) U
	Common factory costs	11,000	10,000	1,000 F
	Total	$85,000	$84,300	$ 700 F

		Performance Budget	Actual	Price, Spending, Efficiency Variances
FORMING DEPARTMENT MANAGER: (See Exhibit 13–11) Monthly cost report detailing costs. Daily nonfinancial data with weekly and monthly summaries.	Direct materials	$16,800	$16,400	$ 400 F
	Direct labor	15,000	14,420	580 F
	Variable overhead	12,000	11,000	1,000 F
	Fixed overhead	11,000	11,300	(300) U
	Total	$54,800	$53,120	$1,680 F

GROUP LEADER OR SUPERVISOR:
No formal reports from accounting system. Primarily nonfinancial data. Very short timing, hour by hour, day by day.

EXHIBIT 13–10 Responsibility accounting and the control process

ager also deals in physical quantities on a day-to-day basis. Many of the objectives of the department are expressed in physical terms, and the technical standards, in physical terms, provide guides for performance measurements. The accounting system should later verify what the department manager already knows. The time horizon of the department manager is limited to a relatively short period, probably the time covered by a production schedule.

At the next level (factory manager in our illustration), the concern of the manager has moved from physical (nonfinancial) measures to financial measures. The factory manager is not responsible for profit, but is involved in a wide range of decisions that are measurable in financial terms.

At the level of top management, the president is concerned with the attainment of objectives and plans for the future. The amount of information needed depends on management style. If decisions are decentralized, top management establishes company goals and objectives and expects subordinates to administer the continuing activities of the company. As long as subordinates are meeting their objectives, the president deals only in summary information. If decisions are centralized, the president needs more information, in greater depth, about the operations of the company.

DEPARTMENTAL PERFORMANCE ANALYSIS

The starting point in any responsibility reporting system is the departmental reports. In this section we will show how these reports are constructed and how the reports for a manufacturing department manager, the vice-president of manufacturing, and the vice-president of marketing culminate in reports for top management.

DEPARTMENTAL COST REPORT—FORMING DEPARTMENT

The departmental budget for the Karl Company's forming department was developed in Exhibit 13–4 as part of the Profit Plan. The departmental budget in the profit plan was a *static budget;* only one level of activity was planned. However, in management reports, the performance budget should be adjusted to show what the costs should be at the *actual level* of activity.

A departmental cost report for the Forming Department is illustrated for the fourth quarter in Exhibit 13–11. The report contains three cost columns: a Performance Budget, actual costs for the period, and the variances of actual costs from the Performance Budget.

The fourth-quarter Performance Budget is based on the actual production of 6,000 small terrariums and 12,000 large terrariums. For example, the Performance Budget for material ($16,800) is the 6,000 small units produced times their standard cost of $.40 per unit plus the 12,000 large units produced times their standard cost of $1.20 per unit (see the standard cost card in Exhibit 13–2).

| | QUARTER 4 | | |
	Performance Budget	Actual	Variance
MATERIAL—Plastic	$16,800	$16,400	
Material quantity variance			$ 400 **F**
DIRECT LABOR	15,000	14,420	
Labor efficiency variance			1,000 **F**
Labor rate variance			(420) **U**
VARIABLE OVERHEAD	12,000	11,000	
Variable overhead spending variance			200 **F**
Variable overhead efficiency			800 **F**
TOTAL VARIABLE COSTS	$43,800	$41,820	$1,980 **F**
FIXED COSTS:			
Depreciation	$ 8,000	$ 8,000	$ 0
Other fixed production costs	3,000	3,300	(300) **U**
Total	11,000	11,300	300 **U**
TOTAL DEPARTMENTAL COSTS	$54,800	$53,120	$1,680 **F**
PHYSICAL DATA:			
Units produced:			
Small		6,000	
Large		12,000	
Actual plastic used (pounds)		41,000	
Actual direct-labor hours		2,800	

EXHIBIT 13–11
Forming Department cost report for Karl Company

For labor, the Performance Budget ($15,000) is the 6,000 small units times $.50 plus the 12,000 large units produced times $1.00.

During the fourth quarter, costs in the Forming Department were $1,680 under the Performance Budget. The total departmental cost line from the Forming Department cost report will be carried into the Factory Cost Report.

FACTORY COST REPORT

The Factory Cost Report focuses on all manufacturing costs. The costs of each subordinate department are shown as a single-line summary. If more information is desired by the factory manager, the individual cost report for any subordinate department may be examined.

The Factory Cost Report is presented in Exhibit 13–12, where actual costs are compared with the Performance Budget. The Performance Budget for the factory is prepared by applying the flexible budget to the actual level of production in the plant as a whole. However, the budget figures for the subordinate departments come from the summary of their departmental reports. Only the costs under direct control of the plant manager are detailed in this report.

| | QUARTER 4 | | |
	Performance Budget	Actual	Variance
COSTS CONTROLLABLE BY SUBORDINATE DEPARTMENTS			
Forming Department	$54,800	$53,120	$1,680 **F**
Packing Department	19,200	20,280	(1,080) **U**
Material price variance	0	900 **U**	(900) **U**
Total	$74,000	$74,300	$(300) **U**
FIXED COSTS COMMON TO FACTORY			
Depreciation	$ 1,000	$ 1,000	$ 0
Other fixed production costs	10,000	9,000	1,000 **F**
Total	11,000	10,000	1,000 **F**
TOTAL FACTORY COSTS	$85,000	$84,300	$ 700 **F**

EXHIBIT 13–12
Factory Cost Report for
Karl Company

DEPARTMENTAL REPORT—MARKETING

The marketing departments are profit centers. Selling more or fewer units than planned will affect the income of the period. The activity variance is the increased contribution margin from the sale of more units than predicted in the Profit Plan or the reduced contribution margin from selling fewer than planned. Because of the activity variance, reports for the marketing area should show the Profit Plan as well as the Performance Budget and actual results.

Exhibit 13–13 illustrates a report prepared for the marketing manager for Quarter 4. In our example, one report is presented for the entire marketing area. This report could be a compilation of reports for responsibility centers such as product lines or territories. The first column in the report, headed *Profit Plan*, is the budget developed for this area, as part of the total Profit Plan (Exhibit 13–8). At that time the sales manager expected to sell 8,000 small and 6,000 large terrariums and prepared a marketing budget for that sales volume. During the quarter 6,000 small and 12,000 large terrariums were actually sold, and the Performance Budget was prepared for this level. Variances from the Profit Plan are presented in the two variance columns. The first variance column, the activity variance, shows the effect on income of selling more or less units than planned. The sale of 2,000 fewer small terrariums and 6,000 more large terrariums than planned resulted in a total increase in contribution margin of $14,200. The sale of 2,000 fewer small terrariums reduced the contribution margin by $5,000 (2,000 × $2.50) and sale of 6,000 more large terrariums increased contribution margin by $19,200 (6,000 × $3.20). Because fixed costs were not increased by the change in sales volume, the change in contribution margin is also the change in income. The second variance column shows the deviations in prices, efficiency, and spending from the Performance Budget. These variances were

	QUARTER 4				
	(a) Profit Plan	(b) Performance Budget	(c) Actual	(a − b) Activity	(b − c) Price, Efficiency, Spending
PRODUCT—SMALL:					
Sales	$40,000	$30,000	$ 30,000	$(10,000) **U**	$ 0
Variable production costs	16,000	12,000	12,000	4,000 **F**	0
Contribution margin from production	$24,000	$18,000	$ 18,000	$ (6,000) **U**	0
Variable selling costs	4,000	3,000	2,600	1,000 **F**	400 **F**
Contribution margin from operations	$20,000	$15,000	$ 15,400	$ (5,000) **U**	$ 400 **F**
PRODUCT—LARGE:					
Sales	$48,000	$96,000	$120,000	$ 48,000 **F**	$24,000 **F**
Variable production costs	24,000	48,000	48,000	(24,000) **U**	0
Contribution margin from production	$24,000	$48,000	$ 72,000	$ 24,000 **F**	0
Variable selling costs	4,800	9,600	12,000	(4,800) **U**	(2,400) **U**
Contribution margin from operations	19,200	38,400	60,000	19,200 **F**	21,600 **F**
CONTRIBUTION MARGIN FROM ALL PRODUCTS:	$39,200	$53,400	$ 75,400	$ 14,200 **F**	$22,000 **F**
Less fixed marketing costs:					
Depreciation	$ 6,000	$ 6,000	$ 6,000	$ 0	$ 0
Other fixed costs	14,000	14,000	16,000	0	(2,000) **U**
Total	20,000	20,000	22,000	0	(2,000) **U**
Marketing contribution	$19,200	$33,400	$ 53,400	$ 14,200 **F**	$20,000 **F**

EXHIBIT 13–13 Marketing Department report for Karl Company

in selling prices and selling costs. Use of two columns to show the variances allows the variances due to sales activity, in the first column, to be separated from the variances due to price, spending, and efficiency, in the second column.

REPORTS TO TOP MANAGEMENT

Reports to top management should do three things: first, for control they should explain the difference between the profit in the Profit Plan and actual profit, drawing management's attention to significant problem areas (management by exception); second, they should show the aggregate data used in financial reports; and third, they should provide feedback about the achievement of goals and objectives.

One way to show why planned and actual profit differed is a summary report called the Report on Profit Plan. The report shows only variances from the plan. To be effective, the differences should be grouped by responsibility centers (manufacturing, marketing, and administration). The report for the Karl Company for the fourth quarter is shown in Exhibit 13–14. The marketing area accounted for $34,200 of additional operating income through additional sales

```
                        KARL COMPANY
                     REPORT ON PROFIT PLAN
                      Fourth Quarter 19X2

Planned income from Profit Plan                          $(15,800)
Variances due to marketing:
   Activity variance                      $14,200
   Selling price variance                  24,000
   Marketing costs                         (4,000)        34,200
Variances due to production:
   Material price variance                 $(900)
   Material quantity variance               (200)
   Labor efficiency variance                 700
   Labor rate variance                      (800)
   Variable overhead efficiency variance     700
   Variable overhead spending variance       300
   Fixed overhead spending variance          900            700
Variances due to administration:
   Administrative costs                   $ 1,000         1,000
Actual income                                            $20,100
```

EXHIBIT 13–14
Report on Profit Plan for
Karl Company

($14,200 activity variance), increased selling prices (shown by the selling price variance of $24,000) less increased marketing costs of $4,000. All factory cost variances accounted for $700 of the variation from plan. Administrative costs under the control of top management were $1,000 under budget. These variances explain the differences between the planned loss of $15,800 developed in the Profit Plan (Exhibit 13-8) and the actual income of $20,100.

In addition to the Report on Profit Plan, top management would receive the traditional financial statements: Income Statement, a Statement of Financial Position, and a Cash Flow Statement. Exhibit 13–15 presents an Income Statement for the fourth quarter. Because this statement is for management, it presents the Profit Plan as developed at the beginning of the year, a Performance Budget reflecting the actual level of sales, and the actual Income Statement. Variances are separated into those caused by increased sales activity and those by price, spending, and efficiency. Because they are not a direct part of the responsibility reporting system, the Cash Flow Statement and the Statement of Financial Position are not shown.

As a final step, top management needs a comparison of the actual results with the original objectives.

SUMMARY AND EXTENSIONS OF PERFORMANCE ANALYSIS

The examples of responsibility accounting reports shown in this chapter are merely representative of possible reports. Depending on management's questions

KARL COMPANY
INCOME STATEMENT
Fourth Quarter, 19X2

	(a) Profit Plan	(b) Performance Budget	(c) Actual	VARIANCES	
				(a − b) Activity	(b − c) Price, Efficiency Spending
Sales	$ 88,000	$126,000	$150,000	$ 38,000 F	$24,000 F
Variable costs:					
Production	$ 40,000	$ 60,000	$ 60,200	$(20,000) U	$ (200) U
Marketing	8,800	12,600	14,600	(3,800) U	(2,000) U
Total	48,800	72,600	74,800	(23,800) U	(2,200) U
Contribution margin	$ 38,200	$ 53,400	$ 75,200	$ 14,200 F	$21,800 F
Fixed costs:					
Production	$ 25,000	$ 25,000	$ 24,100	—	$ 900 F
Marketing	20,000	20,000	22,000	—	(2,000) U
Administration	10,000	10,000	9,000	—	1,000 F
Total	55,000	55,000	55,100	—	(100) U
Income before taxes	$(15,800)	$ (1,600)	$ 20,100	$ 14,200 F	$21,700 F

EXHIBIT 13–15   *Quarterly income statement for management of Karl Company*

and needs, the reports and analyses can be expanded almost infinitely. For example:

> The activity variance could be decomposed to show the deviation in profit caused by selling a different product mix than planned.
>
> The material price variance could be decomposed to show the effect of purchasing substitute materials. This could also affect the material quantity variance.
>
> The labor rate variance could be decomposed to show the labor mix variance that would result because work was performed by a worker in a different pay grade than planned.
>
> Cost variances could be decomposed by product line or territories.
>
> The activity variance could be analyzed by product line or sales territories.

Let's carry our discussion of control systems one more step. We have emphasized that the potency of a control system is always relative to other possible control systems. Comparison of a Performance Budget with actual performance is relatively stronger, at least in theory, than comparison of the planning budget with actual, because the Performance Budget equalizes the activity level between budget and actual. However, the Performance Budget may not be the optimum measure. The Performance Budget is based upon the flexible budget, which was structured upon presupposed operational techniques, pricing structures, cost structures, and market conditions. In this sense the Performance Budget represents an *ex ante* measure; it is a control tool in that its basic structure was determined in advance.

Even more potent would be *ex post* measures, that is, performance measures that *should* have resulted, considering all actual events, both inside and outside the firm. For example, the activity variance could be analyzed by looking at economy-wide or industry-wide events that could be known only after the fact. In a general sense, *ex post* measures are the result of more complete information than *ex ante* measures; therefore, they are relatively stronger.

From this discussion it should be clear that there are no perfect control systems. Each mode of performance analysis can be judged only in terms of its contribution to management. Certainly one principle is that the control system should be no stronger than necessary, given the objectives of management. Control systems should be developed only to the extent that the benefits from the data outweigh the costs of obtaining them.

Finally, it should be emphasized that budgetary and accounting systems are only one component of the complete control system. Generally, accounting systems address themselves to evaluating efficient behavior; they do not focus on organizational effectiveness.

THE COST OF VARIANCE INVESTIGATION

In recent years information theorists have paid increasing attention to when a variance should or should not be investigated further. The basic principle is that variance investigation should be undertaken whenever the expected savings from the investigation outweigh the costs of the investigation.

For example, assume that a milling department has an unfavorable labor efficiency variance of $500 this month, which the manager considers significant. The departmental manager believes that this variance will continue for the next three months unless an investigation is undertaken to discover the cause. There is a 20% chance that the cause is random and that the variance will cease regardless of the action taken. If the investigation is undertaken the department will have to absorb their expenses of $1,000. Past experience has shown there is a 10% chance the investigation will fail to discover the cause of the variance. In this case the company must bear the costs of the investigation ($1,000) plus the cost of the continuation of the variance ($1,500). Based on these data the manager prepared the decision table on page 566. In this example the expected costs of not investigating are $1,200; the expected costs of an investigation are $1,120. Therefore it would be cost advantageous to investigate the variance further.

Possible Outcome	Cost of Possible Outcome	Probability of Possible Outcome	Expected Value
Do Not Investigate:			
Variance is random and will cease	$ 0	.20	$ 0
Variance will continue	$1,500	.80	1,200
		1.00	$1,200
Investigate Further:			
Variance is random and will cease	$1,000	.20	$ 200
Variance cannot be corrected*			
(.80 × .10)	$2,500	.08	200
Variance can be corrected†			
(.80 × .90)	$1,000	.72	720
		1.00	$1,120

*The 10% probability that the variance cannot be corrected applies to only 80% of the possibilities.
†The 90% probability that the variance will be corrected applies to 80% of the possibilities.

HUMAN ASPECTS OF BUDGETARY CONTROL

There is a tendency to overemphasize the mechanical aspects of the budgetary system and to expect it to work without regard to the interpersonal relationships implied therein. However, goals and objectives are achieved through people. It is important that we examine the effects of budgets on people and the effects of people on the budget. The human element is an extremely complex issue; oversimplification is easy in our brief discussion. A review of behavioral research literature reveals that the studies have raised more questions regarding human behavior than they have answered.

Early budgetary literature adopted a mechanical and materialistic view of human behavior. This view of worker and manager behavior assumed that employees were primarily motivated by monetary rewards, that employees would avoid work whenever possible, that employees were ordinarily inefficient and wasteful. These assumptions led to the belief that responsibility had to be established and external pressure applied to achieve the desired results. In practice, a high level of performance through budgets has often been accompanied by several unfavorable consequences, including excessive pressure on employees, hostility toward the budget, and conflict among departments.

EXCESSIVE PRESSURE

Behavioral research has provided some information on the effects of pressure in the management process. It does appear that individuals and groups work best with some kind of pressure. When benchmarks are too loose, motivation diminishes; as they are tightened, motivation increases. However, when a benchmark becomes too tight, motivation becomes poor. There appears to be an optimum amount of pressure, although its limits are not clear and how it affects different types of individuals is not known.

Responsibility accounting identifies individual responsibility for budgeted costs and deviations from plan. Management by exception implies that significant deviations from the plan will cause the superior to exert pressure for correction. Excessive pressure can result in growing antagonism toward the budget. It is possible for a firm to create a situation where budgetary success means failure for worker and managers. In such a situation, the planning and coordinating function of the budget can be completely negated as the budget becomes something to be feared.

INTERDEPARTMENTAL CONFLICT

Responsibility accounting focuses attention on limited areas of responsibility and tends to cause managers to overemphasize departmental goals. The lower-line managers may attempt to direct budgetary pressure away from themselves by shifting the blame to other departments. This departmental overemphasis can operate against the organization's goals and objectives.

PARTICIPATION AND MOTIVATION

Participation by the managers in preparing the budget has been advocated as a way to increase employee motivation and reduce organizational conflict. The call for such participation is widespread in accounting literature. Most current management theorists and management accountants believe that employee initiative, performance, and morale are increased with employee participation. The value of participation rapidly becomes interwoven with the theory of organizational structures.

One indication that an organization encourages active employee participation is the existence of good superior–subordinate relationships fostered by (1) frequent person-to-person contacts; (2) the use of results in performance appraisal; (3) the use of departmental meetings to review actual results; and (4) the creation of a "game" spirit (margin for error, tolerance, and slack).

A closer look at this list provides further insights into the planning and control process. First, participation is achieved on a personal basis. A formal, indirect mode of communication creates the danger of pseudoparticipation. Pseudoparticipation, which pretends to be participation but is not, is a form of deceit; the result can be a decrease in motivation. Second, the achievement of the goal or budget should bear directly upon the reward received by the employee. Further, direct, clear feedback allows the employee to adjust aspiration levels and strive to achieve desired rewards. Finally, a certain amount of leeway, termed *slack,* gives the employee some freedom of movement and action. It keeps employee pressure at an accepted level.

SLACK

An individual in an organization is motivated to achieve two sets of goals: personal and organizational. A manager's personal goals within the organization may relate to income, status, size of staff, or discretionary control over the allocation of resources. Where a budget serves to measure performance, a manager will strive to set the budget so that it can be achieved and still meet top management's objectives. To avoid the stigma attached to failure, a manager will attempt to introduce a cushion, or slack.

Slack can be thought of as a budgetary lubricant. Some slack is necessary to reduce friction between individual and organizational goals and to give managers room to perform. It has been shown that success causes people to raise their levels of aspiration and that failure causes them to lower their aspirations. The provision of slack is one way employees attempt to avoid failure.

Every firm operates with slack; perfection of the traditional economic model is neither possible nor desirable. Resources cannot be perfectly allocated. The treasurer introduces slack by maintaining excessive cash balances; division management understates sales projections; line management requests employee positions that will be filled only as budgetary expectations are met; and manufacturing costs are based on estimates that do not reflect improvements. Slack tends to grow in good years, when satisfactory profits are easily attainable; in bad years slack is voluntarily decreased throughout the firm. Cost-cutting campaigns are attempts to reduce excessive slack that will jeopardize long-run profit objectives of the firm through inefficiency. Too much pressure to reduce slack will create conflict in the system and may result in system failure. The solution is to find a level of slack that maintains efficiency and avoids the conflict caused by excessive pressure.

SUMMARY

The budget serves as a focus of the planning process, as an integrative tool for the many plans, and as the baseline for the control process. The master budget is management's principal vehicle for coordinating the firm's plans. Without the integrating features of the budget, there is a danger that the various responsibility centers will act to optimize their own performance to the detriment of the total firm.

The budgetary process has both a downward and an upward flow of information. Before the budget can be developed upward with management participation, direction through goals and objectives must come from the top. The compilation of responsibility center budgets into the Profit Plan is an iterative process. Responsibility center budgets and, to some extent, company objectives are revised until both the responsibility center managers and top management reach budgets that are perceived as fair and attainable.

To be effective, the budgetary system must be relevant to management needs. Two dimensions of relevancy exist: First, the concept of responsibility accounting requires that the budgetary system be tailored to the organization. This requires that costs and revenues be identified with the manager responsible for their incurrence. Second, the concept of management by exception requires that significant deviations from plan be identified so that the cause may be determined and action taken, if necessary, to prevent future variances.

The proper administration of the budget in a responsibility accounting setting depends not only on the methodology, but also on the impact it has on the persons affected. Paramount here are the problems of pressure, motivation, and slack.

PROBLEMS AND CASES

13-1 *(Expense Estimation in Marketing Department).* The Dunmire Company is attempting to develop a system of responsibility accounting and reporting. The following data for June were selected as a representative month for the marketing area. During June 60,000 units were sold at $5.00 per unit.

Sales salaries (fixed)	$30,000
Sales commissions (6% of sales)	$18,000
Travel (3% of sales)	$ 9,000
Sales ordering costs ($5,000 + $.10 per unit sold)	$11,000
Advertising costs ($30,000 + $.50 per unit sold)	$60,000
Shipping costs ($.20 per unit sold)	$12,000

REQUIRED:

Prepare a budget for the marketing area for July when sales are estimated to be 62,000 units at $5.00 per unit.

13-2 *(Analyzing Changes in Gross Margin).* The Outdoor Equipment Company is surprised to see a decline in gross margin on one of its product lines in 19X3. Data for 19X2 and 19X3 follow:

	19X2	19X3
Units sold	12,000	15,000
Sales	$72,000	$75,000
Cost of Goods Sold	45,600	60,000
Gross margin	$26,400	$15,000

REQUIRED:

Explain as completely as you can the reasons for the decline in gross margin.

13-3 *(Analysis of Sales by Product).* The Fargo Company has established marketing responsibility centers by product lines. Budgeted and actual sales for June were as follows:

Budgeted sales for June:		
Product D	300 units	$ 24,000
Product F	30,000 units	120,000
Total		$144,000
Actual sales for June:		
Product D	330 units	$ 24,750
Product F	32,000 units	121,600
Total		$146,350

REQUIRED:

Prepare an analysis of sales by responsibility center. Your analysis should show price as well as activity variances.

13-4 *(Continuation of Problem 13-3—Analysis of Contribution Margin by Product).* Assume that planned and actual variable costs for the Fargo Company (Problem 13-3) for the month of June were as follows:

Planned variable costs for June:	
Product D	$45 per unit
Product F	$3 per unit
Actual variable costs for June:	
Product D	$50 per unit
Product F	$2.80 per unit

(Assume any deviations were due to efficiency.)

REQUIRED:

Using the sales data from Problem 13-3 and the above data, prepare an analysis of contribution margin for each responsibility center.

13-5 *(Performance Report).* The C and G Pottery Company is attempting to analyze their profitability by product line. For November, Glen prepared a budget that called for production and sales of 100 casseroles priced to sell at $20.00 each. The cost for this product line is estimated at $6.00 variable and $3.00 fixed per unit. The fixed marketing costs, including advertising and booth fees, were budgeted at $500 for the month.

During November 120 casseroles were produced and sold. The selling price was reduced to $18.00 per unit. Variable costs were $5.50 per unit and, fixed marketing costs were $400.

REQUIRED:

Prepare a performance report to show the difference in income between the budgeted and actual income for the casserole line.

13-6 *(Revision of Departmental Report).* The Alford Company has two departments—Casting and Finishing. During the month of March the Finishing Department completed 10,300 units; because of an inferior casting mold 300 units were rejected during the final stress inspection in the Finishing Department. Because only 10,000 were completed the Performance Budget was developed using 10,000 units. The defective units resulted when a new inspector in the Casting Department passed a number of questionable castings. Normally these errors are discovered before the transfer from casting to finishing.

FINISHING DEPARTMENT COSTS

	Performance Budget	Actual	Variances
Direct materials (variable)	$ 60,000	$ 61,710	($1,710) **U**
Direct labor (variable)	50,000	50,800	(800) **U**
Supervision (fixed)	3,000	3,200	(200) **U**
Power (variable)	8,000	8,300	(300) **U**
Indirect materials (variable)	5,000	5,250	(250) **U**
Depreciation (fixed)	6,500	6,500	0
Total costs	$132,500	$135,760	($3,260) **U**

REQUIRED:

Revise the departmental report to reflect only the costs under control of the Finishing Department.

13-7 *(Cost of Variance Analysis).* Charles Crown, the manager of the Personnel Department, received his management report for the month of July, which showed an unfavorable spending variance for computer services of $400. Charles believed that the unfavorable variance was the result of excessive time usage on the computer caused by an inefficient software program that used too many calculational steps. He had to make a choice between continuing to use the program for the next six months until a new computer software package was implemented, or calling in a programmer now to correct the fault. He believed that there was a 20% chance he was wrong about the program and that the cost variance would not occur again and an 80% chance he was correct and that the cost overrun would occur again. He estimated that the computer programmer would cost the department $900 and that even if the programmer was called there was only a 60% chance that the new program would correct the fault.

REQUIRED:

Prepare a decision table indicating what action you believe that Charles should take.

13-8 *(Cost to Investigate).* The milling process is showing erratic results in output. Because the process is not scheduled for major maintenance for some time, the supervisor has called a service company to determine if the process is out of control.

   The service company estimates the cost to investigate process to be $4,000, and, if out of control, the cost to correct the process to be $9,000. If the process is actually out of control, early maintenance at this time should save $45,000 in operating costs between now and the regularly scheduled maintenance. The service company estimates the probability of the process being in control at 80%, and the probability of it being out of control at 20%.

REQUIRED:

Should the process be investigated? Explain.

13-9 *(Preparing Performance Budget).* The March income statement for the paper products division of the High-Performance Company is presented below.

PAPER PRODUCTS DIVISION
HIGH-PERFORMANCE COMPANY
INCOME STATEMENT
Month of March

	Profit Plan	Actual
Units sold	100	90
Inventories	$ 0	$ 0
Sales	$10,000	$9,300
Production costs:		
Direct material	$ 1,300	$1,200
Direct labor	1,600	1,400
Variable overhead	800	650
Fixed overhead	500	525
Total	4,200	3,775
Gross margin	$ 5,800	$5,525
Selling and administrative expenses:		
Variable selling	$ 1,000	$ 920
Fixed selling	800	700
Variable administrative	200	230
Fixed administrative	1,600	1,800
Total	3,600	3,650
Income	$ 2,200	$1,875

REQUIRED:

Prepare a Performance Budget for analyzing the performance of the paper division.

13-10 *(Continuation of Problem 13-9—Preparing Divisional Performance Report).* From the data in Problem 13-9, prepare a report similar to chapter Exhibit 13-10 that analyzes the performance of the paper products division of the High-Performance Company. Assume that any variances in variable manufacturing costs were due to efficiency.

13-11 *(Responsibility Accounting).* Monthly departmental performance reports are prepared by the O'Brien Manufacturing Corporation. A Manager of the Month award is given to the manager who has performed best in relation to his or her budget. A bonus is paid to any department manager whose performance is better than budget. Two departmental reports for the month of May follow.

MARKETING—PRODUCT B
PERFORMANCE REPORT FOR MAY

	Master Budget	Performance Budget	Actual
Sales revenue	$180,000	$200,000	$210,000
Variable costs:			
Production	90,000	100,000	100,000
Selling	18,000	20,000	26,000
Contribution margin	$ 72,000	$ 80,000	$ 84,000
Departmental fixed costs	20,000	20,000	22,000
Departmental margin	$ 52,000	$ 60,000	$ 62,000

PRODUCTION—ASSEMBLY
PERFORMANCE REPORT FOR MAY

	Master Budget	Performance Budget	Actual
Subassemblies (material)	$160,000	$200,000	$190,000
Labor ($5.00 per hour)	80,000	100,000	118,000
Variable overhead	48,000	60,000	67,000
Total variable	$288,000	$360,000	$375,000
Departmental fixed costs	80,000	80,000	75,000
Total departmental costs	$368,000	$440,000	$450,000

One of the goals of the company is customer satisfaction. The marketing manager for Product B received the Manager of the Month award for exceptional customer service. He had received several new orders and was commended by many customers for filling rush orders when competitors refused to do so.

The manager of the Production-Assembly Department is extremely unhappy with the company's accounting system. Her department operated near capacity and completed all orders within the promised delivery schedule but had excessive labor and variable overhead costs. She can show that the labor efficiency variance which was unfavorable by 3,000 hours would have been favorable by 1,000 hours if she had been able to produce at the scheduled level without the rush orders.

REQUIRED:

A. Did the manager of the Production-Assembly Department receive a bonus in May? Explain.

B. Why should the manager of the Production-Assembly Department be so unhappy with the accounting system?

C. Recast the performance reports to reflect responsibility accounting.

D. On the basis of your reports from part *B*, who should receive a bonus? Explain.

13-12 *(Hospital Department Performance Report)*. The Argon County Hospital is located in the county seat. Argon County is a well-known summer resort area. Its population doubles during the vacation months (May–August), and hospital activity more than doubles during these months. The hospital is organized into several departments. Although it is relatively small, its pleasant surroundings have attracted a well-trained and competent medical staff.

An administrator was hired a year ago to improve the business activities of the hospital. Among the new ideas she has introduced are responsibility accounting and quarterly cost reports supplied to department heads. Previously, cost data had been presented to department heads only infrequently. Excerpts from the announcement and the report received by the laundry supervisor follow.

> The hospital has adopted a responsibility accounting system. From now on you will receive quarterly reports comparing the costs of operating your department with budgeted costs. The reports will highlight the differences (variations) so you can zero in on the departure from budgeted costs (this is called *management by exception*). Responsibility accounting means you are accountable for keeping the costs in your department within the budget. The variations from the budget will help you identify what costs are out of line, and the size of the variation will indicate which ones are the most important. Your first such report accompanies this announcement.

The annual budget for 19X3 was constructed by the new administrator. Quarterly budgets were computed as one-fourth of the annual budget. The administrator compiled the budget from analysis of the prior three years' costs. The analysis showed that all costs increased each year, with more rapid increases between the second and third year. She considered establishing the budget at an average of the prior three years' costs, hoping that the installation of the system would reduce costs to this level. However, in view of the rapidly increasing prices, she finally chose 19X2 costs less 3% for the 19X3 budget. The activity level measured by patient days and pounds of laundry processed was set at 19X2 volume, which was approximately equal to the volume of each of the past three years.

ARGON COUNTY HOSPITAL
PERFORMANCE REPORT—LAUNDRY DEPARTMENT
July–September 19X3

	Budget	Actual	(Over) Under Budget	Percentage (Over) Under Budget
Patient days	9,500	11,900	(2,400)	(25)
Pounds of laundry processed	125,000	156,000	(31,000)	(25)
Costs:				
Laundry labor	$ 9,000	$12,500	$(3,500)	(39)
Supplies	1,100	1,875	(775)	(70)
Water and water heating and softening	1,700	2,500	(800)	(47)
Maintenance	1,400	2,200	(800)	(57)
Supervisor's salary	3,150	3,750	(600)	(19)
Allocated administration costs	4,000	5,000	(1,000)	(25)
Equipment depreciation	1,200	1,250	(50)	(4)
	$21,550	$29,075	$(7,525)	(35)

Administrator's comments: Costs are significantly above budget for the quarter. Particular attention needs to be paid to labor, supplies, and maintenance.

REQUIRED:

A. Comment on the method used to construct the budget.

B. What information should be communicated by variations from budgets?

C. Recast the budget to reflect responsibility accounting, assuming the following:

  1. Laundry labor, supplies, water and water heating and softening, and maintenance are variable costs. The remaining costs are fixed.

  2. Actual prices are expected to be approximately 20% above the levels in the budget prepared by the hospital administrator.

(CMA adapted)

13-13 *(Overhead Analysis with Flexible Budget)*. The Jason Plant of Cast Corporation has been in operation for 15 months. Jason employs a standard cost system for its manufacturing operations. The first six months performance was affected by the usual problems associated with a new operation. Since that time the operations have been running smoothly. Unfortunately, however, the plant has not been able to produce profits on a consistent basis. As the production requirements to meet sales demand have increased, the profit performance has deteriorated.

The plant production manager commented at a staff meeting in which the plant general manager, the corporate controller, and the corporate budget director were in attendance, that the changing production requirements make it more difficult to control manufacturing expenses. He further noted that the budget for the plant, included in the company's annual Profit Plan, was not useful for judging the plant's performance because of the changes in the operating levels. The meeting resulted in a decision to prepare a report that would compare the plant's actual manufacturing expense performance with a budget of manufacturing expense based on actual direct labor hours in the plant.

The plant production manager and the plant accountant studied the cost patterns for recent months, and volume and cost data from other Cast plants. Then they prepared the following flexible budget schedule for a month with 200,000 planned production hours, which at standard would result in 50,000 units of output. The corporate controller reviewed and approved the flexible budget.

	Amount	Per Direct Labor Hour
Manufacturing expenses:		
Variable		
Indirect labor	$160,000	$ .80
Supplies	26,000	.13
Power	14,000	.07
		$1.00
Fixed		
Supervisory labor	64,000	
Heat and light	15,000	
Property taxes	5,000	
	$284,000	

The manufacturing expense reports prepared for the first three months after the flexible budget program was approved were pleasing to the plant production manager. They showed that manufacturing expenses were in line with the flexible budget allowance. The report prepared for November, which is presented below, when 50,500 units were manufactured showed that the plant was still not producing an adequate profit.

JASON PLANT
ACTUAL MANUFACTURING EXPENSES
November 19X9
220,000 Actual Direct Labor Production Hours

Variable	
Indirect labor	$177,000
Supplies	27,400
Power	16,000
Fixed	
Supervisory labor	65,000
Heat and light	15,500
Property taxes	5,000
	$305,900

REQUIRED:

Prepare an evaluation of overhead costs for November. Explain where you think management should reduce costs.

(CMA adapted)

13-14 *(Flexible Budgets and Performance Assessment).* The University of Boyne offers an extensive continuing education program in many cities throughout the state. For the convenience of its faculty and administrative staff and also to save costs, the university operates a motor pool. Until February the motor pool operated with 20 vehicles. However, an additional automobile was acquired in February this year, increasing the total to 21 vehicles. The motor pool furnishes gasoline, oil, and other supplies for the cars, and hires one mechanic who does routine maintenance and minor repairs. Major repairs are done at a nearby commercial garage. A supervisor managers the operations.

Each year the supervisor prepares an operating budget for the motor pool. The budget informs university management of the funds needed to operate the pool. Depreciation on the automobiles is recorded in the budgets in order to determine the costs per mile.

The schedule on page 578 presents the annual budget approved by the university. The actual costs for March are compared to one-twelfth of the annual budget.

UNIVERSITY MOTOR POOL
BUDGET REPORT
For March 19X6

	Annual Budget	One-Month Budget	March Actual	Over* Under
Gasoline	$24,000	$2,000	$2,800	$800*
Oil, minor repairs, parts, and supplies	3,600	300	380	80*
Outside repairs	2,700	225	50	175
Insurance	6,000	500	525	25*
Salaries and benefits	30,000	2,500	2,500	—
Depreciation	26,400	2,200	2,310	110*
	$92,700	$7,725	$8,565	$840*
Total miles	600,000	50,000	63,000	
Cost per mile	$0.1545	$0.1545	$0.1369	
Number of automobiles	20	20	21	

The annual budget was constructed upon the following assumptions:

a.   20 automobiles in the pool.

b.   30,000 miles per year per automobile.

c.   15 miles per gallon per automobile.

d. $.60 per gallon of gas.

e. $.006 per mile for oil, minor repairs, parts, and supplies.

f. $135 per automobile in outside repairs.

The supervisor is unhappy with the monthly report comparing budget and actual costs for March. He claims it presents unfairly his performance for March. His previous employer used flexible budgeting to compare actual costs to budgeted amounts.

REQUIRED:

A. Employing flexible budgeting techniques, prepare a report that shows budgeted amounts, actual costs, and monthly variation for March.

B. Explain briefly the basis of your budget figure for outside repairs.

(CMA adapted)

13-15 *(Preparation of Budgets for Responsibility Centers).* Helen Waters, president of Fun Float Boat Company, has operated the company for many years with only an informal cost and budgetary system. She has been elected to the state legislature and would like to place more responsibility with subordinate managers. She has heard about responsibility accounting and wants to install a responsibility accounting and budgetary system.

The company's product is produced in two processes: a fabrication process and a finishing process. Compound A is mixed and sprayed into a mold in the fabrication process. In the finishing process, the molded boat is sanded, sprayed with a finish coat, and buffed.

Helen Waters prepared the following Profit Plan for the first quarter of 19X0.

```
                      FUN FLOAT BOAT COMPANY
                           PROFIT PLAN
                        First Quarter—19X0

                                                      PROFIT
                                                       PLAN

  Number of boats produced and sold                     100

                                        Per Unit       Total

  Sales                                   $750         $75,000
  Variable costs:
    Production costs:
      Material—Compound A                 $100         $10,000
      Material—Finish                       20           2,000
    Direct labor                           100          10,000
    Variable overhead                       50           5,000
    Selling expenses                        75           7,500
      Total variable costs                 345          34,500
  Contribution margin                     $405         $40,500
  Fixed expenses:
    Advertising                                        $ 6,000
    Other marketing                                      4,000
    Factory                                             16,000
    Administrative                                       4,000
      Total fixed costs                                 30,000
  Planned profit                                       $10,500
```

Although there was no standard cost system, she used the following quantities and prices in developing the Profit Plan.

	Fabrication Department	Finishing Department
Cost per finished boat:		
Compound A	100 pounds at $1	
Finish coat		1 gallon at $20
Direct labor	2 hours at $10	8 hours at $10
Variable overhead	2 hours at $5	8 hours at $5
Fixed production costs	$12,000	$4,000

REQUIRED:

Prepare responsibility center budgets for the following areas: purchasing, fabrication, finishing, and marketing.

13-16 (*Continuation of Problem 13-15—Development of Responsibility Center Reports*). Helen Waters, the president of Fun Float Boat Company, asked you to assist her in preparing responsibility center budgets. (These were prepared in Problem 13-15.) Now that the first quarter has ended, she asks you for help in preparing reports for each responsibility center and for the firm.

When Helen Waters made the decision to delegate more authority and responsibility to her subordinate managers, she carefully set out the responsibilities of the managers and informed them that the departmental reports would reflect those items over which they had control.

At the end of the first quarter of 19X0 the accountant prepared the following income statement in much the same as he had done for the last two years.

FUN FLOAT BOAT COMPANY
INCOME STATEMENT
First Quarter—19X0

		ACTUAL
Number of boats produced and sold		120
	Per Unit	Amount
Sales	$800	$96,000
Variable costs:		
Production costs:		
Material—Compound A	$102	$12,240
Material—Finish	21	2,520
Direct labor	90	10,800
Variable overhead	54	6,480
Selling expenses	80	9,600
Total variable costs	347	41,640
Contribution margin	$453	$54,360
Fixed expenses:		
Advertising		$ 4,000
Other marketing		3,000
Factory		18,000
Administrative		4,500
Total fixed costs		29,500
Income		$24,860

The Profit Plan and related data are presented in Problem 13-15. After a study of the records you came up with the following additional data:

Demand far exceeded the expectations in the Profit Plan. Instead of producing and selling 100 boats, 120 boats were produced and sold.

In addition to a selling price increase, advertising and marketing expenses were reduced.

Each boat required the following:

Compound A	102 pounds
Finish coat	1 gallon
Fabrication direct labor	2 hours
Finishing direct labor	7 hours

Wage rates remained unchanged, but the price of finishing material increased to $21 per gallon. Because of increased production more supplies were used resulting in variable overhead of $6 per direct labor hour.

Fabricating and Finishing departments each incurred an additional $1,000 in fixed overhead.

REQUIRED:

A. Prepare a performance report for the fabrication and finishing departments.

B. Prepare a Profit Plan that shows variances from both the Profit Plan and a Performance Budget.

C. Prepare a Report on Profit Plan.

13-17 *(Continuation of Problem 13-15, Independent of Problem 13-16—Development of Responsibility Center Reports with Interdepartmental Conflict).* Helen Waters, the president of Fun Float Boat Company, asked you to assist her in preparing responsibility center budgets. (These were prepared in Problem 13-15.) Now that the first quarter has ended, she asks you for help in preparing reports for each responsibility center and for the firm.

When Helen Waters made the decision to delegate more authority and responsibility to her subordinate managers, she carefully set out the responsibilities of the managers and informed them that the departmental reports would reflect those items over which they had control. However, during the quarter one problem arose that she asked you to handle carefully in the responsibility center reports.

The purchasing agent for the company was offered an excellent price on a new and improved Compound A. The salesperson assured the purchasing agent that the new material would require use of slightly more Compound A and only a little more finishing labor but that it would cut fabrication time markedly. When the new material was used there were significant savings in material cost and fabrication labor as promised. However, it caused a much larger than expected increase in finishing labor. The manager of the finishing department demanded that he be charged only with the costs "over which he has control" as promised when the system was adopted.

The accountant for the company prepared only the traditional income statement for the firm, leaving you with what he considered a mess.

FUN FLOAT BOAT COMPANY
INCOME STATEMENT
First Quarter—19X0

		ACTUAL
Number of boats produced and sold		90
	Per Unit	Amount
Sales	$800	$72,000
Variable costs:		
Production costs:		
Material—Compound A	$ 44	$ 3,960
Material—Finish	21	$ 1,890
Direct labor	110	$ 9,900
Variable overhead	66	$ 5,940
Selling expenses	80	$ 7,200
Total variable costs	321	28,890
Contribution margin	$479	$43,110
Fixed expenses:		
Advertising		$ 7,000
Other marketing		4,500
Factory		17,000
Administrative		4,000
Total fixed costs		32,500
Income		$10,610

The Profit Plan and related data are presented in Problem 13-15. After a study of the records you came up with the following additional data:

> Because of the difficulties with the finishing process, the company produced only 90 boats, all of which were sold. The sales manager lost orders for 10 boats that could not be produced. The price of finished boats was increased, and advertising and other marketing costs were also increased.

> Each boat required the following:

Compound A	110 pounds
Finish coat	1 gallon
Fabrication direct labor	1 hour
Finishing direct labor	10 hours

> Wage rates remained unchanged but material prices were, for Compound A $.40 per pound, for finishing material $21 per gallon. Because of

the production problems more supplies were used, resulting in variable overhead of $6 per direct labor hour.

The Finishing Department also incurred an additional $1,000 in fixed overhead.

All managers agree that if the new material had not been used, production costs would have been "normal," except for fixed overhead.

REQUIRED:

A. Prepare a report for the following responsibility centers: purchasing, fabrication, finishing, factory, and marketing.

B. Prepare a Profit Plan that shows variances from both the Profit Plan and a Performance Budget.

C. Prepare a Report on Profit Plan.

D. Prepare an explanation for Helen Waters of how you handled the conflict over the added costs caused by use of the new Compound A.

13-18 *(Comprehensive Master Budget for Pharmacy).* The James Pharmacy has completed its first year of business in a new shopping center. The owners are very optimistic about the future and plan a number of changes that will expand the business. They plan to develop a budgetary system for planning and control of operations. The following data were accumulated.

1. Sales and merchandise costs for 19X0:

Department	Sales	Gross Margin	Inventory Turnover (Ending Inventory)
Prescription Drugs	$ 60,000	60%	4 times
Patent Medicine	$100,000	40%	6 times
Cosmetics	$ 50,000	20%	10 times
Sundries	$ 90,000	30%	7 times

2. Operating expenses for 19X0:

Expense	Amount	Traceable to Department	Cost Behavior Pattern Fixed and Variable
Salaries	$40,000	40% Prescriptions 20% Patent Medicine	$40,000 + $0
Advertising	$12,000	50% Cosmetics	$12,000 + $0
Rent	$18,000		$0 + 6% of sales
Depreciation of fixtures	$10,000		$10,000 + $0
Miscellaneous	$15,000		$ 6,000 + 3% of sales

3. Statement of Financial Position at the end of 19X0:

Statement of Financial Position			
Cash	$ 3,500	Accounts payable	$15,000
Accounts receivable	12,500	Accrued payables	12,000
Inventory	29,000		
Fixtures and equipment	50,000	Capital stock	40,000
Accumulated depreciation	(10,000)	Retained earnings	18,000
	$85,000		$85,000

4. A number of policy changes have been made that will change the character of the store. The following results are expected.

Department	Percentage Increase in Sales	New Gross Margin Percentage	New Inventory Turnover (End of Year)
Prescription Drugs	100%	60%	4 times
Patent Medicine	50%	40%	6 times
Cosmetics	100%	25%	15 times
Sundries	300%	20%	8 times

5. Other information:

At the end of 19X1, accounts receivable are expected to be $25,000, accounts payable $60,000, and accrued payables $20,000. Salaries will be increased to $50,000 and miscellaneous expense will become $10,000 + 4% of sales. All other cost–volume relationships will be maintained. The stockholders expect the maximum cash dividend possible that will leave a balance of $10,000 in cash.

REQUIRED:

A. Prepare a Profit Plan for 19X1 following a contribution margin approach.

B. Did the changes improve the profitability of the company? Explain.

(Prepared by Jim Jimbalvo)

13-19 *(Performance Evaluation for Pharmacy).* The James Pharmacy has completed its second year of business in a new shopping center and the owners are interested in evaluating operations. (The Profit Plan was prepared in Problem 13-18.) Their actual Income Statement for 19X1 is shown on page 585.

JAMES PHARMACY
STATEMENT
For the Year 19X1

	Total	Prescription Drugs	Patent Medicine	Cosmetics	Sundries
Sales	$760,000	$110,000	$130,000	$120,000	$400,000
Cost of Goods Sold	473,800	66,000	75,400	92,400	240,000
Gross profit	$286,200	$ 44,000	$ 54,600	$ 27,600	$160,000
Rent	$ 45,600	$ 6,600	$ 7,800	$ 7,200	$ 24,000
Miscellaneous variable costs	38,000	5,500	6,500	6,000	20,000
Total	83,600	12,100	14,300	13,200	44,000
Contribution margin	$202,600	$ 31,900	$ 40,300	$ 14,400	$116,000
Direct fixed costs:					
Salary	50,000	35,000	15,000		
Advertising	5,000			5,000	
Product profit	$147,600	$ (3,100)	$ 25,300	$ 9,400	$116,000
Common fixed costs:					
Salary	30,000				
Advertising	5,000				
Depreciation	10,000				
Miscellaneous	11,000				
Profit	$ 91,600				

REQUIRED:

Analyze the difference between planned and actual profit. A good analysis could be organized along the following lines:

> Prescription drugs
> Patent medicine
> Cosmetics
> Sundries
> Total difference between planned and actual profit.

(Prepared by Jim Jimbalvo)

13-20 *(Flexible Budget for Selling Expenses).* Wielson Company employs flexible budgeting techniques to evaluate the performance of several of its activities. The selling expense flexible budgets for three representative monthly activity levels are shown below.

REPRESENTATIVE MONTHLY FLEXIBLE BUDGETS FOR SELLING EXPENSES

Activity measures:			
Unit sales volume	400,000	425,000	450,000
Dollar sales volume	$10,000,000	$10,625,000	$11,250,000
Number of orders	4,000	4,250	4,500
Number of salespersons	75	75	75
Monthly expenses:			
Advertising and promotion	$ 1,200,000	$ 1,200,000	$ 1,200,000
Administrative salaries	57,000	57,000	57,000
Sales salaries	75,000	75,000	75,000
Sales commissions	200,000	212,500	225,000
Salesperson travel	170,000	175,000	180,000
Sales office expense	490,000	498,750	507,500
Shipping expense	675,000	712,500	750,000
Total selling expenses	$ 2,867,000	$ 2,930,750	$ 2,994,500

The following assumptions were used to develop the selling expense flexible budgets.

1. The average size of Wielson's sales force during the year was planned to be 75 people.

2. Salespersons are paid a monthly salary plus commission on gross dollar sales.

3. The travel costs are best characterized as a step-variable cost. The fixed portion is related to the number of salespersons while the variable portion tends to fluctuate with gross dollar sales.

4. Sales office expense is a mixed cost with the variable portion related to the number of orders processed.

5. Shipping expense is a mixed cost with the variable portion related to the number of units sold.

A sales force of 80 persons generated a total of 4,300 orders resulting in a sales volume of 420,000 units during November. The gross dollar sales amounted to $10.9 million. The selling expenses incurred for November were as follows:

Advertising and promotion	$1,350,000
Administrative salaries	57,000
Sales salaries	80,000
Sales commissions	218,000
Salesperson travel	185,000
Sales office expense	497,200
Shipping expense	730,000
Total	$3,117,200

REQUIRED:

A. Explain why flexible budgeting is a useful management tool.

B. Explain why the selling expense flexible budgets presented above would not be appropriate for evaluating Wielson Company's November selling expenses, and indicate how the flexible budget would have to be revised.

C. Prepare a selling expense report for November that Wielson Company can use to evaluate its control over selling expenses. The report should have a line for each selling expense item showing the appropriate budgeted amount, the actual selling expense, and the monthly dollar variation.

13-21 (*Comprehensive Reporting to Different Levels of Management*). The Alberta Manufacturing Company, Ltd. produces a single product and uses a standard cost system. The standards for cost and price for each unit are shown in the following tabulation.

Material: 4 yards of Cloth X at $2.88	$11.52	
3 yards of Cloth Q at $2.16	6.48	$18.00
Direct labor: 5 hours at $2.00		10.00
Factory overhead: Based on direct labor hours (⅓ fixed)		7.50
Cost to manufacture		$35.50
Selling expense (⅔ fixed)		7.20
Total cost		$42.70
Desired profit per unit		5.30
Selling price		$48.00

Materials are recorded in the Raw Materials Inventory account at standard cost, and any purchasing variances, as well as all other variances, are assigned to the operations of the current year as period costs.

For the year ended March 31, 19X2, budgeted production and sales were 12,000 units; actual sales totaled 15,000 out of 18,000 units produced. There were no beginning inventories.

An examination of the accounts disclosed the following:

1. During the year, 250,000 feet of Cloth X were purchased at $1.00 per foot and 180,000 feet of Cloth Q were purchased at $.70 per foot. Materials issued were 230,000 feet of X and 175,000 feet of Q.

2. Direct labor cost was $180,500. Hourly wage rates averaged 5% less than standard.

3. Actual factory overhead was $120,000, of which $35,000 was fixed.

4. Actual selling expenses totaled $107,600, of which $60,000 was fixed.

5. A special sale of 2,000 units was made at a price of $44 each; the other 13,000 units were sold at the planned price.

REQUIRED:

The president of Alberta Manufacturing Co., Ltd. has hired you as a consultant to analyze the operations of the company and explain fully the deviations from plan.

A. Assuming standard variable costing, prepare a report to the purchasing manager, a report to the sales manager, a report to the factory manager, and a report to the president. Each report should deal with the area for which the particular manager has responsibility. In addition, a brief written analysis should accompany each report. Seldom have variances exceeded 5% of standard in the past.

B. Prepare an Income Statement in accordance with generally accepted accounting principles for inclusion in the annual report. You may assume that the standards are accurate.

(Canada SIA adapted)

13-22 *(Flexible Budget for Restaurant).* Pearsons, a successful regional chain of moderate-priced menu restaurants, each with a carryout delicatessen department, is planning to expand to a nationwide operation. As the chain gets larger and the territory covered becomes wider, managerial control and reporting techniques become more important.

The company management believes that a budget program for the entire company as well as each restaurant–deli unit is needed. The budget presented below has been prepared for the typical unit in the chain. A new unit, once it is in operation, is expected to perform in accordance with the budget.

TYPICAL PEARSONS RESTAURANT–DELI
BUDGETED INCOME STATEMENT FOR THE YEAR
Ending December 31
(000 omitted)

	Delicatessen	Restaurant	Total
Gross Sales	$1,000	$2,500	$3,500
Purchases	$ 600	$1,000	$1,600
Hourly wages	50	875	925
Franchise fee	30	75	105
Advertising	100	200	300
Utilities	70	125	195
Depreciation	50	75	125
Lease expense	30	50	80
Salaries	30	50	80
Total	960	2,450	3,410
Net income before income taxes	$ 40	$ 50	$ 90

All units are of approximately the same size, with the amount of space devoted to the carryout delicatessen similar in each unit. The style of the facilities and the equipment used are uniform in all units. The unit operators are expected to carry out the advertising program recommended by the corporation. The corporation charges a franchise fee, which is a percentage of gross sales for the use of the company name, the building and facilities design, and the advertising advice.

The Akron, Ohio unit was selected to test the budget program. The Akron, Ohio restaurant–deli performance for the year ended December 31, 19X8 compared to the typical budget is presented below.

PEARSONS RESTAURANT–DELI
AKRON, OHIO
Net Income for the Year Ended
December 31, 19X8

	ACTUAL RESULTS				Over (Under) Budget
	Delicatessen	Restaurant	Total	Budget	
Gross sales	$1,200	$2,000	$3,200	$3,500	$(300)
Purchases	$ 780	$ 800	$1,580	$1,600	$ (20)
Hourly wages	60	700	760	925	(165)
Franchise fee	36	60	96	105	(9)
Advertising	100	200	300	300	—
Utilities	76	100	176	195	(19)
Depreciation	50	75	125	125	—
Lease expense	30	50	80	80	—
Salaries	30	50	80	80	—
Total	1,162	2,035	3,197	3,410	(213)
Net income before income taxes	$ 38	$ (35)	$ 3	$ 90	$ (87)

A careful review of the report and a discussion of its meaning was carried out by the company management. One conclusion was that a more meaningful comparison would result if a flexible budget analysis for each of the two lines were performed rather than just the single budget comparison as in the test case.

REQUIRED:

A. Prepare a schedule that compares a flexible budget for the deli line of the Akron restaurant–deli to its actual performance.

B. Would a complete report, comparing a flexible budget to the performance of each of the two operations, make the problems of the Akron operation easier to identify? Explain, using an example from the problem and your answer to part A.

C. Should a flexible budget comparison to actual performance become part of the regular reporting system

1. For the annual review?

2. For a monthly review?

Explain your answer.

(CMA adapted)

13-23 *(Complex Variance Analysis Using Standard Costing System).* The Markley Division of Rosette Industries manufactures and sells patio chairs. The chairs are manufactured in two versions—a metal model and a plastic model of a lesser quality. The company uses its own sales force to sell the chairs to retail stores and to catalog outlets. Generally, customers purchase both the metal and plastic versions.

The chairs are manufactured on two different assembly lines located in

	Actual	Budget	Favorable (Unfavorable) Relative to the Budget
MARKLEY DIVISION OPERATING RESULTS FOR THE FIRST QUARTER			
Sale in units:			
Plastic model	60,000	50,000	10,000
Metal model	20,000	25,000	(5,000)
Sales revenue:			
Plastic model	$630,000	$500,000	$130,000
Metal model	300,000	375,000	(75,000)
Total sales	$930,000	$875,000	$ 55,000
Less variable costs:			
Manufacturing (at standard):			
Plastic model	$480,000	$400,000	$ (80,000)
Metal model	200,000	250,000	50,000
Selling:			
Commissions	46,500	43,750	(2,750)
Bad-debt allowance	9,300	8,750	(550)
Total variable costs (except variable manufacturing variances)	735,800	702,500	(33,300)
Contribution margin (except variable manufacturing variances)	$194,200	$172,500	$ 21,700
Less other costs:			
Variable manufacturing costs variances from standards	$ 49,600	$ —	$ (49,600)
Fixed manufacturing costs	49,200	48,000	(1,200)
Fixed selling and administrative costs	38,500	36,000	(2,500)
Corporation offices allocation	18,500	17,500	(1,000)
Total other costs	155,800	101,500	(54,300)
Divisional operational income	$ 38,400	$ 71,000	$ (32,600)

adjoining buildings. The division management and sales department occupy the third building on the property. The division management includes a division controller responsible for the divisional financial activities and the preparation of reports explaining the differences between actual and budgeted performance. The controller structures these reports such that the sales activities are distinguished from cost factors so that each can be analyzed separately.

The operating results for the first three months of the fiscal year as compared to the budget are presented on page 590. The budget for the current year was based on the assumption that Markley Division would maintain its present market share of the estimated total patio chair market (plastic and metal combined). A status report had been sent to corporate management toward the end of the second month indicating that divisional operating income for the first quarter would probably be about 45% below budget; this estimate was just about on target. The division's operating income was below budget even though industry volume for patio chairs increased by 10% more than was expected at the time the budget was developed.

The manufacturing activities for the quarter resulted in the production of 55,000 plastic chairs and 22,500 metal chairs. The costs incurred by each manufacturing unit are presented below.

			Plastic Model	Metal Model
Raw materials (stated in equivalent finished chairs):				
	Quantity	Price		
Purchases:				
Plastic	60,000	$5.65	$339,000	
Metal	30,000	$6.00		$180,000
Usage:				
Plastic	56,000	$5.00	$280,000	
Metal	23,000	$6.00		$138,000
Direct labor:				
9,300 hours at $6.00 per hour			$ 55,800	
5,600 hours at $8.00 per hour				$ 44,800
Manufacturing overhead:				
Variable:				
Supplies			$ 43,000	$ 18,000
Power			$ 50,000	$ 15,000
Employee benefits			$ 19,000	$ 12,000
Fixed:				
Supervision			$ 14,000	$ 11,000
Depreciation			$ 12,000	$ 9,000
Property taxes and other items			$ 1,900	$ 1,300

The standard variable manufacturing costs per unit and the budgeted monthly fixed manufacturing costs established for the current year are presented below.

	Plastic Model	Metal Model
Raw material	$ 5.00	$ 6.00
Direct labor:		
⅙ hour at $6.00 per DLH	1.00	
¼ hour at $8.00 per DLH		2.00
Variable overhead:		
⅙ hour at $12.00 per DLH	2.00	
¼ hour at $8.00 per DLH		2.00
Standard variable manufacturing cost per unit	$ 8.00	$10.00
Budgeted fixed costs per month		
Supervision	$4,500	$3,500
Depreciation	4,000	3,000
Property taxes and other items	600	400
Total budgeted fixed costs for month	$9,100	$6,900

REQUIRED:

A. Explain the variance in Markley Division's contribution margin attributable to sales activities by calculating the

1. Sales price variance.

2. Sales activity variance.

3. Sales volume variance.

B. What portion of sales volume variance, if any, can be attributed to a change in Markley Division's market share?

C. Analyze the variance in Markley Division's variable manufacturing costs ($49,600) in as much detail as the data permit.

D. Based on your analyses prepared for parts A, B, and C:

1. Identify the major cause of Markley Division's unfavorable profit performance.

2. Did Markley's management attempt to correct this problem? Explain your answer.

3. What other steps, if any, could Markley's management have taken to improve the division's operating income? Explain your answer.

(CMA adapted)

13-24 *(Evaluation of Budgetary Control System).* Tom Emory and Jim Morris strolled back to their plant from the administrative offices of Ferguson & Son

Mfg. Company. Tom was manager of the machine shop in the company's factory; Jim was manager of the Equipment Maintenance Department.

The men had just attended the monthly performance evaluation meeting for plant department heads. These meetings had been held on the third Tuesday of each month since Robert Ferguson, Jr., the president's son, had become plant manager a year earlier.

As they were walking Tom Emory spoke:

Boy, I hate those meetings! I never know whether my department's accounting reports will show good or bad performance. I'm beginning to expect the worst. If the accountants say I saved the company a dollar, I'm called "Sir," but if I spend even a little too much—boy, do I get in trouble. I don't know if I can hold on until I retire.

Tom had just received the worst evaluation he had ever received in his long career with Ferguson & Son. He was the most respected of the experienced machinists in the company. He had been with Ferguson & Son for many years and was promoted to supervisor of the machine shop when the company expanded and moved to its present location. The president (Robert Ferguson, Sr.) had often stated that the company's success was due to the high quality of the work of machinists like Emory. As supervisor, Tom stressed the importance of craftsmanship and told his workers that he wanted no sloppy work coming from his department.

When Robert Ferguson, Jr. became the plant manager, he directed that monthly performance comparisons be made between actual and budgeted costs for each department. The departmental budgets were intended to encourage the supervisors to reduce inefficiencies and to seek cost reduction opportunities. The company controller was instructed to have his staff "tighten" the budget slightly whenever a department attained its budget in a given month; this was done to reinforce the plant supervisor's desire to reduce costs. The young plant manager often stressed the importance of continued progress toward attaining the budget; he also made it known that he kept a file of these performance reports for future reference when he succeeded his father.

Tom Emory's conversation with Jim Morris continued as follows:

Emory: I really don't understand. We've worked so hard to get up to budget and the minute we make it they tighten the budget on us. We can't work any faster and still maintain quality. I think my men are ready to quit trying. Besides, those reports don't tell the whole story. We always seem to be interrupting the big jobs for all those small rush orders. All that setup and machine adjustment time is killing us. And quite frankly, Jim, you were no help. When our hydraulic press broke down last month, your people were nowhere to be found. We had to take it apart ourselves and got stuck with all that idle time.

Morris: I'm sorry about that, Tom, but you know my department has had trouble making budget, too. We were running well beyond at the time of that problem, and if we'd spent a day on that old machine, we would never have made it up. Instead we made the scheduled inspections of the forklift trucks because we knew we could do those in less than the budgeted time.

Emory: Well, Jim, at least you have some options. I'm locked into what the Scheduling Department assigns to me and you know they're being harrassed by sales for those special orders. Incidentally, why didn't your report show all the supplies you guys wasted last month when you were working in Bill's department?

Morris: We're not out of the woods on that deal yet. We charged the maximum we could to our other work and haven't even reported some of it yet.

Emory: Well, I'm glad you have a way of getting out of the pressure. The accountants seem to know everything that's happening in my department, sometimes even before I do. I thought all that budget and accounting stuff was supposed to help, but it just gets me into trouble. It's all a big pain. I'm trying to put out quality work; they're trying to save pennies.

Tom Emory's performance report for the month in question is reproduced below. Actual production volume for the month was at the budgeted level.

	Budget	Actual	Variances
MACHINE SHOP—OCTOBER 1978			
T. Emory, Supervisor			
Direct labor	$ 39,600	$ 39,850	$ 250 **U**
Direct materials	231,000	231,075	75 **U**
Depreciation—equipment	3,000	3,000	0
Depreciation—buildings	6,000	6,000	0
Power	900	860	40 **F**
Maintenance	400	410	10 **U**
Supervision	1,500	1,500	0
Idle-time	0	1,800	1,800 **U**
Setup labor	680	2,432	1,752 **U**
Miscellaneous	2,900	3,300	400 **U**
	$285,980	$290,227	$4,247 **U**

REQUIRED:

A. Identify the problems that appear to exist in Ferguson & Son Mfg. Company's budgetary control system and explain how the problems are likely to reduce the effectiveness of the system.

B. Explain how Ferguson & Son Mfg. Company's budgetary control system could be revised to improve its effectiveness.

(CMA adapted)

13-25 *(Hospital Cost Control System).* Valley Community Hospital is a 350-bed nonprofit, general hospital. It operates under a prospective reimbursement system whereby a fixed revenue budget for the hospital is negotiated annually with the State Hospital Commission, a division of the State Department of Health. The Hospital Commission regulates hospital charges and total revenue through a formal budget review and approval process that is mandatory for all hospitals in the state. Each hospital's budget request is based on a forecast of the types of patients it will be treating (called its expected "case-mix"), costs associated with treatment, and associated revenues. Charges for services are regulated, although hospitals are permitted to generate some revenue greater than actual costs incurred.

Each hospital's budget is adjusted periodically for changes in the general level of prices affecting the industry, changes in the type and number of patients expected to be treated, and approved changes in services offered and physical facilities of the institution.

The prospective reimbursement system covers all payors (insurance companies, government programs such as Medicare, etc.) and provides the hospital with a fixed revenue budget that cannot be varied by retrospective adjustment. It may permit prospective adjustment for past over- or underpayments based on established criteria, however.

Valley Community Hospital receives one-twelfth of its total annual approved budget monthly with proportionate shares being paid by the various private insurance companies and government programs based on projected proportions of patients and charges falling under each payment program. For example, if it is expected that 50% of the hospital's expenses will be incurred treating Blue Cross patients, Blue Cross will submit one-twelfth of its 50% share of the total annual budget each month. If during the year the hospital expends less than its annual budget, any savings can be used for appropriate institutional purposes. However, if the hospital exceeds its budget, it must absorb the loss (or discontinue admitting patients).

Because of extensive concern over the rising costs of hospital services during the past decade, prospective reimbursement is being initiated in many parts of the country in an effort to encourage cost containment and more efficient operation of hospitals. The hypothesis is that if hospitals know what their total budgets are in advance, they will make cost minimization choices when faced with potential expenditures. There will be a direct incentive to assure that only necessary services are provided to patients and that only patients who truly need hospitalization are admitted.

Traditionally, hospitals were paid after each patient was discharged based on charges for all costs incurred, with no control by any outside agency or organization of the total hospital budget. There was no incentive in such a system for cost containment, especially because most patients were not directly paying for their own care and therefore were not very concerned about costs. In truth, the incentive in the traditional hospital reimbursement system was for the hospital to deliver more services so more revenue was generated, rather than decreasing use of services.

This is the first year that Valley Community Hospital has operated under a prospective reimbursement system. Therefore, there is a lot of concern and anxiety about expenditures on the part of hospital administrative staff members.

The administrative staff has been working with the director of Management Information Systems to develop a reporting system that will provide comparisons between actual expenditures and projected expenditures that are accurate enough to provide managerial control over costs and revenue during the period covered by the prospective rate. Projected expenditures to a great extent have been based on the previous year's experience.

From the hospital's basic chart of accounts (mandated by the Hospital Commission for budget review purposes), the Accounting Department has established 32 final cost centers.

1. Dietary
2. Admitting
3. Billing
4. Routine room charges
5. Nursing
6. House staff (interns/residents)
7. Medical Records
8. Social Services
9. Newborn intensive care
10. Intensive care
11. Coronary care
12. Operating Room
13. Recovery Room
14. Anesthesia
15. Delivery Room
16. Diagnostic Radiology
17. Radioisotopes
18. Radiotherapy
19. Laboratory
20. EKG, EEG
21. Medical–Surgical Supplies
22. Physical Medicine
23. Respiratory Therapy
24. IV Therapy
25. Pharmacy
26. Renal Dialysis
27. Renal Transplant
28. Urology
29. Emergency Room
30. Clinics

31. Outpatient

32. Miscellaneous

Overhead accounts such as housekeeping, administration, data processing, accounting, and purchasing are dealt with through a special allocation algorithm, which generates a set of linear equations whose solution provides the identified fraction of each overhead account allocated to each final cost center. The direct costs of each final cost center and the portion of overhead costs allocated to each cost center represent the total cost of providing the services associated with each final cost center. Charges are then established for each service within each final cost center and patient bills are generated based on actual services received.

The hospital's managerial accounting system previously provided department managers with basic financial information such as expenditures for salaries, benefits, supplies, equipment, and staff development. However, it did not provide data related to use of departmental resources for patient care. It was not possible to ascertain what types of patients used the department's resources or to evaluate the appropriateness of use of the resources. The administrative staff and departmental managers now feel this type of data is essential for management under the prospective reimbursement system.

John Smith, director of research, identified a "patient classification system" developed at the Yale University Center for Health Studies that he felt might be useful for monitoring resource utilization by groups of patients. The system classifies patients into what are called "Diagnosis Related Groups" (DRG) based on medical and demographic characteristics of the patients (such as age, sex, diagnosis, and surgical procedures). He reported to the administrative staff that the Yale researchers developed the system after statistical analysis of data on approximately 1 million hospital admissions. The system classifies patients into 383 DRG. Here are some examples of DRG.

#165—Pneumonia with age less than 31.

#166—Pneumonia without surgery without secondary diagnosis with age greater than 30.

#167—Pneumonia without surgery with secondary diagnosis with age greater than 30.

#168—Pneumonia with surgery.

#183—Stomach ulcer without surgery without secondary diagnosis.

#184—Stomach ulcer without surgery with secondary diagnosis.

#185—Stomach ulcer with surgical procedure (biopsy, visualization, other).

#186—Stomach ulcer with surgery (removal of portion of stomach, other major operation) without secondary diagnosis.

#187—Stomach ulcer with surgery (removal of portion of stomach, other major operation) with secondary diagnosis.

Based on the analysis performed by the Yale researchers, each DRG consists of a homogeneous group of patients based on expected resource consumption or cost of care.

The administrative staff at Valley Community Hospital, with input from its medical staff, decided that the DRG system could be used to define the "product" of the hospital. Resource use, costs, and charges would be monitored by DRG, and departmental budgets could be established based on expected number of patients to be treated in each DRG and expected resource consumption within each DRG.

Using data abstracted from each patient's medical record and data from each patient's bill, the director of Management Information Systems was able to produce management reports by DRG for use by the administrative staff, medical staff, and department managers.

Mary Brown, assistant administrator responsible for the Obstetrics/Newborn Unit, received the following reports in April:

DRG 282, DELIVERY WITH COMPLICATIONS WITH CESAREAN SECTION

	Volume and Cost 19X0	Volume and Cost 19X1
Number of patients	255	329
Number of days of stay	1752	2200
Average length of stay	6.87	6.69
Total cost	$382,056	$525,602
Cost per case (unit)	$ 1,498	$ 1,598
Cost per day	$ 218	$ 239
Total charges	$447,269	$611,036
Average charges per case	$ 1,754	$ 1,857
Ratio: Costs/Charges	.85420	.86018

REQUIRED:

A. Prepare an analysis of the data found in Tables 1 and 2. Identify key information from each table that may be useful to Mary Brown for management planning and control purposes.

B. Describe constraints of the data and additional data or information that would assist in this analysis process.

C. Discuss the applicability of cost centers, the diagnosis related groups (DRG), and the revenue-generating policies in obtaining the goal of cost containment.

DRG 321, IMMATURITY, HYALINE MEMBRANE DISEASE,
OTHER MAJOR DISEASES OR CONDITIONS OF INFANCY
WITH SECONDARY DIAGNOSIS

	Volume and Cost 19X0	Volume and Cost 19X1
Number of patients	216	202
Number of days of stay	2409	2461
Average length of stay	11.15	12.18
Total cost	$496,707	$719,376
Cost per case (unit)	$ 2,299	$ 3,561
Cost per day	$ 206	$ 292
Total charges	$460,703	$524,979
Average charges per case	$ 2,133	$ 2,599
Ratio: Costs/Charges	1.07815	1.37029

chapter **14**

MEASUREMENT OF DIVISIONAL PERFORMANCE

Under responsibility accounting, costs, revenues, and, in some cases, investment in resources are assigned to the manager who exercises control over them. Our illustrations in the previous chapters were concerned with cost centers and profit centers. An entirely different dimension is added in this chapter when management's responsibilities are extended to cover resource investments.

DIVISIONALIZATION

A **division** (often called an **investment center**) is a responsibility center where the manager is held accountable for both production and marketing operating decisions, as well as the investments in the resources necessary to carry out the above decisions. Divisional management is concerned not only with *how* operations are carried on, but also *what* resources these operations use. All the conditions for overall evaluation of a company are present in a division. Corporate goals and objectives provide constraints on the divisions. However, within those broad constraints, a division may operate as a separate company. It may be identified along geographic lines, as Eastern and Western divisions, along product lines, as Chevrolet and Cadillac divisions, or along separate industry lines, as in food products and leisure-time products divisions.

Business firms establish autonomous divisions for several reasons. The most important reason is to provide a natural separation of activities that will facilitate decentralization of the decision-making activities within the organization. Complementing decentralization is the ability to measure a division's performance in terms of corporate objectives, principally through the measurement of **return on investment** (ROI). Because this measure is compatible with overall corporate objectives, division management may be given a high degree of freedom in the management of resources. The ultimate test of the effectiveness of management decisions is whether they provide the firm with a satisfactory overall rate of return on the assets committed. It is the ability to measure return on investment that makes decentralized administration attractive.

Several conditions should be present, however, for decentralization to operate successfully.[1] First, each division must be independent of other divisions. Unless this separation is possible, performance measurement of an individual division is illusory. The more difficult it is to separate income and investment measures, the less probable it is that a division makes independent decisions. Interdivisional transactions may cause measurement problems but they do not preclude separate divisional status. Second, the decisions of one division to increase its own income should not be allowed to reduce corporate income. It would be dysfunctional to allow a division to compete with other divisions or deal with other divisions in such a way as to cause overall corporate income to decline. This situation may arise if division boundaries are poorly drawn or corporate goals and objectives are not clearly stated. Finally, it is important to decentralization that corporate management refrain from making decisions for the divisions; divisions must be free to make decisions themselves. Corporate management should step in only as an emergency measure.

---

[1]David Solomons, *Divisional Performance, Measurement and Control* (Homewood, Ill.: Richard D. Irwin, Inc., 1965).

RETURN ON INVESTMENT

Simply stated, **return on investment** (ROI) is found by dividing income by some measure of investment. Return on investment analysis relates the income, as determined on the Income Statement, to the resources used to generate the income, as measured on the Statement of Financial Position. There are two components to the return on investment calculation: profit margin and investment turnover. **Profit margin,** sometimes called *profit as a percentage of sales,* is found by dividing income by sales. **Investment turnover** is sales divided by investment in assets. Return on investment is the product of these two components.

$$\frac{\text{Return on}}{\text{investment}} = \frac{\text{Profit}}{\text{margin}} \times \frac{\text{Investment}}{\text{turnover}}$$

In an expanded form, return on investment is

$$\frac{\text{Return on}}{\text{investment}} = \frac{\text{Income}}{\text{Investment in assets}} = \frac{\text{Income}}{\text{Sales}} \times \frac{\text{Sales}}{\text{Investment in assets}}$$

The return on investment may be increased by increasing the profit margin, by increasing the investment turnover, or by some combination of the two. To illustrate the components of return on investment, let's assume that a firm has sales of $500,000, expenses of $400,000, income of $100,000, and investment in assets of $250,000. The return on investment is computed as

$$\frac{\text{Return on}}{\text{investment}} = \frac{\$100,000}{\$250,000} = \frac{\$100,000}{\$500,000} \times \frac{\$500,000}{\$250,000}$$

$$= \quad 40\% \quad = \quad 20\% \quad \times \quad 2 \text{ times}$$

If, through cost reduction, the firm is able to increase the income as a percentage of sales by an additional 3%, the return on investment will increase by 6%. The investment turnover acts as a multiplier. Suppose instead that the firm is able to speed up collection of receivables and reduce inventories through better planning. The turnover component of the return on investment calculation will be increased. If working capital can be decreased by $25,000, the total investment in assets will decrease and the investment turnover will increase to 2.2 times. The return on investment will increase to 44%.

$$\frac{\text{Return on}}{\text{investment}} = \frac{\$100,000}{\$500,000} \times \frac{\$500,000}{\$225,000}$$

$$= 20\% \times 2.2 \text{ times}$$

$$= 44\%$$

When assessing performance, one of the major advantages of analyzing the components of return on investment is in identifying the causes of change. For example, let's assume the return on investment for an older division, in the process of modernizing and expanding, drops from 40.0% in 19X3 to 25.5% in 19X4. Does this represent poor performance? Data for the two years follow.

	19X3	19X4
Sales	$400	$500
Income	$ 40	$ 51
Investment in assets	$100	$200

The return on investment for each year follows.

$$
\text{19X3} \quad \frac{\text{Return on}}{\text{investment}} = \frac{\$\,40}{\$400} \times \frac{\$400}{\$100}
$$

$$
40.0\% = 10.0\% \times 4.0 \text{ times}
$$

$$
\text{19X4} \quad \frac{\text{Return on}}{\text{investment}} = \frac{\$\,51}{\$500} \times \frac{\$500}{\$200}
$$

$$
25.5\% = 10.2\% \times 2.5 \text{ times}
$$

The rate of return for 19X3 was high because of old assets that were nearly depreciated. With the large additional investment in 19X4, the asset turnover dropped from 4.0 to 2.5 times. However, the profit margin increased slightly. It it takes time to start up the new facilities and get them up to a profitable level, it may be that the division has performed well, particularly when the long-run profitability is considered.

MEASUREMENT OF RETURN ON INVESTMENT COMPONENTS

To use return on investment analysis effectively in management assessment, it is important that measures of income and investment be clearly understood by all concerned. There are some variations in practice in both the measurement of income and the measurement of investment.

The income figure used in calculating return on investment is usually taken directly from the financial statements. Income for internal reports used in measuring divisional performance can differ from Generally Accepted Accounting Principles in two important respects. First, when products or other assets are transferred between divisions of the company, proper evaluation of the divisions may require transfer prices. The use of a transfer price based on some measure other than historical cost could result in divisional profit being attached to divisional inventories. Transfer pricing will be discussed later in this chapter. Second, because of its usefulness in short-range decisions, variable costing may be used for inventory valuation and internal income measurement. Therefore, the income principles used in calculating divisional rates of return may or may not conform to Generally Accepted Accounting Principles. It is more important that the income measure be understood and used consistently throughout the firm.

The measurement of investment is even less standardized than the income measure. The most readily available measure of investment is the book value of assets shown on the Statement of Financial Position. However, this measure has an inherent weakness. Over time, the carrying value of the assets decreases through depreciation charges. As long as the income remains relatively constant, the return on investment will increase because of the declining investment base. If a manager holds income reasonably constant and makes no new investments, the rate of return will show improving performance. The ultimate result is a decline in the firm's productive capacity as the assets wear out.

There are several ways to overcome this defect in return on investment analysis. One approach is to use the original cost of the asset before any deduction for depreciation, providing a constant return on investment if earnings are constant. Another approach is to use a method of depreciation with increasing charges over the life of the asset. The result is a constant rate of return on investment; each year a lower income is related to a smaller asset base.

Another difficulty in using ROI as a measure of performance is that any calculation using historical cost (either original or depreciated) to measure the investment base may be overstating the return in a period of inflation. As the asset base increases in value because of a change in the price level, the company may be misled about the rate of return being achieved. As an example, assume that Stagnation, Inc. has reported assets of $100,000 and income of $20,000 in its most recent financial statements. The return on investment, based on original cost, is 20% ($20,000 ÷ $100,000). Let's assume that since the assets were acquired, their replacement cost has doubled, primarily because of an increase in construction costs. In many cases meaningful rates of return can be found by restating the value of the assets on the Statement of Financial Position and the depreciation expense on the Income Statement to reflect their current replacement costs. The following comparison shows return on investment for assets at original cost and at replacement cost.

	Original Cost	Replacement Cost
Assets	$100,000	$200,000
Operating Income	$ 30,000	$ 30,000
Depreciation	10,000	20,000
Income	$ 20,000	$ 10,000
Return on Investment	$\left(\dfrac{\$\,20,000}{\$100,000}\right) = 20\%$	$\left(\dfrac{\$\,10,000}{\$200,000}\right) = 5\%$

To the management of Stagnation, Inc. it appears that a rate of return on investment of 20% is being earned. In reality, the return is only 5% when replacement costs are considered.

The rates of return among divisions within the same company may not be comparable if their asset bases were acquired at different times. The carrying costs of recently acquired assets are usually relatively close to replacement costs, whereas the carrying costs of old assets may be substantially different. For a proper comparison of two different divisions, it may be necessary to restate each unit's assets and depreciation expenses at current replacement costs.

Another adjustment that some firms make in their ROI calculation is to use only **productive assets** in their investment base. Under this method, assets not currently committed to productive use are excluded from the investment base. If any assets are removed from the base, earnings related to them should be excluded from the income. From a performance evaluation perspective, the mere existence of idle resources implies that management may not be using its resources wisely; exclusion of these assets from the investment base may serve as a disguise of inefficient operations.

In many companies with decentralized divisions, the home office centralizes some corporate activities, such as cash management or billing and collection of receivables. In cases where corporate assets are pooled or where assets are shared among divisions, the common, or jointly shared, assets must be allocated to the benefiting divisions for the proper measurement of their individual investments. Difficulty in identification of assets with separate divisions may indicate that the responsibility center should be identified as a cost or profit center rather than an investment center.

The most commonly apportioned assets are receivables and inventories. Where receivables are maintained by the central office, the allocation is often based on receivables turnover. The investment base would include the amount of receivables generated by the firm's credit and collection policies applied to the division's sales. If the inventories and their levels are centrally controlled, they can be apportioned by applying an inventory turnover to actual sales volume or material consumption. Caution should be used in this allocation procedure; the critical assumption is that the allocation procedure realistically represents the operating conditions of the division.

PERFORMANCE ASSESSMENT THROUGH RETURN ON INVESTMENT ANALYSIS

Separation of the overall rate of return into profit margin and investment turnover enables a manager to see the overall effects of decisions. To illustrate this point, let's assume that a corporation has three independent divisions and that top management's overall goal is a total before-tax return on investment of 24%. This goal is illustrated in graphic form in Exhibit 14–1. The vertical scale measures investment turnover (Sales ÷ Investment). Profit margin (Income ÷

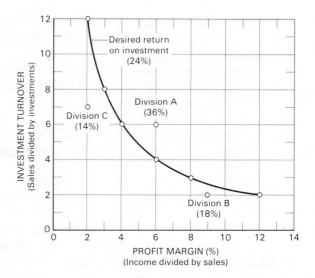

EXHIBIT 14—1
Divisional performance
assessment through return
on investment analysis

Sales) is shown on the horizontal scale. The desired rate of 24% may be attained
by any combination of investment turnover and profit margin shown on the
curve. For example, a 24% return could be achieved with an investment turnover
of 12 and a profit margin of 2%; it could also be obtained with an investment
turnover of 6 and a profit margin of 4%.

Actual rates of return on investment for the three divisions are shown
on Exhibit 14–1. Division A shows a rate of return of 36%. The investment
turnover is six times per year and the profit margin is 6%. Division A achieved
results above the desired rate.

Division B did not achieve the desired rate of return. The division obtained an 18% return with an investment turnover of 2 and a profit margin of
9%. On the surface, the 9% margin seems satisfactory, but the turnover seems
low. If the investment turnover had been increased to 3, the division would
have earned a satisfactory rate of return of 27%. The low turnover indicates that
the division did not utilize its assets properly in relation to sales. The analysis
should begin by studying the asset structure to see if nonproductive assets are
excessive. Perhaps excess inventory, idle cash, or unused plant capacity exists.
It is also possible that division management has misinterpreted the demand for
the product or has not actively pursued additional sales.

Division C's 14% rate of return also did not achieve the desired rate.
The investment turnover of 7 seems to be adequate, indicating good utilization
of the assets. The profit margin of 2% seems low, however. It could perhaps
be improved by a study of the cost structure; a low profit margin may be
indicative of poor cost control. The manager should assess the production facilities in an attempt to lower manufacturing costs, and should test other costs,
particularly those such as advertising, to ensure that they are being incurred
wisely. An analysis of the pricing structure might also prove informative.

This type of analysis is useful in directing the manager's attention toward broad areas for improvement, but it does not determine what should be done. The ability to interpret the profit margin and investment turnover depends on the specific business or industry involved. For example, a retail grocery store typically has a low profit margin and a high investment turnover. A steel mill or a jewelry store, on the other hand, would have a relatively high profit margin and, with a heavy investment in plant and equipment or inventory, a relatively low investment turnover. The rate-of-return analysis must be related to the specific situation.

OVEREMPHASIS ON RETURN ON INVESTMENT ANALYSIS

There is no question that the rate of return on investment is a valuable measure of *overall firm or divisional performance*. It relates the resources to their utilization better than any other single measure. If a given firm consistently earns a rate of return of 5% while another firm earns 25%, we would expect investors to prefer the firm with a 25% return. In the long run, capital investment will flow away from firms with low rates of return toward those with higher return rates.

There are many advantages in using investment centers and return on investment to evaluate performance. First, return on investment is a generally accepted measure of overall performance. As a measure of divisional performance, it is compatible with a firm-wide rate-of-return analysis. In addition, it corresponds to the intuitive view that investments are made with the goal of achieving a desired rate of return.

Second, return-on-investment analysis, because it is a ratio, provides a common denominator allowing comparisons of different activities. Retailing activities can be compared with wholesaling activities, steel companies can be compared with fabrication companies, and one company can be compared with other companies in the same industry.

Third, rate of return can be easily understood and interpreted.

Finally, return-on-investment analysis can provide a solid incentive for optimal utilization of the firm's assets. It encourages managers to obtain assets that will provide a satisfactory return on investment and to dispose of assets that are not providing an acceptable return.

Return-on-investment analysis does have limitations that must be considered. First, many subjective judgments contribute to a measurement of both the income and the investment base. In many firms there are some allocations of the centrally incurred expenses and assets; any apportionment is subject to arbitrary interpretation.

Second, the rate of return represents a single control point that can be manipulated by the manager. Earlier we pointed out that one way to increase the rate of return is to make no new capital investments. Because book values decline due to depreciation, the investment base will continually decrease in value, causing the rate of return to increase. This effect could lead to a situation where the manager's favorable performance assessment is jeopardizing the long-range profit potential of the firm.

A third shortcoming of overemphasizing divisional rate of return in evaluating performance is that it can distort the overall allocation of firm resources. To illustrate, let's assume that a firm is currently earning an overall rate of return of 15%, but that Division A is earning a 20% return. Assume that the manager of Division A has the opportunity to purchase a new asset that would earn an 18% return, which is greater than the overall company return of 15%. However, if the new project is undertaken by Division A, its rate of return will fall. Further assume that the next best alternative use of the funds is a project desired by Division C, whose operations are currently earning only 10%. If Division C can earn 14% on the new investment, it will increase its rate of return but reduce the overall corporate rate of return. Thus, what is good for Division C will be bad for the company as a whole, and what is bad for Division A will be good for the company as a whole.

RESIDUAL INCOME

The concept of residual income was developed as an alternative to the rate of return to measure divisional performance. **Residual income** is the incremental income of a division after deducting an interest charge based on the value of the division's investment in assets. The company's average cost of capital is usually used as a measure of the interest charges. For example, assume that Division S has a budgeted income of $100,000 this year, with a budgeted investment of $500,000. Further, assume that the cost of capital for the corporation is 15%. The income objective for the division, in terms of residual income, is

Divisional income	$100,000
Cost of capital used by division	
(15% × $500,000)	75,000
Residual income of Division S	$ 25,000

A principal advantage of residual income is that it encourages capital investment any time the manager can exceed the firm's cost of capital. Any new investment will increase the division's residual income if it yields an income higher than the cutoff (required) percentage. A second advantage is that it allows different rates of return for different assets. For example, a manager can use a different cost of capital for risky projects than for stable, relatively certain projects. In this way the performance measure can be made consistent with the decision rules employed in capital investment decisions.

Residual income as a performance measure overcomes some of the shortcomings of return-on-investment analysis, but it is not a perfect measure. Most of the problems in measuring divisional income and divisional investment discussed earlier in this chapter are present in the measurement of residual income as are some of the problems of deriving a fair and equitable measure of the cost of capital.

Many companies choose to use both return on investment and residual income in evaluating performance. The understandability of the return-on-investment measure is complemented by the motivation for capital investment provided by the residual income measure.

INTRAFIRM TRANSFER PRICING

Divisional income as a control measure is based on the view that the divisions operate much like independent companies. It is assumed that a division buys its resources in one market and sells its products or services in another. In many decentralized organizations, however, products and services are often exchanged between divisions. For these exchanges it is necessary to establish a **transfer price,** the price at which goods and services are transferred among divisions. *Any price* can be a transfer price. It may be based on a price that would exist in an independent market, the cost to the producing division, or an arbitrarily established price.

There is no simple measure of a transfer price that can meet all the needs of a decentralized firm. Any transfer price that is not the price a division would pay in the open marketplace results in an arbitrary allocation of income among the divisions and weakens the measurement of divisional performance. The task of management is to develop a transfer pricing system that (1) allows a measure of performance to reflect the division's use of resources and (2) allows the optimal allocation of the firm's resources.

Where there is an independent, competitive market and the divisions are reasonably autonomous, open-market prices provide the best transfer price for divisional assessment. However, when corporate policy requires trading among the company's divisions, a portion of the control over resource utilization is removed from the divisions and their profit responsibility is blurred. For decentralization to work in these cases, there must be an arbitration procedure to settle any disputes regarding transfer prices and the subsequent assessment of management performance.

TRANSFER PRICING FOR MEASURING MANAGEMENT PERFORMANCE

The best transfer price for measuring management performance is one that reflects the price in an open, competitive market. These market prices are the best measure of revenue for the selling division and of cost inputs for the buying division. A major drawback in the use of market prices is that few markets are perfectly competitive. Further, in many instances, no outside market exists for the products or services being transferred. One way to establish market prices under these conditions is through bids from outside firms. However, if the supplier is aware that the bid is simply to establish an internal transfer price and will not result in an order, the quoted price may be unrealistic.

For market prices to have maximum effectiveness in management performance measurement, both the buying and selling divisions must be able to act independently. The divisions must be free to buy or sell their products in any market. If there is no outside market for the products or services, or if corporate policy requires interdivisional trading, negotiated market prices may be necessary.

In circumstances where there are no competitive market prices and a negotiated transfer price cannot be established, the company cannot effectively use profit or investment centers. It should only use cost centers for management performance evaluation. By using standard costs as the transfer prices for cost centers, the selling divisions are encouraged to have good cost control. The manager of a selling division would be evaluated as the manager of any other cost center. Performance would be measured by the question, "How well did the division control costs?"

In responsibility accounting, a division's performance should reflect only revenues and costs subject to the control of the division. Artificial prices, such as a constant markup on cost, allow divisional income to be measured but only give an appearance of a profit center. An artificial transfer price with an arbitrary markup does not fit the requisite of controllability. Control over revenue is not present and the divisions are not true profit centers.

TRANSFER PRICES FOR DECISIONS

The ideal transfer price for management decision making is the price that would emphasize the well-being of the company as a whole, rather than of the individual divisions. For decision-making purposes, the transfer price should reflect the opportunity cost of the goods or services transferred between the divisions. An optimal allocation of resources takes place only if the goods or services are priced on transfer at the opportunity cost that would be incurred to obtain the goods or services elsewhere. Where an outside market exists, the goods and services are available from external sources and the open-market price is the best measure of opportunity cost.

Where no external market exists, only top management may be in a position to know the opportunity costs of a particular exchange. It may be necessary for top management to prescribe a transfer price or arbitrate in the negotiations so that decisions reflect corporate objectives. One approach is to use the variable costs incurred by the selling division as the transfer price charged to the buying division. The use of variable costs allows each divisional manager to assess the differential costs more accurately. When used as a transfer price, standard variable costs, representing what costs should be, are preferred over actual variable costs. The selling division is thus prevented from passing inefficiencies on to the buying division.

The manager of the selling division cannot be expected to accept readily a price as a performance measure that will produce a large divisional loss even if it is best for the firm as a whole. In fact, if variable costs are used as the transfer price, the manager of the selling division should be indifferent between selling to another division of the company or closing down. In either case the selling division's loss would be equal to the fixed costs of the division.

Top management support is essential in negotiations between divisions. Each division must be shown the effect of the transfer pricing policy on firm-wide profits as well as the effect on divisional performance. The minimum transfer price is generally the variable unit cost and the maximum is the market price adjusted for any savings of doing business inside the company. The transfer prices used must recognize the economic reality of the division's environment for decision making and at the same time be fair to division managers for performance evaluation.

TRANSFER PRICES FOR EXTERNAL REPORTING

Under Generally Accepted Accounting Principles, assets must be stated at cost, and revenue is not recognized until a sale is completed with an outside party. The only transfer price appropriate for external reporting is an actual cost based on full-absorption costing. In this way the inventory is stated at the full cost required to bring the goods to the condition for sale.

When divisional financial statements are consolidated into financial statements for the firm as a whole, all interdivisional profits resulting from transfer prices must be eliminated from assets on hand. All interdivisional payables, receivables, purchases, and sales must also be eliminated.

TRANSFER PRICING CASE

To illustrate some of the problems of transfer prices, let's assume that the Rex Company produces industrial chemicals. Three divisions are evaluated on the basis of their divisional income and return on investment. Division R extracts material from animal by-products. The resulting product, Product R, is sold to Division E, as well as to outside customers. Division E processes Product R into a number of other products. One of these products, Product E, is sold primarily to Division X. Division X combines one unit of Product E with other ingredients to produce an industrial cleaner, Product X. A diagram of the product flow follows.

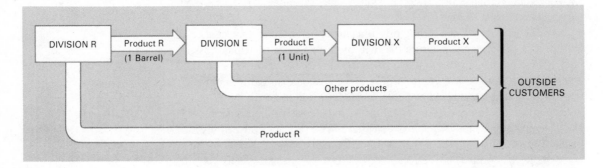

Price and cost information for products R, E, and X follows.

	Product R (per barrel)	Product E (per unit)	Product X (per unit)
Selling price to outsider	$100	$300*	$500
Transfer price	$100	$300	—
Additional variable costs	$ 60	$110	$100
Contribution margin	40%	30%	?

*Limited sales.

Each division buys and sells externally as well as to other divisions. Top management expects each division to operate independently.

Assume that Divisions R and E were satisfied with a market price of $100 per barrel for Product R. There were a number of buyers and sellers in an established market for Product R. The market for Product E, however, was smaller with fewer suppliers. The purchasing agent for Division X requested bids for Product E from Division E and Mohawk Chemical Company, an outside supplier of Product E. The bids were $300 from Division E and $250 from Mohawk Chemical Company.

When asked to match the Mohawk Chemical Company bid of $250, the manager of Division E refused, citing two reasons. First, it was widely known that Mohawk Chemical Company had idle capacity in the plant that manufactured Product E. The Division E manager maintained that Mohawk was "underpricing" Product E and that they would not attain their normal profit margin. Second, the manager of Division E had set a division objective of an average contribution margin ratio of 30%. The price to Division X had to be $300 for Division E to maintain its 30% contribution margin ratio. The 30% contribution margin ratio was determined as follows:

Variable costs of Division E:

Cost of Product R (purchased from Division R)	$100
Variable costs of producing Product E	110
Total variable costs	$210

$$\begin{aligned}
\text{Desired selling price} &= \frac{\text{Variable costs}}{\text{Variable cost ratio}} \\[6pt]
&= \frac{\$210}{(1 - \text{Contribution margin ratio})} \\[6pt]
&= \frac{\$210}{(1 - .30)} = \$300
\end{aligned}$$

When the manager of Division E requested that top management require Division X to pay $300 for Product E, the corporate controller prepared the following tabulation that showed the contribution margins from a company-wide standpoint under the two alternatives.

	Buy Internally	Buy from Mohawk
Selling price of Product X	$500	$500
Variable costs:		
Division R	$ 60	$ 0
Division E	110	0
Division X	100	100
External purchase price	0	250
Total variable costs	270	350
Contribution margin	$230	$150

The contribution margin of $150 when Division X purchases from Mohawk is easy to see. Product X has a selling price of $500 and variable costs of $350 under this alternative. Variable costs of $350 include the external purchase price of $250 added to the $100 variable costs of Division X.

The contribution margin of $230 when Division X purchases internally is more difficult to see. Product X has a selling price of $500 and variable costs of $270 under this alternative. To arrive at the variable costs of $270, add the variable costs of the three divisions without considering any fixed costs or markup ($60 from R, $110 from E, and $100 from X).

Clearly, this analysis shows that Division X, from the company-wide standpoint, should purchase from Division E rather than from Mohawk. The company will earn an extra $80 per unit ($230 − $150) contribution margin.

However, in this case what is good for the company as a whole is not satisfactory to either of the division managers.

As long as Division E refuses to lower its selling price, Division X should want to purchase externally from Mohawk; but top management should want a transfer from Division E to Division X to take place. Division E wants the internal transfer to take place at $300—a transfer Division X should not want. If Division E holds out for $300, it loses most of its market for Product E and Division X purchases from Mohawk at $250. Division manager E's willingness to forego this sale will depend on the marketplace for Product E and the alternative uses of Division E's capacity. If the actual market price for Product E is $250, as bid by Mohawk, and if Division E cannot use the productive capacity for any other purposes, then Division E is in a weakened bargaining position. Actually, unless other alternatives are present that provide a greater contribution margin ratio than that offered by the $250 transfer to Division X, Division E should be willing to sell to Division X at $250 per unit. In fact, if there is enough excessive capacity in Division E, they should be willing to sell Product E at any price greater than its real variable costs of $210 ($100 + $110).

If the manager of Division E has alternative uses other than the manufacture of Product E, the problem changes. Any time the manager of Division E can obtain a contribution margin from outsiders of more than $80 (the difference between $250, Mohawk's price, and $170, the internal variable costs of Divisions R and E) per unit of productive capacity, the firm would want Division E to sell to outsiders and Division X to buy from Mohawk. Any time the contribution margin of Division E falls below $80 per unit of capacity, the firm would want Division X to purchase its materials from Division E.

The ability of division managers to negotiate freely with one another is the heart of responsibility centers. Unless this condition exists, the control system is weakened. It is essential that the organization develop performance evaluation measures that will encourage the individual managers to take the action that is in the best interest of the organization as a whole but still leaves them independent of top management. Only under these conditions can the impact of their decision making be assessed and compared.

The above case illustrates that the question of suitable transfer prices for the two functions of management performance assessment and decision optimization does not have an easy answer. The firm must give serious consideration to its goals and objectives in using transfer prices before adopting a particular measure.

MULTIPLE PERFORMANCE MEASURES

Throughout the previous chapters we have stressed financially quantifiable data for judging the effectiveness of management decision making. Financial measures such as the return on investment and residual income are valid and useful, but they are not the only suitable measures. Many nonfinancial measures are also valuable.

When a method of assessment emphasizes a small number of financial measures to the exclusion of others, the system can be more easily manipulated. This is true even though the measures are inherently valid. There is no question that return on investment and income for the period, as examples, are valid measures of performance. However, reliance on a single control tool can distort the decision-making process. The manager who maximized the rate of return by delaying potentially profitable capital investment is an example.

Many firms prefer multiple goals and multiple performance measures, both financial and nonfinancial. Financial goals could include profitability ROI, and productivity and efficiency measures. Personnel goals could include personnel training and development, and employee morale including turnover and absenteeism measurements. Marketing goals could include product leadership, market penetration, and new product development. Societal goals could include public responsibility measures, community involvements, and charitable actions. Management goals could include participative actions, promotability, and smooth transitions.

Three observations may be made from a close examination of these goals. First, the measures to assess performance are both financial and nonfinancial. Profitability and productivity may be financial measures. Employee morale and personnel development measures are certainly nonfinancial and highly subjective. The mixture of subjective and objective assessment measures taxes the measurement skill of the accountant and the evaluation skills of management.

Second, the goals are somewhat contradictory. For example, increasing profitability through increasing employee productivity may lower employee morale. Also, maintaining product leadership may call for research and development costs that lower short-range profitability. The manager should not emphasize one goal by jeopardizing another; an optimal balance should be sought.

Third, multiple goals will increase pressure upon the managers. An attempt to meet many criteria simultaneously can be frustrating and confusing. The proper balance of goals and performance measures is difficult to set. While many of the concepts presented in this text appear highly quantitative and objective, we can never overlook the fact that the setting of goals, the evaluation of actual performance, and the development of a system to measure management decisions are highly subjective. Management accounting relies on scientific methods, but it always has been and always will be an art.

SUMMARY

A widely used test of the effectiveness of management's decisions is the return on investment. The return on investment is

$$\begin{aligned} \frac{\text{Return on}}{\text{investment}} &= \frac{\text{Income}}{\text{Investment}} \\ &= \frac{\text{Sales}}{\text{Investment in assets}} \times \frac{\text{Income}}{\text{Sales}} \end{aligned}$$

where (Sales $\div$ Investment = Investment turnover) and (Income $\div$ Sales = Profit margin).

While conceptually sound and easy to determine, the rate of return on investment has limitations. It focuses management's attention on a single measure and can result in optimizing the measure rather than optimizing the decisions. For example, failure to make new capital investments will increase the rate of return and simultaneously reduce the company's long-range profit potential. The use of residual income as a measure of divisional performance is one way of overcoming some of the shortcomings of return on investment analysis.

Where there are responsibility centers that rely on each other for their production inputs, the problems of interdivisional transfer pricing exist. With profit centers or investment centers, a firm must develop transfer prices when the divisions exchange goods or services. There are many possible transfer prices. To obtain optimum utilization of company resources, transfer prices based on variable costs seem best. For management performance assessment, transfer prices based on current market prices or standard costs seem best. For external reporting purposes, transfer prices based on full cost with no added profit margin conform to generally accepted accounting principles.

There is no single performance measure that can fulfill all management's needs. Overemphasis upon one measure, although that measure seems appropriate, can be detrimental. The best control system includes many performance measures, such as budgets, cost standards, product leadership, and technical standards; and many nonquantifiable measures, such as personnel attitudes and public responsibility. If a firm is to achieve a goal of long-run profitability and stability, it must consider *all* the relevant factors.

PROBLEMS AND CASES

14-1 *(Return on Investment).* The Mountain Division of Nationwide, Inc. had an average investment of $2 million in 19X0. Sales for the year totaled $500,000, variable expenses were $250,000, and fixed expenses were $150,000.

REQUIRED:

Determine the following:

A. Profit margin.

B. Investment turnover.

C. Return on investment.

14-2 *(Return on Investment, Residual Income).* The Electronics Division of HiTech Company earned $25 million on an investment of $100 million, while the Small Appliance Division earned $12 million on an investment of $120 million. The firm's cost of capital is 16%.

REQUIRED:

For each division, calculate

A. Return on investment.

B. Residual income.

14-3 *(Return on Investment, Residual Income).* An investment center used assets of $300,000 to earn $90,000 of income for the year. Sales revenues for the year were $1,800,000.

REQUIRED:

A. Determine the profit margin, investment turnover, and return on investment.

B. Calculate the residual income if the company has a 25% cost of capital.

14-4 *(Residual Income).* The West Coast Division of the Sunny Corporation has a income of $65,000. The division's investment in assets for the same period was $460,000, and it had a residual income of ($4,000).

REQUIRED:

A. What is the dollar amount of cost of capital for this division?

B. What is the rate of return charged on capital?

C. What is the rate of return on capital that would be required to change residual income to $7,500.

14-5 *(Transfer Price).* Division A transfers all of its production to Division C at 10% over total cost. Division A's transfer price is $330. Variable costs comprise 60% of the total costs of Division A. How much would Division C pay if the price was based solely on variable cost?

14-6 *(Return on Investment).* The NJS Corporation is divided into three investment centers. The following data relate to the divisions.

	Division		
	A	*B*	*C*
Budgeted sales	$1,500,000	$2,000,000	$3,000,000
Budgeted net income	$ 25,000	$ 33,000	$ 42,000
Investment in assets	$ 200,000	$ 300,000	$ 300,000

REQUIRED:

A. Determine the return on investment for each division.

B. Determine the return on investment for the entire company.

C. The manager of Division C is considering a proposal to invest $200,000 in assets that would earn $26,000. Who would be more likely to favor the proposal—the Division C manager or the president? Why?

D. Assume the manager approves the proposal. Determine the new rate of return for Division C and for the corporation as a whole.

14-7 *(Return on Investment).* Compute the unknowns (letters *a* through *i*) for Divisions X, Y, and Z.

	X	Y	Z
Income	*a*	$ 100,000	*g*
Sales	$1,500,000	$2,000,000	$1,200,000
Investment	*b*	*d*	*h*
Return on investment	*c*	20%	25%
Cost of capital	15%	10%	12%
Minimum return on capital	$ 37,500	*e*	$ 36,000
Residual income	$ 12,500	*f*	*i*

14-8 *(Performance Evaluation with ROI).* A division manager for the See-All Eyeglass Company is being considered for a year-end bonus because his divisional return on investment has increased 4%. You have been asked to evaluate the following data and make a recommendation about the bonus.

	Year 1	Year 2
Division sales	$1,200,000	$1,600,000
Division income	$ 60,000	$ 64,000
Division assets (net of depreciation)	$ 500,000	$ 400,000

REQUIRED:

A. Compute the profit margin, investment turnover, and return on investment for both years.

B. Identify the component of return on investment that is responsible for the overall increase in ROI. What may have caused the increase?

C. Based on your findings, should the manager be rewarded for the performance of this division? Explain.

14-9 *(Transfer Price).* The Atlantic Division of Eagle Company sets its selling and transfer price for its low-pressure valve as follows:

	Per Unit
Variable production costs	$20
Fixed production costs	12
Total costs	$32
Profit (20% of selling price)	8
Selling price	$40

The Atlantic Division has been selling 180,000 units, 90% of its output, to the Pacific Division. The Pacific Division has secured an outside bid of $30 for this value and is asking the Atlantic Division for a lower price. The Atlantic Division has no alternative use for its facilities at this time.

REQUIRED:

A. What is the impact on corporate profits if the Pacific Division decides to purchase outside?

B. What is the lowest price the Atlantic Division should charge the Pacific Division just to stay in business?

C. As an arbitrator for the company, what transfer price would you recommend to the company to settle the dispute?

D. What transfer price would the company use in the external financial statements if some of Atlantic Division's production remained on hand at the end of the year?

14-10 *(Return on Investment).* A common measure of a manager's performance is return on net worth. This is a particularly important measure from the stockholder's point of view. This ratio can be expressed as the product of three other ratios as shown below:

$$\underset{\text{net worth}}{\text{Return on}} = \frac{\text{Income}}{\text{Net worth}} = \overset{1}{\frac{\text{Income}}{\text{Sales}}} \times \overset{2}{\frac{\text{Sales}}{\text{Assets}}} \times \overset{3}{\frac{\text{Assets}}{\text{Net worth}}}$$

REQUIRED:

A. Discuss the return on net worth as a management goal and as a measurement of management performance.

B. What management activities are measured by each of the ratios *1, 2,* and *3*?

C. Would separation of the return on net worth into the three ratios and use of these ratios for planning targets and performance measures result in goal congruence (or improvement toward goal congruence) among the responsible managers? Explain your answer.

(CMA adapted)

14-11 *(Graphic Presentation of Return on Investment)*. The Custom Manufacturing Company desired a return on investment of 36%. The following were actual results by sales outlet.

	Investment Turnover	Profit Margin
Outlet A	4 times	6%
Outlet B	9 times	5%
Outlet C	6 times	6%

REQUIRED:

A. Compute the return on investment for each outlet.

B. Illustrate graphically each outlet's return on investment and the company's desired return on investment.

C. List some possible reasons for the performance of Outlets A and B.

14-12 *(Investment by Division)*. The Corn Products Division of Cobb Company has prepared the following Profit Plan for 19X9.

Sales	$5,000,000
Variable expenses	$2,500,000
Fixed expenses	1,500,000
Total expenses	4,000,000
Income	$1,000,000
Assets employed by the division	$4,000,000

The entire company has projected a rate of return of 15%. The cost of capital for the company is 12%.

The division is considering the following investment in new equipment for a new product.

Cost of equipment	$200,000
Expected annual sales	$300,000
Variable expenses	40% of sales
Annual fixed expenses (including depreciation of equipment)	$140,000

Other divisions have submitted proposals for new projects that will provide a return on investment of approximately 15%.

REQUIRED:

A. As manager of the Corn Products Division, would you accept or reject the proposal? Explain.

B. As president of Cobb Company, would you want the division to accept or reject the proposal? Explain.

C. What would you recommend to avoid problems of this nature in the future?

14-13 *(Transfer Price for Decisions).* The Billings Bag Company has several divisions that produce a number of packaging products. The Bag Division purchases fibers from the Finished Fibers Division, as well as from several outside companies, for the production of bags. In May the Bag Division received an order for 1 million bags at $12 per thousand and requested bids for finished fibers from a number of companies, as well as from the Finished Fibers Division. Three bids were considered.

1. The Finished Fibers Division bid will result in a materials cost of $6.00 per thousand bags based on full cost. Finished Fibers Division is operating at 65% of capacity and earning a contribution margin of 40%.

2. A bid resulting in a materials cost of $5.00 per thousand bags was received from the Himalayas Company. This company will buy its raw material from the Import Division of the Billings Bag Company. Raw materials account for $1.50 of the $5.00. The Import Division earns a contribution margin ratio of 50%.

3. The lowest bid, resulting in a materials cost of $4.50 per thousand, was received from the Andes Company, a completely independent company.

REQUIRED:

A. From whom should the Bag Division manager buy if he acts in conformity with his division's goals?

B. From whom should the Bag Division manager buy if he acts in conformity with corporate goals?

C. If you were the president of Billings Bag Company, what would you do to maximize the corporation's income and yet maintain decentralization?

14-14 *(Determining Transfer Prices).* Kenneth Enterprises, Inc. has several divisions that have interdivisional sales of components. The company is fully decentralized. Individual divisions may purchase or sell in any market consistent with the division's goals. The Electronics Division purchases most of its wire from the Metal Products Division. The two divisions are in the process of negotiating the price for the wire the Electronics Division will purchase next quarter. The following information was accumulated for the decision.

1. Costs of Metal Products Division (per spool for 12,000 spools, 60% of capacity):

Material	$30
Direct labor	15
Variable overhead	10
Fixed overhead	20
Fixed selling and administration costs	10
Fixed central corporate costs	6
	$91

2. The Metal Products Division has an income objective of 9% of sales. Pricing has been consistent with this rule.

3. The current market price for the wire has dropped to $75 per spool.

REQUIRED:

A. Determine the selling price that would allow the Metal Products Division to achieve its income objective.

B. What price is the maximum the Electronics Division should offer to pay for wire?

C. What is the minimum price the Metal Products Division could charge and be no worse off than if the Electronics Division purchased from the outside?

D. What price should top corporate management use in evaluating whether to have the wire made by the Metal Products Division or purchase it from the outside?

14-15 *(Return on Investment and Residual Income).*

Part A.

The A and B Manufacturing Company, a decentralized producer of building materials, has a firm-wide goal of 18% return on investment and a cost of capital of 15%. The following data relate to the operating divisions.

	Income	Investment
Division D	$30,000	$200,000
Division E	$50,000	$250,000
Division F	$20,000	$ 80,000

REQUIRED:

1. Compute the return on investment for each division.

2. Compute the residual income for each division.

3. Rank the divisions according to performance.

Part B.

The A and B Manufacturing Company is considering the purchase of a new venture that would be placed in one of the existing operating divisions. The project will have assets of $30,000 and earn $5,400 per year.

1. What will the new project do to each of the performance measures in part *A* above?

2. If the asset is acquired, in which division should it be placed?

14-16 *(Evaluation of Old and New Plants).* The Caustic Chemical Company produces the same chemical in two different plants. New Plant was put into production two years ago and has operated near capacity since opening. The corporate management is very pleased with the operating results for New Plant. Old Plant has been in operation for many years. Because the market cannot absorb the total production of the two plants, production has fluctuated widely at Old Plant and remained at capacity in New Plant. Because of these fluctuations in volume, Old Plant has had unfavorable labor and variable overhead efficiency variances.

Corporate management evaluates the plants on the basis of income and return on investment. Data for the two plants are presented below. Assume a 20% cost of capital.

	Old Plant		New Plant	
Capacity in barrels	1,000,000		2,000,000	
Investment in assets	$2,000,000		$10,000,000	
Selling price of product per unit	$16		$16	
Operating costs:				
	Standard	Actual	Standard	Actual
Material per unit	$5	$5	$5	$5
Labor per unit	$6	$6.40	$2	$2
Variable overhead per unit	$1	$1.10	$2	$2
Fixed overhead per year	$1,000,000		$10,000,000	
Actual level of operations				
(Percentage of capacity)	50%		100%	

REQUIRED:

A. Prepare an income statement for each plant. Compute the return on investment and residual income for each. Comment on the performance of each.

B. How should production be distributed between the plants if the market remains at 2,500,000 barrels per year?

C. Devise a way to evaluate the performance of the plants that will be fair to Old Plant.

14-17 *(Determining Transfer Prices).* The Chemical Division of Southeast Industries produces a chemical product called Gluck used in paints and many industrial products. The Industrial Products Division, another Southeast Industries Division, uses Gluck in several of its products but has always purchased Gluck from outside suppliers.

The internal auditor for Southeast Industries has examined a number of profit improvement ideas and recommends that the Industrial Products Division purchase Gluck from the Chemical Division. At the present time the Chemical Division is operating at 50% of capacity. The annual requirements of the Industrial Products Division have been 3,000 barrels at $180 per barrel. The audit team found that variable selling costs would be reduced to $10 per unit on intercompany sales.

The internal audit team developed the following data concerning the production of Gluck during the past year.

Chemical Division

Capacity	10,000 barrels per year
Unit selling price	$ 200
Variable production costs	$ 116
Variable selling costs	$ 20
Fixed production costs	$200,000
Allocated fixed corporation costs	$ 88,000

REQUIRED:

A. What is the breakeven point for the Chemical Division? How much income did the division earn last year?

B. What is the highest transfer price that can be justified on intercompany sales of Gluck? Explain.

C. What is the lowest transfer price that can be justified on intercompany sales of Gluck? Explain.

D. The Industrial Products Division can purchase Gluck from Bayou Chemicals at $170 per barrel. Should the Chemical Division be required to meet this price? Explain.

E. What is your answer to B and C if the Chemical Division is operating at capacity? Explain.

14-18 (*Alternate Proposals for Transfer Prices*). PortCo Products is a divisionalized furniture manufacturer. The divisions are autonomous segments with each division being responsible for its own sales, costs of operations, working capital management, and equipment acquisition. Each division serves a different market in the furniture industry. Because the markets and products of the divisions are so different, there have never been any transfers between divisions.

The Commercial Division manufactures equipment and furniture that is purchased by the restaurant industry. The division plans to introduce a new line of counter and chair units that feature a cushioned seat for the counter chairs. John Kline, the division manager, has discussed the manufacturing of the cushioned seat with Russ Fiegel of the Office Division. They both believe a cushioned seat currently made by the Office Division for use on its deluxe office stool could be modified for use on the new counter chair. Consequently, Kline has asked Russ Fiegel for a price for 100-unit lots of the cushioned seat. The following conversation took place about the price to be charged for the cushioned seats.

Fiegel: John, we can make the necessary modifications to the cushioned seat easily. The raw materials used in your seat are slightly different and should cost about 10% more than those used in our deluxe office stool. However, the labor time should be the same because the seat fabrication operation basically is the same. I would price the seat at our regular rate—full cost plus 30% markup.

Kline: That's higher than I expected, Russ. I was thinking that a good price would be your variable manufacturing costs. After all, your capacity costs will be incurred regardless of this job.

Fiegel: John, I'm at capacity. By making the cushion seats for you, I'll have to cut my production of deluxe office stools. Of course, I can increase my production of economy office stools. The labor time freed by not having to fabricate the frame or assemble the deluxe stool can be shifted to the frame fabrication and assembly of the economy office stool. Fortunately, I can switch my labor force between these two models of stools without any loss of efficiency. As you know, overtime is not a feasible alternative in our community. I'd like to sell it to you at variable cost, but I have excess demand for both products. I don't mind changing my product mix to the economy model if I get a good return on the seats I make for you. Here are my standard costs for the two stools and a schedule of my manufacturing overhead. [See below for standard costs and see page 626 for overhead schedule.]

OFFICE DIVISION
STANDARD COSTS AND PRICES

	Deluxe Office Stool		Economy Office Stool
Raw materials			
Framing	$ 8.15		$ 9.76
Cushioned seat			
Padding	2.40		—
Vinyl	4.00		—
Molded seat (purchased)	—		6.00
Direct labor			
Frame fabrication (.5 × $7.50/DLH)	3.75	(.5 × $7.50/DLH)	3.75
Cushion fabrication (.5 × $7.50/DLH)	3.75		—
Assembly* (.5 × $7.50/DLH)	3.75	(.3 × $7.50/DLH)	2.25
Manufacturing Overhead (1.5DLH × $12.80/DLH)	19.20	(.8DLH × $12.80/DLH)	10.24
Total standard cost	$45.00		$32.00
Selling price (30% markup)	$58.50		$41.60

*Attaching seats to frames and attaching rubber feet.

OFFICE DIVISION
MANUFACTURING OVERHEAD BUDGET

Overhead Item	Nature	Amount
Supplies	Variable—at current market prices	$ 420,000
Indirect labor	Variable	375,000
Supervision	Nonvariable	250,000
Power	Use varies with activity; rates are fixed	180,000
Heat and light	Nonvariable—light is fixed regardless of production while heat/air conditioning varies with fuel charges	140,000
Property taxes and insurance taxes	Nonvariable—any change in amounts/rates is independent of production	200,000
Depreciation	Fixed dollar total	1,700,000
Employee benefits	20% of supervision, direct and indirect labor	575,000
	Total overhead	$3,840,000
	Capacity in DLH	300,000
	Overhead rate/DLH	$12.80

Kline: I guess I see your point, Russ, but I don't want to price myself out of the market. Maybe we should talk to corporate to see if they can give us any guidance.

REQUIRED:

A. John Kline and Russ Fiegel did ask PortCo corporate management for guidance on an appropriate transfer price. Corporate management suggested they consider using a transfer price based on variable manufacturing cost plus opportunity cost. Calculate a transfer price for the cusioned seat based on variable manufacturing cost plus opportunity cost.

B. Which alternative transfer price system—full cost, variable manufacturing cost, or variable manufacturing cost plus opportunity cost—would be better as the underlying concept for an intracompany transfer price policy? Explain your answer.

(CMA adapted)

14-19 *(Performance Measurement Through Return on Investment).* Two identical small companies, A and B, manufacture cleaning compounds under identical franchises from a larger company. Their franchises give each an exclusive right to sell anywhere within 300 miles of its factory and require each to show substantial increases in sales until a volume is reached that indicates satisfactory cultivation of its entire franchised territory. Each has 10 sales representatives, and each president estimates that 100 sales representatives would provide optimal coverage (measured by return on investment) of his allotted territory.

At the beginning of Year 2 each company had $10,000 cash available for investment. The companies considered various methods of utilizing the

$10,000 available cash to improve their operations. Each company adopted a different plan.

Company A

The president of Company A investigated his costs of raw materials and discovered that his company bought liquid raw materials in carload lots. He estimated a prospective saving of $8,000 per year on raw materials costs if such liquids were purchased in tank cars instead of boxcars, and that an investment of $10,000 would be needed in underground storage tanks to make use of tank cars feasible.

Company A acquired the storage tanks. Liquid raw materials were purchased in tank cars and the predicted $8,000 annual saving on purchased raw materials was realized in all subsequent years.

Company B

Company B, on the other hand, decided to expand its sales force. The $10,000 cash available at the beginning of Year 2 would be used during the year to recruit and train five additional sales representatives. Since the entire $10,000 would be written off as an expense in Year 2, the after-tax profits would be reduced by $5,000. However, in Year 3 and subsequent years, this 50% increase in the sales force would increase sales by 50%, and annual sales could be expected to go to $300,000. Furthermore, because breakeven volume was $100,000 and the company made a $10,00 profit on $200,000 sales, it could be expected to make a $20,000 profit on $300,000 sales. This would defend its territorial rights under its franchise.

The results for both companies are condensed in the following schedule.

	YEAR 1		YEAR 2		YEAR 3	
	A	B	A	B	A	B
Sales	$200,000	$200,000	$200,000	$200,000	$200,000	$300,000
Net income:						
Before taxes	$ 20,000	$ 20,000	$ 27,000*	$ 10,000†	$ 27,000	$ 40,000
After taxes	$ 10,000	$ 10,000	$ 13,500	$ 5,000	$ 13,500	$ 20,000
Total assets	$ 50,000	$ 50,000	$ 59,000	$ 50,000	$ 58,000	$ 50,000
Return on investment	20.0%	20.0%	22.9%	10.0%	23.2%	40.0%
Cash flow (to be paid in dividends)			$ 14,500	$ 15,000	$ 14,500	$ 20,000

Calculation of figures:

*Net income of A in Year 1	$20,000
Add: Reduction in raw materials costs	8,000
	$28,000
Deduct: Depreciation, 10% of $10,000	1,000
Net income of A in Year 2	$27,000
†Net income of B in Year 1	$20,000
Deduct: Expense of training salesmen	10,000
Net income of B in Year 2	$10,000

(Training expenses entirely written off in Year 2)

REQUIRED:

Is the return on investment a good measure of the relative performance of Companies A and B in Year 2 and 3? Discuss fully.

(Canada SIA adapted)

14-20 *(Divisional Bonuses and Transfer Prices).* The owner of the Nibler Equipment Company is nearing retirement age and wants to provide incentives for key employees who hold management positions with the firm. He formally organized the business into three divisions—New Equipment Sales, Used Equipment Sales, and Equipment Repairs—and agreed to pay each manager 50% of the income of the division as a bonus. To measure income by division, Mr. Nibler will charge each division rent based on the value of the space used and a management fee based on divisional sales to cover Mr. Nibler's salary and other administrative costs. Each division is to operate as an independent business with responsibility for purchasing, marketing, and sales. Corporate goals relating to quality of service and fairness to the customer are to be maintained.

Income Statements for the first quarter of operations as separate divisions follow.

NEW EQUIPMENT SALES DIVISION
INCOME STATEMENT
Quarter 1, 19X3

Sales of new equipment		$325,000
Trade-in allowance in excess of appraised		
value of used equipment		25,000
Net sales		$300,000
Operating expenses:		
Cost of equipment sold	$210,000	
Direct operating expenses of division	30,000	
Rent	20,000	
Management fee	18,000	278,000
Income		$ 22,000

USED EQUIIPMENT SALES DIVISION
INCOME STATEMENT
Quarter 1, 19X3

Sales of used equipment		$175,000
Trade-in allowance in excess of appraised		
value of used equipment		15,000
Net sales		$160,000
Operating expenses:		
Cost of used equipment sold	$105,000	
Direct operating expenses of division	20,000	
Rent	8,000	
Management fee	9,600	142,600
Income		$ 17,400

The New England Sales Division and Used Equipment Sales Division take trade-ins from Customers. The Used Equipment Sales Division must establish the appraised price and must purchase the used equipment from the New Equipment Division at the appraised price. If the New Equipment Division manager believes that the appraised price is too low, he may sell the used equipment on the wholesale market. If service is needed on used equipment, the repair manager will estimate the cost and bill the selling divisions at the estimate. If the actual cost exceeds the estimate, the Repair Division must bear the added costs. For years the Repair Division (earlier the Service Department) has provided service work for the selling divisions at cost.

EQUIPMENT REPAIR DIVISION
INCOME STATEMENT
Quarter 1, 19X3

	Repair Work for Outside Customers	Repair Work for Other Divisions	Total
Charges to customers	$75,000	$20,000	$95,000
Variable cost of work performed	52,500	21,000	73,500
Gross margin	$22,500	$ (1,000)	$21,500
Operating costs:			
Direct operating expenses of division			$ 6,000
Rent			6,000
Management fees			5,700
Total			17,700
Income			$ 3,800

The New Equipment Sales Division recently sold a new piece of equipment and accepted a used piece of equipment in trade. The following information relates to the sale.

List price of machine (sales are normally made at list price)	$12,000
Cost of equipment sold	$ 8,400
Trade-in allowed on old equipment	$ 2,000
Appraisal value in present condition (determined by Used Equipment Sales Division)	$ 1,300
Cost of estimated repairs required (determined by Equipment Repair Division)	$ 600

When the repairs were actually performed, additional internal damage not apparent in the estimate raised the repair cost to $1,000. The best price the Used Equipment Sales Division could finally get for the used equipment was $1,800.

REQUIRED:

A. How much did each manager earn or lose on the transaction?

B. When the service manager saw the income statement, he became very angry and said that he had been taken by the other managers for the last time. He will now charge full price for all service. What should the service manager have charged for the service on the trade-in equipment? Using this new charge, recompute the amount each division gained or lost on the transaction.

C. If the internal repair work was performed equally for each sales division, determine the amount of bonus each manager would have earned if the service manager had charged the "full price" for service.

D. The management fee consists of the president's salary, accounting, credits and collections, and other administrative costs of the company. Comment on the manner in which the management fee is charged to each division. How would you establish a transfer price for this "service"?

14-21 *(Contribution Margin Approach and Transfer Pricing).* DePaolo Industries manufactures carpets, furniture, and foam in three separate divisions. DePaolo's operating statement for 19X3 follows below. Additional information regarding DePaolo's operations are as follows:

1. Included in Foam's sales revenue is $500,000 in revenue that represents sales made to the Furniture Division that were transferred at manufacturing cost.

2. The Cost of Goods Sold is composed of the following costs.

	Carpet	*Furniture*	*Foam*
Direct material	$ 500,000	$1,000,000	$1,000,000
Direct labor	500,000	200,000	1,000,000
Variable overhead	750,000	50,000	1,000,000
Fixed overhead	250,000	50,000	–0–
Total Cost of Goods Sold	$2,000,000	$1,300,000	$3,000,000

3. Administrative expenses include the following costs.

	Carpet	*Furniture*	*Foam*
Segment expenses:			
Variable	$ 85,000	$140,000	$ 40,000
Fixed	85,000	210,000	120,000
Home office expenses (all fixed):			
Directly traceable	100,000	120,000	200,000
General (allocated on sales dollars)	30,000	30,000	40,000
Total	$300,000	$500,000	$400,000

4. Selling expense is all incurred at the segment level and is 80% variable for all segments.

John Sprint, manager of the Foam Division, is not pleased with De-Paolo's presentation of operating performance. Sprint claimed,

> The Foam Division makes a greater contribution to the company's profits than what is shown. I sell foam to the Furniture Division at cost and it gets our share of the profit. I can sell that foam on the outside at my regular markup, but I sell to Furniture for the well-being of the company. I think my division should get credit for those internal sales at market. I think we should also revise our operating statements for internal purposes. Why don't we consider preparing these internal statements on a contribution approach reporting format showing internal transfers at market?

DEPAOLO INDUSTRIES
OPERATING STATEMENT
For the Year Ended December 31, 19X3

	Carpet Division	Furniture Division	Foam Division	Total
Sales revenue	$3,000,000	$3,000,000	$4,000,000	$10,000,000
Cost of Goods Sold	2,000,000	1,300,000	3,000,000	6,300,000
Gross profit	$1,000,000	$1,700,000	$1,000,000	$ 3,700,000
Operating expenses:				
Administrative	$ 300,000	$ 500,000	$ 400,000	$ 1,200,000
Selling	600,000	600,000	500,000	1,700,000
Total operating expenses	900,000	1,100,000	900,000	2,900,000
Income from operations before taxes	$ 100,000	$ 600,000	$ 100,000	$ 800,000

REQUIRED:

A. John Sprint believes that the intracompany transfers from the Foam Division to the Furniture Division should be at market rather than manufacturing cost for divisional performance measurement.

1. Explain why Sprint is correct.

2. Identify and describe two approaches used for setting transfer prices other than manufacturing cost used by DePaolo Industries and market price as recommended by Sprint.

B. Using the contribution approach and market-based transfer prices, prepare a revised operating statement by division for DePaolo Industries for 19X3 that will promote the evaluation of divisional performance.

C. Discuss the advantages of the contribution reporting approach for internal reporting purposes.

(CMA Adapted)

14-22 *(Transfer Prices and Profit Centers).* A. R. Oma, Inc. manufactures a line of men's perfumes and after-shave lotions. The manufacturing process is basically a series of mixing operations with the addition of certain aromatic and coloring ingredients; the finished product is packaged in a company-produced glass bottle and packed in cases containing six bottles.

A. R. Oma feels that the sale of its product is heavily influenced by the appearance and appeal of the bottle and has therefore devoted considerable managerial effort to the bottle production process. This has resulted in the development of certain unique bottle production processes in which management takes considerable pride.

The two areas (perfume production and bottle manufacture) have evolved over the years in an almost independent manner; in fact, a rivalry has developed between management personnel as to which division is the more important to A. R. Oma. This attitude is probably intensified because the bottle manufacturing plant was purchased intact 10 years ago, and no real interchange of management personnel or ideas (except at the top corporate level) has taken place.

Since the acquisition, all bottle production has been absorbed by the perfume manufacturing plant. Each area is considered a separate profit center and evaluated as such. As the new corporate controller, you are responsible for the definition of a proper transfer value to use in crediting the bottle production profit center and in debiting the perfume profit center.

At your request, the Bottle Division general manager has asked certain other bottle manufacturers to quote a price for the quantity and sizes demanded by the Perfume Division. These competitive prices are

Volume	Total Price	Price per Case
2,000,000 eq. cases*	$ 4,000,000	$2.00
4,000,000	$ 7,000,000	$1.75
6,000,000	$10,000,000	$1.67
*An *equivalent case* represents 8 bottles each.		

A cost analysis of the internal bottle plant indicates that it can produce bottles at the following costs.

Volume	Total Price	Cost per Case
2,000,000 eq. cases	$3,200,000	$1.60
4,000,000	$5,200,000	$1.30
6,000,000	$7,200,000	$1.20

(Your cost analysts point out that these costs represent fixed costs of $1,200,000 and variable costs of $1.00 per equivalent case.)

These figures have given rise to considerable corporate discussion as to the proper value to use in the transfer of bottles to the Perfume Division. This interest is heightened because a significant portion of a division manager's income is an incentive bonus based on profit center results.

The Perfume Production Division has the following costs in addition to the bottle costs.

Volume	Total Cost	Cost per Case
2,000,000 cases	$16,400,000	$8.20
4,000,000	$32,400,000	$8.10
6,000,000	$48,400,000	$8.07

After considerable analysis, the marketing research department has furnished you with the following price–demand relationship for the finished product.

Sales Volume	Total Sales Revenue	Sales Price per Case
2,000,000 cases	$25,000,000	$12.50
4,000,000	$45,600,000	$11.40
6,000,000	$63,900,000	$10.65

REQUIRED:

A. The A. R. Oma Company has used market-based transfer prices in the past. Using the current market prices and costs, and assuming a volume of 6 million cases, calculate the income for the Bottle Division, the Perfume Division, and the corporation.

B. Is this production and sales level the most profitable volume for the Bottle Division? The Perfume Division? The corporation? Explain your answer.

C. The A. R. Oma Company uses the profit center concept for divisional operation.

1. Define *profit center*.

2. What conditions should exist for a profit center to be established?

3. Should the two divisions of the A. R. Oma Company be organized as profit centers?

(CMA adapted)

14-23 *(Transfer Pricing for Decision Making)*. National Industries is a diversified corporation with separate and distinct operating divisions. Each division's performance is evaluated on the basis of total dollar profits and return on division investment.

The WindAir Division manufactures and sells air-conditioner units. The coming year's budgeted Income Statement, based on a sales volume of 15,000 units, appears below.

WINDAIR DIVISION
BUDGETED INCOME STATEMENT
For the 19X1–X2 Fiscal Year

	Per Unit	Total (000 omitted)
Sales revenue	$400	$6,000
Manufacturing costs:		
Compressor	$ 70	$1,050
Other raw materials	37	555
Direct labor	30	450
Variable overhead	45	675
Fixed overhead	32	480
Total manufacturing costs	214	3,210
Gross margin	$186	$2,790
Operating expenses:		
Variable selling	$ 18	$ 270
Fixed selling	19	285
Fixed administrative	38	570
Total operating expenses	75	1,125
Net income before taxes	$111	$1,665

WindAir's division manager believes sales can be increased if the unit selling price of the air conditioners is reduced. A market research study conducted by an independent firm at the request of the manager indicates that a 5% reduction in the selling price ($20) would increase sales volume 16% or 2,400 units. WindAir has sufficient production capacity to manage this increased volume with no increase in fixed costs.

At the present time WindAir uses a compressor in its units, which it purchases from an outside supplier at a cost of $70 per compressor. The division manager of WindAir has approached the manager of the Compressor Division regarding the sale of a compressor unit to WindAir. The Compressor Division currently manufactures and sells a unit exclusively to outside firms that is similar to the unit used by WindAir. The specifications of the WindAir compressor are slightly different, which would reduce the Compressor Division's raw material cost by $1.50 per unit. In addition, the Compressor Division would not incur any variable selling costs in the units sold to WindAir. The manager of WindAir wants all of the compressors it uses to come from one supplier and has offered to pay $50 for each compressor unit.

The Compressor Division has the capacity to produce 75,000 units. The coming year's budgeted Income Statement for the Compressor Division is shown below and is based on a sales volume of 64,000 units without considering WindAir's proposal.

COMPRESSOR DIVISION
BUDGETED INCOME STATEMENT
For the 19X1–X2 Fiscal Year

	Per Unit	Total (000 omitted)
Sales revenue	$100	$6,400
Manufacturing costs:		
Raw materials	$ 12	$ 768
Direct labor	8	512
Variable overhead	10	640
Fixed overhead	11	704
Total manufacturing costs	41	2,624
Gross margin	$ 59	$3,776
Operating expenses:		
Variable selling	$ 6	$ 384
Fixed selling	4	256
Fixed administrative	7	448
Total operating expenses	17	1,088
Net income before taxes	$ 42	$2,688

REQUIRED:

A. Should WindAir Division institute the 5% price reduction on its air-conditioner units even if it cannot acquire the compressors internally for $50 each? Support your conclusion with appropriate calculations.

B. Without prejudice to your answer to part A, assume WindAir needs 17,400 units. Should the Compressor Division be willing to supply the compressor units for $50 each? Support your conclusions with appropriate calculations.

C. Without prejudice to your answer to part A, assume WindAir needs 17,400 units. Would it be in the best interest of National Industries for the Compressor Division to supply the compressor units at $50 each to the WindAir Division? Support your conclusions with appropriate calculations.

(CMA adapted)

14-24 (Transfer Pricing System).

Birch Paper Company*

"If I were to price these boxes any lower than $480 a thousand," said James Brunner, manager of Birch Paper Company's Thompson division, "I'd be coun-

---

*Copyright 1957 by the President of Fellows of Harvard College. Reprinted by permission.

termanding my order of last month for our salesmen to stop shaving their bids and to bid full-cost quotations. I've been trying for weeks to improve the quality of our business, and if I turn around now and accept this job at $430 or $450 or something less than $480, I'll be tearing down this program I've been working so hard to build up. The division can't very well show a profit by putting in bids that don't even cover a fair share of overhead costs, let alone give us a profit.''

Birch Paper Company was a medium-size, partly integrated paper company, producing white and kraft papers and paperboard. A portion of its paperboard output was converted into corrugated boxes by the Thompson division, which also printed and colored the outside surface of the boxes. Including Thompson, the company had four producing divisions and a timberland division, which supplied part of the company's pulp requirements.

For several years, each division has been judged independently on the basis of its profit and return on investment. Top management had been working to gain effective results from a policy of decentralizing responsibility and authority for all decisions except those relating to overall company policy. The company's top officials believed that in the past few years the concept of decentralization had been successfully applied and that the company's profits and competitive position had definitely improved.

Early in 1957, the Northern division designed a special display box for one of its papers in conjunction with the Thompson division, which was equipped to make the box. Thompson's staff for package design and development spent several months perfecting the design, production methods, and materials to be used. Because of the unusual color and shape, these were far from standard. According to an agreement between the two divisions, the Thompson division was reimbursed by the Northern division for the cost of its design and development work.

When all the specifications were prepared, the Northern division asked for bids on the box from the Thompson division and from two outside companies. Each division manager was normally free to buy from whatever supplier he wished; and even on sales within the company, divisions were expected to meet the going market price if they wanted the business.

In 1957, the profit margins of converters such as the Thompson division were being squeezed. Thompson, as did many other similar converters, bought its paperboard, and its function was to print, cut, and shape it into boxes. Although it bought most of its materials from other Birch divisions, most of Thompson's sales were made to outside customers. If Thompson got the order from Northern, it probably would buy its linerboard and corrugating medium from the Southern division of Birch. The walls of a corrugated box consist of outside and inside sheets of linerboard sandwiching the fluted corrugating medium. About 70% of Thompson's out-of-pocket cost of $400 for the order represented the cost of linerboard and corrugating medium. Although Southern had been running below capacity and had excess inventory, it quoted the market price, which had not noticeably weakened as a result of the oversupply. Its out-of-pocket costs on both liner and corrugating medium were about 60% of the selling price.

The Northern division received bids on the boxes of $480 a thousand from the Thompson division, $430 a thousand from West Paper Company, and $432 a thousand from Eire Papers, Ltd. Eire Papers offered to buy from Birch the outside linerboard with the special printing already on it, but would supply its own inside liner and corrugating medium. The outside liner would be supplied by the Southern division at a price equivalent of $90 a thousand boxes, and it would be printed for $30 a thousand by the Thompson division. Of the $30, about $25 would be out-of-pocket costs.

Because this situation appeared to be a little unusual, William Kenton, manager of the Northern division, discussed the wide discrepancy of bids with Birch's commercial vice-president. He told the vice-president: "We sell in a very competitive market, where higher costs cannot be passed on. How can we be expected to show a decent profit and return on investment if we have to buy our supplies at more than 10% over the going market?"

Knowing that Mr. Brunner had on occasion in the past few months been unable to operate the Thompson division at capacity, it seemed odd to the vice-president that Mr. Brunner would add the full 20% overhead and profit charge to his out-of-pocket costs. When asked about this, Mr. Brunner's answer was the statement that appears at the beginning of the case. He went on to say that having done the developmental work on the box, and having received no profit on that, he felt entitled to a good markup on the production of the box itself.

The vice-president explored further the cost structures of the various divisions. He remembered a comment that the controller had made at a meeting the week before to the effect that costs that were variable for one division could be largely fixed for the company as a whole. He knew that in the absence of specific orders from top management Mr. Kenton would accept the lowest bid, which was that of the West Paper Company for $430. However, it would be possible for top management to order the acceptance of another bid if the situation warranted such action. And although the volume represented by the transactions in question was less than 5% of the volume of any of the divisions involved, other transactions could conceivably raise similar problems later.

REQUIRED:

1. In the controversy described, how, if at all, is the transfer price system dysfunctional?
2. Describe other types of decisions in the Birch Paper Company in which the transfer price system would be dysfunctional.

glossary

A **Absorption Costing** A system of measuring inventory costs that assigns the production costs of material, labor, variable overhead, and fixed overhead to the product. Nonproduction costs are treated as period costs. Also called *Full Costing*.

Accelerated Cost Recovery System (ACRS) A method of depreciation deductions developed by the Internal Revenue Service that uses arbitrary recovery periods instead of useful lives.

Accountability (A) The responsibility of management to protect and increase the assets of the firm for the stockholders. (B) The assignment of delegated duties to individual managers for the development of responsibility accounting.

Accounting Method (See *Accounting Rate of Return*.)

Accounting Rate of Return Another name for the unadjusted rate of return; used in long-run decisions to assess project feasibility where the rate of return is determined by dividing the average annual accounting income by the initial investment.

ACRS (See *Accelerated Cost Recovery System*.)

Activity Accounting Recording data by a specific organizational segment. (See *Responsibility Accounting*.)

Activity Base A measure of an operating activity within a department, division, plant, or company; used to allocate indirect costs.

Activity Variance A measure of the ability of the firm to meet budgeted sales volume; the difference between the period's planned activity in the master budget and the actual volume attained. The variance may be measured in number of units or in dollars of contribution margin.

Actual Costs (A) Historical costs measured by their cash equivalent value on an after-the-fact, arm's-length transaction basis. Also called *Incurred Costs* and *Historical Costs*. (B) Costs measured by consideration given to acquire the resource.

Adjusted Rate of Return The actual rate of return on a long-term project computed by adjusting cash flows for the time value of money. Also called *Discounted Rate of Return*.

Administrative Costs Costs that are not directly associated with production, selling, or distribution.

Allocation   The process of distributing or apportioning costs or revenues to products, departments, divisions, or other organization units on the basis of benefits received or resources used.

Annuity   A series of equal payments or receipts to be paid or received at the end of successive periods of equal time.

Asset Turnover   Sales divided by total assets available.

Assets   The resources currently available to a firm for the benefit of future activities.

Attained Volume   The level of production or sales activity actually reached during the accounting period. Also called *Actual Volume*.

Attention Directing   The accountant's task of supplying information that focuses on those activities of a firm needing corrective action.

Attest Function   The action of the independent CPA who audits the financial records of a firm to reduce uncertainty regarding the accuracy and fairness of reported financial statements.

Average Cost   Fixed costs plus variable costs divided by the units produced.

Average Cost Pricing   (See *Cost-based Pricing*.)

Average Costing   (See *Weighted-Average Costing*.)

Average Revenue   Total revenue earned divided by the total units sold.

Avoidable Costs   Costs that would not be incurred if a particular activity were discontinued.

Average Standards   (See *Currently Attainable Standards*.)

B   **Balance Sheet**   A formal statement of the resources of a firm and their sources at a particular point in time. Also called *Statement of Financial Position*.

Behavioral Accounting   An area of accounting that studies the interactions among individuals, organizations, and the accounting process.

Benefit–Cost Analysis   An evaluation of the relationship between the benefits and the costs of a particular project.

Bill of Materials   A statement of the quantity of raw materials allowed for manufacturing a specific quantity of units.

Blanket Overhead Rate   A method of apportioning overhead to work-in-process that uses only one rate for the entire factory.

Book Value   The carrying value of a resource measured at cost less accumulated depreciation.

Book Value Method   (See *Accounting Rate of Return*.)

Breakeven Graph   A graphic presentation of cost-volume-profit relationships over the relevant range with special emphasis on the point at which total costs equal total revenue.

Breakeven Point   The activity level where total sales equal total costs. Graphically the breakeven point is where the sales line intersects the total-cost line.

Budget   An integrated plan of action expressed in financial terms.

Budget Rollover   Continual revision and projection of a budget by dropping a past period and adding a new period; particularly useful in cash management.

Budget Variance   The difference between actual costs incurred and the flexible budget adjusted to actual activity level. Also called the *Spending Variance*.

Budgeted Capacity   (See *Expected Volume*.)

Budgeted Costs   Future costs (predictions, estimates, forecasts) that are formally combined into an integrated plan of action.

C   **Capacity Costs**   (A) Another term for fixed costs. (B) Costs necessary to provide organization and operating facilities to produce and sell at the budgeted volume level.

Capacity Decisions   (See *Long-range Decisions*.)

Capacity Variance   A variance computed in an absorption costing system showing the overapplication or underapplication of fixed manufacturing costs to products. It is measured as the difference between planned fixed manufacturing costs and applied fixed manufacturing costs. Also called *Volume Variances* or *Fixed Overhead Volume Variance*.

Capital Budgeting   (A) The process of long-range planning involved with adding or reducing the productive facilities of a firm. (B) The process of long-range planning for specific projects.

Capital Expenditure Budget   A formal plan involving the procurement or disposition of productive resources.

Capital Rationing   A ranking of investment proposals for a firm with a shortage of capital to invest.

Capital Turnover   (See *Asset Turnover*.)

Carryback and Carryforward   An IRS tax code provision in which an operating loss may be carried back and/or forward as an offset to operating income.

Carrying Costs   Costs incurred in maintaining an inventory, including storage and warehousing, insurance, and cost of money invested in inventory.

Cash Budget   A formal, integrated plan of cash inflows, outflows, and balances.

Clock Card   A record of an employee's work time; used in determining an employee's pay.

Coefficient of Correlation (r)   A measure of the relationship between two variables. $+1.0$ or -1.0 shows perfect correlation; a zero shows no correlation.

Coefficient of Determination (r^2)   A measure showing the percentage of variation in one variable explained by the variation in another variable.

Committed Costs (A) Fixed costs incurred by the productive facilities and organization maintained to provide a firm's output capacity. (B) Costs treated as fixed costs because they cannot be separated into their fixed and variable components.

Common Costs (A) In multiple-product firms, costs that are not inherently traceable to individual products or product lines (*Joint Product Costs*). (B) Costs applicable to more than one costing objective; they cannot be traced to the objective without using an allocation base. Also called *Joint Costs* and *Indirect Costs*.

Comprehensive Budget (See *Master Budget*.)

Comptroller (See *Controller*.)

Conservatism The practice of undervaluing assets and revenues and overvaluing liabilities and expenses so that financial position is never overstated.

Constant Costs (See *Fixed Costs*.)

Constraint A restriction on the production process limiting the amount of resources that can be committed.

Continuous Budget A technique of budget preparation that adds a new period (such as a month) in the future as the period just ended is completed. (See *Budget Rollover*.)

Contribution Center (See *Profit Center*.)

Contribution Margin Selling price per unit less the variable cost per unit. Also called *Marginal Income*. The contribution margin may be expressed on a per-unit basis, as a total, or as a ratio.

Contribution Margin Approach Income statements that separate costs into fixed and variable components and measure the contribution margin by deducting all variable costs from sales.

Contribution Margin from Operations Sales revenue less all variable costs.

Contribution Margin from Production Sales revenue less variable production costs.

Contribution Margin Ratio Sales percentage (100%) minus the variable cost ratio. That portion of each sales dollar that provides the contribution margin. Contribution margin divided by sales.

Control The process of measuring and correcting actual performance to ensure that a firm's objectives and plans are accomplished.

Control Limit An acceptable range within which costs may deviate from standard or budget. Beyond this limit costs are "out of control."

Controllable Cost A cost that can be regulated by a given manager in either the short run or the long run. A cost that is the responsibility of a specific manager.

Controller A firm's principal accounting officer responsible for planning and controlling the firm's financial data base. Also called *Comptroller*.

Conventional Accounting (See *Absorption Costing*.)

Conversion Costs   The sum of direct labor and manufacturing overhead costs.

Correlation Coefficient   (See *Coefficient of Correlation.*)

Cost   (A) The cash or the cash-equivalent value of the resource obtained or the resource committed, whichever can be measured most objectively. (B) Value foregone to achieve an economic benefit.

Cost Accounting Standards Board (CASB)   A former federal agency of Congress to assist governmental agencies as buyers of goods and services in understanding and negotiating cost-based prices; functions now in the Government Accounting Office.

Cost Accumulation   The process of summing costs within the accounting system.

Cost Allocation   The process of dividing indirect costs among costing objectives such as time periods, products, or responsibility centers.

Cost Allocation Base   The denominator used to make cost allocations. Typical denominators used as a base to allocate overhead to jobs are direct labor hours and machine hours. Typical denominators used as a base to allocate costs between departments are number of employees and square footage.

Cost Application   The accounting process of using an overhead rate to allocate factory overhead costs to individual units of product.

Cost-based Pricing   The process of determining a selling price by calculating the cost of a unit of product and adding a markup. An addition for profit is made to some suitable cost base. Also called *Cost-Plus Pricing* and *Average Cost Pricing.*

Cost Behavior Patterns   An expression of the relationship between a cost and some variable, such as production volume, which affects that cost.

Cost–Benefit Analysis   The systematic process of comparing costs and benefits between possible alternatives.

Cost Centers   Organizational units where costs naturally come together. A natural clustering of costs by functional areas.

Cost Effectiveness Analysis   The measure of the relationship between the incurrence of costs and a nonfinancial criterion.

Cost Flow   The way accountants classify and process accounting data to show product and period costs.

Cost Objective   Any focal point for which the measurement of costs is desired. Typically cost objectives include time periods, products, departments, and responsibility centers.

Cost of Capital   The cost of providing financial resources for the firm.

Cost of Goods Sold   Costs released from the inventory and matched with revenue in the period the products are sold.

Cost of Sales   (See *Cost of Goods Sold.*)

Cost-Plus-Fixed-Fee Contract   A sales contract in which the seller is reimbursed for all reasonable (allowable) costs incurred in fulfilling the contract plus an agreed-upon fee.

Cost-Plus-Percentage Contract   A sales contract in which the seller is reimbursed for all reasonable (allowable) costs incurred in fulfilling the contract plus a profit determined as a negotiated percentage of actual costs.

Cost-Plus Pricing   (See *Cost-based Pricing.*)

Cost Pool   A grouping of similar costs; one function of cost pools is to allow different allocation bases within a department or organizational unit.

Cost Reimburseable Contract   A sales contract in which the seller is reimbursed for all costs incurred in fulfilling the contract. (See *Cost-Plus-Fixed-Fee, Cost-Plus-Percentage,* and *Cost Renegotiable Contracts.*)

Cost Renegotiable Contracts   A sales contract in which the buyer and the seller have opportunities to redefine certain aspects of the contract after production has begun.

Current Assets   Cash plus those assets that are expected to be converted into cash or consumed during the coming year or normal operating cycle.

Current Liabilities   Liabilities that will mature and require payment within the coming year or operating cycle.

Current Ratio   Current assets divided by current liabilities; used as a measure of liquidity.

Currently Attainable Standards   Standards of performance that can be attained in the actual operations with skilled, efficient effort. Also called *Normal Standards* and *Average Standards.*

Cutoff Rate   The minimum desired rate of return.

D **Data Base**   Information available to management for planning, decision making, and control functions.

Decentralization   An organizational approach to making decisions where authority is delegated to lower levels within firm.

Decision Tree   A diagram of the relationship among complex decisions showing the outcome of each possible outcome.

Demand Curve   A graphic curve showing the product quantity that will be sold at different prices. The curve normally slopes downward and to the right, showing that as the selling price increases, customer demand decreases and that as price decreases, customer demand increases.

Departmental Cost Sheet   A basic record for the accumulation of costs in a process-costing system.

Depreciation   The allocation of the original cost of plant and equipment to the time periods benefited by the use of the asset.

Differential Analysis   (See *Incremental Analysis*.)

Differential Benefit   The difference in total benefits between any two acceptable alternatives. Also called *Incremental Benefit*.

Differential Cost   The difference in total costs between any two acceptable alternatives. Also called *Incremental Cost*.

Differentiality   The concept that only costs or benefits that differ between alternatives are relevant to decisions.

Diminishing Returns   The economic concept that increased usage of production facilities requires more productive energy per unit to produce one additional unit.

Direct Allocation Method   A method that allocates the cost of each service department directly to the producing departments.

Direct Costing   (See *Variable Costing*.)

Direct Costs   Costs that are capable of being traced and logically associated with a particular objective such as product, time period, or organizational unit.

Direct Labor   Labor that is expended directly on the final product and traced directly to the product by the accounting system.

Direct Materials   Materials used in the production of the final product and traced directly to the product by the accounting system.

Direct Method   (See *Direct Allocation Method*.)

Discount Rate   The desired minimum rate of return; used in long-run decisions.

Discounted Benefit–Cost Ratio   A method of capital budgeting project assessment that applies a predetermined discount rate to cash inflows and outflows and ranks the alternatives by their ratio of discounted benefits to discounted costs.

Discounted Cash Flow   Any capital investment decision process that adjusts cash flows over the life of the investment for the time value of money. (See *Adjusted Rate of Return, Discounted Benefit–Cost Ratio,* and *Net Present Value*.)

Discounted Rate of Return   (See *Adjusted Rate of Return*.)

Discounting   The process of adjusting cash flows for the time value of money. Also called *Present-value Analysis*.

Discretionary Costs   Fixed costs that arise from specific management decisions to appropriate a specific sum. Also called *Managed Costs* and *Programmed Costs*.

Distribution Costs   Nonproduction costs that arise from ensuring that the proper goods are in the proper place, ready to sell. Also called *Order-Filling Costs*.

Division   A responsibility center where the manager is held responsible for both production and marketing operating decisions and for decisions involving investments in the resources necessary to implement plans; an investment center.

Dual Prices   (See *Shadow Price*.)

Dysfunctional Behavior   Actions that interfere with the accomplishment of the organization's goals.

E   **Economic Income**   (A) A concept that no income exists until all who provided resources are paid for the cost of their resources. (B) The maximum amount that can be paid in dividends and leave the firm with the same economic wealth at the end of a period that it had at the beginning of the period.

Economic Order Quantity (EOQ)   The amount of purchases (or production) that should be made at any one time to minimize the carrying costs and the procurement (or setup) costs.

Economies of Scale   Gains in operating efficiencies due to increases in volume.

Effectiveness   The accomplishment of a desired objective, goal, or action.

Efficiency   The accomplishment of a desired objective, goal, or action with the minimum resources necessary.

Efficiency Variance   (A) A quantity variance for labor determined by the difference between the actual hours worked and the standard hours times the labor wage rate. (B) A variance for overhead determined by the difference between the actual hours worked and the standard hours times the variable overhead rate.

Elasticity of Demand   The responsiveness of consumers to price changes. If consumers are sensitive to price changes, demand is elastic. If consumers are unresponsive to price changes, demand is inelastic.

Engineering Cost Estimates   A method of separating costs into their fixed and variable components by direct estimates based on technical expertise.

Equilibrium Point   The intersection point of the supply and demand curves. At this point the amount that producers provide equals the amount that customers demand, and the market is in balance.

Equivalent Production   The number of whole units of product for which a department or cost center is accountable during the time period.

Ex Ante   A performance assessment measure determined before actual operations.

Ex Post   A performance assessment measure determined after actual operations that includes adjustments for actual operating circumstances.

Excess Material Requisition   A form used to request needed production materials in excess of the standard amount of materials allowed for the output.

Excess Present Value   A technique of discounted cash flow analysis that determines whether the present value of future cash inflows at the desired rate of return is greater or less than the present value of the future cash outflows. Also called *Net Present Value*.

Expected Actual Standard   A standard based on the most likely attainable results; an estimate of what will happen, not what should happen.

Expected Value   The sum of all possible outcomes multiplied by the probability of their occurrence.

Expected Volume   The anticipated level of activity for the coming year. Also called *Budgeted Capacity* or *Expected Capacity*.

Expense   (A) A cost that has been consumed in the production of revenue. (B) An expired cost.

Expired Costs   (A) A cost that has no future revenue-producing potential. (B) An expense.

F   **Factory Burden**   (See *Overhead*.)

Factory Overhead   (See *Overhead*.)

Factory Overhead Rate   (See *Overhead Rate*.)

FASB   (See *Financial Accounting Standards Board*.)

Favorable Variance   (A) A variance where actual costs are less than budgeted or standard costs. (B) A variance where actual revenue exceeds budgeted revenue.

Feedback   The reporting function of accounting concerned with providing information to management so that performance may be evaluated and, if necessary, actions altered.

Financial Accounting   Focus of accounting data for interfirm allocations and for the generation and maintenance of the capital structure of a firm.

Financial Accounting Standards Board (FASB)   An independent decision body concerned with establishing policy for external reporting practices.

Financial Costs   Costs of obtaining financing for an organization's capital requirements.

Finished Goods Inventory   The cost of unsold but completed goods that are held in inventory awaiting sale.

First In, First Out (FIFO)   An inventory costing method where the first costs received are the first costs transferred out.

Fixed Budget   A plan that expresses only one level of estimated activity or volume. Also called *Static Budget*.

Fixed Costs   Costs that in total do not change with changes in output volume. On a per-unit basis, the cost per unit of output will vary inversely with changes in volume.

Fixed Overhead Spending Variance   The difference between actual fixed production costs incurred and budgeted fixed production costs shown in the flexible budget.

Fixed Overhead Volume Variance   The difference between budgeted fixed costs and fixed costs applied to Work-in-Process Inventory.

Fixed Price Contract   Agreement to a price that remains unchanged over the life of a contract.

Flexible Budget   A statement of how costs change with changes in the activity level; often expressed as the formula $y_c = a + b(x)$ where a is the total fixed costs, b the variable rate, and *x* a measure of the activity level. May refer to any specific cost or grouping of costs. Also called *Variable Budget*.

Forecast　A projection of variables, both controllable and noncontrollable, that is used in the development of plans and budgets.

Full Costing　(See *Absorption Costing*.)

Functional Classification　(A) Classification of costs by the department or the responsibility center affected. (B) Allocation of costs to functions performed, such as office expense, warehouse expense, order-filling costs.

Future Benefits　Benefits that are expected to be gained at some future time, based on predictions, estimates, and forecasts.

Future Costs　Costs that are expected to be incurred at some future time, based on predictions, estimates, and forecasts.

Future Value of Money　The value to which an invested sum will grow by the end of a certain period if compounded at a given annual rate of interest.

G　**General Costs**　(See *Administrative Costs*.)

General Price Index　An index showing the change in the purchasing power of the dollar for a broad group of assets.

Goal　The basic plan or direction of a decision maker. The direction toward which all decisions and activities are focused.

Goal Congruence　The process of combining the many diverse, separate goals of firm subcomponents into a unified whole.

Gross margin　Sales less Cost of Goods Sold using absorption costing.

Gross Profit　(See *Gross Margin*.)

H　**Heuristic**　(A) A trial-and-error approach to problem solving. (B) Methods of investigation that lead to further investigation.

High-Low Method　A method of determining fixed and variable costs that utilizes the highest and lowest activity levels and their related costs.

Historical Costs　(See *Actual Costs*.)

Historical Overhead Rate　A method of apportioning overhead costs to work-in-process after production for the period is completed.

Hurdle Rate　A name for the minimum desired rate of return.

I　**Ideal Standard**　A standard that can be achieved only if all conditions are perfect.

Ideal Volume　The maximum plant output (in units) that can be achieved in the short run, with no allowances for repairs, maintenance, or rest periods.

Identifiable Costs   Costs that can be associated with a particular product or department.

Idle Time   (A) Labor time not involved in productive effort; usually treated as indirect labor. (B) Unused plant capacity.

Incentive Contract   A cost-plus contract where there is a bonus incentive if costs are below the budgeted amount. In some cases a penalty is assessed if costs exceed the budgeted amount.

Income Statement   A statement that evaluates operating performance by comparing revenues (accomplishments) with costs (efforts).

Incremental Analysis   (A) The process of measuring the additional costs or benefits of one alternative chosen over another. (B) A method of comparing alternative plans of action by calculating the present values of the differences between *net* cash inflows.

Incremental Benefit   The total additional benefit that will be gained if a particular alternative is chosen over another. The difference in total benefits between two alternatives. (See *Differential Benefit*.)

Incremental Cost   The total additional cost that will be incurred if a particular alternative is chosen. The difference in total costs between two alternatives. (See *Differential Cost*.)

Incurred Costs   (See *Actual Costs*.)

Indirect Costs   Costs that cannot be logically assigned to an objective without allocation. (See *Common Costs*.)

Indirect Expenses   (See *Overhead*.)

Indirect Factory Costs   (See *Overhead*.)

Indirect Labor   Labor included in overhead because it cannot be traced directly to the units of output or to a department.

Indirect Manufacturing Costs   (See *Overhead*.)

Indirect Materials   Minor materials included in overhead because they are not directly traceable to the finished products.

Inflation   The decline in the purchasing power of the dollar.

Information Economics   The study of the costs and benefits of data in the belief that the benefits from using data should exceed the costs of gathering it.

Insolvency   The inability of a firm to meet its debts when they are due. In bankruptcy situations insolvency is defined as liabilities exceeding assets.

Inspection of Contracts   A method of separating costs into their fixed and variable components by examining existing production activities and contracts.

Interfirm Allocations   Allocation of resources among firms in the economy, usually through the capital (stock and bond) markets.

Internal Rate of Return   The discount rate that creates an excess net of present value of zero.

Intrafirm Allocations   Allocation of resources within a firm to the various departments or responsibility centers.

Inventory Turnover   Cost of goods sold or cost of goods consumed divided by inventory value.

Investment Centers   Segments of a firm where resources, revenues, and costs are traced and the rate of return on investment is used as a control measure.

Investment Decisions   (See *Long-range Decisions;* also see *Capital Budgeting.*)

Investment Turnover   Sales divided by investment in assets. One component of return on investment. A measure of activity that shows if assets have generated revenue.

Invoice   A form sent by a supplier billing a firm for materials purchased; serves as a source document for the purchases entry.

Iterative Process   An approach to budgeting where the budget is developed through a sequential series of steps.

J   **Job Cost Sheet**   A basic record for the accumulation of product costs in a job-costing system. Also called *Work Order* or *Job Order*.

Job Costing   A system of determining production costs that traces the materials, labor, and other factory costs to specific units or batches.

Joint Costs   (See *Common Costs.*)

Joint Process   A production process in which a single input results in more than one output.

Joint Product Cost   (See *Common Costs.*)

Just-in-Time Inventory (J-I-T)   A method of inventory control where materials arrive in a department just as they are used, thereby reducing inventory levels.

L   **Labor**   (See *Direct Labor* and *Indirect Labor*.)

Labor Efficiency (Quantity) Variance   The variance that measures the efficient or inefficient use of labor; the difference between standard hours in actual production and actual hours worked priced at the standard wage rate.

Labor Rate (Price) Variance   The variance that measures the ability to control wage rates and labor mix; the difference between actual wage rate and standard wage rate multiplied by the actual hours worked.

Last In, First Out (LIFO)   An inventory costing method where the last costs received are the first costs transferred out.

Lead Time   The interval between the time a purchase order is placed and the time materials are received and available for use.

Learning Curve   A mathematical expression of the fact that labor time will decrease at a constant percentage over doubled output quantities.

Least-squares Regression   A statistical tool for fitting a straight line to data, providing a systematic and reliable method of estimating fixed and variable costs. Can also be used in projecting sales. Also called *Statistical Regression Analysis* or *Regression Analysis*.

Leverage   (See *Trading on the Equity*.)

Liabilities   Economic obligations of a firm to outsiders.

Limiting Factor   (See *Constraint*.)

Line-Item Budget   A budget in which accountability for expenditures of money is identified with specific expenditure lines in the budget.

Linear Programming   A mathematical method used in a number of business decisions (including optimum product mix problems), where many interacting variables are combined to use limited resources to maximize profits or minimize losses.

Liquidity   The amount and composition of a firm's assets with emphasis on their conversion to cash.

Liquidity Ratio   A ratio of liquid assets to current liabilities, computed as (Cash + Marketable securities + Receivables) ÷ Current liabilities.

Long-range Decisions   Decisions adding to or reducing the productive capability of a firm. These decisions affect the cash flows of more than one accounting period so that the time value of money is a significant variable.

Long-range Excess Capacity   A measure of capacity held in reserve to meet fluctuations in demand; long-term growth determined in units as the difference between practical capacity and normal capacity.

Loss   A cost that has been consumed without providing a benefit or revenue.

M   **Managed Costs**   Fixed costs whose amounts are determined by management, not by their direct relationship to production output. (See *Discretionary Costs*.)

Management Accounting   The focus of accounting data for intrafirm allocations through the planning and control process.

Management by Exception   The practice of focusing attention only on those activities where actual performance differs significantly from planned performance.

Management by Objectives   A management style where the superior and the subordinate jointly establish the subordinate's goals and objectives for the coming period.

Manufacturing Expenses   (See *Overhead*.)

Manufacturing Overhead   (See *Overhead*.)

Margin of Safety   The amount (or ratio) by which the current sales volume exceeds the breakeven volume, either in units or dollars.

Margin on Sales   Income divided by net sales. Also called *Profit Margin*.

Marginal Costing   (See *Variable Costing*.)

Marginal Costs   The cost of one additional unit of output. The cost incurred to move from output n to output $n + 1$.

Marginal Income   (See *Contribution Margin*.)

Marginal Revenue   The increment in total revenue obtained when output is increased by one additional unit.

Master Budget   An integrated plan of action for a firm as a whole, expressed in financial terms. Also called *Planning Budget* and *Comprehensive Budget*.

Matching   The accounting process of comparing costs and revenues for a period in the determination of income.

Material Price Variance   A measure of the ability to control material prices incurred; the difference between the actual material cost and the standard material cost multiplied by the actual quantity purchased.

Material Purchased Price Variance   (See *Material Price Variance*.)

Material Quantity Variance   (See *Material Usage Variance*.)

Material Requisition   A request for release of material held in the storeroom to authorized personnel. The source document to record raw material issues.

Material Usage Variance   A measure of the efficient or inefficient use of materials; the difference between the standard quantity required for actual production and the actual quantity used priced at the standard cost per unit of material.

Materials   Physical commodities consumed to make the final product.

Mixed Cost   A cost that has both fixed and variable cost attributes.

Monopolistic Competition   An economic marketplace where there is a large number of firms. Each firm has little control over price except to create product differentiation.

Monopoly   An economic marketplace characterized by a single firm as the sole producer of a product for which there are no close substitutes.

Motivation   The internal and external factors that influence an individual to act.

Multiple-Regression Analysis   A mathematical method of measuring the change in the dependent variable (cost) with changes in two or more different independent variables (measures of volume).

N   **Natural Classification**   Classification of overhead costs by the nature of the expense, that is, utilities, insurance, depreciation, rent or taxes.

Negotiated Market Price   A transfer price negotiated between the buying and selling divisions where no open-market price is established.

Net Book Value   The unexpired cost of an asset carried on the financial records of the firm. Historical cost of an asset less accumulated depreciation to date.

Net Present Value   A method of selecting capital investment projects. Proposals are assessed by the difference between discounted cash inflows and discounted cash outflows using a predetermined desired rate of return. (See *Present Value*.)

Net Working Capital   The excess of current assets over current liabilities. Also called *Working Capital*.

Noncontrollable Costs   Costs that a given manager cannot affect by his or her decisions.

Nonproduction Costs   The costs of selling and distributing the final product and of general administration.

Nonrelevant Benefits   Benefits that are not affected by a decision and will not change as a result of the decision.

Nonrelevant Costs   Costs that are not affected by a decision and will not change as a result of the decision.

Normal Distribution   The bell-shaped curve where 68.27% of the observations fall within ± 1 standard deviation, 95.45% within ± 2 standard deviations, and 99.73% within ± 3 standard deviations of the mean.

Normal Overhead Rate   An overhead rate based on normal volume.

Normal Standard   A standard that can be achieved if activities are efficient. (Also called an *Average* or *Currently Attainable Standard*.)

Normal Volume   The level of output necessary to meet sales demands over a span of years (usually three to five), encompassing seasonal and cyclical variations.

O   **Objective Function**   A mathematical statement used in linear programming that relates production output to contribution margin.

Objectives   Specific quantitative and time-performance targets to achieve a firm's goals.

Oligopoly   An economic marketplace where a few firms control a significant share of the market. Firms are mutually interdependent and often follow the dominant firm in pricing and production volume decisions.

Operating Budget   (Also called the *Profit Plan*.)

Operating Cycle   The period involved from the time cash is invested in inventory until the time cash is recovered from sale of the goods.

Operating Decisions   (See *Short-range Decisions*.)

Opportunity Cost   (A) Benefit that would have been obtained from an alternative if that alternative had been accepted. (B) The cost of foregone revenue by choosing a particular alternative.

Order-Filling Costs   (See *Distribution Costs*.)

Order-Getting Costs   (See *Selling Costs*.)

Out-of-Pocket Costs   Costs that will require an expenditure of cash as a result of a decision.

Overabsorbed Overhead   The excess of overhead cost applied to the product over the actual overhead costs incurred. Also called *Overapplied Overhead*.

Overapplied Overhead   (See *Overabsorbed Overhead*.)

Overhead   All costs of operating the factory except those designated as direct labor and direct material costs. Also called *Factory Burden, Manufacturing Expenses, Indirect Factory Costs, Manufacturing Overhead, Indirect Expenses, Indirect Manufacturing Costs*, and *Factory Overhead*.

Overhead Efficiency Variance   (See *Variable Overhead Efficiency Variance*.)

Overhead Rate   A method of allocating the indirect factory costs to the products, creating an average overhead cost per unit of production activity.

P   **Payback Period**   The length of time necessary to recover the initial investment of a project; investment cost divided by annual net cash flow.

Performance Budget   An adjusted budget prepared *after* operations to compare actual results with revenues and costs that *should* have been incurred at the actual level attained.

Performance Report   A report to a manager comparing actual results with planned results in his or her area of responsibility.

Period Costs   Costs that are not inventoried and are treated as an expense in the period in which they are incurred.

Planning   The process of selecting goals and objectives and the actions required to attain them.

Planning Budget   (See *Master Budget*.)

Plant-wide Overhead Rate   (See *Blanket Overhead Rate*.)

Practical Capacity   (A) The most efficient operating level if fixed costs remain constant and output levels per unit of effort do not diminish; ideal capacity less allowances for repairs, maintenance, and rest periods. (B) Maximum sustainable long-run capacity.

Predetermined Overhead Rate   An overhead rate determined in advance of production by dividing estimated (budgeted) overhead costs by an estimated (budgeted) volume base.

Preferred Stock   Capital stock with priority over other shares in the areas of dividends and distribution of assets upon liquidation.

Present Value   The concept that a sum invested today will earn interest and be worth more at a later date; a dollar in the hand today is worth more today than a dollar to be received (or spent) in the future.

Present Value of Money   The amount that must be invested now to reach a given amount at some future given point of time, assuming it is compounded at a given rate of interest.

Price Variance   A measure of how well actual prices agreed with planned prices; the difference between the actual prices and the standard (budgeted) prices multiplied by the actual quantity purchased.

Prime Costs   The sum of direct material and direct labor.

Prior Department Costs   Used in process costing, the costs incurred in a preceding department that have been transferred to a subsequent department.

Probabilities   The likelihood of a specific event occurring.

Procedures   Detailed instructions specifying how certain activities are to be accomplished.

Process Costing   A method of determining the unit cost of manufacturing where production costs are divided by units produced during a given time period.

Producing Departments   Departments or organizational units that contribute directly to the conversion of raw materials into finished products. Departments that come in physical contact with the products.

Product Costs   Costs that attach to the unit of product and remain as an asset in the inventory until the goods to which they are attached are sold.

Product Margin   The contribution margin of a particular product less directly identifiable fixed costs.

Production Base   A common denominator that equates all units produced. The most common measures of production base are units of product, machine hours, labor hours, and labor cost.

Production Budget   A component of the master budget that establishes the level of production planned for some future period.

Production Costs   Costs that are necessary to produce a finished product. Also called *Manufacturing Costs*.

Productive Assets   Assets committed to production, storage, or distribution of a firm's products or services.

Profit Centers   Organizational units where both revenue and costs naturally come together and income or contribution margin are used as control measures.

Profit Margin   Percentage of income on sales. One component of the return on investment calculation. Income divided by sales.

Profit Plan   A budgeted income statement.

Profit-Planning Chart   (See *Breakeven Graph*.)

Profit–Volume Chart   A graphic technique that shows breakeven analysis by plotting only the contribution margin on the chart.

Pro Forma **Statements**   Financial statements prepared before actual occurrence of events. Also called *Budgeted Statements*.

Profitability Accounting   (See *Responsibility Accounting*.)

Program Budgeting   A budgetary system used in the public sector that focuses on the output of the organization rather than on specific inputs.

Programmed Costs   (See *Discretionary Costs*.)

Projected Statement of Financial Position   A projected balance sheet prepared to reflect expected financial position at the end of the planning period.

Purchase Order   A form sent to a supplier by the purchasing department requesting the shipment of material.

Purchase Requisition   A form issued by the storeroom requesting the purchasing department to procure some specific material.

Purchasing Budget   A component of the master budget showing planned purchases for some future period.

Purchasing Costs   Used in EOQ formulas, the additional costs of placing a purchase order.

Pure Competition   An economic marketplace where a large number of independent firms produce a standardized product. No single firm can influence the market price; the price equals marginal revenue; a firm's demand schedule is horizontal.

Q   **Quantity Variance**   A measure of how well actual quantities agreed with planned quantities; the difference between the actual quantities used and the standard (budgeted) quantities for actual production, multiplied by the standard price.

R   **Rated Capacity**   Equipment capacity determined by its designers.

Rate Variance   (See *Price Variance*.)

Raw Materials Inventory   Production materials on hand but not yet processed.

Reciprocal Allocations   A method of allocating service department costs with the use of simultaneous equations.

Regression Analysis   (See *Least-squares Regression*.)

Relevant Benefit   A benefit that is cogent to the alternative being considered and will be affected by the decision.

Relevant Cost   A cost that is cogent to the alternative being considered and will be affected by the decision.

Relevant Data for Decision Making   Future differential costs or benefits related to a particular decision.

Relevant Range   The span of volume over which the cost behavior (or management plans) can be expected to remain valid.

Reorder Point   The inventory level where an order must be placed to provide adequate lead time to ensure delivery when needed.

Replenishment Point   The point in time when the physical inventory is restocked by deliveries.

Report on Profit Plan   A management report explaining the differences between the Profit Plan and the actual Income Statement for a particular time period.

Required Rate of Return   The minimum desired rate of return used in long-run, discounted cash flow analysis.

Residual Income   A measure of divisional performance; the cost of capital deducted from divisional income or contribution.

Residual Sum of Squares   The sum of the variation of each y value from the corresponding predicted value given by the regression equation.

Responsibility Accounting   (A) A system of recording costs and revenues where each manager is assigned only those factors that he or she can affect by his or her decisions. (B) A system that attempts to assign and match authority and responsibility.

Responsibility Centers   A broad term that implies the development of an organizational structure where there is identifiable responsibility for each cost, revenue, and resource.

Return on Investment (ROI)   The most widely used single measure of an operation's performance; (1) profits divided by assets committed or (2) margin on sales times asset turnover.

Revenue   The inflow of economic values from company operations. Also called *Sales* or *Sales Revenue*.

Revenue Center   Responsibility centers where only revenues are traced directly.

Risk   An exposure to loss because of inability to control conditions on which the firm is dependent.

Rolling or Moving Average   A method of calculating an average; the oldest data are dropped and the newest data added each time the average is calculated.

S   **Safety Stock**   The minimum inventory level that provides a cushion against running out of stock because of changes in demand or changes in lead time.

Sales Budget   A formal statement of planned sales levels for the coming period.

Sales Forecast   A projection of sales for a particular future period of time.

Sales Mix   The relative combination of the quantities of each type of product sold in a multiproduct firm.

Sales Volume Variance   (See *Activity Variance*.)

Scattergraph   A graphic representation showing the general relationship of cost to some base of activity; used in segregating costs into their fixed and variable components.

Scattergraph Method   A method of segregating fixed and variable costs by plotting cost and activity data on a graph and then fitting a line by visual inspection so that half the plots lie above the line and half lie below the line.

Scheduled Production   A production plan that identifies the specific quantity and type of goods to be produced in the next period.

Segment   A subcomponent of a firm; a responsibility center.

Segment Margin   The contribution margin of a subcomponent, segment, or division of a firm less all separable, identifiable fixed costs.

Selling Costs   Nonproduction costs that result from marketing activities. Also called *Order-Getting Costs*.

Semifixed Costs   (See *Semivariable Costs.*)

Semivariable Costs   Costs that are neither completely fixed nor completely variable, changing with changes in production volume, but not in direct proportion. They may be stepped, mixed, or curvilinear.

Sensitivity Analysis   A method of showing how outcomes would differ if the actual cash inflows or outflows differ from those planned.

Separable Costs   (A) Costs that can be identified with a specific segment of the firm. (B) Costs that would be avoided if a product line or segment of the firm were dropped.

Service Department   A department that supports the producing departments in their activities but is not directly in contact with converting the raw materials into finished products.

Setup Costs   Costs incurred to prepare a factory for a production run.

Shadow Price   How much contribution margin will increase if one more unit of a limiting resource is available.

Short-range Decisions   Decisions involving production output, pricing, and product mix. They are concerned with the optimum use of existing resources and, typically, the time value of money is not considered significant.

Simplex Method   A mathematical method of solving simultaneous equations that, because of bulk and size, would be impractical to solve graphically or manually.

Simulation   A method—usually computerized—that uses a mathematical statement of the interrelationships of variables to test the effects of changes.

Slack   (1) The difference between organizational goals and individiual goals that give managers room to perform. (2) In linear programming, the amount of an unused, or available constraint.

Solvency   Ability of a firm to pay its debts when due.

Source Document.   A form that serves as a basis for an accounting entry; an original record.

Specific Cost of Capital   The cost of a specific source of capital.

Specific Price Index   An index showing the change in the purchasing power of the dollar for a specific group of assets.

Spending Variance   The difference between actual overhead and budgeted overhead in the Performance Budget for the actual level of operations. Also called *Budget Variance*.

Split-off Point   The point in the production process where products with joint costs are separated and become individual products.

Stairstepped Cost   A semivariable cost that increases in discrete intervals.

Standard   A precise measure of what should occur if performance is efficient.

Standard Absorption Costing   A system of product costing that focuses on management planning and control; product cost is determined by the sum of the standard costs for materials, labor, and both variable and fixed overhead. The variances between actual and standard are treated as period costs.

Standard Cost   A predetermination of what a unit of product *should* cost; a planning and control reference.

Standard Error of the Estimate   A measure of how well a regression line fits the actual data when using least-squares regression analysis. The further the observations from the regression line, the larger will be the standard error.

Standard Overhead Rate   A predetermination of what overhead *should* cost per unit of output.

Standard Variable Costing   A system of product costing that focuses on management planning and control; product cost is determined by the sum of the standard costs for materials, labor, and variable overhead. The fixed overhead costs and the variances between actual and standard costs are treated as period costs.

Statement of Financial Position   (See *Balance Sheet.*)

Static Budget   (See *Fixed Budget.*)

Statistical Regression Analysis   (See *Least-squares Regression.*)

Step Costs   A semivariable cost that changes abruptly at intervals.

Step-down Allocation Method   A technique of assigning costs of service departments to revenue-producing departments where costs of the most widely used service are allocated first to all remaining departments, and so on, until the costs of all service departments have been allocated.

Sunk Cost   A cost that has already been incurred and will not require a future expenditure of cash.

Supplementary Fixed Overhead Rate   An overhead rate calculated at the end of the accounting period to adjust the inventories from variable costing to absorption costing.

Supply Curve   An economic concept that relates market prices to the quantity of product that suppliers or producers are willing to supply.

T   **Target Rate**   (Also called *Desired Rate of Return.*)

Tax Shield   Recognition that a cost shields income of future years against tax to the extent that the cost may be deducted against income. The most common example is a depreciable asset.

Time-adjusted Rate of Return The rate of interest at which the present value of budgeted cash inflows for a project equals the present value of budgeted cash outflows for the project.

Time Ticket A factory record of how the employee spends his or her time.

Time Value of Money The difference between the value of a dollar today and its value at some future point in time of invested.

Total Contribution Margin The contribution margin per unit times the number of units sold.

Total Cost The sum of all fixed costs and all variable costs.

Total Revenue The quantity sold times the price per unit.

Traceable Cost (See *Controllable Cost*.)

Trading on the Equity Using borrowed money with a fixed interest cost to invest in a project with a higher rate of return so that the return on the stockholders' equity is increased.

Traditional Costing (Also called *Absorption Costing*.)

Transfer Price The price charged by one segment of an organization when it supplies a product or service to another segment of the same organization.

Transferred-in Costs (See *Prior Department Costs*.)

U Unadjusted Rate of Return A rate of return that has not been adjusted for the time value of money. (See *Accounting Rate of Return*.)

Unavoidable Costs Costs that will be incurred whether a project is continued or discontinued.

Uncertainty A lack of information about the probability of alternative results.

Uncontrollable Costs Costs that are unaffected by the decisions of a specific manager.

Underapplied Overhead The amount by which actual overhead exceeds overhead applied to the products.

Unexpired Costs Assets; costs carried forward to future periods where they have the potential of contributing to future revenues.

Unfavorable Variance (A) A variance where the actual costs are greater than the budgeted or standard costs. (B) A variance where actual revenue is less than planned or budgeted revenue.

Usage Variance (See *Quantity Variance*.)

V Variable Budget (See *Flexible Budget*.)

Variable Costs Costs that vary in total dollar amount in direct proportion to changes in production volume. The cost per unit of output is constant over the relevant range of activity.

Variable Cost Ratio   Variable costs divided by sales.

Variable Costing   A system of measuring inventory costs that assigns variable production costs of material, labor, and variable overhead to the product unit cost. Fixed overhead costs and nonproduction costs are treated as period costs. Also called *Marginal Costing* and *Direct Costing*.

Variable Overhead Efficiency Variance   The variance that measures the effect of inefficient or efficient use of labor on variable overhead costs; the difference between standard hours in actual production and actual hours worked, priced at the variable overhead rate.

Variable Overhead Spending Variance   The difference between actual variable costs incurred and the amount that the flexible budget allows for variable costs for the actual volume worked.

Variable Profit Ratio   (See *Contribution Margin Ratio*.)

Variance   The difference between actual results and planned results.

Volume Variance   (See *Fixed Overhead Volume Variance*.)

W   **Weighted-Average Costing**   A method of inventory costing where total dollars of goods available during the period are summed and divided by the total units available.

Work-in-Process Inventory   The cost of uncompleted products still in the factory.

Working Capital   The excess of current assets over current liabilities.

appendix A

Present Value of \$1 $PV = (1 + r)^{-n} = \dfrac{1}{(1 + r)^n}$

Period	2%	4%	6%	8%	10%	12%	14%	16%	18%
1	.980	.962	.943	.926	.909	.893	.877	.862	.847
2	.961	.925	.890	.857	.826	.797	.769	.743	.718
3	.942	.889	.840	.794	.751	.712	.675	.641	.609
4	.924	.855	.792	.735	.683	.636	.592	.552	.516
5	.906	.822	.747	.681	.621	.567	.519	.476	.437
6	.888	.790	.705	.630	.564	.507	.456	.410	.370
7	.871	.760	.665	.583	.513	.452	.400	.354	.314
8	.853	.731	.627	.540	.467	.404	.351	.305	.266
9	.837	.703	.592	.500	.424	.361	.308	.263	.225
10	.820	.676	.558	.463	.386	.322	.270	.227	.191
11	.804	.650	.527	.429	.350	.287	.237	.195	.162
12	.788	.625	.497	.397	.319	.257	.208	.168	.137
13	.773	.601	.469	.368	.290	.229	.182	.145	.116
14	.758	.577	.442	.340	.263	.205	.160	.125	.099
15	.743	.555	.417	.315	.239	.183	.140	.108	.084
16	.728	.534	.394	.292	.218	.163	.123	.093	.071
17	.714	.513	.371	.270	.198	.146	.108	.080	.060
18	.700	.494	.350	.250	.180	.130	.095	.069	.051
19	.686	.475	.331	.232	.164	.116	.083	.060	.043
20	.673	.456	.312	.215	.149	.104	.073	.051	.037
21	.660	.439	.294	.199	.135	.093	.064	.044	.031
22	.647	.422	.278	.184	.123	.083	.056	.038	.026
23	.634	.406	.262	.170	.112	.074	.049	.033	.022
24	.622	.390	.247	.158	.102	.066	.043	.028	.019
25	.610	.375	.233	.146	.092	.059	.038	.024	.016
30	.552	.308	.174	.099	.057	.033	.020	.012	.007
35	.500	.253	.130	.068	.036	.019	.010	.006	.003
40	.453	.208	.097	.046	.022	.011	.005	.003	.001
45	.410	.171	.073	.031	.014	.006	.003	.001	.001
50	.372	.141	.054	.021	.009	.003	.001	.001	

20%	22%	24%	26%	28%	30%	35%	40%	45%	50%
.833	.820	.806	.794	.781	.769	.741	.714	.690	.667
.694	.672	.650	.630	.610	.592	.549	.510	.476	.444
.579	.551	.524	.500	.477	.455	.406	.364	.328	.296
.482	.451	.423	.397	.373	.350	.301	.260	.226	.198
.402	.370	.341	.315	.291	.269	.223	.186	.156	.132
.335	.303	.275	.250	.227	.207	.165	.133	.108	.088
.279	.249	.222	.198	.178	.159	.122	.095	.074	.059
.233	.204	.179	.157	.139	.123	.091	.068	.051	.039
.194	.167	.144	.125	.108	.094	.067	.048	.035	.026
.162	.137	.116	.099	.085	.073	.050	.035	.024	.017
.135	.112	.094	.079	.066	.056	.037	.025	.017	.012
.112	.092	.076	.062	.052	.043	.027	.018	.012	.008
.093	.075	.061	.050	.040	.033	.020	.013	.008	.005
.078	.062	.049	.039	.032	.025	.015	.009	.006	.003
.065	.051	.040	.031	.025	.020	.011	.006	.004	.002
.054	.042	.032	.025	.019	.015	.008	.005	.003	.002
.045	.034	.026	.020	.015	.012	.006	.003	.002	.001
.038	.028	.021	.016	.012	.009	.005	.002	.001	.001
.031	.023	.017	.012	.009	.007	.003	.002	.001	
.026	.019	.014	.010	.007	.005	.002	.001	.001	
.022	.015	.011	.008	.006	.004	.002	.001		
.018	.013	.009	.006	.004	.003	.001	.001		
.015	.010	.007	.005	.003	.002	.001			
.013	.008	.006	.004	.003	.002	.001			
.010	.007	.005	.003	.002	.001	.001			
.004	.003	.002	.001	.001					
.002	.001	.001							
.001									

appendix B

Present Value of an Annuity of \$1 $PV = \dfrac{1 - (1 + r)^{-n}}{r}$

Period	2%	4%	6%	8%	10%	12%	14%	16%	18%
1	0.980	0.962	0.943	0.926	0.909	0.893	0.877	0.862	0.847
2	1.942	1.886	1.833	1.783	1.736	1.690	1.647	1.605	1.566
3	2.884	2.775	2.673	2.577	2.487	2.402	2.322	2.246	2.174
4	3.808	3.630	3.465	3.312	3.170	3.037	2.914	2.798	2.690
5	4.713	4.452	4.212	3.993	3.791	3.605	3.433	3.274	3.127
6	5.601	5.242	4.917	4.623	4.355	4.111	3.889	3.685	3.498
7	6.472	6.002	5.582	5.206	4.868	4.564	4.288	4.039	3.812
8	7.325	6.733	6.210	5.747	5.335	4.968	4.639	4.344	4.078
9	8.162	7.435	6.802	6.247	5.759	5.328	4.946	4.607	4.303
10	8.983	8.111	7.360	6.710	6.145	5.650	5.216	4.833	4.494
11	9.787	8.760	7.887	7.139	6.495	5.938	5.453	5.029	4.656
12	10.575	9.385	8.384	7.536	6.814	6.194	5.660	5.197	4.793
13	11.348	9.986	8.853	7.904	7.103	6.424	5.842	5.342	4.910
14	12.106	10.563	9.295	8.244	7.367	6.628	6.002	5.468	5.008
15	12.849	11.118	9.712	8.559	7.606	6.811	6.142	5.575	5.092
16	13.578	11.652	10.106	8.851	7.824	6.974	6.265	5.668	5.162
17	14.292	12.166	10.477	9.122	8.022	7.120	6.373	5.749	5.222
18	14.992	12.659	10.828	9.372	8.201	7.250	6.467	5.818	5.273
19	15.678	13.134	11.158	9.604	8.365	7.366	6.550	5.877	5.316
20	16.351	13.590	11.470	9.818	8.514	7.469	6.623	5.929	5.353
21	17.011	14.029	11.764	10.017	8.649	7.562	6.687	5.973	5.384
22	17.658	14.451	12.042	10.201	8.772	7.645	6.743	6.011	5.410
23	18.292	14.857	12.303	10.371	8.883	7.718	6.792	6.044	5.432
24	18.914	15.247	12.550	10.529	8.985	7.784	6.835	6.073	5.451
25	19.523	15.622	12.783	10.675	9.077	7.843	6.873	6.097	5.467
30	22.396	17.292	13.765	11.258	9.427	8.055	7.003	6.177	5.517
35	24.999	18.665	14.498	11.655	9.644	8.176	7.070	6.215	5.539
40	27.355	19.793	15.046	11.925	9.779	8.244	7.105	6.233	5.548
45	29.490	20.720	15.456	12.108	9.863	8.283	7.123	6.242	5.552
50	31.424	21.482	15.762	12.233	9.915	8.304	7.133	6.246	5.554

20%	22%	24%	26%	28%	30%	35%	40%	45%	50%
0.833	0.820	0.806	0.794	0.781	0.769	0.741	0.714	0.690	0.667
1.528	1.492	1.457	1.424	1.392	1.361	1.289	1.224	1.165	1.111
2.106	2.042	1.981	1.923	1.868	1.816	1.696	1.589	1.493	1.407
2.589	2.494	2.404	2.320	2.241	2.166	1.997	1.849	1.720	1.605
2.991	2.864	2.745	2.635	2.532	2.436	2.220	2.035	1.876	1.737
3.326	3.167	3.020	2.885	2.759	2.643	2.385	2.168	1.983	1.824
3.605	3.416	3.242	3.083	2.937	2.802	2.508	2.263	2.057	1.883
3.837	3.619	3.421	3.241	3.076	2.925	2.598	2.331	2.109	1.922
4.031	3.786	3.566	3.366	3.184	3.019	2.665	2.379	2.144	1.948
4.192	3.923	3.682	3.465	3.269	3.092	2.715	2.414	2.168	1.965
4.327	4.035	3.776	3.543	3.335	3.147	2.752	2.438	2.185	1.977
4.439	4.127	3.851	3.606	3.387	3.190	2.779	2.456	2.196	1.985
4.533	4.203	3.912	3.656	3.427	3.223	2.799	2.469	2.204	1.990
4.611	4.265	3.962	3.695	3.459	3.249	2.814	2.478	2.210	1.993
4.675	4.315	4.001	3.726	3.483	3.268	2.825	2.484	2.214	1.995
4.730	4.357	4.033	3.751	3.503	3.283	2.834	2.489	2.216	1.997
4.775	4.391	4.059	3.771	3.518	3.295	2.840	2.492	2.218	1.998
4.812	4.419	4.080	3.786	3.529	3.304	2.844	2.494	2.219	1.999
4.843	4.442	4.097	3.799	3.539	3.311	2.848	2.496	2.220	1.999
4.870	4.460	4.110	3.808	3.546	3.316	2.850	2.497	2.221	1.999
4.891	4.476	4.121	3.816	3.551	3.320	2.852	2.498	2.221	2.000
4.909	4.488	4.130	3.822	3.556	3.323	2.853	2.498	2.222	2.000
4.925	4.499	4.137	3.827	3.559	3.325	2.854	2.499	2.222	2.000
4.937	4.507	4.143	3.831	3.562	3.327	2.855	2.499	2.222	2.000
4.948	4.514	4.147	3.834	3.564	3.329	2.856	2.499	2.222	2.000
4.979	4.534	4.160	3.842	3.569	3.332	2.857	2.500	2.222	2.000
4.992	4.541	4.164	3.845	3.571	3.333	2.857	2.500	2.222	2.000
4.997	4.544	4.166	3.846	3.571	3.333	2.857	2.500	2.222	2.000
4.999	4.545	4.166	3.846	3.571	3.333	2.857	2.500	2.222	2.000
4.999	4.545	4.167	3.846	3.571	3.333	2.857	2.500	2.222	2.000

index